COERCION
AND GOVERNANCE

*The Declining Political Role
of the Military in Asia*

Coercion
and Governance

---

*The Declining Political Role
of the Military in Asia*

EDITED BY

MUTHIAH ALAGAPPA

Stanford University Press
Stanford, California
2001

Stanford University Press
Stanford, California
©2001 by the Board of Trustees of the
Leland Stanford Junior University

Printed in the United States of America on acid-free,
archival-quality paper.

Library of Congress Cataloging-in-Publication Data
Coercion and governance : the declining political role of
   the military in Asia / edited by Muthiah Alagappa.
        p.   cm.
   Includes bibliographical references and index.
   ISBN 0-8047-4226-X (alk. paper) — ISBN 0-8047-
4227-8 (pbk. : alk paper)
      1. Civil military relations—Asia I. Alagappa,
Muthiah.
JQ26.C64 2001
322'.5'095—dc21   2001020988

Last figure below indicates year of this printing:
09   08   07   06   05   04   03   02   01

CONTENTS

TABLES AND FIGURES

TABLES

FIGURES

ACRONYMS AND ABBREVIATIONS

ABRI	Angkatan Bersenjata Republik Indonesia
ACC	Appointments Committee of the Cabinet
ACSA	Acquisition and Cross-Servicing Agreement
AFC	Allied Forces Command
AFD	Armed Forces Division
AFP	Armed Forces of the Philippines
AFPFL	Anti-Fascist People's Freedom League
AMC	Army Medical Corps
ANSP	Agency for National Security Planning
ASC	Army Security Command
ASEAN	Association of Southeast Asian Nations
AWT	Army Welfare Trust
Bayan	Bagong Alyansang Makabayan
BJP	Bharatiya Janata Party
BNP	Bangladesh Nationalist Party
BSF	Border Security Force
BSPP	Burma Socialist Program Party
Bulog	National Logistics Board
CAO	Civil Affairs Office
CBCP	Catholic Bishops Conference of the Philippines
CCP	Chinese Communist Party
CCPA	Cabinet Committee on Political Affairs
CDF	Ceylon Defense Force
CDNS	Council for Defense and National Security
CENTO	Central Treaty Organizaton
CGS	chief of the general staff
CHDF	Civilian Home Defense Forces
CHT	Chittagong Hill Tracts
CIA	Central Intelligence Agency
CIC	Counterintelligence Corps
CMC	Central Military Commission
CMPC	Central Military Party Committee
CPM	Communist Party of Malaya
CPP	Communist Party of the Philippines
CPT	Communist Party of Thailand
CRP	Central Reserve Police
CSC	Chief of Staff Committee

CVF	Chosun Volunteer Forces
DCIC	Defence Coordination and Implementation Committee
DGFI	director-general of Forces Intelligence
DILG	Department of the Interior and Local Government
DNS	Department of National Security
DPC	Defense Planning Committee
DPP	Democratic Progressive Party
DPR	Dewan Perwakilan Rakyat
DPRD	Dewan Perwakilan Rakyat Daerah
DPRK	Democratic People's Republic of Korea
DRP	Democratic Republican Party
DRV	Democratic Republic of Vietnam
EDCOR	Armed Forces Economic Development Corps
EDSA	Epifanio de los Santos Avenue
FPI	Front Pembela Islam
FULRO	United Front for the Liberation of Oppressed Races
FWO	Frontier Works Organization
GAM	Gerakan Aceh Merdeka
GDP	gross domestic product
GNP	gross national product
GOC	general officer commanding
GPWD	General Political Warfare Department
GSH	General Staff Headquarters
HDO	Higher Defense Organization
IAF	Indian Air Force
IAS	Indian Administrative Service
IB	Intelligence Bureau
IBHI	Independent Bureau of Humanitarian Issues
IDF	Indigenous Defense Fighter
IISS	International Institute for Strategic Studies
IJI	Islamic Jamhoori Itihaad
IMET	International Military Education and Training
INA	Indian National Army
INC	Indian National Congress
INP	Integrated National Police
IPKF	Indian Peacekeeping Forces
IRBM	Intermediate Range Ballistic Missile
ISI	Inter Services Intelligence
ISOC	Internal Security Operations Command
ITBP	Indo-Tibetan Border Police
JCSC	Joint Chiefs of Staff Committee
JRB	Jatiyo Rakkhi Bahini
JUSMAG	Joint U.S. Military Advisory Group
JVP	Janatha Vimukthi Peramuna
KBL	Kilusang Bagong Lipunan
KCIA	Korean Central Intelligence Agency
KMT	Kuomintang

KODAM	Regional Military Commands
KODIM	District Military Commands
Kopassus	Special Forces Command
Kopkamtib	Command for the Restoration of Security and Order
KORAMIL	Subdistrict Military Commands
KOREM	Resort Military Commands
Kostrad	Army Strategic Reserve Command
KPA	Korean People's Army; also North Korean People's Armed Forces
KWP	Korean Workers' Party
LDP	Liberal Democratic Party
LTTE	Liberation Tigers of Tamil Eelam
MAC	Mainland Affairs Council
MAF	Malaysian Armed Forces
MDPC	Ministry of Defense Party Committee
Metrocom	Metropolitan Command
MILF	Moro Islamic Liberation Front
MINDEF	Ministry of Defense
MND	Ministry of National Defense
MNF	multinational force
MNLF	Moro National Liberation Front
MoD	Ministry of Defence (India)
MOD	Ministry of Defense (Bangladesh)
MOEs	military-owned enterprises
MOFA	Ministry of Foreign Affairs
MoU	Memorandum of Understanding
MPAF	Ministry of People's Armed Forces
MPC	Military Party Committee
MPR	Majelis Permusyawaratan Rakyat
MPS	Military Planning Staff
MQM	Movement of the Mohajirs
MRD	Movement for the Restoration of Democracy
MTCs	military trial courts
MTDP	Mid-Term Defense Program
NAMFREL	National Movement for Free Elections
Napolcom	National Police Commission
NDC	National Defense Commission
NDPO	National Defense Program Outline
NDSC	National Defense Security Command
NGO	Nongovernmental Organization
NICA	National Intelligence Coordinating Authority
NISA	National Intelligence Security Agency
NKCP	North Kalimantan Communist Party
NLC	National Logistics Cell
NLD	National League for Democracy
NLL	Northern Limitation Line
NPA	New People's Army
NSB	National Security Bureau

NSC	National Security Council
NSI	National Security Intelligence
NUF	National United Front
OPM	Organisasi Papula Merdeka
OSS	Office of Strategic Studies
PA	People's Alliance Party
PACC	Presidential Anti-Crime Commission
PAF	Pakistan Air Force (Chapter 3)
PAF	Philippine Air Force (Chapter 6)
PAP	People's Action Party
PARAKU	Pasukan Rakyat Kalimantan Utara
PBF	Patriotic Burmese Forces
PC	Philippine Constabulary
PCJSS	Parbattya Chattagram Janashonghoti Samity
PDI-P	Partai Demokrasi Indonesia-Perjuangan
PERISTA	Perkembangan Istimewa Angkatan Tentera
PGRS	Pasukan Gerila Rakyat Sarawak
PK	Pusan-Kyungnam
PKI	Partai Kommunis Indonesia
PKP	Partai Keadilan dan Persatuan
PLA	People's Liberation Army
PLOTE	People's Liberation Organization of Tamil Eelam
PMA	Philippine Military Academy
PNI	Partai Nasionalis Indonesia
PNP	Philippine National Police
PPP	Pakistan People's Party
PPP	Partai Persatuan Pembangunan
PPR	political party regulations
PRC	People's Republic of China
PSB	Presidential Security Battalion
PSC	Presidential Security Command
PSO	principal staff officer
PSU	Presidential Security Unit
PVL	Philippine Veterans Legion
RAM	Reform the Armed Forces of the Philippines Movement
RAW	Research and Analysis Wing
RMAF	Royal Malaysian Air Force
RMN	Royal Malaysian Navy
ROC	Republic of China on Taiwan
RPKAD	Army Para-Commando Regiment
RUCs	Regional Unified Commands
SAF	Singapore Armed Forces
SAS	Special Air Service
SCAP	supreme commander for the Allied Powers
SDC	Subcommittee on Defense Cooperation
SDF	Self-Defense Forces
SDP	Social Democratic Party

SEATO	Southeast Asia Treaty Organization
SEC	Second Economy Commission
SLFP	Sri Lanka Freedom Party
SLORC	State Law and Order Restoration Council
SOEs	state-owned enterprises
SPDC	State Peace and Development Council
TADA	Terrorists and Disruptive Activities Act
TNA	Tamil National Army
TNI	Tentera Nasional Indonesia (Indonesian National Defense Forces)
UMEH	Union of Myanmar Economic Holdings, Ltd.
UMNO	United Malays National Organization
UNP	United National Party
UNTAET	United Nations Transitional Authority for East Timor
USAFFE	U.S. Armed Forces in the Far East
USAMGIK	American Military Government (in Korea)
USVA	U.S. Veterans Administration
VCP	Vietnamese Communist Party
VFA	Visiting Forces Agreement
VPA	Vietnamese People's Army

PREFACE

Who guards the guardians?
—Plato, *The Republic*

A CENTRAL PARADOX AND QUINTESSENTIAL CIVIL-MILITARY PROBLEM of the modern state is how a country can create a military strong enough to protect the political community from internal and international threats and, at the same time, ensure that the military does not dominate the state or become an instrument for internal repression. Very few countries have been able to overcome the perennial problem relating to the accountability of rulers as well as the control of the institutions of state coercion. In many countries, including a large number in Asia, the military has intruded on and dominated politics. The October 1999 military coup in Pakistan; the actions of the Burmese and Chinese militaries in crushing prodemocracy protests in Rangoon and Beijing in 1988 and 1989, respectively; and the continued military stranglehold on the Burmese state are manifestations of military intrusion upon and domination of politics in Asia. However, as demonstrated by developments in the Philippines (1986), South Korea (1987), Taiwan (1987), Bangladesh (1991), Thailand (1973, 1992), and most recently in Indonesia (1998), the military has also been dislodged from the political helm. The relationship between the soldier and the state in Asia, as elsewhere, has undergone and continues to undergo change—more fundamentally in some countries than in others. In this study we investigate and explain key changes and continuities in civil-military relations in sixteen Asian countries and anticipate future trajectories.

A key finding of the study is that from a long-term and regional perspective, the political power and influence of the military and its participation in governance, though still considerable in some countries, is on the decline. At the founding moments in fifteen of the sixteen countries investigated, civil-military interaction was characterized by military subordination to civilian authority. However, beginning in the mid-1950s, the number of Asian countries under military domination increased, reaching a peak in the early 1980s. Since 1986, civilian control of the military, especially democratic civilian control, has been on the rise. At the time of writing, only two countries (Burma and Pakistan) are under military rule, and the military is the central pillar of the totalitarian regime in North Korea. Although the number of countries under civilian rule has increased dramatically, the relationship between the state and soldier is not a settled issue even in countries that have reasonably well established political systems. In countries that are undergoing democratic transition, civilian control of the military is far from established. Civil-military relations in these countries are still a contested domain that is being redefined only incrementally and often through struggle. Some setbacks and even reversals cannot be ruled out. From a long-term perspective, however, the scope and jurisdiction of the military in governance has decreased and will likely continue to do so, with a corresponding increase in civilian supremacy.

A related finding is that civilian supremacy does not equal democratic civilian control. In the foreseeable future, civil-military interaction in Asia will continue to be characterized by multiple patterns. Subjective civilian control is likely to continue in Malaysia, Singapore, and Sri Lanka. The Leninist pattern is likely to persist in the People's Republic of China and Vietnam in the short to medium term but, along with the totalitarian pattern in North Korea, appears unsustainable. It is difficult to anticipate the civil-military trajectories in these latter countries except to state that with the increasing inability of the communist parties and supreme leaders to monopolize political power, the symbiotic relationship between party, leader, state, and military is likely to become more diluted, with the state assuming greater control over the military. A military regime appears unlikely in either China or Vietnam. The Burmese military may be able to continue its stranglehold on the state through sheer force and terror, but it is unlikely that the Pakistani military can dominate the political helm indefinitely. Some form of power sharing that eventually paves the way for more durable civilian rule is likely though not inevitable.

Though the Leninist and military rule patterns will persist for some time, democratic civilian control is emerging as the dominant mode of civil-military interaction in Asia. Japan and India, both of which have experienced uninterrupted democratic civilian control during the past five decades, are likely to continue in this pattern. Democratic civilian control is consolidating in Taiwan, South Korea, and to a lesser degree in the Philippines and Thailand. In Bangladesh and Indonesia, such control is still in an early stage and could suffer setbacks. Civil-military interactions in Malaysia, Singapore, and Sri Lanka, though of the subjective type, do exhibit some features of democratic civilian control. For reasons explored in this study, the trends toward civilian control and the growing dominance of democratic civilian control appear to be durable.

The key to understanding civil-military relations in Asia, as elsewhere, is the significance and role of coercion—the key asset of the military—in state and nation building and in the exercise of political authority. As the significance of coercion in these processes increases or decreases, so does the political power and influence of the military. Although the salience of coercion in the international consolidation of the state is important, the significance and role of coercion in domestic governance is the more crucial variable in explaining the relationship of the soldier to the state. The weight of coercion in securing the loyalty and obedience of citizens is directly linked to and is a reflection of the legitimacy of the nation-state, its political system, and its government. The relationship between the international deployment of the military and political legitimacy is not as clear cut. This said, the political power and influence of the military is greatest when coercion plays a crucial role in both domestic governance and in ensuring international security.

The several propositions that have been advanced to explain developments in civil-military relations—push-pull, institutional imbalance, military professionalism, corporate interest, congruence of interests, and others—suffer certain shortcomings and at best can provide only a limited explanation. Our proposition that the power and influence of the military varies with the salience of coercion in governance has much greater power in explaining the full cycle of military politics. It also connects civil-military interaction to the larger processes associated with state and nation building, construction of legitimate political order, and change in the international system. The weight of coercion in governance is correlated with success or failure in the internal and international consolidation of the nation and state, the legitimacy of the political system and incumbent government, the level of economic development, and the institutional and resource capacity of the government to address the challenges confronting it through political, social, and economic measures. As nations and states become better consolidated, as institutions and procedures for the acquisition and exercise of state power become more widely accepted, and as the economy and state capacity develop, there will likely be a corresponding decline in the weight of coercion and in the power and influence of the military in governance. Much therefore hinges on the consolidation of nation and state, development of a legitimate political system and state capacity, economic development, and the material and normative structure of the international system.

In Asia, as elsewhere, postcolonial and postrevolutionary governments faced enormous challenges in state and nation building as well as in constructing legitimate political systems. Although experiences varied, in many countries power and authority were not concentrated in the state, state institutions were unable to dominate the entire country, minorities resisted integration into national communities, political systems were challenged by groups espousing rival organizing ideologies, legitimacy of governments was contested by competing elite, and in several cases the new states were confronted with severe international threats to their very existence. Internal and international security were prime concerns of many Asian countries. In many cases, state coercion played a dominant role in most if not all these processes and resulted in military role expansion and a dramatic increase in the coercive, organizational, economic, and political power and influence of the military. Though Asian countries still continue to face major challenges—and in some cases the challenges have become more acute—during the past five decades or so, several have made substantial progress in the internal and international consolidation of nation and state and in the development of widely accepted systems and institutions for political domination. In these countries, the resort to coercion, especially the private, partisan, and repressive use of force in governance, has declined, and so has the political power and influence of the military.

A large number of Asian countries, particularly those in East Asia and Southeast Asia, have also experienced high rates of economic growth for well over two decades. The highly successful export-led growth strategies of these countries integrated their national economies into the global capitalist economy, instituting new rules and procedures for the countries' management with spillover social and political effects. Sustained economic development in the capitalist mode made for a more complex economy that demanded sophisticated management that was well beyond what could be provided by the military. It also set in train the development of new domestic forces—an independent private sector, growth of middle and working classes, strong and vibrant civil societies—making for much more complex states and societies, with the latter demanding greater welfare, accountability, and participation in governance. Such development also strengthened other state institutions. The social and political mobilization engendered by sustained capitalist development tilted the distribution of power against the military and altered the norms and rules of governance.

Simultaneously, and especially since the mid- to late 1980s, the international context altered decidedly in favor of democracy, human rights, and the market economy. International organizations and key external actors condemned military coups and ostracized military governments. Not only have these developments altered the normative structure and distribution of power in favor of civilian institutions, with a corresponding decline in the political influence of the military in several countries, they have also generated close domestic and international scrutiny of military institutions and their activities. The interplay of coercion, political legitimacy, and economic development in the context of a changing international system, we argue, explains long-term change and continuity in Asian civil-military relations.

Our central argument borne out by the experiences of the past several decades suggests that enhancement of civilian supremacy requires strengthening the legitimacy, capacity, and roles of civilian institutions; sustained economic development; and reduction of the salience of coercion in governance. These hinge on forging agreement on the political identity of the nation-state and the system for political domination, success in economic growth and development, and development of appropriate political and socioeconomic policies and processes to address political and social problems. This does not imply that coercion is irrelevant for governance, only that its role should be limited and indirect and be viewed as the ultimate sanction, not the first recourse.

Turning more explicitly to civil-military interaction, consolidation of civilian supremacy entails mobilization of superior political, ideational, moral, and economic power on the part of civilian authorities and the translation of such power into strong institutions to regulate matters pertaining to the military and its role in governance. By compelling political, bureaucratic, and military actors to interact in accordance with specified rules and procedures in the development of policy, institutions condition all actors to operate under a civilian framework and reduce (though not eliminate) the salience of brute power. The cross-cutting alliances and cleavages made possible by interaction through institutions also contribute to the development of understanding and respect for different perspectives, leading to moderation and compromise. These developments enhance the legitimacy of the civilian-dominant political system.

As it becomes accustomed to operating in such a framework, the military in the long run internalizes the norm of civilian control. Further, institutional design—in terms of issues, jurisdiction, and actors—can affect policy outcome, which is the substance of civil-military relations. By being able to influence the substance of policy as well as the power and interests of competing actors, institutions can affect the civil-military balance in favor of civilian authority. The goal should be to limit the military role to external defense. When it is necessary to deploy the military in an internal security role, it must remain under the close oversight of civilian authorities who themselves must be legitimate and accountable. Ultimately, civilian leaders and officials must have the jurisdiction to define and control the role of the military in governance and manage the military as a state institution, although certain powers may be delegated to the military in the interest of operational and administrative efficiency. To be durable, the deepening and consolidation of civilian supremacy must span the domains of power, ideas, and interests and be reflected in institutions, policy outcomes, and sustained practice.

ACKNOWLEDGMENTS

COVERING 16 COUNTRIES; INVOLVING 19 CONTRIBUTORS, 42 senior scholars, and 38 readers; and spanning more than three years, this project, like its predecessor, *Asian Security Practice,* has been a major undertaking and intellectually very demanding. The challenge was made more formidable by the absence of a widely accepted body of concepts, propositions, and theories in the subfield of civil-military relations as well as the paucity of theoretically informed studies of civil-military relations in Asia. The authors and I often found ourselves operating in relatively poorly mapped terrain, compelling us to cover much more new ground, both theoretically and empirically, than would be normal in this kind of enterprise. The challenges have certainly broadened and deepened our intellectual horizons, but the experience also has been humbling. Through interaction in two rigorous workshops, reading and rereading each other's papers, and continuous interchange through E-mail, the authors and I have learned a great deal from the project. We hope this book and the several policy papers that resulted from the project can make a modest contribution to the study and practice of civil-military relations in Asia and elsewhere. Also, we hope the reader will find the book as stimulating and rewarding as it has been for us to write it.

In keeping with my goals of promoting theoretically informed study of Asia-Pacific politics and security and fostering the development of a new generation of scholars who can engage in more rigorous scholarship that straddles theory and area studies, I invited mostly younger scholars to contribute the country chapters and involved more established scholars—theorists and regional and country specialists—to review, discuss, and comment on their work. Also, in light of the considerable work that has been done on civil-military relations in South America, Southern and Eastern Europe, and Africa, I invited experts on these regions to participate in the project. The authors and senior scholars drawn from South, Southeast, and East Asia, the United States, Australia, Latin America, and Europe met in two stimulating and productive workshops: first in October 1998 in Honolulu and then in Bangkok in April 1999.

From inception of the idea in late 1997 through the appearance of the book in print, the intellectual journey—described by the late Michel Oksenberg as a "long march"—has benefited enormously from interaction with and input from many scholars and practitioners. Felipe Aguero, Samina Ahmed, Suchit Bunbongkarn, Chu Shulong, Donald Crone, Harold Crouch, David Pion-Berlin, and Maj. Gen. Noboru Yamaguchi participated in both workshops. Zakaria

Haji Ahmad, Gen. Jose T. Almonte, Michael Aung-Thwin, Richard Baker, Thomas Berger, P. R. Chari, Maj. Gen. Bunchon Chawansin, Yun-han Chu, Sumit Ganguly, Mel Gurtov, Stephan Haggard, David Kang, James Kelly, Kwa Chong Guan, Lam Truong Buu, Robin Luckham, Ron May, Chung-in Moon, Charles Morrison, S. D. Muni, Koji Murata, Michel Oksenberg, Mochtar Pabottingi, Lt. Gen. V. R. Raghavan, Gowher Rizvi, Salim Said, Andrew Scobell, Takashi Shiraishi, Jeffrey Simon, Dae-sook Suh, Tin Maung Maung Than, Carlyle Thayer, Harold Trinkunas, and Iftekhar Zaman participated in one of the two workshops. All these scholars gave generously of their time and expertise. They read and reread several chapters, and some commented on the penultimate draft chapters. Itty Abraham, Vinod Aggarwal, Dewi Fortuna Anwar, Surachart Bambrungsuk, Maj. Gen. Dipankar Banerjee, Chua Beng Huat, Stephen Cohen, Frank deSilva, Narayanan Ganesan, Thomas Gold, Selig Harrison, Tim Huxley, Ellis Joffe, Kim Byung Kook, Kim Yung Myung, Sankaran Krishna, Carl Lande, William Liddle, Albert McCoy, Andrew Nathan, Jeremy Paltiel, T. J. Pempel, Susan Pharr, Ahmed Rashid, Hasan Askari Rizvi, Saeed Shafqat, David Shambaugh, James Shinn, John Sidel, Joseph Silverstein, David Steinberg, Jonathan Stromseth, Akihiko Tanaka, Robert Taylor, William Turley, Thongchai Winichakul, Richard Yang, and Yu Bin read one or more penultimate draft chapters. Larry Diamond read and commented on the entire manuscript and provided many helpful suggestions. To these scholars I would like to express my deep appreciation and thanks. They made an enormous contribution to the project. It has been my privilege—professionally and personally—to interact with them. Cristina Eguizabal and Marin Strmecki, though they were not direct participants, provided strong support for the project.

I would also like to thank the highly talented and hard-working contributors to this book. Their expert knowledge of the countries as well as of key issues in comparative politics greatly aided the intellectual refinement of the project as it progressed. Also, their willingness to ground their inquiry in a common framework and rework the chapters several times is admirable and has made for a more coherent book. Several contributors participated in open briefings on the subject for U.S. Congressional members and staff and for the Pentagon staff in February 2000. These and other more informal briefings conducted in Asia, as well as the five policy papers and another book on military professionalism in Asia from the project, are part of the East-West Center's attempt to make research at the center relevant for the policy community in Asia and the United States. Samina Ahmed, Dewi Fortuna Anwar, Surachart Bambrungsuk, Maj. Gen. Dipankar Banerjee, Gen. Sun Chin-ming, Christopher Collier, You Ji, J. Kristiadi, Lee Min-yong, Andrew Scobell, Tin Maung Maung Than, Carlyle Thayer, Harold Trinkunas, and Maj. Gen. Noboru Yamaguchi contributed to the military professionalism of the book and the policy papers.

Thanks are also due to the Ford Foundation and the Smith-Richardson Foundation for providing funding support; the Institute for Strategic and International Studies, Chulalongkarn University in Bangkok, for co-hosting the second workshop; the Woodrow Wilson International Center for Scholars for co-hosting the briefings in Washington; Charles Morrison, president of the East-West Center, for his support of the project; Jeanne Hamasaki for so ably organizing the two workshops; Christopher Collier, Yoshihisa Amae, Iati Iati, and Rosevelt Dela Cruz, who served as research assistants for the project; Don Yoder for his copyediting; Elisa Johnston, Sharon Yamamoto, and Carol Wong for overseeing the production of the policy papers; Phyllis Tabusa for assisting with the bibliography; Laura Moriyama for handling all the correspondence in relation to the project and simultaneously providing excellent support for my myriad activities as director of studies; and Lillian Shimoda for her efficient secretarial services in the past six months. Special thanks are due to Ann Takayesu, who again so efficiently word processed the entire manuscript and prepared it for submission to the Stanford University Press.

From a personal perspective, the past two years have been among the busiest in my life. This project along with two others had to be managed at the same time as reorganizing, integrating, reorienting, recruiting for, and managing the Research Program at the East-West Center in my capacity as director of studies. Without the understanding, patience, and support of my wife, Kalyani, I could not have performed the numerous and rewarding, though at times onerous, duties as director of studies. My research would have suffered and this book would not exist. I would like to express my deepest appreciation to her as well as to my children Radha, Shanthi, and Padma. I would like to dedicate this book to Vikram, who has brought a new meaning and perspective to life.

Muthiah Alagappa

CONTRIBUTORS

MUTHIAH ALAGAPPA is Senior Fellow and Director of Studies at the East-West Center in Honolulu. He has a Ph.D. in International Affairs from the Fletcher School of Law and Diplomacy, Tufts University. His research interests include international relations theory, international politics in the Asia-Pacific, and comparative politics in Asia.

MARY P. CALLAHAN is Assistant Professor at the Jackson School of International Studies, University of Washington. She has a Ph.D. in Political Science from Cornell University. Her research interests include military politics, historical memory, and ethnic politics.

SUNIL DASGUPTA is a Ph.D. candidate at the University of Illinois at Urbana-Champaign. Previously, he was defense correspondent for *India Today* magazine (in New Delhi). His research interests include civil-military relations, military history, nationalism, ethnic conflict, and foreign policy.

GEETHA GOVINDASAMY is Lecturer at the Department of East Asian Studies, University of Malaya, Kuala Lumpur, Malaysia. She has an M.Phil. from Queens' College, Cambridge (U.K.) and an M.A. from the International University of Japan. Her research interests include politics, foreign policy, and security issues in the Asia-Pacific.

EVA-LOTTA E. HEDMAN is Millennium Research Fellow in the Department of Politics, School of Oriental and African Studies at the University of London. She has a Ph.D. from the Department of Government at Cornell University. Her research and writing focuses on the politics of social movements and civil society, as well as the mobilization of "uncivil" society and political violence in Southeast Asia, with a particular emphasis on the Philippines.

JINSOK JUN is Researcher at the Center for International Studies and Lecturer at Inha University, Incheon, Korea. He has a Ph.D. in Political Science from the University of Kentucky. His research interests include civil-military relations and security and intelligence institutions.

EIICHI KATAHARA is Associate Professor, Faculty of Law, at Kobe Gakuin University. He has a Ph.D. in Asian and International Studies from Griffith University. His research interests include Japan's foreign and security policies and Asia-Pacific political, economic, and security issues.

CHIH-CHENG LO is Associate Professor in the Department of Political Science at Soochow University (Taipei). He has a Ph.D. in Political Science from the University of California, Los Angeles. His current research interests include international relations theory, U.S. foreign policy, cross-Strait relations, Asian regional security, and game theory.

AMENA MOHSIN is Professor in the Department of International Relations at University of Dhaka. She received a Ph.D. from the Faculty of Social and Political Sciences at Cambridge University. Her research interests include ethnicity, minority, and gender issues.

CHUNG-IN MOON is Professor of Political Science and Director of the Institute for Korean Unification Studies at Yonsei University, Seoul, Korea. He has a Ph.D. in Political Science from the University of Maryland. He is currently writing a book on the political economy of defense industrialization in South Korea.

JAMES MULVENON is Associate Political Scientist at RAND. He has a Ph.D. in Political Science from the University of California, Los Angeles. His research interests include Chinese military affairs, information warfare, and missile defenses.

K. S. NATHAN is Professor of International Relations at University of Malaya, Kuala Lumpur, Malaysia. He has a Ph.D. in International Relations from Claremont Graduate School. His teaching, research, and publications are in the areas of strategic studies, big power relations in the Asia-Pacific region, ASEAN regionalism, and Malaysian security and foreign policy.

JAMES OCKEY is Senior Lecturer at Canterbury University, Christchurch, New Zealand. He has a Ph.D. from the Department of Government, Cornell University. His research interests include poverty and democracy, crime and politics, and culture and leadership.

DARINI RAJASINGHAM-SENANAYAKE is Senior Fellow at Social Scientists' Association and International Centre for Ethnic Studies, Colombo, Sri Lanka. She has a Ph.D. from the Department of Anthropology, Princeton University. Her research interests include multiculturalism, nationalism, armed conflict, women in conflict, migration, refugee studies, minority rights, and the humanitarian regime.

GEOFFREY ROBINSON is Associate Professor of History at the University of California, Los Angeles, where he teaches and writes about Indonesia and Southeast Asia generally. He has a Ph.D. in Government from Cornell University. Before coming to UCLA, he worked for six years at Amnesty International's research department in London. From June to November 1999 he served as a Political Affairs Officer with UNAMET (United Nations Mission in East Timor) in Dili, East Timor.

BABAR SATTAR is a graduate student at the University of Oxford, United Kingdom. He has an M.Sc. in International Relations from Quaid-i-Azam University, Islamabad, Pakistan. His area of research and interest is law.

HIDESHI TAKESADA is Professor and Chief of the Third Research Department at the National Institute for Defense Studies, Japan. He has an M.A. in Political Science from Keio University. His research interests include politics and international relations of Korea.

TAN TAI YONG is Associate Professor and Acting Head in the Department of History at National University of Singapore. He has a Ph.D. in History from Cambridge University. His research interests include partition and its impact in South Asia and the international history of South and Southeast Asia.

THAVEEPORN VASAVAKUL is currently Southeast Asia Regional Director at the Council on International Educational Exchange and Resident Director of Study Center at the Vietnam National University in Hanoi. She has a Ph.D. from the Department of Government at Cornell University. Focusing mainly on Southeast Asia, her research interests include transition from authoritarianism and socialism, politics of institution building, and identity politics.

COERCION AND GOVERNANCE

The Declining Political Role of the Military in Asia

Introduction

Muthiah Alagappa

My dear countrymen. The choice before us on October 12 [1999] was between saving the nation and the constitution. As the constitution is but part of the nation, I chose to save the nation.... This is not martial law, only another path toward democracy. The armed forces have no intention to stay in charge any longer than is absolutely necessary to pave the way for true democracy to flourish in Pakistan.

—Chief Executive Gen. Pervaiz Musharaf

The [Indonesian military] knows the whole society is changing [and] that [it] has to change its attitude toward society. We have a strong military and we need it.... Some of our generals are good, some are bad, like in any other society.

The problem is that we have to take a very gradual approach to [the military].... I waited for the results of the National Commission on Human Rights investigation of alleged military violation of human rights in East Timor.... If [General Wiranto] is implicated, [I will say to him] it is better to save the institution, the Indonesian Armed Forces, so you have to resign.

We must not act like we did in the past. Our soldiers went to Aceh and attacked the people. It must not happen again...the people are not our enemy.

We need a strong military to defend our country. But that does not mean we want to return to a military state.

—President Abdurrahmand Wahid

IN A LIGHTNING COUP D'ÉTAT ON OCTOBER 12, 1999, Pakistan's army chief Gen. Pervaiz Musharaf ousted democratically elected prime minister Nawaz Sharif. Citing the crumbling economy, the diplomatic isolation of Pakistan and its loss of international credibility, the destruction of state institutions by civilian political leaders, cracks in the federation, and an alleged intrigue by Sharif to sow discord and dissension within the armed forces, Musharaf, promising good governance, proclaimed himself the chief executive of the country. He instituted a system of government comprising the sitting president, a six-member National Security Council (NSC) headed by Musharaf himself and supported by a think tank, and a cabinet of ministers who will work under the guidance of the NSC, and he appointed provincial governors who will function through a small cabinet. Although Musharaf pledged to free the people of

Pakistan from the "yoke of despotism" and move Pakistan from "sham democracy" to "true democracy," he refused to indicate how and when he will return power to an elected civilian government. However, following the May 12, 2000, ruling of the reconstituted supreme court that validated the October coup and gave him sweeping powers to amend the 1973 constitution, Musharaf has committed himself to the mandate of the court to carry out the necessary social and political reforms and announce a date for national elections 90 days before the expiry of the three-year period in October 2002.[1] There is no guarantee that national elections will be held by this date.

About the same time that the military was taking control of the political helm in Pakistan, the Indonesian military (Tentera Nasional Indonesia [TNI])—which had been part of the political leadership for more than 30 years and which many observers at home and abroad depicted as a crucial player in the ongoing political transition in that country—was unexpectedly and rather deftly being dislodged from the corridors of power.[2] Following the last-minute withdrawal of sitting president B.J. Habibie from the presidential competition, in a dramatic development the People's Consultative Assembly elected Abdurrahmand Wahid, a moderate Muslim cleric, and Megawati Sukarnoputri, daughter of the first president, as the fourth president and vice-president of Indonesia, respectively. Successive unexpected developments, especially the formation of a "national unity cabinet" with representation from a wide range of political parties spanning almost the entire Indonesian political spectrum, dramatically undercut the military's political power and influence, which was already on the wane since the ouster of Suharto in May 1998. Instead of playing a kingmaker role, as widely anticipated in the run-up to the presidential election, the military, at least in the short term, has been sidelined under a democratically elected civilian leadership. General Wiranto, chief of the thitherto powerful TNI, had to pull out of the vice-presidential race, resign his TNI position, and accept a less powerful appointment as coordinating minister for political and security affairs in Wahid's national unity cabinet. (Four months later he would be forced to resign from this position for alleged involvement in the TNI's human rights violations in East Timor.) For the first time, a civilian was appointed defense minister, and the position of TNI commander went to a naval officer.

Though highly dramatic, the developments in Pakistan and Indonesia are not unique to these countries. Throughout much of Asia, the military is still a crucial actor in domestic and international politics, playing key roles in state and nation building, in political domination, in maintaining internal order, and in ensuring international security. However, the political role of the military and more generally the patterns of civil-military relations in Asia span a wide spectrum, ranging from firm democratic civilian control of the military in Japan and India through consolidation of such control in South Korea and Taiwan; transition to democratic civilian control in the Philippines, Thailand, Bangladesh, and Indonesia; subjective (ethnic and dominant party) civilian control of the military in Singapore, Malaysia, and Sri Lanka; communist party control of the military in China and Vietnam; totalitarian dictatorship control of the military in North Korea; and military domination of the state in Pakistan and Burma.

Further, the relationship of the soldier to the state in Asia is not a settled issue. Substantive change is occurring in nearly every country. Though change has been more fundamental in Taiwan, South Korea, the Philippines, Thailand, Bangladesh, and Indonesia, the basis and content of civil-military relations in established democracies like Japan and India are also experiencing change. Change is also occurring in party-military relations in the Asian socialist states of China and Vietnam, and in the totalitarian regime in North Korea. In fact, because of the ongoing economic transitions in China and Vietnam and the likely political changes that may follow, civil-military relations in these countries may be in for more far-reaching change in the years ahead.

Looking to the future, although the military in a number of countries continues to wield considerable political influence that may even increase, the long-term trend in Asia is toward a reduction in the political power and influence of the military and strengthening of civilian control, especially democratic civilian control of the military. Compared to the 1960s and 1970s, when seven or eight countries were under military rule or military-backed rule, at the time of writing there are only two or three (Burma, Pakistan, and perhaps North Korea). This number could increase, but a throwback to earlier periods appears highly unlikely. The states, societies, and economies in Asia are becoming more vibrant and complex, and the international context has altered decidedly in favor of democracy, capitalism, and human rights. The balance of power is increasingly tilted against the military. In any case, military intervention, as proven time and again, does not provide the solution to the many multifaceted and complex political and economic challenges confronting the Asian countries. In earlier times, an economic crisis like the one that occurred in 1997 would have been an opportunity for the military to intervene. This time, however, the South Korean and Thai militaries stood on the sidelines while civilian political leaders, bureaucrats, and technocrats managed the crisis. Even so, the reduction in the military's political role and consolidation of democratic civilian control of the military are likely to be gradual and complex and prone to violence and occasional setbacks. And, "ultimately," there still will be substantial variations across Asia in the relationship of the soldier to the state.

The continuing political salience of the military, the enormous diversity in state-soldier relations, and the trend in Asia toward democratic civilian control raise several important questions: Why do some militaries dominate the state or continue to exercise considerable political influence while others have abstained from or terminated their political roles? Why have militaries with a similar background (India, Pakistan, Bangladesh, and Sri Lanka, for example, and China and Taiwan) behaved so differently? Why have some militaries (South Korea and Taiwan) disengaged almost completely from politics while others (Pakistan and Burma) find it difficult to kick this habit? Can the communist parties in China and Vietnam continue to monopolize political power and maintain control over the military while liberalizing their economies? Such questions are explored in this comparative study of civil-military relations in Asia.

PURPOSE AND PROPOSITIONS

Seeking to illuminate the relationship between the soldier and the state in sixteen Asian countries, this study explores and explains ongoing changes and anticipates future trajectories in this relationship. Specifically, it investigates the following questions.

1. What is the relationship between the military and the other institutions of the state—particularly those that are the containers of political power?

2. Has this relationship changed over time? How and why?

3. What is the anticipated trajectory of civil-military relations in Asia? And, why?

Civil-military relations covers not only the relationship of the military to the state but also its relationship to the political and civil societies—and civil-military relations are influenced by state-society relations as well. But to keep the study manageable, we shall not deal with military-society and state-society relations except as they bear upon the relationship between the soldier and the state. Thus, although the "civil" component of the term "civil-military" normally refers to the state (minus the military), political society, and civil society,[3] it is used more narrowly in this study to refer to the nonmilitary apparatus of state—especially the political, administrative, and juridical institutions. In communist states, the term "civil" refers to the communist party and associated institutions. The army, navy, and air force (and the marine corps where applicable) form the core of the term "military." It also includes police and paramilitary forces whose tasks are to maintain internal order and border security, as well as security and intelligence agencies. In all these civil and military institutions our concern is with the leadership, especially those individuals and groups who formulate and execute policy on issues relating to military-civilian interaction. The individuals may or may not hold the most senior positions in their organizations; the groups may be formal or informal.

Further, although the focus of the study is on the relationship of the military as an institution to the other state institutions, it is investigated in the broader context of the connection between coercion (which includes but is not limited to force) and governance (which in this study includes nation and state building, the structure and process of political domination, the maintenance of internal order, and safeguarding the international security of the state). This approach is premised on the belief that the relationship of the soldier to the state is strongly influenced by the weight of coercion in governance. We believe that such a broad inquiry, which has not been common in the study of civil-military relations, will provide new insights and connect the subfield of civil-military relations to the larger issues in comparative politics.

The study advances two sets of explanatory propositions. The first set is rooted in the fact that state coercion plays a key role in building national political communities, in the structure of political domination, in extending the reach of government, in maintaining law and order, and in preserving international security. As the primary (though not exclusive) repository of state coercion, the military is a key institution in governance. Participation in governance endows the military with power and influence, the magnitude of which varies with the importance or weight of coercion relative to norms, rules, law, and custom in the practice of governance. The argument here is that as state coercion becomes more prominent, especially in domestic politics, the size of the military as well as its scope and jurisdiction expands, usually to the detriment of other institutions of the state, tilting the distribution of power in favor of the military. The weight of coercion in governance in turn is influenced by two key factors: one is the domestic and international legitimacy of the nation-state and the political system, and the second is the level of economic development. Rooted in the interplay of coercion, legitimacy, and economic development, the first set comprises three interconnected propositions.

1. The main proposition is that as the weight of coercion in governance rises (or declines), so does the political power and influence of the military. When the weight of coer-

cion in governance is low, civilian supremacy is likely to be the norm. Conversely, military or military-backed rule is highly likely when coercion is the mainstay of political domination.

2. The weight of coercion in governance is inversely proportional to the legitimacy of the nation-state and political system and the capacity of the noncoercive institutions of the state to address the challenges confronting the country. If the nation-state and political system are widely accepted and the political, administrative, and legal institutions of the state are capable of addressing the problems confronting the country through political, economic, and social measures, then coercion will not figure prominently in governance and vice versa.

3. The weight of coercion in governance declines with increasing levels of economic development. Sustained economic development in the capitalist mode makes for a complex economy (that is highly integrated into the global economy) as well as for a more complex state and society. The noncoercive institutions of the state, the capacity of which should increase with sustained economic development, assume greater prominence in the political and administrative management of the state. Coercion becomes less central to the management of the challenges that confront the country.

Together, the three propositions above can explain long-term changes in civil-military relations, but they are less useful (though not irrelevant) in explaining specific developments. Their primary function is in setting structural constraints. Explanation of specific developments must focus on the level of agency—institutions and personalities. This leads to the second set of propositions. Because an array of causal factors may be at work and their salience and mix may be case specific, the focus of the second set of propositions is on the intervening variables of beliefs, interests, and power of the key actors as well as the nature and strength of the political system. The concern is not the numerous (uncontrollable) factors but how they may affect the three intervening variables and with what consequence for civil-military relations. The three propositions that comprise the second set are enumerated below.

4. The pattern and content of state-soldier relations are the outcome of the interaction of the interests, power, and beliefs of the civilian and military institutions mediated by the power and influence of civil society and the international community.

5. Where the political system is widely accepted, the principles and norms of that system will determine the pattern of civil-military relations. The specific content, however, will be an outcome of the interplay of the competing interests of the relevant key actors and the distribution of power among them.

6. In situations where the political system is contested sharply or is in transition, then the distribution of power becomes crucial. Explanations of specific developments in civil-military relations in this context must necessarily turn on the distribution of power among the key actors and their competing interests. As the configuration of power among the key state institutions as well as their beliefs and interests are affected by the state of civil society and the key external actors, they must also feature in the analysis of civil-military developments.

These two sets of propositions, fleshed out in greater detail in Chapter 1, are particularly relevant to Asia, where most of the states are postcolonial and relatively recent in origin. State coercion figured prominently in the early years in the internal and international consolidation of these states as well as in political domination. The high salience of coercion increased the power and influence of the military in a large number of countries, leading in several cases to military intervention and domination of the state. Over time, with success in economic development and the development of noncoercive state institutions, as well as the construction of legitimate political systems for the acquisition and exercise of state power, the salience of coercion and by extension the power and influence of the military declined in some countries. In countries that failed in economic development and that have not had much success in developing a widely accepted political system, as well as in those that alienated or have been unable to integrate minority communities, coercion has continued to figure prominently in governance. In these countries, the power and influence of the military have remained unaltered or even increased. We explore and develop these themes fully in the concluding chapter of the book. Next, we discuss the nature of the civil-military problem in conceptual terms and its manifestation in the countries investigated in the study.

THE NATURE OF THE CIVIL-MILITARY PROBLEM IN THE MODERN STATE

Force is a critical feature of the modern state. Max Weber claimed that monopoly over the legitimate use of force was as essential a characteristic of the state as compulsory jurisdiction and continuous organization in a territory (Weber 1964: 156). Though critical of Weber in several respects, including his backward generalization of the state, Anthony Giddens acknowledges territoriality and control over violence as key features of the state.[4] Defining a state as a political organization "whose rule is territorially ordered and which is able to mobilize the means of violence to sustain that rule," he posits that only in the modern state can the state apparatus lay successful claim to the monopoly of the means of violence (Giddens 1987: 20, 120). Centralized control over the means of violence is one of the four "institutional clusterings" that Giddens identifies with modernity.[5] Though force was a feature of the traditional state, it is the monopoly mechanism and centralized control that distinguish the modern state (Elias 1998). Chronic threats to the monopoly of force do exist in certain contemporary states, but as noted by Giddens (1987: 121), the modern state is nevertheless different from the traditional state in that "armed groups or movements today are almost always oriented to the assumption of state power either by taking over an existing state's territory or by dividing up a territory and establishing a separate state." Monopoly of coercion has become an essential component of definitions of the modern state in the Weberian tradition, which is the dominant contemporary perspective on the state.[6]

The quest for monopoly over coercion was a driving force in the formation of Western European nation-states. Charles Tilly (1975, 1985, 1992) traces the origins of European states to "the effort to monopolize the means of violence within a delimited territory adjacent to a power holder's base" (1989: 172). His argument is that state making in Europe was shaped by the interaction of war making, resource extraction, and capital accumulation. To secure the benefits of power within a fixed or expanding territory, European rulers engaged in war with their competitors. War making required bureaucratic organization and the extraction of resources from subjects as well as the promotion of capital accumulation by those who could finance the acquisition of war-making capability by the rulers. According to Tilly (1992: 90–91), the capital-intensive and coercion-intensive methods of resource extraction were less successful than the capitalized-coercion method; the latter had a decided advantage in warfare. Consequently, the national state—the product of the capitalized-coercion method—won out over other forms of state, including city-states, empires, and urban federations.

Apart from its central role in the consolidation of European states, force featured prominently in political domination and the maintenance of internal order. Weber, however, makes clear that "domination of men by men" in the modern state rests on rational-legal authority— "on a belief in the 'legality' of patterns of normative rules and the right of those elevated to authority under such rules to issue commands" (Weber 1964: 131, 328). Laws and custom are the primary means of regulating society in the modern state. The abstract availability of physical violence, however, is necessary to ensure their efficacy (Luhmann 1985: 169). By ensuring that those who violate the socially accepted rules will be punished, physical force leads to clear outcomes, increases the security of expectations, and makes for greater regularity of social interaction. Force is thus the ultimate sanction and an integral part of state authority. It is legitimate only when "permitted by the state or prescribed by it" (Weber 1964: 156). The use of force by other entities is illegal. In a similar vein, Giddens (1987) notes that although force still plays a role in the internal administration of the modern state, force-related sanctions have become attenuated and indirect. He distinguishes between internally directed policing power to maintain law and order and externally directed military power to protect the state from outside aggression. Monopoly by the state removes force as a factor in domestic politics and shifts attention to the international domain, where force is still a legitimate means to achieve political ends.

Notwithstanding this shift and the indirect role of force in political domination and the maintenance of internal order, force continues to be a central feature of the modern state. Claiming supreme jurisdiction and autonomy in decision making, governments seek monopoly over coercion within defined territorial boundaries. This quest gives rise to two interconnected problems. The first stems from the goal of concentrating force in the state and denying it to nonstate groups. Only a few states have been successful in this quest. In many countries, the quest for state monopoly of coercion has been challenged by groups that do not subscribe to the nation, state, and political system as presently constructed and who reserve the right to use force in pursuing their political ends. Not only may governments be subject to violent challenges in such situations, but a lack of monopoly over coercion may also undermine the effectiveness of their governance, including control over their own militaries. The inability of the state to monopolize force and the possession of the means of organized violence by nonstate groups pose a problem that is usually not labeled as a civil-military problem. However, it is a problem with consequence for civil-military relations. The state has to deal with a military organization over which it has no authority and that challenges the very existence and authority of the state. Further, the existence of nonstate organized violence intensifies the role of coercion in governance, complicating the relationship between the state and its military as well as between them and society.

The second, more conventional civil-military problem relates to the control of the managers of violence. Having concentrated force in the state, the challenge then is to prevent the coercive institutions from dominating the state and society and to ensure that state coercion is used in the service of the public interest, not for private and partisan purposes. As the primary repository of the ultimate means of state violence, the military is a key institution of the state, comparable to the civilian bureaucracy and the judiciary. However, because of the brute force at their disposal, the institutions that manage state coercion—the military, paramilitary, police, and intelligence agencies—can become powerful actors with potential to trump the other institutions. They may seek to deploy the power at their disposal to curb liberty, impose their own will on the state and the community to be protected, or further their own corporate and individual interests. Preventing military domination of the state, promoting control by a civilian government that itself is legitimate and accountable to its citizens, limiting the deployment of state coercion for public purposes, defining the proper role and jurisdiction of the military, and regulating the military as an institution are among the key concerns that lie at the heart of the civil-military problem. The resolution of this problem and related issues requires the development of civilian supremacy or civilian control. Civilian supremacy is "government control of the military," and the criteria for civilian control is "the extent to which military leadership groups, and through them the armed forces as a whole, respond to the direction of the civilian leaders of the government" (Huntington 1956: 380). Huntington identifies two types of civilian control: objective and subjective. In objective control, there is a clear divide between the government and the military, and the latter obeys the former not because it shares the social values and political ideologies of society but "because it is its duty to obey." In subjective control, there is no clear divide between the government and military. The military embodies the values and ideologies in society, and it obeys the government because it agrees with it. The military's loyalty is not to any government in power but to a specific government or a specific type of government. Under subjective control, the divisions in society are reflected in the military. And, civilian control is usually associated with the maximization of the power of "particular social classes, and particular constitutional forms" (Huntington 1956: 382).

The nature of the civil-military problem and the issues to be addressed vary by political system. In the democratic system, the concern is to ensure a professional and apolitical military that acknowledges civilian authority and executes the orders of a democratically elected government. Though there may be variations, at base civilian authority is supreme in a democratic system. In a communist system, the concern is to indoctrinate and secure the political loyalty of the military and mobilize its support for the party and its goals. The goal is to ensure party supremacy over the military. Ensuring the loyalty of the military, maintaining tight control over it, and deploying it to serve the goals of the dictator are the concerns in a personal dictatorship, especially of the totalitarian type. Even a military regime is not free of the problem. Here the challenge is for the "military as government" to control and retain the loyalty of the "military as an institution."[7] These are generic problems. Specific problems will vary by country and stage of development.

In Western Europe and the United States, for the most part, states have monopoly on force, the role of force in domestic politics and governance has become indirect and attenuated, and the institutions that manage state coercion are under the control of legitimate governments. The militaries in these countries acknowledge civilian authority and act in the service of the state and society as directed by democratically elected governments primarily, if not exclusively, in the international security role. As observed by Michael Howard (1959), the civil-military problem in these countries "is not over [political] power but priorities." It centers in large part on interdepartmental contentions over matters of defense, including strategy, force posture, budget allocation, operational autonomy, and commitment of troops. Democratic civilian control of the military is the norm in these countries, although concerns continue to be raised from time to time about the military's increasing influence, the rise of militarism, and the growing cultural divide between the military and society.[8]

In South America, where military juntas were common, there has been a rise in democratic civilian rule since the late 1970s. Following the elections in Ecuador in 1979, Peru, Argentina, Brazil, Chile, and other South American countries elected civilian leaders, including opposition figures to government. Most of the democratic transitions occurred under constitutional frameworks devised by the military-authoritarian rulers, but the latter were not able to control the pace of liberalization or the outcomes (Aguero 1997). However, the militaries still managed to retain certain prerogatives, and there are several major challenges to be overcome in establishing civilian supremacy and consolidating democracy in the South American countries. Nevertheless, civilian control of the military has been on the rise. In Brazil, for example, contrary to the expectation that the military would continue to be an extraordinarily powerful force in the post-transition era, elected politicians have been able to considerably narrow its sphere of influence (Hunter 1997). Recent developments, such as the ouster of the civilian government in Ecuador in January 2000, the earlier election of former military officers to power in Bolivia, Venezuela, and Guatemala, and the Fujimori government's increasing reliance on the Peruvian military, however, have raised concerns about the resurgence of military political influence on that continent. These developments notwithstanding, the failure of the attempt to create a National Salvation Junta in Ecuador suggests that a return to the earlier military junta era appears unlikely. In general, military attitudes toward politics in South American countries are more likely to be defensive to protect their institutional autonomy than to be proactive to destabilize civilian regimes (Pion-Berlin 1992). However, more subtle forms of military influence, such as backing for specific governments, are still in the cards.

The situation in Asia is unlike that in Western Europe. In some ways, it is similar to that in South America, but the situation in Asia is much more diverse and complex. State coercion plays a crucial, direct, and visible role in Asian countries: in state and nation building, in political domination, in maintaining internal order, and in ensuring international security. State formation in Asia is still in an early stage and differs sharply from the West—in some ways, the process is the inverse of that in Western Europe. Competition, elimination, monopolization, and development of centralized control are occurring but within internationally recognized political units whose boundaries, for the most part, have been fixed. With a few exceptions (Japan, Thailand, China, Nepal), contemporary Asian states have colonial origins, and their territorial boundaries were demarcated by colonial powers. Asian states entered into and exist in an international system that naturalizes the norms associated with the Westphalian state, and Asian leaders aspire to the normative ideal of the modern nation-state. They seek to build nations and states on the basis of the colonial units they inherited. And, to consolidate their positions as well as their constructions of state and national identity, they seek to eliminate rival ideas, leaders, and groups.

Force plays a crucial role in their efforts to achieve internal consolidation. It has been deployed quite freely and on a massive scale in support of nation building—especially in relation to segments of minority communities that resist "national" integration. Force is a key component of the policies and strategies of Beijing vis-à-vis the Tibetans and Uighurs; Manila vis-à-vis the Moros; Bangkok vis-à-vis the Malay Muslims in southern Thailand; Jakarta vis-à-vis the East Timorese, West Papuans, and Acehnese; Yangon vis-à-vis the many minority nationalities in Burma; Dhaka vis-à-vis the Chittagong Hill tribal people; Colombo vis-à-vis the Tamils; and New Delhi vis-à-vis the Muslim Kashmiris and the Assamese, Naga, Mizo-ram, and Manipur peoples in northeastern India.

Coercion plays a central role as well in the structure and process of political domination. Rulers in a number of Asian countries rely on coercion to maintain their position and secure compliance from their citizens and subjects. State coercion was a crucial pillar of the Syngman Rhee, Park Chung-hee, and Chun Doo-hwan governments in South Korea; Mao Zedong's rule in China; the Kuomintang (KMT)-led governments in Taiwan until 1987; the Marcos dicta-torship in the Philippines; and the military governments in Thailand, Pakistan, Bangladesh, and Indonesia. This is still the case in North Korea, Burma, and Pakistan and, in some respects, in Indonesia, Sri Lanka, Bangladesh, Vietnam, and China as well. Even in countries like India, Malaysia, and Singapore, where political systems have become more firmly established, state coercion continues to be a critical feature that is not far removed from direct application.

The tension and conflict arising from nation-state building and political legitimation proj-ects—together with the ethnic, sectarian, caste, and class conflicts endemic in many of these societies—make the maintenance of law and order in Asian countries a formidable task requir-ing routine deployment of state coercion, sometimes on a massive scale. This is evidenced in the vast array of internal security legislation and the dramatic growth in paramilitary forces and security/intelligence agencies throughout Asia (Collier 1999).

Force is also crucial in the international relations of Asian states. North Korea, South Korea, and Taiwan confront acute political and military threats to their survival. India and Pakistan have an acute conflict over Kashmir that goes to the heart of the political identity of these two states. Many states including China, India, and Japan have territorial conflicts with neighboring states. And, too, there are deep-seated apprehensions and rivalries among most of the Asian states. The threat and use of military force play a central role in all these conflicts and rivalries. Regional cooperation is commanding increasing attention, but it is unlikely to become the mainstay of national security policy. Most Asian states rely on their own national military capabilities; a few (South Korea, Japan, Taiwan) rely on their allies as well.

Because of the centrality of coercion in political domination (including regime security), in nation building, and for international security, governments in Asia, like their counterparts elsewhere, seek exclusive control over the means and use of coercion within their territorial boundaries and allocate a substantial percentage of state revenues to institutions that are the repositories of state coercion. This claim to monopoly of coercion is challenged in several coun-tries—especially by minority communities that challenge the legitimacy of the nation-state and the political system as constructed. They too seek to acquire and deploy force in pursuit of their goals, which often run counter to those of the state. The Sri Lankan case where the Liberation Tigers of Tamil Eelam (LTTE) have the ability to engage the government forces in major bat-tles is the most dramatic example. But many other nonstate groups, including several guerrilla groups in Kashmir and the northeastern states of India, the Moro Islamic Liberation Front (MILF) and the Abu Sayyaf group in the Philippines, the Gerakan Aceh Merdeka (GAM) and the Organisasi Papua Merdeka (OPM) in Indonesia, and the several minority insurgent forces in Burma, also pose serious challenges to the authority of the state. The possession of organized violence by these nonstate groups and the challenge they pose to state authority expose the affected countries to the first type of civil-military problem.

The second, conventional type of civil-military problem is even more widespread in Asia. The militaries in several Asian countries are not subordinate to civilian authority. They have entered the structure of political domination. In Burma, Pakistan, and North Korea (and until recently in Indonesia), the military dominates the political process and determines national goals and agenda. In the Philippines, Thailand, and Bangladesh, although the military has formally disengaged from politics, it continues to wield substantial informal influence in the political process. Even in countries like South Korea and Taiwan where military disengagement from politics is more complete, the militaries still seek to preserve institutional autonomy as well as a key role in the formulation (as opposed to limiting themselves to implementation) of security policy. The militaries in these and other countries still have substantial off-budget revenues through their extensive commercial interests and ventures. Some seek to legitimate their developmental role. Many also engage in illegal activities for personal and corporate profit.

The specific nature of the civil-military problem varies by country. In Japan, the challenge is in determining how to move toward a more normal democratic pattern of civil-military relations. In India, Sri Lanka, and the Philippines, a key challenge is to prevent the abuse of state power and erosion of democratic rights at the local level when the military is deployed in the internal security role. In Taiwan, a remaining challenge relates to the need to shift the loyalty of the military from the KMT to the Taiwanese state and the incumbent government. Another challenge in Taiwan and also in South Korea and Thailand is to delineate the proper role of the military in security policymaking. The divestment of military-owned enterprises in all these countries is another major concern. In Indonesia and Bangladesh, the concern is to ensure civilian supremacy across a broad spectrum of issues and, even more urgently, to prevent a military coup. In China and to a lesser degree in Vietnam, the concern is with maintaining military loyalty and party supremacy over the military. Divesting the military from its business enterprises is also a major concern in China.

The problem in Pakistan is multifaceted and centers on the military's overwhelming domination of state and society. In Burma, there is no civil-military problem in the conventional sense, but there is the concern of the military government to maintain control over the military institution, especially the field commanders. There is, of course, a larger civil-military problem rooted in the conflicting desire of the military to continue its dominant political position and that of a large segment of the population to move toward a democratic political system. The above list is not exhaustive, and the nature of the civil-military problem in each country is much more complex and multifaceted than depicted. The purpose here is to provide an indication of the salience and diverse nature of the civil-military problem in Asia.

THE CHANGING NATURE
OF CIVIL-MILITARY RELATIONS IN ASIA

As demonstrated by developments during the past two decades in Pakistan, Indonesia, North Korea, Taiwan, South Korea, Bangladesh, the Philippines, Sri Lanka, and China, the relationship between and among the institutions that are the containers of state political power

and those that manage state coercion are in the midst of substantive and in some cases fundamental change. Change is more pronounced in states undergoing political system transformation. In these countries, the redefinition of civil-military relations is in many ways a struggle
among competing political and military elites over the scope, jurisdiction, and role of the military in the structure of political domination as well as the issue of civilian control over the military in other key arenas. Though less dramatic, civil-military relations are also undergoing
change in the other countries, including established democracies such as India and Japan. As
the chapters in this book make clear, the nature and intensity of the struggle and change vary
from country to country and span a wide spectrum.

Change in Democratic States

The military establishments in Japan and India continue to submit to democratic civilian control. Political changes in these countries as well as changes in the missions and roles of the military, however, appear to be altering the basis for this subordination as well as the content,
though not the pattern of their civil-military relations. In Japan, the changing domestic political landscape as well as the altered international security situation and the growing role of the
Japanese Self-Defense Forces (SDF) in coping with natural disasters, in international peacekeeping, in the defense of Japan, and in providing international security in the Far East are
contributing to the rehabilitation of the military, increasing its legitimacy, and possibly also raising its social and political standing, thus altering the purpose and basis for civilian control of
the military. Eiichi Katahara (see Chapter 2) identifies three important changes in civil-military
relations in Japan: from bureaucratic to political control of the SDF, the increasing stature and
power of the SDF vis-à-vis other ministries and agencies, and popular acceptance of the SDF.
Based on these changes, he argues that civil-military relations in Japan are moving from containment of the military to a more normal democratic pattern of civil-military relations.

In the case of India, it is argued that weakening political institutions and the increased
internal security role of the Indian armed forces are altering and possibly eroding the basis for
civilian supremacy and that concordance or subjective civilian control rather than objective
civilian control increasingly characterizes civil-military relations in India (Cohen 1990a; Ganguly 1991a; Kukreja 1991; Schiff 1995). Sumit Ganguly (1991a) argued that repeated use of the
army to quell communal violence would politicize it and erode the army's long-standing tradition of political neutrality. Sunil Dasgupta (see Chapter 3) argues that the military's growing
internal security role has undermined democratic civilian control at the local level and increased
the friction between the civilian bureaucracy and the military. As examples of civil-military
friction he cites the dismissal of naval chief Admiral Bhagwat and the military's efforts to reject
domination by the civilian bureaucracy. He goes on to argue, however, that friction with the
civilian bureaucracy and the growing internal security role are unlikely to undermine civilian
control over the military at the national level, which is shifting from bureaucratic control to
control by democratically elected political leaders. In his view, the growing "militarization" of
the political, technical, and administrative leadership, which blurs the civil-military divide, poses
the greater threat to substantive (as opposed to formal institutional) democratic civilian control
of the military in India.

Consolidation of Democratic Civilian Control

Civil-military relations in South Korea and Taiwan have been fundamentally transformed from an authoritarian to a democratic pattern. The military in South Korea has almost completely disengaged from politics, and the prospect of a coup appears rather remote. The election of long-time opposition leader Kim Dae-jung as the first minority president in 1997 and the military's support for his sunshine policy, which it initially viewed as appeasement of North Korea, are indicative of the distance that has been traveled in a short time. President Kim Young-sam, the first elected civilian prime minister of South Korea, took a series of decisive measures that effectively discredited the military and reduced its power and prerogatives (Luckham 1996a: 220–22). These measures included the purge of a large number of the senior members of the powerful Hana faction; removal of more than twenty senior generals, including the chief of staff, for alleged corruption; and the prosecution of Chun Doo-hwan and Roh Tae-woo, former generals turned president, for their role in the suppression of the 1980 Kwangju "prodemocracy" uprising. The military promotion and assignment system has also been overhauled, although regional and school ties still continue to be a factor. The power and role of the various security and intelligence agencies, which now come under the control of civilians, have been seriously curtailed. Nevertheless, there are still a few issues—the strong influence of the military in making security policy, for example, and the institutions and procedures for civilian oversight of the military—that must be redefined and developed (Moon 1989) (see Chapter 4). The continuation of the North Korean threat and lack of civilian expertise explain in part the continued domination of the security policy arena by serving and retired generals. However, even here there has been substantial change. The making of security policy is no longer the exclusive turf of the military. It is now the responsibility of the National Security Council (NSC) chaired by the president. Half the NSC members are civilian ministers, and the other half are retired generals in ministerial appointments.

Similarly, in Taiwan, democratic civilian control of the military has been strengthened since 1987. There has been a definite though still incomplete shift from Kuomintang (KMT) party control to control of the military by the democratically elected state executive and legislature (Chapter 5). Concurrently, the mission and role of the military have altered as well. The internal security role (which included protecting the KMT's political dominance) came to an end with the lifting of martial law in 1987 and the dissolution of Taiwan Garrison Command in 1992. The primary military role now is in external defense. Military penetration of state and society has decreased as well, and the military is also gradually disengaging from several key business enterprises, including that in mass media. Notwithstanding the advances made in democratic civilian control of the military, there are still a number of challenges, primarily in the areas of security policymaking and oversight of the military as an institution. The military has resisted the appointment of a civilian defense minister, and it has been reluctant to submit to legislative oversight on matters like arms procurement. Nevertheless, as pointed out in Chapter 5, considerable progress has been made to increase the transparency and accountability of the military and its activities. The National Defense Law that came into force on January 29, 2000, should help further streamline and strengthen democratic civilian control of the military.

There is still the concern as to whether the military would be subservient to a non-KMT government. The election and inauguration in May 2000 of President Chen Shui-bian of the proindependence Democratic Progressive Party (DPP) and the pledge of allegiance of the military to the democratically elected president have ameliorated this concern but not eliminated it. Chen could not make major changes to the national security team. All senior national security positions—premier, secretary-general of the National Security Council, defense minister, and head of the National Security Agency—went to former military officers. Seeking to enhance confidence in his government and control the prounification military, Chen appointed Tang Fei, a retired general who had been chief of the general staff and defense minister in the Lee Teng-hui government, as premier. Though Chen was not pressured to make these appointments, the induction of former senior military officers underscores the privilege still enjoyed by the military establishment and the president's keenness to retain the loyalty of the military. In Taiwan, as in many other consolidating democracies, enhancement of democratic civilian control of the military has progressed in an incremental fashion. Continued consolidation, however, would require more institutional reform, further redefinition of the military mission and role, and development of civilian expertise to enable elected and bureaucratic civilian officials to exercise effective oversight over military institutions and activities.

Transition to Democratic Civilian Control

The military in the Philippines, Thailand, Bangladesh, and Indonesia has also disengaged from politics. However, in contrast to South Korea and Taiwan, military disengagement from politics in these countries is still incomplete and tentative.

In the Philippines, the structure of civilian control of the state's coercive apparatus underwent dramatic change following the ouster of President Ferdinand Marcos in 1986. The Aquino era was characterized by a spate of unsuccessful coups by politicized agents within the state coercive apparatus and by widespread militarization of society. In the latter part of the Aquino administration and the succeeding Ramos administration, a number of politicized officers entered electoral politics. This trend "peaked and then subsided in tandem with the rise and fall of the Ramos administration" (Chapter 6). The military as an institution became resubordinated to democratic institutions. Orlando Mercado, an anti-Marcos activist and environmentalist with no military background, was appointed defense minister by President Joseph Estrada, and civilian-political considerations appear to dominate security policymaking. The Police Constabulary has been removed from the Armed Forces of the Philippines (AFP) chain of command. Redesignated the Philippine National Police, it is now under the control of the Department of the Interior and Local Government. The national legislature has reinstituted the Commission on Appointments and other congressional committees to exercise oversight of the military and police forces. Concurrently, the AFP's role has been redefined. Though it still has the responsibility to fight the remnants of the Maoist and Muslim armed rebellions, its primary responsibility now is external defense. The Philippine military as an institution seemed to be firmly under the control of elected officials. Democratic civilian control of the military in the Philippines seemed to be more advanced than in the other countries investigated in the democratic transition category.

This notion was quashed by the dramatic defection of the entire leadership of the Philippine armed forces to join the massive protest rally—dubbed People Power II—of the middle class, the radical left, and the poor that led to the ouster of President Estrada on January 20, 2001. Estrada, the populist ex–movie star and alienated vice-president of President Fidel Ramos, was elected to the presidency in 1998 with a huge majority. Beginning in mid-2000, his administration was beleaguered by allegations of corruption. Estrada himself was impeached by the House of Representatives on charges of corruption. The Senate trial that began in December was brought to an abrupt halt on January 16, 2001, when the Senate refused to consider evidence that Estrada had amassed funds under a false name. This sparked a massive "People Power" rally that was joined by the leadership of the armed forces. Gen. Angelo Reyes, chief of the armed forces, declared to the protesters: "On behalf of the 130,000 members of the Armed Forces, I would like to announce that we are withdrawing support from the president."[9]

The Philippine military leadership, in collusion with retired generals such as former general and president Fidel Ramos, claims to have acted in a guardian role "to protect the people and the state" from Estrada, who the military alleged was ruining the country. The failure of the constitutional process to deal with the charges leveled against Estrada and the defection of the military leadership raise serious questions about the state of democracy and civilian control of the military in the Philippines. Vice President Gloria Macapagal Arroyo—who was sworn in as president on January 20, much like Corazon Aquino was sworn in after the ouster of President Marcos in 1986—stands on shaky ground, with the competing forces that put her in office demanding payoffs. For example, to accommodate former president Ramos, Arroyo fired the national security advisor she had appointed only four days earlier and replaced him with Gen. Lisandro Abadia, who is a close ally of Ramos. This appointment sparked the resignation of Defense Secretary Orlando Mercado, who had been a close ally of Estrada and a member of his cabinet but subsequently defected. Mercado had initiated investigations against Abadia for improperly securing interest-free loans for two firms at which he was a board member. There is also an internal struggle within the military to determine the successor to General Reyes.

Meanwhile, concerned with plots inside and outside the military to destabilize her government, Arroyo has been courting the military with tax exemptions, bigger budgets, and other benefits in an effort to consolidate military support for her fledgling and troubled administration.[10] Though expedient, the unconstitutional role played by the military in the ouster of Estrada and its subsequent muscle flexing are major setbacks for democracy and democratic civilian control of the military. However, a reversal of democratic rule is unlikely. There still is strong public opposition in the Philippines to any form of authoritarian rule in which the military can play a key role.

The Thai, Bangladesh, and Indonesian militaries continue to retain formal or informal political influence and, in varying degree, seek to preserve institutional and professional autonomy, limit civilian involvement in security policymaking, and preserve their commercial interests. In Thailand, after the 1992 shooting of prodemocracy demonstrators and the showdown that led to the resignation of Gen. Suchinda Kraprayoon (briefly the unelected prime minister), the military vowed not to launch another coup. It responded to the 1997 economic crisis not by launching a coup, as in earlier eras, but by facilitating the passage of a new constitution in September 1997 and helping to bring about a change in government in November of that year. It was reported that Gen. Chetta Thanajaro played a key role in the resignation of

Prime Minister (and former army chief) Chavalit Yongchaiyuth in favor of Chuan Leepkai, leader of the Democratic Party, and his respected economic team. The military is seeking new ways of influence. Though direct intervention will be opposed, there is considerable public support for "behind the scene roles" as in 1997. Also, retired generals are entering politics by contesting elections. More than 30 former senior military officers contested the January 6, 2001, election, and the new Thaksin Shintawara cabinet has a few ex-generals, including retired general and former prime minister Chavalit Yongchaiyuth, who has been appointed defense minister.

Democratic civilian control of the Thai military has been on the ascendance and, in contrast to earlier periods, this process has been considerably aided by the 1997 economic crisis. For the first time, the post of defense minister was held by a civilian (Prime Minister Chuan Leepkai), and active duty officers and bureaucrats have been barred from holding cabinet positions. The Thai military has begun to submit to civilian (executive and parliamentary) scrutiny of promotions, budgets, and procurement. Its illegal cross-border trading activities have been substantially curtailed through the liberalization of trade with neighboring countries, and its off-budget revenues are coming under greater scrutiny. However, the military is far from giving up its institutional and professional autonomy, its influence in security policymaking, its developmental role, or its business interests. It is pertinent to observe here that although the Thai military facilitated the passage of the new constitution, it also lobbied hard to ensure that the new constitution authorized and legitimized its developmental role and excluded a specific clause that would have made coups illegal. It is quite possible that these and other reforms may be stalled under the Thaksin government. Defense Minister Chavalit had been previously opposed to what he termed "civilian interference in military matters" like arms procurement. Redefinition of the relationship of the military to the state, which began in 1973 and became more marked after 1992, as observed by James Ockey (Chapter 7), has been a struggle, punctuated by periodic contestation, including resorting to violence.

In Bangladesh, the military has chosen to steer an apolitical course since the ouster of President (formerly general) H. M. Ershad in 1990. The relationship of the soldier to the state, however, is still unsettled as civilian governments attempt to increase their control over the military and the latter seeks to ensure its corporate interests are protected. The deep cleavages in political society and the volatile nature of politics in Bangladesh, as well as the efforts of political parties to attract military support, provide the military with leverage and opportunity to reassert itself in politics as it did in the 1996 incident. On the other hand, the development of civil society and changes in international norms constrain the Bangladesh military—giving rise to a situation in which the military is unlikely to intervene directly but exercises considerable influence informally. There is clear indication of increasing civilian control of the military: the position of defense minister is held by a civilian (the prime minister), the prime minister appoints the service chiefs, and civilians now control the intelligence agencies. However, civilian governments have had to adjust their policies as well to accommodate the institutional interests of the military and its policy demands—leading to a situation characterized by Amena Mohsin (Chapter 8) as "uneasy accommodation."

In the case of Indonesia, as noted earlier, the civil-military balance has tilted against the military, and state-soldier relations are in the midst of substantial change. President Wahid was initially able to increase civilian control of the military well beyond most optimistic assessments through a series of measures, including rotation and appointment of reform-minded officers to key senior positions in the TNI, emphasis on political as opposed to military solutions in dealing with regional problems and grievances including secession, separation of the police force from the military and placing it under the office of the president, initiating a review of the 1982 law on defense and security, and capitalizing on the strong domestic and international demands for investigation and action in regard to the abuses committed under Suharto. A key indicator of the distance traveled was the forced resignation of General Wiranto from the cabinet in February 2000 after a two-week-long power tussle with the president over the military's human rights violations in East Timor.

With its legitimacy seriously undermined and facing investigation and trial for human rights abuses in East Timor and elsewhere, the once-unquestioned military is now searching for a new role in the Indonesian state and society. In line with a "new paradigm" that de-emphasizes the security approach of the Suharto era, the military committed itself initially to reducing its military's sociopolitical role. Confronted with a continuing barrage of public criticisms and accusations of past and ongoing abuses, army chief Tyasno Sudarto, after a meeting of senior military officers in April 2000, apologized to the nation for past mistakes and promised to terminate the military's sociopolitical role altogether. A couple of months later the TNI stated its readiness to dismantle its territorial structure if so required by the civilian authority and after the Peoples Consultative Assembly (Majelis Permusyawartan Rakyat [MPR]) had defined the roles and mission of the TNI. However, it defended the need for maximum troop presence in the troubled areas of Aceh, Riau, Irian Jaya, and other remote areas for security reasons.

Though it is on the defensive and a Pakistan-like coup is highly unlikely in the short term, as observed by Geoffrey Robinson in Chapter 9, the army is not a spent political force. The TNI still has several cards to play—especially in matters of defense and security. The executive and administrative agencies of government do not have the capacity to deal with regional unrest and rebellion. Although the police force has been assigned this responsibility, for a number of reasons the military is likely to continue to figure prominently in dealing with internal security. Further, the TNI is still the most cohesive national institution and has an extensive presence throughout Indonesia. Until it is fully dismantled or substantially reconfigured, the territorial structure gives the army enormous influence. Able to use its power and influence for mischief making and subverting civilian control, the military still can reemerge as a key player in the event of national or regional instability.

Although initial progress in democratic civilian control of the military has exceeded expectations, many challenges still remain. Dissatisfaction in some military and civilian quarters over political interference in military promotions and appointments, shortfall in the defense budget, future military representation in the MPR, policy differences over addressing internal security problems, dealing with the past abuses of the TNI, redefining the role of the TNI and restructuring its relations with other state institutions, and developing the necessary civilian institutions and expertise to ensure civilian oversight of the military are among the issues that still have to be addressed. Infighting among political leaders, the weakening position of Wahid, and the temptation to fall back on the military for support are also causes for serious concern.

From the foregoing discussion, it is evident that civil-military relations in the Philippines, Thailand, Bangladesh, and Indonesia are in new terrain. The prospect of a return to military rule or military-backed rule is still a distinct possibility, especially in Bangladesh and Indonesia. The basis for submitting to civilian control, the division of responsibilities and roles, and the substance and mechanism for civilian control of the military are still being negotiated, sometimes violently. This struggle is likely to be protracted and contested and prone to setbacks, possibly even reversals.

Ethnic and Dominant Party Civilian Control

Unlike the countries discussed in the preceding two sections, no dramatic change has occurred in civil-military relations in Malaysia and Singapore. Civilian control of the military continues to characterize civil-military relations in both these countries. Driven by the perceived need to maintain ethnic political domination or political domination by a single party, civilian control of the military in these countries is of the subjective genre. In Malaysia, the overwhelmingly Malay-dominated police and armed forces have remained subordinate to civilian authority in a political system designed to ensure the political supremacy of the Malay community that makes up about 55 percent of the population. Though it has no explicit political role, the military has an implicit role to defend Malay political dominance in that country (Chapter 10). This role became more pronounced in the wake of the May 1969 elections, the results of which were perceived to jeopardize the special position of the Malay community. The military was called out to restore law and order in the ensuing racial riots. In the post–May 1969 era, the Malay character of the armed and police forces became even more pronounced. Since then, however, the political power of the Malay community has become well entrenched. During the past two decades, the economic power of that community has also increased dramatically. In the context of these developments, the political salience of the military has receded further into the background.

As in Malaysia, the composition of the Singapore armed forces, especially the composition of its senior ranks, firmly reflects the dominant political position of the majority Chinese community in that country (Bedlington 1981). The military, shaped and controlled by the ideas and structures put in place by the People's Action Party that has dominated Singapore since 1959, functions as an integral part of the political-bureaucratic structure for political domination in the highly centralized state. There is little doubt that the military, like every other institution in that country, is under the firm control of the political and administrative elite. However, for a number of reasons outlined by Tan Tai Yong in Chapter 11, the distinction between civil and military in Singapore is blurred, leading to what he describes as a fusion model. One important cause of this blurring of the distinction between civil and military is the practice of lateral transfer of senior military officers to fill key political and administrative positions. Although some have argued that this practice erodes civilian control and enhances the influence of the military, Tan argues that this is part of the "government's pragmatic approach to optimizing the country's talent pool" and that this would not lead to an increase in the military's political influence. Service in the Singapore military, he posits, is a duty and vocation, not a professional calling. Hence, it has not generated regimental pride and interests and the associated corporatist behavior that is common in several other Asian countries.

In contrast to Malaysia and Singapore, civil-military relations in Sri Lanka have undergone two critical changes. One, the progressively ethnicized and politicized Sri Lankan military has become an instrument for Sinhala domination of the state. In addition to democratic principles, the basis for military subordination to civilian authority now includes a strong subjective dimension. This change in the basis for military subordination is reflected in the fact that the Sri Lankan military prosecutes the war in the north and east of the island not as a conflict between the government and insurgent forces but as a war between the Sinhalas and Tamils. The second critical change is that although the military remains subservient to the civilian government at the national level, the "war machine" is out of control in the north and east of the country as well as in the border war zones where the military has been fighting the LTTE for the past seventeen years (Chapter 12). The military is the state and the law in these areas. Further, the state has ceded monopoly over legitimate violence in the conflict areas to state-funded nonstate paramilitary groups and the LTTE. In conjunction with state-supported paramilitary groups, the military has also resorted to illegitimate violence—torture, rape, kidnapping—as well as extortion, smuggling, and other activities that have blurred the divide between state and nonstate groups and activities. The state and segments of society in these areas have become militarized, giving rise to a culture of violence that perpetuates the armed conflict as an end in itself. The unrelenting internal war and the political leaders' inability to devise political and sociocultural solutions to the conflict have had dramatic consequences for state-society interaction and for civil-military relations in Sri Lanka, especially in the zones of conflict.

Communist and Totalitarian Civilian Control

Subjective revolutionary type of civilian control continues to characterize civil-military relations in Asia's communist states, although here too changes are underway. The military in China, still under the control of the top leadership of the Chinese Communist Party (CCP) through the Central Military Commission (CMC), appears to be emerging as an autonomous actor in the political process. With the passing of the revolutionary generation, political leadership and military leadership have become separate and quite distinct. With bifurcation, the top political leadership can no longer take the military's subordination and support for granted, leading to an authority relationship that is described by James Mulvenon (Chapter 13) as conditional compliance. For example, in return for suppressing the 1989 democracy uprising, military modernization was elevated in priority and the People's Liberation Army (PLA) budget was increased. Conditional compliance is also a function of the importance of PLA support to the consolidation of postrevolutionary political leadership (Shambaugh 1993; Joffe 1993) (see Chapter 13). At the same time, however, CCP leaders (Jiang Zemin and his anointed successor Hu Jintao) are trying to consolidate their control of the PLA through filling key positions in the state and party CMCs with loyalists or politically neutral officers, and limiting the PLA's nonbudgetary revenue. In July 1998, Jiang Zemin ordered the military to divest its business enterprises, but with the understanding that the military would be compensated by an increase in its budget. The actual amount of compensation and military dissatisfaction with it have been the subject of much speculation, reflecting the altered nature of civil-military relations in China.

Overall, the scope and jurisdiction of the nondefense roles of the PLA have declined. Presently, its formal internal role is limited to upholding the supremacy of the communist party and maintaining internal stability. Informally, it continues to be a key player in factional struggles. The importance of the PLA in this regard is evident from Mao Zedong's use of the CMC during the Cultural Revolution and the fact Deng Xiaoping retained control of the CMC even after he gave up the state and party positions.[11] Now there is speculation that Jiang Zemin may try to follow in this path after he steps down from the positions of party secretary-general and state president in October 2002 and March 2003, respectively. Because the chairman of the CMC (not the party secretary-general or the state president) commands the military, this position is viewed as critical to the exercise of power from behind the scene as a state elder. With the erosion of the ideological legitimacy of the CCP and the passing of the revolution generation political leadership, the PLA is potentially a powerful determinant of Chinese domestic politics. However, its influence is also constrained by the bureaucratic orientation of the new generation of PLA leaders, the growing complexity and internationalization of the Chinese economy and society, and the dramatically altered international context. As such, although control of the military by the top CCP leadership is unlikely to alter any time soon, the relationship between the party, state, and military will continue to change, becoming more complex and bureaucratic. Because of the generation change in party and military leadership, the ongoing changes in both these institutions, and the ongoing transformation of the economy and state-society relations, the past is unlikely to be good indicator of future civil-military relations in China (Gurtov and Hwang 1998: 17–18).

Unlike in China where party control of the military in reality has been control of the military by the paramount leader, the Vietnamese military has indeed been commanded by the Vietnamese Communist Party (VCP). Greater continuity characterizes party-military relations in Vietnam, although changes are discernible in the role of the military as well as in its political position and influence. Though defense is still important, Thaveeporn Vasavakul (Chapter 14) argues that the emphasis in the role of the military appears to have shifted to maintaining regime security and domestic stability as well as promoting economic development in the *doi moi* era. When compared to the 1980s, the political and economic role of the Vietnam People's Army (VPA), as well as its influence, appears to be on the increase. The VPA's political prominence may be traced to its historic role in state building and the increasing concern among the Vietnamese leadership with ideological security; its economic role is linked to the early revolutionary period as well as the financial crisis precipitated by the withdrawal of Soviet aid in the late 1980s. Redefinition of roles and increased military representation in the party hierarchy, however, have not led to any fundamental change in party-military relations. Although military representation in the party hierarchy has increased, this still does not compare with the high level (more than 20 percent) of representation in the 1960s and 1970s. Further, unlike the situation in China, the seniormost military leaders in Vietnam have remained political generals. The dual role elite is still a feature in Vietnam. Thus, although the military appears likely to continue to play an important role in shaping the post–*doi moi* political, economic, and social order, it still operates under the leadership of the VCP. Still subject to strong party control, the VPA must advance its policy goals and corporate interests in competition with other voices within the party and the state.

Party-military relations in totalitarian North Korea are quite distinct if not unique. They have evolved in three distinct stages. In the immediate postliberation period, institutional conflict characterized party-military relations; in the second post–Korean War phase, the Korean Workers' Party (KWP) under the leadership of Kim Il Sung exercised absolute control over the

Korean People's Army (KPA); in the third and current phase the military has the upper hand, playing dominant roles in the state and the party. As Chung-in Moon and Hideshi Takesada (Chapter 15) point out, the military's power and influence have grown substantially under Kim Jong Il. The KPA has 15 percent of all seats in the Supreme National Assembly, and generals occupy top positions in the KWP and in government. Unlike China, where the party, state, and military are becoming more distinct, in North Korea there is growing fusion with the military as the dominant partner. Kim Jong Il has assumed the office of head of state in his capacity as chairman of the National Defense Commission and not the KWP. The KPA also plays a paramount role in economic development. Despite and in some ways because of the dire economic situation in North Korea, the KPA's economic role has become even more significant in recent times. Reflecting its growing power and influence, the military was declared in 1998 to be "the party, the state and the people."

However, despite its growing salience in the political, economic, and security spheres, Moon and Takesada posit that the military would appear to be still under the firm control of the great leader—Kim Jong Il, who dominates the KWP as well. The younger Kim's control of the military was evident both during the North-South Korea summit meeting and in the major reshuffle of senior military officers that he initiated in October 2000. The dominant influence of the KPA in the context of the personal dictatorship of Kim Jong Il looks set to continue because only the military can guarantee the position of Kim and North Korea's national security. With a very high military participation ratio (more than six million under arms),[12] a closed economy, and an obsession with security, North Korea, one of the few remaining totalitarian states, is turning into a garrison state. However, as Moon and Takesada note, the military's dominant position may well change if the North-South Korea dialogue that began with the June 2000 summit leads to an easing of the security situation and the international isolation of North Korea and as Kim Jong Il begins to address the economic slide that has characterized North Korea for well over two decades, reaching crisis proportions in the past decade.

Military Domination of State

The military continues to dominate the state in Pakistan and Burma. After almost 25 years of military rule, civilian leaders in Pakistan acceded to power in 1988, but the relationship between generals and political leaders was tenuous and contentious. Given the weakness of civilian governments, the military, as the most respected national institution, continued to wield enormous political influence. Its backing was crucial for the survival of civilian leaders, especially in situations of impasse among them. In November 1997, for example, military backing saved Prime Minister Nawaz Sharif in his confrontation with the president and chief justice. In addition to being a tacit referee, the military views itself as a national guardian with responsibility to define and protect the Pakistani nation and state and the right to criticize and remove the government when necessary.

In October 1998, army chief Gen. Jehangir Kramat criticized the "destabilizing effects of polarization, vendettas, and insecurity-driven expedient policies" of the Sharif government and identified the problems facing the country and the actions that must be taken (Ahmed 1998: 19–20). Although Sharif compelled Kramat to resign, the general's statement, given the country's chaotic political and economic situation, had wide support across the political spectrum.

Further, because of the breakdown of the civilian bureaucracy, the army's role in civil affairs has grown. It has been called upon to perform law-and-order functions, including setting up military courts to deal with terrorism, assisting in rebuilding crumbling utilities (water, power, railway), and aiding the education department. The military continues to have almost total control over security policy. Thus, although there was a civilian government at the political helm and the prime minister had the power to dismiss military chiefs, the military continued to be a powerful institution in Pakistan. It retained complete control over security policy as well as institutional and professional autonomy and many of the prerogatives and privileges it acquired during the era of military rule.

In October 1999, therefore, when the Pakistani military judged the Sharif government to be corrupt, inept, intruding into the security arena, and sowing discord within the military, it launched a coup to save the nation. Today the military is at the political helm. Babar Sattar (Chapter 16) argues that even though it is attractive and may be justified in the short term, military rule is no solution to the many deep-seated ills facing Pakistan and that, unlike the earlier martial law governments, the present one faces greater problems of legitimacy. The longer the military stays in power, the greater the chance of it discrediting itself. At some point, the military will have to return power to an elected civilian government. The supreme court comprising judges appointed by Musharaf validated the coup, but it has also mandated national elections and return to democratic rule. It is unclear if, how, and when this will happen and how the military will define its relationship to the state and government in the subsequent era.

In Pakistan, there have been interregnums of civilian rule. In Burma, however, the Tatmadaw (the Burmese military), which seized power in 1962, continues to dominate the stage. More than a decade after the 1988 massive public uprising and the May 1990 elections in which detained leader Aung San Suu Kyi's National League for Democracy (NLD) won an overwhelming victory, the military shows no sign of sharing power with elected civilian leaders, let alone relinquishing political power. A new generation of military officers under the leadership of Lt. Gen. Khin Nyunt, committed to perpetuating military rule, took power in a silent coup in late 1997, replacing the State Law and Order Restoration Council (SLORC) with the new State Peace and Development Council (SPDC). The military, which has been engaged in state building since the 1950s, is now reportedly seeking to legitimize its hold on power through a new constitution (drafted without input from the NLD) and the establishment of the Union Solidarity and Development Association, a quasi-political party not unlike the Indonesian Golkar during the Suharto era (Crispinin 1998: 26). Although the Tatmadaw's control on political power appears absolute and unshakable, Mary P. Callahan (Chapter 17) asserts that it is also beset by weaknesses—tension between the Rangoon-based junta and the regional commanders, and unprecedented discipline problems in all ranks, reducing combat effectiveness—that represent a crack in the edifice of military rule.

SIGNIFICANCE OF THE STUDY
OF CIVIL-MILITARY RELATIONS

The foregoing overview of the diversity of the civil-military problem in Asia and the changing nature of the relationship between the soldier and the state highlights the central role of the military in the domestic and international politics of the Asian countries. It is thus crucial to understand the relationship of the military to the state. As noted by Andreski (1971), military organizations can be a critical determinant of political organization, with consequences for the size and cohesion of states, the administrative hierarchy, and the extent of government regulation of society and the economy. Recognition of the centrality of coercion and the institutions that manage state coercion "opens the way to an understanding of the growth and change in governmental forms" (Tilly 1985: 172). Political systems—democratic, autocratic, authoritarian, Marxist-Leninist, totalitarian, absolutist, traditional, monarchic, theocratic, oligarchic, sultanistic—vary widely. A key distinguishing feature among them is the place and role of force in state surveillance, in securing compliance, and in maintaining internal law and order. As noted by Rapoport (1962: 97), "military and political institutions are inseparable" and in some ways mutually dependent. Change in the character of one produces a change in the other. The study of comparative politics can thus be aided by studies of civil-military relations.

The latter can provide important insights into the dynamics of domestic politics and governance as well as the international behavior of states. Certainly it can illuminate the relationship between the state, its security forces, and society. How does the military relate to the state and society? What is the basis for this relationship? What is the nature of the military's role and influence? Is the military's role expanding or contracting? Who commands, controls, and oversees the military? Answers to such questions are useful in understanding the dynamics of domestic politics—especially in states where the military's role exceeds the traditional security function. The changes in government in Pakistan and Thailand cannot be explained without reference to civil-military relations in these countries. Similarly, civil-military relations explain in substantial measure the political developments in Indonesia—including the legitimacy crisis and ouster of Suharto, the civilian resentment of the military, the outcome of the 1999 presidential election, the crisis in East Timor, and the separatist movements in Aceh and West Papua.

Studies of civil-military relations also help to explain regime persistence, change, and consolidation; the nature of the military regime in Burma, the reasons for its persistence, and the prospects for political change in that country; the dynamics and trajectory of the political transition occurring in Indonesia; the scope and depth of democratic transitions in South Korea, Taiwan, Thailand, the Philippines, and Bangladesh and the prospects for democratic consolidation in these countries; the dynamics of the economic and political transformations under way in China and Vietnam and their likely trajectories; and the persistence and changes in the democratic regimes in India and Japan and the quasi-democratic regimes in Malaysia, Sri Lanka, and Singapore. Understanding such issues is aided substantially by the systematic study of civil-military relations in these countries.

Similarly, the study of civil-military relations can make substantial contributions to our understanding of the international behavior of states. The differences in the international orientation and behavior of prewar and postwar Japan; of the Sukarno, Suharto, Habibie, and Wahid governments in Indonesia; and of China during and after the Cultural Revolution, as well as the international behavior of Pakistan and the nuclear policies of India and Pakistan, can all be illuminated by studies of civil-military relations.

Despite its importance, the study of civil-military relations in Asian countries has not commanded much attention among Asian or Western scholars. In the early decades of the postindependence period, there were a few single-country studies and later a few regional and sub-regional studies. (See Ahmad and Crouch 1985; Olsen and Jurika 1986; Djiwandono and Cheong 1998; Kennedy and Louscher 1991; Selochan 1991; Kukreja 1991.) Then, even this limited effort petered out. The exception here is the study of party-military relations in China, which has commanded considerable attention on the part of China scholars.[13] Even here, David Shambaugh (1999: 3–4) points out that the number of PLA specialists is very small and that many gaps exist in our understanding of Chinese civil-military relations. He asserts (1999: 14): "Civil-military relations (in China) still remains a black hole, with woefully inadequate data, which forces us to often speculate beyond what hard evidence is available." To the extent that civil-military relations in other Asian countries have received attention, it has been largely in the context of Third World studies and, more recently, studies of democratic transition in postauthoritarian states (Crouch 1997; Hernandez 1996). In other regions of the world, especially Central and South America, the study of civil-military relations has commanded more attention.

Many reasons may account for the lack of interest in Asia. First, the subject's importance and the contributions it can make to the study of domestic and international politics appear not to be widely appreciated. The role of force has been perceived essentially in the functional context of managing internal and international security. The relationship of the institutions of coercion to the structure of governance has been perceived primarily in terms of military intervention in politics. As the incidence of military coup d'état has declined in Asia, so too has interest in civil-military relations. The broader relationship of force to state-making and governance in all types of societies—and the many insights into domestic and international politics that can flow from the study of civil-military relations—appear to be overlooked. This has been the case in the theoretical literature as well. Until recently, for example, definitions of democracy, as observed by Harold Trinkunas (1998: 9), made no reference to civilian control of the military as an essential condition. The focus was on civilian leadership and social consensus to preserve democracy. Terry Karl was among the first to include civilian control of the military as part of the definition of democracy (Karl 1990). For Samuel Fitch (1989: 134), consolidation of democracy entails not just political subordination of the military to a democratic government, but also "the professional subordination to constitutionally designated state authorities."

Second, the critical study of domestic politics is not encouraged in many Asian states. In the name of security and stability, certain issues including civil-military relations have been labeled sensitive by the government and removed from the arena of public discourse. Along with the difficulty of conducting research in such areas, concerns of censorship and fear of repression have kept some scholars, especially indigenous ones, away from this subject and indeed from the study of domestic politics. The situation has improved somewhat but not in all countries. (Such considerations were cited by several Asian scholars who declined invitations to contribute to this study.)

Third, the economic dynamism that characterized East and Southeast Asia for the better part of three decades until the crash of 1997—as well as the changing international politics of the region, including the development of regional cooperation—have attracted a disproportionate number of scholars from what is already a small pool. Studies on these topics have been in great demand and highly rewarding—politically, financially, and professionally.

Finally, the elevation of economics and regional cooperation has been accompanied by a deprecation of the role of force and an unstated disdain among Asian scholars for the study of institutions associated with the management of force. For different reasons, there still is a strong disdain in postwar Japan for the military and, by extension, the study of civil-military relations. The situation in Japan and elsewhere is beginning to change, though only gradually. This study is a modest effort to correct the situation and stimulate greater interest in the subject.

STRUCTURE OF THE BOOK

Mapping and explaining the diversity and change in the relationship of the soldier to the state in Asia is the focus of this study. It is organized in eight parts. Part I develops an analytical framework and sets the context for the country-specific chapters that follow. Parts II to VII investigate civil-military relations in sixteen Asian countries. To facilitate comparison, the country studies have been grouped by type and stage of civilian or military control: democratic civilian control (Japan and India); consolidating democratic civilian control (South Korea and Taiwan); transition to democratic civilian control (the Philippines, Thailand, Bangladesh, and Indonesia); subjective (ethnic and dominant party) civilian control (Singapore, Malaysia, and Sri Lanka); subjective (communist party) control of the military (China and Vietnam); totalitarian dictatorship control (North Korea); and military domination of the state (Pakistan, Burma). Addressing common questions and deploying a common framework developed in Part I, these sixteen studies investigate the relationship of the military to the state (especially its political leaders and organs); how and why this relationship has changed; the implications of change for the dynamics of domestic politics; and the likely trajectory of civil-military relations in the country.

Although the country studies address common questions and conform to a common framework, the authors have been allowed wide latitude in expanding and enriching the core approach in a manner they consider appropriate to their countries of study. Based on the findings of the studies in Parts II to VII and other published works, Part VIII takes a regional perspective. It explains the key developments in civil-military relations in Asia, the different patterns that exist, and the similarities and differences across countries within each pattern. It also anticipates the future trajectory of civil-military relations on a regionwide basis.

It is useful at this juncture to define three key terms: state, regime, and government. The term "state" has many meanings. Indeed, some view it as an abstract fiction or a meaningless concept (Benjamin and Duvall 1985: 22–28). In this book, "state" is used in the generic sense to mean "a structure of domination and coordination including a coercive apparatus and the means to administer society and extract resources from it" (Fishman 1990: 428). It does not refer to the system of political domination or the relationship among the various institutions of the state. The normative-legal-institutional order of the state is the domain of the term "regime," which in this book refers to "the formal and informal organization of the center of political power, and of its relations with the broader society. A regime determines who has access to political power, and how those in power deal with those who are not" (Fishman 1990: 428). In operational terms, "regime" refers to the principles, institutions, and procedures that constitute the political system. "Government" refers to the actual exercise of political power within the framework of the regime—specifically, the agency through which the state's purposes and policies are formulated and realized. It comprises the executive (political and administrative), the legislature, and the judiciary.

PART I

Conceptual Perspective

CHAPTER 1

Investigating and Explaining Change: An Analytical Framework

Muthiah Alagappa

Covenants without swords are but words.
—Thomas Hobbes

Monopoly over the legitimate use of force is as essential a characteristic of the state as compulsory jurisdiction and continuous organization in a given territorial area.
—Max Weber

An armed, disciplined body is, in its essence, dangerous to liberty; undisciplined, it is ruinous to society.
—Edmund Burke

The wonder . . . is not why [the military] rebels against its civilian masters, but why it ever obeys them.
—Samuel Finer

A CENTRAL PARADOX OF THE MODERN STATE—and its quintessential civil-military relations problem—is how to create a military strong enough to protect the nation-state from external and internal threats but at the same time prevent it from dominating the state or becoming an instrument for internal repression. Monopoly over coercion, as noted in the Introduction, is a defining feature of the modern state. The theoretical justification for this monopoly is the claim to sovereignty: supreme jurisdiction within territorial boundaries and decision-making autonomy in international affairs. In functional terms, monopoly over coercion is deemed essential for ensuring domestic sociopolitical order, for protecting the political community (its ideals, autonomy, and territorial integrity) from external threats, and for creating an international environment conducive to the fulfillment of national goals and purposes. The concentration of the ultimate means of violence in a single institution, however, endows that institution with enormous brute power that can be deployed to dominate the state, curb liberty, or serve partisan purposes.

The conflicting demands of creating a potent institution and preventing it from dominating the state are resolved in the abstract by treating coercion and its institutional containers as instruments of state policy under the direction of a legitimate civilian government. Further, based on the assumption that the state is internally pacified, the military's primary role is deemed to be in the international arena. Although the military's role and its relationship to the government may differ with the political system, in the logic of the modern state the military is at bottom an instrument of the state and subordinate to a legitimate government that is accountable to its citizens. However, practice often departs, at times radically, from this ideal.

To begin with, there is no clear divide between domestic affairs and international affairs. In a number of states, including many in Asia, force is as much an instrument of policy in domestic affairs as it is in international affairs. Second, nonstate political groups often seek to acquire and deploy coercion in pursuit of goals that conflict with those of the state and the incumbent government. Consequently, the government's claim to monopoly over the means and use of coercion within territorial boundaries has seldom been realized. Third, governments themselves are not always legitimate. In fact, the development of a durable, legitimate political system is a major challenge confronting many Asian states (Alagappa 1995). Fourth, the military is not necessarily subordinate to government. Instead of serving as an instrument of state policy, in several countries the military intrudes into the political arena and in some cases dominates the state. Finally, the role of the military often extends beyond the matter of international security to include internal security as well as political and socioeconomic functions. With state coercion deployed for a variety of private, corporate, and partisan purposes, militaries have engaged in activities ranging from political domination of the state to participation in commerce to extortion and smuggling. In the process, militaries have robbed, persecuted, and killed the very people it is their duty to protect. For many countries, therefore, the civil-military problem arising from the concentration of force in the state is a serious concern.

The nature of this problem, as noted in the Introduction, and its management vary widely from country to country—at times even within a country depending on the issue and the level of government. The military, for example, may have a low political profile but nevertheless control security policymaking, exercise autonomy over its own institutional matters, and have access to extrabudgetary revenue. Similarly, it may be subject to civilian control at the national level but not at the provincial level. Moreover, the military-civilian relationship is dynamic. Contestation over the basis for political legitimacy, economic growth and development (or the lack thereof), and changes in the international context, among other forces, affect the interests, power, and beliefs of civilian and military leaders and can alter the content and pattern of civil-military interactions. Civil-military relations in Asia, as in other developing countries, are complex and dynamic and subject to periodic negotiation and change, at times through confrontation and violence.

The term "civil-military relations" implies a sharp dichotomy between two sharply bounded and coherent institutions. This is not the case in practice. Except in autocracies, the civil comprises many actors. And although the military may be more cohesive, better organized, and hierarchical, there may be several military actors because of factionalism, interservice rivalry, and other considerations. There are cleavages within each component, too, as well as linkages and alliances across the civil-military divide. Civil-military interaction, moreover, is not always antagonistic and focused on control. Description and analysis of civil-military relations must be nuanced and sensitive to these possibilities.

This chapter develops an analytical framework for investigating and explaining change in civil-military relations in Asia. Although the term "civil" comprises political and civil societies as well, for reasons advanced earlier the focus of this study is the relationship of the military as an institution to the political and administrative institutions of the state. Political, civil, and international societies are elements in this framework as well, depending on their impact on the state-soldier interaction. The chapter is organized in three parts. The first develops a framework for investigating change. The framework seeks to identify change in civil-military interaction through alterations in the breadth of military participation in governance (scope) and decision-making power (jurisdiction) and deploys the combination of these two indicators to ascertain if civilian (or military) supremacy is on the rise or decline. The second section critically reviews the major propositions that have been advanced in the study of civil-military relations with a view to identifying key building blocks for a comprehensive explanatory framework. The focus in this section is on three issues pertinent to this inquiry: military intervention and nonintervention in politics, problems of military rule and military exit from politics, and civil-military interaction in the postauthoritarian phase. The final part elaborates on the two major propositions advanced in the Introduction. One, the significance and weight of coercion in governance is the key to explaining long-term change and continuity in civil-military relations. And second, specific developments in civil-military relations are best explained by the interaction of the interests, power, and beliefs of the civilian and military institutions mediated by the influence of civil society and the international community.

INVESTIGATING CHANGE:
JURISDICTION, SCOPE, AND SUPREMACY

Investigations of change must answer three questions: Change from what? What is the content and direction of change? And how is change to be measured? Change can only be investigated with reference to a baseline—a set of initial conditions. In this book, the baseline is the state of civil-military relations at the founding moment: independence from colonial rule (Philippines 1946, India 1947, Pakistan 1947, Sri Lanka 1948, Burma 1948, North Korea 1948, South Korea 1948, Malaysia 1957), founding revolution (Republic of China 1912 and 1949, Thailand 1932, Vietnam 1945, Indonesia 1949, People's Republic of China 1949), liberation from American occupation (Japan 1952), or separation or secession (Singapore 1965, Bangladesh 1971). This baseline is significant for two reasons. First, for most states it marks the formal break with traditional and colonial rule and the beginning of the effort to construct a modern nation-state. (This does not mean, of course, that features of traditional and colonial rule ceased to exist at that moment.) Second, the baseline provides a sufficiently long time horizon—four or five decades—making it possible to distinguish durable change from interludes and to discern patterns and trends. Because it is impossible to cover every change over a period of four or five decades, in each country study the focus is on key turning points or defining moments in state-soldier relations.

Civil-military interaction can vary along two dimensions: scope and jurisdiction.[1] Scope indicates the breadth of military participation in governance. This participation may range from narrow concerns over institutional matters to broad political and social goals (Colton 1978: 63–65; Pion-Berlin 1992: 84–86; Trinkunas 2000). Though important, scope does not reveal the true nature of military participation in governance and may, in fact, be misleading. Military involvement in internal security and socioeconomic development, for example, does not necessarily constitute role expansion. For the latter to be the case, an increase in scope must be accompanied by a change in jurisdiction—the power to make decisions—in such matters. If the military itself decided on these roles or coerced the government into authorizing them, one might argue a case of role expansion and an increase in the military's influence. Such a case cannot be argued, however, if the civilian government authorized these roles on its own and retains the power to retract them. Engagement in internal security and developmental roles might well have the consequence of increasing the military's power and influence, which in turn could affect the power to make decisions. The crucial indicator, however, is a change in jurisdiction, irrespective of how it came about. The key point is this: the combination of jurisdiction and scope provides a good basis for ascertaining the content of civil-military interaction and whether the civilian (or the military) role and supremacy are on the rise or decline. Civilian supremacy is the ability of a government to conduct general policy free of military interference and to set the limits of military role and behavior. The three concepts—jurisdiction, scope, and civilian supremacy—are elaborated next.

Jurisdiction

Jurisdiction refers to the authority to make and implement policy. It is possible to distinguish two types of jurisdiction: ultimate and divided. An institution with *ultimate* jurisdiction has overall responsibility and is the final authority deciding policy. It may delegate decision-making power over specified issues to others. It may also determine the rules that should be followed in exercising delegated power and how oversight is to be achieved. Although ultimate jurisdiction does not imply exclusive control over decision making, this is sometimes the case. In *divided* jurisdiction, policymaking power is divided among institutions by issue and even within an issue area, with each institution exercising ultimate authority within the defined area.[2] The security issue area, for example, may be the preserve of the military, although it defers to civilian authority in other matters. Even within the security issue area, the military may have ultimate jurisdiction only over certain issues. In Thailand before the mid-1990s, for example, the military controlled Burma and Cambodia policy while deferring to civilian authority on other security matters. Divided jurisdiction is most likely during periods of political transition.

Jurisdictional boundaries, therefore, may vary across issue areas and over time—especially in states undergoing political and economic change. In postauthoritarian states, for example, civilian authority to make policy may initially be limited to the political arena, whereas the military retains control over security and other functions as well as institutional matters. In time, jurisdictional boundaries may shift according to the success of the competing institutions in mobilizing support and increasing their store of power, and in due course altering the normative beliefs of society in matters of governance, including the role of the military. Even in states not undergoing regime change, jurisdictional boundaries may alter along with changes in specific circumstances or the military's mission. In communist states, for example, moments of leadership succession may increase the military's political salience, whereas periods of consolidated political leadership may diminish it. In democratic states, likewise, growing internal turmoil and the involvement of the armed forces in maintaining law and order may lead to an increase in the military's jurisdiction over internal security policy. Assessments of civil-military relations, therefore, must take a close look at jurisdictional change in critical areas of governance.

Scope

Scope, as noted, refers to the breadth of military participation in governance. The aspects of governance in which there is military involvement—and whether the involvement is broadening or narrowing—are among the issues that should be investigated. Five areas are crucial here: the structure of political domination and the military's place in it; the control, organization, and management of the military as an institution; security policymaking; the military's socioeconomic role; and the military's engagement in illegal activities such as smuggling and drug trafficking. Military participation in governance is at its broadest when the military dominates politics; it is narrowest when limited to purely institutional matters. Participation in socioeconomic and illegal activities is often a means to political and institutional ends rather than a goal in its own right. The content of these five areas of governance and the questions to be investigated are elaborated below.

Political Participation.   Politics is about using power and influence to dominate the state and make policy on its behalf. The military's place in the structure of political domination is the starting point for investigations of civil-military relations. It determines, in large measure, the scope and jurisdiction of military participation in other areas of governance as well. Of particular interest here are the military's weight in political governance, the form of its participation in politics, and its self-conception.

With regard to the military's political salience, inquiry should focus on the importance of coercion and the military's role in sustaining the political system. The key question is whether the survival and functioning of the incumbent government—and, by extension, the political system—are predicated on military support and acquiescence. If the government is legitimate and can stand on its own with coercion playing only a limited, indirect, and supportive role in the domestic and international politics of the state, then the military is likely to have little political clout. Its role in governance—including the arrangements for organizing and managing the military—will be determined in large measure by the civilian government. The military will be confined to providing professional advice and lobbying for its interests through defined institutions and procedures under the control of civilian authority. If coercion is a highly visible and consequential factor in governance, however, military support is likely to be crucial for the government's survival and functioning—in which case it is necessary to investigate the degree and nature of dependence, the political power and influence that accrues to the military from such dependence, how that power and influence are utilized, and whether the military's importance is increasing or decreasing. Constitutional and legal provisions, as well as interviews with officials, are a good starting point for inquiry but may not reveal the whole story.

Often it is necessary to investigate actual military participation—its type and extent—at the national and provincial levels as well as the means employed by the military in seeking to exercise influence (Giddens 1987: 249; Colton 1978: 64–65).

Military participation in "councils of government" may range from backing a civilian government to dominating the state. Four types of participation may be distinguished: referee, guardian, participant-ruler, and praetorian rule.[3] If the military has the ability to decisively alter the distribution of power, it can act as a referee among competing political groups; in this role the military may not be part of the government, but has the power to influence which civilian group governs and to define its decision-making powers. In the guardian role as well, the military may not be a direct participant in government; in this role the military, with the power to intervene and displace governments that stray from "national ideals," may back a specific government on ethnic, class, or ideological grounds. In the participant-ruler category, the military is a direct participant in government; it may be a junior or equal partner occupying positions of authority in governing councils at the national, regional, and local levels; it is likely to have ultimate jurisdiction in specified areas. In the final category—praetorian rule—the military is the dominant player and has ultimate authority in all areas of governance. There are different types of military regimes. The most extensive is that which seeks to perpetuate military rule through the creation of a single-party structure. Although the military regime is the most extreme form of military participation in politics, there is no strict hierarchy among the others. A military in a guardian role may well be politically more powerful than a military in the participant-ruler category. The utility of these categories is primarily to demonstrate the type of participation and secondarily to indicate, in a general way, whether participation is on the rise or decline.

Military participation in policymaking may take the form of professional advice, lobbying, alliance with certain political and administrative interests, blackmail (including withdrawal of political support), and threat and use of force. The means deployed depend on the type of military participation in politics and jurisdictional boundaries. Blackmailing, withdrawal of political support, and the threat and use of force may be more common in situations where the military plays the referee or guardian roles or is a participant-ruler. Professional advice and lobbying are more likely when civilians have ultimate authority; alliances and cross-institutional links are more likely in situations of divided jurisdiction. The connection between type of participation and means, however, is a loose one subject to variation. More significant from the perspective of this study is the connection between the means employed and supremacy. An emphasis on institutions, expert advice, lobbying, and alliances is indicative of civilian predominance; blackmailing, withdrawal of support, and threat and use of force are signs of weak civilian authority and significant military power and influence.

Closely related to the military's political salience and the extent of its participation in politics is the military's self-conception of its responsibilities toward the state. Committed to certain ideational and physical definitions of the state and viewing the protection of these values as their responsibility, some militaries may see themselves as "servants of the state rather than of the government in power" (Finer 1975: 22). In such cases, military self-conception is a key factor in its approach to civil-military relations. The military may make its subordination to civilian authority conditional upon the pursuit of these ideals. Alternatively, it may seek to legitimate its participation in the political process and its nonsecurity functions in terms of these ideals. Self-conception is particularly salient to militaries that arrogate to themselves a national guardian role. A change in self-conception may reflect a change in political orientation and goals. Investigating the discourse among military leaders on national goals and the role of the military—as well as the content of military doctrine and curricula at senior military colleges—is particularly useful in understanding changes in the military's attitudes and orientation (Stepan 1988: 45–54).

In addition to providing concrete signs of change in civil-military relations in the political arena, these three indicators—increase or decrease in the military's political salience; changes in the extent and means of military participation in politics at the national, provincial, and local levels; and changes in the military's self-conception—may indicate actual or impending change in other arenas of governance as well. But change in other areas is not inevitable. In the initial stages of democratic transition, for example, in exchange for reducing its political role the military may seek to preserve and possibly even strengthen its prerogatives in institutional and security matters. And the civilian authorities for a number of reasons, including lack of expertise or a desire to consolidate their hold in the political realm, may willingly concede to such demands.[4] Such pacts are viewed by some analysts (O'Donnell and Schmitter 1986: 37–48) as an essential element of democratic transition. Movement beyond this bargain—and the increase of civilian control over other areas of governance—hinges on the civilian political elite's ability to engender power and ideational shifts in its favor.

Institutional Autonomy.   Control over the military's organization and management as an institution is an important aspect of civil-military relations. Because of its roles and missions—and the belief that the profession demands its own distinct command, control, administrative, and legal structures—the military often seeks autonomy over its organization and management. As a corporate body the military also strives for internal control of its profession on the grounds that it alone is competent "to judge on such matters as size, organization, recruitment, and equipment" (Finer 1975: 23). The desire to maximize autonomy may push the military to limit civilian intrusion in these matters. From the perspective of the civilian government, however, civilian supremacy entails jurisdiction over some of these issues and the consequent need to limit military autonomy. The outcome of this interaction is a key indicator of the direction and depth of change in civil-military relations, especially in the post-authoritarian phase of government.

In this area of governance, one needs to investigate the chain of command, control over senior promotions and appointments, control over the defense budget, and the relationship between the civilian and military legal systems. With regard to command and control of the military, there are two key questions: Who commands the military? And how deep and effective is this command? Answers to these questions can be derived from investigation of the following: Who is the commander in chief? Who holds the position of defense minister? How broad and how deep is this person's authority? Is there a joint chief of staff, or do the services operate independently? Who defines the military's missions and strategic objectives? What is the procedure for and who has ultimate authority on choice and acquisition of major weapons systems? Who authorizes large-scale deployment? Who controls the deployment and use of weapons of mass destruction?

On the issue of promotions and appointments, political leaders of all hues normally seek to fill senior positions with politically loyal or neutral officers in order to consolidate their position in office and ensure that their policies are carried out. The ability of civilian leaders to regulate promotions and appointments to senior positions is especially critical in fledgling democracies and in political systems (including autocratic, military, and communist regimes) where there is no orderly process for political succession. Here the key concern is: Who has the final say on these matters? If responsibility is shared, on what basis? Similar questions must be explored with regard to the allocation and supervision of the defense budget, including the development of force posture and weapons procurement. An important issue in this connection is whether the military has access to off-budget revenue. If it does—and if the off-budget revenue is not subject to civilian oversight—the civilian authority has lost an important control mechanism and the military has gained considerable flexibility in the activities it can undertake.

Except for a few countries like Germany and Japan, militaries usually have their own legal systems. These systems are generally rooted in and subordinate to the nation's legal system. Barring situations of martial law, military courts cannot try all cases and usually cannot try civilians. Changes in these norms may signal changes in the degree of autonomy enjoyed by the armed forces. A key issue to investigate here is the jurisdiction of civilian courts over infractions committed by the military in the course of discharging its mission and operations (Pion-Berlin 1992). Does the military, for example, accept trial by civilian courts of human rights abuses committed by its personnel, or does it seek to exclude such matters from the civilian domain by seeking immunity?

Security Policymaking. Closely linked to institutional autonomy and crucial both to the state and to the military is the security function. Providing security for its citizens is perhaps the primary rationale for government; protecting national security is the fundamental role of the military. Even when the military does not participate directly in political domination, its role in formulating and implementing security policy obliges it to participate in the political process. Some militaries, viewing security as their home turf, may go further and seek to control policymaking in this area. Jurisdiction over security matters is an important indicator of the relationship between soldier and state—especially in countries where the military is not at the political helm or countries in the process of democratic transition. Continued military control of security policymaking in postauthoritarian states, for example, is indicative of partial civilian control and the lack of democratic consolidation. Increasing civilian control in this area, by contrast, is a firm indicator of the subordination of the military to civilian control and democratic consolidation. Growing military control over national security policymaking in consolidated democracies and communist states signals the erosion of a key feature of these systems.

Change in civil-military interaction in this area may be discerned by investigating who has ultimate authority in defining national security problems, in assessing threats to national security, and in formulating national security policy, doctrine, and strategy. Threat assessment is particularly salient. The institutional arrangements for intelligence collection and threat assessment, the provisions for oversight of these agencies, and whether the government has access to alternative sources of intelligence or is the captive of agencies dominated by the military—all are key considerations.

A second issue to investigate is the military's internal security role. Although protecting the state from international military threats is the military's primary rationale in the modern state, militaries in Asia are frequently deployed in the internal security role. Here the questions to explore include, Who defines the military missions in this role? What is the relationship among military, paramilitary, and police forces in discharging this role? How does the military relate to the civilian authorities in discharging this role? Does the civilian government have the authority to rescind this role? What is the military role in domestic intelligence agencies? Does the military's involvement in internal security enhance its power vis-à-vis civilian authorities? Civil-military interaction in matters of security may best be ascertained by investigating specific cases in the management of domestic and international security problems.

Socioeconomic Role.   Apart from their security role, militaries in Asia and elsewhere frequently engage in socioeconomic activities, including nation building. In the latter role, the military may be viewed as a national school where citizens "can learn appropriate civic virtues and important technical and administrative skills that may contribute to the maintenance or improvement of their community" (Rapoport 1962: 71). This role may be couched in the context of national integration and modernization. The military's economic activities span a wide spectrum, including the management of defense production, manufacturing of commercial goods, ownership of television and radio broadcasting networks and newspapers, management of national airlines, shipping corporations and utilities, farming, and rural development. The military's social service activities include rural health, education, and relief work during natural disasters.

These activities may be undertaken in a nonpartisan manner as part of national development at the behest of civilian governments. Governments may also encourage the military to undertake such activities in order to redirect scarce resources to other sectors—as was the case in China and Vietnam in the early phases of their modernization and renovation programs. Alternatively, the military may engage in these roles on its own initiative in order to strengthen its power and influence vis-à-vis other state institutions as well as to secure off-budget revenues. Whatever the purpose, military involvement in socioeconomic activities is usually justified in the name of national development and security. These activities occupy an intermediate place between political involvement and the military's effort to preserve institutional autonomy and determine its security role. In postauthoritarian states, while conceding the political sphere, militaries may seek to retain security-related and budget-generating socioeconomic activities both to preserve their institutional autonomy and to influence security policymaking. As in other areas of governance, the key issues to investigate are the range of activities, their purpose, who authorized them, and whether the range of activities is broadening or narrowing. Also worth exploring are how these activities affect the distribution of power between civilian and military actors as well as the tensions, cleavages, and alliances they create in civil-military interactions.

Illegal Activities.   A number of Asian militaries also engage in illegal activities such as drug trafficking, smuggling, and extortion. At times they collude with local militias, bosses, and thugs to carry out political intimidation while bolstering their own personal fortunes. Sometimes undertaken with the blessing of the national government, at other times on the military's own initiative, these activities do affect civil-military relations. Issues to investigate include, What is the scope and why does the military engage in these activities? Why do governments tolerate them? Does the government seek to control such activities? How, and with what success? What are the consequences of these activities for civil-military relations?

Civilian Supremacy

Changes in the military's jurisdiction and scope signal changes in state-soldier relations. Figure 1.1 captures the possible combinations of these two dimensions. Box A is the ultimate in civilian supremacy. In this situation the jurisdiction of the civilian government applies across all areas of governance, including oversight of key military institutional matters. Box B is the opposite: military jurisdiction prevails across the spectrum. Most countries in Asia are somewhere in between, with jurisdiction varying across issue areas. In a country like Thailand that is in the midst of democratic transition, the military has withdrawn from direct political participation but retains a good measure of informal political influence and exercises considerable control over security policy and the military's organization and management. The elected civilian government has begun to exercise control in areas that were once the preserve of the military, however, such as budget items and senior promotions and appointments. Democratic consolidation in such countries will entail further reductions in the scope and jurisdiction of the military and a corresponding increase in that of civilian authorities, ultimately culminating in Box A.

The scope/jurisdiction scheme outlined in Figure 1.1 is particularly useful because jurisdictional boundaries are likely to vary across issue areas and over time. Instead of forcing analysis into false and untenable dichotomies, this scheme makes it possible to investigate division and delegation of authority in different issue areas, the interaction of different institutions with interest in policy formulation in a specific issue area, internal differentiation within institutions, and cross-institutional links. It permits greater nuance in analysis as well by allowing for gradations in civil-military relations and incremental changes and, moreover, indicates the direction of change, toward civilian or military supremacy.

The term "civilian control," frequently associated with Samuel Huntington (1956), has been the subject of much discussion. Timothy Colton (1978: 62–63) rejects the term "control" because in his view it implies antagonistic relations between sharply bounded institutions and it forces analysts to think in dichotomous terms. Because of the gradations in Soviet party-military relations, the subject of his inquiry, he prefers the term "participation." Though recognizing the usefulness of the term "civilian control," Aguero (1995) contends that subjective civilian control is inappropriate to the task of his inquiry (democratization) and maintains that the connection between professionalism and objective civilian control posited by Huntington does not always hold true. Aguero prefers the term "civilian supremacy," which he defines as "the ability of a civilian, democratically elected, government to conduct general policy without interference from the military, to define the goals and general organization of national defense, to formulate and conduct defense policy, and to monitor the implementation of military policy" (p. 19).

This definition of civilian supremacy, as Aguero acknowledges, is essentially the same as the definition of civilian control advanced by Claude Welch. Arguing that civilian control is a matter of degree, that all armed forces participate in politics in some fashion, and that civilian control is a set of relationships, Welch (1976: 1–3) takes the cue from Huntington that civilian control is "government control of the military" and states that civilian control is "one of setting limits within which members of the armed forces, and the military as an institution, accept the government's definition of appropriate areas of responsibility." Although these three terms—participation, control, and supremacy—have been advanced as competing alternatives, each is quite distinct and has its own relevance for the study of civil-military relations. "Par-

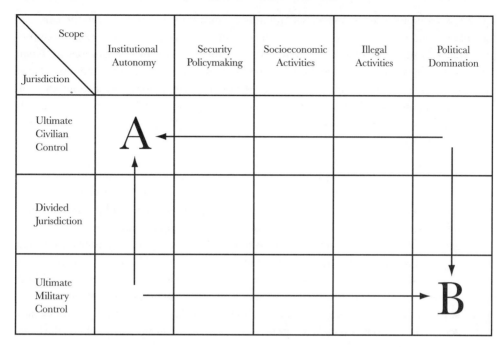

FIGURE 1.1.   Civil-Military Relations: Scope, Jurisdiction, and Supremacy.

ticipation" is useful for the reasons cited by Colton, but it does not obviate the need for the term "control," which is essential to indicate who defines the framework for such participation. There is greater overlap between "control" and "supremacy," and, contrary to Aguero, both terms may be defined and operationalized to convey gradations in civil-military relations. Thus, although it is possible to argue that supremacy is distinct from control, the two terms are used interchangeably in this book because of the overlap in common usage.

Decision-making power and breadth of participation, as noted earlier, are the key indicators of change and continuity in civil-military relations. Expansion and consolidation of civilian supremacy, therefore, entail an increase in the decision-making power of civilian authorities and a corresponding reduction in the jurisdiction and scope of military participation in governance. Aguero envisages a two-step process here: first, military withdrawal from "power positions outside the defense area and, second, the appointment and acknowledgement of civilian political superiors in the defense and military areas" (1995: 19). Civilian control, however, does not only mean democratic civilian control. It may also mean party control of the military, as in Leninist states, and may also develop in the process of institutionalizing authoritarian rule.

How does one measure consolidation of civilian control? Much attention has focused on changes in constitutions, laws, and the chain of command; on civilian control of promotions, appointments, and budget; and on policy outcomes. If political leaders repeatedly get their way despite military objections on questions of military policy, it is possible to argue that civilian control is on the rise (Pion-Berlin 1997: 1). While certainly important, these are simply short-term measures. Long-term consolidation of civilian control requires durable change in

the distribution of power between civil and military institutions of the state, in the beliefs of
the military, and in the beliefs of the political community as a whole on the military's appropriate place in state and society—as well as the legitimacy of political institutions and their
capacity to address the political and socioeconomic problems confronting the country. These
matters are taken up later in the chapter. Here let us simply note that consolidation of civilian control can only be achieved through power and ideational shifts, development of widely
accepted institutions and processes for the management of civil-military interaction, and prolonged experience.

Civil-Military Relations in Communist States

Although our discussion thus far has not explicitly focused on the state-soldier relationship in
communist states, suitably modified much of the discussion is applicable to these states as well.
It will be useful at this juncture to briefly focus on the peculiar nature of civil-military relations
in the socialist states. In theory, the Marxist-Leninist state is governed by the dictatorship of the
proletariat. As the "vanguard of the proletariat," the communist party is the "bearer of truth
and legitimacy" and the leading organ that initiates and implements policy in all areas of governance. It penetrates and dominates all institutions of state and society from the national to
local levels. All institutions and movements in the country are dedicated to upholding the hegemonic position of the party.

In this party-state system, the civil component of the term civil-military relations for all
intents and purposes is the communist party, and the study of civil-military relations is in fact
the study of party-military relations. Several models have been advanced for the study of civil-
military relations in communist states. These include the totalitarian model (Huntington 1957),
the party-military conflict model (Kolkowicz 1967, 1982), the institutional congruence model
(Odom 1978), the participatory model (Colton 1978), the interest group model (Kolkowicz 1978),
the bureaucratic model (LeoGrande 1978), the political socialization model (Volgyes 1978), the
revolutionary soldier model (Perlmutter 1977), the contingency model (Albright 1980), and the
historical development model (Adelman 1982). Our purpose here is not to evaluate these models but to draw on them to highlight the issues pertinent to our investigation of change in civil-
military relations in communist states in the five areas of governance.

With respect to the place and role of the military in political domination, the norm in communist states is not an apolitical military but a distinctly political institution that is committed to
upholding the communist ideology and the supremacy of the party. Though it is a separate institution, the military is not independent from and does not stand apart from the party. There is a
certain symbiosis between party and military, and the military is an active participant in the political process—both in making and implementing policy. It is not illegitimate for the military to
intervene in factional political struggles or for military personnel to assume senior party positions as long as the military does not seek to replace the party as the dominant political force.
Perhaps it is because of this symbiotic relationship and the opportunity available for military
men to assume senior party positions that there has not been a military coup in communist states.
The symbiotic and participatory aspects of civil-military relations in communist states are well
captured by the institutional congruence, participatory, and bureaucratic models. The revolutionary model is useful in understanding the ideological commitment of the military.

These models, however, do not reflect the tensions that may arise from party penetration and control of the military. The conflict model is useful here, although the "red versus expert" argument that underpins this model usually rests implicitly on the Huntingtonian conception of apolitical professionalism. Military professionalism in communist states, however, does not exclude political participation. It also does not imply that the military is removed from internal security or economic development roles. As guardian of the regime, it is the duty of the military to protect the regime from internal and international political, military, and economic threats. Similarly, as a key institution of the state, it is also expected to partake in socioeconomic development.

Thus, although civilian control of the military is the norm in communist states, it is a version of subjective, not objective, civilian control. Change in civil-military relations in communist states should be investigated in the context of the pattern and norms outlined above. Often change may be only a matter of degree with little or no consequence for the overall pattern. However, the policy of the Asian socialist states to move toward a market economy and internationalize their economies while maintaining Leninist political systems may challenge and have far-reaching consequences for the relationship of the party to the state and the military, taking civil-military relations into new terrain. Investigation should therefore focus on within-system change as well as change that may be transforming the political system and pattern of civil-military relations.

CIVIL-MILITARY EXPLANATIONS: STATE OF THE ART

A review of current explanations of civil-military relations leads to three observations. First, numerous factors have been advanced to explain developments or nondevelopments in civil-military relations: historical legacies, political culture, ideology, strength of civilian institutions, development of civil society, advantages of military institutions, sociological background and motives of military leaders, factionalism in the military establishment, military professionalism, the military's missions and roles, levels of economic development, and changes in the international context. As observed by Donald Horowitz (1980), the emphasis has been on producing competing single-factor explanations. There have been few serious attempts to link these variables in a comprehensive explanatory framework, let alone develop a parsimonious theory of civil-military relations. Despite more than four decades of effort, cumulation in the subfield of civil-military relations has been weak. The subfield has not "produced a large body of findings that enjoy widespread support and that would apply with equal force to a wide range of countries" (Feaver 1999: 236).

Second, explanations have been development specific. They have sought to explain the military coup d'état, military nonintervention in politics, the military as an agent of modernization, the performance of military regimes, military and economic development, or the military's exit from politics. There have been few attempts, however, to develop a framework that can explain not only intervention but also military rule and withdrawal—and more generally the rich diversity in pattern and content of civil-military relations that can be found in Asia and elsewhere. As noted in the Introduction, there are several patterns of civil-military relations in contemporary Asia, including military domination of politics in Burma, Pakistan, and possibly North Korea; various stages of military disengagement from politics in South Korea,

Taiwan, the Philippines, Thailand, Bangladesh, and Indonesia; continued democratic civilian control of the military in Japan and India; subjective civilian control of the military in Malaysia, Singapore, and Sri Lanka; and continued Communist Party control of the military in China and Vietnam. Further, civil-military relations in most of these countries have undergone changes—more dramatically in some than in others. South Korea, Thailand, Bangladesh, and Indonesia have experienced the full cycle of military politics: intervention, domination, and now disengagement. In Asia the trend appears to be toward greater civilian control of the military. Theories of civil-military relations should be able to explain such multiple patterns, changes, and trends. Otherwise, their utility is distinctly limited.

And third, with a few exceptions (Tilly 1985, 1992; Porter 1994; Downing 1992; Burke 1997), civil-military explanations have not been connected to the broader political dynamics and processes like those associated with state formation and political legitimation as well as to change in the international material and normative context. Admittedly, the development of over-arching theories has made little headway in the social sciences. There is also the danger that the high level of abstraction required to explain multiple and conflicting developments may distance analysis from reality. These considerations should temper our expectations, but they should not impede the development of explanations that have a wider reach.

Before undertaking this task in the next section, it will be useful to have an overview of the civil-military explanations that have been advanced on issues pertinent to this inquiry. This section reviews the major propositions on three issues: military intervention and nonintervention in politics; problems of military rule and military withdrawal or disengagement from politics; and civil-military interaction in postauthoritarian states (with an emphasis on civilian supremacy). In addition to a critical appraisal of the major propositions, the purpose is to identify key building blocks that can aid in the development of propositions to explain the different patterns as well as change in the relationship of the soldier to the state in Asia and elsewhere.

Military Intervention and Nonintervention

Among the numerous explanations that have been advanced to explain the politicization of the officer corps and military intervention or nonintervention in politics, those focused on the nature of the military profession, the military's mission and roles, the weakness of political institutions, and the government's performance have been influential.

The Military Profession.   Three competing propositions connect the nature of the military profession and the propensity of the military to intervene in politics.[5] One, professional militaries are apolitical and do not intervene in politics. Second, professionalization breeds corporate interest, the preservation of which leads to civil-military conflict and military intrusion in politics. Third, the "new professionalism" of the militaries in developing countries encourages political intervention.

The first thesis advanced by Huntington (1957) has been most influential—especially among policymakers. Seeking to explain the political orientation of the officer corps in terms of the degree of military professionalism, Huntington asserts that a highly professional military (in terms of expertise, corporateness, and responsibility) will be "politically sterile and neutral," concentrating on strategic matters and leaving political decisions to civilian authorities. This situation constitutes his "objective" civilian control. An unprofessional military, by contrast, is politicized and disposed to intervene in politics. There is a circularity to this argument, however, in that the outcomes to be explained—politicization and intervention—are also the evidence for explanation. Further, Huntington's proposition would imply that military disengagement from politics after it has intervened would hinge on the development of military professionalism. Although the tension between the military's roles in governance and the management of violence is important, it is difficult to argue that such tension must necessarily lead to military disengagement in politics.

In practice, it is possible for professionalism and military intervention in politics to coexist, as they have in Pakistan during the past forty years. By any standard, the Pakistani military is a professional body, but it also has been interventionist. The dramatic changes in civil-military relations in that country have not been driven by considerations of military professionalism. Professionalism and praetorianism also coexisted in South Korea from 1961 through 1987. Change in South Korean civil-military relations, including the military's disengagement from politics, was driven by several considerations—all of which reduced the salience of coercion in governance. It had little to do with professionalism. Similarly, it is difficult to argue that the Indonesian military's disengagement from politics is a consequence of the development of professionalism. In the twilight years of the Suharto era, there was a debate within the armed forces over the future role of the military (Honna 1999). The proponents of reform, however, were of many hues, with one group advocating greater emphasis on the development of military professionalism (expertise). However, even this group argued for a modified sociopolitical role, not complete disengagement from politics. The Indonesian and the earlier Philippines experiences, however, do suggest that the tension between the military as government and the military as an institution is fertile ground for the development of reform groups, which, in conjunction with other societal forces, can play an important role during the transition to democratic rule, particularly in the lead up to and in the immediate aftermath of the breakdown of the authoritarian regime.

As noted by Pion-Berlin (1997: 15), the behavior of the more professional Third World armies does not support Huntington's claim. Most scholars, he says, believe that Huntington "has greatly overemphasized the salutary effects of professionalism." In a similar vein, Feaver (1999: 235) asserts that inquiry into the linkage between professionalism and military subordination to civilian authority has not been fruitful and should be abandoned. Nevertheless, given its simplicity and a lack of credible alternatives, Huntington's proposition continues to hold sway in policy circles. One manifestation of its continuing influence is the emphasis placed on military professionalism by Western and some Third World governments as a tool for depoliticization of the military and a criterion for measuring consolidation of civilian control in Third Wave democratic transitions.

The second and third propositions challenge Huntington's thesis. Abrahamsson (1972) and Perlmutter (1977) highlight the corporate interests and characteristics of the military that may motivate it to intervene in politics. They posit that professionalization breeds corporate interests—and the better defined these interests become, the greater the chance they could lead to civil-military conflict if they collide with civilian interests. In this postulation the military's propensity to intervene in politics and policy formulation is linked to its corporate and bureaucratic roles (as opposed to its expertise role). It is argued that the corporate orientation of the modern military determines its political behavior and that a high degree of corporatism is cor-related with military praetorianism (Perlmutter 1977: xvi). According to this line of argument, the military will intervene to protect its corporate interests—including control over recruitment, doctrine, training, promotions, salaries, and arms procurement. In this scheme, the civilian gov-ernment accommodates the interests and demands of the military in order to prevent a coup.

The corporate-interest driven proposition, unlike Huntington's professionalism thesis, does not suffer the problem of circularity. Addressing the corporate concerns of the military is also an important consideration in civil-military relations, especially during periods of transition to civilian rule. However, though important, corporate interest is a subsystemic level factor that is hardly a necessary or sufficient cause for military intervention. At best it may, in Finer's (1975) terminology, constitute a push factor. Where it does fuel intervention, such intervention is likely to be reactive and defensive—to protect its institutional autonomy and prerogatives—and short-lived (Pion-Berlin 1992). Once the situation has been corrected and jurisdictional boundaries established, the military is likely to return power to civilians. For more extensive and proactive military domination of the state and politics, the military project must go beyond that of cor-porate interest.

The third proposition connecting military professionalism and political orientation is that of Stepan (1973). In contrast to Huntington's thesis that a professional military is apolitical, Stepan claims that the new professionalism that emphasizes internal security and national devel-opment politicizes the military and contributes to its role expansion. Noting the simultaneous increase in the professionalism and politicization of the Brazilian and Peruvian militaries—and contending that this is part of a wider phenomenon—Stepan develops an alternative formu-lation of professionalism focused on internal security and national development. The broad expertise required to deal with internal security problems narrows the skill differentiation between the military and political elite, leading to the belief that there is "a fundamental inter-relationship between the two spheres, with the military playing a key role in interpreting and dealing with domestic problems owing to its greater technical and professional skills in dealing with internal security issues." In the process the new professional, according to Stepan, becomes highly politicized, leading "inevitably to some degree of role expansion." The extent of role expansion, however, is a function of the legitimacy of the civilian government. The weaker the civilian government, the greater the military's role expansion, and vice versa.

Though frequently interpreted as such, Stepan's formulation of a new professionalism and his thesis are not antithetical to those advanced by Huntington. The new professionalism and its presumed consequences are in fact one version of Huntington's subjective control. Hunt-ington says that professionalism as he defines it is impossible in situations of domestic conflict, that the military is politicized in situations where the government's legitimacy is challenged, and that under subjective civilian control, political and military skills and roles are inter-changeable. The new professionalism concept is useful, however, in highlighting a point made earlier: a high degree of military professionalism does not preclude politicization. As for the proposition that the new professionalism politicizes the military and leads to its role expansion, earlier I argued that the military's internal security role need not lead to these consequences. There are many instances in which the military has engaged in the internal security role with-out becoming politicized. The Indian military, for example, has been massively involved in internal security roles for several decades. Although this role has contributed to the erosion of democratic rights at the local level, it has not led to role expansion of the military at the national level. In Malaysia, too, the military was deeply involved in countering domestic insurgencies, but this mission was carried out under an elaborate framework of control by elected and bureaucratic civilian authority at the national and state levels. As noted in earlier discussion, what is critical is not the role itself but the decision-making power. In the Indian and Malaysian cases, ultimate jurisdiction rested with a legitimate civilian government. The key—which Stepan notes but does not accord due weight—is the legitimacy of civilian government and its capacity to determine and oversee the use of state coercion in maintaining the internal and international security of the state. Though the ideology of a new professionalism may lend itself to military role expansion, there is no inevitable link between the two.

Military Mission and Roles. The second set of explanations link military intervention and nonintervention to continuous threat of war, mission and roles of the military, and mobilization for war. One hypothesis is that the continuous threat of war blurs the civil-military distinction and leads to the political ascendance of the military. This garrison state hypothesis was advanced by Lasswell (1941, 1962) as the antithesis of the civilian (democratic) state. Positing a continuous threat of war and emphasizing the technological revolution, he argued that the specialists on violence are in the ascendant and will come to dominate the political stage. In his view, the civilian (that is, the democratic) state is not viable "under conditions of chronic war and threat of war or violent revolution." Mills (1956) posited that the United States was engaged in a permanent war economy and argued that a centralization of power by a homogeneous elite comprising political, corporate, and military leaders (the military-industrial complex) would subvert democracy. Lang (1972: 117) argued that with the growing salience of science and technology in national security, the distinction between strategy and policy and between military and civilian entities has become blurred in the advanced industrialized countries. Strategy is intricately connected to policy. And as the military component in foreign policy gains ground, so too does the weight attached to the counsel of soldiers—leading to the rise of the garrison state. All three argue that rather than constituting a restraint, military professionalism provides the impetus for expansion of military influence in the context of a continuous threat situation.

A second proposition is that the specific mission of the nation's military has a major impact on civil-military relations. However, there is disagreement over which mission is conducive to civilian or military control. Desch (1996: 12–13) argues that international combat missions are the "most conducive to healthy patterns of civil-military relations [by which he means the democratic model], whereas nonmilitary, internal missions often engender various pathologies." Diamond and Plattner (1996: xvi) argue the contrary: they cite the absence of large-scale interstate conflict as one of the key reasons for the retreat from military rule in Latin American countries. Still others (Stepan 1973; Ganguly 1991a; Desch 1996) posit a connection between the military's internal security roles, erosion of democracy, and the political ascendance of the military.

The third set of propositions link mobilization for war and civil-military relations. Here too, there are conflicting propositions. Downing (1992) argues that what matters is not exposure to violent conflict per se but the extent of domestic mobilization of resources. Light domestic mobilization of human and economic resources in combination with the "numerous institutions, procedures, and arrangements" that existed in medieval Europe, according to him, provided the basis for the emergence of democracy while "extensive domestic resource mobilization" contributed to the rise of military-bureaucratic authoritarianism. Tilly (1985: 186) advances an opposite argument: the availability of external resources for Third World states (and hence the absence or minimal need for domestic mobilization) makes for "unconstrained [military] organizations that easily overshadow all other organizations within their territories"— thereby increasing the advantage of military power and the incentive to seize control of the state.

More than 50 years have lapsed, but the garrison state proposition has not come to pass in the advanced industrialized democracies. The militaries in these countries continue to be subordinate to civilian authority. Lasswell and others ignored the vitality of the democratic ideas and the checks and balances instituted by democratic institutions in these countries. As observed by Friedberg (2000: 5–6), in the case of the United States, the fragmented nature of the American political system, especially the separation of powers among the different branches of government, and the pervasive antistatist ideology with the concomitant interest in limiting state power, prevented the development of a stronger, more centralized state like that posited by the proponents of the garrison state hypothesis.

Evidence can be found to support as well as contradict each of the other propositions. The military did dominate politics in countries such as South Korea, Taiwan, and Thailand that were confronted with acute international threats. This is still the case in Pakistan. However, the presence of acute international threat has not always led to the military's political ascendance as illustrated by the experience of India and, to a lesser degree, that of Singapore. Further, despite the continuation of grave international threats to state survival, the militaries in South Korea, Taiwan, and Thailand (1973) were compelled to disengage from politics. Finally, the military has intervened in politics in countries such as Burma and the Philippines that do not confront major international threats to security. There is no clear causal connection between grave external threats and political ascendance of the military. In some cases, external threats have enhanced the power of the military, whereas in others they have not.

Evidence can also be found to support or contradict the posited connections between the internal security role and the political ascendance of the military. However, as pointed out earlier, the key is not whether the role is internal or external, but who has the power to make decisions. Nevertheless, the likelihood for military role expansion is greater in the internal than in the international role. In the internal role the military is deployed within the country. Such deployment provides the military with the opportunity to build organizational, administrative, and economic resources and capacity that can more readily be deployed to increase the power of the military to the detriment of other state institutions. Further, the involvement of the military in internal security and socioeconomic roles demystifies government, exposes the weaknesses of civilian leaders and institutions, and enhances the confidence of the military in its ability to govern. It is more difficult though not impossible to translate the assets of the international role (external defense as well as deployment in foreign countries in an occupation role or in a developmental capacity) into domestic power and authority—which is the key to civil-military relations. This said, the political salience of the military is greatest when political legitimacy of the civilian government is weak and coercion plays a crucial role in both domestic governance and safeguarding the international security of the country, as for example in Pakistan.

As with the other two propositions, evidence can be found to support or refute the posited connection between light or heavy domestic mobilization and the pattern of civil-military relations. As observed by Porter (1994: 10–11), although the centralizing tendency of war (internal and international) may promote autocratic rule, modern war has also promoted democratic rule because of the need for mass mobilization and capital.

Although the experience of the advanced industrialized democracies during the past five decades refutes the garrison state hypothesis and none of the other propositions is conclusive, this particular set of explanations focused on the threat of war and the mission and roles of the military serves a useful purpose in highlighting, if only indirectly, the functional connection between coercion (the primary endowment of the military) and the internal and international consolidation of the nation-state, and its implication for civil-military relations. We will argue later that alteration in the weight of coercion in governance is a crucial variable in the explanation of change in civil-military relations.

The Weakness of Political Institutions.   The third set of explanations shifts the focus from the military to the state and society—especially the weakness of political institutions in developing states. The major proposition here is that of Finer (1976), who links the propensity to intervene to the level of political culture. He asserts that countries with a high level of political culture are less prone to military intervention and vice versa. Finer explains military intervention in terms of push and pull factors, attributing greater weight to the latter. Though the military's strengths, motives, and disposition are important, he says, the opportunity to intervene is critical. Finer links the decision to intervene and the form of military intervention to the level of political culture. A high level of political culture inhibits military intervention, while a low level provides the opportunity for intervention. Finer (1976: 78) defines political culture in terms of the legitimacy enjoyed by rulers and the degree of public support for and participation in the "complex of civil procedures and organs" that constitute the political system. In a similar vein— and departing from his professionalism argument—Huntington (1968: 194) states that "the most important causes of military intervention in politics are not military but political, and reflect not the social and organizational characteristics of the military establishment, but the political and institutional structure of the society."

Riggs (1964) takes this argument a step further by maintaining that military intervention is a function of unbalanced institutional development. According to Riggs, the institutions of state control—bureaucratic and military institutions—were more highly developed than the institutions for political participation and governance. As politicians and political institutions failed, the military and bureaucracy were compelled to intervene. A similar but class-based explanation is advanced by Alavi (1972). His argument is that at the moment of independence, the weak and underdeveloped indigenous bourgeoisie was unable to subordinate the highly developed colonial state (military-bureaucracy) apparatus through which the metropolitan power had exercised dominion. Further, the military-bureaucratic oligarchy is well placed to mediate the competing but no longer contradictory interests of the indigenous bourgeoisie, the metropolitan neocolonial bourgeoisie, and the landed class. Because it is not the instrument of a particular class, the state acquires a relatively autonomous position and role in the neocolonial state. He deploys this argument to explain the political dominance of the military in Pakistan and Bangladesh. Also in the institutional mode of analysis, Tilly (1992: 218), seeking to explain the rise of military regimes in the Third World, advances three possibilities: the failure of civilian-dominated institutions leading to takeover by the military; the disproportionate support for Third World militaries provided by outside powers, which strengthens them vis-à-vis their civilian competitors; and the greater autonomy of Third World states (and by extension the militaries) from their societies because they acquire their resources not from the people but from outside the country.

A second society-based explanation of military politicization and intervention is that the military intervenes to protect and advance the interests of a specific class or ethnic/religious group (Enloe 1981). Unlike the institutional weakness and imbalance arguments, this proposition views the military not as an institution separate and aloof from society but as an extension of it and hence not immune from the conflicts and tensions that beset it. According to this argument, an ethnically homogenous or class-based military may intervene to protect the interests of that community or class. Alternatively, in a military that is not homogenous, the office corps may be factionalized along ethnic, class, regional, or ideological lines. Reflecting the divisions in society, such factionalization can precipitate military involvement in the political conflict and power struggle among civilian groups.

This of propositions has several merits. One, it focuses not just on the military but also on the relative strength of military and civilian institutions. This is important, as the nature and content of civil-military relations are outcomes of the interaction of these institutions. Second, it draws attention to the issue of political legitimacy, which is central to political domination. This critical issue is discussed later in this section. Third, it draws attention to the systemic motive and rationale for military intervention—the weakness and inability of civilian government to preserve the unity of the country, maintain law and order, and improve the economic welfare of the people. Fourth, the institutional imbalance argument draws attention to the crucial variable of power. Although power by itself does not dictate behavior, the balance of power between different institutions and groups, including the civilian and military institutions of the state, is especially important in societies where the normative framework for the acquisition and exercise of state is still in the process of construction. Finally, the society-based proposition may be helpful in explaining civil-military relations in ethnically plural societies such as Sri Lanka, Malaysia, and Singapore when one particular community seeks to dominate the state.

The propositions in this set of explanations also suffer some drawbacks. One, the coercive institutions of the state, including the military, were not as highly developed as presumed in these propositions. As it will become clear from the discussion in the concluding chapter of the book, when compared to the political leadership and institutions, the military at independence was weak in stature, organization, and resources and, in many instances, a disunited and faction-ridden institution. Only later did it become more cohesive and stronger. How and why this occurred cannot be explained by the institutional arguments. Second, they miss the functional connection between the military and the state, for example, on the role of coercion in governance. Such function-based analysis can provide critical insights into the reasons for increase (or decrease) in the military's political power and influence that is not available from straight institutional analysis. High reliance on coercion for political domination, for example, would necessitate the development of strong coercive structures and institutions that could inhibit the development of noncoercive state capacity and tilt the distribution of power in favor of the military. A third related shortcoming is that the factors that may enhance or undermine the power and legitimacy of the competing institutions are not an integral part of the propositions. Without a dynamic element, their ability to explain change and diversity is limited. Finally, these propositions ignore the international context. As observed by Tilly (1992: 223), great power competition during the cold war significantly affected civil-military relations in the developing countries. Similarly, the end of the cold war, the dominant position of the United States, and the ascendance of democracy, capitalism, and human rights to near hegemonic status have significantly undermined the power and influence of militaries while strengthening that of civilian leaders and institutions, with consequence for civil-military relations.

The Government's Performance.   Closely linked to the political, institutional, and cultural explanations is the final set of explanations focused on government performance and level of development. One proposition is that performance failures on the part of civilian governments—especially those that precipitate crisis situations and slow economic development—provide the impetus for military intervention (Fossum 1967; Hoadley 1975). The second proposition, advanced by Huntington (1996: 9), is that coup is a function of underdevelopment. He posits a connection between the level of economic development and the propensity for coups and their success or failure. According to Huntington, successful coups occur in countries with per capita gross domestic product (GDP) under $500. Countries with per capita GDP of $1,000 or more do not have successful coups, and in those where the per capita GDP exceeds $3,000, there are no coup attempts.

Scholars like Janowitz (1963: 18–22), however, are skeptical about the relationship between level of economic development and the military's propensity to intervene. Yet others like Putnam (1967), who investigated the correlation between economic growth, social mobilization, and military intervention in Latin America, have hypothesized that the short-run effect of economic growth is to encourage military intervention. In the long term, however, the social mobilization resulting from economic growth will reduce the military's political role. Putnam also noted the growing autonomy of the political sphere, however, and the habituation to military rule in some countries.

Though attractive, these two propositions in and of themselves suffer several shortcomings. First, much depends on the nature and legitimacy of the political system and government as well as the public perception of what brought about the economic failure and crisis. Until recently, economic growth in India, for example, has been rather slow, and its per capita income is still around the $500 level. And India has suffered many crises of governance, but transfer of power has always occurred through the ballot box. Despite its many failings, the democratic political system enjoys broad support in that country. Similarly, the democratic systems in South Korea and Thailand have gained in legitimacy. Hence, the response to the 1997 economic crisis in these two countries was not a coup d'état as in earlier times but change of government through the democratic process.

The economic crisis in Indonesia also did not result in military intervention. In fact, the crisis discredited the Suharto government and put the military on the defensive. The economic crisis brought into sharp relief the legitimacy problem that had confronted the Suharto government since the late 1980s and precipitated the democratic transition in that country. It is possible that failure on the part of the Abdurrahmand Wahid government to address the many problems confronting Indonesia may undermine its legitimacy and bring about a change in government. However, it is not a foregone conclusion that this must lead to military intervention and rule. The point here is that failure to perform (a condition that is difficult to determine objectively except in the more extreme situations) by itself is not a determinant of military coup.

Although one can find exceptions to the proposition that coups become more difficult as countries move up the ladder of economic development, it does have value in explaining change in civil-military relations, particularly the declining importance of coercion in governance and by extension the reduction in the political power and role of the military. Sustained economic growth in the capitalist mode engenders the growth of new socioeconomic and political forces that alters the distribution of power among state institutions as well as among state, society, and the private sector. By building state capacity, especially of its noncoercive institutions to address the problems confronting society, capitalist development reduces the salience of coercion in governance. It also promotes the rule of law and respect for private property rights and increases transparency and accountability. A strong private sector and civil society usually accompany economic growth and development with a corresponding reduction in the role of the state in the allocation of economic goods. The state and society become much more complex and less vulnerable to management or change by force. To be sure, economic growth poses its own tensions, contradictions, and challenges, but increasingly these cannot be dealt with by coercion. Because of the impact it has on the salience of coercion in governance as well as on the distribution of power among the different institutions and groups in the state and society, the economic development variable can be useful in explaining change in the content of civil-military relations.

The Inherent Instability of Military Rule

A dominant view in the literature is that military governments are inherently unstable and military regimes are not durable—very few have exceeded twenty years (Nordlinger 1977: 138–39). Our discussion in this section focuses on the legitimacy problem confronting military governments and the military exit from politics.

Legitimacy Problem.　　The core explanation advanced for the relatively short life span of military regimes is the problem of legitimacy—acknowledgment of the right to rule by the public, especially the politically powerful groups. Even if not acknowledged as fully legitimate, the military needs a measure of acceptance by civil, political, and international societies. It cannot rule by coercion alone. Drawing on the current literature, four interconnected propositions can be constructed to explain the short life span of military regimes. One, performance legitimacy, the basis on which the military usually stakes its claim to rule, is not durable. Second, the values and goals cherished by the military make it impossible for it to construct a widely accepted political framework. Third, the military is unable to overcome the succession problem. Finally, the tension between military as government and military as institution is fundamental and inescapable, leading to fissures and ultimately the breakdown of military regimes.

To begin with, military governments usually enjoy negative legitimacy (Huntington 1991: 49–50). But this is not enduring, and military governments often stake their claim to legitimacy on promise of performance—restoration of order and stability, protection of national security, and delivery of economic well-being. Although failure to perform undermines the military's claim to legitimacy, successful performance may also undermine the military's legitimacy, resulting in what Huntington has characterized as the performance dilemma. Success in restoration of order removes the security and stability rationale, although military governments may exploit the danger of potential chaos and disorder in the event of change in government. Sustained economic growth, for its part, creates new forces and interests, especially strong middle and working classes that become dissatisfied with the political status quo, demanding political participation and change, particularly if the fruits of economic growth are not widely shared. Sustained economic growth also makes for a more complex and internationalized economy that is more vulnerable to international crisis and pressure. Thus, while good performance may have legitimating potential in the short run, its negative consequences become more salient in the long run.

The legitimacy problem of the military, however, is more deep-seated. It lies in the military's distaste for politics, distrust of politicians, preference for stability, order, and efficiency, lack of linkage to political and civil societies, and its unwillingness to accommodate change. All of these attributes contribute to the military's inability to construct an acceptable political framework for the management of the state, including the acquisition and exercise of state power. Military governments often seek to de-politicize the political and administer the country through a techno-bureaucratic alliance—sometimes co-opting political leaders favorably disposed toward the military. The preference is for a strong government suspended above society on the assumption that people do not know what is best for them. Military governments close off or severely limit opportunities for political participation and competition, casting political opponents as subversives who threaten order and security. The exclusionary approach and reliance on coercion polarizes society, uniting alienated political groups whose sole purpose then becomes the ouster of the military government by all means available—both internal and international. Further, once the military assumes power, it often suffers the same limitations as the civilian government it displaced. In the absence of checks and balances, a military government that stays long in power becomes the captive of a narrow section of the elite and is prone to corruption and cronyism. The image of the military government, blind to and unable to correct its weaknesses, becomes tarred, undermining its right to rule and strengthening opposition demand for return to civilian rule.

Two other related problems that confront military rulers are political succession and retaining control over the military. Given the manner in which the military appropriates political power and its inability to develop an acceptable framework for governance, often the only available option for leadership and government change is through another coup or counter coup. Coups perform the role of elections in military and authoritarian regimes. As observed by Clapham and Philip (1985: 24), succession in military regimes is "like paths through the jungle: there are various trails, all of them pretty rough going... and most of them not leading to where you want to go anyhow." Succession in military regimes is unpredictable and can be violent.

Further, once the military rulers begin to govern, fissures usually develop between those who govern and those who command the troops, especially the field commanders. The conflicting demands of the two vocations, field commanders' disenchantment with the institutional and policy paths chosen by those at the political helm, unhappiness with the division of spoils, factionalism, and concern to preserve the unity, integrity, legitimacy, and effectiveness of the military are among the reasons that contribute to the development of such fissures. To consolidate their control and prevent counter coups, military leaders at the political helm may hold on to senior positions, appoint loyalists, create counter-balancing factions, develop patronage networks, develop extensive surveillance and intimidation mechanisms, or remake the political center by co-opting potential challengers. Despite these measures, the contradiction between military as government and military as an institution is a fundamental and inescapable contradiction that ultimately leads to disunity and breakdown of the military regime (Ricci and Fitch 1990: 68).

The legitimacy problem of military governments is compounded by the fact that military rule is no longer an accepted form of government in the contemporary era. Much of the international community has outlawed military intervention in politics. At best, they accept military intervention as temporary, and they demand policies and measures for a quick return to civilian rule. For example, the United States, the European Union, and the Commonwealth have all condemned the ouster of democratically elected governments in Pakistan (1999) and Fiji (2000) and imposed political and economic sanctions, limiting their interaction with the military or military-backed governments and demanding a return to democratic rule. Moreover, most militaries do not view themselves as permanent rulers. Usurpation of political power is often accompanied by declarations to the effect that military rule is temporary and that power will be returned to civilian leaders once the political, social, or economic ills have been rectified. Inability to legitimate and institutionalize its rule, increasing reliance on coercion, and difficulties associated with retaining the support of the military as an institution are among the key factors that explain the inherent instability and the relatively short life span of military governments. As observed by Ricci and Fitch (1990: 70), "the essence of government is politics rather than administration." The deficiency of the military in this arena cannot be compensated by "tinkering with organizational charts or substituting one set of leaders for another." However, once they have enjoyed the privileges, military rulers find it difficult to give up political power.

Military Exit from Politics.   In seeking to explain the military's exit from politics, Finer (1985: 23–24) posits that "what applies to military intervention... can also be 'played back' to explicate its extrusion." Although he cites certain military and social motivations and necessary conditions for military abdication, he does not venture to explain the origin of these changes in motivations and conditions. There is no dynamic content to his explanation. In any case, voluntary withdrawal is rare, and such withdrawals in Burma (1960), Pakistan (1985), and Thailand (1973) were followed by another round of military intervention. In most cases, authoritarian leaders and militaries have been compelled to exit from politics. Here explanations of military withdrawal merge with those of democratic transition.

The literature on democratic transition is vast and the issues covered are many. Much of the conceptual and theoretical work on this subject has been done by scholars working on Latin America and Southern Europe. Of particular significance is the multiyear *Transitions from Authoritarian Rule* project directed by O'Donnell, Schmitter, and Whitehead (1986), which systematically and comparatively focused on democratic transitions in Latin America and Southern

Europe by investigating cases of transition from bureaucratic authoritarianism, military populism, and sultanistic despotism. Given the political predominance of the military in these two regions as rulers or backers of authoritarian rule, civil-military relations are an important though not the primary focus of this literature. Also significant from the perspective of this study is the 26-nation study *Democracy in Developing Countries* undertaken by Diamond, Linz, and Lipset (1989) in the 1980s. As military regimes belong to the genre of authoritarian regimes, in this section we shall try to glean from this literature explanations relating to the breakdown of authoritarian regimes paying particular attention to military regime collapse.

A multiplicity of propositions have been advanced to explain the impetus for liberalization, the breakdown of authoritarian regimes, and the onset of democratic transition. (See O'Donnell and Schmitter 1986: 15–21; Stepan 1986: 64–84, Przeworski 1986: 47–63; Huntington 1991: 37–40.) These explanations fall into two categories: international factors (defeat in war, conquest, changes in the global material and normative structure, changes in the global economy, changes in the foreign policy of major powers), and domestic factors (economic crisis, loss of legitimacy, conflict within the ruling bloc, growing public opposition, civil war, internal conflict).

While accepting the salience of international factors—that a regime's survival is influenced by international norms and that a downturn in the global economy can have negative consequences—analysts have in the main viewed them more as constraints on action rather than drivers of change. According to O'Donnell and Schmitter (1986: 18), international factors did not "compel authoritarian rulers to experiment with liberalization, much less... cause their regimes to collapse." In their view, domestic factors played the crucial role in liberalization initiatives and the collapse of authoritarian regimes. Kaufman (1986) contends that bureaucratic-authoritarian governments in Latin America "have shown significant ability to survive prolonged periods of diplomatic isolation and a ruthless capacity to crush opposition from below" and believes that change is more likely to come about through disintegration from within than overthrow from outside.

In emphasizing the predominance of domestic factors, the bulk of this scholarship agrees that the onset of transition and military withdrawal from politics can be traced to cracks within authoritarian regimes. O'Donnell and Schmitter (1986: 19) assert: "There is no transition whose beginning is not the consequence—direct or indirect—of important divisions within the authoritarian regime itself, principally along the fluctuating cleavages between hard-liners and soft-liners." Imminent death of the regime's founder, conflict over succession, loss of legitimacy issuing from mass unrest or mass noncompliance, impending economic crisis, strong foreign pressure—these are among the developments that can produce cracks in an authoritarian regime (Przeworski 1986: 55). And when cracks do appear, competing groups within the ruling bloc seek to bolster themselves by enlisting the support of elements that have been excluded from politics. Such openings usually produce "a sharp and rapid increase in general politicization and popular activation—the resurrection of civil society" (O'Donnell and Schmitter 1986: 26, 48–56).

Division within the military was a key element in the military exit from politics in Thailand (1973), the Philippines (1986), Bangladesh (1990), and Indonesia (1998). In 1973, Gen. Krit Sivara, commander in chief of the Thai army, refused to allow major army units to come to the aid of the military government led by Thanom Kittikachorn and Praphat Charusathien,

leading to its collapse (Samudavanija 1982). In the Philippines, the defection of defense minister Enrile and acting chief of staff Fidel Ramos and the mutiny by the Reform the Armed
Forces of the Philippines Movement (RAM) played a crucial role in the ouster of President
Marcos. Had a segment of the military not mutinied, it is unclear if the 1986 People Power revolution would have succeeded (Mackenzie 1987). The refusal of the Bangladesh military to
back the government in the face of a massive public uprising led to the ouster of President (formerly general) H. M. Ershad in 1990. Rivalry between General Wiranto (Suharto loyalist and
ABRI chief) and General Prabowo (Suharto's son-in-law) appears to have been a key part of
the drama that led to and followed the ouster of Suharto. Withdrawal of backing by Wiranto
was a critical factor in Suharto's decision to step down. In contrast to these cases, the Burmese
military, notwithstanding persistent rumors of rivalry and rift, appears to have preserved unity;
and, despite the 1988 massive public protest, the overwhelming victory of the Aung San Su-u
Kyi–led National League for Democracy in the 1990 military organized elections, and continued international pressure, it has continued cling to power.

However, as the "revolutions" in Thailand, Bangladesh, the Philippines, and Indonesia as
well as that in South Korea (1987) indicate, division within the military alone is not sufficient.
A confluence of domestic and international factors—serious legitimacy deficit on the part of
the military or military-backed government; inability of the military government to address
the mounting challenges; disunity within the military and emergence of reform-minded officers; growth, unity, and mobilization of political and civil society in opposition to military rule;
growing vulnerability to and a changing international context—all coalesced to compel the
military to exit from politics in the above cited countries.

Military-State Relations in the Postauthoritarian State

Unlike the literature on the intervention, domination, and exit phases of military politics that
emphasize the development of propositions and theories, however weak, that on the postauthoritarian phase is markedly different. It is much more normative and applied in character.
Much of the writing is on the nature of the civil-military problem and how to promote democratic civilian control. Other issues discussed include the role of power and ideas in the consolidation of civilian control and the level of explanation.

Postauthoritarian Civil-Military Problem.   The key civil-military problem in the postauthoritarian state is the need to curb the military's political power and define its institutional status
within the emerging democratic framework. Civilian control of the military has been identified as critical for successful democratic transition (O'Donnell and Schmitter 1986: 32). Recognizing that the civil-military problem during the transition process varies from country to
country, Huntington (1991: 231–38) links it to the type of authoritarian regime that was displaced. In the case of one-party dictatorships, the civil-military problem is to separate the military from the dominant party and transfer its loyalty and subordination to the democratic institutions of the state. The problem is much greater, he says, in dealing with the military after a
personal dictatorship because officers or groups down the chain of command are likely to be
politicized. These disgruntled officers are likely to engage in "transitional coups." The civil-
military problem is likely to be protracted in democracies that follow a military regime. Here

the problem is one of dealing with the military as an institution and reducing its power to make it compatible with democratic norms.

Promotion of Democratic Civilian Control.   Militaries in the postauthoritarian phase usually try to negotiate their role in governance. They may demand special provisions in the new constitution—including the right to administer the country or parts of it in situations of emergency—and demand the continuation of laws and decrees passed during the period of military rule as well as jurisdiction in certain areas of governance. Most likely they will seek guarantees of the military's autonomy in institutional matters and amnesty for past human rights abuses and other atrocities. Several guidelines have been recommended for democratizers (Huntington 1991: 243–53): professionalizing the armed forces (based on the argument that a professional military is politically neutral and will serve the government of the day); reorienting the military toward international military missions; restructuring the defense establishment and replacing the top leadership of the armed forces; reducing the size of the armed forces; and becoming sensitive to the military's status concerns.

While supportive of immediate measures—like changes in the constitution and laws, changes in the chain of command, and civilian control over promotions, appointments, and budgets—especially because they can buy time, O'Donnell and Schmitter argue that they are not likely to have a quick impact on the deeply rooted self-images and attitudes of the officer corps. The military must somehow be "induced to moderate its messianic self-image and must be given a creditable and honorable role in accomplishing (but not setting) national goals." Further, political leaders must be made to play by democratic rules and prevent the military from being drawn into politics in the service of disgruntled politicians. These long-term goals can only be achieved through education, prolonged experience with democratic governments, and new thinking on the part of military officers. Reducing the power of the military and returning it to normal status requires the development of political institutions, the management of internal conflict through political and socioeconomic means, attenuation in the direct application of force in governance, and the development of a socioeconomic pact among all interested parties. In a similar vein, Goodman (1990: xiv) asserts that incremental change—rather than immediate and full civilian control of the military—has been characteristic of successful transitions. For democracy to take root, he says, "both military men and civilian leaders must take on new roles" that permit the building of trust and cooperation.

Role of Power and Ideas.   The importance of a favorable balance of power for successful transition and for promoting civilian supremacy over the military has been stressed by several scholars. Aguero (1995), for example, asserts that the military's attitudes (motivations and ideological consent) are not an essential component of civilian supremacy, although he concedes they may be desirable in the long run for democratic consolidation. Emphasizing the distribution of power during the democratic transition, he argues that "democratization and civilian supremacy can be secured without prior voluntary support of the democratic credo by members of the armed forces" (1995: 21). The central issues for Aguero in civil-military relations in this period are issues of power. The outcome of democratic transition, he states, will be determined by the relative empowerment of civilians and the military. According to him, the "initial conditions are critical in shaping the first transition outcome," which in turn has a powerful influence on the subsequent process (1995: 39). Aguero cites certain conditions that may empower civilian authorities in their pursuit of civilian supremacy: civilian control over the transition agenda, civilian coalescence around fundamental aspects of democratization, public support for government, civilian expertise on national defense, and the absence of military resistance to democratization (1995: 35–36).

Similarly, Rueschemeyer and colleagues (1992: 50–51), writing on democratic transition, recognize the role of "ideas, values, and nonmaterial interests," but they too do not assign ideational factors a key role in their analysis of democratization. Given their power-oriented conception of democracy, they prefer to consider only those ideas that are socially powerful and organizationally grounded. This approach, while useful in some ways, downplays the significance of ideas in democratization and by extension in civil-military interaction. The distribution of power is certainly important, especially during crisis situations, but civil-military interaction is based on more than power differentials. Interests and beliefs are also crucial. In fact, power differentials are salient only insofar as they constrain or facilitate certain developments. And the immediate causes of these developments are rooted in interests and beliefs that should be treated as variables in their own right. Ideational shifts in society at large, as well as in the military, are critical for democratic transition and consolidation. As observed by Dahl (1971: 50), polyarchy is impossible unless the military is sufficiently depoliticized to permit civilian rule. He writes, "the crucial intervening variable" affecting the chances for polyarchy is "the strength of certain beliefs not only among civilians but among all ranks of the military."

The explanatory framework developed in the next section is based on the conviction that interests, beliefs, and power—each in its own right and in combination—inform the behavior of civilian and military actors and their interaction.

Level of Explanation.   Another issue of contention is the level at which democratic transition and by extension democratic civilian control should be explained. Because of the uncertainty and indirection that characterize democratic transition, O'Donnell and Schmitter (1986: 4–5) maintain that "the 'normal' social science concepts and approaches" are inadequate for the study of democratic transition. Though not denying the long-term impact of structural factors such as macroeconomics and social class, they assert that "short-term political calculations . . . cannot be deduced or imputed to such structures." Democratic transition, they say, should be analyzed with "distinctly political concepts, however vaguely delineated and difficult to pin down they may be." Adopting a political economy perspective and distinguishing themselves from the structural-functional explanation of the modernization school, Rueschemeyer and colleagues (1992: 5) employ a comparative historical approach that focuses on actors "whose power is grounded in control of economic and organizational resources and/or coercive force and who vie with each other for scarce resources in the pursuit of conflicting goals." To orient their analysis, however, they develop a theoretical framework that is essentially structural. This framework helps to identify conditions favoring or inhibiting democratization but not the immediate cause for specific transitions. The latter is the task of historical case studies that focus on sequencing.

Despite differences in the causal analysis, Huntington's explanation for democratization operates at essentially the same level as that of Rueschemeyer and colleagues. There is an implicit connection in Huntington's analysis between structural factors and the behavior of agents. Both structure and agency are relevant in explaining change in civil-military interaction. Although a focus on agency might be more suitable to explain a particular development, the long-term success or failure of that development hinges on structural conditions and trends. The short-run success of the 1991 coup d'état in Thailand but the military's ultimate failure to perpetuate its rule, for example, cannot be explained without invoking the changes that have occurred in the country's normative and material structures. Explanatory frameworks, therefore, should incorporate both structure and agency and their recursive interaction. Having reviewed the major propositions and identified some key variables that must inform explanation of civil-military relations, we now proceed to the third and final task of this chapter—the construction of a comprehensive and integrated explanatory framework.

EXPLANATORY FRAMEWORK: TWO BROAD PROPOSITIONS

An obvious point that emerges from the preceding discussion is that the civil-military relations are not just the consequence of the attributes of one institution. They are the outcome, rather, of the interaction, among other things, of the interests, beliefs, and power of political, administrative, and military institutions of the state. Therefore, explanations rooted only in the attributes and strengths of the military (like professionalism or corporate interests) or civilian institutions (legitimacy and capacity) are not satisfactory. At best they provide partial explanation. More useful are Finer's "push and pull" and Riggs's relative institutional strength explanations, which highlight the need to focus on both sets of institutions. As observed earlier, even these explanations suffer a number of shortcomings. Further, the relationship of the soldier to the state is intricately connected to several larger processes, like those associated with the nation- and state-building projects, construction of the structure for political domination, the mode and pace of economic development, safeguarding the international security of the state, and the international context. Explanation of civil-military relations must be rooted in and take account of these considerations.

This study advances two sets of propositions. The thrust of the first set of propositions rooted in the interplay of coercion, political legitimacy, and economic development is that the weight and role of coercion in governance is the crucial determinant of the nature and content of civil-military relations. It is crucial for two reasons. One, coercion is the key asset of the military, whose primary rationale and function are the concentration and application of force. Second, coercion in governance provides the key functional connection between the military and the state. As observed in the Introduction, coercion is a critical component of governance. In the ideal type modern state, political domination and, more broadly, domestic governance rest on rational legal authority, with coercion playing an attenuated and indirect role. It is more salient in the external defense of the political community. In this ideal type state, the political (executive and legislative), administrative, judicial, and economic institutions of the state are well developed. The beliefs underlying governance as well as the distribution of power are clearly in favor of civilian domination of the state and the military. However, an increase in the salience of coercion in governance makes for an expansion in the size, capacity, and role of the military (and other institutions of coercion). And such expansion is usually (though not always) to the detriment of the other institutions of the state, inducing a change in the distribution of power in favor of the military and contributing to a rise in its political power and influence. This leads to our first proposition. As the weight of coercion increases (or decreases), so does the power and influence of the military relative to the noncoercive state institutions. The military's political influence, which may take the form of intervention and domination, is high when coercion becomes the mainstay of governance and vice versa.

This raises the question as to when and why the salience of coercion increases or decreases. The weight of coercion in governance is determined by two key factors—political legitimacy and level of economic development—and this leads to our next two propositions. If the government, regime, and nation-state are contested domestically and internationally, and if the state does not have the political, diplomatic, administrative, and economic capacity to address the challenges confronting the country through noncoercive means, the weight of coercion in governance and the political power and influence of the military would increase. This especially would be the case if the challenges to the state include a coercive dimension. Alternatively, if the government, regime, and nation-state enjoy widespread legitimacy, then the salience of coercion and by extension the power and influence of the military would decline. This is the second proposition. The third proposition links the salience of coercion to the level of economic development. Increasing levels of economic development, as noted earlier, would make for a more complex state, society, and economy and strengthen the noncoercive capacity of the state, reducing the salience of coercion and by extension the power and influence of the military. Civilian supremacy would be the more normal condition in state-soldier relations in a state that is widely perceived as legitimate as well as highly developed both politically and economically.

The thrust of the second set of propositions is that the pattern and content of state-soldier relations are outcomes of the interaction of the interests, power, and beliefs of key civilian institutions (political executive, legislature, bureaucracy, communist party) and military institutions (armed forces, paramilitary forces, intelligence, and security agencies) mediated by the beliefs and power of civil society and the international society. In situations where the structure of political domination is well established, the beliefs of that system (principles and norms) determine the pattern of civil-military relations. Explanation of the specific content of civil-military relations, however, must rely on the interests of the relevant actors and the distribution of power among them. If, on the other hand, the political system is the object of struggle, explanation of civil-military relations must turn on the distribution of power among key actors and their interests, which are also likely to be affected by the power and beliefs of civil society and the international community, particularly that of the major powers. Obviously the two sets of propositions are interconnected, but they are also distinct. The first set is more structural and useful in explaining long-term continuity and change, whereas the second set is more relevant in explaining specific developments in civil-military relations. These two sets of propositions, especially the causal connections, are elaborated below.

Coercion, Governance, and Civil-Military Relations

State coercion, as observed earlier, plays a key role in governance: in building an integrated national political community as envisioned by the national elite, in constructing the structure of political domination, in extending the reach of the government to all parts of the country, and in defending the political independence and territorial integrity of the state against international threats. As a key repository of state coercion, the military plays a role in all these areas of governance under the labels of internal and international security. Participation in governance endows the military with power and influence.

The primary contention of this set of propositions is that as the weight of coercion in governance increases (or decreases), so does the power and influence of the military relative to other state institutions. Increased reliance on coercion has several consequences: build-up in the size of the military with a corresponding increase in defense expenditure diverting resources away from other priorities and institutions, development of a unified military command structure that reaches to all parts of the country, increased military control over security policymaking, the enactment of emergency legislation that limits the authority of other institutions as well as curtails the activities of political and civil society, military control of public administration in troubled areas, military involvement in economic and commercial activities in the name of security, and the generation of off-budget revenues for the military institutions and for individuals. The net consequence is to strengthen the military as an institution and increase its power and influence relative to the other state institutions, making for a transformation in the structure and process of governance at the national and/or provincial levels.

The weight of coercion in governance is inversely proportional to the legitimacy of the nation-state and its political system as well as the capacity of noncoercive state institutions to address the problems confronting the country. If the nation-state as constructed and the system of political domination are legitimate—and the political, legal, and administrative institutions, processes, and policies of the state are capable of addressing the political, social, and economic problems confronting it—coercion will not figure prominently in governance. The military's role and power will be limited and it will be subordinate to the civilian government. If, however, state coercion is crucial for political domination as well as for preserving the country's unity, independence, and territorial integrity, then the military's power and influence vis-à-vis the political and administrative leaders will increase, contributing to role expansion (see Figure 1.2 and Table 1.1).

This proposition is similar to the demand or pull theories advanced by Finer and Huntington. In their theories, however, the military intervenes because the civilian government is weak and incapable while the military enjoys some advantages and may be disposed to intervene. Explanation of the increase in the power and influence of the military in our proposition is rooted in the increasing reliance of the civilian leadership on the state coercive apparatus to maintain their positions of power and to deal with the challenges confronting the state. It is this reliance on coercion that requires the expansion of the military and other coercive institutions in size as well as of their scope and jurisdiction in governance. This proposition differs sharply from the push theories advanced by Perlmutter, Nordlinger, and Abrahamsson. The coercive asset of the military only becomes important in the context of a civilian government that suffers legitimacy problems and relies increasingly on state coercion to address the challenges confronting it. Increased reliance on coercion further undermines the legitimacy of civilian authority, which in turn further increases the salience of coercion resulting in a vicious cycle. Less encumbered in deploying its brute power, the military may deploy its coercive asset to exploit this situation by inhibiting the development of rival institutions and in the process hinder the development of political, administrative, and judicial arms of government. Such developments that constitute the supply or push factor, however, come into play only in the

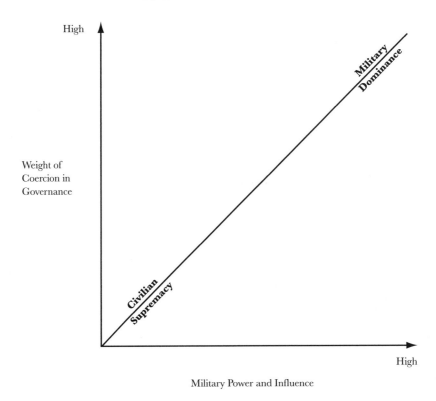

FIGURE I.2.   Coercion in Governance and the Military's Political Influence.

later phase of the cycle. The initial precipitating condition that draws the military in is the shortcomings of civilian authority and the attempt to redress them by relying on the state coercive apparatus.

Increasing reliance on coercion need not always lead to a military takeover, however. There can be situations characterized both by a high degree of political legitimacy as well as high salience of coercion in governance, as for example in post-1987 Korea and Taiwan. Force continues to be critical in safeguarding the international security of these states, but this has not led to an increase in the military's political influence because both these countries now have widely acknowledged democratic governments, and public opinion is strongly against military involvement in domestic politics. The massive deployment of force by the legitimate governments to protect their countries from external threats is not domestically contested, although there are differences over strategy and force posture. Similarly, the massive deployment of coercion in the pursuit of internal and international security in India has not led to an increase in the political influence of the military at the national level, although, as noted earlier, it has increased the power and influence of the military at the local level. The key here is to distinguish between legitimate use of state coercion that is within the law and in the pursuit of goals and purposes of the political community, and the illegal and repressive use of state coercion for private and partisan purposes that are considered illegitimate by key segments of the pub-

TABLE 1.1   Coercion, Legitimacy, and Political Influence of the Military.

State Coercion / Legitimacy	Low	High
High	Military power and influence low. Civilian control of the military is the norm.	Civilian control at the national level but military influence is high in provinces/areas where coercion dominates governance.
Low	State is a contested or failed entity. Government does not have monopoly over coercion.	Military power and influence high. High probability for military dominance of politics.

lic. The former situation would not lead to an increase in the power and influence of the military, whereas in the latter case there is much likelihood that this will occur.

The proposed inverse relationship between the salience of coercion and legitimacy runs the risk of circularity. To avoid this, it is important to develop indicators for coercion and legitimacy that are independent of each other. Among others, the following are useful indicators of the weight of coercion in governance: increase or decrease in the expenditure for internal security and defense; increase or decrease in the size of military, paramilitary, police, and intelligence forces, as well as change in their command structure and deployment pattern; the nature and extent of security legislation; declarations of emergency and martial law; and the weight attached to coercive measures relative to political, diplomatic, economic, and sociocultural measures in addressing the challenges confronting the state. The legitimacy of a political system may be determined through investigation of the existence of shared norms and values, their translation into widely accepted institutions, conformity with established rules in the acquisition and exercise of state power, and consent of the governed (Alagappa 1995: 14–24). The presence (or absence) of groups with substantial and growing support that advocate different ideologies for political organization may be viewed as evidence of the lack (or existence) of shared norms. The degree of public participation in the political system and the public's compliance with the commands of the incumbent government is another indicator of the level of support for the system. Similarly, the acquisition of state power through established institutions, rules, and procedures and its exercise for public purpose in accordance with the law are indicators of legitimacy. Indicators of consent of the governed will vary by political system. Consent is critical in a participatory type of political system but not unimportant in others. In a participatory system, consent includes the activities related to the election of government at different levels and recognition of the authority of that government to issue commands as well as the duty to obey them.

The dynamic aspect of this proposition stems from the fact that coercion cannot form the indefinite basis for governance, compelling governments—especially of the military and authoritarian varieties—to bolster their legitimacy and build noncoercive state capacity through the construction of acceptable political frameworks and economic development. Governments may negotiate political solutions to internal problems like secession as well as to some international conflicts like that over territory. They may also negotiate with competing groups a more widely accepted system for political domination. If successful, these and other political efforts can considerably enhance the internal and international legitimacy of the nation-state, the incumbent government, and the political system it represents. This should be accompanied by a corresponding decline in the weight of coercion and by extension a reduction in the role of the military in governance. Often, however, authoritarian governments seek to construct pseudo-democratic political frameworks that control participation and exclude potential challengers. And, because of the inherent contradictions noted earlier, the legitimacy of military regimes is short lived. Consequently, military governments continue to rely on coercion to maintain their hold on power. Military rulers may cling to power by using coercion to suppress opposition from political and civil society—and they may be temporarily helped in this effort by success in economic development, which is their preferred mode of legitimation.

However, sustained economic development in the capitalist mode has several consequences that tilt the distribution of power against the military: the state's reduced salience in allocating values and material goods, the development of middle and working classes that strive for political equality and participation, the development of civil society, the development of administrative and legal institutions to guarantee property rights and transactions, a new emphasis on transparency and accountability, and integration into the global economy. The net effect of sustained economic development is a complex state, society, and economy, the management of which requires political, administrative, and technical skills that are well beyond the expertise and capacity of institutions that manage state coercion.

Authoritarian/military rule, as observed earlier, cannot be institutionalized and is therefore untenable in the long run—leading to crisis and the transfer of power to civilian leaders. But if the civilians cannot forge a legitimate political system and play by its rules, and if they fail to address the country's political, economic, and social problems, the military may reintervene, possibly with public support, making for a cycle of coups and withdrawals. Only prolonged economic growth in the capitalist mode—combined with the development of political norms and institutions fostering broad political participation—can break the vicious cycle of coups and civilian rule. Capitalist development alone is not sufficient. It must be accompanied by shifts in ideas about political governance, including the proper role of the military, and by organization and mobilization of the new interest groups in society. Such changes may be encouraged by international norms and the policies and actions of major powers as well. Change in the distribution of power in favor of the civilian political and administrative leadership as well as consolidation of norms that favor broad political participation promote civilian control and increase the barrier to military role expansion and intervention. A failure of checks and balances, a breakdown of political consensus, growing internal conflict, and increasing reliance on coercion to address political problems, on the other hand, can increase the power and influence of the military and undermine the norm of civilian control at the national or provincial levels of government. The dynamic of change in our propositions issues from sustained economic development, from ideational shifts, and from changes in the degree and content of political agreement in society.

The above set of propositions rooted in the interplay of coercion, political legitimacy, and economic development is of the historical-structural genre. It can explain long-term change and trends but is less useful in explaining particular developments. Here explanation must focus on the level of agency. This leads to our second set of propositions, which claim that specific developments in civil-military relations are the outcome of the interaction of the beliefs, interests and power of the key civilian and military actors tempered by the power and beliefs of civil society as well as the policies and actions of key external actors.

Interests, Power, and Beliefs

As observed in earlier discussion, there may be an array of causal factors; the salience and combination of factors will in all likelihood vary by case; and in one or more ways each case is *sui generis*. However, what matters in analysis is not the factors themselves or how they combine, but their impact on the interests, beliefs, and power of key actors and how this in turn affects civil-military interaction. Take the variable of historical legacy, for example. That a military did or did not participate in the struggle for national liberation or won or lost a war is by itself unimportant as an explanation. There is no clear casual connection. For example, the Indian and Pakistani militaries did not participate in the struggle for independence; yet one (the Pakistani) has tended to dominate politics, whereas the other has steadfastly stayed away from politics. Similarly, the TNI, the Tatmadaw, the People's Liberation Army (PLA), and the Vietnamese People's Army (VPA) all played crucial roles in the success of their respective national liberation/independence struggles. The TNI and the Tatmadaw deployed the historical legacy to enhance their political positions. The PLA and the VPA, on the other hand, despite their many advantages at the outset and during subsequent periods of political crisis, have continued to submit to the supremacy of their respective communist parties. Of consequence, however, is whether and how participation in an event shaped or altered the interests, power, and beliefs of key civilian and military actors as well as the society at large and the consequence of such change for civil-military interaction. This approach shifts the focus of analysis away from the (uncontrollable) numerous factors to their impact on three key intervening variables—interests, beliefs, and distribution of power among the salient actors. In addition to integrating the consequences of multiple factors, this framework also facilitates explanation of a wider range of developments in civil-military relations.

The three intervening variables—interests, beliefs, and power—are interconnected, and each is subject to change as well. Interests may be defined by personal, institutional, or professional concerns as well as by beliefs about governance including the place and role of the military. Power may be economic, coercive, or organizational. It also has a political and ideational component that merges with beliefs. Beliefs (principles and norms) often reflect and advance the interests of actors, and the salience of specific beliefs in society rests on the power of the group espousing them. For its political beliefs to become dominant, however, the group espousing them must not only secure preponderant power but gain wide acceptance of the beliefs through practice by other significant actors. In the Gramscian conception, successful hegemony—the production of a shared idea or norm—rests on a synthesis of all elements of society into a "collective will" forging ideological unity. Only on the basis of this common worldview can the dominant group exercise political, intellectual, and moral leadership (Mouffe

1979). When this situation prevails, beliefs become institutionalized, internalized, consequential for political behavior, and less amenable to exploitation at will. Such autonomous political beliefs in turn influence the definition of political interests and the distribution of power in society. A fundamental and almost insurmountable weakness of authoritarian and military governments is their inability to develop hegemonic beliefs and translate them into widely accepted institutions that would legitimize their hold on state power. Political beliefs, hegemonic or otherwise, are subject to change as well, though hegemonic beliefs change only gradually. Beliefs may be transformed by new ideas as well as by changes in interests and the distribution of power.

A political belief can be an independent or a dependent variable. How it is deployed will depend on one's judgment of the autonomy of specific beliefs and the purpose of inquiry. If political beliefs attain hegemonic status, they will be crucial in explaining the pattern of civil-military relations. If ideological unity is not achieved, political relationships will hinge on raw interests and power. And explanations of civil-military relations will have to rely on these two dimensions. Even when political beliefs are widely accepted, the content of civil-military relations is likely to be shaped by the political interests of the various actors in the system and the distribution of power among them. Thus, the content of civil-military relations may vary from country to country and over time even when they have a similar political system.

As indicated in Table 1.2, the salience of beliefs, interests, and distribution of power in explaining the pattern and content of civil-military relations will vary with the degree of consolidation in the political system. In consolidated political systems, political beliefs—institutionalized and internalized by key actors, including the military—are critical in explaining the pattern and trajectory of civil-military relations and their durability. Political and corporate interests and the distribution of power are important, too, especially in detailing the content of civil-military relations. Explanations based only on political beliefs, without due consideration of the underlying political interests and distribution of power, are of doubtful value—especially when the political system is contested or in transition. When there are substantial differences in beliefs, the distribution of power becomes crucial. The military's decision to intervene, play a behind-the-scenes role, or stay out, for example, will be influenced to a considerable extent by its judgment of the interests and distribution of power among competing institutions and groups. Success is predicated on whether this judgment accords with reality. Similarly, success in consolidating civilian control over the military during a democratic transition hinges on the ability to increase civilian power vis-à-vis the military and over time to institutionalize norms that promote civilian supremacy. Interests and distribution of power are particularly salient in Asian countries, whose political systems are not yet consolidated. The domestic arena in these countries is characterized not by "administration, law, and order" but by competition and conflict, and a struggle for power among competing groups.

Further, as noted earlier, the relationship of the soldier to the state is not determined solely by the interaction among the institutions of the state. Civil society and international actors may play a crucial role as well, especially during moments of transition. The importance of civil society in the state-soldier equation depends on several factors: the autonomy of the state, the links between state and society, and the density of civil society. Civil society will have little impact if the state is highly autonomous, does not depend on society for revenue or legitimacy, and is strong enough to dominate society. A well-developed and mobilized civil society, on the other hand, can be a counterweight to the state and also affect power differentials among state insti-

TABLE 1.2 Beliefs, Interests, Power, and Explanation of Civil-Military Relations.

Intervening variables	*Political system*		
	Consolidated	Transitional	Contested
Beliefs (principles and norms)	Explain existing pattern of civil-military relations	Explain projected normative goals	Beliefs are the object of contestation
Interests and power	Explain the detail content of contemporary civil-military relations	Explain actual pattern and content of civil-military relations	Explain the issues of contestation in civil-military relations

tutions, exerting influence in defining the military's proper role and the norms that govern civil-military interactions. Particularly salient here are civil society organizations like the church, labor unions, media, and student movements; their political interests and beliefs; and how they relate to the different institutions of the state.

Domestic configurations of interests, beliefs, and power are affected too by changes in the international context. States do not exist in isolation. This has become especially evident in the post–cold war era in which democracy, human rights, and capitalism have attained near-hegemonic status. The United States, the European Union, and multilateral agencies such as the International Monetary Fund (IMF) and the World Bank actively promote these values. The integration of national economies into the global economy and the massive and rapid financial flows between countries have increased the vulnerability of developing economies, as demonstrated by the 1997–99 Asian financial crisis. Weak countries and economies have become more vulnerable to international crisis, pressure, and intervention. Although the international factors may not be the primary driving forces of domestic change, they can reinforce domestic institutions and groups seeking change. Major powers can also play supportive and watchdog roles in the posttransition phase. Explanations of civil-military relations should focus, therefore, on not only the interaction among key civilian and military institutions but also the way this interaction is shaped by civil society and the international system.

Thus far the framework has rested on the assumption that the countries in question are internally pacified and the state has a monopoly over the means and use of coercion. This, however, is not the case in most Asian countries. Groups other than the government also seek to develop and deploy coercive organizations in pursuit of goals that run counter to the state's. The possession of organized violence by nonstate groups implies that the civil-military problem confronting the state is a question not only of managing institutions that are the repositories of state coercion but also of dealing with coercive organizations that are not under its control. The common government response has been to label such groups as terrorists or insurgents and deal with them as threats to national security. Apart from creating a different type of civil-military problem, the existence of nonstate groups with the means of organized violence complicates the relationship of the state to its own institutions of violence as well as to society. As such, the existence of nonstate political actors with the means of organized violence must feature in the analysis of civil-military relations.

The two sets of propositions advanced in this chapter are particularly relevant to developing countries in Asia and elsewhere that are still in an early stage in the state-formation process. Despite their long histories, most Asian countries are relatively new and weak as modern nation-states. With the exception of Japan and Thailand, they have colonial or quasi-colonial origins. Their break with the colonial and traditional past came only in the twentieth century, in most cases after World War II. Their physical boundaries, national identities, and political systems, which in most cases did not have firm indigenous roots, have been contested internally and in some cases internationally. The domestic arenas have been characterized by struggle for political power and the right to rule as well as the right to define the ideational bases of the fledgling nations and the basis for inclusion and exclusion from the political communities under construction.

Postindependence and postrevolutionary political leaderships have been intent on building strong modern nation-states on the basis of the territorial units inherited from colonial rule while simultaneously consolidating their hold on power. Consolidating political authority at the center, extending the reach of government to all parts of the country, and consolidating the national identity, sovereignty, and territorial boundary are key concerns driving the state-building process. The military has figured prominently in this process because of the centrality of coercion. In some countries, the military has been a competitor for political power in its own right or in support of a group. Apart from coercion, economic development and construction of legitimating frameworks are the two other key measures deployed by governments in their effort to consolidate the state and their own authority. The interplay and consequences of these three instruments—coercion, economic development, and political legitimation—have to a considerable extent shaped civil-military relations in Asian countries.

PART II

Democratic Civilian Control

CHAPTER 2

Japan: From Containment to Normalization

Eiichi Katahara

SINCE THE END OF WORLD WAR II, civil-military relations in Japan have been characterized by civilian political domination over the Japanese armed forces, euphemistically called the Self-Defense Forces (SDF). With the devastating defeat of Japan in the war and the subsequent Allied Occupation reforms aimed at demilitarization and democratization, the prewar pattern of civil-military relations came to an end. The prewar system of "dual government"—in which legal authority was divided between civilian and military elites—allowed the military not only to play an independent role in national security affairs but also to expand its political influence into the civil sphere, culminating in the militarization of domestic politics and society on the one hand and reckless aggression and war on the other (Huntington 1957; Katzenstein and Okawara 1993; Tobe 1998). The terrible memories of the war and the strong distrust of the military became deeply entrenched in the minds of the Japanese. Even today, more than 50 years after the end of the Pacific War, the strength of pacifism is manifested in Japan's continued commitment to the "peace constitution" and an array of self-imposed restraints on the SDF—including *senshu boei* (exclusively defense-oriented policy); the ban on sending military units for combat abroad; the denial of the right of collective self-defense; political constraints on defense spending; the ban on conscription; the ban on the export of arms; the three non-nuclear principles that prohibit Japan from possessing, manufacturing, and introducing nuclear weapons into Japan; and the commitment to the peaceful use of space.[1] As Thomas Berger puts it, Japan's postwar culture of antimilitarism is "one of the most striking features of contemporary Japanese politics and has its roots in collective Japanese memories of the militarist takeover in the 1930s and the subsequent disastrous decision to go to war with America" (Berger 1993: 120). And one of the bitter lessons the Japanese have learned from the wartime past is that "the military is a dangerous institution that must be constantly restrained and monitored lest it threaten Japan's postwar democratic order and undermine the peace and prosperity that the nation has enjoyed since 1945" (Berger 1993: 120). During much of the postwar years, therefore, problems of civilian control over the military remained a central issue in the building of the Japanese democratic state. Under these circumstances, the SDF was rigidly constrained by an intricate web of political, legal, and social restraints. The strict abstention of the SDF from politics has become the norm in the postwar Japanese political order.

This chapter argues that civil-military relations in Japan have been shifting from containment to normalization in the postwar period. In the early postwar years, the SDF was the object of containment through legal, political, and social restrains so that it would never again control Japan's national security policymaking. The roles and missions of the SDF, therefore, remained unclarified and largely delegitimized. From the mid-1970s through the 1990s, Japan's civil-military relations gradually became normalized in three important respects. First, there has been a shift in civilian control of the SDF from a bureaucratically managed system to a system of political control in which elected officials set the national security agenda and govern policymaking processes (Nagao 1996). Second, there has been a shift in the civil-military balance of power in that the power and stature of the Defense Agency vis-à-vis other ministries and agencies have been upgraded along with the SDF's increased standing. Third, popular attitudes toward the SDF have shifted from fear and distrust to recognition that the SDF is a necessary institution not only for Japan's security needs but also for a variety of international activities such as UN peacekeeping operations. In the normalization of civil-military relations we see a reflection of the successful institutionalization of civilian democratic control over the Japanese armed forces. The overall pattern and content of civil-military relations in Japan are therefore approaching those of other advanced industrial democracies in that the problem of reconciling democratic control with the technical expertise of military men has become a legitimate concern (Huntington 1957).

Specifically, the chapter argues that the normalization of civil-military relations took place in two distinct periods in the postwar years. During the first phase, the mid-1970s and early 1980s, the legitimacy of the SDF was gradually established with the emergence of a greater public consensus on the fundamentals of Japan's security policy—namely, its maintenance of the SDF and the Japan-U.S. security arrangements. This change was due largely to the success of the government's policy initiatives in articulating the roles and missions of the SDF through the adoption of the National Defense Program Outline (NDPO) and the Guidelines for Japan-U.S. Defense Cooperation to reassure the concerned Japanese public on the one hand and to respond to the changing security environment on the other. Nevertheless, the profile of the uniformed officers of the SDF throughout the 1970s and 1980s was distinctly low-key, and their dissenting voices were substantially suppressed in the context of postwar Japanese pacifism and antimilitarism.

The 1990s, the second phase, have seen further normalization of civil-military relations. First, there has been a gradual shift from bureaucratic to political control of the SDF manifested in the growing policymaking role of the politicians. Second, the expanding roles and missions of the SDF through the adoption of a series of revised or new security policies—including the SDF's participation in UN peacekeeping, the new NDPO, and the new Guidelines for

Japan-U.S. Defense Cooperation—have led to the enhanced stature and power of the Defense Agency (the SDF included) in relation to other bureaucracies, along with the SDF's improved standing in the civil-military balance of power. Third, wider public support for the SDF's new roles and missions has been another reflection of the normalization process.

The chapter argues further that if there is no fundamental change in Japan's domestic politics and its security environment, the basic pattern of civilian supremacy over the SDF is likely to remain intact. The growing policymaking power of the politicians in relation to the bureaucrats, the enhanced ability of the National Diet for oversight of the SDF, and the emerging "civil society" in Japan, as well as growing international expectations for Japan's greater security role, will contribute to a further strengthening of civilian supremacy over the Japanese armed forces.

The first section of this chapter provides a historical context for analyzing civil-military relations in postwar Japan, focusing on the legal and social norms that circumscribe these relations. The second section explores the changes in civil-military relations that took place during the mid-1970s and the early 1980s. The third section investigates newly emerging patterns and contents of civil-military relations in the 1990s. In each case, we shall examine the jurisdictional boundaries between civilian authorities (defined here as civilian-controlled institutions of the state, including the political leadership) and the military (the uniformed officers of the SDF) in two areas: the structure of political domination and national security policymaking.[2] The fourth section presents a case study on the impact of the Persian Gulf War on Japan's civil-military relations in order to elucidate the delicate tension between the political leadership and the SDF at a time of crisis when Japan's civil-military relations were put to the test. Finally, the chapter addresses the implications of the changing character of civil-military relations for domestic politics generally and for national security policy in particular.

The literature on civil-military relations in Japan, it should be noted, is surprisingly sparse.[3] This is partly a reflection of Japan's postwar culture of antimilitarism—even in academic circles, where the study of military history and strategy was deliberately shunned—and partly because postwar Japan has concentrated exclusively on economic development and left much of its own security burden to the United States.

HISTORICAL CONTEXT

To place this analysis of postwar Japanese civil-military relations in a proper historical context, it is necessary to trace their history back to the pre-1945 period. Indeed, the prewar Japanese civil-military relations stand in stark contrast to those of the postwar period (Huntington 1957; Katzenstein and Okawara 1993; Tobe 1998; Gow 1993). First and foremost was the legal structure of military independence. In 1878, when the General Staff was created after the Prussian model, a separation between matters of military strategy and operations (*gunrei*) and administrative matters (*gunsei*) was established, and the General Staff was made independent of the government, thus enabling the chief of the General Staff to report to the emperor directly.[4] The Meiji Constitution of 1889, which stipulated that the emperor had "supreme command of the army and navy," allowed the military authorities to assert the "independence of the supreme command" to prevent the cabinet from interfering in military affairs. Second, the prewar military played an active role not only in military matters but in education, economic affairs, and foreign policy as well. A case in point was the composition of cabinet posts since the inception of the cabinet in 1885: before 1913 and after 1936, only military leaders on active duty could become army and navy ministers. Between 1913 and 1936, the appointment of reserve or retired officers was allowed (with the exception of Prime Minister Hara, who temporarily substituted for the navy minister in 1921). Military officers, however, were appointed to civilian cabinet posts quite frequently. Hence "the fact that the military's cooperation was indispensable for forming and maintaining Cabinets gave it great leverage in Japan's political life" (Katzenstein and Okawara 1993: 13). Third, the prewar military's relations with society, buttressed by its institutional links and widespread nationalism, were extensive. The conscription system, introduced in 1873, revised several times, and continued until its abolition in 1945, helped to develop a pervasive link between the military and society—especially the lower-middle-class and peasant elements. The military's link with society was also manifest in its organizations: the Imperial Military Reserve Association, the Greater Japan National Defense Women's Association, and the Greater Japan Youth Association (Katzenstein and Okawara 1993: 14–16).

Following the defeat of Japan in the Pacific War, the Allied Occupation began in September 1945 and lasted until April 1952. Gen. Douglas MacArthur was appointed supreme commander for the Allied Powers (SCAP). Demilitarizing Japan was the immediate objective of the occupation reform so that Japan would never again become a menace to the United States and world peace. To this end, the Japanese imperial armed forces were demobilized, their weapons were destroyed, war criminals were brought to trial, and many were executed.

By the late 1940s, however, the emerging cold war forced the Allied occupation to shift its focus from demilitarization and democratization to political stability, economic recovery, and rearmament for Japan. The sudden invasion of South Korea by Communist North Korea on June 25, 1950, proved to be a decisive event that reversed the course of occupation reforms. The U.S. occupation forces stationed in Japan were immediately sent to fight the Korean War. To maintain internal security in Japan, MacArthur ordered on July 8, 1950, the establishment of the Police Reserve Force of 75,000 men.[5] The vanquished Japan was now viewed by the United States as an ally and a crucial forward base of operations in Asia and the Pacific. Yet American pressure on Japan to rearm faced considerable difficulties. During the Yoshida-Dulles talks in January and February 1951, Prime Minister Shigeru Yoshida rejected John Foster Dulles's demand for major rearmament on three grounds: fears of Japanese militarism in Asia, the overriding need for economic recovery, and terrible memories of the devastating consequences of the Pacific War. However, in a secret memorandum submitted to the United States on February 3, 1951, Prime Minister Yoshida conceded to Dulles to create "security forces, land and sea, totaling 50,000" (Hosoya et al. 1999: 89). In August 1952, the National Safety Agency was established, followed by the inauguration of the National Security Force in October. With the enactment of the two defense laws in 1954, the Japanese Defense Agency and the SDF came into being (Weinstein 1971; Welfield 1988; Auer 1973; Tanaka 1997).

Japanese security policy in the postwar period has been based on two fundamental legal documents: the constitution and the Japan-U.S. Security Treaty. While the former was a product of U.S. occupation reforms, the latter stemmed from the realities of the emerging cold war. The constitution has long been a major source of controversy in postwar Japanese politics. The fundamental problem derives from the ambiguous status of the Japanese SDF, Japan's de facto armed forces, whose existence is not provided for in the constitution. Article 9 of the constitution reads as follows:

> Aspiring sincerely to an international peace based on justice and order, the Japanese people forever renounce war as a sovereign right of the nation and the threat or use of force as a means of settling international disputes.
>
> In order to accomplish the aim of the preceding paragraph, land, sea, and air forces, as well as other war potential, will never be maintained. The right of belligerency of the state will not be recognized.

Despite the ambiguous constitutionality of Japan's possession of armed forces, successive governments since the 1950s have interpreted Article 9 of the constitution as not precluding the exercise of the right of self-defense.[6] Hence, the SDF was established in July 1954—Tokyo's response to the geopolitical realities of the international situation.

The other pillar of postwar Japanese security policy is the Japan-U.S. security arrangements. The Japan-U.S. Treaty of Mutual Cooperation and Security, signed in 1960 as a revised version of the Japan-U.S. Security Treaty of 1951, continues to function as an integral element of Japan's defense policy. Given the constitutional limits on defense posture and capabilities and the perceived necessity to cope with all levels of contingencies, including a global war, Japan relies extensively on American nuclear as well as conventional deterrent capabilities.

The legal basis for civilian control of the SDF is provided by the constitution and two laws regarding the Defense Agency and the SDF: the Law on the Establishment of the Defense Agency (the Defense Agency law) and the Law on the Self-Defense Forces (the SDF law), both enacted by the government on July 1, 1954. These two laws make functional provisions for the structure, the scope, and the location of authority (Miyazaki 1977). The constitution stipulates that the prime minister and other ministers of state must be civilians (Article 66) and that the prime minister appoints state ministers, a majority of whom must be chosen from members of the National Diet (Article 68). The Defense Agency law establishes the Defense Agency as an external bureau of the Prime Minister's Office (Article 2) and stipulates that the director-general of the Defense Agency must be a state minister (Article 3). Hence, the director-general of the Defense Agency must be a civilian and a member of the National Diet, and his appointment must be made by the prime minister. The annual defense budget is prepared by the cabinet and shall be determined by the National Diet (Articles 83 and 86 of the constitution).

The Defense Agency report "On Civilian Control," submitted to the National Diet in 1965, describes specific jurisdictional boundaries in relation to civilian control at three levels: the relation between the National Diet and the SDF, the relation between the government and the SDF, and the relation between civilian officials of the internal bureaus (*naikyoku*) of the Defense Agency and uniformed officers of the Joint Staff Council and the three staff offices (Nishioka 1988: 97–102).

On the relation between the National Diet and the SDF, the cabinet (which holds jurisdiction over the administration of national defense) is responsible to the National Diet. The National Diet makes legislative and budgetary decisions on such matters as the authorized strength of the SDF and its main organization and monitors the administration of national defense. The prime minister, in issuing orders to mobilize all or part of the SDF in case of external aggression (or when there is a danger of such aggression), must obtain prior (or ex post facto) approval from the National Diet (Article 76 of the SDF Law). The mobilization of the SDF in cases where the police force cannot maintain public order requires the ex post facto approval of the National Diet (Article 78 of the SDF Law).

On the relation between the government and the SDF, the administration of national defense is subject to the cabinet's control. The prime minister, on behalf of the cabinet, exercises supreme control and supervision over the SDF (Article 7 of the SDF Law).[7] The prime minister gives orders to the director-general of the Defense Agency, who in turn gives the orders to the chiefs of staffs of the three services (Articles 8 and 9 of the SDF Law). Moreover, the prime minister must consult with the Security Council of Japan that is established within the Cabinet (Article 2 of the Security Council Establishment Law).[8] The principle of civilian supremacy over the military is thus embedded in the command structure for the operations of the SDF.

On the relation between the civilian officials of the internal bureaus (*naikyoku*) of the Defense Agency and the uniformed officers of the Joint Staff Council and the three staff offices, the principle of civilian supremacy over the military is institutionalized within the Defense Agency.[9] The Defense Agency has responsibility for administrative control of the SDF. The director-general, who is a civilian state minister, is assisted by two vice-ministers, one from the ruling party (parliamentary vice-minister) and the other from the Defense Agency (administrative), and civilian counselors. The chiefs of staff of the Ground, Maritime, and Air Self-Defense Forces, as the highest professional advisers to the director-general, are subject to his direction and supervision. The Joint Staff Council, composed of the chairman and the chiefs of staff, assists the director-general in formulating defense plans and coordinating the command and operations of the SDF (Article 26 of the Defense Agency law). Specifically:

1. The internal bureaus draft legislative bills as well as the orders of the cabinet and the Prime Minister's Office.

2. Communication and negotiation with the Diet and the various organs of the central government are handled exclusively by the internal bureaus. The staff offices engage in such activities only on minor matters and only with the approval of the director-general of the Defense Agency.

3. All plans concerning the SDF's operations and organization are drafted by the Joint Staff Council and the staff offices under the director-general's instructions. The internal bureaus draft these instructions and examine the drafts of the plans before sending them to the director-general for final approval. (See Nishioka 1988: 97–102; Katzenstein and Okawara 1993: 50.)

Perhaps no issue has been the site of greater controversy in postwar Japanese civil-military relations than the question of preparing to respond to a military contingency. Because of Japan's bitter experiences with the military running amok in the 1930s and 1940s, more than any other democratic society Japan since 1945 has given greater priority to retaining control over its armed forces than to maintaining military readiness. Consequently, the legal framework for mobilizing the SDF has been inadequate from a military point of view. As Robert Horiguchi (1989: 7) explains:

> Under Article 76 of the SDF Act, the Prime Minister can order the mobilization of the Force in the event of imminent external military attack. However, under existing laws, the SDF is required to ask

permission from central government agencies and local authorities before it can take action. For instance, for a military convoy to pass through a community, unhindered by traffic lights, authorization is required of the local Public Safety Commission. The setting up of a command post in a potential combat zone would be subject to approval by the Construction Ministry under the Building Standards law. Similar restrictions apply to the establishment of field hospitals, which come under the jurisdiction of the Ministry of Health and Welfare, as well as the burial of men killed in action at places other than legally designated cemeteries.

Clearly, this state of affairs has been the object of much criticism from the SDF. The first major challenge came in 1965. The revelations of the so-called Mitsuya (Three Arrows) exercises by Haruo Okada of the Japan Socialist Party at the House of Representatives Budget Committee on February 10, 1965, was an episode illustrating the political sensitivity of civil-military relations in the early postwar years (Nishioka 1988: 263–75; Welfield 1988: 204–5; Maeda 1995: 127–34). Indeed, it stirred up considerable criticism not only in the opposition parties but in the media. The "top secret" paper exercises, conducted in 1963 by uniformed officers of the SDF and civilian staff of the Defense Agency, assumed various military contingencies developing on the Korean peninsula that would require combined military operations with the United States, mobilization of the SDF to ensure domestic security, and the expedited enactment of a host of emergency legislation through the National Diet. Shocked by the sudden revelations in the National Diet, Prime Minister Eisaku Sato declared that "this kind of thing is impermissible. I believe it is regrettable that this kind of planning has been undertaken without the government's knowledge." Several days later, however, Prime Minister Sato justified the exercises by saying, "It is absolutely natural for a defense authority to conduct the type of exercise being performed. I am more concerned that top secret documents have been leaked" (Maeda 1995: 128–29; Welfield 1988: 205). Subsequent government explanations claimed that the exercises were just "studies" and had nothing to do with an actual defense plan. Nevertheless, the Mitsuya exercises aggravated public distrust of the SDF and reinforced the perception that civilian control of the SDF should be strengthened.

On July 19, 1978, Gen. Hiroomi Kurisu, chairman of Joint Staff Council, told a press conference that "since there are many inadequacies in the present Self-Defense Forces Law, it is possible that the forces might be obliged to take extralegal action (*chohokiteki kodo*) in time of emergency" (Welfield 1988: 404; Otake 1983). The remark was taken by some as a challenge to the principle of civilian control over the SDF. Defense Agency director-general Shin Kanemaru, with Prime Minister Takeo Fukuda's approval, immediately removed Kurisu from office. Nevertheless, the problem of the inadequate legal system for mobilizing the SDF attracted the wider attention of the media. After the dismissal of General Kurisu, Prime Minister Fukuda gave an order to facilitate studies on emergency legislation—studies that the Defense Agency had, in fact, already begun in August 1977 (Otake 1983). The Defense Agency released interim reports on the progress of the studies in April 1981 and October 1984.[10] Nevertheless, successive governments have failed to initiate legislation on emergencies. The lack of emergency legislation exemplifies not only the persistent political sensitivities involved but also the weakness of Japan's political leadership, compounded by an array of jurisdictional problems cutting across ministries and agencies and local governments.

Along with the legal norms that inform Japan's defense and national security policy, the social norms have played an important role in shaping the pattern and content of civil-military relations in postwar Japan. Indeed, Japan's culture of antimilitarism, with its roots in the haunting memories of the disastrous war, has proved to be an enduring fact of life with far-reaching implications for its defense policy and civil-military relations (Berger 1998). Many Japanese have long viewed the SDF with distrust and disdain, if not overt hostility, and the SDF has been isolated from society at large. Indeed, Japanese have referred to the SDF as "*zeikin dorobo*" (tax thieves) or "*hikagemono*" (social outcasts) (Tahara 1978; Sugiyama 1995). Above all, for a long time public opinion on national security was sharply divided into two camps: the "conservatives," represented by the bureaucracy and the Liberal Democratic Party (LDP), supporting the gradual growth of the SDF, and the "progressives," represented by the opposition parties and the mass media, vociferously opposed to the government move toward rearmament (Otake 1983).

Japan's postwar history has seen pacifism and antimilitary sentiment and the institutionalization of antimilitarism and civilian control of the military in the legal and social norms. The overall pattern and content of civil-military relations have therefore been conditioned by the system of civilian political domination, characterized by strong bureaucratic power and authority, thereby ensuring civilian supremacy over the SDF.

ESTABLISHING THE SDF'S LEGITIMACY

During the mid-1970s to the early 1980s, significant changes took place in civil-military relations, marking the first critical period in the postwar history of the SDF. Most important was the emergence of a national consensus on the fundamentals of Japan's security policy—namely the desirability of maintaining the SDF and the Japan-U.S. security arrangements, thereby contributing to the legitimation of the SDF. The public image of the SDF was improved as well, reflecting wider recognition that the SDF would be necessary for the defense of Japan and particularly useful in times of natural disasters.[11] This change was due largely to the success of the government's policy initiatives in articulating the roles and missions of the SDF through the adoption of the NDPO and the Guidelines for Japan-U.S. Defense Cooperation, thereby reassuring the concerned Japanese public (Katahara 1990; Mochizuki 1983–84). A combination of international and domestic factors compelled Japan to adopt these new national security policies in the 1970s. On the domestic front, Japanese defense policymakers wished to alleviate public fears about the growth of the SDF and the ever-increasing defense spending. On the international front, they became concerned about the changing international circumstances, including the growing military threat from the Soviet Union and the increasing U.S. pressure for Japan's greater defense efforts. The intensifying informal consultations between the uniformed officers of the SDF and their American counterparts compelled Japan's political leadership to formulate guidelines in order to ensure the civilian control of the SDF's interactions with the United States, thus enhancing the transparency of civil-military relations.

Structure of Political Domination

With the entrenched system of civilian political domination over the SDF intact, a symbiotic relationship between the bureaucrats and the politicians had emerged by the early 1980s, marking a gradual shift in the well-established patterns of bureaucratic domination. The rising prominence of LDP policy experts, or *zoku* (policy tribes), led to a convergence of policymaking roles of bureaucrats and LDP politicians. In the defense budget making, for example, the LDP's *kokubozoku* (defense tribe) became increasingly embroiled in the process. The Defense Agency remained distinctly low-key vis-à-vis other ministries, and its role was circumscribed by seconded officials from more powerful ministries occupying important posts of the internal bureaus.[12] The Ministry of Foreign Affairs (MOFA) played a central role in policy formulation and implementation pertaining to security arrangements with the United States.[13]

During the mid-1970s and the early 1980s, the political leadership found itself having to exert considerable power in making security policy decisions of critical importance. In the mid-1970s, Defense Agency director-general Michita Sakata took crucial initiatives in formulating the NDPO and the Guidelines for Japan-U.S. Defense Cooperation. In the late 1970s, Prime Minister Masayoshi Ohira introduced the concept of comprehensive security, which provided useful guidelines for Japan's multifaceted strategic planning and engagement in the international community. In the early 1980s, Prime Ministers Zenko Suzuki and Yasuhiro Nakasone played decisive roles in directing Japan's defense policy. Prime Minister Suzuki's remark about a thousand-mile sea-lanes defense was understood by Washington as Japan's official policy. Prime Minister Nakasone took a leading role in promoting the defense buildup and modifying aspects of Japan's defense policies, including abolition of the 1 percent of gross national product limit on defense spending.

It was also during the mid-1970s and the early 1980s that the role of the uniformed officers was gradually strengthened—not only because of their expertise in technical matters but, more significantly, because of their close links with American counterparts through consultations, joint studies, and joint military exercises. In other words, they were put in the forefront of receiving U.S. demands, requests, and expectations about Japan's defense roles and missions. They naturally saw American "pressures" as a useful argument in putting forward a case for a substantial defense buildup (Katahara 1990).

The early 1980s saw efforts to strengthen the cabinet's role in the structure of political domination. In December 1980, the Council of Ministers Concerned with Comprehensive Security was established. In July 1986, the National Defense Council was replaced by a more comprehensive Security Council of Japan as a new apparatus for deliberating national security issues and thrashing out "countermeasures for serious emergencies." This step was prompted by a series of international incidents—including the MiG-25 landing and defection at Hakodate airport in September 1976, the Dhaka hijacking incident in September 1977, and the shooting down of a Korean airliner by Soviet fighters near Sakhalin in September 1983.[14] And in July 1986, the Cabinet Secretariat was reorganized to include the new post of cabinet public relations officer and newly established offices: the Cabinet Counselors' Office, responsible for general policy coordination; the External Affairs Coordination Office, responsible for coordinating action on international issues not related to defense; the Internal Affairs Coordination Office, responsible for coordinating government response to domestic crises; the National Security Office, secretariat for the National Security Council; and the Information Research Office, responsible for coordinating government-wide information collection, analysis, and distribution.[15]

National Security Policymaking

Political and bureaucratic leaders played central roles in the adoption of new national security policies in the 1970s in order to reassure the concerned Japanese public as well as to cope with the changing international environment. The NDPO, adopted in October 1976, defined basic defense doctrines and set out SDF procurement goals in clear terms. It provided the basis for subsequent defense buildup programs until the mid-1990s. The adoption of the Guidelines for Japan-U.S. Defense Cooperation in November 1978 marked an important shift in the Japan-U.S. alliance in that they established, for the first time in postwar history, an institutional framework for joint defense planning and close security consultations. Clearly, the government initiatives in articulating the SDF's roles and missions contributed to the emergence of a wider consensus on Japan's national security policy, culminating in the legitimization of the SDF (Katahara 1990).

Chief architects of the NDPO were Michita Sakata—a senior LDP politician and "dovish" Defense Agency director-general—and civilian officials of the Defense Agency, most prominently Takuya Kubo, an intellectual and scholarly bureaucrat (Otake 1983; Chuma 1985; Tanaka 1997). Kubo stayed at the center of the policymaking mechanism of the Defense Agency, and his status as civilian chief of the Defense Agency and Sakata's strong political leadership helped to create a political climate for adoption of the NDPO. At the stage of policy initiation, Kubo and other civilian bureaucrats of the Defense Agency vigorously prepared the groundwork. In early 1971, Kubo circulated his controversial "KB paper" around the Defense Agency, arguing for the adoption of his concept of the "standard defense force" (*kibanteki boeiryoku*) as a guiding strategic basis for Japan's long-term defense force development—as opposed to the "required defense force" (*shoyo boeiryoku*). The concept of a standard defense force was predicated on a set of political judgments about likely military contingencies; it was aimed at developing a small but well-equipped defense force capable of repelling "limited and small-scale aggression." The required defense force concept, by contrast, called for a defense force capable of matching the military forces in the vicinity of Japan's strategic environment, including those of the USSR. Given Japan's political and economic conditions, as well as its profound strategic vulnerabilities, Kubo deemed it neither practical nor desirable to develop the required defense force. Though top uniformed officers expressed skepticism about the viability of the standard defense force, the domestic political climate was such that some "brakes" (*hadome*) would need to be applied to Japan's ever-growing SDF. In March 1975, Sakata established an ad hoc private advisory commission, the Forum on Defense Issues, thus facilitating the formulation of a new defense policy outline.

Kubo's ideas won the support of the LDP leadership, including Prime Minister Takeo Miki, Defense Agency director-general Sakata, the bureaucracies such as the powerful Ministry of Finance, and, more generally, the mass media (Otake 1983; Chuma 1985). On October 29, 1976, the National Defense Council and the cabinet formally adopted the NDPO, a new guideline for Japan's defense buildup programs. Throughout the formulation process, the role of SDF uniformed officers remained singularly low-key. Dissenting voices of top officers about Kubo's ideas were overshadowed by the forceful civilian leadership. The uniformed officers' demands for larger force levels also met resistance from civilian officials of the Defense Agency and the Ministry of Finance (Hirose 1989). The principle of civilian supremacy over the military, therefore, was observed in the formulation process of the NDPO.

The formulation process of the 1978 Guidelines for Japan-U.S. Defense Cooperation confirmed the basic pattern of civilian leadership in national security policymaking as well, although the initial impetus came from growing apprehensions about the efficacy of civilian control of the SDF as they interacted with the U.S. forces for security policy consultations. By the mid-1970s, prompted by the growing military threat from the Soviet Union, both Japanese and American uniformed officers had initiated close consultation on joint planning for the defense of Japan and its sea lanes. These consultations were conducted apparently without the full knowledge of Japan's highest political leadership—casting doubt on the efficacy of the civilian control of the SDF. Further, Japan's potential role in the U.S. global strategy—a role the U.S. Navy would expect Japan to assume in the contingency of a major war with the USSR—was such that it could not simply be left to informal military-to-military consultations, unauthorized and possibly unknown by Japan's political leadership. Some observers thought that strategic issues of this magnitude should be dealt with at the highest political level so that the SDF would be subject to civilian authorities.[16]

The issue was promptly and opportunely taken up by Tetsu Ueda, a Socialist Party Diet member, on March 8, 1975, in the Budget Committee of the House of Councillors. Ueda asked in the Diet interpellation period if there were "secret agreements" between the SDF and the U.S. Seventh Fleet regarding division of labor in the defense of sea lanes in an emergency (Ueda 1983, 1997; Murata 1997).[17] Defense Agency director-general Sakata was uncertain about the matter and promised to look into it and provide an answer as soon as possible. Sakata declared later that there had been no such "secret agreements," but he admitted that the Joint Staff Council and the staff offices of the three services were conducting close consultations on the defense of Japan with their American counterparts without the knowledge of the political leadership. It was a rude awakening for Sakata, a layman on defense issues who strongly believed in the importance of civilian control of the SDF (Sakata 1975, 1980, 1986).

Sakata, therefore, felt the need to exercise some form of political control over military affairs involving the SDF and the U.S. forces in Japan. By establishing formal mechanisms for such consultations, he thought the government could authorize and monitor military consultations. On August 29, 1975, Director-General Sakata met U.S. Defense Secretary Schlesinger in Tokyo. Sakata explained to Schlesinger three basic requirements for the defense of Japan: to cultivate the strong will of the people to defend the nation, to improve the minimum level of defense capability within the constraints of the constitution, and to rely on the United States in case of a large-scale attack on Japan or nuclear threat. Sakata then made two important suggestions: to establish an official forum for close consultations within the Security Consultative Committee and to hold an annual meeting, in principle, between Japan's director-general of the Defense Agency and the U.S. secretary of defense.[18] The Americans responded quickly and positively to Sakata's suggestions. Schlesinger remarked in the press conference:

> Proper mechanisms for consultations between the U.S. and Japan, where both countries seriously examine important security questions of the Western Pacific, should have existed a long time ago. Japan has so far been a too passive partner. I think this Japanese attitude has changed. On the American side, also, it has been increasingly recognized that there should be more balanced roles allocated in the security relations.[19]

Consequently, the Subcommittee on Defense Cooperation (SDC) was established as a sub-ordinate organ of the Japan-U.S. Security Consultative Committee (SCC) on July 8, 1976. Although Director-General Sakata played a vital role in the decision, the subsequent process of formulation was dominated by civilian officials of the Defense Agency and the MOFA and uniformed officers of the SDF. The SDC began formulating the guidelines in August 1976.[20] The SDC met on eight separate occasions between August 1976 and November 1978, when the final draft of the guidelines was completed. The draft was accepted by the Seventeenth SCC on November 27, 1978, and subsequently approved by the National Defense Council and the cabinet on November 28.[21] Civilian officials of both governments (primarily the Defense Agency and the MOFA for the Japanese) supervised the formulation process, while the Joint Staff Council of the SDF and the headquarters of the U.S. forces in Japan played a major role in draft-ing the guidelines.[22]

Implementation of the guidelines not only strengthened the Japan-U.S. alliance but also increased the transparency of civil-military relations. First, Japan and the United States rein-forced formal mechanisms for consultation on security matters through regular talks, both at the top political level and at the working levels of relevant bureaucracies and military forces. Since then, for the first time in the history of the Japan-U.S. alliance, various studies on joint defense planning have been conducted by uniformed officers of the SDF and the U.S. forces in Japan under the aegis of the guidelines. Finally, joint military exercises with U.S. forces became routine with the active participation of the SDF, which developed into a modern mil-itary force equipped with increasingly advanced weapons.

IN SEARCH OF WIDER SECURITY ROLES

Japan's civil-military relations underwent further incremental but significant changes in the 1990s. The changing character of civil-military relations in this period can be measured in three important respects. First, there emerged a shift from bureaucratic to political control of the SDF, manifested in the growing policymaking role of the politicians, especially since the mid-1990s. Second, the expanding roles and missions of the SDF through the adoption of a series of new or revised security policies—including the SDF's participation in UN peace-keeping, the new NDPO, and the new Guidelines for Japan-U.S. Defense Cooperation—led to the enhanced stature and power of the Defense Agency (the SDF included) in relation to other bureaucracies, along with the improved standing of the SDF in the civil-military bal-ance of power. Third, wider public support for the SDF's new roles and missions was another reflection of the normalization process. The growing public consensus favoring the limited use of Japan's armed forces in response to external threats (such as the incursion of North Korean ships into Japan's territorial waters in 1999) signaled a sea change in the Japanese per-ception of the SDF. Four factors contributed to the normalization of civil-military relations in this period: the changing Japanese political landscape (such as the end of one-party rule by the LDP and the emergence of bipartisanship on security issues), the changing post–cold war security environment surrounding Japan, the strengthening of Japan-U.S. security arrange-ments, and the enhanced expertise of Defense Agency officials and the professionalism of uni-formed officers of the SDF.

Changing Political Landscape

The defeat of the LDP in the July 1993 general election marked the end of its uninterrupted domination of Japan's postwar politics since 1955 and led to recurring patterns of coalition and realignment throughout the 1990s. The Hosokawa government, which broke with the LDP's long-term one-party rule, was replaced in June 1994, after a two-month rule by the Hata Cabinet, by a coalition government formed by the LDP, the Social Democratic Party (SDP), and the Sakigake Party. The SDP's chairman, Tomiichi Murayama, led this previously unthinkable coalition until January 1996, when Murayama suddenly announced his resignation. The LDP leader Ryutaro Hashimoto took over the government, managed to gain seats in the October 1996 lower house elections, held for the first time under the new electoral system, but still fell short of a majority in the lower house and therefore needed support from the opposition, namely the SDP and Sakigake. Hashimoto's mishandling of the deepening economic and financial crisis led to a major defeat for the LDP in the July 1998 upper house elections, forcing him to resign. The newly elected LDP president, Keizo Obuchi, took over the government and in January 1999 formed a coalition government with the conservative Liberal Party, headed by Ichiro Ozawa, marking a resurgence of the LDP-centered conservative dominance.

The end of the LDP's one-party rule in the early 1990s meant a shift in the power balance between politicians and bureaucrats in the structure of political domination: the political leadership was weakened and bureaucratic power enhanced in relative terms. Yet by the mid-1990s, the bureaucracy itself had become the focal point of criticism for policy failures, scandals, and cover-ups, leading to calls for administrative reform and deregulation. Under these circumstances, Prime Ministers Hashimoto and Obuchi took the lead in pursuing key policy issues, including defense and national security.

It was also in the early 1990s that a greater consensus emerged on defense and national security, leading to greater bipartisanship on these issues (Nagao 1996). After the 1991 Persian Gulf War, the Japanese people came to recognize that Japan would have to contribute to international peace and order not just in terms of money but in terms of manpower; hence, the new role for the SDF in UN peacekeeping received wider acceptance. The opinion polls conducted by the Prime Minister's Office in 1995 showed that more than 70 percent of the respondents considered the SDF's participation in UN peacekeeping as successful (Asagumo Shimbunsha 1998: 700). In July 1994, the SDP reversed its long-held goal of unarmed neutrality and recognized the constitutionality of the SDF, although it remained highly critical of Japan's deepening military ties with the United States. The major opposition parties such as the Democratic Party (under the joint leadership of Hatoyama and Kan) and the Komei Party held the centrist view as to the necessity of the SDF and the Japan-U.S. security arrangements. Consequently, the ability of the National Diet to monitor the SDF was enhanced to a considerable extent.

Despite its status as an agency within the Prime Minister's Office and not yet a fully fledged ministry, the Defense Agency (including the SDF) increased its power and stature in relation to other ministries and agencies (Nagashima 1998). In particular, the Defense Agency became a key player in Japan-U.S. security arrangements, an area where the MOFA holds the primary jurisdiction. Indeed, the Defense Agency, assisted by uniformed officers of the SDF, played a central role in formulating a series of new security policies adopted in the 1990s—namely, the new NDPO and the new Guidelines for Japan-U.S. Defense Cooperation. Moreover, the Defense Agency actively promoted security dialogues and defense exchanges with neighboring states, including China, South Korea, Russia, and Southeast Asian countries—a reflection of the enhanced expertise of Defense Agency officials and the uniformed officers of the SDF.

Accordingly, the standing of the SDF was gradually but remarkably on the rise in the 1990s, contributing to the normalization process of Japan's civil-military relations. The question of sending the SDF abroad remained highly controversial, but the Kaifu government managed to send Maritime SDF minesweepers to the Persian Gulf in April–October 1991, after the war was ended. The SDF was granted wide recognition for its contributions to UN peacekeeping operations in Cambodia in 1992–1993, in Mozambique in 1993–1995, on the Golan Heights since 1996, and in relief operations in Zaire in 1994 (to rescue refugees in Rwanda). Prime Minister Hashimoto was notably instrumental in raising the SDF's standing. His government dispatched C-130s to Thailand to prepare for a possible evacuation of Japanese nationals from Cambodia in July 1997.[23] Unlike Prime Minister Kaifu, who shunned seeing Defense Agency officials and SDF uniformed officers in the prime minister's official residence during the Persian Gulf War, Prime Minister Hashimoto willingly invited SDF uniformed officers to his official residence on various occasions (Funabashi 1999: 117–20). In June 1997, Hashimoto abolished the 1952 National Safety Agency order that had prohibited uniformed officers from speaking in the National Diet, thereby allowing SDF uniformed officers to contribute to deliberations on defense and security issues in the Diet. Further, the Hashimoto Cabinet included uniformed officers of the SDF in the staff of the Cabinet National Security Affairs Office (Nagashima 1998). These developments were a testimony to the normalization of civil-military relations in that the political leadership embarked on engaging the SDF in a wide variety of activities including humanitarian and disaster relief operations, international peacekeeping, and bilateral and multilateral security dialogues and defense exchanges with other countries.

The 1990s saw important changes in the institutional arrangements for defense and national security that contributed to the enhanced standing of the Defense Agency. The first was the reorganization of the SCC, a consultative forum for facilitating Japan-U.S. security arrangements. Throughout the 1960s, 1970s, and 1980s, the U.S. ambassador to Japan and the commander in chief of the U.S. Pacific Command had been the chief participants from the U.S. side, whereas the Japanese side was represented by the minister for foreign affairs and the Defense Agency secretary-general. In December 1990, U.S. representation was upgraded to include the secretary of state and the secretary of defense, and in September 1996 the reconstituted SCC (the so-called Two Plus Two) was held for the first time in Washington. This in turn had the effect of equalizing the standing of the Defense Agency vis-à-vis the MOFA, which had long been in charge of Japan-U.S. security arrangements.[24] Further, the reorganization within the Defense Agency upgraded the SDF's standing in relation to the civilian internal bureaus of the Defense Agency. In January 1997, the Defense Intelligence Headquarters was established under the SDF Joint Staff Council, not within the internal bureaus of the Defense Agency. The headquarters is led by a uniformed officer of the SDF; the deputy is a civilian official of the Defense Agency.[25]

The need to strengthen the role of the prime minister and the cabinet in times of crisis became the subject of intense debate in the 1990s—especially after a series of international and domestic crises such as the 1991 Gulf War, the 1995 Great Hanshin-Awaji Earthquake in Kobe, and the 1995 Aum Shinrikyo gas attacks on Tokyo subways. In December 1997, the Hashimoto Cabinet endorsed the government's Administrative Reform Committee report calling for a reduction in the number of central government bodies from 22 ministries and agencies to 13, including the Prime Minister's Office, by 2001. Along with streamlining the bureaucracy and strengthening the prime minister's leadership role in strategic decision making on a variety of policy issues, a key objective was to strengthen the functions of the cabinet so that Japan's political leadership might respond effectively to emergencies—a further step toward normalization of Japan's civil-military relations.[26]

National Security Policymaking

The geopolitical imperative behind Japan's adoption of new security policies in the 1990s—the Law Concerning Cooperation for UN Peacekeeping and Other Operations (international peace cooperation law) and the Law Concerning the Dispatch of Japan Disaster Relief Teams (disaster relief law) in June 1992, the new NDPO in November 1995, and the new Guidelines for Japan-U.S. Defense Cooperation in September 1997—was the potential for instability and conflict in the post–cold war world. With the end of the cold war, the possibility of global war diminished. Yet the world continued to be bedeviled by regional conflicts, the proliferation of weapons of mass destruction (and their means of delivery), and diverse problems such as refugees and international terrorism. In the Asia-Pacific region, the prospect of great instability on the Korean peninsula, North Korea's military capabilities and provocative behavior, uncertainty about America's long-term commitment to East Asian security, and the rise of China as a great power began to loom large in the minds of Japanese policymakers.

The initial impetus for Japan's awakening to the realities of the post–cold war world came from Washington's call for contributions to its efforts in resolving the Persian Gulf War in 1990–1991. Japan's $13 billion contribution, however, earned it neither credit nor gratitude from Western and Arab countries. The disappointing experience of the Gulf War prompted Tokyo to galvanize support for the dispatch of SDF units for UN peacekeeping operations, culminating in the enactment of the international peace cooperation law in June 1992. The law represented a significant expansion of the SDF's roles and missions. Yet there remained substantial restrictions on the size and the modality of its participation in UN peacekeeping activities. For political and constitutional reasons, the government set five conditions: a cease-fire must be in place; the parties to the conflict must have given their consent to the operation; there must be strict maintenance of neutrality; should any of the foregoing conditions cease to be satisfied, Japan may withdraw its contingent; and use of weapons shall be limited to the minimum necessary for self-protection. The law stipulated that the maximum number of personnel allowed to participate in these activities at one time would be 2,000. The principle of civilian control was secured in that an implementation plan would require cabinet approval, and decisions on the implementation plan (as well as changes and termination of activities) would be reported to the National Diet. Further, the SDF's peacekeeping operations would be limited to logistic support assignments: medical care, transportation, communications, and construction services. The "core missions of peacekeeping forces," such as monitoring disarmament, patrolling cease-fire zones, and inspecting the disposal of abandoned weapons, were to be frozen until new legislation was enacted.[27]

In addition to establishing a legal basis for UN peacekeeping and international relief operations, Japanese policymakers also felt the need to formulate new national security policies.
Among their concerns about the evolving situation of the post–cold war period, two security
issues in particular had occupied their minds by early 1994. One was Tokyo's recognition of the
inadequate system of crisis management and its inability to assist the United States in the event
of regional contingencies. The North Korean nuclear crisis in the spring of 1994 sensitized both
Tokyo and Washington to the singular lack of political assurances about defense cooperation
between the two governments. During the crisis, the U.S. forces in Japan sent to the SDF Joint
Staff Council a list of 1,900 specific items the U.S. forces would need from Tokyo in the event of
an emergency on the Korean peninsula. Apparently for domestic political reasons, the Japanese side was noncommittal. In April 1994, the U.S. Seventh Fleet sounded out the Defense Agency
on the possibility of dispatching SDF minesweepers for a Korean contingency. The Defense
Agency replied in the negative: such operations, it said, would be deemed an execution of the
right of collective self-defense and therefore unconstitutional (Funabashi 1999: 282).

Tokyo's other concern had to do with the worrisome perception, growing on both sides of
the Pacific, that the Japan-U.S. security alliance had lost its sense of direction (Funabashi 1999).
Japan felt compelled to revitalize the alliance with the United States to make it more relevant
to the new demands of the post–cold war world.

In February 1994, Prime Minister Hosokawa, on his own initiative, laid the groundwork
for revising the 1976 NDPO by creating a special advisory group for the prime minister (Boei
Nenkan Kankokai 1996). In August 1994, the advisory group submitted its report, *The Modality of the Security and Defense Capability of Japan: The Outlook for the 21st Century*, to Prime Minister
Murayama, who had replaced Hosokawa in June 1994 (Boeimondai Kondankai 1994). The
report argued that "Japan should extricate itself from its security policy of the past, that was,
if anything, passive, and henceforth play an active role in shaping a new order." The report
presented a comprehensive list of security policy initiatives focusing on the importance of "multilateral security cooperation," the need to enhance the "functions of the Japan-U.S. security
cooperation relationship," and the necessity for the "maintenance and operation of a highly
reliable and efficient defense capability."

The report's elevated emphasis on "multilateral security cooperation" and unilateral security measures relative to the bilateral security arrangements with the United States, however,
aroused criticism from Japan watchers in the United States. Cronin and Green (1994: 2), for
example, observed that "there are growing signs in Japan's policy planning of renewed attention to the United Nations, to regional multilateral mechanisms, and to stronger independent
capabilities as means of hedging against possible U.S. withdrawal or fatigue." What became
increasingly clear to both Tokyo and Washington was the imperative to redefine the Japan-U.S.
alliance by developing new policy guidelines and mechanisms. In Washington, these concerns
led to the "Nye initiative," an effort by the newly appointed assistant secretary of defense, Joseph
Nye, to reconstruct U.S. security strategy for the East Asia–Pacific region. The "Nye Report,"
released in February 1995, served as a useful model for the formulation of the new NDPO (Funabashi 1999: 248–79).

In November 1995, the Murayama Cabinet adopted the new NDPO. The new NDPO
substantially expanded the SDF's roles and missions to include response to large-scale disasters, terrorist attacks, and "various other situations that could seriously affect Japan's peace and

security" (which could mean regional military contingencies), as well as participation in UN peacekeeping operations. Based on the NDPO, a Mid-Term Defense Program (MTDP) for fiscal years 1996 through 2000 provided for a substantial increase in defense capabilities.

In April 1996, Prime Minster Hashimoto and President Clinton launched the Japan-U.S. Joint Declaration on Security, which reaffirmed the importance of the Japan-U.S. alliance as a stabilizing factor in the Asia-Pacific region and formally endorsed a review of the 1978 guidelines.[28] In June 1996, Tokyo and Washington reconstituted the SDC under the auspices of the SCC to review the guidelines on the basis of the new NDPO and the Japan-U.S. Joint Declaration on Security. To achieve a degree of transparency in the formulation process of the new guidelines, the two governments released a progress report in September 1996 and an interim report in June 1997.

In September 1997, the governments of Japan and the United States issued the new guidelines. The new guidelines provide a comprehensive framework for defense policy consultation and coordination between Tokyo and Washington both in peacetime and during contingencies. The core of the new guidelines remains the same as the 1978 guidelines: in the case of an armed attack against Japan, the Japanese SDF would conduct defensive operations, whereas the United States would take care of offensive measures. Yet it can be argued that the new guidelines constitute part of the normalization of Japan's civil-military relations in the 1990s. First, the new guidelines emphasize the need for active peacetime cooperation aimed at stabilizing an international security environment—promoting security dialogues in the Asia-Pacific region, participating in UN peacekeeping operations, and conducting emergency relief operations. This represents a substantial expansion of the roles and missions of the Defense Agency (including the SDF). Second, in conducting bilateral operations in the case of an armed attack against Japan, the new guidelines incorporate the concept of joint operations of their respective forces' ground, Maritime, and air services—a step that could very well lead to a substantial upgrading of the standing of the Joint Staff Council. Third, the scope of the SDF's non-combat support operations in the case of regional contingencies was clarified and expanded to include logistic support for U.S. combat forces, enhanced surveillance operations, minesweeping, interception of contraband on the high seas, measures to deal with refugees, and non-combatant evacuation operations. As we have seen, these changes in security roles and missions are a crucial measure of the changing character of civil-military relations in Japan. Fourth, Tokyo and Washington began to establish two institutions envisaged in the guidelines: "a comprehensive mechanism" for joint defense planning and the establishment of common standards and procedures and "a bilateral coordination mechanism" for specific activities in times of crisis. The prominent role of the Defense Agency (including uniformed officers of the SDF) is institutionalized in these mechanisms.

The formulation of the new NDPO and the new guidelines—led by officials of the Defense Agency and the MOFA with little input from politicians—was exceedingly bureaucratic. Yet, the subsequent policymaking in the National Diet highlighted the shift of civilian control from the bureaucracy to the politicians. In April 1998, the Japanese government submitted to the National Diet bills to establish a legal basis for implementing the new guidelines.[29] On May 24, 1999, after a heated debate in the National Diet, the guidelines legislation was enacted with the support of the LDP, the Liberal Party, and New Komeito. One of the key questions was whether basic plans to support U.S. military operations in case of contingencies in "areas surrounding

Japan" should require Diet approval. The government bill only stipulated that the government "report such plans to the Diet," meaning that the Diet's approval would not be mandatory. The Democratic Party and New Komeito, however, insisted that in light of the cardinal principle of civilian control Diet approval should be required in principle before initiating SDF operations, though the government could seek ex post facto Diet approval in the event of an emergency. The ruling LDP, which lacked a majority in the upper house even with its coalition ally, the Liberal Party, had no choice but to accommodate the views of the main opposition parties.

In sum, then, Japan's civil-military relations in the 1990s were leading toward normalization in important respects. The shift of civilian control over the SDF from bureaucrats to politicians, the expanding roles and missions of the SDF through the adoption of a series of new or revised security policies, and the widening public support for the SDF's new roles and missions were crucial measures of the changing character of civil-military relations in Japan.

IMPACT OF THE GULF WAR: A CASE STUDY

The Persian Gulf War in 1990–1991 engendered an intense debate in Japan over Japan's role in maintaining a stable international order in the post–cold war world. The crux of the issue had to do with the fundamental tension between Japan's adherence to pacifism and the potential use of the SDF for international peace and security. The impact of the Gulf War on civil-military relations was twofold. First, the war prompted Tokyo to adopt the international peace cooperation law in June 1992, thereby paving the way for the SDF to take part in UN peacekeeping operations for the first time in Japan's postwar history—a significant expansion of the SDF's roles and missions that contributed to the enhanced stature of the Defense Agency and the SDF in the civil-military balance of power. Second, the Gulf War had an impact on Japanese public attitudes toward the SDF. Along with the emergence of a greater public consensus that Japan should play a proactive role in international affairs, public support for the SDF's role in UN peacekeeping increased to a considerable extent. As noted earlier, the SDF's subsequent contributions to UN peacekeeping in Cambodia, Mozambique, the Golan Heights, and relief operations in Zaire improved the public image of SDF officers and helped them to shed their outdated image as social outcasts.

The major focus in this case study is on the delicate tension between the political leadership and the SDF in these defining times, which can be divided into three distinct periods.[30] The first covers the period from Iraq's aggression against Kuwait in early August to mid-September 1990, when Tokyo announced a series of policy responses to support the U.S.-led coalition effort in the Persian Gulf. The second period, from mid-September to mid-November, was the height of political struggle, when Tokyo drafted the controversial UN Peace Cooperation Bill (the UNPC Bill). The third period, from mid-January to late April 1991, was a time in which Tokyo made decisions of consequence to the SDF, including the dispatch of SDF transport aircraft to rescue war refugees and the dispatch of SDF minesweepers to the Persian Gulf after the war had ended.

"Bush Phones"

Although Tokyo's initial response to the crisis in the Persian Gulf—a strong condemnation of Iraq's aggression and an announcement of economic sanctions against Iraq—came on August

5, only three days after Iraq's invasion of Kuwait, events over the subsequent six months confirmed the familiar pattern of Japan's foreign policy being "too little, too late." American pressures, including the "Bush phones"—the push-button telephone calls from President Bush to Prime Minister Kaifu requesting Japan's visible, timely, and substantial contributions—proved to be a driving force behind Tokyo's sporadic decisions on measures to support the U.S.-led coalition efforts in the gulf. On August 29, the Kaifu government announced a host of measures, including material and financial contributions to the multinational forces as well as economic aid to frontline states such as Egypt, Turkey, and Jordan. The following day, Tokyo announced its financial contributions, including $1 billion for the multinational forces in the gulf. All of these measures, however, fell short of America's expectations and engendered negative reactions in the U.S. Congress as well as in the Western mass media. With U.S. displeasure reaching the boiling point, Tokyo announced on September 14 an additional $3 billion package of aid for peace-restoring activities in the Persian Gulf region and for economic development and evacuee relief in frontline states.[31] Japan's checkbook diplomacy was thus played out against a backdrop of strong U.S. pressure.

Most notable in this phase of the policy process was the SDF's abstention from involvement in Japanese policymaking on the Gulf Crisis. Indeed, despite U.S. requests for the dispatch of SDF minesweepers, Prime Minister Kaifu was adamant in refusing such requests on political and constitutional grounds. Hence, Japan's contributions were confined exclusively to nonmilitary matters such as transport of nonlethal materials and financial assistance.

Demise of the UN Peace Cooperation Bill

Amid mounting foreign pressures for Japan's contributions to the coalition's effort in the Persian Gulf, the Kaifu government began seeking a legal basis for supporting UN-sponsored peacekeeping operations. The initial idea was to create a civilian corps: a "UN Peace Cooperation Corps" composed of volunteers recruited from a wide range of fields, including private citizens. Prime Minister Kaifu stressed, at a press conference on August 29, that he would not consider a new security role for the SDF. Top officials of the MOFA, including Vice-Minister Takakazu Kuriyama, supported this view. And it was the MOFA that took a leading role in drafting the bill. The Defense Agency was excluded from the policy process in the beginning. The political drama over the subsequent two months highlighted the tension between the deep pacifist sentiment and antimilitary feelings of many Japanese elites, including Prime Minister Kaifu, and their growing recognition that Japan, as a responsible member of the international community, must contribute more positively to the efforts to maintain world peace and order. Hence, the policy process became highly politicized: turf battles between the MOFA and the Defense Agency, political maneuverings by LDP's defense-oriented politicians (*kokubozoku*, or defense tribe), behind-the-scenes pressure emanating from uniformed SDF officers, highly charged opposition parties criticizing the bill—and high-powered officials of the U.S. government (including President Bush and Ambassador Armacost) and the U.S. Congress calling for Japan's substantial contribution to the multinational forces in the Persian Gulf.

Prime Minister Kaifu's idea of not including the SDF in the volunteer corps clashed with views favoring a prominent role for the SDF in the corps. The Defense Agency was concerned that the corps, if created as an organization under the jurisdiction of the MOFA, would have a debilitating impact not only on the standing of the Defense Agency but, perhaps more seriously, on the morale of the SDF officers. The LDP's defense-oriented politicians, who felt sympathy for the low standing of the Defense Agency, shared these concerns. Younger officials of the MOFA had few reservations about making use of the skills and capabilities of the SDF for the corps, provided that its work would be confined to nonmilitary fields. But it was President Bush's remark in his meeting with Prime Minster Kaifu on September 29 that had a decisive impact: Bush reportedly suggested that if the "Japanese forces" could perform nonmilitary functions in transportation, logistics, and medicine, this contribution would be welcomed by the world. Kaifu now realized that the corps would require the SDF's military expertise and experience.

By early October it had become clear to the Kaifu government that the SDF would form the core of the corps. Yet several delicate issues emerged. One issue concerned the status of SDF officers joining the corps. The MOFA argued that personnel joining the corps would have only the status of a civilian servant; hence, SDF officers would lose their original status. The Defense Agency, however, claimed that SDF officers joining the corps should retain their original status so that they would be categorized as military officers under international law. Related to this issue was a battle between the MOFA and the Defense Agency over the jurisdiction regarding the corps. The MOFA wanted SDF officers joining the corps to be removed from the command and control of the Defense Agency director-general, making them subject to the prime minister, whereas the Defense Agency sought to retain the director-general's jurisdiction over the SDF as units. As the MOFA's position on this matter was unyielding, the Defense Agency held a meeting on October 4 to thrash out a policy option that might be acceptable to both sides. The outcome, however, was a byzantine solution: ground SDF officers would be seconded to the corps with their original status retained but falling under the direct command of the prime minister, whereas Maritime SDF and air SDF would be mobilized as units and assigned transport operations on the basis of the SDF law stipulating that only SDF officers are permitted to operate their ships and aircraft. This policy was subsequently accepted by the MOFA. Prime Minister Kaifu, on tour to the Middle East at the time, had little input in these decisions.

On October 9, following his return from the trip, Prime Minister Kaifu met with the LDP's "big three"—Secretary-General Ichiro Ozawa, chairman of the Executive Council Mutsuki Kato, and chairman of the Policy Affairs Research Council Takeo Nishioka—in order to decide on the draft bill that was worked out by officials of the MOFA and the Defense Agency. What happened at this final phase of the policy process attested to Kaifu's lack of leadership. It was not the prime minister but LDP politicians at the apex of power who twisted the draft bill and injected the fully fledged participation of the SDF as units into the bill. Kaifu thus proved to be a weak and vacillating leader, because his earlier resistance to the use of the SDF as units in the corps was overridden by the views of politicians favoring more salient participation. LDP Executive Council chairman Kato, a graduate of the Army Academy, was offended by the separation of the ground SDF from other services in the draft bill, because he feared this would undermine their morale. Kato was well aware of the dissenting voices of uniformed ground SDF officers, including retired generals.

On October 16, the Kaifu Cabinet approved the bill and submitted it to the National Diet. The final bill stipulated the involvement of the SDF as units or personnel in the corps. One issue emerging in the course of the debate concerned the concept of collective security. In Ozawa's view, the notion of "collective security," based on the UN charter, was different from the concept of the right of "collective self-defense" and thus was consistent with the ideals of the constitution. Hence, Ozawa believed that Japan's military contribution under the auspices of the United Nations was constitutional. In effect, therefore, Ozawa was pressing the government to reinterpret the constitution so that Japan could cooperate more positively with UN activities through the dispatch of the SDF abroad. This move, however, was stopped by the Cabinet Legislation Bureau, which deemed the dispatch of the SDF for roles involving the use of force, even under UN auspices, to be unconstitutional.

Amid much confusion and obfuscation, displayed in the government's responses to the opposition parties' interpellation in the Diet, it became clear that the bill would fail. The Komeito, a centrist party that had the swing votes in the upper house, strongly opposed the bill. Even among the LDP, older-generation leaders such as Masaharu Gotoda and Kiichi Miyazawa expressed reservations about an expanded security role of the SDF.[32] And, fundamentally, the Japanese people did not support the bill. According to an opinion survey conducted in November by *Asahi Shimbun*, 78 percent of those interviewed opposed the dispatch of the SDF abroad, 58 percent opposed the UNPC Bill, and only 21 percent expressed their approval of it.[33] In early November, the government decided to drop the bill. The demise of the bill meant that public concerns about the SDF's new role represented a formidable constraint on the government's effort to dispatch the SDF abroad for collective security.

Aftermath of the Gulf War

Following the multinational force's military operation in January 1991, Tokyo decided to provide an additional $9 billion to support operations in the Persian Gulf. Tokyo also announced it would send SDF aircraft to the gulf to rescue war refugees. Prime Minister Kaifu was initially hesitant about the idea, but again he succumbed to pressures from LDP secretary-general Ozawa and LDP general council chairman Nishioka. But this announcement caused much controversy even within the LDP, due to the absence of a provision permitting such action in the SDF law. The SDF law provides for the transport of "state guests and others at the request of the government," but refugees were not included in the category of "others" in the SDF law's enforcement ordinance. The government therefore decided to add a clause permitting the transfer of refugees in the enforcement ordinance, thereby establishing a legal basis for such action.

On April 24, 1991, after the Gulf War was over, the Kaifu government decided to send Maritime SDF minesweepers to the Persian Gulf to clear waterways for the first time since the inception of the SDF. The opposition parties, except for the Democratic Socialist Party, attacked the government because the dispatch of the SDF was problematic in light of the constitution and because the government had bypassed a parliamentary debate on the issue. The government's decision on the dispatch of minesweepers to the Persian Gulf came only after the war was over, but it nevertheless attracted considerable public attention (though not much criticism at this time).[34]

The foregoing analysis suggests the progression from containment to normalization in Japan's civil-military relations. Although Prime Minister Kaifu lacked policy leadership during much of the crisis, it was not the bureaucrats but the civilian elected officials such as the LDP's senior politicians who played a decisive role in policymaking. The demise of the UNPC Bill meant that the decision to dispatch the SDF for collective security was still premature at the time. But subsequent political developments pointed to a shift from containment to normalization in civil-military relations. Indeed, the unhappy experience of the Gulf War turned out to be a critical turning point in that it triggered the Japanese political elite to adopt the international peace cooperation law in June 1992—thereby enabling the SDF to take part in UN peacekeeping for the first time in Japan's postwar history. This step represented a substantial expansion of the SDF's roles and missions and contributed to the enhanced stature of the Defense Agency (including the SDF) in the civil-military balance of power. The experience of the Gulf War also affected Japanese attitudes toward the SDF. Public support for the SDF's role in UN peacekeeping increased considerably, leading to a growing political consensus favoring the limited and defensive use of the armed forces as a legitimate instrument of foreign policy.

The Trajectory and Its Implications

Throughout the postwar years, Japan's civil-military relations have been characterized by civilian political domination over the SDF. A critical measure of the normalization of civil-military relations has three elements. The first is the gradual shift in security policymaking power from the bureaucrats to the politicians, along with the enhanced ability of the National Diet for monitoring the SDF. The inclusion of uniformed SDF officers in key institutions of decision making and their greater interaction with political leaders suggest that the overall pattern and content of civil-military relations in Japan are approaching those of other advanced industrial democracies where the problem of reconciling democratic control with the technical expertise of military personnel remains a formidable challenge. Second, the proposed roles and missions of the SDF have been the main battlegrounds for the Japanese debate over civil-military relations. The SDF's enhanced roles and missions suggest that the power and stature of the Defense Agency have been upgraded in relation to other bureaucracies, along with the improved standing of the SDF, thus redressing the civil-military balance of power. And third, greater public acceptance of the SDF has been another critical measure of the normalization of civil-military relations. Indeed, the growing political consensus favoring the limited and defensive use of the armed forces as a legitimate instrument of foreign policy signals a major change in the Japanese attitude toward the SDF.

The normalization of civil-military relations in Japan can be interpreted in various ways. It may be regarded, for example, as part of the broad process of the Japanese state becoming a "normal state"—an idea advanced by Ichiro Ozawa (1994) and new-generation neoconservatives. Proponents of the idea of Japan as a "normal state" consider military force as a legitimate instrument of foreign policy to achieve political objectives in a society of states. They argue for a reinterpretation or revision of the constitution to enable Japan to play a more prominent role in resolving international security problems under the banner of the United Nations. Specifically, this "normal state" thesis argues that the SDF should participate actively in collective security and collective self-defense.

The normalization of civil-military relations may also be interpreted as a reflection of the successful institutionalization of civilian democratic control over the Japanese armed forces. The public fear that the SDF would run amok unless constrained by an array of political, legal, and social checks has largely receded. In its place there has emerged a new pattern of civil-military relations whereby the political leadership assigns the SDF a wide variety of roles and missions, cautiously but proactively, including defense cooperation with the United States, humanitarian and disaster relief operations, international peacekeeping, and security dialogues with the militaries of other countries. The growing policymaking power of the politicians, along with the enhanced ability of the National Diet for monitoring the SDF, testifies to Japan's efforts to establish a system of responsible government accountable to the public. The current Japanese debate on the necessity of emergency legislation, moreover, reflects the Japanese search for a proper legal basis for mobilization of the SDF in time of emergency—a critical step to be taken in order to strengthen civilian control of the SDF. The emerging "civil society" in Japan (Yamamoto 1999), the powerful international mass media, and the growing international expectation for greater transparency of Japan's security policy processes will also contribute to a strengthening of civilian supremacy over the Japanese armed forces.

It can be argued, then, that the normalization of civil-military relations will place Japan in a better position to play the role of "global civilian power" (Funabashi 1991). The proponents of this perspective call for Japan to assume global responsibilities in tackling a host of issues such as regional conflicts, the proliferation of weapons of mass destruction and missile delivery systems, environmental problems, and human rights violations. They argue for increasing Japan's proactive role in UN peacekeeping and humanitarian operations and for strengthening regional and global arms control and confidence-building mechanisms. They think it prudent for Japan to refrain from using offensive military forces for settling international conflicts, while recognizing the importance of strong political leadership and the SDF's expertise and input in policymaking and implementation—main ingredients of the normalization of civil-military relations. The "global civilian power" thesis emphasizes the continued relevance of the two pillars of Japanese postwar security policy: the constitution and the Japan-U.S. alliance. The constitution, which embodies Japan's postwar ideals of peace and democracy, decidedly defines a democratic and nonmilitarist orientation of the Japanese state. The Japan-U.S. alliance not only buttresses Japan's commitment to democratic ideals but also conditions its pursuit of an exclusively defense-oriented security policy.

The normalization of civil-military relations, therefore, does not necessarily mean that the basis for civilian supremacy over the military has been eroding in Japan. Nor does it necessarily propel Japan into the status of a normal state. On the contrary, the normalization of civil-military relations signals a welcome upward progression in the larger process of the institutionalization of democratic governance of the Japanese state.

CHAPTER 3

India: The New Militaries

Sunil Dasgupta

IN 1947, THE BRITISH HANDED OVER THE INSTITUTIONS OF GOVERNANCE on the Indian subcontinent to the independent states of India and Pakistan. The British Indian armed forces were divided between the two new states. Since then, Pakistan has had four military governments; India's military, by contrast, has remained under the control of civilian authorities. Indeed, a poor, fractious India has been a surprising example of democracy in the developing world. The key factors contributing to the survival of democracy in India have been the conceptual and institutional British legacy of civilian control over the military, the strategic choices made by nationalist leaders, the comparatively higher stature of the nationalist leadership, the success of civilian institutions, and, finally, the restraint of the military. (For details of these arguments see Cohen 1988, 1990; Ganguly 1991b; Kukreja 1991; and Kundu 1998.) In recent decades, however, British traditions have faded, the military is seen as the most nationalist of institutions (raising the legitimacy of the armed forces), and civilian institutions that held the military in check are weakening. The military's growing internal security role has given rise to concerns about the future of civilian control over the military.

This chapter argues that despite the seeming breach in the postindependence civil-military balance, the military as an institution is not becoming more powerful than civilian authorities. The increased use of the armed services is, in fact, led by civilian authorities who could theoretically cut back that role at will. In Latin America and Africa, this has not been the case; once militaries get a taste of power, they are unlikely to remain secondary players. This is clearly a worrisome prospect for India, but the character of its militarization—led up front by civilian groups and paramilitaries—has kept the principle of civilian control in place. Instead, what we see is civilian militarism. Politicians and civilian bureaucrats are willing to use force more often and earlier on, increasingly through paramilitary forces and intelligence agencies. There has been a striking increase in the strength of paramilitary forces. By and large, the public has supported the internal use of force, which is seen as being necessitated by foreign subversion.

In external security, this "new militarism" can be seen in India's nuclearization, which has been led, significantly, by a civilian scientific bureaucracy. The scientists who control India's nuclear program and the civilian bureaucrats and police officers who lead the paramilitary forces have direct access to the decision-making process, something the armed forces have not systematically enjoyed. Not only does this strain the principle of control, the role played by these unelected actors in national security decision making also detracts from what Muthiah Alagappa has called "democratic civilian control," that is, the exercise of political imperatives by elected officials (see analytical framework, Chapter 1).[1]

Viewed from this perspective, India faces a greater worry: the erosion of democratic civilian control over its men-at-arms, both the formal military and other armed organizations.[2] Not only is control over state coercion in the hands of those who execute it (thus subverting the idea of control), but excessive use of force often violates the democratic rights of about 40 million people, or about 5 percent of the population (Cohen 1988: 100). The increased internal security role of the military has institutional and strategic implications as well. The army risks ethnic conflict. Following an Indian Army attack on a Sikh holy shrine in 1984, about 2,600 Sikh soldiers mutinied (Kundu 1996: 69). Strategically, army officers worry that if several divisions are tied down fighting rebellions, India's conventional superiority over Pakistan will be reduced.[3] Even the growth of paramilitary forces has not taken the pressure off the army. Caught in protracted counterinsurgency operations, military officers blame incompetent civilian bureaucrats and paramilitary forces for their domestic overdeployment and declining effectiveness.

The difficult relationship between armed forces and civilian bureaucracy can also be attributed to the bureaucratic domination of the military. In independent India, the armed services have had little control over the development of strategy, they wield negligible influence on the budget and procurement processes, and they have been unable to interact directly with the parliament. The service chiefs are supervised by the defense secretary on policy matters and further down the bureaucratic chain on routine affairs. The military brass shares with (and is often dominated by) the civilian bureaucracy in the making of policy and procedures. Unit movements across command lines and promotions over the rank of major require approval from the civilian Ministry of Defence (MoD). Lately, however, the military has been trying to shake off bureaucratic domination. The armed forces have registered victories following two recent incidents. First, a military-bureaucracy showdown that led to the dismissal of a navy chief has forced the bureaucracy to treat service chiefs with greater respect. Second, the battle for Kargil in 1999 has given new urgency to the demands made by the military. Today, the two sides compete for control (manifested in issues of deployment, promotion, and protocol) and resources (budgets, pay, and procurement).

The first section of this chapter traces the evolution of civil-military relations in India after independence. Rather than look minutely at institutional arrangements, which have remained largely unchanged since 1947, this section traces the underlying philosophies and competition between the players. The second section explores civilian militarism in India—manifested in the increased domestic deployments of the armed forces, the growth of paramilitaries, and the erosion of democratic rights. The third section examines the more visible military-bureaucracy conflict caused by bureaucratic domination of the armed forces. Recent gains by the military and the pressures of internal security duties have worsened the conflict. The two case studies in the fourth and fifth sections—the dismissal of Vishnu Bhagwat as navy chief and India's nuclearization—demonstrate the growing military-bureaucracy tensions and support the contention that civilian groups dominate the military at the high end of the conflict spectrum as well. In conclusion, the chapter explores the implications of current trends for continued civilian control of the military and the management of national security in the future.

CIVIL-MILITARY RELATIONS SINCE 1947

The bureaucratic domination of the military was the result of the unique circumstances of Indian independence—a legal transfer of power that kept most British institutions alive. Thus, on August 15, 1947, India adopted the collaborationist armed forces as its national military and with it accepted the concomitant problems of legitimacy and trust. Nationalist leaders such as Jawaharlal Nehru, who became the first prime minister of the country, made strategic choices at this critical juncture. First, in recognition of the importance of an effective national army, the British armed forces were allowed to exist as they had before independence. The army even continued to employ British officers for a period. Second, the decision was made against politicizing the military—nationalist leaders refused, for instance, to rehabilitate members of the Indian National Army (INA), a force raised by the Japanese from British Indian Army prisoners of war in Southeast Asia. Led by the charismatic nationalist leader Subhas Chandra Bose, INA units fought with the Japanese against Allied Forces in Burma. Rehabilitating INA members would legitimize political soldiers—a dangerous precedent, as Pakistan's four military coups have shown. And third, because the nationalist leadership distrusted the military leaders, they monitored the armed forces very closely via the civilian bureaucracy. A civil-military manual in 1952 set the stage for later bureaucratic domination (Nalapat 1999: 10). Lacking the legitimacy to protest, the military services accepted the situation.

The nationalist leadership was generally averse to the use of force in foreign policymaking. National security issues were ignored at the cabinet level and dominated by V. K. Krishna Menon, the defense minister and a close confidante of Nehru (Ganguly 1991b: 13). Menon is said to have interfered in the internal matters of the military and contributed to India's defeat in 1962 by China. The formal civil-military arrangement survived the war and continues to exist today—the recent creation of the National Security Council (NSC) promises changes in the future, though there are serious doubts about its success.

At the apex of a three-tier structure is the Cabinet Committee on Political Affairs (CCPA)—previously the Defence Committee of the Cabinet. The CCPA comprised all senior ministers of the prime minister's cabinet and was responsible for policymaking on a wide variety of subjects including foreign affairs and defense. Below the CCPA, the Defence Planning Committee (DPC)—previously the Defence Minister Committee—consisted of the cabinet secretary; the prime minister's special secretary; the secretaries of finance, external affairs, planning, defense, defense production, and defense research and development; and the three service chiefs. The Chief of Staff Committee (CSC) was the military component of the third tier. The other half was the MoD's Defence Coordination and Implementation Committee (DCIC), chaired by the defense secretary. The DCIC coordinated defense production, defense research and development, finances, and the requirements of the services (see Kundu 1998: 76–80; Ganguly 1991b: 13; Thomas 1986: 119–34).

The 1962 defeat resulted in a massive expansion of the Indian armed forces. The Indian Army doubled over the next ten years. Defense expenditure as a percentage of gross national product doubled between 1961 and 1965. The Indian Air Force acquired MiG-21 fighters and production technology from the Soviet Union. The Indo-Tibetan Border Police (ITBP) was raised to patrol the Indo-Chinese border. In 1965, the Border Security Force (BSF) was raised for border patrol duties in western deserts and around East Pakistan (which later became Bangladesh).

A more deep-rooted legacy of the 1962 debacle was an arrangement whereby the armed forces were given unprecedented operational freedom. Senior army officers vociferously protested political interference, especially Menon's early role. Unequivocally blamed for the defeat, the political leadership thought it prudent to stay away from micromanaging the armed forces (for an analysis of the blame for 1962, see Palit 1991: 1–2, 68–110). This led to a Clausewitzian division of labor between the military and the political leadership. The armed forces were allowed a high degree of operational freedom so long as they followed the strategic directions of the political leadership. Thus, national leadership gained control of the "logic of war," which according to Clausewitz lies in the political realm, while the "grammar of war" rightfully remained the preserve of the armed forces.

This arrangement worked quite successfully in the 1965 and 1971 wars against Pakistan. The downside, however, was that operational freedom aggravated the civilian (both political and bureaucratic) mistrust of the military. The lack of regular political involvement with the armed forces meant that the political leadership never quite knew what was happening inside the military. Thus, operational freedom came at the cost of increased bureaucratic monitoring. Over the years, bureaucratic domination reached a level where all service-originated proposals require MoD approval.

By the early 1980s, starting with the Sikh rebellion in Punjab, the armed forces became increasingly deployed in internal security. This process came to a head in the early 1990s when the Indian Army and paramilitaries were simultaneously fighting insurgencies in Punjab, in Jammu and Kashmir, and in at least three northeastern states. The other services, normally not involved in internal security, were also called to duty. The Indian Navy was asked to patrol the Palk Straits between India and Sri Lanka to prevent gunrunning, and Indian Air Force transports were flying security forces across the country on rapid deployment.

The increased internal duties of the military signals a hardening of the Indian state. Not only has New Delhi responded to increasing internal violence, but it has initiated the violence itself in an effort to establish authority in a highly mobilized political environment (Mathur 1992: 337–48). Internally there is social, economic, regional, and religious churning. Internationally the country has continued to live in a hostile region even as it was cut adrift by the cold war's unexpected end. The absence of the lightning rod of charismatic leadership—and the unraveling of the Congress Party that ruled 40 of India's 50 years—exaggerates the external and internal drift. Problems seem irresolvable, and violence is the instrument of choice more often (and much earlier). The external manifestation of the hardening of the state came in May 1998, when India declared itself a full-fledged nuclear power.

All this does not mean that civilian control over the military in India is institutionally threatened. It indicates a high level of contestation that is likely to remain within the bounds of democracy. Indeed, elsewhere contestation between the civilian and military leaderships is seen as a commitment of the military to democracy (Pion-Berlin 1997: 19). Moreover, as S. E. Finer has suggested, the military must absorb the principle of civilian supremacy (Finer 1988: 24). This much is complete in India. Its institutional democracy and formal civilian control over the military appear to be safe. At the same time, however, the erosion of democracy in states and districts, especially in the insurgency-hit regions, is worrisome for what it does to the substance of Indian democracy. Democracy is not just about institutions. It is about values as well. Democracy protects individual rights and minority communities. As much as democracy is said to lead to peace, without peace democracy is devalued. Today the core of the Indian state—politicians, bureaucrats, and the public generally—have become militaristic. This widespread sanction does not absolve militarism from what it does. The majority of India's people may approve of the use of excessive force in Kashmir and the Northeast, but that does not make it right or democratic.

Most studies on India's civil-military relations have not taken this perspective, though some have worried about the problem (see, for instance, Cohen 1988; Ganguly 1991b). The primary concern in the literature has been to explain the institutional success of civilian control over the military in India and, by comparison, the failure of civilian control in other developing countries, especially Pakistan (see, for instance, Kundu 1998; Jalal 1995).[4] This chapter, however, suggests a shift in the study of Indian civil-military relations from an instability model (which is applied to developing countries and investigates the survivability of institutions) to a stability model (which is usually applied to developed countries and examines contestation and meaning). Rather than focusing on institutional and formal civil-military arrangements at the national level, we must investigate the undergrowth of ethnic problems, the new role of paramilitaries, the erosion of local democracy, and the reality of civilian control.

RISE OF CIVILIAN MILITARISM

Though the Indian Army primarily focuses on external threats, twelve of its seventeen major campaigns between 1947 and 1995 were internal (Jaswant Singh 1999: 142–43). In the period 1982–89, the army was deployed in "aid to civil power" 721 times (Rosen 1996: 263). In the twenty years from 1951–70, the army had been called out 476 times (Sinha 1985: 30). Since the mid-1980s, there were three major domestic deployment locations for Indian security forces: the Northeast, where a series of existing insurgencies became urgent; Punjab, where rebellion threatened the heart of India; and in the Jammu and Kashmir, where India's very identity was in doubt.[5] Although they do not formally involve martial law, domestic military operations display several of its features, such as the suspension of civil liberties, press censorship, and search and arrest without warrants. These campaigns have been longer and bloodier and have stretched the security forces to exhaustion. They have involved large forces: about thirteen brigades in the Northeast, 100,000 troops in Punjab, and 200,000 regular troops in Kashmir. About 30 to 40 percent of the army is currently devoted to internal security duties.

To supplant the internal role of the army, large numbers of paramilitary forces have been raised under the command of civilian police officers.[6] The Central Reserve Police (CRP) force has doubled since 1986 to 165,000, and the BSF, which was raised in 1965 and in 1986 numbered about 100,000, now has a strength of 180,000 (Kuldip Singh 1998: 63).[7] States have their own armed constabulary and riot control battalions. One estimate pegs the total strength of

Indian paramilitary forces at about 1 million (Ganguly 1991b: 22; see also International Institute for Stategic Studies [IISS] 2000: 157). Senior paramilitary officers have used a higher figure of 1.4 million in a symposium discussion (Arya and Sharma 1991: 31). That would make the paramilitary forces larger than the regular armed services. Since 1947, the paramilitary has grown tenfold while the army has quadrupled, and most of the increase came after the military defeat in 1962 (Kukreja 1991: 223–24, n. 69). Assuming a conservative deployment ratio of 50 percent, about 1 million men-at-arms are fighting warlike situations in India. "Between 1974–75 and 1996, the level of internal 'paramilitarization,' as measured by the ratio between paramilitary forces and population, rose… 71 percent in India" (Collier 1999: 8–9). India comes in second, after war-torn Sri Lanka, of all the countries studied in this volume.[8]

This vast increase in the number of men-at-arms—presumably in reaction to an equally impressive growth in societal violence—indicates significant militarization of Indian society. What has caused this dramatic growth and increased use of security forces? First, New Delhi has often resorted to the use of force in support of its developmental agenda. This has been attributed to the "powerlessness" of the Indian state to deliver on its objectives (see, for instance, Mathur 1992: 337–48 and Kohli 1994: 89–107). Referring in particular to Indira Gandhi's prime ministership, Kuldeep Mathur (1992), for instance, writes,

> (h)er inability to get people to adopt the state's codes and norms led her to new responses—authoritarianism and harsh methods—that still ran headlong against the same brick wall. What is alarming is that this pattern of state response, in the face of its inability to enforce social control, is becoming more frequent. A vast state coercive apparatus has been built up and state power is linked to it through laws that may be authoritarian in character. (Mathur 1992: 340)

Second, there has been a remilitarization of society through the increased availability of AK-47 imitations and plastic explosives (Rao 1999: 36–41).[9] Stringent gun control laws have not been able to prevent the diffusion of small arms. Indian security forces in Kashmir between 1990 and 1998 recovered around 18,000 AK series rifles, 7,000 pistols and revolvers, and 500 rocket launchers (Rao 1999: 38). In Punjab, an estimated 10,000 AK series rifles were captured in the period 1988–1994 (Kasturi 1999: 53). The extent of diffusion owes much to the end of the Afghan war in the north, Tamil Tiger gunrunning in the south, and the armed groups on the India-Burma border (see, for instance, Rao 1999: 36–41).

Third, there is a broad pattern of institutional decay and polarization of Indian society. Political institutions are no longer able to respond to massive mobilization across the country. To simplify drastically, the educated, urban, Muslim youth in Kashmir came to see secessionism as the only way to political influence. In Punjab, an agricultural elite looking for political power outside the Congress Party system chose the Sikh temple management committees as its vehicle. When the Indian state resisted this alternative mode of mobilization, they organized in armed groups. In the far Northeast, a semiautonomous region under the British, the local elite protested the transformation and modernization efforts of the Indian state (which wanted a well-knit nation) almost immediately after 1947. In the valley of Assam, this has meant ethnic Bengali domination—the crux of the Assamese revolt.

At the root of the remilitarization in the mainland is a lower-caste challenge against a centuries-old social Brahmanical system that did not alter sufficiently in the first three decades of independence. Private armies—gangs, really—operate with considerable impunity in the

North Indian states of Bihar and Uttar Pradesh, in the Northeast, and now even in Delhi and Mumbai.[10] New local elites have emerged under the leadership of "backward-class" figures such as Laloo Prasad Yadav and Mulayam Singh Yadav. (For the processes that brought these outcomes see Duncan 1997: 979–96.) Established elites have tried to regain the initiative through appeals to Hinduism and have had considerable political success. The gathering Hindu movement—and its implications for some 150 million Indian Muslims—has added a new dimension of insecurity. Though overall statistics are hard to find, an appendix in a book published by the government's Indian Institute of Public Administration lists 210 major incidents of collective violence—mostly caste- and religion-inspired rioting—in the period 1951–1985. Of these incidents, 58 occurred in 1951–1970 and 152 in 1971–1985 (Shukla 1988: 309–28). Since then the trend is believed to have intensified.

Fourth, television has united the core of this besieged state and solidified the consensus for militaristic options. The battle for Kargil in summer 1999 culminated this process. Earlier, for instance, it was believed that South Indians did not care about Kashmir. The Northeast was often conflated with the state of Assam. But as India's first television war, Kargil brought expected results. As people watched the war unfold on their television screens—first with despair but ultimately with the jubilation of victory—there was an upsurge of nationalism across the country not seen since 1962. The dissemination of images of war, glory, and martyrs—especially the telecast of funeral ceremonies—has led to long lines outside recruitment centers. Contributions to the National Defence Fund have poured in from across the country.[11]

What does this mean for civil-military relations? An increasing number of civilians (bureaucrats, policemen, and opposition groups, including secessionist forces) behave like the military. In Punjab, for instance,

> an undue emphasis on military type operations with total neglect of police work of investigation and prosecution of terrorist crime, coupled with [state police chief] K. P. S. Gill's open advocacy of the "killer instinct," had weakened the civil complexion of the police and produced an authoritarian streak in its psyche at all levels of command.... This resulted in making the Punjab police...a law unto itself—out of control of its own officers except a handful who commanded personal loyalty. (Lal 1999: 20)

The presence of these "new militaries" in the decision-making system subverts the idea of control itself. The concept of control requires separation between those who undertake coercion and those who sanction it. The concept of civilian control further requires that civilians sanction the use of force—the presumption here is that civilians are less likely to allow the use of force and the consequent erosion of democratic rights. If civilian groups behave like the military, however, violating the democratic rights they are mandated to protect, they could be described as the de facto military, and democratic civilian control could be jeopardized. Indeed, police officers are appointed as special secretaries in the Internal Security Division of the Ministry of Home Affairs. As the functional lines between the civilian and military blur, the institutional separation between execution and control is compromised, and civilian control becomes problematic.

The conventional wisdom on this issue is that civilians use force less often, but when they do they are more ferocious. Thus, the civilian-authorized use of force does not necessarily violate the principle of civilian control over the military. Moreover, control implies the ability to choose between using force and refraining from the use of force. A distinction needs to be made, perhaps, between the command of the military and control over the military. Clearly, in India political command over the services is not in question. The armed forces and even the civilians who act as the "new militaries" take their commands from the political leadership. Instead, it is the control function that has become problematic. Will loss of control eventually lead to loss of command? Unlikely, but the loss of control is troubling itself.

Reflecting similar concerns, scholars have argued for the inclusion of effective civilian control over the military as a requisite of democracy (Karl 1990: 2). The process of democratization is considered incomplete if the military continues to exercise independent power behind the scenes. In India, the problematic democratic civilian control over the military equally diminishes democracy. The liberal foundation of the Indian state and constitution guards against militarism by mandating a democratic process—and not coercion—for the resolution of disputes. The internal use of force—irrespective of whether civilian or military leaders make the decision—has the impact of encouraging militarism. By electing to use force, civilian authorities become the de facto military. That the civilian leadership has raised paramilitary forces that equal the size of the armed forces reinforces this notion.

At the practical level, democracy—the purpose of civilian control—is eroding not just in the peripheral regions of Kashmir and the Northeast but also in the heartland: in Punjab, Bihar, western Uttar Pradesh, the jungles of Orissa and Madhya Pradesh, the Telegana region of Andhra Pradesh, and in coastal Gujarat and Maharashtra. We can see evidence of increases in the number of complaints filed with the National Human Rights Commission, which increased from 496 in 1993–1994 to 6,947 in 1994–1995 and 20,514 in 1996–1997 (Kochanek 2000: 15). Though there is no way of verifying how many of the allegations are frivolous, a police officer who served in Punjab during the height of the Sikh rebellion, for instance, found most complaints he received to be true (Lal 1999: 23). The subversion of control described here has led to a slew of laws—often put in place by executive ordinance—legitimizing the erosion of democracy and potentially tipping the constitutional civil-military balance in favor of a military mindset, if not the military as an institution. Moreover, the explosion in the size of the paramilitary—the new militaries—creates organizational friction, compromises unity of command, and reduces the effectiveness of security forces.

Erosion of Democracy

During insurgencies, the Union government in New Delhi can use the special provisions of President's Rule to dismiss elected state governments—and parliamentary extension of President's Rule can put the electoral process on hold for years. In Jammu and Kashmir, for instance, following the dismissal of the state government in 1990, there were no local and state elections for more than seven years. The Union government nominates an executive governor (normally governors are ceremonial; executive power in the states is vested in the office of the elected chief ministers). More often than not, retired army generals and senior police and intelligence officers are appointed as emergency governors. Former senior military and police officers, it is hoped, will be more adept at managing violence and will enable better coordination between the state administration, police, paramilitary forces, and army troops. Where the governor is a civilian, a military advisor is appointed to assist him. The appointment of an army general as advisor to the governor of Punjab, according to Elkin and Ritezel (1985: 489), signaled de facto military control over a state government. "Ajai Singh [the military commander during Operations Bajrang and Rhino in Assam in 1990–1991] ended up dominating the [Central Command Coordination] Council as the officials turned to him for advice on tackling the rebellion" (Hazarika 1994: 216). The presence of generals in what would be civilian positions consolidates the view that large sections of the Indian population actually live under military administration.[12]

The imposition of President's Rule in a state is followed closely by induction of federal security forces—paramilitary and army—into the state. Local commanders of these forces, both military and paramilitary, are given powers to declare curfews, conduct searches without warrants, and take potential troublemakers into preventive custody.[13] During this period, the army runs a semblance of district administration and maintains law and order—indeed, it is the inability of civilian administration to function that leads to the army being called out.[14] The rapid induction of large-scale security forces does not allow adequate retraining for counterinsurgency operations. Soldiers en route to Kashmir receive a few weeks of retraining (depending on how urgently they are needed) in the newly established Udhampur, Jammu, branch of the Army's College of Insurgency and Jungle Warfare. The pressure of internal security duties takes its toll when a tired, sleep-deprived soldier sitting in a bunker loses control by firing into a hostile crowd of protesters, some of whom might be carrying guns.[15] According to Khusro Rustamji, "the expansion of the BSF and the CRP has created numerous problems of training and control which tend to affect performance" (1992: 82). In 1993–1994, army chief Bipin Chandra Joshi felt compelled to issue his "ten commandments"—a list of dos and don'ts that soldiers were ordered to carry in their pockets at all times.[16]

Though most human rights violations are command and control failures that are punished upon discovery, some have the tacit approval of the military high command and the civilian leadership. Unable to meet the high burden of law—evidence is rare and witnesses very few— and frustrated by the slow legal process, security forces are known to summarily execute suspected militants in fake encounters.[17] Another popular tactical method is the use of "cats," captured militants who have been persuaded to identify other members of their groups. In one version the "cat" is driven through his old neighborhood in an unmarked vehicle to pick out suspects who are then arrested by supporting teams. Although the entire procedure is open to abuse, "cats" are often forced to identify innocent people as militants. More ambitious "cats" might even conduct their own operations—which then opens the opportunity for extortion in what is cynically called a "game of cats and mice."

A remarkably frank but somewhat self-serving account of the methods used by police and security forces is provided by Chaman Lal, a police officer who has led counterinsurgency operations in Punjab and the Northeast. He believes, for instance, that the "shooting of terrorists in 'hot-chase' situations is justified," but decries the "cold-blooded killing of terrorists after taking them into custody." According to Lal, "the extra-judicial killings and torture in custody place a question mark on the authenticity of even real encounters" (Lal 1999: 22). Though he says he followed a "hearts and minds" policy, others in the police and security forces displayed a "killer instinct." The internal rivalries within the police and security forces result in similar "outing" of the obviously egregious methods employed by security forces. Militant groups are also known to use similar methods: executing informers and those who work with the government, declaring their own curfews, and collecting "taxes." (For the abuses of militancy in Punjab and Kashmir, see Human Rights Watch 1994.)

The ultimate result is visible in the casualty figures. Despite the possible underreporting, official figures are astounding. An Indian Army officer writes that until March 1999, "the army had killed 7,994 militants and another 24,251 had been apprehended in J&K [Jammu and Kashmir].... Army casualties included 1,005 killed and 3,017 wounded" (Kanwal 1999: 19). These figures do not include the even greater losses inflicted and suffered by paramilitary forces, which are in charge of policing cities and towns and face the brunt of militant activity. In all, says the officer, terrorism in Kashmir caused the deaths of 29,000 civilians and made 280,000 homeless (Kanwal 1999: 19). Militancy in Punjab in 1983–1992 is estimated, conservatively, to have caused 12,000 deaths, including 1,400 police, 300 paramilitary, and 50 army personnel.

Overall casualty figures used by the government and secessionist groups differ widely and have not been independently verified. Both Amnesty International and Human Rights Watch reports tend to be microlevel documentation of human rights violations. Certainly, no systematic counting of casualties is available in the public domain. The last census conducted in the state of Jammu and Kashmir was in 1981. The state missed the 1991 census, and New Delhi ordered another round of census taking in summer 2000. To arrive at a reasonable match between incidents and casualties, I undertook a preliminary analysis of a selected list of major incidents in a book on insurgency by a senior police officer.

The list contains a total of 413 major incidents in the period 1991–1995. In all, 3,223 persons had died and 2,223 were wounded (the figures include militants, security forces, and civilians). The average number of persons killed in an incident was 8, which is a high figure, but also perhaps to be expected since the list comprises major incidents only. The largest number, 1,065 persons, died in four Northeast states (579 wounded); 954 died in Punjab (449 wounded); 747 died in Jammu and Kashmir (412 wounded). Left-wing violence resulted in the death of 174 persons, mostly in Central India (43 wounded). In Kashmir, a large number of militants were killed (172). Comparatively, in the Northeast there were fewer (66) and in Punjab none (probably a reporting error, given that the Sikh insurgency is believed to have been tamed). Four left-wing militants were also reported killed. The largest number of civilians died in Punjab (887), followed by the Northeast (729), Jammu and Kashmir (398), and left-wing violence (69). The most security forces were killed in the Northeast (270), followed by Kashmir (177), left-wing violence (91), and Punjab (67).

Legal Sanction

The use of excessive force by the security forces is sanctioned by a plethora of emergency laws. These draconian laws are mostly introduced through executive ordinances but have been ratified later by legislatures and are often upheld by the judiciary (for an extensive though slightly out-of-date survey of legally sanctioned violations of democratic rights, see Desai 1986). These statutes provide cover and legitimacy for the erosion of democratic rights—and, as systematic violations of the constitution's original intent, are more dangerous than the human rights abuses themselves. Even more worrisome is the fact that civilians, rather than the military, have sought to impose draconian laws. Constitutional civilian control is based on the belief that civilians would prevent—not encourage and shelter—the loss of democracy. These laws, then, defeat the purpose of civilian control. They indicate the willingness of civilian authorities to use violence as a political tool and, moreover, mark a shift toward militarism in the constitutional civil-military balance.

The Armed Forces Special Powers Act was originally passed in 1958 to aid pacification efforts in Nagaland and Mizoram in the Northeast. The law has been extended to other areas as required. The special powers allow military personnel to enter and search without warrant, make arrests, and use lethal force without fear of prosecution, so long as these actions were carried out in good faith. A series of "disturbed areas" acts allow the Union government to deploy security forces without the continuous supervision of the district magistrate, who would normally authorize every step of "aid to the civil" operations.[18]

The National Security Act of 1980 (which replaced the Maintenance of Internal Security Act of 1971, the primary legal cover used during the emergency of 1975–1977) allows preventive detention of up to two years of persons believed to be prejudicial to the defense of India, public order, or maintenance of essential services. The Terrorists Affected Areas (Special Courts) Act of 1984 was the first attempt to establish a separate judiciary for trying militant rebellion. The special courts were not only aimed at short-circuiting the criminal justice system; they allowed extensive witness protection, in-camera court proceedings, and trials in absentia (Sinha 1995: 145–46, 147–49, 153, 180–84).[19]

The most notorious law is the Terrorists and Disruptive Activities (Prevention) Act of 1985, which is applied to selected areas for specific periods of time. The law requires periodic extension by the national parliament.[20] TADA, as it is better known, allows a year-long preventive detention, special in-camera courts, witness protection (even to the extent of denying the accused the right to cross-examination), the use of confessional statements as evidence as a matter of norm, presumption of guilt, establishment of guilt by association, and punitive seizure of property. A news report finds that between June 1985, when TADA was enacted for Punjab, and April 1992, some 13,225 persons had been detained. Only 78 were finally convicted, despite its easy rules of evidence.[21] Also indicative of the misuse of TADA is the fact that there were 65,000 detainees in 1993, including politicians in opposition, lawyers, and journalists (Karan 1997: 131, 133–34, app. 1, 220–22).

The record of the judiciary in legally sanctioning government authoritarianism has been mixed. Though the courts have generally allowed emergency laws to stand and special courts to be constituted for militants' trials, judges have also increased access to the public by allowing more class action suits and writ petitions. On the one hand, the courts seem to have accepted the special circumstances of insurgencies and permitted lax evidence rules, longer preventive custody, and erosion of democratic rights (see, for instance, Ramanathan 1996: 46–47). On the other, for the rest of the country, the judiciary has expanded constitutional provisions to include due process and equal treatment under law. The courts have allowed public interest litigation on behalf of "bonded labor, tribals, women, the homeless and defendants held in custody for years waiting trial." The National Human Rights Commission, set up in 1993 to "ward off" international and domestic criticism, has actively investigated complaints, intervened in court proceedings, reviewed existing human rights laws, and undertaken human rights education (Kochanek 2000: 13–14). As yet, the commission can only pursue complaints against the police and the paramilitary forces; the army is excluded from its jurisdictional purview.

An activist judiciary that seeks to investigate the army's actions might in the future cause civil-military tension. Either this conflict will be manifested as an executive-judiciary standoff, where the civilian government tries to defend its authorization of excessive force, or, more likely, the civilian government might abandon the "new militaries," letting the leaders of counterinsurgency campaigns take the fall. This could lead to widespread disenchantment in the security forces and, perhaps, encourage former security personnel to enter the electoral fray in order to defend themselves. Thus, the civil-military tension might be brought into the political arena. At the very least, it would lead to considerable agitation among security forces.

Military-Paramilitary Friction

The protocol in internal security deployment requires that state police forces must fail before the paramilitary is inducted. It is only after the paramilitary fails that the Indian Army is called in. Ideally this would mean that the various organizations do not have to work with each other or step outside their command structures. In practice, however, the large forces required for counterinsurgency campaigns necessitate the concurrent deployment of police, paramilitary, and army. The institutional arrangement that has evolved is a statewide unified command headed by an executive governor (appointed under the provisions of President's Rule). On the ground, the "disturbed area" is divided up among the operating agencies. Paramilitary forces are deployed inside cities, and the army takes charge of the small towns, rural areas, jungles, mountains, and borders where the separatists hide out.[22]

The system does not ensure proper coordination, however, especially at the company level, where most counterinsurgency operations are fought. Senior officers of the different security organizations may sit together at the state capital, but unity of command is a mirage. Despite the existence of joint interrogation centers, for instance, there is almost no interagency intelligence sharing—the crux of counterinsurgency warfare. Usually run by the state police, the joint interrogation centers are considered quite ineffective. By the time a militant is brought to the center, the arresting agency has already obtained and perhaps acted on all possible information.

In an effort to establish unity of command, control, and intelligence, the Indian Army has often taken command of other forces in the designated area. The Assam Rifles, the oldest paramilitary force, has been under the command of the military in the Northeast even though the Ministry of Home Affairs has jurisdictional control over the force (Chibber 1979: 7). Assam Rifles is an exception, however. In 1999, the army sought direct control over the BSF and CRP units fighting the insurgency in the state of Jammu and Kashmir. Although the move had New Delhi's tacit support, it was turned down by the Kashmir state government, which normally controls the paramilitary forces, exacerbating relations between the federal and state government apparatus.

By and large, army officers view the paramilitary forces as incompetent at best and counterproductive at worst. The paramilitary forces are known to panic more quickly while controlling crowds, for example, and are prone to exact severe retaliation for losses in their ranks. One retired army brigadier suggests that "for [the] smooth functioning of a paramilitary force, in conjunction with the Army, it should be officered wholly or partly by Army officers" (Kuldip Singh 1998: 64). Indeed, after the 1962 and 1965 wars, a significant number of emergency commission officers demobilized from the army were recruited back into the paramilitary forces. Since then, however, the paramilitary organizations have grown apart as older paramilitary officers who had served in the army have retired.

Senior paramilitary officers, many of whom belong to the elite Indian Police Service cadre, resent the army's charges of incompetence and present countercharges. According to a senior police officer who has been involved in counterinsurgency campaigns,

> The use of the security forces, particularly the army, in aid to civil power to deal with grave situations of internal security invariably creates serious problems of command, control, and coordination.... Army officers, particularly those at junior levels of command, often lack an understanding of the parameters of the army's role in aid to civil authority. Instead of accepting their deployment as assisting civil power in dealing with a particular emergency, they generally insist on assuming command [of the area or the situation], making the civil authorities redundant. Their advocacy of a unified command is a clever ploy to make the civil administration, particularly, the police, subordinate to the army which is not implied in the principle of aid to civil power. (Lal 1999: 20)

A retired senior police officer who has led a paramilitary organization believes the solution to the coordination and command problem is to induct a police member into the service Chiefs of Staff Committee—a demand completely unacceptable to the military (Rustamji 1992: 84). In defense of their relatively poor performance, paramilitary officers point to the army's substantially superior resources and training system against their own continuous use.[23] Moreover, paramilitary soldiers are deployed inside cities and towns, where most of the fighting occurs. If their soldiers are frazzled and sometimes commit human rights violations, they argue, it is because of having to live in the thick of rebellion with far less training than the army. K. Subrahmanyam, one of India's leading defense analysts, says: "When trouble breaks out there is a continuous buck-passing from the District Police to the Provincial Armed Constabulary to CRP to BSF and the Army" (Subrahmanyam 1990: 110).

According to Khusro Rustamji (1992: 84), "The army seeks help in conflicts, gets it, and then turns around to denigrate it, even accusing it of failure to cover up its own faults." Police officers, anticipating the army's attitude, refuse to cooperate from the beginning. In any case, police officers say, the army is deployed only in the later stages of the rebellion—by which time the paramilitary has done the dirty work of eliminating the hard-core insurgents.

The Role of Intelligence Agencies

The new role played by paramilitary forces is almost matched by the "militaristic" activities of another set of civilian institutions, the intelligence agencies. Under the direction of prime minister Indira Gandhi in the mid-1970s, India's intelligence organizations began to develop an aggressive—and, some say, politically motivated—program. The first major example of this new role could be seen in Punjab, where Mrs. Gandhi wanted to divide the local opposition Akali Dal party. She is reported to have used the Intelligence Bureau (IB), India's domestic intelligence organization, to support a radical Sikh leader, who would go on to lead the Sikh separatist movement that cost her her life. The second example, from the early 1980s, was the involvement of India's external intelligence organization, the Research and Analysis Wing (RAW), in support of separatist Tamil groups in Sri Lanka, the island nation off India's southern coast. Mrs. Gandhi saw her support for the Tamil groups both as destabilizing what she believed was an antagonistic government in Colombo and as shoring up her position in the Indian state of Tamil Nadu, which had strong ties with the Sri Lankan Tamils.

The RAW "recruited, trained, armed, and provided intelligence and logistical support to Sri Lankan Tamil militants" (Gunaratna 1993: xviii). Among them was the Tamil Tigers, or the LTTE (the Liberation Tigers of Tamil Eelam), which would become the nemesis of both the Sri Lankan Army and the Indian Peacekeeping Force (IPKF), sent in 1987 to implement a peace deal brokered by New Delhi. The RAW had helped the LTTE set up its headquarters in the city of Madurai in southern India, closely supervising its operations and training until the Tigers got out of hand. The RAW had provided money, weapons, and communication equipment to the Tamil groups. The agency set up training camps in Tamil Nadu and up along India's east coast in the states of Andhra Pradesh and Orissa. RAW agents actively trained Tamil militants and, according to some accounts, even wrote manuals and standard operating procedures. After 1987, when the IPKF began fighting the LTTE, the RAW would raise yet another force, the Tamil National Army (TNA) to combat the Tiger menace. The move failed miserably. The LTTE overran a number of TNA positions and captured RAW-supplied weapons (Mehta 1999: 45; for a Sri Lankan indictment of the RAW's role in Tamil militancy, see Gunaratna 1993).

Similarly, in Punjab, the IB had a significant role in the way Sikh militancy developed. "Evidence now emerging on the 'secret war' against terrorism points conclusively to the direct involvement of sections of the security and counterinsurgency intelligence agencies in the setting-up, control, and actions of certain militant organizations" (Gurharpal Singh 1996: 417; see also Pettigrew 1995). In the late 1970s, even before Sikh militancy had taken off, the IB had allegedly worked hand in glove with Mrs. Gandhi, her son and heir apparent, Sanjay, and Zail Singh, then a Sikh leader in the Congress and later a president of India. They wanted to use Sikh extremism to cut public support for the Akalis (Tully and Jacob 1985: 54–58, 60). Significantly, there is a strong view within the army that Sikh militancy was in part created by Mrs. Gandhi's politics (see, for instance, Kundu 1996: 55). Through the Punjab "think-tank," a group of senior advisors, Mrs. Gandhi maintained contact with militants inside the temple complex until a month before the June 1984 army action. The IB is believed to have played a critical role.

Intelligence agencies are also known to conduct their own internal security campaigns, often arming rival groups in a divide and rule formula. Today in Kashmir, the Ikhwan-e-Muslimoon is known to work with security forces against other militant groups (Bose 1999: 28). In the Northeast, the central government has supported Kuki groups against Naga insurgents. Even among the implacable Naga militants, the government is known to have used the Khaplang faction against the more hard-core Muivah organization (Hazarika 1994: 110).

The aggressive part played by civilian intelligence agencies not only points to civilian militarism, it has also contributed to the growing distrust between civilian and military institutions. Though the antipathy can be traced back to the 1962 war, when, the military charges, the IB failed to detect Chinese troop movements across the border and provide reliable estimates of Chinese military strength, much of the damage is recent (for the 1962 debacle, see Palit 1991). The 1971 war against Pakistan saw some fruitful interaction between the military and intelligence agencies, but this was short-lived. In Sri Lanka, the RAW could not provide the IPKF with significant intelligence on the LTTE despite its "long and sustained alliance" with the organization. According to an Indian Army general who served in the IPKF, "Not even once, at least in the Batticaloa sector [where he served], did any intelligence agency provide any worthwhile intelligence to the field formations over the 30 months [of deployment]. If anything, [the] RAW's presence and influence in the field was the source of friction and confusion among Tamil groups, leading to operational dissonance" (Mehta 1999: 45).

Earlier, in June 1984, when the military was ordered to attack the Golden Temple in Amritsar, the IB had been unable to provide any information on militant activity inside the temple complex. The army, for instance, did not know that the militants had armor-piercing weapons. When the army used searchlights mounted on tanks to blind the militants inside the temple, they became ready targets (Akbar 1985: 205; Tully and Jacob 1985: 166). It has been reported that militants have even managed to infiltrate the intelligence agencies and local police, to the consternation of the security forces (Tully and Jacob 1985: 80, 129–30, 146). More recently, India's intelligence agencies failed spectacularly in the summer of 1999, leading to the Kargil battle. Independent observers have reported on the military-intelligence conflicts in the counterinsurgency campaigns in the Northeast and in Kashmir. Since the intelligence agencies are staffed primarily by bureaucrats and policemen, the military's problems with them are part of the larger military-bureaucracy competition that is the subject of the next section.

THE MILITARY-BUREAUCRACY CONFLICT

Despite the recognition of the military's importance, the initial impact of independence was the political neglect of the services. This neglect reflected the political predilections of leaders such as Nehru, who wanted the armed forces to work for peace, while they busied themselves with the real work of development.[24] Mahatma Gandhi demanded that the army "plough the land, dig wells, clean latrines and do every other constructive work that they can, and thus turn the people's hatred of them into love."[25] Foreign policy was largely devoid of military content. Even the initial operations in Kashmir, Hyderabad, and Junagadh in 1947–1948 did not bring political attention to the military. (For details of these operations see Praval 1990: 21–93.) The conflict with China in 1962 further demarcated the spheres of civilian and military influence. The 1962 defeat was blamed on political interference, and when hostilities broke out against Pakistan in 1965, chief of army staff J. N. Chaudhuri asked for and was granted operational freedom (Cohen 1988: 113). Indira Gandhi accepted a nine-month wait before starting the 1971 war. Army chief Sam Manekshaw had wanted the time to build up reserves and supplies on the main battlefront in the east (Rosen 1996: 248).

Under this essentially Clausewitzian bargain, the political leadership set the goals—that is, provided the grand strategic vision—and then left the military alone to achieve the objectives. The arrangement gave military leaders their realm—of operations—and removed the politicians from the locus of blame. As a result, the armed forces could manage their internal affairs but would not have direct representation in higher defense planning organizations: the latter would ensure continued civilian control over the military. The success of the 1965 and 1971 wars against Pakistan solidified operational freedom as the optimum civil-military balance for India.

The Upshot of Operational Delegation

Partly because civilian leaders remained distrustful of the military, independence and the post-1962 operational delegation were accompanied by intrusive monitoring of the armed forces by the civilian bureaucracy (Ramdas 1999). As early as 1952, an office manual of the Ministry of Defence put forth that "three wings of the armed forces [would] report, not directly to the political authority but [to] the civilian bureaucracy" (Nalapat 1999: 10). The manual provided that service chiefs work under the supervision of the defense secretary (Ravinder Pal Singh 1999: 12). Since then, a "thick layer of civil servants [was] interposed between the Defence Minister and the three Service headquarters, preventing direct interaction between the Minister and the Services" (Sinha 1980: 10).

The civilian official in the Ministry of Defence, who routinely clears service proposals, is a joint secretary or at best an assistant secretary (Chawla and Joshi 1999: 24). Civilian bureaucrats have become the front-end of the defense establishment, negotiating with the rest of the government and the legislature, exercising control and supervisory functions, and acting as gatekeeper for service-generated proposals. All promotions above the rank of major are approved by the MoD. (Promotions in lower ranks are based on time served without any real evaluation of merit.) Appointments of brigade, division, and corps commanders are made in consultation with the civilian bureaucracy. Army commanders are picked by the Appointments Committee of the Cabinet (ACC). The service chief might provide a seniority-based slate of candidates, but his role is largely one of persuasion. "As a result," says an observer, "the respect of the men below for their Chiefs has diminished, and the command and control system within the Services has [been] weakened" (Nalapat 1999: 10).

There is no formal interaction between the military and members of parliament (except when a legislative committee asks military leaders for depositions).[26] The armed forces have negligible influence over the budget process except to make representations to the MoD. The military has little discretion over how it spends its budget. Amiya Ghosh, a former financial adviser in the MoD, finds that ultimately the budget process needs to be connected closely with political and national security decision-making processes, allocation of priorities, and procedures of procurement (Ghosh 1996: 13). But for the most part these issues are out of military hands. All acquisition committees, for instance, are headed by civilian authorities with little technical ability (Ramdas 1999).

Military officers have slipped in precedence—even following wars in which the services were

> called upon to make the supreme sacrifice in the service of the nation. Service Chiefs became junior to Judges of the Supreme Court after the 1971 war, Lieutenant Generals were made progressively junior to secretaries in the Government of India, to Members of the Railway Board, to Chief Commissioners, and to Chief Secretaries. Similarly, Major Generals became successively junior to Chief Secretaries, Director of the Intelligence Bureau, General Manager of Railways, and to the Inspector General of the Police in the States. (Sinha 1984)

Because of their pyramidal structure the armed forces have fewer opportunities of advancement. While all officers in the Indian Administrative Service (IAS)—the primary civil service—

reach the equivalent rank of major general, most army officers retire two ranks below at lieutenant colonel. The IAS cadre, which is one-tenth the size of the army's officer corps, has more than 100 appointments equivalent to the rank of chief of army staff. It also takes longer for army officers to reach the same ranks as IAS and even police officers. Further, since states have their own order of protocol for ranks of brigadier and below, anomalies exist across the country (Cohen 1988: 106).

Military pay compares poorly with the bureaucracy, let alone the private sector. In 1947, the Indian Army was one of the best paymasters in the country. It ranked favorably with the civil service, the police, and the private sector. Following independence, the new government implemented a 40 percent pay cut for the army officer corps and the civil services. Though inflation has since taken the biggest bite out of the paychecks, it is noteworthy that military pay has slipped below equivalent civil service positions. In the arena of bureaucratic politics, the civil service has won out over the military (Rosen 1996: 225). By one calculation, the total benefits of company and battalion commanders fell between 60 and 70 percent in real terms from 1947 to 1982 (Rosen 1996: 224).

Among the group where military service should be most popular—the children of officers—few consider joining up. Though the children of junior commissioned officers and noncommissioned officers are still entering officer ranks, the shortage of officers is acute. According to Jaswant Singh, the Indian Army is short 13,000 officers—about 30 percent of the officer corps (Jaswant Singh 1999: 112). The Indian Navy and the Indian Air Force have to deal with shortages in their rank-and-file as well because they require recruits with more education: while an army *jawan* can be handed a rifle and sent off to a unit with minimal training, airmen and sailors must handle sophisticated equipment.

The Military Gains

In the 1980s, a generational change brought the political and military leadership closer—and worsened military-bureaucracy relations. The first generation of postindependence service officers, almost entirely trained within the country, were free of the baggage of having served a colonial power. (For career patterns of military officers see Cohen 1988: 104.) Rajiv Gandhi's tenure as prime minister became the instrument and symbol of this change on the civilian side. The new generation of civilian leaders seemed to be more trusting of the military. Arun Singh, a close aide of Rajiv Gandhi, became minister of state for defense. Though only a junior minister, Singh had full access to the prime minister. On the military side, an equally exceptional general officer, Krishnaswami Sundarji, became the army's chief of staff. Together they initiated pathbreaking modernization efforts. Though theirs was a personal and chance partnership, the Singh-Sundarji legacy remains. It is seen within the armed services as something of a model political-military relationship.

The Indian Army was reorganized around two mechanized strike corps that could penetrate to the rear of the Pakistan Army and mountain warfare divisions that could defend a Chinese attack over the Himalayas. Combined arms doctrines were introduced, and in 1987 they were tested in India's largest military exercise, Brasstacks. The scope and location of Brasstacks almost led to a war with Pakistan (Bajpai et al. 1995: 56–60). On the India-China border in the Northeast, the Singh-Sundarji team conducted Chequerboard, an exercise intended to test

Chinese defenses, quite dangerously.[27] In the mid-1980s, at what appears to be the Indian Army's behest, the Siachen Glacier in northwestern Kashmir became the world's highest battleground (Chibber 1990: 146–52).

The growing political-military nexus also provided the impetus for the large arms imports undertaken by India in the 1980s—and has since been accused of corruption in the acquisitions.[28] The most prominent scandal erupted over the purchase of the Bofors howitzer and contributed to Rajiv Gandhi losing the 1989 general elections. Bureaucrats played a key role in investigating the case after a non-Congress government came to power. The fact that sections of the civil service routinely side with political factions encourages the services to question the legitimacy of the bureaucracy's supervision and, in turn, encourages the civil servants' distrust of the armed forces.

Not surprisingly, in the 1980s the armed forces were able to reverse some of the pay and status rollbacks. In 1987, the Fourth Pay Commission doubled salaries and provided free food distribution for officers and their families up to the rank of colonel. The Fifth Pay Commission in the mid-1990s substantially increased military pay again—though civil service salaries remain higher. The Fourth Pay Commission also elevated the rank of service chiefs above the defense secretary and precipitated a "war of precedence in the South Block" (home of the MoD). The service chiefs have been unwilling to accept direction from the civilian defense secretary, but they are hamstrung by the routine clearances they require from the MoD. A news report states that "matters have taken such a ridiculous turn that meetings between the defense secretary and the military top brass are held in the neutral venue of the MoD's conference room" (Chawla and Joshi 1999: 24). The petty squabbling creates serious consequences when critical meetings are avoided or misunderstandings escalate, leading in 1998 to the dismissal of a service chief.

The Bhagwat controversy, the latest showdown between the military and bureaucracy, which is explored in greater detail later, has resulted in the unprecedented bureaucratic acceptance of the military's imperatives. "Today, nobody would dare question a [service] chief; can any government fire two chiefs in its tenure? The *babu* [bureaucrat] in the Raksha Mantralaya [MoD] has never been more inconsequential" (Gupta 2000). Coupled with a sense of urgency brought by the Battle of Kargil, the military seems to be getting the upper hand. Indeed, as the next section shows, the increased use of the military in internal security has improved its bargaining position vis-à-vis the civilian bureaucracy.

The Impact of Internal War

The urgency of internal security has brought even greater bureaucratic attention to military matters. Military officers are resentful of losing operational freedom, especially in the context of their extended deployment in internal security duties. The post-1962 solution of operational delegation worked well in the short wars of 1965 and 1971 (and even during the 1980s peacetime arms buildup), but it has become increasingly thin in the lengthy counterinsurgency campaigns of the 1980s and 1990s. The actual use of force and the exigencies of war demanded greater congruence and continual dialogue between strategy and operations—that is, between the civilian and military realms.

The first collateral impact of the increasing domestic deployment was the Sikh mutiny following a June 1984 army attack on Amritsar's Golden Temple, the holiest Sikh shrine. More than 1,400 men mutinied at the Sikh Regimental Center in Ramgarh, killing the regimental commandant and wounding three officers. In all, 2,600 Sikh soldiers mutinied (Kundu 1996: 46–69; Cohen 1988: 132–38). The armed Sikh soldiers then headed for Punjab in army vehicles, necessitating a major operation across north-central India to apprehend them. The Golden Temple was being used by Sikh separatists as their headquarters of military operations.[29]

The mutiny showed the dangers of the Indian Army participating in internal security duties—especially without reforming its single class unit system (a continuation of the British "martial races" policy of recruitment from collaborating communities and maintaining regiments based on caste, religion, and language. The objective was greater control and unit cohesion. A recent survey found that 44 percent of army officers still believed the "martial races" policy was acceptable—and 20 percent thought it was a good idea. In a control question that betrayed a still wider latent support for the policy, almost 70 percent said the "martial races" policy had served its purpose of helping military effectiveness, presumably through small-unit cohesion based on caste homogeneity (Kundu 1991: 74 table, 75 table). That the army could follow its discriminatory separate-but-equal policy—in the face of the universalist values of civilian India—was only possible because operational delegation allowed the military to remain at a distance from the rest of society. With increased internal deployment, the separate-but-equal policy quickly became a liability.[30]

The biggest shock for the Indian Army was the loss of command, control, and intelligence during its peacekeeping campaign in Sri Lanka in 1987–1990. (For details see Sardeshpande 1992: 137–44, 153.) The Sri Lankan deployment has often been compared to the U.S. involvement in Vietnam—a tough, thankless set of battles the military won on the ground while losing the war. (For an extensive comparison, see Indian Defence Review [IDR] Team 1990: 78–87.) As discussed in the section on the role of the intelligence agencies, a long-term institutional result, periodically reinforced by other failures such as the battle for Kargil in 1999, has been the hostile relations between the armed forces and civilian intelligence agencies (which are controlled by bureaucrats). Interagency mistrust has crippled the Joint Intelligence Committee—the national node for intelligence collection and analysis—and reduced the efficacy of national security planning.

Further, counterinsurgency deployments necessarily involve paramilitary forces, state police, intelligence agencies, civilian bureaucrats, and politicians on an everyday basis. Unified commands are the norm rather than the exception. In the multi-institutional environment of counterinsurgency campaigns, the logic of operational freedom compounds military-bureaucracy tensions. As the last bulwark preventing the country's disintegration, army officers see themselves as making amends for the mistakes of the civilian authorities. The military also blames the bureaucracy for interfering—an unreasonable charge, because the civilian bureaucracy is intricately involved with governance before the military is introduced and continues to have a role in the resolution of the crisis.

Quite smug about their indispensability—"if we have to do this, just leave us alone"—military officers treat bureaucrats (and even politicians) with contempt at the local level, only to reap distrust at the national level, where decision making is controlled by the civil service. A reserve officer of the Territorial Army, for instance, writes,

> the loneliness of being away from home for long periods of duty in counter-insurgency areas, coupled with a growing sense of dismay at the callousness of the civilian administration and political

authority, produce a frustration that is virtually complete. While trying to clean up the mess created by bureaucratic and political ineptitude, the soldier is also putting his own neck on the line. The sense of honour that has been instilled in soldiering prevents him from walking away and leaving the mess as it was. (Manavendra Singh 1999b: 26)

Moreover, service officers often find themselves outmaneuvered in New Delhi politics. All this adds up to where military officers find the bureaucrats crafty, undependable, self-serving, and incompetent. In turn, civilian bureaucrats display a disregard for the military's starchiness, vainglory, and indispensability. "The Service Chiefs have always tended to behave as prima donnas, especially when dealing with the civilian bureaucracy" (Deshmukh 1999). This attitude has, arguably, contributed to the growth of civilian-controlled paramilitaries. The civilian bureaucracy claims its right of civilian control (a suspect contention because civilian control really means political rather than bureaucratic control).

CASE STUDY 1: L'AFFAIRE BHAGWAT

The most aggravated case of military-bureaucracy collision culminated in the dismissal of the chief of naval staff, Vishnu Bhagwat, on December 31, 1998. Bhagwat was the first sitting chief of staff to be fired in independent India. In the past, Nehru and Defence Minister Menon forced an army chief to resign in the 1950s, Indira Gandhi routinely picked politically pliant officers (in appointments below the chiefs as well) over the more deserving, and in 1990 Prime Minister Chandra Shekhar considered the removal of a service chief. But Bhagwat was the first to be dismissed. (See Cherian 1999; Deshmukh 1999; Cohen 1988: 129.) What led to this drastic action?

The immediate cause for the dismissal was Bhagwat's refusal to appoint Vice-Admiral Harinder Singh as the deputy chief of naval staff. Bhagwat claimed it was the chief of naval staff's prerogative to choose the deputy chief because the "morale and fighting efficiency of the navy" were his responsibility. He seemed willing only to allow the civilian authorities (especially the Appointments Committee of the Cabinet, the highest political body making personnel decisions) the right to confirm or reject a candidate nominated by the navy chief rather than propose names of officers for the position. As it turned out, the prime minister and the defense minister agreed with the defense secretary, the seniormost civilian bureaucrat in the MoD, that Bhagwat had defied "the established system of cabinet control over the defense forces."

In an unprecedented press conference held at the Press Club of India in New Delhi on February 21, Bhagwat responded. Calling his dismissal "a politico-military coup,"[31] he accused Defence Minister George Fernandes (the final object of his ire) of corruption, treason, favoritism, and illegal behavior. Bhagwat charged that Fernandes had removed him at the behest of arms dealers who wanted the navy's indigenization program to fail and claimed that Fernandes had knowingly undercut the efforts to check shipments of illegal arms from reinforcing the insurgents in northeastern India—a highly contentious interservice operation, codenamed Leech.[32] Though details of this operation are scanty, obviously there were problems with the assignment of duties, coordination, and the apportionment of blame and credit. Bhagwat even accused the chief of the army staff, Ved Prakash Malik,[33] as well as Harinder Singh, Fernandes, and Ajit Kumar, then defense secretary, of being communally motivated. Harinder Singh had attacked Bhagwat personally—calling his wife, Niloufer Bhagwat, a "half-Muslim, card-carrying member of the Communist Party"—in a letter to the MoD seeking redress for Bhagwat's actions against him.

Civilian authorities—political and bureaucratic—retaliated by charging Bhagwat with compromising national security interests. Apparently Bhagwat had disclosed details of Operation Leech. Moreover, Bhagwat had reportedly gone beyond his brief in talking publicly about the Sagarika antiship missile currently under development and by communicating directly with the Pakistan High Commission about a violation of Indian airspace.

The basic issue in the Bhagwat controversy is control—though charges of corruption, favoritism, political maneuvering, and even treason traded openly in January–April 1999 indicate other sources of military-bureaucratic tensions as well. As noted earlier, senior military appointments (as well as in the civil bureaucracy and public-sector industry) are made by the ACC. The cabinet does not have the time, however, to review the hundreds of candidates in the running. Usually the cabinet depends on recommendations from senior civil servants who do the initial legwork. At that stage, Bhagwat is said to have fought the bureaucracy six months over Harinder Singh's inclusion in the list of candidates for deputy chief (Chawla and Joshi 1999: 19–24). Because of the institutional arrangement, senior military officers routinely lobby ministers and bureaucrats. Not only does this system lead to informal rent-seeking networks (where, it has been alleged, appointments are sold for future advocacy for a weapons system that a minister might want to acquire), but, by Bhagwat's reasoning, it subverts the chain of command—something he himself precipitated on a grander scale.[34] Upon receiving his dismissal notice, Bhagwat went to the president's official residence, the Rashtrapati Bhavan, to appeal to the supreme commander of the armed forces, the president (Chawla and Joshi 1999: 19–24). Even though the president refused to intercede on his behalf, Bhagwat had potentially involved a constitutional figurehead and threatened the civilian political domination of the military.

Most of the military-bureaucracy tension is couched in the rhetoric of civil control. B. G. Deshmukh, a cabinet secretary in the 1980s, strongly criticized Bhagwat for contemplating defiance:

> It must be categorically and unambiguously stated that the armed forces of India are under full and effective control of the elected Union government. It means that they shall carry out all the legal and constitutional orders passed by such a government. There are definite procedures and conventions laid down or implicitly accepted when the Service Chiefs want to represent against such orders and decisions. . . . It is not expected of them to make or to start a public controversy on any issue. (Deshmukh 1999)

Admiral Ramdas, a Bhagwat supporter, argues for balance:

> Every one of us in the Services understands and respects "civil control" over the military. [But] implicit in this is the principle that the civil authority [that is, political power vested in the people's representatives and the cabinet] treats the armed forces with respect. The customary compliments paid to the Services during the annual defence debate appear to be just lip-service when seen against the backdrop of recent events—in the context of the unprecedented insult to the office of the Chief of Naval Staff. (Ramdas 1999)

For observers of the Indian armed forces, the Bhagwat incident not only exemplified the military-bureaucracy friction, it breached the military's institutional insularity as well.[35] As issues of bureaucratic domination and corruption in the defense establishment came out in the open, public scrutiny of the civil-military relationship has increased.[36] The military has gained ground in its competition with the bureaucracy. "The Defence Ministry bureaucracy has been rolled over; at least that much Admiral Bhagwat has achieved through his kamikaze act" (Gupta 2000). On January 6, 1999, Defence Minister Fernandes ordered the integration of the service headquarters with the MoD—a long-standing demand of the armed forces. Along with the May 1998 nuclear tests, then, the Bhagwat controversy has led to reorganization of higher defense planning—though, critics say, the success of these changes remain uncertain.

CASE STUDY 2: INDIA'S NUCLEAR WEAPONIZATION

India's rejuvenated nuclear program not only illustrates the militarism of Indian society: it also places responsibility for the militarization in civilian hands. The tests, originally considered by the thirteen-day Bharatiya Janata Party (BJP) government in 1996, were finally implemented in May 1998 when the BJP returned to power. Apart from a conservative political party, the tests were advocated by defense and atomic scientists led by A. P. J. Abdul Kalam, scientific adviser to the defense minister, and R. Chidambaram, head of India's nuclear bureaucracy.[37] Though the Indian military supported the tests—in principle and logistics—the services do not appear to be institutionally occupied with weaponization. (See, for instance, the comments of army chief Ved Prakash Malik in Chengappa 1999: 41–43.) The navy has no delivery system and is unlikely to possess one in the near future. The army has a ballistic missile—but its 150-kilometer range makes it useless as a strategic weapon. Moreover, frontline army troops do not carry elementary nuclear equipment such as gas masks, precluding theater use of nuclear weapons. The air force, which was reportedly handed possession of nuclear devices in the early 1990s, has the only viable delivery option. But a couple of squadrons of fighter-bombers are hardly credible against an enemy with long-range missiles, such as China.[38] Against Pakistan, India's nuclear deterrent is more credible, but given India's conventional superiority it is of less use as well (for a contrary view of what is possible, see Manavendra Singh 1999a: 59–63).

Though there are at least three different schools of thought that influence India's nuclear weapons program (for an excellent review of the various positions and counterpositions, see Bajpai, n.d.), the real impetus is technology and those who procure or produce it.[39] The Agni Intermediate Range Ballistic Missile (IRBM) will only be useful if its boosted version (Agni II) is successfully tested, produced, and inducted into the military (Chari 1999). The feasibility of a nuclear button at 7 Race Course Road (the prime minister's official residence) or the Prime Minister's Office in the South Block—and a communication node at a fallout-safe distance from New Delhi—depends on India upgrading electronic locking and coding technology and communication infrastructure. The government is also trying to buy a Russian S-300 air defense system to protect the capital from enemy attack.[40]

As a group, defense scientists appear to be more knowledgeable than service chiefs about India's nuclear doctrine.[41] V. S. Arunachalam, a former scientific adviser to the defense minister, is reported to have said a few years before the nuclear tests: "If New Delhi goes up in a mushroom cloud, a certain theater commander will go to a safe, open his book, and begin reading at page one, paragraph one, and will act step by step on the basis of what he reads" (Rosen 1996: 252). No service chief has ever been so definitive. An emergency nuclear group designed to be the conduit for authorizing use of nuclear weapons reportedly comprises representatives of the Defence Research and Development Organization and the Department of Atomic Energy as well as members of the armed forces. In the future, possession of the weapons might be in the hands of designated missile regiments and air force squadrons, but civilian scientists should be present on-site with the weapons.[42]

After the May 1998 tests, the government revived the NSC; in early 1999, it ordered the integration of the service headquarters with the MoD. The NSC replaces the CCPA as the primary defense and foreign policymaking body. Not unlike the CCPA, the NSC constitutes a core ministerial group—with the ministers of defense, home affairs, external affairs, finance, and the deputy chairman of the Planning Commission—plus a national security adviser located in the Prime Minister's Office.[43] The ministerial NSC is supported by a Strategic Policy Group comprising the three service chiefs; key bureaucrats in charge of defense, defense production, foreign affairs, home affairs, finance, atomic energy, and space; the governor of the Reserve Bank of India; the directors of domestic and foreign intelligence; the chairman of the Joint Intelligence Committee; and the cabinet secretary.[44]

The likely failure of the institutional changes in higher defense planning should lead the military to complain about bureaucratic domination yet again—though the sensitivity of the nuclear weapons issue will probably push the actual expression of grievances to other matters. The CCPA system—which the NSC mimics—did not work well. Overly powerful prime ministers used the body as a kitchen cabinet. Without direction from the CCPA, the lower echelons of the three-tier system were in entropy. An earlier attempt to constitute an NSC in 1990 is believed to have failed because the entrenched bureaucracy did not want to share power. The current instability in the government, with parties coming in and out of power, makes the bureaucracy even more powerful now. For the same reasons, senior military officers say, recommendations by high-level committees headed by former defense ministers Arun Singh and K. C. Pant remain lost in the labyrinth. Others have expressed doubts that the defense minister's proposal of bringing six general officers into the MoD will succeed in its purpose of integrating the ministry and the service headquarters (Chari 1999: 21).

A long-standing demand from the army to create a position of chief of defense staff has proven prescient in the recent call for an Indian nuclear triad complete with sea-, air-, and land-based delivery systems.[45] The lack of a defense chief, who could strike a sensible balance in the triad, might revive old issues of interservice rivalry. Since independence, civilian leaders have deliberately equalized the three services, taking no chances with intervention (Cohen 1988: 118–21). Obviously the two smaller services, the navy and the air force, have aided the civilian cause—a reduction in the army's influence has implied an increase in their own.[46] In addition to abolishing the post of commander in chief, held by the army chief, the chiefs of staff of the three services were made equal in rank (Kukreja 1991: 209–10). Before independence, the army chief served as commander in chief of all armed forces in India. In the ten-year period 1970–1980, the Indian Army's share of the defense budget fell from 74 percent to 66 percent (Smith 1994: 115).

Nuclear weaponization has brought the first opportunity for the navy and the air force to replace the army as the premier service. Though the navy does not have a delivery system, the air force does—and, like other air forces, wants to become the country's strategic arm. Jasjit Singh, a former air force officer (and later the director of the government's Institute of Defence

Studies and Analyses in New Delhi), makes a forceful case for an Indian strategic air command comprising an integrated strike capability of intermediate-range ballistic missiles, long-range bombers, strategic reconnaissance including satellites, and electronic warfare aircraft. Jasjit Singh has observed: "Any longer range system [than the 120-km to 150-km Prithvi] with the Army would be suboptimal....If and when Agni [the IRBM] is developed, it should also be integrated in with the Strategic Air Command (SAC)" (1990: 38). The army has already claimed the Agni IRBM by forming a missile regiment—currently equipped with the Prithvi—and providing personnel for conducting the Agni test flights.

Defense scientists are likely to resolve this interservice competition by providing technology. If the Agni II does not become available soon, or if it is handed to the air force, the army might lose its status as the preeminent service. The many ways in which civilian groups control India's nuclear policy—as other civilian groups control internal security policy—supports the chapter's general hypothesis of continued civil control over the military. It may be argued that all countries follow this model of nuclear evolution where control in the primary stages of the program is in the hands of scientists. This claim might be exaggerated somewhat. In the United States, for instance, the services acquired actual possession of the weapons once they became available. At that point, it becomes useful to think about civilian control over the military (for details of the U.S. case, see Feaver 1992). From all indications, the services and the scientists share actual possession of weapons in India. The defense scientists also have privileged access to the controlling political authority and institutions, raising questions about the quality of civilian control. Democratic civilian control would require that elected officials subject to electoral pressures best represent the interests of the public. As I have said before, when civilian groups become too powerful, they might as well be the de facto military. Moreover, as holders and arbiters of national security outcomes, defense scientists are civilians, but they are unelected. By acting as the de facto military they raise concerns about true civilian control over the military.

IMPLICATIONS

Two significant aspects of Indian national security policy—internal security and nuclear weapons (both nonconventional)—are seemingly in the hands of unelected civilian groups. Internal security policy is the bailiwick of bureaucrats in the Ministry of Home Affairs. The impetus for nuclear policy is with scientists in the Defence Research and Development Organization (under the MoD) and the Department of Atomic Energy (controlled by the Cabinet Secretariat and eventually the Prime Minister's Office). Elected representatives sit at the head of these organizations and make the big decisions, but they are circumscribed by the routine policymaking, the everyday monitoring, and the creation of the menus by bureaucrats and scientists. By and large, these unelected civilian groups seem to have more real power than they should (under ideal civilian control) and the elected political leadership has less than it should. A news report, for instance, said that A. P. J. Abdul Kalam, the defense minister's scientific adviser, was assessing the services' claim for a budget increase of $2.8 billion in 1999.[47] This threatens to violate democratic civilian control—that the public's wishes are carried into government through the electoral process by political leaders susceptible to defeat in the next election.

The danger is exacerbated by the subversion of the control function as the makers of policy become its executors and vice versa. Growing paramilitaries, overactive intelligence agencies, police officers as special secretaries in the Ministry of Home Affairs, defense scientists on site with the nuclear forces—all are blurring civil-military lines. More equivocal, but no less valid, is the impact of a military mindset among the bureaucrats and scientists. Civilian militarization, therefore, is eroding the meaning of civilian control. Optimistic descriptions of Indian civil-military relations analyze the seemingly intact institutional arrangement, not the underlying dynamics of the actors.

As the social and state militarization evident in Kashmir and the Northeast bleeds into the mainland through caste wars and Hindu-Muslim conflicts, its impact will become openly visible. Beyond a certain threshold—and a qualitative estimation of this level can be based on the experiences of the insurgency-hit states—we can expect a loss of public support for violence irrespective of political preferences. Until India's heartland is subject to the perils of militarization, however, support will no doubt solidify behind the use of violence and suspension of democratic rights, especially in the peripheral regions. Rebellions as in Kashmir have become synonymous with external aggression. The sense of domestic and international drift, remilitarization of society, social churning, rising crime and violence—all have increased public support for militaristic measures. The BJP, a conservative political party representing middle-class fears rather than long-term interests, has been doing well in the polls. The party has given expression to current public support for militarization—most clearly by precipitating India's nuclearization.

The use of force, internal and external, has always led to intense conflict between fighters and those who control them: both Churchill and Hitler fought their generals, as did Lincoln and Ben Gurion. The national security environment is thus a contributor to and a consequence of civil-military relations. In India, the defeat of 1962 brought operational freedom and bureaucratic domination for the military. The internal security threats of the past two decades stretched the security forces domestically, precipitating tensions between the military and the paramilitary and between the military and the civilian bureaucracy. As the level of violence increases, we can expect civil-military relations to become more contentious over control, resources, and the apportionment of credit and blame.

Since the 1980s, politicians have been weighing in gradually on behalf of the military. Jaswant Singh, the BJP's point-person for national security and foreign affairs, has written that the armed forces are seriously unprepared.[48] According to Singh, the inability of the armed forces to lobby the public and parliament has cost them budget allocations and eventually reduced their effectiveness. When they are not capricious, bureaucrats in the civilian MoD appear ill prepared for increasingly technical military planning. The arrangement itself—with the military tasked with national security but having little power in the policymaking process—creates an accountability hole that can be blamed for the lack of military preparedness.

The growing political/military nexus should bring small victories for the services: the paramilitary forces might be put under army command more often, and nuclearization might compel the politicians to allow greater service participation in defense planning. But the bureaucracy is not going to become impotent in the future, and the politicians are unlikely to give the house away. Instead, as the Bhagwat incident showed, military-bureaucracy wrangling might be the most visible aspect of civil-military relations in India. And despite the politicians being generally sympathetic to the military's antibureaucracy arguments, they are unlikely to allow the civil-military balance to tilt the other way significantly.

Thus, the question of civilian control of the military stands resolved institutionally, but not in spirit. That is, the military continues to be dominated by civilian institutions, but the purpose of such control stands defeated. The narrower question of political domination of the armed forces is resolved in spirit—there is no serious challenge—but not in practice. Bureaucrats and scientists are more powerful than they should be in a democratic system. The autonomy enjoyed by the services is not going to increase dramatically. Indeed, the future is likely to be more contentious, which in itself is not all bad. Contestation, even in the management of national security, is an essential part of democratic practice. But since this contestation is limited to the national level and the urgency of war compels a degree of consensus on militarization at the local level, there will be further erosion of democratic rights in insurgency-hit areas.

PART III

Consolidating Democratic Civilian Control

CHAPTER 4

South Korea: Consolidating Democratic Civilian Control

Jinsok Jun

THE MILITARY USED TO BE A DOMINANT POLITICAL ACTOR in South Korea. Indeed, the military has left profound impacts on contemporary Korean politics not only through two major cycles of military intervention in civil politics, in 1961 and 1980 respectively, but also by interacting with civil society in diverse forms. Despite its paramount importance, very little scholarly attention has been paid to the dynamics of civil-military relations in South Korea. This chapter is designed to fill the lacunae by exploring critical elements of civil-military relations in South Korea: changes and continuities in the military's role in political domination, the making of security policy, the command and control of security agencies, and the military's socio-economic role.

The chapter begins by tracing the genesis of the Korean military from the angle of state formation, history, and culture and then examining the two cases of military intervention in South Korea's civil politics. As we shall see, the diverse origins of the military and a proliferation of intramilitary factionalism, coupled with political misuse of the military, were responsible for the military's intervention in civil politics. The second section looks into the evolving patterns in civil-military relations since 1948. The South Korean military has intervened twice in civil politics. Unlike its counterparts in Southeast Asia and Latin America, however, its intervention was not institutionalized, and military-turned-civilians have controlled politics through a quasi-military format. Moreover, democratic transition and consolidation terminated the quasi-military rule and eventually led to civilian control of the military. Despite the progress made in democratic civilian control of the military, the latter retains strong influence in the making of security policy. But there has been a change in the command and control of security agencies that used to serve as instruments of military intervention in civil politics, as well as military surveillance and control of civil and political society, under the previous military regimes. Democratic changes have placed security agencies under civilian control and have curbed their maneuvers in civil politics. Finally, the military in South Korea has played an important role in the process of modernization through manpower training, dissemination of modern methods of organization and management, and active participation in the construction of physical infrastructure. But as South Korea has graduated from the stage of modernization, the military's socioeconomic role has become significantly curtailed. The third section explores change and continuity in the evolution of civil-military relations in South Korea. Though economic development and democratization have broadened civilian control of the military security agencies, the persistence of military threats from North Korea and institutional inertia have justified the military's continuing dominance in the management of national security affairs.

As we shall see, civil-military relations in South Korea illustrate both changes and continuities. Although the military role in political domination and the control of security agencies have undergone profound changes in favor of the civilian sector, the military's primacy in national security policymaking and management continues regardless of changes in patterns of political governance. Notwithstanding this mixed picture, democratization and economic development have reinforced civilian control of the military. And despite continuing military threats from North Korea, the trend is likely to continue.

GENESIS OF THE SOUTH KOREAN MILITARY AND PATTERNS OF POLITICAL INTERVENTION

As its coercive apparatus, the military is an inseparable part of the state's machinery. Thus, it is impossible to understand the military without elucidating the state's formation and its evolutionary dynamics. Contemporary state formation has long been the subject of extensive debate (Choi 1993; Sohn 1998; Cho 1998). Despite diverse interpretations, a new consensus has emerged in recent years, defining the South Korean state as "overdeveloped" (Alavi 1972). The South Korean state was overdeveloped vis-à-vis civil society not only because of its centralized decision-making structure, hegemonic ideology, corporative organization, and control of civil society but also because of its monopolization of physical power (Choi 1993). In South Korea the overdeveloped state was manifested in terms of a formidable coercive apparatus in which the military and the police constituted the two primary forces. No other social forces could challenge them. They became the two principal agents of state domination over civil society.

Understanding Contemporary State Formation in South Korea

The origin of the overdeveloped state can be traced back to the Japanese colonial period, during which effective bureaucracy and oppressive police were developed for colonial domination. This state structure was left intact even after the Japanese colonial period ended in 1945. The U.S. military government and later the Syngman Rhee regime strengthened the colonial legacy by building an overdeveloped state through the absorption of Japanese colonial bureaucrats, the police, and the military. Several factors explain this continuation of the colonial legacy: pervasive social and political chaos followed by national liberation; time and resource constraints in building new institutions; and scarcity of administrative human resources amid acute social and political crises resulting from the ideological confrontation of left and right.

The colonial legacy was not the sole determinant of the overdeveloped state, however. Two additional factors must be taken into account: long-term historical legacies and the Korean War. The institutional inheritance from Japanese colonialism was critical, but old authoritarian ideologies and values of the Chosun dynasty were deeply merged in the process of institutionalization and profoundly affected the already centralized state power structure. The Chosun dynasty was a kingdom with a centralized power hierarchy that maintained a political system based on Confucian philosophy. Confucianism as political philosophy emphasizes the idea of discriminative social orders and classification. Thus, centralized political power and social hierarchy were regarded as universal laws of nature, which in turn justified the dominance of the ruling elite over the rest of society (Man-kyu Kim 1982). In view of this, the Confucian state is inherently authoritarian. It is ironic to note that although the Japanese colonial system completely destroyed the state structure of the Chosun dynasty, its authoritarian features lived on precisely because the ideological tendencies of the Japanese empire were compatible with those of Chosun.

The Korean War, too, contributed to the birth of the overdeveloped state in South Korea. As in other war-stricken nations, the Syngman Rhee regime was forced to strengthen its state apparatus not only to fight North Korean invaders, but also to deal with social and political instability during and after the Korean War. As a result, three major components of the state—namely bureaucrats, the police, and the military—showed an exponential growth, whereas civil society itself was in disarray. Thus, the state's prevalence over civil society and its subsequent growth and expansion can be seen as an unavoidable outcome of the Korean War.

Genesis of the Korean Military

The central role of the military in Korean politics and society emanated from the very nature of the overdeveloped state. Since the inception of the Republic of Korea, the military was the best-organized social force. Neither bureaucrats nor the police could match the military in terms of size, group cohesion, institutionalization, and mobilization. It was also the most modernized state institution with a conservative ideology. Several factors influenced the rise of the contemporary military institution in South Korea.

First and most immediate was the American influence. Following the end of the Pacific War, American occupation forces liberated the southern part of Korea, and the American Military Government (USAMGIK) ruled it from 1945 to 1948 under a trusteeship arrangement. The modern form of the South Korean military was created with the guidance of the American Military Government. (For USAMGIK and the 1945–1948 period, see Song 1979, Dong-a Ilbosa 1988, and Meade 1951.) The American Military Government wanted to establish a traditional Western-style military just like the one in the United States, which is nonpolitical and professional. Creating and maintaining a professional and nonpolitical military was not easy, however. Despite an outright transplantation of the American military institution in South Korea, local dynamics prevented the South Korean military from keeping its professionalized and nonpolitical stance.

Moreover, the Japanese imperial tradition had left a deep impression on the South Korean military. When Korea was liberated from Japanese colonial rule in 1945, several groups joined together to form the contemporary South Korean military: returned independence fighters, Koreans who had served in the Japanese imperial army as officers and student recruits, and those who now joined the military without any previous experience (Han 1984: 30–47). Of this assemblage, those with a Japanese military background were the best organized and constituted the lion's share of the newborn South Korean military. They became the dominant faction in the military and were responsible for shaping its nature, ideology, and operational logic. Thus, though the military's institutional structure was shaped by American influence, its ethos was a product of the Japanese imperial military tradition with its nondemocratic, authoritarian, and militaristic, not to mention brutal, values (Dong-hee Lee 1993: 226).

If American and Japanese influence shaped the form and contents of the South Korean military, two major traits of traditional political culture were also responsible for its internal dynamics as well as its interactions with civil society. One of these influences is the enduring tradition of the Chosun dynasty, which had downgraded the military in Korean society. Although military officers (*mugwan* or *muban*) were often included in the ruling coalition, they were very much subject to the command and control of the scholar-gentry class (*mungwan* or *munban*). Thus, civilian control of the military was widely institutionalized during the Chosun dynasty. In addition, high military positions—like other high government positions—were normally set aside for the scholar-gentry class. Apart from enjoying a few privileged supreme commanding positions, the scholar-gentry class did not have to serve in the military. The peasant class, however, was mobilized to serve whenever needed if they were between the ages of 16 and 60 (Dong-hee Lee 1993: 184–86). Although it is difficult to find any links between the military system based on social classification and that of the modern Korean military, the primacy of the scholar-gentry class over military officers had long shaped popular perceptions of the military. Such perceptions later became the primary source of tension between civil politics and the military.

The other influence is factionalism—still the dominant template of political culture in South Korea. This factionalism originated in the recruitment system under the Chosun dynasty, during which only *yangban* were entitled to obtain high-level government positions—through a state examination called the *gwageo*.[1] Intra-elite competition within the Chosun dynasty was quite fierce, partly because of the competitive recruitment system and partly because of the limited number of positions (Ki-baek Lee 1982: 210). The political power struggle inside the ruling bloc went on for centuries, resulting in various factions based on different regions. The ruling class normally had a regional power base built upon two major elements: one was an economic establishment through landownership; the other was a regional education system called the *seowon*. The *seowon* became the place for recruiting the ruling elite through education, and specifically for the recruitment of regional faction members (Ki-baek Lee 1982: 249–50). Factional politics, grounded in regional origins and school ties, was the most powerful game in the Chosun dynasty. Such legacies were not limited to civil society, but extended as well to military organization. Despite the facade of unity, the South Korean military was deeply divided by regional and school ties that often served as an impetus for military intervention in civil politics.

If the genesis of the South Korean military can be attributed to the dynamic interplay of American institutional structure, Japanese colonial ethos, and Confucian tradition, its expansion was a product of the Korean War. The war's outbreak and the subsequent protracted military confrontation with North Korea resulted in an asymmetric growth of the military vis-à-vis other elements of the South Korean state and society. By the mid-1950s, the South Korean military had evolved into an institution with more than 650,000 personnel consuming more than one-third of the government's expenditures. Such physical expansion had elevated the military to the apex of the overdeveloped state in the post–Korean War period.

Patterns of Military Intervention

If the South Korean military had been apolitical and professional as its American creators envisioned, it would have not become the subject of extensive debate. The problem was its notorious track record of intervention in civil politics. There were two cycles of military intervention in South Korea's politics: the May 16 military coup in 1961, staged by Maj. Gen. Park Chung-hee, and the military seizure of political power in 1980 by Maj. Gen. Chun Doo-hwan. Military intervention in South Korea's civil politics had been shaped by the interaction of four forces: pull, push, ecological, and conversion factors (Jun 1996). Although the military's factionalism and institutional interests constituted the vital push factors, the pull factors were an unstable political society and inducement effects. The push and pull factors were by and large the necessary conditions for military intervention. The sufficient conditions came from ecological factors such as socioeconomic instability and conversion factors such as civilian control over the military through effective use of the security and intelligence agencies.

The first military intervention, by Park in 1961, can be seen as a dialectical outcome of the four variables. Fierce infighting between old generals and Young Turks over issues of promotion and corruption as well as new threats to the military's institutional interests in the form of sharp reductions of the defense budget under the Chang Myon regime pushed the Young Turks led by General Park to venture into civil politics. Political society was fragmented and chaotic due to the immature parliamentary system and factional struggles within the ruling coalition— forces that in turn pulled the military into civil politics. At the same time, problems of pervasive political instability, economic crisis, and social turmoil followed by the April student revolution of 1960 prompted General Park and his clique to engage in a long cycle of military intervention in civil politics. (See Auh 1971, Chai 1972, Han 1974, and Se-jin Kim 1971 for discussions of the 1961 coup.) If there had been effective surveillance over the military through a security and intelligence apparatus, Park's coup could have been prevented. But this apparatus was very much paralyzed, and some of its leaders gave tacit approval of the coup by ignoring intelligence reports on Park's plotting.

The second cycle of military intervention in civil politics, by Chun in 1980, can be understood from a similar perspective. Certainly military factionalism constituted the most critical push factor. The assassination of President Park on October 26, 1979, led to a power vacuum in the military, which in turn triggered a power struggle between old generals (graduates of the old Korean Military Academy) and new generals (graduates of the new four-year Korean Military Academy). Chun staged a mutiny on December 12, 1979, and took control of the military. But Chun's intervention in civil politics was pulled by the deformity of political society in 1980. Despite political *albertura* in 1980, political society was severely divided—and subsequent political instability offered an ideal rationale for military intervention in the name of national security. As in the 1961 military coup, an economic downturn, social unrest, and extensive labor disputes enabled Chun and his followers to stage a mutiny first and then to take over the civilian government. More critical was General Chun's strategic positioning in the security and intelligence apparatus. As commander of the National Defense Security Command at the time of mutiny and military intervention, Chun virtually monopolized the flow of information and kept Choi Kyu-ha's caretaker government from monitoring the military's movements. (See Chung 1987, Han 1993, Roh 1995, and Song 1994 for the 1979–1980 coup.)

There was ample chance for the military to reintervene in civil politics prior to the democratic transition in June 1987. As the end of Chun Doo-hwan's presidential tenure approached, there were intense debates on a constitutional amendment for direct presidential elections. In the process, Chun announced his decision to sustain the constitutional order of April 1987 allowing indirect election of the president through an electoral college. Chun's decision infuriated opposition political parties and indeed civil society at large. Mass street demonstrations under the initiative of students followed. The middle class, which had traditionally shown a conservative stance and political apathy, now joined the rank and file in public protests. Initially, Chun deliberated over declaring martial law and reinforcing military intervention in the form of a progovernment coup. But the intensity of public protest, American opposition, and polarization of the ruling coalition into soft-liners and hard-liners averted such a move and led to the June 29 declaration on democratization by Roh Tae-woo, the ruling party's presidential candidate and one of the generals who had staged the mutiny of 1979 (Hak-joon Kim 1991; Man-woo Lee 1990). The declaration and its implementation led to democratic opening and transition in South Korea, resulting in direct presidential elections in December 1987. Roh won the election primarily because of a three-way split in the opposition bloc. Although the Roh government was a legitimate democratic government, it was viewed by the majority of South Koreans as a continuation of the past military legacy.

Since then South Korea has been under the rule of two civilian presidents: Kim Young-sam and Kim Dae-jung. Kim Young-sam was elected president in 1992 and labeled his government as a "*mun-min*" government (roughly "civilian" government). The emphasis on "civilian" was meant to differentiate his regime from the past military authoritarian regimes, and Kim is generally regarded as the first elected civilian president since 1961. The election of current president Kim Dae-jung is more meaningful, however, not only because he is the first minority-party presidential candidate to get elected through democratic and peaceful elections, but also because he was elected despite an alleged veto by the military.

In sum, then, the genesis and expansion of the South Korean military cannot be separated from the historical context of state formation. Japanese colonial legacy, American military occupation, and the Korean War transformed the military into the most powerful element of the contemporary South Korean state. And despite the American intent to create a professional military, it has made two significant interventions in civil politics that shaped and reshaped the horizons of civil-military relations in South Korea. Historical tensions based on civil discrimination against the military—as well as rivalry among military factions and sociopolitical instability—have all contributed to creating a politicized military in South Korea. Thus, it can be argued that the politicized military was embedded in the very creation of the South Korean state.

EVOLVING PATTERNS OF CIVIL-MILITARY RELATIONS

From its inception to the present, the South Korean constitution has consistently stipulated civilian control over the military. No uniformed officer may be elected or appointed president of the republic, and the president is the supreme commander of the armed forces. From a constitutional point of view, therefore, the military had no place in the civilian political arena. The military did intervene in civil politics, however, altering the contour of civil-military relations. In fact, the military in South Korea has long been the dominant political actor even though it has not always prevailed over civil politics. The course of civil-military relations depends on the overall power configuration of South Korean politics as well as social and economic changes. This section elucidates the patterns of civil-military relations by looking into four empirical domains: political domination, security policymaking, command and control of security agencies, and the socioeconomic role of the military.

Changing Patterns of Political Domination

Who has dominated the political arena in South Korea? Under the First Republic (1948–1960), civilian leadership reigned and ruled while the military remained a submissive agent of civilian government. President Syngman Rhee maintained his dictatorial rule by relying heavily on the Liberal Party and coercive state machinery. The police and the military constituted the core of his rule. He was able to absorb the old Japanese police structure and personnel after he became president, and the police had nationwide branches and a highly centralized command structure (Han 1983: 11–16). Rhee used the police extensively in monitoring and controlling civil society. Indeed, the police were directly tied to the ruling Liberal Party and therefore became that party's instrument of political domination.

Along with the police, the Rhee regime utilized the military. Following the Korean War, as we have seen, the South Korean military expanded rapidly and came to outnumber the police (Se-jin Kim 1971: 39–40). But it was not easy for Rhee to control and manipulate the military for his political purpose. Both in peacetime and wartime, the South Korean military was technically under the operational command of the U.S. commander in South Korea, who also held the position of UN commander in chief (Ministry of Defense 1956: 422–23; Han 1983: 50).[2] Although the American command of the South Korean military ensured civilian control of the military, delimiting its scope of political maneuver, Rhee took advantage of factional struggles within the military, especially among high-ranking officers, to consolidate his power. He created competition for loyalty among contending military factions and pursued a divide-and-rule policy in the military. Since Rhee was a charismatic figure and founder of the nation, it was easy for him to trigger such competition in his favor (Se-jin Kim 1971: 57–58).[3] Military intervention in civilian politics took place during the Rhee era, but only "by invitation." President Rhee himself maneuvered the military into taking his side by engaging in civil politics (Se-jin Kim 1971: 108–9).[4]

Although the South Korean military was under the American forces, Rhee was able to exploit the military for his political purposes. As we shall see, he utilized the military police and the Special Task Command (Teukmoodae), a military counterespionage unit, in monitoring and controlling opposition political leaders. The most notable example was the mobilization of the military police to prevent the opposing Democratic Party from blocking a constitutional amendment that would extend the presidential term in 1951. On other occasions, too, Rhee relied on the military to oppress his political opposition. Thus, there was civilian control over the military during the Rhee period, but that civilian leader himself violated the principles of objective civilian control. The Rhee regime exemplified a civilian-led authoritarian rule in which he controlled the military through his own charisma as well as his exploitation of factional struggle within the military.

Civilian domination of politics and the military continued through the Second Republic after the Rhee regime was overthrown by the student revolution of April 19, 1960. During the transition period, martial law was declared and the military had a decisive moment of political domination. But even though there was a growing dissatisfaction with civilian politics, the military restrained itself. The Second Republic, under Chang Myon, which lasted less than a year, appointed a civilian defense minister and attempted to reduce the size of the military and the defense budget. This period of civilian control came to an abrupt end in 1961, however, with Park Chung-hee's May 16 military coup. After overthrowing the Second Republic, Park declared martial law, dissolved the National Assembly and political parties, and banned political activities. The Supreme Revolutionary Council for National Reconstruction—all of its members were active military officers—took over executive, legislative, and judiciary functions and ruled South Korea by decree. The military government lasted for two years until it transferred political power to the civilian sector in 1963 under immense pressure from the United States and the South Korean public. During this period, however, there was absolute domination of civilian politics by the military.

But the transfer of political power to civilian government did not signal the end of military intervention. Park and his associates retired from the military, organized the Democratic Republican Party (DRP), and ran a presidential campaign. Park narrowly won the election. During the Park regime (1963–1979), the military as an institution stayed out of civilian government and politics. Officers who got involved in the civilian sector were forced to retire from active service. Nevertheless, recruitment of retired military officers into civil politics and administration became very active during this period. During the First Republic, for example, the National Assembly had no representation at all from retired military officers. During the Second Republic, the proportion of military-turned-assemblymen was less than 4 percent. In Park's reign, the portion rose to 16 percent. The ratio of retired military officers in the cabinet also increased: from 7 percent in the First Republic and 3 percent in the Second Republic to 28 percent during the Park period (Yong-ho Kim 1990: 288–89). Thus, the Park regime can be characterized as a quasi-military rule in which retired military officers penetrated and controlled civilian politics and government.

Interactions between civil politics and the military during this period were mixed, however. Park was sensitive to political moves by the military and was successful in depoliticizing the military through several means. First, he patronized the formation of the Hana faction and positioned its members in strategic posts within the military. Second, he mobilized security and intelligence agencies in detecting links between retired and active officers and preventing political moves by military officers. Finally, Park minimized potential grievances from the military by co-opting retired military officers through extensive rewards. During the Park period, managerial positions of state enterprises and ambassadorial posts were to a great extent staffed by retired military officers. Likewise, Park used both stick and carrot in taming and depoliticizing the military.

Nevertheless, Park made extensive use of the military for domestic political purposes. During the Third Republic (1963–1972), Park was cautious in using the military for domestic politics. Although he created and ruled through the DRP as the hegemonic party, in Sartori's terms (Sartori 1976: 230–38), he was still in the process of consolidating his power in civil politics and the military. In the second phase of his rule, the Yushin period (1972–1979), however, Park gave up the idea of ruling through the hegemonic party by consolidating his personal power over the state and ruling party. The Yushin regime was nothing but a dictatorship in which the president exercised absolute political power. The president had the authority to dissolve the National Assembly, but the legislature did not have the right to impeach the president. The president also had the right to appoint up to one-third of the National Assembly's members. Nor were there any presidential term limits. The presidential election was indirect and conducted by the electoral college (Ahn 1990: 117–18). In order to maintain his authoritarian regime, Park relied heavily on the military security apparatus. The National Defense Security Command (NDSC) rivaled the Korean Central Intelligence Agency (KCIA) in monitoring and controlling civil society. Indeed, the NDSC was Park's most oppressive machinery in repressing political opposition to the Yushin regime. In addition, Park invented a system of Yushin cadres through which young civil service officers were recruited from the military and positioned in strategic government posts to monitor and control the government from within. During the Park period, therefore, the military as an institution did not intervene in civil politics. Although he himself had seized political power through a coup, Park was able to depoliticize the military and maintain control over it. Yet his rule would not have been possible without extensive military support. Retired military officers constituted the backbone of civil politics and government. Thus, despite its civilian facade, the Park regime was in fact a military regime.

Chun Doo-hwan and his followers in the military took political power by staging a mutiny against the old generals on December 12, 1979, and then mounting a quasi-coup in May 1980. Like Park, Chun established a strong authoritarian regime. Although the constitution itself was not exactly like the Yushin constitution, the president could still dissolve the National Assembly and install an interim institution that would perform its function. Moreover, the new constitution provided for strong presidential power over the legislative and judicial bodies. The Chun regime was highly personalized, and in this sense it resembled the Yushin system (Ho-jin Kim 1990: 228).

There are striking similarities between the two regimes in the way they managed civil-military relations. Chun, like Park, retired from the military, formed a political party, and became a civilian president as the constitution stipulated. A great majority of those associated with Chun's coup also retired from active military service and joined either the new ruling Democratic Justice Party or the government. And like the Park regime, the Chun regime was successful in controlling and depoliticizing the military. Nevertheless, there are some differences between the two regimes. While Park recruited heavily from the military, Chun purposefully limited the participation of military officers in civil politics and the government. The ratio of retired military officers in the National Assembly was reduced from 16 percent under Park to 9 percent under Chun. For cabinet positions, too, the ratio was curtailed from 28 percent under Park to 21 percent under Chun. The trend can be attributed to Chun's efforts to give a flavor of civilianized politics to his regime in order to enhance its political legitimacy. More important, Chun relied heavily on the Hana faction as an elite in both military and governmental institutions throughout his regime (Chung 1987; Han 1993; Roh 1995; Song 1994). Both the mutiny on December 12, 1979, and the takeover of political power in May 1980 were undertaken through the concerted efforts of the Hana faction. Critical political decisions were made in consultation with them, and administrative and technical decisions were left to bureaucrats. In a sense, Chun's political power rested upon two pillars: the state bureaucracy and the Hana faction (Choi 1989: 208). His controlling the military presented few obstacles. After all, he was the leader of the Hana faction, and its members held the key positions in the military throughout his reign.

In sum, then, under the Chun regime the military was very much fused into civil politics, creating a new form of civil-military symbiosis. While the National Defense Security Command was monitoring both military and civil political matters, the ruling Democratic Justice Party's leadership was dominated by retired military officers who belonged to the Hana faction. Its members also prevailed over the state apparatus by occupying strategic positions in the presidential office and the Agency for National Security Planning. In this sense, there was no clear boundary between the military and civilian politics. But, as under Park, the military as a whole was kept aside from civilian politics by the security and intelligence apparatus.

Although Chun suffered a persistent legitimacy problem throughout his reign due to his illicit takeover of political power and brutal suppression of the Kwangju Uprising in 1980, Roh Tae-woo was in much better shape. Roh was known to be responsible for the democratic opening through his June 29 declaration. He was also elected through a relatively fair and free electoral competition. Although the legitimacy problem involving his military background was resolved through direct presidential elections, Roh's regime was not much different from Chun's.[5] Although Roh tried to separate his regime from Chun's and to maintain his newfound public support, for example, he was unable to change the elite group framed around the Hana faction. The Hana faction, of which Roh himself was a member, continued to be the dominant element in the military. Nevertheless, after the democratic opening in 1987 the military's influence over civilian politics and government affairs was substantially reduced. In this sense, then, civil-military relations underwent a major change under Roh.

The election of Kim Young-sam as president in 1992 marked a fundamental watershed in South Korean politics. Although he formed an alliance with Roh and other conservative politicians with a military background, he was the first truly civilian president since 1961. To emphasize the difference of his regime from previous military regimes, Kim labeled his government as "*mun-min*" (civil) government and began implementing extensive democratic reforms (Han 1994: 474–87). The most notable of these reforms involved a purge of the military. The principal target, of course, was the Hana faction. The Kim Young-sam government began penalizing its members in various ways.

Kim relieved Gen. Kim Jin-young, the army chief of staff, and Maj. Gen. Seo Wan-soo, the commander of the NDSC, both of whom were Hana faction members, from their posts on March 8, 1993, just a few days after his inauguration. Within a year, more than twenty generals were either discharged from active service or transferred to less significant posts (Han 1998: 12; Jae-hong Kim 1994: chap. 10). The purge drive led to the discharge of eight lieutenant and full generals. Kim also discharged four generals for the charge of their implication in the mutiny on December 12, 1979.[6] Kim officially declared the mutiny as a "coup-like accident," thus justifying his military purification measures and forced discharge of generals as a "historically correct" act. Following Kim's initial take on the Hana faction, other military issues such as intra-military corruption involving weapons procurement programs and personal management became targets of the military reform. Interestingly enough, once the government showed the will to reform the military, military officers themselves began to voice their criticism on these issues. Thus, the military reform continued on with the inspection of personnel management corruption in the army, the navy, and the air force and with the special inspection of the weapon procurement program called "Yoolgok," eventually resulting in discharge or jailing of more generals (Don-sik Joo 1997: 39–40). Although the purge and the subsequent reform provoked some resistance in military circles, the measures were needed not only for disciplining the military but for the sake of Kim's publicity and his own political maneuvering (Joon-hyeong Lee 1994a: 18).[7]

The Kim Young-sam government learned an important lesson through the reform: civilian control over the military is feasible only through the elimination of the politicized faction in the military and the exercise of executive prerogatives over personnel management such as promotions and assignments. Indeed, military involvement in civil politics was led by politicized military factions that were framed around common interests of promotion and assignment. The success of the reform, including the purge of the Hana faction, was possible partly due to his decisive leadership style and partly due to popular support of his reform.

The removal of the Hana faction did not, however, end military factionalism. Before long, a new faction—framed around the Pusan-Kyungnam regional tie and the Kyungbok High School tie—emerged as the dominant element. Cases of two generals with successful military careers under the Kim Young-sam government exemplified this trend. Gen. Kim Dong-jin, the army chief of staff, who later became the chairman of the Joint Chiefs of Staff and eventually the minister of national defense, was a graduate of Kyungbok High School. The Third Army Commander Yoon Yong-nam, who later became the army chief of staff and then the chairman of the Joint Chiefs of Staff, was from Pusan province (Don-sik Joo 1997: 42). These two generals formed dominant factions in the military, one representing the regional tie, and the other the school tie. This was probably a grim limitation of Kim Young-sam's military reform policy. This is not to underestimate Kim's military reform efforts. Despite his reform drive, however, the old practice of factionalism still remained, replacing one faction with another. What made the situation worse was his second son Kim Hyun-chul's deep involvement in military politics. Often known as "little president," Kim Hyun-chul exercised powerful influence on governmental policies, especially on the military personnel management. One of Kim Hyun-chul's close friends is known to have stated that most of the high positioned military generals under the Kim Young-sam government contacted him and vowed their loyalty to Kim Young-sam and himself.[8] In view of this, civilian control and command over the military under the Kim Young-sam government was quite firm, and there was no sign of reversing that process. Nevertheless, it leaves the question whether that was an institutionalized and democratic control or a personalized process.

Despite public concern that the military would veto Kim Dae-jung as South Korea's next president, his election in December 1998 provoked no opposition from the military—a sign of the South Korean military institution's continuing neutrality. Unlike Kim Young-sam, Kim Dae-jung has not undertaken to reform the military. On the contrary, his government has taken a more conciliatory step by announcing that it will not discriminate against former members of the Hana faction in promotions and assignments. Despite a growing concern that another form of military factionalism might arise favoring officers from Cholla province, Kim Dae-jung's support base, Kim has so far managed to pacify civil-military relations and ensure civilian control over the military.

The Kim Dae-jung government was well aware of political repercussions of regional favoritism in the military. In conjunction with this, Chun Yong-taek, new national defense minister, submitted a report to president Kim Dae-jung at the end of February 1998. This report contained an evaluation of the military management policy under the Kim Young-sam government that emphasized two points; first, Kim Young-sam's military reform drive resulted in low morale among military officers, and second, promotion and assignment based on regional and personal ties continued despite the reform. The report also suggested taking reconciliatory actions for members of the Hana faction in order to utilize their expertise.[9] Military personnel management under the Kim Dae-jung government seemed so far balanced. Army corps commanders have been drawn from Cholla, Kyungki, and Kyungbuk provinces in equal number (one each), and division commanders have been appointed with regional balance in mind: four division commanders from the Kyunsang province, three from Cholla, and two from Choongchung in 1998.[10] Promotion in 1999 seemed to pose no serious problem either. In the case of lieutenant generals, one was from Kyungsang, one from Cholla, and two from Seoul. At the brigadier general level, six were from Seoul, ten from Choongchung, fifteen from Cholla, and seventeen from Kyungsang.[11]

However, the latest promotion and assignment in 2000 seems to be a bit troublesome. At the full general level, three were from Cholla and one each from five different other provinces. This presents a stark contrast with the beginning of the Kim Dae-jung government, during which there were four from Kyungsang and two from Cholla, one from Seoul, and one from Pyungnam. It is also important to note that the key positions such as the chairman of the Joint Chiefs of Staff, the Third Army commander, the army vice-chief of staff, the commander of NDSC, and the commander of Special Warfare Command are now filled with those from the Cholla province.[12] Nevertheless, this does not necessarily mean that there is a certain faction in the military now as there was before, like the Hana faction or Pusan-Kyungnam (PK) faction. This is because the trend of promotion and assignment under the Kim Dae-jung government maintained overall balance with an emphasis on career experiences and professional training. The Kim Dae-jung government appears to have learned lessons from the military management of the past regimes.

Security Policymaking

In a country like South Korea where threats to national security are genuine and acute, the domain of national security policymaking becomes an important vantage point for evaluating civil-military relations. In principle, civilian control over the military is predicated not only on preventing military intervention in civil politics but also on ensuring civilian supremacy in national policymaking. Thus, one would expect civilian control over the military to correspond to civil control over national security policy. But the South Korean case reveals an unusual continuity of military supremacy over national security policymaking despite democratization and the institutionalization of civilian control over the military. This section explores change and continuity in national security policymaking in South Korea by looking into three major areas: ideology, decision making, and recruitment (Moon 1989).

Security ideology is important because it shapes the foundation of national security management by influencing the norms, beliefs, and values of decision makers and ordinary people alike (Moon 1998). Security has been always a serious issue in South Korea. After all, South Korea is still in a state of military confrontation with North Korea despite the truce agreement. Memories of the Korean War are deeply entrenched in the minds of older generations, and a sharp sense of military tension with the North is widely shared in the South. As Moon notes, however, there was no explicit formation of security ideology in the 1950s and early 1960s (Moon 1989: 12). Nonetheless, people feared communist threats and accepted anticommunism as a guiding ideology for national security. Rhee actively exploited the anticommunism because it served a dual purpose. Externally, the ideology could be expected to draw American support. Internally, anticommunism drew public support and justified Rhee's dictatorial rule (Jin 1981). At the same time, anticommunism served as an ideological guide as well as a unifying force of the military.

Park adopted a similar pattern. When he staged the military coup in 1961, he cited anticommunism as his ideological base. Under his Yushin regime, the security ideology finally developed in full scale. The Yushin system advocated national interests over personal interests (including freedom) and state dominance over individual civil life. The national interests under the Yushin regime were defined in militaristic terms; thus security maintenance became the ultimate national goal (Ahn 1990: 128). The concept of *chongryok anbo* (total security), the leading ideology, consisted of such core values as military self-help, anticommunism, modernization, economic growth, and national survival. The ideology was imposed on every social organization through security education (Moon 1989: 13). In a sense, the primacy of the military over national security affairs was justified with this ideological orientation.

After the departure of Park, however, national security ideology framed around *chongryok anbo* no longer appealed to the public—not only because of its misuse for domestic political purposes, but also because there had been no major military conflicts with North Korea for quite a long period of time. The Chun regime, therefore, emphasized threats rather than security ideology per se. The following passage epitomizes the rationale behind the primacy of the military over civilians in the management of national security affairs under Chun: "We are in a special situation where 700,000 North Korean military forces threaten the half of South Korea's population within only 30 km distance. We cannot just blindly emphasize civilian control over the military in this situation. Given the heightened political role of the military in many developing countries even without a vivid external threat, we need to redefine proper civil-military relations in the South Korean context" (Hong 1993: 68).

Kim Young-sam vigorously engaged in purging the military, but security appeared to draw less attention from him.[13] In reaction to past military rule that had misused national security for domestic political purposes, Kim distanced himself from emphasizing security issues. Incumbent president Kim Dae-jung went even further. Upon his inauguration, President Kim declared his "sunshine policy" emphasizing exchanges, cooperation, and reconciliation in inter-Korean relations. As part of his new policy initiative, the Kim government also proposed dismantling the old cold war ideology and institutions (Moon and Steinberg 1999). A realigning of cold war ideology is yet to be seen, however. Although the military has remained silent, conservative forces have staged major attacks on Kim Dae-jung's new national security ideology. Nonetheless, democratization, along with a new ideological orientation, has reinforced civilian control over the military even in the arena of national security. Indeed, since the democratic transition in 1987, the national security ideology has lost its power and the military can no longer manipulate security ideology in advancing its institutional and political interests. Under the Kim Dae-jung government, the trend is likely to continue, profoundly affecting national security management.

Two further aspects of national security are decision making and personnel recruitment. After the military takeover of civil politics in 1961, national security decision making was virtually monopolized by the military as a sacred domain. Strategic and tactical doctrines, weapons choice and acquisition, resource mobilization, articulation of foreign and defense policies—such matters were rarely subject to legislative checks and balances or to public accountability. The defense budget was exempted from ordinary budget processes. Civilian participation was fundamentally restricted, and public debate on national security issues was not tolerated. Even scholarly debates on confidence-building measures and arms control were banned in the 1970s and 1980s. The Ministry of National Defense and the National Intelligence Service (formerly the KCIA), both of which were controlled by the military, always prevailed over other bureaucratic agencies and dictated the nature and direction of national security policy. This top-down monolithic structure of national security management had long been sustained by the military (Moon 1989: 14–16).

Since the inauguration of the Kim Dae-jung government in 1998, however, there has been a major institutional change. Following the American example, the Kim government established the National Security Council (NSC) under the president to deliberate on a broad range of national security issues, to assist the president in making security decisions, and to ensure interagency policy coordination. The NSC comprises the minister of unification, the minister of foreign affairs and trade, the minister of national defense, the director of the National Intelligence Service, and the senior presidential secretary for national security and foreign affairs; the minister of unification serves as chair. Civilian dominance in the council has become pronounced. Although there was an institution similar to the NSC as early as 1963 under Park Chung-hee, it was under the prime minister, and its main purpose was to assist cabinet ministers rather than deliberate and coordinate national security policies. In the absence of a formal institution such as the NSC, former presidents utilized unofficial meetings with military and intelligence personnel in making major security decisions (Min-young Lee 1996). As a result, national security decision making under previous regimes was rather personalized.

Democratic opening and transfers of political power, however, have brought about major changes in national security decision making. The legislative branch has become more active in monitoring and influencing national security policy. Nongovernmental organizations (NGOs) have also emerged as new actors in national security policymaking—especially in matters of unification policy and the defense budget. The most notable trend is the new importance of the mass media. Under previous authoritarian regimes, the mass media were tightly controlled and public opinion played no significant role. But democratic opening and new freedoms of expression have turned the mass media into the most important element in the process of national security policymaking.

This does not mean that the military no longer has a role in designing national security policy. The military is still a powerful player, and its influence in national security policymaking is closely associated with patterns of personnel recruitment. Since the Park regime, the military has virtually monopolized positions related to national security. Since 1961, for example, no civilian has ever held the position of defense minister, and key decision-making posts have been occupied by active or retired military officers. Civilians have held only supporting positions in budgeting, accounting, and auditing within the Ministry of National Defense (Moon 1989: 17). Under the current Kim Dae-jung administration, the trend continues. Of the five NSC members, the ministers of foreign affairs, trade, and unification are authentic civilians. The other three members are all retired army generals. Clearly, then, national security policymaking under the Kim Dae-jung government still comprises significant military elements.

Nevertheless, it must be emphasized that active-duty military officers are under civilian command in the process of managing national security policy. All military personnel, including the chief of the Joint Chiefs of Staff, are under the defense minister, who is a general-turned-civilian cabinet minister. The same can be said of the National Intelligence Service, where no uniformed officers can be posted. Two recent examples confirm civilian control over the military in national security policymaking. One is Kim's adoption of the sunshine policy. Initially, the military viewed it as an appeasement doctrine that could undercut the country's security posture. The initial disenchantment has disappeared, however, and the military has been incorporating the sunshine policy in its own strategic doctrines. Another example is the naval clash with North Korea in June 1999, when North Korean fishing boats and a navy escort crossed the Northern Limitation Line (NLL) and violated South Korea's territorial waters. Despite the South Korean Navy's warning, the North Korean provocation continued. When the South Korean military recommended a more offensive posture, including immediate retaliation, President Kim gave a restraining order and the military complied. Although a naval cross fire took place, dealing a critical blow to the North, the incident stands as an example of civilian control over the military during an acute security crisis.

However, the real litmus test of civilian control over the military is yet to come. On June 13, 2000, president Kim Dae-jung held a historic summit meeting with Kim Jong Il of North Korea. Both Kims produced the June 15 Joint Declaration, which contains five points of mutual agreement: North-South Korean initiative in steering Korean unification; mutual understanding of commonalities of modes of national unification between the South Korea proposal of confederation and North Korean proposal of federation; reunion of separated families; economic, social, and cultural exchanges and cooperation; and resumption of official dialogue.[14] If both Koreas abide by the joint declaration, peaceful co-existence between the two Koreas might become more feasible than ever before. Such developments will eventually lead to military confidence-building, arms control, and arms reduction. It is yet to be seen whether the military will comply with civilian decisions on arms control and reduction, even risking its own institutional interests.

In sum, then, the South Korean case illustrates that civil control over the military in the arena of national security management has varied from regime to regime. Although national security policymaking under authoritarian regimes was dominated by the military, the democratic opening and consolidation have ensured firm civilian control, and no uniformed officers have been placed in decision-making positions. It must be noted, however, that the number of retired military officers in national security management has increased significantly.

Control of Security and Intelligence Agencies

Although security ideology provided a justification for military intervention in civil politics under the authoritarian regimes, the security and intelligence agencies represented an instrument for maintaining regime stability by controlling links between the military and civilian politics. Even dating back to the Rhee regime, South Korea's security and intelligence agencies worked more for regime security than national security.

Rhee was notorious for utilizing the military police and the Counterintelligence Corps (CIC) as his political instruments. Rhee placed the military police headquarters under the Ministry of Defense, not under the army, in order to keep it under his direct command for political purposes (Ministry of Defense 1956: 373). The CIC unit dates back to the Intelligence Division under the U.S. Military Government in Korea in 1945. During the Korean War, it became a special service unit under the direct control of army headquarters.[15] Under Rhee the unit became a powerful military security agency—as its Korean name, Teukmoodae (Special Task Command), implies. Its stated mission was to engage in counterespionage against North Korea. But in reality it became a politically influential organization since Rhee used the Special Task Command extensively not only in monitoring the military, but also in penalizing his civilian political foes. Chang's short-lived regime attempted to change this negative image by realigning its function to pure counterespionage and renaming it the Bangchupdae (Counterintelligence Corps).

When Park came to power through a military coup, the power of the CIC grew once again, for Park wanted tight control over the military.[16] In the late 1960s, the CIC was expanded into the Army Security Command (ASC) and Kim Jae-kyu, the man who assassinated President Park in 1979, was appointed as its first commander. Throughout the 1970s, the ASC grew more powerful. It was the ASC that unveiled the Yoon Pil-yong scandal and arrested the commander of the Capital Defense Command and other officers.[17] In 1977, Park consolidated the army, air force, and navy CIC units into one, resulting in the establishment of the National Defense Security Command. The NDSC was designed to eliminate redundancy among multiple CIC units and to establish effective counterespionage against North Korea while making maximum use of the military budget and personnel.[18]

As Park himself had seized political power by a coup, he was well aware of the dangers of military intervention in civil politics. Thus, he made enormous efforts in depoliticizing the military. Ironically, the military was most depoliticized under his reign. He divided military positions into two levels: one consisted of command structure positions, including the army chief of staff and the joint chief of staff; the other consisted of intelligence/security positions such as commander of the Defense Security Command and commander of the Capital Defense Command. He then had the defense security commander report directly to him rather than to the minister of defense or the army chief of staff. Park used this dual structure to ensure a system of checks and balances just as Rhee had utilized the military police headquarters (Byoung-ki Yang 1993: 118–19). In other words, Park made use of the military security/intelligence apparatus for monitoring and controlling the military. The paradox of the Park regime is that Park politicized the military security apparatus in depoliticizing the entire military. Although the NDSC was aimed at engaging in counterespionage and other forms of intelligence operations within the military, its activities were not limited to the military domain. The NDSC engaged in intelligence operations against civilians too. Officially, the NDSC was under the control of the minister of defense, but its commander was able to report directly to Park—an important sign of the power and prestige vested in the NDSC.[19]

Chun was in charge of the NDSC when he staged his mutiny and coup in 1979 and 1980. In fact, the success of these moves can be attributed to his control over the security apparatus. Thus, he was well aware of the instrumental value of using the security agencies for regime security. Chun and Roh appointed their own Hana faction members to command the NDSC throughout their presidential tenures and allowed them to bypass the ordinary chain of command in reporting. In a sense, both Chun and Roh used the security and intelligence apparatus as the vital control mechanism over the military and civil society. Nevertheless, there was an anomaly. In April 1987, it was widely known that Chun was deliberating on the declaration of martial law in order to quell popular protest. But such a move was delayed and eventually aborted. American pressures played a role in this change of mind. But more critical was the division between hard-liners and soft-liners within the ruling bloc (Przeworski 1991). Ironically, the military was backing the soft-liners while politicians from the ruling party, the police, and the Agency for National Security Planning were taking the hard line. The military, especially the NDSC, Chun's most trusted security unit, recommended that since violent suppression of popular protest could worsen the situation, it would be wiser to seek a political compromise rather than impose martial law. Chun took the NDSC's recommendation seriously and urged Roh to announce the June 29 Declaration (Moon and Kang 1995). The episode reveals that the development of civil society had placed enormous constraints on military ventures into civil politics. In the face of social and political crisis, the civil-military symbiosis began to weaken.

Under the Kim Young-sam government, the military in general and the NDSC in particular were targets of reform. As a result, the NDSC became weaker. But around 1996, the NDSC regained its power and began reporting to the president again.[20] It is hard to figure out exactly what Kim Young-sam's intention was in re-empowering the NDSC. But several facts suggest that Kim Young-sam might have been trying to use it for regime security. In 1995, the ruling Democratic Liberty Party lost local governmental election by gaining only five of fifteen governor and mayor seats. Congressional election was due in 1996, and the presidential election was scheduled in 1997. Kim might have been trying to use the old trick of using security and intelligence agencies for influencing electoral outcomes. Another piece of data somewhat confirms this. The telephone eavesdropping by security and intelligence agencies, including the NDSC, rose sharply during the period 1995–1997. There were 1,794 cases in 1995, and its frequency rose to 2,443 cases in 1996 and to 6,002 cases in 1997.[21]

Another important security unit is the National Intelligence Service—previously the Agency for National Security Planning (ANSP) and the KCIA. The KCIA was the leading national intelligence organization and combined both security (FBI) and intelligence (CIA) functions. In principle, the KCIA was supposed to coordinate civilian and military security and intelligence. In reality, however, its role depended on who was in charge and that person's relationship with President Park. Originally, the KCIA was modeled after the CIA of the United States. Kim Jong-pil, nephew-in-law of Park and key architect of the May 16 coup in 1961, was responsible for the creation of the agency and expanded its functions to counterespionage and domestic security. Thus, despite its similarity in name to the American CIA, in organization and functions it was closer to the Soviet KGB. Not just an intelligence-gathering apparatus for security, it was an institution created for "terminating possible indirect communist attacks and removing obstacles of the revolutionary goal."[22] Essentially the KCIA could investigate, free from interference, any case in the name of national security and intelligence gathering (Choong-sik Kim 1993: 44). It was also entitled to investigate and arrest without a court warrant.

Under Park, the KCIA was quite an extensive organization. It was composed of three major wings: management, security, and intelligence. While the management wing was involved in planning, budgeting, and personnel affairs, the intelligence wing took charge of gathering intelligence on North Korea through human sources based overseas as well as technical intelligence. These two wings were not directly involved in domestic politics. More troublesome was the security wing. In principle, the security wing was supposed to engage in counterespionage against North Korea. In actuality, however, it paid more attention to domestic political affairs and was vital to the security of Park's regime. The security wing operated branch offices in all the provinces and major cities. Its agents penetrated virtually every segment of society, from students and churches to labor and the military. It was the security wing that monitored anti-regime activities, arrested and interrogated democratic activists, and engaged in covert political operations to divide and rule opposition parties. This was the physical arm of Park's political rule (Han 1993: 259). It was through the KCIA that Park could sustain his regime by overcoming domestic opposition. It served as an ear as well as a fist for Park's Yushin regime.

The KCIA was created and operated by uniformed officers. After the Yushin regime in 1972, however, the military's presence in the agency was radically reduced. All the active officers in the agency were required to retire from the military or accept active military service. At the same time, monitoring of the military was transferred from the KCIA to military security, and agents recruited from the military were subject to discrimination in promotion and assignments. Such developments indicate that the agency was increasingly being brought under civilian control.

Chun dismantled the KCIA after he seized power, reorganized it into the ANSP, and staffed its key posts with close associates, mostly from the military. Under Chun, however, the ANSP's role was very much limited to the civilian sector; monitoring and control over the military were left to the NDSC. This division of labor continued throughout the Roh Tae-woo regime. Upon his inauguration, Kim Young-sam tried to weaken the ANSP's power, but toward the end of his incumbency he seemed to rely on it for his regime's security, like the case of the NDSC.[23] The Kim Dae-jung government is again attempting to depoliticize the intelligence agency. As a token of this effort, Kim restructured the agency to give more emphasis to international intelligence gathering while downgrading internal security functions. Since the advent of civilian government, the military's presence in the agency has been fundamentally curtailed.

In sum, then, the management of national security agencies in South Korea appears to be a mixed blessing with respect to civil-military relations. On the one hand, security/intelligence organizations can serve as effective tools for monitoring the military and eventually preventing its intervention in civil politics. On the other hand, failure to control the apparatus by executive leadership could encourage military intervention in civil politics. Thus, effective use of the security/intelligence apparatus represents an important aspect of civil-military relations. More important, control of the security and intelligence apparatus should be democratic and objective. Authoritarian regimes have maintained arbitrary control over this apparatus in order to ensure their security. Democratic regimes, however, have power to prevent the personalization of the security/intelligence apparatus through proper institutional arrangements.

The Military's Socioeconomic Role

The military in South Korea has left several painful scars on society. Not only has its political intervention retarded the country's political development, but the transmission of military culture to civilian life has made South Korean society more rigid and hierarchical. Above all, the military's brutal suppression of the Kwangju Uprising critically tarnished its image and created tensions in the military relations with society.

However, the military has made an enormous contribution to South Korea's modernization and socioeconomic development. From the late 1950s to the late 1970s, the military played an important role in resocializing and training (Gwang-sik Kim 1998: 17). The compulsory draft forced nearly all of South Korea's young men into the military, where they not only got technical training but also learned organized social life through military discipline. In fact, it was this technical training that enabled South Korea's successful pursuit of labor-intensive industrialization. The military has also made a profound contribution to the country's physical infrastructure in the form of roads, highways, bridges, and cultivation of farmland and woods (Han 1998: 17). Although this positive role is sometimes forgotten as South Korean society develops, the military continues to make social and economic contributions. Nowadays its socioeconomic role is geared toward national disaster recovery and rescue missions. And the South Korean government is deliberating on more effective socioeconomic use of the military during peacetime (Han 1998: 19).

ACCOUNTING FOR CHANGES IN CIVIL-MILITARY RELATIONS

Despite a constitutional stipulation that prescribes civilian primacy over the military, the military has intervened more than once in South Korea's civil politics. Two cycles of military domination over civil politics have come to an end, however, and today there is firm civilian control over the military. Civil-military relations in national security policymaking have changed as well. Although the military's influence over national security policy has not completely vanished—it still exercises critical influence through retired generals in key decision-making posts—the management of national security has become increasingly civilianized and there are no institutional links between retired generals and active military officers. The most notable change can be seen in the security/intelligence apparatus. Both the military security agency and the national intelligence organization have become increasingly depoliticized, and today the military would find it nearly impossible to intervene in civil politics through the security and intelligence apparatus. Indeed, South Korea is now entering a new landscape of civil-military relations that is radically different from the past.

What accounts for such changes? Certainly the process of democratic opening and consolidation is significant. The democratic opening in 1987 was instrumental in expelling military elements from South Korean politics. Furthermore, the imprisonment of former presidents Chun and Roh and their associates on charges of treason and corruption has created new deterrents to military intervention in civil politics. The court decision that even successful military coups are subject to the rule of law sent a stern warning to the military. At the same time, institutional inertia has played an important role. Since 1987, the process of democratic consolidation has brought civilian leaders back into a political arena once dominated by the military. Although former president Roh's plan to promote democratic transition is ambiguous and the subject of intense debate, his decision to accelerate democratic opening turned out to be a valuable bridge between the former authoritarian regimes and the civilian regimes to come. Once the civilian political domination was consolidated, it has become extremely difficult to reverse it. Civilian and military segments of state and society have begun to accept civilian control as the norm.

Equally important is the expansion of civil society and its increased deterrent role. The civilian sector has grown strong and well organized since the 1980s. Horizontal solidarity among the NGOs, which have proliferated since the democratic opening, has kept the military out of civil politics. The NGOs did not want another authoritarian regime led by military leaders and were eager to support civilian leaders like Kim Yong-sam and Kim Dae-jung. As exemplified by Chun's aborted martial law in 1987, civil society became explosive in resisting military intervention in civil politics. At the same time, South Korean society has become differentiated in a structural and functional sense. Today the military is no longer the best-organized and most advanced element in society.

The military's exit from civil politics was feasible not simply because of democratic changes in civil society but also because of a changing political calculus in the military itself. Military politics in South Korea is sharply differentiated from that in Latin America and Southeast Asian countries such as Indonesia. In South Korea, the military has never intervened in civil politics as an institution. In South Korea, military interventions were a product of risky adventures by a handful of politicized officers. Spoils of the military coups were monopolized by those involved in the venture. Those who stayed behind in the barracks did not get any benefits. On the contrary, they fell prey to the public's harsh critiques along with the politicized officers. Such uneven returns of benefits among officers triggered internal frictions in the military, posing yet another deterrent to politicization of the military. Under democratic regimes, furthermore, the practice of rewarding nonpoliticized officers through promotion while punishing politicized officers has encouraged the political neutrality of the South Korean military.

Meanwhile, the military's continuing influence over national security policymaking can be attributed to two factors. The first is the constant military threats emanating from the North. Although there have been no major escalations on the Korean peninsula, North-South relations have remained tense and from time to time erupt into skirmishes. This environment has elevated the military to a position of preeminence in the field of national security management. Democratic consolidation notwithstanding, the military is likely to continue playing a significant role in security policymaking. The other factor is the availability of experts on national security affairs. Even though South Korea has cultivated a number of civilian experts on national security, their representation in the national security community is very limited. Retired military officers constitute the lion's share, and they can be said to be more experienced in the actual management of national security. Thus, a combination of threats from the North and a preponderance of security experts with a military background explain the persistence of military influence in national security policymaking.

But one caveat is in order. It is hard to predict whether the North-South summit talk in June 2000 would be just another futile attempt to establish peace between two countries like in the past, or a true historical turning point for two countries. One thing for sure is that if indeed this summit talk develops into a fruitful inter-Korean peaceful co-existence, then it would certainly reduce influence of the military in national security policymaking.

Civilian control over the security and intelligence apparatus has helped in depoliticizing the military. Kim Young-sam and Kim Dae-jung have deprived the military security agency of its functions of monitoring civil and political society. This limitation of political roles by a security agency has further reduced the chances of military intervention by realigning civil-military relations in favor of civil society. Kim Young-sam's purge of the military, focusing on Hana faction members who were strategically positioned in the military security apparatus, is particularly noteworthy. Kim was able to tame the military by removing officers from strategic posts. This implies the importance of political leadership in controlling military security agencies. In fact, it is the new democratic mandates and the commitment of leaders that have put the military security apparatus under firm civilian control.

Finally, changes in the military's socioeconomic role can be explained by evolutionary dynamics. Simply put, the passage of time has altered the military's role in society. In the 1950s and 1960s, the military was the most effective agent of modernization. But as South Korea has graduated from the stage of modernization, the military's role has been correspondingly curtailed. Nowadays, more than 80 percent of those who are drafted have a college-level education. These draftees do not need any technical training. Most of the physical and social infrastructure has been completed and no longer needs the military's involvement. Social infrastructure such as the information highway goes beyond the purview of the military. Likewise, the military's socioeconomic role in peacetime has been substantially limited.

Thus, the changes in civil-military relations can be ascribed to the dynamic interplay of several factors: political regime change; a strong, vibrant, and alert civil society; a shifting calculus of interest within the military; and threats from North Korea. Of these, it can be argued that political regime changes involving democratic opening and consolidation are the most critical variable in accounting for changes in civil-military relations.

PATTERNS AND IMPLICATIONS

We can draw several interesting theoretical implications from this examination of civil-military relations in South Korea. The most important is that civil-military relations cannot be aggregated: as done elsewhere in this volume, they should be disaggregated into several dimensions and approached from a contextualized analysis of the components. The South Korean case reveals that civilian domination over the military does not necessarily guarantee civilian domination over national security policy. Another important point emerging from this analysis is the pattern of military intervention in politics and its impact on civil-military relations. In South Korea, the military has never intervened in civil politics as an institution—a fact that has made it easy for the military to exit from politics and has also made it easy for the military to prevent its intervention. This leaves us with an important puzzle, however, involving the role of retired military officers. Should retired officers be viewed as military or civilian actors? Until this issue is resolved, debates on the military nature of Korean politics and national security policymaking are likely to continue.

While each aspect of the civil-military relationship is shifting in new directions, there is one persistent trend in South Korea—namely factionalism. From the Rhee regime to the Kim Young-sam regime, even under Kim Dae-jung, the patron-client relationship based on factionalism has shaped the dynamics of political domination. Whether under a civilian-controlled or a military-controlled regime, factionalism and personalization of political power have prevailed. Indeed, the lack of institutionalized political power has brought two rounds of military intervention and authoritative regimes. Even under the civilian government of Kim Young-sam, it is suspected that Kim was trying to control the military by placing officers of his PK faction in key positions (Joon-hyeong Lee 1994b: 216–19). Under Kim Dae-jung, officers from Cholla province, his strongest support base, have occupied strategic posts. Unending patron-client relationships based on regionalism and factionalism could become a major obstacle to normalizing civil-military relations.

The South Korean case also reveals that one of the prerequisites for normalized civil-military relations is a well-developed and institutionalized political society. A balanced political party system and stable democracy could lead to the institutionalization of civilian control over the military, which in turn would minimize the opportunities for personal abuse of the military by political leaders. Along with this, socioeconomic stability is critically important in ensuring healthy civil-military relations. Indeed, military intervention in civil politics has always taken place in the twilight zone of social chaos and economic crisis.

Moreover, we need to note the importance of the security/intelligence apparatus. Although it has been misused by past military regimes, they were right in understanding that effective control of this apparatus is necessary not only for the prevention of military intervention in civil politics but also for normalized civil-military relations. But as the interventions show, politicizing this apparatus brings nothing but trouble. Thus, it seems essential to institutionalize, rather than personalize, civilian control over these organizations. Otherwise, there is no effective way to monitor and control the military.

Aside from the tendency of factionalism based on patron-client relationships, there is one more problematic aspect of the civil-military relationship. Although institutionalizing a new civil-military relationship is always a difficult task, it is an even greater challenge in areas the military has traditionally considered its own private turf—institutions such as the Ministry of Defense, for example. A future task for civilian leaders, therefore, is to ensure civilian control in such areas by developing its own civilian experts with military expertise. Although this is no easy undertaking, it is essential for the future health of the civil-military relationship.

CHAPTER 5

Taiwan: The Remaining Challenges

Chih-cheng Lo

THE POLITICAL SITUATION IN THE REPUBLIC OF CHINA (ROC) on Taiwan has undergone a significant but smooth transformation. After 40 years of authoritarian rule, Taiwan's transition to democracy began in 1987 when the ruling Kuomintang (KMT) Party lifted martial law and was completed ten years later with the historic direct presidential election of 1996. In March 2000, this process took another major step forward with the election of President Chen Shui-bian and the first transfer of political power in the highest elected office to an opposition party. As Taiwan moves into the important phase of democratic consolidation, some are beginning to warn of factors contributing to a possible breakdown of the new democracy: economic crisis, leaders' foibles, political polarization, ethnic conflict, external threat, legitimacy crisis, and more. Given that the military often represents a threat to the effective exercise or even the survival of civilian rule, one of the foremost tasks of any new democracy is to bring the military establishment under civilian control. To be sure, the question of civil-military relations has been and remains high on the political agenda of democratic leaders in Taiwan.

Article 140 of the ROC constitution promulgated in 1947 stipulates: "No person in active military service shall concurrently hold a civil office." Moreover, the three services of the armed forces "shall stand above personal, regional, and party affiliations and shall be loyal to the State and love and protect the people" (Article 138), and "no political party and no individual shall make use of armed forces as an instrument in the struggle for political power" (Article 139). Notwithstanding such crystal-clear ordinances, a democratic civil-military relationship is yet to be fully established in Taiwan. Future developments will depend in large part on the actions and reactions of the civilian and military leaderships in this consolidating democracy.

Since the late 1980s, civil-military relations in Taiwan have undergone significant changes, with the general trend toward greater civilian control over the military. Given their long-standing ideological indoctrination and distinct ethnic composition, however, the armed forces, particularly the mainlander-dominated officer corps, have demonstrated hostility toward certain political ideas, especially the claim for Taiwan's separation from the Chinese mainland. The possibility that the military might have prevented independence-minded opposition parties (mainly the Democratic Progressive Party [DPP]) from coming to power troubled many people on the island (Tien 1997). Indeed, military-turned-civilian premier Hau Pei-tsun once claimed loudly in the Legislative Yuan that "the army will not protect Taiwan Independence." Clearly, then, the primary danger to Taiwan's democracy and sound civil-military relations emanates from the military's "conditional loyalty." Since this is the key test of democratic consolidation in Taiwan, the question of civil-military relations merits careful investigation.

This study explores the changing face of the Taiwanese army over the years—from a party-dominated military to an increasingly state-controlled armed forces. Taiwan, as we shall see, has made progress in recent years toward greater civilian supremacy over the military, or what Huntington (1957) calls "objective civilian control." We begin by delving into the military's changing relationships with the state, the party, and society. On the one hand, the increasing civilian control of the military reflects the process of political democratization on the island: the ebbing of external threats and the emergence of civil society have created an environment conducive to restructuring civil-military relations. On the other hand, against this backdrop, the interactions between the political elite (both inside and outside the regime) and the military establishment have shaped the direction of changing civil-military relations. In other words, the military's gradual disengagement from politics in Taiwan can be attributed to the shrewd and careful process of bargaining initiated by civilian leaders, especially President Lee Teng-hui. With unprecedented legitimacy and popularity, Lee skillfully exploited crises, manipulated support, reshuffled military leadership, and accordingly expanded civilian control over the military.

Two cases are investigated here to demonstrate this skillful manipulation. The first case deals with personnel changes in the upper echelons of the armed forces—especially the elimination of Gen. Hau Pei-tsun as a political force and the efforts to civilianize the defense ministry. The second case explores the incremental transparency of defense policies and the greater supervisory role assumed by the legislative branch and public opinion on arms procurement. Taking as given the necessity of establishing the primacy of elected civilian authorities (executive and legislative) in all areas of national defense policy, this study emphasizes executive and legislative supremacy over the military. In general, reformers within the authoritarian regime gained power and took the initiative, with the cooperation of the opposition, in bringing about the transition. Finally, the chapter explores the prospects for democratization and the establishment of fully democratic civil-military relations.

CHANGE AND CONTINUITY

Despite its importance, the subject of civil-military relations has scarcely been touched upon by scholars in Taiwan. This paucity of relevant studies is understandable, though, given the short time since Taiwan's transition from authoritarian rule. Moreover, the exceptional security situation distinguishes Taiwan from other countries. The core task of the government, according to some, is to ensure the country's survival in the face of threats from the People's Republic of China—and for that purpose, all necessary means should be utilized. Accordingly, protecting the secrets most critical to the national security from public awareness (and theoretically from enemies) is surely justified (Lo 1999: 1). Thus, the government's right to classify national defense information—encompassing the security policymaking process, military operations, military personnel, weapons technology, and arms procurement—has rarely been questioned. As a consequence, efforts to explore the interactions among civilian and military authorities have been very cursory.

Since the late 1980s, however, Taiwan's democratization has generated greater public and academic interest in opening up the black box of national defense. As a result, civilian officials and the public in general are better informed on military issues today than they were under the authoritarian regimes. This section examines the changing face of the military's relations with state, party, and society. Overall, Taiwan has gradually reduced the military's power and standing, incrementally diminished military prerogatives, and professionalized the armed forces.

After its retreat to Taiwan in 1949, the KMT had to restructure civil-military relations to meet the imminent threat from the Chinese Communist Party. The ultimate goal, therefore, was to ensure the party's control over the state, military, and society. The KMT regime did everything it could to ensure that the military was controlled by the party and divided against itself for the purpose of keeping a tight party grip on power. In the aftermath of a series of party reforms in the 1950s, a Leninist party-state system was firmly established—and was not seriously challenged until the late 1980s. During the authoritarian rule of Chiang Kai-shek and Chiang Ching-kuo (1949–1988), the paramount leaders dominated the party and through it controlled the state, military, and society. In this party-state system, the military was viewed as the party's instrument, military officers had to be party members, political commissars and party cells paralleled the normal military chain of command, and ultimate loyalty was to the party rather than the state. Given the military's importance in guaranteeing the regime's survival in the face of internal and external challenges, it was granted a key role in the country's development and economy. Not only did defense long consume the lion's share of the government's budget, but the military penetrated society in a variety of ways—including the setup of the Taiwan Garrison Command, which was in charge of domestic security issues and the execution of martial law.

In the Leninist party-state system, state control over the military is usually indirect, even when there is a legal basis for the chain of command. In the case of Taiwan, however, an even more ambiguous (and sometimes contradictory) legal arrangement of state control over the military has long existed. Article 36 of the ROC constitution stipulates that the president "shall have supreme command of the army, navy, and air force of the country," and Article 3 of the Organization Law of the Executive Yuan states that "the Executive Yuan shall establish [among others] a Ministry of National Defense [MND]." According to the Organization Law of the MND, the ministry shall be in charge of the defense affairs of the whole country. Within the MND is the General Staff Headquarters (GSH), and under it the various services. In charge of military affairs, the GSH is headed by a chief of the general staff (CGS): in the military command system, the CGS acts as chief of staff to the president for operational matters; in the administrative command system, he serves as chief of staff to the defense minister and is therefore also responsible to the premier.

Whereas the MND has jurisdiction over such issues as defense policy and budget formulation, the GSH, being responsible to the president, commands military education, mobilization, training, arms production and procurement, intelligence, and other war-related activities. This dualistic and in most cases parallel system of civilian control over the military was never a serious problem during the authoritarian era: the paramount leaders controlled both lines of command. As Taiwan turns into a democratic polity, however, problems have begun to surface. Several difficulties could result from divided civilian control over the military: coordination or even confrontation problems between the two lines of command; interactions between the president and premier that could have an impact on the military's role; and the independence of the military from the Executive Yuan, constitutionally the highest administrative organ of the state (Article 53 of the ROC constitution). Moreover, the obvious lack of checks and balances by the Legislative Yuan could pose challenges for the functioning of Taiwan's democracy (Cheng 1997: 93–94).

One of the major problems associated with possible conflicts between the military command and administrative command systems is the lack of accountability in defense policy-making. Until recently, the MND had consistently ignored the demand of the Legislative Yuan to invite the chief of general staff and commanders in chief of the three military forces to appear before the Defense Committee of the Legislative Yuan to report on defense affairs.[1] A clear restructuring of the command system is crucial to healthier civilian control over the military. The long-awaited National Defense Law, which was finally signed into law on January 29, 2000, is the first concrete legal step towards this goal. It, for the first time, clearly places the minister of defense above the CGS in the chain of command, thus in principle unifying the military command and administration systems under the MND. This change is further substantiated by the shifting of several subsidiary departments from the GSH to the MND. Since implementation of the law is to take place over three years, realizing all its goals will pose a significant challenge to the new administration; however, in the long run, it promises to resolve this major issue. The de jure command of civilian authority over the armed institutions of the state was stipulated in the ROC constitution, but until now the functioning of de facto civilian control of the military has rested upon the KMT party's control. Accordingly, the "party-in-control approach" or "Chiang-in-command model" characterized relations between party, state, and military before democratization took place on the island.

One of the most important ramifications of democratic transformation in Taiwan is the growing public demand for greater de facto civilian control over the military. The most symbolic development in building democratic civilian-military relations is the nomination of civilian defense ministers. In practice, most ROC ministers of national defense have been discharged from the military just before they took office. The appointments of Dr. Chen Lu-an in May 1990 and later Dr. Sun Chen in May 1993, both civilians, as defense ministers proved to be unsatisfactory. There were rumors that high-ranking military officers had difficulties adapting themselves to civilian control. The disagreement and coordination problems between the civilian defense ministers and military chief of general staff were quite evident during these two recent attempts to increase civilian control by appointing civilian defense ministers. The military's disinclination to accept a civilian defense minister left President Lee Teng-hui with no choice but to appoint Chiang Chung-ling—another discharged general—to succeed Dr. Sun as the thirteenth minister of defense. As a consequence, the trend toward civilian control over the defense establishment faced a setback. Chiang in turn was succeeded by Tang Fei, who had previously served as CGS; Tang frankly admitted that given the current defense organizational structure, no civilian defense minister can survive his job. In fact, defense issues are so complicated that the defense minister cannot do without a capable and supportive staff. Yet almost all the staff working under the MND are military personnel, so the civilian defense minister clearly will have difficulties moving a policy forward by himself.[2] The new government of President Chen, proceeding with utmost delicacy in military matters, has not taken the risk of naming a civilian defense minister. Only current or recently retired generals were considered for the post, and finally the decision was made simply to promote Vice-Minister Wu Shih-wen (from the navy, and a close associate of Tang Fei). Thus, the expectation, now formally embodied in the National Defense Law, that the minister should be a civilian continues to only be met through a technicality.

Currently, the ROC's national security policy and defense decision-making system is concentrated in the National Security Council (NSC), under the presidency, and in several ministries under the Executive Yuan, such as the MND, the Ministry of Foreign Affairs (MOFA), and the Mainland Affairs Council (MAC). The NSC is the constitutional advisory body to the president and relies on its subordinate, the National Security Bureau (NSB), for collection and analysis of intelligence. The chief of general staff as well as the director of the NSB also attend the NSC meeting. The president's policy and strategy statements, prepared by the NSC, often establish basic conceptual guidelines that assist the MND, MOFA, and MAC in developing assessments and strategies. According to the 1991 Organization Law of the National Security Council, both the NSC and the NSB are checked by the Legislative Yuan. Moreover, the law clearly stipulates that the number of military personnel shall not exceed one-third of the total staff working under the NSC. At present, both the general secretary of the NSC and the director of the NSB are from the military. In short, although recent years have witnessed its gradual disengagement from politics, the military still plays a predominant role in shaping the country's security policy as well as its political development.

During the period of strongman authoritarian rule, defense policy was the exclusive province of the political and military elite. The asymmetry of power between the executive and legislative branches of government was most apparent in the matter of national defense. In the aftermath of democratization, the growing demand for checks and balances has reinforced the legislative monitoring of the military establishment and defense policymaking. Although democratization in Taiwan has gradually empowered the legislative branch in regulating military affairs, the mechanisms for parliamentary oversight of the military in general and the MND in particular have not been effective. Clearly, the parliament should play the key role in ensuring the political and financial accountability of the executive, but many constitutional experts in Taiwan argue that the present constitution favors the executive branch. With respect to political accountability, Additional Article 3 of the ROC constitution stipulates: "The Executive Yuan has the duty to present to the Legislative Yuan a statement on its administrative policies and a report on its administration. While the Legislative Yuan is in session, its members shall have the right to interpellate the president of the Executive Yuan and the heads of ministries and other organizations under the Executive Yuan." Article 3 also points out that "should the Executive Yuan deem a statutory, budgetary, or treaty bill passed by the Legislative Yuan difficult to execute, the Executive Yuan may . . . request the Legislative Yuan to reconsider the bill.... Should the Legislative Yuan not reach a resolution within the said period of time, the original bill shall become invalid." The same article says that "the Legislative Yuan may propose a no-confidence vote against the premier of the Executive Yuan" and points out that "should the no-confidence motion fail, the Legislative Yuan may not initiate another no-confidence motion against the same president of the Executive Yuan within one year."

To hold the executive branch accountable for its policies, then, interpellation of public officials appears to be the only available tool in the hands of legislators. Other mechanisms—such as a no-confidence vote or overriding, executive veto—are almost unthinkable in Taiwan's current political setting. Moreover, the Legislative Yuan's power to oversee the work of the executive by questioning ministers and cross-examining state personnel is deemed ineffective. Without the constitutional powers of impeachment, censure, appropriation, and auditing, the Legislative Yuan is not much more than "a dog barking at a train." This is especially true in the case of parliamentary oversight of the military.

Other problems, as well, can be traced to the present framework of legislative checks and balances. Information asymmetry between the executive and legislative branches, for example, has resulted in the Legislative Yuan's inability to oversee defense decisions and budgets. One of the main difficulties is the lack of a general statutory right of access to official records and information. The executive branch (specifically the MND) has enjoyed great discretionary authority in deciding which information should be classified and which can be disclosed. In response to pressure from opposition legislators and the public at large, the MND published the first-ever *National Defense Report* in 1992 and since then has published three more editions. Although it was long overdue, the report's publication indicated a significant move toward a more transparent and accountable defense organization. The National Defense Law now specifically obligates the MND to prepare these reports. Moreover, closed-door sessions will now be held in the Legislative Yuan to examine defense proposals such as arms procurement, and legislators can now gain access to certain classified defense documents. In general, however, the MND has demonstrated a reluctant or even hostile attitude toward the public's desire for greater openness on defense issues. In short, it is still difficult for the Legislative Yuan and the general public to scrutinize the decisions and conduct of defense officials and therefore to ensure that they are indeed answerable for their actions.

In the matter of budgetary accountability, too, the legislative branch has shown its inability to hold the executive answerable for its defense budgets. Article 59 of the constitution stipulates that "the Executive Yuan shall, three months before the beginning of each fiscal year, submit to the Legislative Yuan a budgetary bill for the following fiscal year." And Article 70 states that "the Legislative Yuan shall not propose any increase in the budget estimates submitted by the Executive Yuan." Clearly, three months is not enough time for the legislators to examine the proposed defense budget thoroughly. In addition, compared to the huge number of staff working under the MND to compile the data and propose the budget, the Defense Committee of the Legislative Yuan has only a small research staff to analyze the defense budget. As a result, facing the MND's defensive or even hostile attitude, legislators sometimes have to rely upon whistle-blowers to uncover the military's hidden budgets or expose scandals in the military establishment. Once the budget bill is passed, the Legislative Yuan, without appropriation power, can only wait for the auditor general's report on the MND's spending. Although the auditor general is accountable to the Legislative Yuan, the Audit Ministry is institutionalized under the Control Yuan.

According to Additional Article 7 of the constitution: "The Control Yuan shall be the highest control body of the State and shall exercise the powers of impeachment, censure, and audit." Article 95 of the constitution further stipulates that "in exercising its power of control, the Control Yuan may request the Executive Yuan and its ministries and commissions to make available to it any orders they have issued and all other relevant documents." Since the Control Yuan may request "all relevant documents" it considers necessary, it would appear that the transparency of the government's conduct and decisions is ensured. The National Defense Law for the first time provides a statutory foundation for the systematic classification of documents, including a time limit, but the executive is the one who decides which information can be disclosed. Given the military's general resistance to disclosure and possible self-incrimination, the Control Yuan's efforts at inspecting military wrongdoing are in most cases less than vigorous. Still, as evidenced by the rising number of impeachment and censure cases initiated by the Control Yuan, there have been improvements. During the period 1993–1998, for example, 36 of the 128 cases of impeachment (28 percent) were against the MND. During the same period, the defense and intelligence sector of the government accounted for 13 percent of the total cases of censure initiated by the watchdogs (84 of 656 cases).

In terms of financial accountability, Article 60 of the constitution stipulates: "The Executive Yuan shall, three months after the end of each fiscal year, submit to the Control Yuan a final financial statement of the year." Article 105 further states that "the Auditor General shall, within three months after submission by the Executive Yuan of the final financial statement, complete the auditing thereof in accordance with law and submit an audit to the Legislative Yuan." Again, given its small staff and time pressures, the Ministry of Audit cannot function effectively in scrutinizing detailed defense expenditures. Furthermore, even in the auditing stage, "black budgets" may still be classified on national security grounds. Accordingly, in the current institutional setting it remains extremely difficult to hold the MND accountable financially.

In short, then, democratization has produced an impetus for more legislative oversight and therefore civilian control of the military. In this regard, there is indeed a trend toward greater transparency and accountability of defense decisions and the military establishment. But institutional constraints pose a serious obstacle to consolidating democratic civilian control over the military. Without adequate information, the executive branch cannot be properly scrutinized and held accountable legally, politically, or financially. In Taiwan, as we have seen, the military establishment and defense policies usually fall into the distinct category of national security secrets. The primacy of secrecy over accountability is the defining feature of the ROC military's power to withstand more civilian control.

The military's incremental withdrawal from politics can also be evidenced by the changing relationship between the former ruling party, the KMT, and the military. Before the lifting of martial law in 1987, the "party within the military" (*junzhong youdang*) and the "military within the party" (*dangzhong youjun*) had long been the two flip sides of the same coin in the KMT's "party control over the military" (*yidang lingjun*). The integration of military and party proved successful in ensuring the KMT's political dominion. Over the decades, the KMT developed party cells parallel with the organizational structure of the military. Publicly or privately, it recruited, trained, and organized party members in the armed forces. Through its party cells and the political commissar system, the KMT successfully monitored and controlled the military (Cheng 1990a: chap. 6). As a consequence of the KMT's deliberate penetration, the military establishment became highly partisan and politicized (Cheng 1990b).

The other direction of this two-way street was the military's active participation in the decision-making process within the KMT. Before 1987, the military occupied two to five seats in the KMT's Central Standing Committee, while in the full Central Committee the military controlled at least one-seventh of the seats (Su et al. 1997: 8). Moreover, many civilian posts—Taiwan provincial governor, defense minister, many ambassadors—were staffed by ex-military persons, and the major security agencies such as the NSC and the NSB were under the military. Still, in the authoritarian period the Chiangs had the final say on the country's security and other important policies.

The democratization process also triggered a transformation in the party-military relationship. Although there were still representatives from the military in the KMT's Fourteenth Party Congress selected in September 1993, the defense minister was the only military representative to hold a seat on the Central Standing Committee. Since then, all active-duty military personnel have been removed from the party's major decision-making organs such as the Central Committee. General Hau—a dominant military as well as political figure who could have posed a serious threat to civilian control—was eventually removed from the core of political power with his resignation as premier in 1993.

Apart from greater state control over the military and the military's gradual disengagement from the party, Taiwan also witnessed gradually normalized military-society relations. As an integral part of the Leninist party-state system, the military establishment had penetrated deeply into Taiwanese society in a variety of ways. During the authoritarian period, the Taiwan Garrison Command represented the highest domestic security and police authority. In addition, the military played an important role in Taiwan's economic life. Through the Veteran's Association and its subsidiary industries and corporations, the military involved itself extensively and intensively in the island's economic activities (Chen et al. 1991). The military also got involved in the mass media business through the ownership of television and radio stations, newspapers, and publishing companies. More important, the military was long active in Taiwan's electoral politics, endorsing candidates with strong military connections (mostly KMT-nominated candidates). In the past, moreover, through special examination privileges, active-duty or retired military personnel could easily occupy positions in the administrative and judicial systems. And, finally, the implementation of compulsory military service for all men at the age of twenty reinforced the integration of army and society. In short, the past five decades have witnessed the military's deep penetration into Taiwan society.

In July 1992, the Taiwan Garrison Command was dissolved—leading to a clear separation of power between the army and regular police forces. Other spheres of interest long monopolized by the military were also challenged around that time by opposition parties and by forces outside the military establishment. In the face of fierce criticism and public pressure—the result of liberalization and democratization—the military involuntarily had to redefine its role in the society and gradually give up its power and vested interests. These positive developments included the military's disengagement from the mass media, waiving of examination privileges, withdrawal from the school systems, and yielding of many special business interests (Su et al.

1997). In addition, military bashing and scrutiny of national defense are no longer taboo in Taiwan. Today there are many books and magazines and radio and television programs providing expert information on what used to be the black box of the military community.

The dissolution of the Taiwan Garrison Command in 1992 elevated the role of the police in domestic security. Moreover, when the Coast Guard Administration was established in January 2000 under the Executive Yuan, there was a consensus to appoint a civilian to serve as its director.[3] In addition to these reforms, the Legislative Yuan passed the Civil Organizations Law in October 1992 and revised the University Law in 1993, prohibiting political party activities in the army and on college campuses.[4] Despite these regulations political activities have continued (both by ruling and opposition parties), but in a more subtle and competitive way. The growing consensus that a diminishing military role in the island's social and political life would be a welcome development is reflected in the National Defense Law, which explicitly forbids active-duty soldiers from political activities.

In sum, then, the military's influence over political decisions in general and security policy in particular is in decline. Since the late 1980s, the military has been disengaging itself from politics, and democratic principles and norms are gradually emerging as the foundations of civil-military relations. Nonetheless, the development of sound civil-military relations has never been a one-way street in new democracies—witness the military's reluctance to accept the authority of civilian defense ministers. Moreover, there are still important institutional deficiencies in holding the military accountable for its conduct and decisions.

Throughout the 1990s, many scholars warned that the ultimate test of military obedience to civilian control would come when the ruling KMT had to one day hand over power to one of the opposition parties. Given the military's traditional position against Taiwan's independence, the possibility of electing a DPP president, in particular, raised doubts about whether the military would remain loyal. With the inauguration of President Chen, these fears have been allayed for the time being. Although no grave crisis has occurred, and Chen has at least superficially been accepted as commander in chief, Taiwan needs to continue to work hard to redefine the roles and missions of its military establishment.

Former premier Hau Pei-tsun, as noted, once claimed that the ROC's armed forces would not protect Taiwan independence. However, in his debut in the Legislative Yuan as chief of the general staff, then CGS Tang Fei stated: "The army supports the ROC and the name of the country is the ROC, not Taiwan. If some day the name of the country is changed according to the constitution into Taiwan, we will safeguard Taiwan."[5] His statement indicated a significant departure from previous attitudes generally held in the military establishment. Although Tang's attitude probably earned him the premiership, and the transition thus far has been reasonably smooth, it remains to be seen whether this reorientation of the military's mission is dominant among the military leadership.

Certainly efforts to diminish military prerogatives and vested interests could encounter resistance from the military establishment. Many have worried that a military-industrial complex has gradually taken shape in Taiwan—especially in the matter of arms procurement. For years the military has been charged with arms procurement irregularities and scandals—for example, active-duty officers have leaked confidential procurement information to arms dealers in exchange for kickbacks. Although the Legislative Yuan and the general public have called for greater transparency and accountability in the matter of arms procurement, civilian supervision of such processes is still inadequate. In short, although a broad acceptance of the norms of military professionalism and civilian control is emerging in Taiwan, it will take time to deflate a bloated officer corps, to define new missions, and to civilianize defense policymaking.

EXPLAINING THE TRANSFORMATION
OF CIVIL-MILITARY RELATIONS

Although there are a few studies on civil-military relations in Taiwan, almost all of them are either descriptive or normative (Li 1993; Chen and Ko 1993). None of these studies has traced the causes of the military's gradual withdrawal from politics. Though we have witnessed a great deal of research on political democratization in Taiwan, the changing contours of civil-military relations have received only minimal treatment. Although the factors contributing to democratic transition may have been the driving forces behind the transformation of civil-military relations on the island, the causes of democratization provide only a macro-illustration of political change in Taiwan. To explain the pattern and dynamics of changing civil-military relations, we need more research—preferably an integration of both macro and micro levels of analysis. How do we account for the gradual transformation of civil-military relations in Taiwan?

Though the institutional mechanisms conducive to greater civilian control have only just begun to be established, interactions among the civilian and military elites have undergone important changes. Military strongmen who could mobilize military power and exert political influence are absent from the scene today. More important, the norm of civilian control appears to be increasingly accepted in the society. We should never assume, however, that the issue of civil-military relations has been taking care of itself. The transition in civil-military relations has been the result of negotiations between civilian and military leaders.

The ebbing of external threats—especially the relaxation of cross-strait tensions in the early 1990s—and the rise of a vibrant civil society as a consequence of liberalization during the same period have created an environment conducive to the restructuring of civil-military relations. Against this backdrop, the reform-minded civilian elite within the ruling party, in cooperation with opposition leaders, initiated reforms that gradually advanced civilian control over the military. At many historical junctures, President Lee, with unprecedented legitimacy and popularity, skillfully took advantage of public pressure to reform military affairs and reshuffle military personnel. In other words, the military's incremental disengagement from politics in Taiwan can largely be attributed to bargaining among the civilian and military elites and to the domestic and international environments. In this section, we examine the removal of military strongman Hau Pei-tsun from the political scene and the normalization of arms procurement.[6]

At the time Lee succeeded Chiang Ching-kuo as president of the ROC, General Hau had already served as chief of the general staff for six years, a record-breaking and law-bending appointment. To consolidate his power, President Lee initially had no choice but to rely on General Hau for political support. Indeed, Hau's explicit support played a determining role in the outcome of Lee's struggle to assume the KMT chairmanship in 1988. As the first native Taiwanese president, Lee enjoyed unprecedented popularity on the island. Even opposition groups developed strong feelings for him.[7] Still, Lee's shaky political base forced him to make concessions to Hau—as demonstrated by Lee's full endorsement of Hau's proposed reshuffle of high-ranking military officers in May 1988. Among the 35 important military posts rearranged at that time, members of the Hau faction filled 21 of them (or 60 percent). Moreover, Hau's major competitors such as Chiang Chung-ling, Liu Ho-chien, and Kuo Ju-lin were all relegated to insignificant positions—a sign of Hau's growing ambition and expanding power in Taiwan's politics (Chang 1992: table 2).

During the Thirteenth KMT Party Congress, the military representatives, most of them belonging to the Hau faction, captured 21 seats in the Central Committee. It was widely believed that Hau was becoming increasingly dissatisfied with the president's mainland policy and with his tolerance of those advocating Taiwan independence. It was also reported that Hau had attempted to ally himself with marginal factions in the KMT to check the power of Lee (Chang 1992: chap. 2). Observing such a development and the gathering of anti-Lee forces in the Thirteenth Party Congress, Lee decided in November 1988, one month before Hau's term came to an end, to reappoint Hau for another term as chief of the general staff. Although this decision generated wide criticism, President Lee realized the necessity to establish a united front against imminent challenges within his own party.

Sitting next to an aspiring military strongman had put the president in an uneasy position. The relationship between Lee and Hau further deteriorated when Lee visited Singapore in March 1989 as "president from Taiwan" and the finance minister, Shirley Kuo, led a delegation to the Chinese mainland to attend the Asian Development Bank meeting in May. In order to assert his authority, the civilian president needed to disconnect General Hau's close ties with the military establishment. This, however, could only be achieved with very shrewd strategies. Several events that occurred in 1989 gave the president opportunities to remove Hau from his long-held position as chief of the general staff.

In July 1982, mainly in response to the U.S. reluctance to sell FX aircraft to Taiwan, Taipei decided to build its own advanced fighter planes, later known as the Indigenous Defense Fighter (IDF). As chief of the general staff, Hau had been deeply involved in developing the plane and proudly claimed it as one of his greatest achievements. In October 1989, however, Lee, together with many civilian and military officials as well as domestic and foreign observers, witnessed the failure of the IDF's test flight in Taichung—an incident that created much criticism of Hau. Nevertheless, despite the incident, Lee decided to proceed with production of the IDFs and use the completion of the IDF program as a legitimate excuse to displace Hau. Moreover, in the same month, Lee, for the first time without the company of the GSH officers, convened high-ranking officers from the three services stationed in the southern part of Taiwan to clarify his political orientation.

Lee's obvious attempt to get rid of Hau faced direct opposition from the general himself. Lacking a legitimate reason to continue in office, Hau began to manipulate high-ranking military posts in his favor before he left—demonstrating once again his recalcitrance and strength. In the end, Hau was nominated defense minister in November 1989. More important, the military under Hau's leadership mobilized resources to support certain candidates in the December legislative elections. The result was quite satisfactory for the military in general and for Hau in particular: among the fourteen candidates backed by the military, eleven were elected. The KMT as a whole, by contrast, suffered an unprecedented electoral defeat. On December 5, 1989, Hau assumed the post of defense minister.

Events at the special plenary session of the KMT Central Committee held in February 1990 hastened Lee's determination to curb Hau's influence in the military. The primary purpose of the meeting was to nominate the KMT's presidential candidate. Those who supported or opposed Lee's nomination were divided along the lines of the nominating procedures. Pro-Lee groups favored the method of "standing up"; the anti-Lee camp preferred the method of "casting votes." Although the "standing-up" faction eventually defeated the "vote-casting" faction, the military's reservations about Lee's leadership were becoming clear. Among the 21 central commissioners representing the military, 12 seconded the method of vote casting, 7 abstained, and only 2 supported the procedure preferred by Lee. Backed by reformers in the party, however, Lee's will eventually prevailed. He was nominated as the KMT's presidential candidate and was elected to the eighth presidency (after finishing Chiang's term of 1983–1990) one month later. From then on, Lee's legitimacy was boosted, and he gained greater social support for his political agenda.

With his Taiwanese ethnic background, Lee had a better chance to win the sympathy of the general public, who had great antipathy or even hostility toward the mainlander KMT regime. In April 1990, for the first time ever, Lee invited Huang Hsin-chieh, chairman of the opposition DPP, to the presidential office to discuss national affairs. The meeting was a symbolic but nevertheless important move, because Lee began to garner support from the opposition. With the cooperation of forces outside the regime, this newly elected president gained additional resources in removing obstacles within the party and the government—a significant aspect of Lee's reform initiatives.

In May, President Lee's decision to nominate Hau as the next premier of the Executive Yuan was a great shock to the public. Scholars, students, and opposition leaders took to the street, with banners declaring "Oppose Military Intervention in Politics." Moreover, the overwhelming majority of newspaper editorials and articles opposed Hau's nomination. Despite public pressure, the Legislative Yuan eventually approved Hau's premiership—revealing how much support the president could mobilize when needed. As premier, Hau was now obliged to act center stage rather than behind the scenes, and he was scrutinized intensely by the general public. More important, putting Hau in this position made him responsible and accountable to the Legislative Yuan, where the opposition was taking shape. Apparently Lee felt it was better to have Hau scrutinized as premier rather than have him shelter behind the shield of national security as chief of general staff or defense minister.

To take advantage of the momentum, in June Lee convened a National Affairs Conference outside the regular administrative system. More than a hundred representatives from Taiwan and abroad participated. One of the major goals of this conference was constitutional and political reform of the country. Constitutional reform has been an important aspect of Taiwan's democratization because it involves sensitive issues such as sovereignty, ethnicity, forms of government, representation of the people, and legitimacy of the regime. Since February 1991, constitutional reform in Taiwan has gone through five phases, and each phase has accomplished certain ends. In general, the trend has been toward greater accountability of the government and better mechanisms for regulating civil-military relations. More important, political democratization and social liberalization have produced a vibrant civil society that has been the driving force for political reform in general and democratic civil-military relations in particular. Against this backdrop, it was time for Lee to eliminate Hau's residual influence in the military.

At the end of 1990, Lee's decision to terminate the Period of National Mobilization for Suppression of the Communist Rebellion in May 1991 indicated the relaxation of tensions in the Taiwan Strait and therefore the necessity to redefine the military's roles and missions in society. The outbreak of the Persian Gulf War in 1991 provided great opportunities for Lee to exercise his power as supreme commander of the ROC armed forces. He made use of this. opportunity by examining troops and giving orders and developing closer ties with military leaders. Lee also kept himself closely informed about military affairs, which enabled him to initiate defense reform.

Further tension between Lee and Hau was generated by the premier's attempt to regain his influence in military affairs. In July 1991, DPP legislator Yeh Chu-lan made an urgent interpellation, criticizing Hau for holding secret meetings with high-ranking military leaders, which obviously intruded upon the power of the president. This news caused great concern among the opposition and sparked a good deal of public criticism. In response, when receiving eight recently promoted high-ranking military officers on August 1, 1991, Lee urged them to "look to the country, not to individuals"—a remark that provoked a lot of public discussion about the potential conflict between the military strongman and the rising political strongman.

Another opportunity for Lee arrived when the chief of the general staff, Chen Miao-lin, decided to retire after his term expired in November. Against the wishes of Hau, who favored Yeh Chang-tung, Lee decided to appoint Admiral Liu Ho-chien—a long-standing opponent of Hau's "Big Army" doctrine of concentrating resources on land forces. This arrangement served two purposes. On the one hand, it reflected Lee's emerging strategy of emphasizing air and naval forces. Whether a strong army or a dominant navy and air force would be more effective in ensuring national security had long been a matter of hot debate in Taiwan. Hau's eight-year service as chief of general staff and his tenure as defense minister had resulted in the triumph of the "Big Army" doctrine and, moreover, had led to a significant distortion in the allocation of defense resources, both human and material. This defense doctrine, however, contradicted Lee's strategic thinking, which stressed the deterrent power of air and naval forces. Liu's appointment revealed Lee's endeavor to redress the imbalance in the country's security strategy and defense resources.

On the other hand, naming Liu as the new chief of general staff also had the virtue of helping Lee establish close ties with military leaders loyal to him. The appointment also helped to correct the long-term power imbalance among different services in the armed forces. In the aftermath of Liu's appointment as the new chief of general staff and as a consequence of Lee's sweeping promotion of high-ranking military officers, the president deftly removed Hau's influence and consolidated his own power in the military (Chang 1992: 83–84). In late 1992, Paris's decision to sell 60 Mirage 2000-5 fighter planes and Washington's announcement that it would sell 150 F-16A/B fighter planes to Taiwan further boosted Lee's leadership as supreme commander of the armed forces.

Finally, the KMT's losses in the legislative elections of December 1992 gave Lee an opportunity to oust Hau from his final political post. With its strong showing in the elections, the opposition party called for Hau's resignation. At first, the presidential office neither affirmed nor dismissed the possibility of Hau's leaving the premiership. But as the public's demand for Hau's removal continued to grow, events began to turn against him. On January 30, 1993, invited to report at the closing session of the National Assembly, Hau was humiliated by DPP assemblymen carrying banners urging his resignation. Especially worth noting was the attitude of KMT assemblymen belonging to the mainstream faction (that is, Lee's supporters). When Hau was verbally attacked by the DPP, the KMT mainstream faction either stood idly by or even echoed the DPP's demands. In response, Hau raised his hands and shouted back emotionally and angrily, "Long live the ROC!" and "Smash Taiwan independence!" That afternoon Hau announced his resignation. In February he finally stepped down.

The rise and fall of Hau revealed an important lesson in civil-military relations in Taiwan. Lee's exploitation of the internal and external political and social changes, his manipulation of competing groups inside and outside the military establishment, and his cooperation with reform forces inside and outside the ruling party and government all contributed to the relatively smooth transformation of civil-military relations in Taiwan. It has been a delicate process of bargaining. The most distinctive feature of Taiwan's transition toward healthier civil-military relations is its smooth development at little social, economic, or political cost—again demonstrating the importance of civilian leaders' strategies in gaining the support of reform forces and deflating the possible opposition of conservative groups. Future trends in civil-military relations will continue to depend on such initiatives.

The slow but visible progress in greater civilian oversight of the military has manifested itself as well in the matter of arms procurement. Just as the ROC's armed forces are in a period of transition, so too is the arms procurement process.[8] Over the years, defense policy in general and arms procurement in particular have long been the private preserve of insiders, namely, the military establishment. The lion's share of the defense budget—which itself had accounted for approximately 25 percent of annual government expenditures (although the proportion has recently declined to around 15 percent)—goes to arms procurement and defense-related construction projects. Before the 1990s, however, there had been no tradition whatsoever of open debate about defense spending and military procurement. As a result of democratization and liberalization in the late 1980s, the public demand for more accountability has grown. Today, the public demands not only more rationalized defense spending, but also more cost-efficient and scandal-free arms procurement. In response to the increasing public awareness, as well as the growing public anger produced by a series of procurement scandals, the military establishment was forced to reform itself. Although the incremental transparency of defense policies and a greater supervisory role by the Legislative Yuan have become norms well accepted by both the civilian and military sectors, the deficiencies in the present institutional framework, the civilian sector's inability to supervise, and the military's resistance to change have created difficulties in normalizing civil-military relations with regard to arms procurement.

During the authoritarian period, the nation's decision-making process in defense procurement had long been viewed as a black box. The party-state mechanism dominated every aspect of policymaking. Without full elections of both the executive and legislative branches of government, the public had no means of holding the military accountable for its doings. Before the lifting of martial law and the beginning of political reforms, the Legislative Yuan was nothing but a rubber stamp. It was not until democratization began in the late 1980s that the nation's arms acquisition policy became a target of public criticism. Still, the process toward greater civilian supervision of defense procurement has been very slow and sometimes frustrating. The public's call for a more transparent arms procurement policy has not generated a proactive response from the military. Only in response to strong pressure and relentless criticism of its arms-related wrongdoings did the military begin to take incremental (and mostly ineffective) reform measures.

The dual system of government control over the military, as we have seen, has caused problems for normal civil-military relations. Although Taiwan's defense minister, as head of the military administration system, was supposedly in charge of all defense policymaking, it is the chief of general staff, as head of the military command system, who made the final decision on arms procurement. The agencies under the GSH function as the planning and execution arms of weapons acquisition. They survey the needs of the armed forces, postulate the weapons demanded by certain security considerations, evaluate alternatives, inform legislators, and implement the project once it is ratified. This system has created problems for civilian defense ministers trying to supervise the process of arms procurement executed by the military. For instance, it was reported that the final decision to purchase the French-made Mirage 2000-5 was made not by the defense minister but by the chief of general staff. During a hearing held by the Defense Committee of the Legislative Yuan, former defense minister Sun Chen admitted that he had no control over arms procurement decisions. It was an unpleasant fact, he said, that very few arms procurement projects actually came to his office.

The conflict between the administration and command systems of the military has made proper civilian supervision of defense acquisition almost impossible. The MND's lack of oversight power over the GSH has put defense ministers, especially civilians, in a very tough position. At a hearing held in the Legislative Yuan on March 20, 1998, former defense minister Chen Lu-an admitted that corruption in the military could be prevented by an efficient supervisory system.[9] Such statements reveal the institutional weakness in holding the military accountable for its defense decisions. A major goal of the recently passed National Defense Law is to improve the MND's capacity to oversee the process by unifying the two systems. Over the next few years, as the MND consolidates its authority over the command system, the impact of this change will become clear.

If the MND faces difficulties in supervising the military's arms procurement process, matters are even worse in the legislative branch. Indeed, effective checks and balances appear to be absent in the current institutional framework. The Legislative Yuan does not have the capability to oversee arms procurement, although it has the legal power to approve the budget sent by the MND. The Legislative Yuan gets its information from reports provided by the MND and the Audit Ministry—reports that never reveal the details of arms acquisition. Therefore, members of the Legislative Yuan find it next to impossible to supervise acquisition programs.

And although the Audit Ministry of the Control Yuan is responsible for auditing the budget, it too is incapable of supervising arms acquisition activities. The Audit Ministry has the authority to inspect and audit the procurement of arms and other military equipment, but it has failed to do so—largely because the MND often decides not to submit procurement projects to the ministry for inspection, on the grounds that the information is classified. Under Article 29 of the Statute for Inspection Procedures Governing Construction Works, Procurement of Products, and Disposal of Properties by Government Agencies, whenever the considerations of "highly confidential," "emergency," or "ensuring the quality of military equipment" are involved in the procurement process, military units are allowed to bypass certain requirements and explain the reasons for the purchase later. The MND has been using its own interpretation of the word "later" to keep arms procurement secret for a certain period of time before the classified information is released and the purchase can be checked by the audit agencies. As a consequence, civilian supervision over the military budget has failed.

Moreover, it is clear that the Audit Ministry does not have enough trained people to audit defense spending. The ministry's Second Department is responsible for auditing the defense budget, but it lacks the staff to evaluate the more than 400,000 projects per year. It takes great expertise to audit these projects, and the ministry cannot send officers to each of the 400,000 projects to conduct careful auditing. As a consequence, most of the supervising work of the Legislative Yuan and auditing work of the Control Yuan ends up as mere paperwork. Clearly, then, both internal and external checks and balances are ineffective in holding the military responsible.

In short, there are serious problems with regard to the institutional framework of Taiwan's arms procurement process. The first pitfall is the predominance of executive power over legislative checks and balances—characterized by the Legislative Yuan's inability to oversee arms procurement decisions and budgets. Moreover, there is an imbalance in the information received by the executive and legislative branches—and the latter is in a very disadvantageous position. The major difficulty in holding arms procurement officials accountable to the public is the lack of a general statutory right of access to official records and information. The executive branch (specifically the MND) enjoys discretionary authority in deciding which information should be classified and which can be disclosed. Without sufficient knowledge and institutional power, therefore, citizens and indeed legislators simply have to accept the decisions made by the military. Moreover, the independence of military courts from the civilian judicial system exonerates the military from proper legal accountability. All these factors contribute to the opaqueness of Taiwan's arms procurement decisions and undermine civilian supremacy over the military.

But the most serious problem in the supervision of arms procurement is that those who supervise and those being supervised are mostly from the same military establishment. Almost all of them are military officers who may have worked together at one time or another or at least have indirect connections. Within this closed community there are tacit or even explicit old boy networks, and the traditions of mutual cover-up and back-scratching seem to prevail. To be sure, without civilian scrutiny of the military's procurement activities, the monitoring mechanisms initiated by the defense establishment itself are not very likely to achieve significant results. Indeed, defense procurement activities conducted under this system were replete with examples of improper decisions, official misconduct, scandals, overspending, and cover-ups. Observers have complained that while legislators have trouble gaining access to arms procurement information, arms dealers are often able to acquire the relevant classified documents.

The lack of civilian supervision has opened the door to corruption. Many irregularities have been exposed in Taiwan's arms procurement system. In some cases, retired senior officers have translated their experience and expertise into new careers in key positions in defense industries. The old boy network extends not only to defense industries but also to private firms representing arms manufacturers in Taiwan and abroad. High-ranking officers' relatives who worked for foreign defense contractors also engaged in activities helping their firms obtain arms deals. In April 1994, the head of Taiwan's navy, Admiral Chuang Ming-yao, was forced to step down because of irregularities in the navy's arms procurement process. Eight air force generals were impeached in June 1994 by the Control Yuan for negligence in connection with the acquisition of S-2T antisubmarine helicopters. The most notorious case happened in December 1993, when Captain Yin Ching-feng, who was in charge of the navy's then newly established arms procurement office, was murdered. It was speculated that Yin was killed because he was about to expose a pattern of bribery among retired and active-duty officers and arms dealers.

The lifting of martial law and the liberalization of the press in the late 1980s have made the wide exposure of such scandals possible. Not only has the Taiwanese public been outraged by the military's misconduct and corruption in the process of arms procurement, but many other cases are under investigation, and each may involve shocking scandals. As a result, even then premier Vincent Siew was forced to admit to serious flaws in the country's arms procurement procedure. Against the background of democratization and liberalization, the public has gradually pressed for more transparency and accountability of the military.

As democracy began to take root in Taiwan, opposition parties launched fierce attacks on the military for arms procurement scandals and demanded more openness in the management of defense programs. In 1993, for instance, opposition lawmakers questioned the wisdom of purchasing medium-sized rather than light tanks for Taiwan's ground defense (Opall 1994: 1; Chen 1995: 38). But few took the scandals seriously before Yin's murder in 1993. Under pressure from the public and the Legislative Yuan, the MND began studying ways to improve the arms acquisition process and eventually presented its report, "Review and Improvements in Armed Forces Arms Procurement," to the Legislative Yuan in October 1994. Defense Minister Chiang Chung-ling submitted an updated report to the Legislative Yuan in December 1996.

Moreover, eight study groups were organized in January 1995 to study the whole issue of arms purchasing, including personnel, education, purchasing, planning, political warfare, the comptroller, the judge advocate, and clerical work. In July 1995, a variety of purchasing units were integrated into the newly established Procurement Bureau of the MND. In November 1995, the MND amended the regulations known as the "Operating Procedure and Regulations on Arms Acquisition and Major Construction." The MND also published a handbook entitled *Questions and Answers on How to Participate in the Purchasing of Military Hardware* to guide those wishing to do business with the military. Under sharp criticism and strong public pressure, therefore, the military began to reform itself.

Although it was generally agreed that the ROC's military had indeed taken serious steps to improve accountability and transparency in the arms acquisition process, a further series of procurement scandals in early 1998 indicated the inadequacy of these reform measures. The core of the problem lies in the absence of genuine civilian participation in the process. In fact, the military has revealed a reluctant or even hostile attitude toward the public's desire for civilian oversight of defense issues. Although the MND has introduced some supervisory mechanisms in the aftermath of arms procurement scandals, the institutional rearrangement has taken place mainly within the present military establishment, and the absence of outside scrutiny is still apparent: the mechanisms of internal audit and program review, for example, are still shrouded in secrecy. Again, without independent oversight from the outside, the military's supervisory mechanisms and improvement measures are not likely to achieve significant results.

In view of the public's anger and frustration toward the arms scandals disclosed in early 1998, the government had to implement further reforms. On March 20, 1998, Premier Siew instructed the country's top prosecutor to form a task force to investigate the alleged scandals—

the first time a top civilian prosecutor had led an investigation into a scandal concerning the military. Then Defense Minister Chiang pledged his full support to civilian investigators probing into the alleged scandals.

With the National Defense Law, responsibility for procurement has now been shifted clearly from the GSH to the MND. Further, other measures have been taken to hold military officers financially accountable just like civilian officials. Military personnel responsible for procurement or construction projects are now strictly required to report their assets regularly and avoid conflicts of interest. In the summer of 2000, a fresh investigation into the still unresolved Yin Ching-feng case opened, led by a high-level task force. Given President Chen's previous strong stance on the case as a legislator, some observers were optimistic of a breakthrough. However, the continuing military resistance to the investigation remained in evidence.

PATTERNS AND FUTURE TRAJECTORIES

If democratic transition is not a one-way street, neither is the transformation of civil-military relations. The process of political reform has already opened up all kinds of possibilities. Although Taiwan has certainly crossed an important threshold of democratic transition, the question remains whether the incipient democratic institutions will grow and endure. Changes outside or inside the island may create sudden crises that could reverse the course of civil-military relations. Scholars have cited numerous factors contributing to the breakdown of democracy: economic crisis, leaders' foibles, political polarization, ethnic conflict, external threat, legitimacy crisis, and more. Unfortunately, none of these factors is totally absent in Taiwan today.

We have seen how skillfully the civilian leadership took advantage of domestic and external crises and mobilized power both inside and outside the regime to reshuffle the military leadership and expand civilian oversight of the arms procurement process. In general, since 1990, Taiwan has experienced greater state control of the military and has seen the norms of military professionalism and civilian control increasingly accepted in society. It should be noted, however, that the military's gradual yielding to the civilian leadership has been taking place under the same ruling party—namely the KMT—and under the same leadership—namely President Lee.

On the face of it, the election and inauguration of President Chen has shown that the anxieties of those who thought that the military would somehow intervene were overblown and that the issue of political neutrality was not as grave as had been believed. It is true that no immediate crisis occurred, but several important qualifications are necessary to this rosy assessment. First, although CGS Tang Yao-ming made a very strong statement on election night, before the results were announced, that the military would support the victor, the fact that such a reassurance was considered necessary is itself an indicator of fragility. Second, the post-election period saw a steady stream of rumors about high-ranking officers' unwillingness to serve their new commander in chief; just before the inauguration, a small number resigned. Third, not only could Chen not appoint a civilian as defense minister, but he selected Tang Fei as premier. This eerie (and to many DPP supporters, very irksome) replay of President Lee's appointment of Hau Pei-tsun was obviously felt to be necessary to ensure a smooth transition. Finally, and most importantly, it was Chen himself who made a strong effort to win over the military, not only by taking pains to personally visit many military elders, but significantly by shifting his political rhetoric. In other words, although the KMT no longer controls the presidency, the taboo on certain political ideologies has not actually been clearly broken. Time will tell if Chen is able, through his power of appointment and promotion, especially given the restructuring called for by the National Defense Law, to skillfully cultivate loyalty as Lee was able to do; however, it is also possible that many in the military hope to slow down any reforms and try to wait out Chen's term.

The military's "conditional loyalty" to certain ideological beliefs continues to be a serious challenge to the consolidation of Taiwan's democracy. Whether the armed forces will stand on the sidelines or take part in any political infighting for the definition of Taiwan's political status will continue to be the key test of Taiwan's civilian supremacy. The imperative, therefore, is to redefine the role and mission of Taiwan's military establishment. Taiwan needs to redouble its efforts toward the military's professionalism and depoliticization—inculcated through the service academies and military schools and formalized in military doctrine. But given that the military's mission and role are determined in large part by the threat environment that the nation faces, cross-strait relations will continue to shape the dynamics of civil-military relations in Taiwan. As long as there is no cross-strait crisis, and Chen makes no radical policy shifts, civil-military relations should continue to make incremental progress.

The dualistic system of separating military administration from military command, for example, has made it very difficult for civilians to hold the military responsible and accountable. The new National Defense Law should solve this problem, if it is implemented properly. The fact that many top-ranking officials in the MND were directly involved in drafting the law raises hopes that this multiyear project will proceed smoothly.

Nevertheless, civilian supremacy depends not only on the actions but also the expertise of the civilian leadership in Taiwan. If civilian leaders are to win the military's acceptance of their control and supervision, they must have a substantial knowledge of defense policy and the military's needs. Only then can civilian authorities exercise effective oversight of the military's decisions and activities. The failed attempts to civilianize the defense minister in Taiwan have revealed the lack of civilian expertise in defense matters as a key problem in normalizing civil-military relations. There is a need for what Alfred Stepan (1973) calls "civilian empowerment," whereby civilians develop the competence to manage and monitor military affairs effectively and responsibly. In the case of Taiwan, building up sufficient civilian expertise to staff the defense ministry and the related committees of the Legislative Yuan is a task of great urgency. To assert civilian control of the military, in short, Taiwan must reform the institutional mechanism, redefine the military's mission and role, and improve civilian expertise on defense issues.

PART IV

Transition to Democratic Civilian Control

CHAPTER 6

The Philippines:
Not So Military, Not So Civil

Eva-Lotta E. Hedman

AFTER FERDINAND E. MARCOS WAS FORCED FROM POWER IN FEBRUARY 1986, repeated military attempts to seize the state and widespread militarization of society marked the subsequent transitional regime of Corazon C. Aquino. Between July 1986 and December 1989, Marcos loyalists and "reformist officers" within the Armed Forces of the Philippines (AFP) supported military adventurism that ranged from the 37-hour occupation of the Manila Hotel to the strafing and bombing of Malacañang Presidential Palace (Davide et al. 1990[1]). Meanwhile, with the breakdown of peace talks and cease-fires with the Communist Party of the Philippines (CPP) and its New People's Army (NPA), as well as the Moro National Liberation Front (MNLF), Aquino declared "total war" in February 1987 and, with critical support from the AFP and the U.S. government (Bello 1987; Porter 1987), ushered in a new era of counterinsurgency campaigns to be characterized, according to the president, less by social and economic reform than by police and military action.[2] As the Aquino government moved to endorse "civilian volunteer organizations" during this time, moreover, the mobilization of anticommunist vigilantes and paramilitary groups further contributed to the widespread militarization of Philippine politics and society in the late 1980s (Amnesty International 1988; Lawyers Committee for Human Rights 1988).

A decade later, the primacy of civilian political competition, whether through regular elections or the "People Power" interruption to Joseph Estrada's presidency in January 2001, has severely circumscribed the influence of the military in Philippine politics and society. Since 1990 there has been no further sign of yet another "season of coups" (Nemenzo 1987). Similarly, the "day of the vigilante" has come to a close (Van der Kroef 1988). Although government forces still encounter pockets or factions of communist revolutionaries and Muslim sep-

165

aratists in armed struggle, a widespread demobilization of military troops and paramilitary groups across the country has replaced the intense militarization of the 1980s.

In the wake of the acute challenges posed to state and society by *kudeta* and militias in the late 1980s, it comes as no surprise that concerns about civil-military relations have, once again, tended to fade into the background of Philippine politics and studies alike. To date, the demobilization of putschist officers and state-sponsored vigilantes has yet to attract the intense scrutiny prompted by their prior activation. (See, however, Rutten 1992.) As a result, analysts have largely remained focused on the significance of martial law and its corrupting influences—notably the militarization of government bureaucracies and the politicization of military organizations—upon the difficult (re)democratization of state and society after Marcos (Davide et al. 1990; Hernandez 1985, 1987; Hilsdon 1995; May 1992; McCoy 1988). Conversely, the reintroduction of democratic institutions and procedures in accordance with new constitutional provisions strengthening civilian authority under Aquino has been credited with the declining fortunes of military adventurism, thus reversing the perverse logic set in motion during martial law (Hernandez 1997).

With the advantage of hindsight, this chapter situates the recent rise and fall in military and paramilitary mobilization in broader historical perspective. To that end, it reexamines the relationship of soldier, state, and society at the inauguration of the Philippine republic in 1946. Beyond the consequences of martial law emphasized in the literature, I want to underscore the significance of colonial legacies and postcolonial conditions in shaping relations between the civilian and military branches of governance in the Philippines. Informed by this historically grounded perspective, the chapter offers a critical corrective against easy reification of "civil-military" relations in the Philippines where, notably, election as well as counterinsurgency campaigns have blurred such distinctions in the past.

I wish to reexamine both the "military" and the "civil" aspects of such relations. On the one hand, the chapter underlines the extent to which the AFP, when compared to its Burmese, Indonesian, or Thai counterparts, has remained "not so military" on at least three counts. First of all, according to bilateral treaties between Manila and Washington, the United States has retained primary responsibility for external defense well into the postcolonial era—thus leaving the AFP concerned largely with internal policing. Second, ever since the formation of coercive state apparatuses during the colonial period, Philippine Constabulary (PC) police forces have dominated the rest of the armed forces—thus making law enforcement the bread and butter of the AFP. Third, due to the far-reaching prerogatives of elected officials over military appointments and resources, the PC/AFP has enjoyed little institutional autonomy vis-à-vis Filipino politicians.

On the other hand, the chapter also underscores the significance of "not so civil" forms of political domination on the part of civilian politicians in the Philippines. As documented in numerous studies, the political careers of provincial warlords and urban bosses have depended in no small part on their manifest capacity for violence and coercion. Similarly beyond the pale of civility, moreover, the mobilization of paramilitary formations such as the Civilian Home Defense Forces under Marcos and the so-called vigilante groups under Aquino has enjoyed critical support from civilian government officials. While gaining the presidency in the national elections of 1965 and then again in 1969, Marcos established himself as the country's longest-reigning president through his unprecedented political manipulation of the agents of coercive state apparatuses.

In taking seriously such "not so military, not so civil" dimensions, the chapter draws inspiration from the literature on the Philippine military, including seminal works on the extent of civilian control over the military (Hernandez 1979) and subsequent explorations of "the normalization" of such relations in the post-Marcos period (Hernandez 1997). In particular, I wish to recover important insights about the significance of politics and history for shaping—rather than "distorting," as argued by more formalistic perspectives on civil-military relations—the roles and relations of the AFP. Instead of focusing on the issues of professionalization versus politicization examined in studies on military intervention in and withdrawal from politics in the Philippines, however, I highlight the peculiar configuration of coercive state apparatuses that emerged under American colonial and early postcolonial auspices.

In this vein, the following pages reveal the significance of enduring colonial legacies and neocolonial linkages in shaping the trajectory of civil-military relations—most notably the pattern of militarization in the 1970s and 1980s and then the demilitarization in the 1990s. The success of Ferdinand E. Marcos in consolidating his martial law regime in the 1970s, for example, is shown to reflect the culmination of trends with domestic and international antecedents in civilian politics that strengthened the hand of the executive branch over the legislature (notably in the realm of law enforcement and military affairs). The martial law regime, moreover, is characterized not so much by the ascendancy of the military as an institution as by a more narrowly presidential pattern of civilian control over the AFP. Against this backdrop, the rise of the armed forces reform movement, the failed coup that precipitated the fall of Marcos in 1986, and the repeated putschist attempts on Aquino's transitional regime (1986–1992) are shown to be the outcomes less of military adventurism than the protracted uncertainty surrounding the mechanisms of (civilian) presidential succession during this period. In this context, the fading of active military officers from political center stage in the 1990s and their reemergence in minor supporting roles in the "People Power" drama of early 2001 confirms the primacy of civilian political competition—both electoral and, occasionally, extraelectoral—for shaping the nature, extent, and direction of military involvement in Philippine politics. As in the late 1940s and early 1950s, the colonial legacies of civilian supremacy and the neocolonial context of anticommunist mobilization combined in powerful ways to shape the broad parameters of civil-military relations before, during, and after martial law.[3]

LEGACIES OF EMPIRE

Viewed in comparative regional perspective, the Philippines stands alone in its experience of both colonial rule (1901–1946) and then postcolonial "special relations" (1946–1992) under the auspices of the United States, the twentieth century's dominant military, economic, and political world power. Due to this double whammy, American neocolonialism left peculiar and enduring imprints on the forces of law and order in Philippine politics and society. In particular, four neocolonial legacies have had lasting consequences in the organization and function of the state's coercive apparatuses: subordination to elected officials; formation of the postcolonial armed forces; provision for internal versus external defense; and mobilization of anticommunist cold warriors.

Subordination to Elected Officials

Within a decade of the first nationalist revolution in Asia ending Spanish colonial rule and the savage Philippine-American war reimposing foreign control, the new imperial regime in the archipelago had already installed its first elected (by restricted franchise) municipal mayors (1901), provincial governors (1902), and national assembly representatives (1907) in the islands (Paredes 1989). These elected local officials in turn were granted extensive powers over police and constabulary forces at both municipal and provincial levels of governance under Philippine colonial democracy (Baja 1933; Wolters 1989). Congressmen, moreover, enjoyed significant formal (through the Commission of Appointments) as well as informal (by lobbying the president) influence over the appointments and rotation of constabulary officers (Campos 1983). Finally, at the national level, the Nacionalista senate president (1917–1935) and Philippine commonwealth president (1935–1941) Manuel Quezon also exercised considerable, at times decisive, discretion over the PC as part and parcel of the noted accumulation of executive powers through his skillful manipulation of government bureaucracy and constitution as well as his repeated intervention in provincial politics (McCoy 1989; Trota 1992; Golay 1998: 357). As noted by other scholars, this pattern reflected—and reproduced—a peculiarly American experience of state formation distinguished by the subordination of a weakly insulated bureaucracy (including the police) to elected local and national politicians (Anderson 1988; Sidel 1995).

In the absence of a strong colonial bureaucracy, the Philippines thus developed a "highly decentralized, politicized, and privatized administration of law enforcement" where, notably, police and constabulary appointments, promotions, renumerations, and reassignments rested with municipal and provincial politicians (Sidel 1995: 62). Due to the PC's centrality to the AFP from the latter's formation in 1936, such dynamics have long characterized civil-military relations as a whole. In terms of relative numerical strength, for example, PC forces "constituted the bulk of the army's troops in 1936" and, on the eve of martial law, remained the single largest service within the AFP, counting 23,500 regulars compared to the army's 17,600.[4] Although the Philippine Army saw a dramatic absolute increase in troops during martial law, the majority of which were deployed in Mindanao, the PC retained a relatively central role as suggested by the successive appointments of PC careerists Romulo Espino, Fabian C. Ver, and Fidel V. Ramos as AFP chiefs of staff under Marcos.[5]

As a result, Philippine democracy remained inhospitable to the emergence of a military institution beyond the purview of elected officials. By the same token, local politicians' vast powers over police and constabulary forces allowed them to deploy agents of coercive state apparatuses in support of private election campaigns and criminal rackets well beyond the pale of civil society or civilian politics as commonly conceived. The peculiar colonial-era mechanisms that subordinated state coercive apparatuses to elected (if not necessarily civil) officials survived the Pacific War and independence in such a way as to secure marked continuity with postcolonial relations of power in Philippine politics and society, especially when considered in comparative regional perspective. In terms of mayoral control over the municipal police, for example, one contemporary participant-observer noted that during the American period "the local police has been more or less a toy in the hands of shrewd local politicians and administrative bosses on whom the appointment to the force depend" (Baja 1933: 281). As for constabulary appointments, moreover, the same report argued that since 1917, when the first Filipino, Brig. Gen. Rafael Crame, assumed the post of insular constabulary chief, "scores of transfers have been ordered for no other laudable reason than pleasing the political bosses of the party in power" (Baja 1933: 281).[6] In the postcolonial period, such practices remained the norm as municipal mayors retained the power to appoint and remove municipal chiefs of police and members of police forces; provincial governors enjoyed similar discretion over constabu-lary assignments.[7] "Through its 90 years of law enforcement," another insider noted in the early 1990s, "the PC had to confront the ugly specter of political meddling" (Gutang 1991: 80). With the notable exception of martial law, the Commission of Appointments retained control over the promotion of all officers to the rank of colonel and above in the AFP.[8] Through more informal channels, congressmen exerted considerable influence over assignments and rota-tions—as well as opportunities for "special benefits" associated with smuggling, illegal gam-bling, and other lucrative activities (Kessler 1988: 215). These various forms of political lever-age by elected civilian officials not only undermined the doctrines of military professionalism and national interest studied (and no doubt celebrated) at military academies at home and abroad but, perhaps more important, weakened the institutional autonomy of coercive state apparatuses in the Philippines (however, see McCoy 1995, 1999).

Formation of the Postcolonial Armed Forces

The crucial bridge between prewar forces and wartime mobilization in the archipelago—the U.S. Armed Forces in the Far East (USAFFE)—also served as a launching pad for the new AFP after liberation (Hedman 1997). Officially declared "an umbrella military command" for U.S. and Philippine Army units in July 1941, USAFFE emerged as a mobilizational effort charac-terized by hurried mass promotions of regular and reserve officers alike; mass inductions of reserve forces into USAFFE; and, at best, crash-course training in military camps (Trota 1992: 201–10). Although, officially, U.S.-Philippine resistance ended shortly after the American sur-render in Bataan in April 1942, in reality such efforts continued in a decentralized form as guer-rilla groups proliferated locally and, to various degrees and extents, reestablished ties with the allied forces in the Pacific—especially toward the end of the Japanese occupation (Mojica 1965; Willoughby 1972). Thus, if the Pacific War constituted an external threat that forced greater military spending, expansion, and planning in the Philippines, USAFFE provided the key insti-tutional mechanism for effectuating the mobilization of resources, deployment of troops, and coordination of command.

Viewed in comparative regional perspective, the mobilization of USAFFE guerrillas under-scored two trajectories that have characterized soldiers and state alike in the postcolonial Philip-pines. First of all, the USAFFE phenomenon revealed the peculiar impact of Japanese occu-pation in the Philippines and its significance in shaping the soldiers and the state that emerged out of the rubble of the Pacific War. Notably, the Japanese Imperial Army made no effort to mobilize new social forces along the lines of the *Pembela Tanah Air* (Defenders of the Father-land)[9] in occupied Indonesia (Anderson 1972) or, for that matter, to replicate its policies in occu-pied Burma where, "through the midwifery of the Japanese, the Burma Independence Army (BIA)...was born" (Taylor 1985: 133). Instead, collaboration and resistance alike remained a matter of "politics by other means" in much of the occupied Philippines (McCoy 1985). That is, while resistance against the Japanese occupation was arguably more widespread in the Philip-pines than elsewhere in Southeast Asia (Wurfel 1988: 12), it also reflected enduring patterns of local factional struggles associated with electoral politics in the American period. With the anti-landlord Huk guerrillas in Central Luzon as the exception to prove the rule (Edgerton 1975; Kerkvliet 1977), the Japanese occupation of the Philippines neither fundamentally displaced what has been referred to in the context of the Western Visayas as "the paradigm of parochial factional struggles with local rivals" (McCoy 1985: 158) nor significantly encouraged a process observed elsewhere of "state-building through war-making" (Tilly 1985, 1992).

Against this backdrop and with vast USAFFE discretion over appointments to municipal and provincial government offices under Gen. Douglas MacArthur's liberation regime, the peculiar dynamics of guerrilla recognition—promising "back pay" and pensions in U.S. dollars—and political patronage helped to jump-start the political careers of many successful veteran claimants (among them Ramon Magsaysay and Ferdinand E. Marcos) in the early postwar elections. As guerrilla status and networks translated into electoral machines and campaigns in the young Philippine republic, so-called new men and old commonwealth politicos alike channeled their considerable energies into local factional politics rather than national—and nationalist—movements (Edgerton 1975).

Second, consistent with the pattern of conservative electoral rather than radical nationalist mobilization that linked prewar commonwealth to postwar Philippine politics, USAFFE emerged according to a process of neocolonial linkages instead of anticolonial struggles. Although hardly exempt from charges of imperialism, American rule in the Philippines since the turn of the century had proved fairly insulated from such mounting nationalist mobilization as the Sarekat Islam and the Partai Nasionalis Indonesia (PNI), the Thakins, and the Indochinese Communist Party against Dutch, British, and French colonialism, respectively. With independence provided for in the 1935 commonwealth constitution, which also introduced a small conscript army of regulars with a large reserve force, the Philippines thus presented a stark contrast to the wartime emergence of nationalist armies mobilized against colonial troops elsewhere in the region. With the landing of liberation forces in Leyte in October 1944, the Philippine Army was officially reconstituted as a section of USAFFE Headquarters before resuming its 1941 separate status and eventually gaining organizational autonomy from the U.S. Army within a week of the independent republic's inauguration—but, importantly, only after the first postwar elections (Hartendorp 1958: 347–48). Furthermore, if changing local conditions associated with factional politics intruded upon the nature and direction of armed resistance during the Japanese occupation, there was little ambiguity about USAFFE's significance in the postwar scramble for official guerrilla recognition to secure back pay and other benefits from the U.S. Veterans Administration (USVA)—the largest such American operation overseas (Hartendorp 1958: 169).

Internal versus External Defense

Under the rubric of the Military Bases Agreement of March 1947 and the Military Assistance Agreement signed a week later, the United States assumed de facto responsibility for securing the Philippine Republic against external threats or challenges. As a result, neither national interests of security nor the political dynamics of reconstruction favored a military buildup of army, navy, or air force after independence. Instead, internal security was the main concern in the young republic as reflected in the formal separation of the Philippine Constabulary from the Armed Forces of the Philippines in 1947 and the transfer of some 12,000 troops from the AFP to the PC the following year. Reconstituted from the wartime Military Police Command and placed under the Department of Interior, the constabulary also received some additional 8,000 troop transfers in 1948 to enable it "to carry out the restoration of peace and order more effectively" (Hartendorp 1958: 349). With the bulk of regular troops under constabulary command and the Joint U.S. Military Advisory Group (JUSMAG) taking an evident interest in internal as well as external security (Shalom 1986: 74–82), local politics and communist containment constituted lasting influences on the nature and direction of police and military forces in the Philippines after independence as demonstrated during election and counterinsurgency campaigns.

Mobilization of Anticommunist Cold Warriors

If the organization and function of state coercive apparatuses revealed enduring legacies of U.S. colonialism for civil-military relations after independence, the early and increasingly comprehensive anticommunist counterinsurgency campaigns mobilized under JUSMAG auspices in the young republic further shaped the AFP under conditions of Pax Americana. With the cold war enveloping Asia by the late 1940s, the virtual reign of terror that dominated the first "unrefereed" presidential elections in the Philippines (Anderson 1988: 15) and the mounting extraelectoral peasant and communist mobilization in Central Luzon threatened to undermine America's Showcase of Democracy at a time when its geostrategic significance was increasing in the region. Against this backdrop, a distinctly neocolonial dynamic developed as U.S.-backed counterinsurgency campaigns encouraged greater accumulation of powers and resources by the executive branch—with important consequences for the agents of state coercive apparatuses and their role in Philippine politics and society.

This dynamic can be discerned in the early 1950s with the United States supporting extensive counterinsurgency measures, economic development assistance programs, and pressures for reformist legislation as well as "free and fair elections" in the former colony. Meanwhile, the Philippine executive branch merged the constabulary with the army—thus removing the PC from the political discretion of provincial governors—and, moreover, suspended the writ of habeas corpus in what was widely decried as "the hallmark of totalitarian dictatorships" at the time (cited in Hartendorp 1958: 301). In 1950, as the Philippine Army began to extend its anti-Huk campaigns to include "civic activities," Secretary of Defense (and former USAFFE guerrilla turned congressman) Ramon Magsaysay, in close collaboration with JUSMAG officers (notably Lt. Col. Edward G. Lansdale), had assumed control over the anticommunist propaganda from the Civil Affairs Office (CAO) and the Huk resettlement programs under the Armed Forces Economic Development Corps (EDCOR).[10] With the specter of communism haunting Asia in the early 1950s, the CAO and EDCOR aimed at carrying "pacification activities from the map rooms and council tables to both field and town plaza, churches and class-rooms" (Crisol 1954: 223). In the 1951 senatorial and 1953 presidential elections, moreover, such "soft" counterinsurgency efforts received further impetus with the mobilization of the first National Movement for Free Elections (NAMFREL) in the Philippines by, notably, former USAFFE guerrillas with assistance from the armed forces as well as ROTC cadets (Coquia 1957; Valeriano and Bohannan 1962: 240). Although the Huks faded into the background in the early 1950s, the rise of former USAFFE guerrilla and recent defense secretary Magsaysay to the Philippine presidency signaled the successful culmination of a peculiarly neocolonial venture involving JUSMAG (especially Lt. Col. Lansdale, aka "General Landslide"), pro-American and anti-communist war veterans, as well as an allegedly reformist armed forces, in soft and hard counter-insurgency campaigns alike (Hedman 1999).

With the advantage of hindsight, three developments during this period in the 1950s appear to be a sneak preview of things to come. First of all, Quirino's expansion of executive powers in tandem with stepped-up counterinsurgency efforts directed against mounting radical mobilization (and sanctioned, at the very least, by the United States) anticipated similar dynamics behind the transformations of state and soldier under Marcos in the 1970s. Second, the evident show of U.S. support for reformist initiatives in the armed forces as well as in the electoral arena—where something of a Trojan horse emerged to challenge the incumbent president from within Magsaysay's Department of Defense—suggested familiar patterns when Juan Ponce Enrile and the so-called RAM boys (Reform the Armed Forces of the Philippines Movement), as well as the second incarnation of NAMFREL, captured the limelight in the mid-1980s. Third, the incorporation into Magsaysay's civilian government of certain reformist elements of military backgrounds and careers—before their (eventual) disappearance into the background of Philippine politics and society—traced a trajectory that seems to resonate with the post-Marcos period. When considered within the broad parameters set by colonial legacies of civilian rule and neocolonial conditions of anticommunist mobilization, these three phases of crisis and resolution illuminate powerful dynamics shaping relations between the civilian and military branches of government in the Philippines.

THE MAKING OF MARTIAL LAW

Although the usurpation of presidential powers under Quirino set an illuminating precedent of sorts in the late 1940s and early 1950s—the suspension of the elected mayors of Manila, Cebu, and Iloilo; the removal of PC forces from the political discretion of provincial governors; and the abolishment of the writ of habeas corpus—political and institutional developments during Marcos's first and second elected terms nonetheless signaled a qualitative departure in the nature and direction of executive *continuismo* by the late 1960s and early 1970s. Like Quirino before him, Marcos first assumed tenure in Malacañang during a period of mounting popular pressures for expanded political participation that, in contrast to the relatively successful containment of the Huk rebellion in the early 1950s, only seemed to escalate in the overall momentum of such threats from below by a new generation in the early 1970s. As in the Quirino era (when the "loss" of China and the Korean War loomed large in the Asian cold war), the Philippine government of the late 1960s enjoyed intensified support for internal security measures from its counterpart in Washington—which, in the context of broad shifts in U.S. foreign policy during this period (with the escalation of the Vietnam War and the declaration of the Nixon Doctrine), further exacerbated the expansion of presidential powers under Marcos. Yet compared to Quirino, who ultimately failed to transcend the provincial strongman politics of which he remained, in ambition as well as style perhaps, but a national-level broker, Marcos succeeded in transforming civil-military relations to a far greater degree than previously observed and with far more serious consequences for Philippine politics and society.

Political stability in the Philippines of the late 1960s faced new threats from below—threats associated with a decline in "the integrative capacity of political machines" (Nowak and Snyder 1974: 1151) and the increased cost of "particularistic rewards" (Scott 1969: 1144) and thus reflective of seemingly more persistent modernization dilemmas than the temporary dissolution of "prewar vertical ties" between landlord (patron) and tenant (client) prompted by the

Japanese occupation (Edgerton 1975; Kerkvliet 1977). By the time of Marcos's first presidential inauguration, the challenges to law and order following on the heels of fairly rapid socio-economic change already anticipated—and, in some quarters, justified—organizational innovation and role expansion in coercive state apparatuses. In this regard, the presence of a highly decentralized system of local policing and the absence of a nationally coordinated law enforcement structure appeared distinctly out of step with continued economic differentiation and internal migration as unprecedented numbers of people were leaving agricultural production and entering, especially, the national capital region during the course of the decade (Pernia et al. 1983: 58).[11] Against the increasing notoriety of organized crime and political violence during this period, two developments stand out as important institutional responses. First of all, the Police Act of 1966 provided for the establishment of a National Police Commission (Napolcom) charged with investigating local policing and then making national policy recommendations to the executive office (Campos 1983). Second, the following year saw the organization of the constabulary's Metropolitan Command (Metrocom) as a "centralized command with jurisdiction over all riot control and internal security operations" (Campos 1983: 214), which would serve as the launching pad for subsequent integration of police forces under Napolcom.[12] In February 1968, Metrocom was expanded further into the Metropolitan Area Command by executive order (Gutang 1991: 88).

Beyond questions of criminality, new threats to law and order extended into the realm of internal security during the late 1960s. In this regard, the resurgence of the Huks in Central Luzon, the founding of the new Communist Party of the Philippines and its New People's Army, and the declaration of the Muslim Independence movement all signified extraparliamentary challenges to the parameters of political integration and stability. By the mid-1960s, embryonic efforts at channeling social mobilization into alternative political institutions were under way, as evidenced by the organization of a workers' party supported by national labor federations, a peasant association backed by former Huks, and a student movement endorsed by radical nationalists—all three of which were identified with prominent Filipino socialists or communists. As the "increased volatility of a radical intelligentsia in the 1960s helped politicize worker and peasant discontent," moreover, these sectors began mobilizing demonstrations, launching strikes, and battling court cases (Nowak and Snyder 1974: 154). Student demonstrations similarly added to the wave of collective action and political protest with the so-called "First Quarter Storm" of rallies and marches in early 1970 (Lacaba 1982). Although Marcos suspended the writ of habeas corpus after the grenade attack on the Liberal Party senatorial rally held at Plaza Miranda, Manila, in August 1971, this period witnessed an overall escalation of student demonstrations and urban bombings until, on the eve of the alleged assassination attempt upon Defense Secretary Juan Ponce Enrile a year later, martial law was declared.

Marcos appeared especially well positioned to consolidate presidential control over the AFP in view of his own professed personal history and long-standing political involvement with military men and matters. Before his reputation as the Pacific War's most decorated Filipino soldier finally backfired in the fake medals exposé of the mid-1980s (Bonner 1987: 400–401), Marcos had cultivated stories of his legendary guerrilla exploits with the 21st Division of USAFFE and the Maharlika unit in northern Luzon. Perhaps of less ambiguous veracity and significance for his postwar political career, Marcos was appointed civil affairs officer of the U.S. Army's Fourteenth Infantry Division and, thereafter, judge advocate general of the Second Infantry

Division of the Philippine Army under the auspices of American liberation and de facto occupation in the months leading up to formal independence in July 1946. Upon his appointment as Manuel Roxas's presidential assistant on veterans affairs, Marcos played a role in the organization and accreditation of guerrilla groups, including the formation of the umbrella federation, the Philippine Veterans Legion (PVL), and the lobbying of the U.S. Congress on veterans benefits. In view of his skillful manipulation of guerrilla war exploits and postwar politics alike, it is perhaps unsurprising that, upon his first election to the Philippine Congress in 1949, Marcos gained a seat on the Committee on National Defense chaired by Magsaysay (Berlin 1982: 181) and continued to cultivate close and lasting ties with military officers throughout his career in the House of Representatives (1949–1959) and the Senate (1959–1965).

If Marcos developed particularly strong linkages within the military establishment during his long years in Congress, the broad context of domestic and international political change contributed to the shifting of greater powers from the legislature to the executive branch by the mid-1960s (Shantz 1972; Doronila 1985). After all, Marcos's election to the presidency coincided with the dramatic escalation of direct U.S. military intervention in Vietnam—which, in turn, heightened the geostrategic import of American naval and air force facilities in the Philippines and increased the amount of U.S. assistance to the Philippine national government (Thompson 1975: 79–82). Such assistance not only supplemented congressional budget appropriations but also allowed for greater executive centralization of patronage resources (Doronila 1985: 115) and thus the relative weakening of the legislature's leverage and restraint vis-à-vis the incumbent president. This trend was further strengthened by the Philippine government's increasing reliance on loans from international financial institutions and foreign banks during this period (Baldwin 1975: 65–75). Meanwhile, the process of industrialization and the opportunity to take over American corporate assets divested in anticipation of the impending expiration of the Laurel-Langley Agreement in 1974 (which guaranteed de facto parity rights to American citizens and corporations in the Philippine economy) increased the reliance of Filipino magnates on state loans and regulatory breaks at the discretion of the president and his subordinates.

Marcos succeeded in manipulating military appointments to a far greater degree than any of his predecessors had ever achieved. In 1965, for example, a well-publicized exposé of smuggling orchestrated by Senator (and presidential aspirant) Marcos anticipated a major shake-up in the military hierarchy (Sidel 1993: 141). Though a changing of the guard typically accompanied the electoral turnover of provincial and national politicians, Marcos prompted an unprecedented reshuffle of military assignments within weeks of his arrival in Malacañang.[13] During the first thirteen months of his presidency, moreover, Marcos refrained from appointing a new secretary of national defense. Instead, he retained this portfolio for himself, thus encouraging frequent and direct contacts with the top military brass (Berlin 1982: 186–87). In yet another key example of his considerable muscling of presidential prerogative over military assignments, Marcos had promoted the meteoric rise through the ranks of Fabian C. Ver who, despite a rather lackluster service record, advanced from mere captain in 1965 to brigadier general by 1970 (Wurfel 1988: 149). Finally, as noted by other observers, Marcos ushered in a new era of institution building—ranging from the activation of the National Defense College in 1966 to the centralization and augmentation of national intelligence and presidential security (Hernandez 1979).[14] Significantly, such initiatives allowed Marcos to consolidate control as they drew into his orbit a peculiar but powerful combination of, on the one hand, an older generation of Magsaysay-era "Amboys" (such as José Crisol) and their latter-day professional coun-terparts (such as Alejandro Melchor) with strong linkages and constituencies in the JUSMAG as well as Washington and, on the other hand, "an informal, clandestine, command structure within the armed forces to execute special operations" (McCoy 1993: 16).[15]

In the swift cabinet reshuffle that followed the student protests at the gates of the presi-dential palace on January 30, 1970, Marcos made two executive appointments that enhanced his maneuvering room vis-à-vis any military and civilian opposition to the strengthening of presidential powers. First of all, Marcos's choice for executive secretary—Alejandro Melchor (then undersecretary of defense, once an academy-trained navy lieutenant commander, and seemingly always eager to promote a greater developmental role for the military-as-institution)—underscored a public alignment of the presidential office with the "technocrat professionals" and their "apolitical expertise" but also, more specifically, with the "military as manager" of national development writ large.[16] Second, by consolidating in the hands of Juan Ponce Enrile the two cabinet posts of justice and defense, Marcos resorted to a virtually unprecedented practice (with the notable exception of Oscar Castelo holding both positions simultaneously under Quirino) that, at least with the advantage of hindsight, appeared to one longtime political opponent designed to ensure that "a suspension of the writ of habeas cor-pus would be supported with legal expertise."[17] Enrile, it is worth noting, was the very first sec-retary of defense who did not have a record of guerrilla activity under USAFFE and subse-quent AFP linkages; he remained, at the time, entirely Marcos's man. As for military assignments, Marcos undertook his next major revamping in January 1972, in the aftermath of the August 1971 suspension of the writ of habeas corpus and the November 1971 electoral defeat for the Nacionalista Party (Berlin 1982: 196).[18]

Martial law thus appeared a distinct possibility—in political as well as logistical terms. After all, in view of the mounting threats from below posed by radical students, workers, and peas-ants mobilized in collective action and the declining "absorptive capacity" of existing mecha-nisms for political participation and representation, Marcos confronted virtually no immediate opposition to the declaration of martial law from other powerful forces in Philippine society (or in Washington, D.C., which deemed a return to "law and order" of paramount interest). In par-ticular, Marcos's careful cultivation of the military as institution—and the commanding officers personally loyal to him—prefigured not merely the formal acquiescence of the top brass, after they were briefed at the infamous "Rolex Twelve" meeting more than a week before the actual declaration of martial law, but also the prior critical collaboration in drawing up de facto oper-ational plans by lower-ranking officers commanding the strategically important troops of the First PC Zone, the Metrocom, and the Rizal PC, who were also accompanied by Enrile, secre-tary of defense, and Ver, head of the Presidential Security Guard (Brillantes 1987). As in the late 1940s under Quirino, mounting social mobilization had provided a useful justification and per-haps also a convenient cover for the strengthening of (civilian) presidential control over the AFP.

THE ANTINOMIES
OF CONSTITUTIONAL AUTHORITARIANISM

In comparison with the return to regular electoral competition and presidential turnover that followed in the wake of Magsaysay's barrio-stomping, mambo-jingling victory over Quirino in

1953, the fall of Marcos in the aftermath of the much-contested snap presidential election of 1986 left an ambiguous legacy for the restoration of Philippine democracy. If the threat from below under Quirino had all but dissipated in the face of a counterinsurgency campaign that combined selective repression with softer reformist efforts focused on land issues and free elections, martial law only postponed—and exacerbated—the ongoing political polarization that, by the mid-1980s, had reached an unprecedented scope and momentum with the mass mobilization of urban activists, peasant guerrillas, radical students, and militant workers under the umbrella of the CPP/NPA. Increasingly, the U.S. government sought to promote the revitalization of democratic institutions and to court the traditional opposition. And as in the case of Magsaysay (albeit through more circumspect postcolonial mechanisms), the United States encouraged the emergence of a reformist presidential candidate—Corazon C. Aquino—as well as the formation of a "free elections movement" to spearhead the transitions from authoritarian rule in the Philippines (Thompson 1988–1989). Yet compared with the 1953 electoral turnover that sealed the arrival of Magsaysay in Malacañang, the termination of *continuista* rule in 1986, within a markedly different postcolonial context, involved much greater military participation—which, in turn, anticipated the ensuing "season of coups" that threatened the survival of Aquino's transitional regime (Nemenzo 1987).

As noted by observers, the declaration of martial law in September 1972 did not signal the installation of the military as government but, rather, the significance of the military as an institution with notably expanded powers and resources (Hernandez 1979). With the suspension of Congress, the relative autonomy of military officers vis-à-vis local politicos increased, though with important qualifications. With the abolition of Congress and, notably, the Commission on Appointments, there was a commensurate reduction in Marcos's reliance on local and provincial politicians—and, as a result, the latter also found their discretion over the military/police considerably circumscribed. An anecdote from the early days of martial law offers an apt illustration of such shifting dynamics and expectations as it recounts how a member of the recently abolished Congress "burst into the waiting room, and after taking in the crowd, strode to Enrile's aide-de-camp, and asked to see the defense secretary":

> "My business is urgent," he said. "I have to see Enrile at once." The aide-de-camp protested and said that he had to wait for his turn. The man's face flushed, and he said in a loud voice, "Don't you know who I am? I am Congressman So-and-So." "I'm sorry, sir," the aide-de-camp replied, politely but firmly. "But we have no more congressmen today. Everybody is equal. We now live in a new society." (De Quiros 1997: 317)

With the activation of an Integrated National Police (INP)—"with the Philippine Constabulary as the nucleus and the local police forces, fire departments and jails as components"—by presidential decree in 1975, the PC/AFP received additional license to expand its administrative and operational control down to the municipal level, further undermining the possibilities of civilian government officials (governors and mayors under martial law) for making or breaking the loyalties (and careers) of the very men tasked with policing their former bailiwicks (Campos 1983: 218–20). Beyond the revival of paramilitary formations such as the Barrio Self-Defense Units during Marcos's second term (1970–1972), martial law saw the formal inception of the so-called Civilian Home Defense Forces (CHDF) under PC command by 1976. As a consequence of such evident expansion, military officers found themselves well positioned to venture into various forms of racketeering previously controlled by local politicians (Tesoro 1986; Sidel 1995). In addition, the top brass gained greater influence in formal terms—notably through the supervisory powers accorded high-ranking generals over "a few strategic private enterprises and public utilities" and the unprecedented jurisdiction granted to military tribunals (Abueva 1979: 36; Hernandez 1979: 21).

Perhaps the most commonly cited evidence for the expansion of the PC/AFP under martial law stems from figures on military troops, budgets, and assistance. In terms of manpower, the AFP more than doubled its forces during the first three years of martial law.[19] A decade later, the AFP counted about four times as many troops as in 1972.[20] Behind such significant increases in the sheer size of the Philippine military was an escalating military budget, which in part was made possible by growing U.S. security assistance. Between the years 1972 and 1977, for example, the Philippines' military budget more than tripled compared to the initial $136 million. Four years later, in 1981, it had doubled again, now totaling $863 million.[21] When translated into military expenditures per capita, the figures for the Philippines were, in fact, the highest for any Association of Southeast Asian Nations (ASEAN) state in the period between 1972 and 1980 (Miranda 1985: 95). The significance of U.S. support for the dictatorship and its military machine is evident from the more than 100 percent increase in military aid to the Philippines during the first four years of martial law, as compared to the period between 1968 and 1972.[22] Total U.S. military assistance to the Philippines reportedly amounted to more than $519 million between 1973 and 1984 (Zwick 1982).

This expansion of the military notwithstanding, the Marcos regime remained profoundly civilian—if not civil—with the AFP still weakly insulated from the powers associated with distinctly political controls and pressures. For example, some provincial politicians close to Marcos retained marked discretion over the appointments, transfers, and promotions of local PC commanders and their subordinates (Bentley 1993; Cullinane 1993). Moreover, senior officers assigned to the twelve Regional Unified Commands (RUCs) introduced under martial law often enjoyed little relative autonomy from the regional chairmen of Marcos's one-party machine, Kilusang Bagong Lipunan (KBL), such as close cronies Eduardo "Danding" Cojuangco in Region III, Roberto Benedicto in Region VI, and Antonio Floirendo in Region XI. More important perhaps, at the national level presidential favoritism governed senior military appointments as evidenced by the rise of palace pet Fabian C. Ver to the rank of general and AFP chief of staff in 1981 and the long service of Marcos cousin Lt. Gen. Fidel V. Ramos as chief of the PC and, after 1975, the INP. As noted by many observers, political and especially presidential prerogatives frequently transgressed the formal chain of command: Defense Minister Juan Ponce Enrile found himself regularly bypassed, for example, and favored generals overstayed, if not their welcome in Malacañang, then clearly their officially prescribed terms of military service.

Perhaps emblematic of such trends, martial law saw the Presidential Security Unit (PSU) transformed under Ver into the larger and more powerful Presidential Security Battalion (PSB) of some 2,000 troops and eventually expanded into an even larger independent command, the Presidential Security Command (PSC), under Ver (Davide et al. 1990: 52). As head of the PSC, Ver commanded forces from all four services, as well as the Metro Manila police, with formal authority equal to that of a deputy chief of staff of the AFP (Wurfel 1988: 149). On August 15, 1981, Ver became the first military officer in Philippine history without a degree from the Philippine Military Academy, or one of its international counterparts, to be appointed chief of staff, thus bypassing Ramos, a West Point graduate senior in rank to Ver. The creation of the Regional Unified Commands in 1982 further contributed to consolidate Ver's power, also at Ramos's expense, by establishing a direct link in the chain of command between the chief of staff and provincial commanders of such composite divisions of PC, Philippine Air Force (PAF), Philippine Army (PA), and Philippine Navy (PN), as well as marine units (Davide et al. 1990: 53). In addition, the operational control of the INP was transferred from the PC chief into the hands of Ver on August 1, 1983. In the eyes of many observers, the AFP looked more like Marcos's praetorian guard than a properly professional military.

During martial law, moreover, the higher echelons of the military showed remarkable staying power due to Marcos's discretion over military appointments and disregard for regular promotions. Whereas Marcos hardly invented the retention of generals beyond retirement age, he extended this practice far beyond anything previously known in the history of the Philippine Armed Forces. Upon declaring martial law in September 1972, for example, Marcos prolonged the careers of a number of senior officers by retiring only 22 out of 47 overstaying generals in June 1978 (Hernandez 1979: 244). Even after martial law was officially lifted, moreover, the upper ranks of the military were filled with overstaying generals, reportedly 30 by early May 1985, of whom 28 were extendees and two were recalled into active service.[23] Many of these appointments were extended more than once— in at least seven cases as many as ten times. In addition, the service of the following three officers was on indefinite extension: Gen. Fabian C. Ver, Lt. Gen. Fidel V. Ramos, and Brig. Gen. Mamarinta B. Lao. Despite considerable internal and external pressures to reform the armed forces in the mid-1980s, there remained a total of 22 extendee generals in the Philippine military at the time of the Epifanio de los Santos Avenue (EDSA) revolt in February 1986 (Davide et al. 1990: 63).

The rumblings of discontent among the junior officer corps were perhaps unsurprising. After all, martial law failed not merely to deliver on the lofty promises of a "Revolution from the Center," but also to insulate the military as an institution from political—rather than professional—considerations intruding upon the recruitment, promotion, and rotation of serving officers. Meanwhile, junior officers had opportunities to develop horizontal solidarities and, eventually, a certain esprit de corps under the RAM banner.

Two important reasons can be discerned for the emergence of such sentiments at the junior officer level, particularly among graduates from the Philippine Military Academy (PMA). First of all, during the four years spent in military training deep loyalties are forged between classmates (Hernandez 1985: 179; McCoy 1995). At the academy, the small class size and the fact that all men live in PMA barracks for the duration of their training combine to create exceptionally strong bonds among classmates.[24] Second, after four years in class together at the PMA, a network developed that facilitated future communication between former classmates. Each class had three members who performed three different leadership functions—the class president, the baron, and the valedictorian— and would serve as contact persons for the class once it left the academy and entered the armed forces.

As for the emergence of the constellation of self-professed reformist forces known as RAM, it is important to reexamine the role of a handful of 1971 graduates and their patron at the head of the Ministry of Defense. The class of 1971 has been depicted as unique in terms of its proclivity for political activism due to formative experiences of social ferment in society, open debate at the academy, and the unprecedented defection to the NPA of 1967 graduate and instructor Victor Corpus.[25] Moreover, coincidence and personal ties played an important role for the emergence of 1971 graduates Col. Gregorio "Gringo" B. Honasan, Col. Oscar "Tito" B. Legaspi, and Lt. Col. Eduardo "Red" E. Kapunan as the hard core of RAM from within the Defense Ministry's security detail—which, in turn, underwent a notable buildup precisely as Minister Juan Ponce Enrile saw his own influence progressively curtailed as a result of power struggles in the Marcos regime.[26]

By the mid-1980s, the class of 1971 graduates who had reached the ranks of major and colonel had direct operational control over significant troop units to an extent far greater than more junior and senior officers. (Col. Victor Batac was PC Provincial Commander in Albay by 1986, for example, and Col. Jake Malajacan was then commanding officer of the Sixteenth Infantry Battalion in Laguna.) Thus, like Young Turks elsewhere, this echelon of middle-ranking officers enjoyed a strategic advantage in terms of eventual mobilizational action. Even where higher-ranking officers did exert direct control over enough troops to allow for a move against the Marcos regime, it would hardly have been in their interest to do so because "they were either too high to be nonpartisan (owing their positions to the powers that be), too comfortable to be interested, or too wealthy to care" (Arillo 1986: 166–67).

Beyond the bonds forged at the military academy, other formative experiences encouraged this clustering of ambitious 1971 graduates and their fellow travelers to develop a sense of shared solidarities and grievances. First of all, they fought together in Mindanao against the MNLF and, in due course, the NPA. Perhaps the most celebrated example of enduring loyalties thus forged is the rescue of a wounded Honasan from behind enemy lines in Sultan Kudarat province by some classmates led by Kapunan, who had joined the air force (Yabes 1991: 13). Second, these young officers tortured together (McCoy 1999: 195–217). In serving the dictatorship, it has been argued, they "personified the violent capacities of the regime"—detention, interrogation, torture, and "salvaging" of unprecedented scope and brutality—and, in a perverse reversal of the military as professional, "these young officers, future RAM leaders included, were superstars in a theater of terror" (McCoy 1988: 30).

Third, they watched the growth of corruption in the higher ranks of the officer corps while the troops on field assignments typically lacked in morale as well as materiel (Danguilan-Vitug 1990). Although corruption was hardly a novelty, the slow pace of rotation at the top of the military implied that the rewards of such activity were savored by the same small clique of senior officers over an extended period of time. Three "Ver generals"—Maj. Gen. Tomas Dumpit, Brig. Gen. Jaime C. Echevarria, and Maj. Gen. Josephus O. Ramas—allegedly amassed millions under Marcos's patronage.[27]

Fourth, they counted the growing number of overstaying generals clogging up the path to promotion while retirement pensions for lower-ranking officers remained but a pittance (Javate de Dios et al. 1988: 304). That is, once martial law was in place and Congress was abolished, the maneuvering room for ambitious younger officers became severely restricted as they could no longer lobby for favorable positions with local politicians (congressmen, senators, and governors) but instead were left at the mercy of politicos at the national level, who were fewer in number and lasted longer than in the pre–martial law period (Javate de Dios et al. 1988: 304). Although the military's expansion in terms of personnel, budget, and prescribed roles in Philippine society had effectively transformed certain high-ranking officers into politicos in their own right, competition among them was severely constrained. Aside from Marcos, Ver, and a handful of other big players such as Imelda R. Marcos, Eduardo "Danding" Cojuangco, and, notably, Enrile, no alternative patrons were available. Thus, mobility was restricted for young and middle-ranking officers.

In the early 1980s, RAM started crystallizing. By May 1985, it was giving official media interviews and, more quietly, exploring possibilities for a coup (Johnson 1987).[28] In addition to support from within the armed forces, RAM also enjoyed de facto protection from the U.S. government, whose ever-increasing flow of special envoys came calling upon Marcos to promote the "professionalization of the military" as part of a broad strategy for economic and political reform (Bonner 1987). Although RAM's overtures in the summer of 1985 failed to secure U.S. backing for the launching of a coup, American intelligence officers refrained from sharing this sensitive information with Marcos and Ver at the time. Meanwhile, conservative businessmen and opposition leaders courted RAM in their homes (Joaquin 1990). By the time of the 1986 snap presidential election, RAM, while publicly campaigning for free elections, was busily plotting a coup—perhaps in anticipation of a postelection cabinet reshuffle and internal military purge by Marcos.

Yet it would be mistaken to view RAM as a phenomenon purely internal to the military—the product of a gradual coming of age, in terms of solidarities, consciousness, and collective action, of these young officers in the armed forces. Indeed, RAM had emerged and flourished within the corridors of the Defense Ministry and under the leadership of Col. Gregorio Honasan who, after his initial fortuitous assignment to Defense Minister Enrile's security unit, not only remained in this post for an extended period but also actively recruited class of 1971 mates Lt. Col. Eduardo E. Kapunan and Col. Oscar B. Legaspi. Enrile, moreover, had amassed a vast personal fortune and a diversified business empire in the course of his long tenure as defense minister (Manapat 1991: 163–205). As a result, he commanded ample resources that, among other things, allegedly financed the import of sophisticated and expensive weapons as well as two retired instructors from the British Special Air Service (SAS) in order to equip and train his men led by Honasan and Kapunan (Arillo 1986: 137; Davide et al. 1990). Despite such apparent wealth and power, Enrile had seen his influence progressively curtailed and, although not officially removed from the chain of command until 1983, he later claimed that he "had been coasting since 1977" (Burton 1989: 228). In this context, Enrile's patronage of RAM promised not only to enhance his ratings in Washington but also to strengthen his hand for any eventual contest for power during the twilight years of the Marcos dictatorship.

The Marcos era thus saw significant change not so much in civil-military relations per se as in the structure of civilian control over the agents of coercive state apparatuses. As shown elsewhere, the AFP's new institutional reach extended far into the civil courts, mass media, and national economy under martial law as Marcos mandated special military tribunals, the early control and subsequent monitoring of media and public utilities by the military, as well as the establishment of "two military-related investment corporations" and the implementation of presidential development programs (Hernandez 1985: 186–88). But as we have seen, the more powerful dynamic set in motion by the declaration of martial law stemmed from the centralization of power over patronage and personnel in the hands of Marcos and those personally loyal to him, together with the shifting relationship between the military and local politicians in the former's favor. In this context, RAM emerged not simply due to internal military developments but as a result of the extraelectoral contestation between rival civilian politicians over the succession to Marcos in the mid-1980s.

STATE AND SOLDIER AFTER MARCOS

Compared to the muted legacies of Quirino's interrupted *continuismo* for the relations of state and soldier under his immediate successor to the presidency, guerrilla-politico Ramon Magsaysay (1953–1957), the post-Marcos resurrection of Philippine democratic institutions under the auspices of widow-*hacendada* Corazon C. Aquino's transitional regime involved much greater challenges for the restoration of electoral politics and elected civilian control over the armed forces. Within months of Marcos's ouster from power, influential elements within both the AFP and the Reagan administration were calling for stepped-up counterinsurgency measures, and opposing the Aquino government's early conciliatory approach signaled by the release of jailed communist leader José Maria Sison and other political prisoners. Before a year had passed, the civilian government began to embrace publicly the military's preferred solution as indicated by Aquino's "total war" declaration against the insurgent forces (Bello 1987; Porter 1987). Meanwhile, the Aquino administration faced down six separate coup attempts by so-called rebel soldiers and Marcos loyalist troops during its first eighteen months in power (Davide et al. 1990: 21). But thanks to the unflagging loyalty of Chief of Staff Ramos, the continued support of the U.S. government, and the manifest endorsements of constitutional rule indicated by local and congressional elections and national plebiscite, the embattled Aquino regime managed to outlast this flurry of putschist activities. More important, even as certain military officers succeeded in making the transition to second careers in electoral politics, the military as an institution underwent a decisive resubordination to the national legislature and local politicians as well as a marked reorientation from an internal political role to a narrowly defined external defense role by the early 1990s.

Inasmuch as martial law deepened, rather than resolved, the political polarization of the late 1960s and early 1970s, it also prompted the gradual development of a range of counterinsurgency strategies and mechanisms—formal and informal—which, in turn, paved the way for further military expansion (if not exactly as a unified institution) into Philippine politics and society by the mid-1980s (Porter 1987). Once Marcos had been safely escorted out of Malacañang and country alike in February 1986, moreover, the military infrastructure and subculture associated with counterinsurgency campaigns received added impetus with the rejuvenation of "U.S.-sponsored low-intensity conflict" under Aquino (Bello 1987). As a result, military deployments and operations intensified in many parts of the country, starting with the massacre of peasant demonstrators by Manila security forces and the activation of the National Capital Region District Command for purposes of establishing "an effective territorial defense" in Metro Manila in January 1987 (AFP General Headquarters, cited in Ziga 1989: 242). In addition to such stepped-up police and military action, Philippine government officials, both civilian and military, issued public endorsements of what they officially designated as Civilian Volunteer Organizations while their local counterparts provided instrumental (if at times more circumspect) support for these essentially paramilitary or vigilante formations (Philippine Senate Committee 1988; Lawyers Committee 1988). Despite frequent government disclaimers, the peculiar dynamics of such vigilante mobilization relied in large part upon—and helped perpetuate—a heightened political role for commanding officers of local military detachments in areas identified as CPP/NPA strongholds (such as Davao, Samar, and Negros Occidental).

Moreover, within just a few months of the much-celebrated "People Power" revolt in February 1986, the threat of military adventurism besieged the Aquino government. The first attempted *kudeta*, while undoubtedly the most bizarre, remains particularly instructive: the occupation of the Manila Hotel (promptly proclaimed the temporary seat of government) by Marcos loyalist politicians and armed military men in July 1986 (Davide et al. 1990: 135–46). Before the end of the same year, the unraveling of another putschist plot, "God Save the Queen," once again linked civilian political ambitions to disgruntled officers—this time from within the

Aquino administration's own cabinet, where Enrile had been well positioned to continue cultivating his old ties with RAM until his forced resignation in November 1986 (Davide et al. 1990: 146–58). Subsequent attempts and plots included the occupation of a national television station in Quezon City (the January 1987 "GMA Incident") and the Philippine Army headquarters in Fort Bonifacio (the April 1987 "Black Saturday Incident"); the planned seizure of the country's main international airport (the July 1987 "MIA Takeover Plot"); the coordinated moves on the presidential palace, military camps, regional commands, and broadcast networks (in the August 1987 coup); and, after a lull, the most serious threat to oust the Aquino government by *golpe* in December 1989 (Davide et al. 1990: 221–469).

Despite their bewildering number and marked diversity in terms of tactics, targets, and outcomes, these putschist attempts to seize the government reveal certain patterns. In the first instance, they remained intimately linked to political ambitions for *civilian* rule without Aquino— that is, the return of Marcos or the revival of the Batasang Pambansa (National Assembly) or a more nebulous junta perhaps headed by former defense minister Enrile. Moreover, there is evidence of considerable *civilian* involvement in the planning and execution of all the coup attempts and plots listed here (Davide et al. 1990). As for internal military backing, the claims by the media-chic RAM boys that they represented the military as an institution remained rather more dubious—not least in view of the emerging factionalism within the junior officers corps itself and the shifting positions evident higher up the chain of command.

Indeed, none of these plots succeeded in ousting the government or, ultimately, in sustaining a putschist esprit de corps in the armed forces. First of all, the various incidents listed here attracted little popular support. Second, a strong core of Aquino loyalists remained in key positions within the AFP which, furthermore, counted many younger officers who openly disagreed with RAM's goals and methods. Third, high-ranking police officers and troops under their command got in the way of more than one of these urban putschist operations (Gen. Alfredo Lim, for example, commander of the Western Police District in Manila). Fourth, upon the discovery of the "God Save the Queen" plot, a cabinet reshuffle replacing Enrile with Gen. Rafael Ileto at the Ministry of Defense strengthened AFP support for Aquino and her most loyal soldier, chief of staff Fidel V. Ramos. Fifth, some Defense Intelligence Agency behind-the-scenes wavering to the contrary, the U.S. government signaled its continued support for Aquino—most visibly so during the rebel air strafing of Malacañang on December 1, 1989, when several U.S. Air Force Phantom jets conducted "persuasion flights" above Metro Manila (Davide et al. 1990: 495).

After the high drama of the late 1980s, the 1990s witnessed the return to elections as the central mechanism for political contestation—thus reaffirming the subordination of state coercive apparatuses to regularly elected civilian politicians and reorienting the armed forces to new roles. First of all, the abolition of the Philippine Constabulary and the establishment of the Philippine National Police (PNP) under the Department of the Interior and Local Government (DILG) removed police personnel as well as policing functions from the AFP's military chain of command (Gutang 1991). The provisions of the 1990 Police Act and the 1991 Local Government Code, moreover, mandated the discretionary powers of municipal mayors and provincial governors over the rotation and activities of local police superintendents, even as the restoration of the national legislature reinstated the Commission on Appointments and other congressional committees as mechanisms for the exercise of formal as well as informal political influence over military and police forces alike. For example, all PNP appointments at the level of senior superindendent and above are subject to confirmation by the Commission on Appointments. Moreover, powers to select PNP provincial directors are vested in the hands of provincial governors. Finally, operational supervision and control over local police forces rest with municipal mayors as does the authority to choose local police chiefs (Republic of the Philippines 1990). As the political opposition to Estrada gained momentum in the fall of 2000, Cabinet Secretary Alfredo Lim conducted repeated DILG 'loyalty checks' on governors, mayors and local police. Meanwhile, under the command of close Estrada associate and chief of police Panfilo Lacson, the PNP remained publicly supportive of the embattled president until the day before his successor was sworn in. Indeed, Lacson only broke with his president after the chief of staff of the armed rorces, Gen. Angelo Reyes, and the secretary of national defense, Orlando Mercado, had announced their defections from Estrada and joined the civilian political opposition and broader protest movement at the Edsa Shrine on January 19, 2001.

Against this backdrop, the Ramos administration (1992–1998) provided something of a denouement as (retired) military men returned to expanding career opportunities on the jagged edges of Philippine politics or in the inner corridors of power. During this period, for example, "the rise in criminal activities... particularly kidnapping and drug-related crimes, was attributed to the involvement of AFP and Philippine National Police (PNP) personnel with various criminal syndicates in the country" (Romero 1998: 199). At the same time, this administration saw the appointment of dozens of retired military officers in a wide variety of civilian positions, including "many strategic and therefore powerful positions in such agencies as the Department of Defense, National Security Council, Department of Interior and Local Government, Department of Transportation and Communication, Department of Public Works, and many ambassadorial posts" (Hernandez 1997: 56–57).[29] A major power broker under Ramos, for example, retired brigadier general José Almonte, served as head of both the National Security Council (NSC) and the National Intelligence Coordinating Authority (NICA). Moreover, even renegade RAM officers ran for public office with some notable successes (such as Senator Honasan) in the aftermath of the 1994 peace agreement between the Philippine government and this putschist faction. In a similar vein, the government's accord with the MNLF in 1996 has seen its long-time leader Nur Misuari elected (without opposition and with backing from the Lakas-NUCD party) as governor of the Autonomous Region Muslim Mindanao. Rather than signaling a new militarist trend in Philippine politics, however, this pronounced development ended with Ramos who, significantly, refrained from extending to his own defense secretary and former chief of staff, Gen. Renato de Villa, the much-coveted presidential endorsement—and associated release of executive resources—which, under Aquino, had helped launch his own bid for Malacañang in 1992 (Putzel 1995).

Furthermore, Ramos's successor to the presidency, Joseph "Erap" Estrada, worked to establish his own network of supporters in the PNP and the AFP, favoring officers marginalized in the previous post–martial law administrations with plum posts. In this regard, Estrada had forged a close alliance with Senators Enrile and Honasan, whose network of "mistahs" from the Philippine Military Academy's class of 1971, etc., had been sidelined under both Aquino and Ramos. Notably, Estrada appointed Chief of Police Panfilo "Ping" Lacson as the director of the PNP, thus confirming a pattern of control by civilian politicians over coercive apparatuses of the state. Lacson, after all, had served as Estrada's right-hand man in the Presidential Anti-Crime Commission (PACC) in the early 1990s and is known to be a trusted lieutenant of the president. Under Lacson, "[p]arallel promotion of three classmates—Ruben Cabagnot, Tiburcio Fusilero, and Reynaldo Acop—to key PNP regional commands made them the most powerful cohort in the police" (McCoy 1999: 335).[30]

Yet, Estrada's civilian political enemies proved equally astute in their cultivation of clients within the Philippine military and police. Notably, Gloria Macapagal Arroyo, elected to the vice presidency in 1998 as an opposition candidate, worked to establish links with key figures among the top brass in the AFP and PNP for much of 2000.[31] Thus, when Estrada found himself increasingly besieged by popular protests in Manila and by the televised impeachment hearings in the House of Representatives, the possibility of a military clampdown against these challenges to his presidency remained beyond reach. Instead, with the prosecution walking out in protest from the Senate trial, the defection of civilian political allies from Estrada culminated with most of his cabinet resigning and joining the street parliamentarians for a "People Power" showdown. In the event, Estrada's close allies in the military—Reyes and Lacson—eventually abandoned their president and commander in chief in the face of persistent pressures from influential businessmen, politicians, and retired officers, and amidst signs of rapidly eroding support for the president among active AFP and PNP officers.[32]

Thus, the ouster of Estrada from the presidential palace on January 20, 2001, and the simultaneous swearing in of his former vice president, Gloria Macapagal Arroyo, to the highest political office of the land, saw an immediate changing of the guard in the military and police establishments. First of all, AFP chief of staff Angelo Reyes, whose tenure had been extended by Estrada into the year 2002, has confirmed his timely resignation from the armed forces upon reaching official retirement age in March 2001. Moreover, PNP director Panfilo Lacson promptly turned in his "courtesy" resignation and has been replaced by Leandro Mendoza as acting national police chief. Finally, with all eyes focused on the May elections, the most important political battles ahead involve candidates associated with the new Macapagal Arroyo and old Estrada administrations, rather than the "word wars" and "coup talks" within military ranks.[33]

As suggested by the following retrospective of the aborted Estrada administration, civilian political considerations have clearly continued to shape the broad contours of national security and law enforcement policies from the 1990s up to the early years of the new century. The much-touted modernization program to upgrade the armed forces' operational capabilities after the closure of U.S. military bases in the Philippines in 1992, for example, remained in virtual limbo under the tenure of Defense Secretary Mercado. Despite legislation passed under the Ramos administration to implement such modernization over a fifteen-year period, Estrada declared a one-year moratorium on government funding of this program during his first month in office in 1998, citing as more pressing problems the Asian financial crisis and the Philippine budget deficit. Not until the following April did Manila earmark an initial $150 million toward this modernization program—"to supplement the 1999 defence budget, which had effectively been frozen at 1998 levels in US-dollar terms" (Huxley and Willet 1999: 18).

Estrada waited until July 1999 before he "pledged to allot P10 billion for the acquisition of military hardware and weaponry to speed up the modernization of the poorly equipped Armed Forces," with specific reference to the Philippine Air Force as "the initial beneficiary of the military upgrade."[34] Although incidents in the South China Sea have provided an important backdrop to such pledges,[35] the modest gains promised to the prioritized air force (still the smallest of the three services) pale against the political maneuvering of Estrada and his supporters to introduce a new chapter in Philippine-U.S. "special relations" by way of the controversial Visiting Forces Agreement (VFA), ratified by the Senate in Manila on May 27, 1999.[36] The possibilities for politically and otherwise useful VFA spinoffs are presumably many—ranging from the investment in heavy infrastructure associated with developing harbor and airport facilities to the boost to local economies due to the influx of dollar-salaried servicemen and -women on R&R.[37]

Meanwhile, the AFP has been relegated to a comparatively circumscribed domestic role: fighting the remnants of Maoist and Muslim armed rebellions in the hinterlands. Whereas the Netherlands-based leadership of the National Democratic Front declared an end to the peace talks with the Philippine government in 1999 and added that "it expected fighting in the country to pick up,"[38] only pockets of NPA guerrillas remain in the mountains of Bicol, the Cordilleras, and in the rural hinterlands of "the Visayas island of Samar and the three southwestern provinces of Mindanao."[39] As the integration of former MNLF guerrillas in the armed forces proceeds apace, moreover, other armed Muslim groups have been confined to local pockets of influence— whether the small Abu Sayyaf, associated with terrorist tactics in Sulu and Basilan, or the much larger Moro Islamic Liberation Front (MILF), anchored in the backwater Mindanao provinces of Magindanao, North Cotabato, and Sultan Kudarat. In March 2000, Estrada launched an "all-out" war against the Abu Sayyaf and the MILF, capturing about 40 of the latter's camps, including its main base, Camp Abubakar. Within a month of resuming the presidency in January 2001, however, his successor, Gloria Macapagal Arroyo, ordered the suspension of military operations against the MILF so as to pave way for a new round of peace talks.[40]

Finally, in the wake of the end of the cold war and after the Senate vote blocking renewal of the Military Bases Agreement with the United States in 1991, the AFP has, for the first time, assumed primary responsibility for external defense. Although the Mutual Defense Treaty of 1951 survived these far-reaching changes in Philippine-U.S. security relations, this agreement remains concerned with threats to either party stemming from "external armed attack in the Pacific"—thus precluding overt U.S. assistance in the (domestic) Mindanao conflict and, at least to date, in the (multilateral) Spratly dispute. The territorial dispute over the Spratly Islands in the South China Sea—contested as well by Taiwan, Vietnam, Malaysia, and Brunei—intensified with the discovery in 1995 of Chinese structures and troops on Mischief Reef some 135 miles west of Palawan and thus well within the 200-mile Exclusive Economic Zone claimed by the government in Manila (Storey 1999).[41] This dispute has highlighted the extent to which, owing to the colonial legacies and neocolonial linkages examined here, the AFP has remained an organization characterized by its land-oriented service in this nation-state of some 7,000 islands, its counterinsurgency mission on the imperial frontiers of the cold war, and its old navy and air force fleets developed in the shadows of the American bases at Subic and Clark.[42]

Although the Visiting Forces Agreement, ratified by the Philippine Senate in May 1999, does not constitute a formal return to the security treaties of the 1947–1992 period, it nonetheless signals another chapter in the long history of Philippine-American "special relations"—or, in the words of the commander in chief of the U.S. Pacific Fleet, Admiral Dennis Blair, "a necessary step into restabilizing a good military-to-military relationship with the Republic of the Philippines."[43] Under the auspices of the VFA, it has been noted, the resumption of large-scale Philippine-U.S. "joint military exercises" appears a distinct possibility.[44] In February 2000, for example, U.S. troops arrived in Luzon for so-called "war games" and, for U.S. and Philippine military officials, a "seminar workshop in preparation for the joint military exercises."[45] Presumably the nature and direction of Philippine-U.S. security relations will continue to hold considerable significance for the AFP's planned "modernization" with respect to the future restructuring of (air and naval) forces, the responsibility for (external) defense, and the procurement of (upgraded) fleets. But contrary to the predictions of RAM supporters in the middle to late 1980s, in the Philippines today the supremacy—if not always the civility—of elected civilian politicians is matched by the subordination—if not necessarily the professionalism—of a properly military armed forces.

CONCLUSION

If scholars analyzing state and soldier in the Philippines have focused largely on martial law and its consequences for the transitional regime, this chapter points to a set of neocolonial legacies and linkages that situate the distinctive trajectory of the Philippine military within a wider context compared to other postcolonial armies in the region. This discussion of the martial law period has focused particularly on patterns of change and continuity with regard to these links and legacies. Viewed in comparative perspective, however, not even martial law appeared properly militarized in the Philippines, and Marcos himself in many ways remained an exceptionally civilian authoritarian. That is, martial law saw the strengthening of presidential powers rather than the enhancement of the military's autonomy. In a similar vein, the coup attempts against the Marcos and Aquino governments reflected not so much the influence of military adventurism as the extraelectoral contestation by rival civilian contenders for the highest political office under conditions of marked uncertainty about the mechanisms for presidential succession. This pattern stands in marked contrast to the entrenchment of a military authoritarian regime in Burma, and the enduring significance of the military-as-institution in Indonesian as well as Thai politics and society.

Two key developments in the 1990s contributed to the marginalization of the military in Philippine politics and society and confirmed the perspective on civil-military relations sketched above in this chapter. First of all, in the wake of the end of the cold war and the demobilization of the CPP/NPA, a Philippine Senate vote blocked the renewal of the Military Bases Agreement—thus signaling a turning point in neocolonial relations and a diminution of the Philippines' geostrategic importance as host to U.S. forces and (nuclear) weapons. Second, the creation of the Philippine National Police under the Department of the Interior and Local Government has removed PNP troops from the AFP's military chain of command. Against this backdrop, there is little evidence of the militarization of Philippine politics and society witnessed in the 1980s. Instead, former putschist officers, retired military generals, and disbanded paramilitaries have resurfaced in second careers in electoral politics, civil administration, and, reportedly, criminal racketeering. Thus, the dramatic "People Power II" that punctuated Estrada's presidency in early 2001 saw key military and police officials taking their cues from civilian politicians, with mounting popular mobilization and impending midterm elections—rather than the possibility of a coup—looming large on the horizon. Although such experiences constitute a telling military legacy of sorts, they seem to have peaked and then subsided in tandem with the rise and fall of the Ramos administration. Today the military as an institution remains firmly under the control of elected officials, and civilian politicians continue to use their clients in the police and military establishments in pursuit of personal ambitions in Asia's oldest democracy.

CHAPTER 7

Thailand: The Struggle to Redefine Civil-Military Relations

James Ockey

So many people were maimed or died as a result of Thanom's military suppression, and the present government has the cheek to honour such a person!

—Lamiad Boonmak, wife of a victim

The public should not mix politics with military sentiments about an old commander.

—Lt. Gen. Kittisak Ratprasert

Outdated, short-sighted and thoughtless attitudes are at play at a time in which the country is just beginning to embrace the principles for which so many shed blood in 1973. The military is no longer a law unto itself and should look to the future and refrain from making kindly gestures to those who sought to deny the people the rights and freedoms that are theirs today.

—*Bangkok Post* editorial, March 23, 1999

THESE COMMENTS FROM THAILAND, which emerged when the military sought an honorary title for a disgraced former commander in 1999, represent some of the different attitudes toward the contemporary Thai military and its past. Demonstrators in Bangkok have been killed by military and paramilitary forces on three separate occasions in the last three decades, so it is little wonder that feelings run high. Neither civilians nor soldiers have forgotten these traumatic events, and the struggle over their meaning continues to haunt civil-military relations.

The most recent massacre had its origins in a military coup in February 1991. According to coup leaders, the military takeover was necessary to purge Thai democracy of corruption. A better democracy would be restored, they promised, within a year—along with a new constitution and without the corrupt politicians who had tainted the old democracy. When the constitution proved a disappointment and then, after elections, coup leader Gen. Suchinda Kraprayoon became prime minister, demonstrators took to the streets.

Although the demonstrations began peacefully, eventually they proved embarrassing and, to the military, provocative. In the early morning hours of May 18, 1992, heavily armed Thai soldiers attempted to disperse the crowd. Protesters refused to disperse; some resisted and troops opened fire. The bloodletting continued for three days as demonstrators repeatedly gathered, then dispersed when fired upon, only to gather again. The demonstrations, and the shooting, gradually eased off after Thailand's respected monarch called for an end to the violence. This intervention by the king no doubt saved many lives. In his newscast to the nation, however, we can see the seeds of the current conflict in civil-military relations. Both General Suchinda and Chamlong Simuang, the principal leader of the demonstrators, were brought before the king and placed on an equal footing. Both were told to stop the fighting, as if both were equally to blame. Thus although the demonstrators clearly came out on top in the struggle, much scope remained for interpreting the events of 1992. Struggles over this interpretation have proved more controversial than the military budget, the military structure, and even the shrinking military role.

When the shooting ended, 44 civilian protesters were dead and another 38 were missing. Gen. Suchinda Kraprayoon, the prime minister, and Gen. Issaraphong Nunphakdi, the army commander, resigned from their posts. Gen. Chainarong Nunphakdi, the regional commander, was transferred to a staff post. The army found itself disgraced and, moreover, the target of considerable civilian resentment. Slowly and, at least for some soldiers, reluctantly, the military began a retreat from its involvement in politics. At the same time, the struggle over interpretations of the past became, for some in the military, a struggle over honor.

Many commentators see the 1992 uprising as a turning point in civil-military relations. Although the massacre may indeed have been the harbinger of change, that change was neither sudden nor complete. As in the earlier democratic uprising of 1973, another important transition, the change has come gradually, with some resistance and occasional backsliding. Some soldiers have been more supportive of change than others. And the struggle to limit military prerogatives is ongoing.

Civilian pressure on the military to continue its withdrawal from politics—and military resistance—have led to a number of controversies since 1992. Significantly, three major controversies in civil-military relations at the turn of the millennium were concerned not primarily with the future of civil-military relations but with interpretations of the past.[1] First, in October 1998, Gen. Chainarong Nunphakdi became a candidate for the post of army commander in chief. In an effort to make him a more attractive candidate,[2] a media campaign was launched by his supporters to absolve him of blame for his role in the 1992 massacre. Civilian opposition to the appointment of the controversial general quickly arose, however, and after a prolonged deadlock between the retiring army commander in chief and the supreme commander, mediated by the civilian prime minister, an alternative candidate was chosen.

Early in 1999, a second controversy developed over the historical role of the military. At that time, the media learned that retired field marshal Thanom Kittikachorn, the authoritarian prime minister at the time of the 1973 democratic uprising, had been appointed as a special royal guard—a purely nominal and honorary position that would allow him to wear a uniform and the insignia of the 31st Infantry Regiment. Again, controversy erupted as civilians protested granting military honors to a man who had been involved when demonstrators were killed; meanwhile, supporters of Thanom sought to clear him of blame. Ultimately he resigned the appointment.

The third controversy erupted shortly afterward when it was revealed that the only copy of the classified official investigation into the May 1992 massacre had disappeared. Although the report was later found, the controversy continued—first over its continued security classification, then over the defense ministry's failure to clear up the mystery surrounding the 38 protesters still missing and the failure to declassify about 60 percent of the report, and then over the contents of the report, which absolved the military and blamed protestors for the violence. The intensely political nature of these conflicts in civil-military relations is clear: the civilian prime minister acting as defense minister, Chuan Leepkai himself, defended both the appointment of Thanom and the continued classification of the investigation into the 1992 massacre. (The army's commander in chief, however, favored declassification, indicating that the military itself was not of one mind.) If indeed the military is being pressured to withdraw from any future role in politics, it may seem paradoxical that the primary controversies have been struggles over the interpretation of the past. In this chapter I explore the relationship between the past and the future of the Thai military. I begin by examining the military's role in the past, its missions, its successes and failures, and the consequent sense of military honor. Changes in role, structure, attitudes, and supply all indicate that the military's slow, reluctant withdrawal from politics is ongoing. The chapter concludes with a look at current trends and the relationship of the past to the future. Until the military can come to terms with its past, it may continue to struggle with its future.

HISTORY AND THE THAI MILITARY MINDSET

History and tradition have been shaping the mindset of the Thai military for more than a century. Much has been written of the military mind since Samuel Huntington defined it as "the values, attitudes, and perspectives which inhere in the performance of the professional military function and which are deducible from the nature of that function" (Huntington 1957: 61). Useful as it might be, Huntington's definition is too abstract. Each military is a unique institution, with its own historical memory, and its mindset is shaped by that memory.[3] The military's memory, like the memory of an individual, is not always historically accurate in emphasizing accomplishments, forgetting failures, and casting actions in the most favorable light. Institutional memories are particularly powerful in a military in which socialization begins in the academy and continues throughout the career of an officer. It is these memories, embodied in military tradition, that must be outlined in order to understand the Thai military mindset, its missions, and the reasons for its attitudes toward history. I begin with a brief history of civil-military relations in Thailand—focusing particularly on military attitudes toward democracy, development, and security—before turning to the military's retreat from politics in recent years. This history can be usefully divided into periods based on the military's perceptions of its role and its enemies (see Table 7.1).

TABLE 7.1   The Military's Shifting Mission

Period	Enemy	Mission	Legacy
Absolute monarchy (1880–1932)	Domestic threats	Protect the king	Professional and political
Promoters (1932–41)	Royalists and colonialists	Promote democracy and independence	Democratic, nationalist, business involvement
World War II (1941–45)	Non-Thai (especially colonialists)	Unite all Thais	Extreme Thai nationalism
Early cold war expansion (1948–57)	Foreign communists	Oppose communism in Southeast Asia	Anticommunism, expanded business role
Counterinsurgency through development (1957–73)	"Foreign" communists in Thailand	Rural development and harsh suppression to fight communism	Promoting development
Counterinsurgency through politics (1973–91)	Misguided Thai communists	Destroy communism through political development	Promoting "democracy"
Post–cold war (1991–)	None	None	Unclear

The Military under Absolute Monarchy

The origins of the modern Thai military can be found in the military science of the West and the colonial militaries of Thailand's neighbors (Anderson 1978). Thai kings were employing Western military advisers at least by the early seventeenth century, although the quality of this training has been questioned (Battye 1974: 82–86, 245–46; Sukunya 1991: 41). Modernization along European lines began in earnest in the 1880s. By then the military budget had climbed to nearly 23 percent of the total budget, and it would remain among the top three budget items each year until 1910 (Sukunya 1991: 57; Seksan 1989: 431–42; Ingram 1971: 192). Part of this budget went to the establishment of two military academies, staffed by both Thai and Western instructors, to train future officers. Those who left the academies, either prematurely or by graduation, were often posted to the bureaucracy, creating close ties between these two institutions.

Over the next 25 years, with the assistance of these foreign advisers, the Thai military was structured along Western lines and trained according to Western techniques. Western military ethics, including ideas of professionalism and the need to avoid political involvement, were instilled into cadets. Yet these ethics were undermined by the factors that made the Thai military similar to the colonial militaries of neighboring countries. Despite the Western structure, discipline, and ethics being taught at the academies, the emerging modern Thai army resembled Western militaries of an earlier era in certain respects: promotion and even admission to the officer corps depended on status.[4] In 1887, King Chulalongkon made the crown prince the commander in chief of the army by statute. Because the crown prince at the time was just ten years old, the king's brother was placed in command and given responsibility for reorganizing and modernizing the armed forces (Sukunya 1991: 72–73; Battye 1974: 272–73). He created a new academy, Saranarom Cadet School, and submerged two earlier academies into it. For the first ten years, entrance was allowed only to the sons of the royal family, of government officials, and of commissioned officers—reinforcing military ties to the monarchy and government officials (Sukunya 1991: 77). Even after admission was opened to commoners, the highest positions in the military were restricted to members of the royal family, creating a conflict with the ethic of merit-based promotion. This conflict would inspire coup attempts in 1912 and in 1932.

The Thai military in its formative years resembled the colonial armies of its neighbors in several respects. One of its purposes was to demonstrate to the colonial powers that Thailand was "modern." Another purpose was to serve as a partial deterrent against them—an attempt to show that the colonization of Thailand would not come without a price (Sukunya 1991: 53; Battye 1974: 262–63). Yet it was clear that the Thai military could not win a war against neighboring colonial powers. Its primary purpose lay elsewhere. The first unit to be developed was the Royal Pages Bodyguard, whose role was to protect King Chulalongkon. Only after the king had become secure in his power—but before he embarked on the extensive administrative reforms that characterized his reign—did he strengthen the rest of the military to support him in those reforms. Finally, the military was intended to strengthen central power in distant provinces by establishing local garrisons.[5] Thus, like the colonial armies of its neighbors, the Thai military was explicitly political, was modernized to protect the regime from domestic enemies and enforce its policies, and was not intended for external defense (Anderson 1978: 200–206). The military was commanded by members of the royal family, promotion was explicitly not based on merit,[6] and the military reforms were to some extent an attempt to enhance prestige. These partly professional, partly colonial, partly aristocratic, highly political origins shaped the attitudes and character of the Thai military throughout its history.

The Military and the 1932 Uprising

The 1932 overthrow of the absolute monarchy was not the first coup attempted. In 1912, a generation after the military reforms, a group of young lieutenants began to organize with the intention of opening up the higher ranks of the military to commoners and instituting some form of democracy (Acharapon 1997). Although the plot was discovered and the lieutenants arrested, it is important to note the dual aims of this coup: one professional, one political. This duality can be attributed to the contradictions inherent in the way the Thai military was modernized, as it was given professional training but political purposes.

The overthrow of the absolute monarchy in 1932, in the midst of the worldwide depression, embraced those same aims. The "revolution" was actually a military coup planned together with government officials. Although the details of the events are not important here,[7] the military's role in carrying out the coup, and its success, had a lasting impact on the attitudes of the Thai military. First, it cemented the relationship between the bureaucracy and the military. This cooperative relationship has endured. The Thai military never attempted to colonize the civilian bureaucracy. Second, it brought the military directly into politics, where it was making the decisions itself. This occurred at a time that coup leaders perceived a crisis for the Thai nation. Third, the military entered politics in support of democracy, and the military

came to believe itself a democratic force. Although these factors have been important separately, they have also been important in combination: they help explain why the military has
frequently interfered in politics without entrenching itself in the political system as in Burma
or Indonesia. Even the Sarit regime, as we shall see, came to power promising democracy and
continued to act as if it would eventually restore it. These legacies were soon reinforced in 1933,
when the military twice rescued the parliamentary regime—first from the high-ranking bureaucrats invited to head the interim government and then from a proroyalist rebellion. The second rescue effort further contributed to the centralization of the military in Bangkok. The proroyalist rebellion gathered its strength in the provinces, even among the military stationed there.
Battles were fought between Bangkok-based troops and provincial troops. After the victory of
the Bangkok troops, weapons were moved from the provinces to Bangkok, and many officers
in the provinces were transferred back to Bangkok where they could be closely watched
(Sukunya 1991: 227–28).

As the regime began to stabilize, the new rulers, both military and bureaucratic, found that
political power was not enough to govern effectively. In order to gain control, they needed financial power. From this point military leaders began to build factions that included not only other
officers and officials but also financial leaders (Sungsidh 1983). The assets generated by these factions were distributed as patronage—further binding the factions together and allowing them to
increase their size and influence. This process contributed to the centralization of the military
in Bangkok, of course, where resources were concentrated. In the late 1930s, the military entered
more fully into politics when the army commander and a key leader of the 1932 coup, Plaek Phi-
bunsongkhram (Phibun), became prime minister in 1938. He not only strengthened the military's role in politics but, with war on the horizon, also sought to militarize Thai society.

The Military and World War II

Phibun's efforts to militarize society immediately prior to and during the war had important
long-term impacts, particularly in the countryside. Phibun used the new technology of the radio
broadcast to bring his militant nationalism directly to rural people. His nationalism during this
period was aggressive: Thailand, he argued, should expand to include all Tai people. During
the war he sent troops to carry out this objective, taking over parts of Cambodia, Laos, and
Burma. This was the first battle experience for Thai troops against non-Thais in some 50 years.
Phibun also developed paramilitary organizations, bringing aspects of militarism greater esteem
in society—aspects such as discipline, respect for uniforms, and formal hierarchical authority.
Here we see the beginnings of a link between the military and a significant group of admirers
throughout the country. This tie would grow during the cold war as the Bangkok-centered military depended on local allies to help fight the communist insurgency.[8]

Although militarism in the countryside can be traced to the military and the Phibun regime,
the role of the resistance movement should not be neglected. Much of the recruitment to armed
resistance units took place in the countryside, spreading the martial spirit there. The Thai resistance movement had close ties to resistance movements in neighboring countries, particularly
Cambodia and Laos, and, like them, was anticolonial and antigovernment because the Phibun
government was on the side of the Japanese. Thus during World War II, we see the Thai military lined up, not with the independence armies, but with the colonial militaries (Anderson

1978: 196, 199). Unlike neighboring Burma, where the two armies were integrated, in Thailand the resistance movement was disarmed and demobilized. Although the pro-Ally resistance benefited in the political realm, as a military institution it went unrecognized.

The Military and Cold War Expansion

The military emerged from World War II in disarray. Civilians, most of them members of the resistance movement, briefly took over the government. All this changed when the cold war began in Thailand. In three short years the military, still highly factionalized, returned to power through a coup. The subsequent return to power of Phibun, earlier tried for war crimes, could only have come about in the context of the cold war. Because Phibun came out in support of the West in its fight against communism—Thailand was thought by U.S. policymakers to be a crucial state in the cold war—the West accepted his return. Furthermore, having accepted his return, the West provided military aid to the Thai armed forces and paramilitary forces to construct an anticommunist force. The goal was to build up Thai forces to the point where they could protect Thailand and provide support to neighboring countries (Fineman 1997: 173). The distribution of this political support and financial aid exacerbated the factionalism in the military, however, as gradually two large vertically organized factions developed to contest for both foreign and domestic resources.

These two vertically oriented factions—one under the control of army commander Sarit Thanarat, the other under the command of Police Director-General Phao Siyanon—competed in all fields: in business and finance, for military aid and weapons, for promotion, in the lucrative narcotics trade, and through the press, for public opinion.[9] The competition added impetus to the militarization of rural society. The expansion of paramilitary forces in the countryside was aimed as much at obtaining American aid as at gaining more armed supporters. Above these two factions, Phibun balanced precariously until September 1957. At that point, army commander Sarit carried out a coup, and Phibun and Phao were sent into exile.

The Military and Development

When Sarit took over, he quickly consolidated the power of his faction, effectively ending the competition for commercial power as he became the sole patron. On taking power, Sarit controlled a military in which both promotion and commercial gain were distributed according to factional loyalties. It was a military with a tradition of taking power, yet it was also a military that believed itself to be prodemocratic: interfering only when necessary and restoring democratic forms when possible. Confronted with a slowly developing counterinsurgency, Sarit maintained a close relationship with the United States, which saw Thailand as the keystone of its defense of Southeast Asia, and had a strong stratum of supporters in the countryside and also in the cities. Finally, Sarit had the blessing of the monarchy.

Three months after taking power, Sarit restored limited democracy. He then went to the United States for medical treatment. With many speculating that he would not live long, he soon found himself losing control of the military. Under these conditions, Sarit decided to abandon democracy. Upon his return he led a coup. Sarit then sought other means of legitimacy for his government and settled on four elements. First, he announced an eventual return to democracy when Thailand was ready and a new constitution had been written. (This constitution was not completed for ten years.) Second, he promoted the monarchy and restored many of its ceremonial functions (Thak 1979). Third, he entered the cold war in great earnest and refocused attention from democracy to anticommunism. This meant continued growth for the armed forces and an expanded role as the military took over much of the counterinsurgency efforts from the police. Fourth, he sought to refocus legitimacy away from democracy to development by insisting on the need to combat communism. He did this to placate the Americans as well as his own supporters. For the military, then, the Sarit period strengthened certain traditions, especially the role in internal security, and weakened others, particularly support for democracy and any lingering antiroyalist sentiment. He also gave the military a war to fight, against "the communists," who were perceived as un-Thai. Above all, Sarit added a new element to the mix: development. Development efforts led to even greater cooperation between the military and the bureaucracy in the ensuing period.

Development was seen by U.S. and Thai policymakers as crucial to counterinsurgency: they believed it would remove the grievances that allowed the Communist Party of Thailand (CPT) to expand. Consequently many programs aimed at rural development in areas where the CPT was strong. Roads were built for strategic purposes; education included heavy doses of anticommunist propaganda; and the military became involved in development projects. In these same hot spots, paramilitary forces were trained and armed to fight "the communists" (that is, their "un-Thai" fellow villagers). The curriculum at Chulachomklao Military Academy was temporarily streamlined, and class size increased, to produce more officers. Nevertheless, the CPT continued to grow. In 1965, the first armed clash occurred. Subsequently, the military fought the cold war not just through development and propaganda but with guns and blood.

During this period, the military fought "the communists" at home and in neighboring countries. In addition to supplying many of the troops for the secret war in Laos, the Thai military sent soldiers to Vietnam. Most of the officers who went to Vietnam were fairly recent graduates. There they were exposed to the American "hearts and minds" and "search and destroy" approaches to counterinsurgency.[10] They were also witnesses to Vietnam's victory over a superpower. Later, in the mid-1970s, based on the conclusions they drew from their experience in Vietnam, these officers were influential in reshaping Thai counterinsurgency policies and the role of the military. For them "the communists" were Thai people deceived by a misguided ideology. Thus communist ideology had to be countered with democracy, and the war had to be fought not just militarily but also through economic and political development.

During the 1970s the debate over counterinsurgency policy intensified. A popular uprising brought about civilian rule in 1973, when the army commander refused to support the Thanom military dictatorship in suppressing demonstrators. During the ensuing period of civilian rule the left organized rapidly, especially among the lower classes, in quite visible ways. Those who thought communists should be suppressed struck back in a massacre by military-supported paramilitary forces at Thammasat University in 1976. When suppression then strengthened the left even more dramatically, moderates returned to power, and a new round of controlled democratization began. Only in the 1980s, after the defeat of the CPT, was the counterinsurgency debate resolved, as the belief that suppression of armed insurgents must be accompanied by political development became part of the military mindset. This process was under way at the same time that civilian society was evolving toward greater political participation.

Civilian Actors and Military Reactions

Although 1992 has been characterized as a watershed in civil-military relations, it cannot be fully understood without reference to the earlier democratic uprising of 1973. Since the 1970s no military government has lasted for much more than a year, whereas civilian rule has increasingly endured for longer periods and been more stable. In turn, the emergence of stable civilian rule has, for the first time, brought the issue of civil-military relations to the fore.

The 1973 demonstrations marked the emergence of new actors onto the Thai political stage: civilians who could no longer be pushed aside. Sarit and his successor, Field Marshal Thanom Kittikachorn, had presided over a period of rapid development, both in Bangkok and the provinces. The communications and transport infrastructure grew, the educational system expanded, cities swelled, many factories were built, and the service sector flourished. All this development also brought about changes in the social structure; labor, the provincial business elite, and middle-class strata all expanded rapidly (Anderson 1977).

The emergence of civilian rule is generally attributed to the advent of a middle class, but it is impossible to understand military reactions without recognizing that all classes and social strata became more politically active in the 1970s (Ockey 1999). Although the students who led the demonstrations in 1973, and later in 1976, were drawn largely from the middle class, the demonstrators themselves came mostly from the lower classes. The fear of communism behind the reaction of the military and its paramilitary allies during the next three years can only be understood as genuine fear of this element. When students began to organize workers and peasants outside the political system, military fears were exacerbated.

Morell and Samudavanija (1981) have argued that the military continued to play a preeminent role behind the scenes during the 1973–1976 period of civilian rule. Although this is undoubtedly true, it overlooks certain crucial changes in civil-military relations. First, with three leading officers forced into exile, the military had lost leaders of large vertical factions; when the defense minister, Gen. Krit Sivara, died unexpectedly in 1976, it lost another. At the same time, members of the first large military academy classes, beginning with Class Five (Table 7.2), were being promoted to major and lieutenant colonel, whereby they occupied important positions in the command structure.[11] Struggles over promotion intensified, and some of these classes forged strong ties that would make up the basis for horizontal factions. Second, with civilians in charge of the government, the potential existed for politicization of promotion, and certain high-ranking generals did seek alliances with political parties. With these two changes, the large patronage-based vertical factions declined in importance, and the influence of top generals in politics and over other officers was reduced. Third, with the advent of parliamentary rule the struggle against "the communists" became more open and expanded into Bangkok. Many military officers saw the emergence of left-wing political parties, labor unions, and radical student groups as evidence of the growth of communism. Counterinsurgency became not just a battle fought in isolated border regions, but a battle that had to be fought in the university, in the workplace, and even in the parliament itself. In this way, politics became subordi-

TABLE 7.2   Military Academy Class Sizes[a]

1946	159	1956	139	1966	196	1976	277
1947	19	1957	165	1967	192	1977	311
1948	6	1958	137	1968	198	1978	283
1949	28	1959	135	1969	188	1979	268
1950	33	1960	168	1970	240	1980	365
1951	57	1961	147	1971	238	1981	257
1952	59	1962	178	1972	276	1982	333
1953	148	1963	141	1973	267	1983	314
1954	170	1964	181	1974	286	1984	329
1955	136	1965	183	1975	371	1985	325

[a]Thailand adopted the West Point curriculum in 1949 and designated that cohort as Class One. Class Five entered the military academy in 1953.

Source. Counted from list of names in *100 Pi rongrian nairoi phrachulachomklaeo* (100 Years of the Chulachomklaeo Military Academy) n.d.

nate to counterinsurgency for some in the military: politicians and their decisions had to be vetted for reasons of national security. Fourth, the battle against "the communists" became more open to scrutiny.[12] Thus as the battle expanded, paramilitary forces and other local influential figures became involved in the killing of suspected communists, undermining the military monopoly over the use of war weapons. Indeed, the general pattern for the military during this period, when viewed from within, was a weakening of influence and a fragmentation of power, especially at the center.

In 1976, the brief experiment with parliamentary rule ended at Thammasat University in a bloody massacre of "communist" students by paramilitary forces and border police armed with heavy weapons. For the next year, a highly oppressive rightist regime under Prime Minister Thanin Kraiwichian governed in Thailand and placed top priority on defeating "the communists" through heavy-handed suppression. Instead, large numbers of noncommunists on the left felt obliged to leave the country or join the communist insurgency in the jungles. The ranks of the CPT swelled; and many of the new recruits were highly educated leaders from student and labor organizations. Many young officers who had fought in Vietnam believed that the repressive policies that had lost the Vietnam War were going to lead to a similar fate in Thailand. Two factions of this opinion—the Young Turks, organized around Military Academy Class Seven, and the Democratic Soldiers, organized ideologically and drawing mainly on staff officers—were particularly important in their support for a coup that overthrew the repressive regime in 1977.[13]

Counterinsurgency and Democracy

The Young Turks and the Democratic Soldiers provided crucial support for the two army generals who became prime minister during the 1978–1988 period. They were also largely responsible for the counterinsurgency policy that followed. The new policy, later formalized in Prime Ministerial Order 66/2523, was based on the belief that the best way to fight communism was through democracy. Along with development and suppression, building democratic institutions became a key pillar of the counterinsurgency strategy. Although this can be seen as a return to the tradition of democracy established in 1932, it is important to keep in mind that in the late 1970s, democratization was not occurring out of any military commitment to democratic principles. Democracy was a policy, a weapon in a war. Prime Ministerial Order 66/2523 was fundamental, not democracy and not the constitution. Democracy was subordinated to counterinsurgency. Perhaps the most important impact of this focus on counterinsurgency rather than democracy was the emergence of an extremely conservative polity. The new constitution discriminated against left-of-center parties, and the military continued to infiltrate and suppress the left, especially in the early 1980s. Because democracy was a weapon, the military sought to control it. They did so by maintaining control over key positions in the cabinet until the late 1980s. At the local level, they built up conservative militarist mass-based institutions such as the Thai National Defense Volunteers, the Military Reservists for National Security, and the Thahan Phran to promote the military's version of democracy. Military television and radio broadcasting facilities were employed to promote military ideas of democracy. The new democracy was to be conservative and representative rather than participatory: there was to be no active participation by the lower classes.

Although democratization was initially limited, it was nonetheless a considerable change from the Thanin period. This, combined with an amnesty to CPT defectors and a concerted attack in the field, constituted the military's counterinsurgency policy. By about 1984, the military was able to declare victory over the CPT.[14] It is difficult to overestimate the importance of this victory to the Thai military. For them it was a war that had been going on for 30 years. Thailand had been so often characterized as another Vietnam, as the next domino to fall, that the military had come to see counterinsurgency as the key to national survival, even though the insurgents never numbered more than about 11,000 (Saiyud 1986: 188). And, of course, the military in Thailand had succeeded where the U.S. military had failed in Vietnam, Laos, and Cambodia. Not only was it a great victory but it combined many of the earlier military roles—including development, democracy, and national security—and demonstrated to the military its own expertise. Moreover, by defeating its longtime enemy, the military had completed the domestic phase of a mission begun nearly 40 years earlier. Left without a battlefield mission at home after the destruction of the Thai communist party, the military actually increased its role in development with such high-profile projects as Isan Khieo (Green Northeast) for drought relief in the arid northeast and Harapan Baru (New Hope) for the south.

Of course there were differences within the military concerning the appropriate nature of democracy. Indeed, the two coup attempts in the 1980s both resulted in part from differences over the nature and pace of democratization (Samudavanija 1982). Other officers, such as retired army commander Gen. Prem Tinsulanon, who was prime minister from 1979 to 1988, his successor Chavalit Yongchaiyuth, and others like them, helped to prevent military takeovers during the 1980s, allowing the parliament as an elected institution to gain some degree of continuity. Meanwhile, civilian politicians in the parliament proved themselves more adept than military officers in the political arena and gradually took over many of the positions the military had used to maintain political dominance. The number of military seats in the senate slowly diminished, and civilian politicians, especially provincial entrepreneurs, gradually took over cabinet ministries that had earlier gone to (retired) military officers (Anek 1988). Public pressure for change also played an important role. Perhaps the most important transition occurred in 1988, when General Prem, under pressure from the press and the public, stepped down as prime minister and was replaced by an elected member of parliament, Chatchai Chunhawan, a long-retired army general who retained little influence in the military. Although on the surface this looked like a victory for civilian politicians, just three years later Chatchai was overthrown.

When Chatchai became prime minister, he took over the defense portfolio. In practice, however, almost all decision making under the defense ministry was delegated to military leaders. Thus at the same time that the cabinet was demilitarized, the military was gaining greater control over internal military affairs. Furthermore, while Prem had carefully balanced factions against each other in military promotions, by the end of the 1980s, continuing to do so was becoming impossible. Many members of Class Seven had been discharged after involvement in two failed coup attempts in 1981 and 1985, and the large and powerful Class Five had no real rivals. When General Chavalit retired in 1990, Class Five was left in control of the military. Shortly thereafter, Class Five carried out a coup, the first in fourteen years, to prevent the dismissal of its leader, army commander Gen. Suchinda Kraprayoon. Class Five promised to clean up the corruption in the political system and restore a better democracy within one year.

During its brief period of political dominion, Class Five set out to undermine the power of civilian politicians and restore the military's preeminence. A new constitution was written that would return most of the power the military had gradually lost during the 1980s. A military-supported political party was organized and given enough financial backing to ensure victory. In 1992, elections were held, the military-backed party won, and General Suchinda left the army to become prime minister. Some of the politicians the military had accused of corruption were named to the cabinet. This attempted reversal of the democratic process led to the bloody events of May 1992, disgraced the military, and led to the ongoing withdrawal. This withdrawal, however reluctant, has been much different from the military's withdrawal from the cabinet and the senate in the 1980s: it has been much more wide ranging. Unlike in the 1980s, when the military actually took greater control of its internal affairs and expanded its economic and social role, in the 1990s civilians have begun to exert control over military activities. Nevertheless, despite reforms, many of the characteristics of the military version of democracy remain.

CURRENT TRENDS: AULD LANG SYNE?

In the aftermath of the 1992 massacre, the constitution was amended to increase civilian control. However, pressure for constitutional reform continued. Eventually the government agreed to appoint a committee to write a new constitution. The politics of reform have been detailed elsewhere (McCargo 1998) and need not concern us here. The results of the reform indicate the continuation of many characteristics of the military version of democracy. The new constitution rewards large existing parties, primarily through a party list system, making it more difficult for new left-wing parties to form. More importantly, the new constitution retains the emphasis on representation, limiting opportunities for lower-class participation, especially in national politics. This is accomplished in at least two ways. First, to join the cabinet, members of parliament have to resign from the parliament. This ensures that no minister is directly responsible to local constituents. Second, and more directly, under the new constitution, all candidates for the parliament must have at least a bachelor's degree. This effectively removes the lower classes, indeed the vast majority of the population, from direct participation in national politics. Ironically the carefully controlled democracy initiated by the military thus remains, although it is no longer controlled by the military, but rather by middle-class reformers. Meanwhile, the role of the military in politics has changed greatly during this same period.

The Thai military entered the post-1992 era thoroughly discredited in the political arena. Yet much of the role expansion that occurred in the 1980s continued into the 1990s. The military was active in rural development, in propagating democracy, in disseminating information through its control of radio and television stations, and in foreign policy. Both the military as institution and its members had extensive business interests, and some were involved in illicit activities. In addition, it had almost complete control over its own internal structures and over promotions within its ranks. Another member of Class Five was named the new army commander in chief—an indication of the power of Class Five, and the lack of alternatives. Unlike his predecessor, the new commander Gen. Wimon Wongwanit was considered to be a highly professional soldier. Under his command, the military began to move away from direct involvement in politics. This resolution to disengage was not without a certain reluctance, however, and not without considerable regret. This process of increasing professionalism and decreasing politicization continues within the context of military tradition—particularly regarding the military's role, its past traditions and victories, its structure, its past business activities, and the cumulative military mindset. If we wish to examine the military's withdrawal from politics, we must consider changes in the structure of the military and issues of supply, especially the budget and personnel. Under supply we must also consider the business interests of the military, both public and private. Perhaps most important are changes in the role of the military given its historical role, not only in politics but in development, in the propagation of democracy, in the media, and in foreign policy.

Structural Changes

During his term as minister of defense in 1996–1997, retired general Chavalit instituted a study of the structure of the military to improve efficiency and civilian oversight. The study was undertaken by a committee composed primarily of military officers, along with some civilians, and the results were submitted by General Chavalit to the Defense Council in September 1997.[15] No further action was taken, however, until civilian prime minister and defense minister Chuan Leepkai had his defense adviser, an army general, present the plan to the chiefs of staff in July 1998. At that time the plan was also reported in the press, giving it greater urgency. The restructuring would place the supreme commander (and the chiefs of each force) under the defense permanent secretary, who had been outside the chain of command. This proposal would have brought the Ministry of Defense into line with the structure of other government ministries. A second proposal would have reduced the size of the Defense Council from 33 members to 22; in the process, the representatives of the Supreme Command and the three branches of the armed services would have been reduced by more than half, from 20 to 8, leaving them with less than a majority of the council.[16] When the plan proved controversial, Defense Minister Chuan insisted that it was only a report and no proposal had yet been submitted. He also took the opportunity, however, to state that "civilians in the future would play a role in security matters."[17] When the plan finally emerged in January 2000, much of the focus was on reducing the size of the military, a goal of military leaders. The command structure was not as Chuan wished. Instead, the Defense Council opted for the structure preferred by military leaders, a joint chiefs–style structure, with the supreme commander acting as chair. Although this new structure will increase the power of the supreme commander and help unify the armed forces, the service commanders will still retain considerable power and autonomy. Thus far, Chuan's claim of a civilian role in national security has not yet been extended to the level where major restructuring can take place over the objections of the military.

Supply: Budget

The most pressing issues in civil-military relations are questions of supply. The economic boom of the late 1980s and early 1990s allowed the Thai government to expand the military budget at a rapid enough rate to keep the military happy. The economic crisis of the late 1990s left the military with little choice but to sacrifice its budgetary interests for the good of the nation.

To understand the subsequent changes in the budget and their importance, it is first necessary to look at the sources of funding for individual officers and their factions. Until the end of the decade, there were lucrative opportunities for officers and factions to support themselves through various private dealings—particularly in protection for illegal activities, in the border trade, and through commissions on arms sales. Moreover, at least three somewhat more legitimate sources were available—special allowances, unaudited profits from military enterprises such as radio stations, and the military secret fund. During the 1990s, each of these sources of income was threatened.

In the 1980s, there was a thriving business in smuggling goods across the Burmese and Cambodian borders. Along both these borders, during most of the 1980s, trade was restricted and military officers were in a position to exert a great deal of control. Where officers were not directly involved in trade, they could demand protection money from those who were. This trade helped to finance the development of military factions and enriched individual officers. In 1988, however, when Chatchai Chunhawan became prime minister, he announced a policy of "turning battlefields into markets." Not only were trade restrictions lifted along Thai borders with Burma, Laos, and Cambodia, but trade was actively promoted. In the short term, this policy may have increased the ability of the military to make money from their powerful position along the border. In particular, certain officers took advantage of their positions to sign contracts with the Burmese government—at the expense of the insurgents. Over the long term, however, as trade became better regulated and procedures standardized, as concessions were locked up, and as politicians became increasingly active in border trade, opportunities for military officers narrowed.[18] This limited important sources of finance for military factions. As military influence in the political system waned in the late 1980s, criminals turned increasingly to politicians for protection—especially after the Ministry of the Interior came under the control of civilian politicians. The leaders of the 1991 coup made a major effort to restore their influence in this area. The Ministry of the Interior was placed under the control of a top general, and the most powerful Bangkok "godfather" was assassinated immediately after the coup. Then coup leaders cracked down on underground casinos and threatened criminals with exile to a remote island. Success was limited, however, because civilian politicians returned a year later.

The economic crisis focused attention on the corrupt activities of individuals, including some in the military. The prime minister and the army's commander in chief sought to crack down on narcotics trafficking, extortion rackets, illegal bookmaking, unsecured loans from the Thai Military Bank, and corruption in the conscription process.[19] The crackdown on the military mafia has been blamed for a spate of bombings in Bangkok and Chiangmai. Although it may have made General Surayud unpopular with some in the military, attacking corruption during the economic crisis certainly made him popular with the public and, should he succeed, may enhance the prestige of a "new" military.

Prior to the economic crisis, the secret funds and income from military enterprises remained unaudited and outside the sphere of civilian control. Furthermore, as the military budget rose, arms sales expanded and, along with them, so did commissions. Proposed arms deals reached a peak in 1996 when the military put together a list of essential weapons acquisitions: for the army, new tanks; for the navy, two submarines; for the air force, F-18s; for the Ministry of Defense, a satellite. The cost would have been 75 billion baht ($3 billion), at a time when the current accounts deficit was high. When civilians questioned the purchases, defense minister General Chavalit declared, "Arms acquisitions are an internal affair of the military. Outsiders stay away. It's not right for them to get involved."[20] The commissions paid on those purchases, had they been completed, would have amounted to hundreds of millions of U.S. dollars.

With the economic crisis, the government budget had to be pared. The military found itself facing rather large cuts and very specific cuts. The prime minister called on the military to cut the number of military attachés posted overseas, for example, and specified how many could be retained and in which countries. Combat allowances were cut back, which provoked considerable anger: some military men even suggested that the concurrent spate of bombing might be in retaliation for the cuts and in frustration with the civilian minister of defense.[21] Cuts were resisted, sometimes successfully, yet civilians more than ever before were directly involved in the allocation of resources in the military budget. This is particularly evident in the decision of the civilian government to take back proceeds from military-owned radio stations, which may amount to as much as 10 billion baht ($265 million) a year. This decision has been strongly resisted by the military, however, which is allowed to use these funds for the welfare of soldiers under a martial law decree issued in 1972.[22] The government is also seeking to audit military secret funds. Furthermore, the civilian prime minister has revived a committee in the Ministry of Defense with the responsibility to oversee the purchase of all weapons, thus removing decision-making authority from the services. But with most of the military budget committed to salaries, budget cuts leave little room for weapons purchases in any case. Thus the military itself has been calling for cuts in personnel so that more money will be available for modernization.

Finally, the economic crisis and political pressure presented an opportunity for the budget scrutiny committee of the parliament to increase its control over the defense budget. Prior to the May 1992 uprising, the debate on the military budget was largely pro forma, and military budgets were approved with little change (Satha-anan 1996; Panitan 1998). Although the debate became more contentious after 1992, it was not until the economic crisis that the committee finally managed to pressure the service commanders to appear in person to defend their budget.

Information is still less comprehensive than that from other departments, however. For the 1999 budget, Defense Minister Chuan managed to convince military leaders that they must set an example by allowing defense cuts at least equal to the average of other ministries. They complied voluntarily, allowing for a shorter debate and less controversy than usual.[23] In the 1999 budget, the military received a slight increase over 1998, which was still well below the overall average increase.

Supply: Personnel and Promotions

Even before the economic crisis, the military was considering its future level of personnel. Some had proposed that the military be radically reduced in numbers and the budget spent instead on sophisticated modern weapons systems.[24] The shortage of engineers and other technicians in Thailand, as well as the sheer scope of such changes, would make this transition difficult and no doubt expensive. Smaller though still substantial cuts are now planned: the military has announced its intention to reduce the number of troops by 20 percent, from 236,000 to 190,000, by 2007.[25] This is in addition to troop cuts made in the mid-1990s.

More controversial has been the issue of promotion, especially to the rank of general. Back in the mid-1960s, as the CPT built strength and the Vietnam War escalated, Thai leaders decided to expand the military at a faster rate. The curriculum at the military academy was streamlined to allow some to graduate more quickly, and more cadets were admitted. Now, some 30 years later, that cohort of officers is at the age where promotion to general is to be expected.[26] Promotions have been based not on military need or qualification, but on time in service. The result is a military that had, by 1997, far too many generals: about one-quarter of all generals had no responsibilities. To reduce the number of generals with no duties, Prime Minister (and Defense Minister) Chuan extended an early retirement scheme put in place by his predecessor, Prime Minister (and Defense Minister) Chavalit. As a further indication of the degree to which promotion has come to be viewed as an entitlement, the incentive package for early retirement included a promotion.[27] By July 1998, only 65 officers had applied for early retirement. At that time, according to the military, there were 1,859 generals—616 of them without responsibilities.[28]

Prime Minister Chuan proposed two other methods of limiting the number of high-ranking officers. He proposed a longer time in rank for major generals and lieutenant generals, and he said that in the future only 75 percent of retiring generals would be replaced. Whereas this was the case in the September reshuffle, when only about 75 percent were replaced, the number of generals promoted earlier in the year in two smaller reshuffles left the military with about the same number overall. If we look at class sizes at the time of entry to the military academy (Table 7.2), it is clear that there is no relief in sight: in fact, class sizes expanded further in 1972, and those officers will soon reach the age where they should be promoted to the rank of general. Class size remained large at least until the mid-1980s, with particularly large intakes in 1975 and 1980. Officers from the 1985 entering class will not reach mandatory retirement until approximately 2025. The plans to reduce troop numbers will exacerbate the problem. Pressures for promotion, therefore, will intensify. Another incentive plan has been adopted to encourage retirement of senior officers, but it may not be enough unless some sort of provision is made to force the retirement of less capable officers.

A shift in the nature of promotion—from an entitlement mentality to institutional need—would contribute substantially to the civilianization of the military. Certainly the idea of an entitlement to the rank of general limits the ability of civilians to control promotions (and thus the rank hierarchy in the military). More importantly, the idea of entitlement indicates a focus on the prestige of individual officers rather than the efficiency of the institution. This self-interest in promotion has been a major incentive in past coups. Yet the ability and willingness to curb promotion has so far been limited.

Role

Perhaps the most important changes have been those affecting the role of the military. Earlier we considered changes in the military's role in politics and the military's role in the economy. But at least three more areas, all of them deemed important to national security, have seen changes. In terms of foreign policy, the military has come to play an important role in relations with Cambodia, Laos, and Burma because of shared borders where insurgencies have long been in existence and because of the Thai battle against communism. Two other areas where the military has taken on a key role are development and democracy: the key pillars of the counterinsurgency policy aimed at protecting Thailand from internal enemies.

Although the military began to employ democracy as a counterinsurgency weapon and restored limited democracy in 1978, generals and retired generals continued to control the Ministry of Foreign Affairs for the next decade. During this period Thai generals developed close personal and economic ties with antigovernment leaders in Cambodia and with Burmese and Laotian generals. These links helped the military to dominate relations with Cambodia and Burma—and, to a lesser degree, with Laos—long after the foreign affairs portfolio passed to civilian hands. Relations between the Thai and Burmese generals remained so close that when the Burmese government arrested some Thai and other foreign protesters in 1998, it was not the Ministry of Foreign Affairs but the army commander General Chettha who successfully negotiated their release.[29] When Gen. Surayud Chulanont was named army commander in 1998, he reportedly insisted that the military must leave the conduct of foreign affairs to the Ministry of Foreign Affairs.[30] Whatever his intentions, General Surayud soon found this impossible. Less than a month later, he stated that personal relationships remained necessary in dealing with Burma, although he still wanted the Ministry of Foreign Affairs to play the leading role.[31] Within the first five months of his tenure, he visited Burma, Cambodia, Singapore, and the Philippines. The Senate Military Affairs Committee lent sanction to the ongoing role in foreign policy, arguing that for some neighboring countries with a strong military influence, there were opportunities for the military to form relationships rapidly and efficiently, and such opportunities should be pursued. The military was to cooperate with the Ministry of Foreign Affairs in carrying out government policy (Samnakngan lekhathikan wuthisapha 1997: 35–36). Although the military's role in foreign affairs may be externally driven, in the short term it is set to continue.

During the 1990s, development work and the propagation of democracy continued at the village level, but with little publicity.[32] This low-level but pervasive participation has been paired with an occasional high-profile offer to provide assistance, such as the offer in the fall of 1998 to take over the installation of a telephone network that had been stymied by charges of price fixing. By refusing all such offers, civilian politicians have limited the ability of the military to take advantage of its efforts at a national level, as it did in the late 1980s. Nor is it clear just how effective the military has been at influencing civilians at the local level. What is clear, however, is that these efforts continue to reinforce in soldiers the idea that development and the propagation of democracy are proper military roles and part of national security. Indeed, the military's role in development has been enshrined in the constitution (Article 5, Section 72) and encouraged by the monarchy.[33] Military participation in development and propagation of democracy also serve as a reminder of the great victory over the CPT through Prime Ministerial Order 66/2523.

Interpretations of History

With such conflicts over compensation and budget, over personnel and promotion, over role and structure, it is indeed curious that the greatest controversy has been stirred over interpretations of history. Earlier I outlined three conflicts in the interpretations of the past. Here I focus on one of them—the controversy over the appointment of the former prime minister Field Marshal Thanom Kittikachorn as a royal guard—in the hope of explaining this struggle over history.

Thanom's career encompasses all of the military's major missions except the most recent. He entered the military academy in 1920, when the mission of the Thai army was to defend the monarchy from internal threats and all senior officers were members of the royal family. At the time the military overthrew the monarchy and established itself in its own eyes as a democratic military, Thanom was just eight years out of the academy. He participated in the nation building of the 1930s and 1940s. Thanom rose rapidly during the 1950s as a protégé of strongman Sarit Thanarat, who later refocused the military on development as a counterinsurgency policy. After the death of Sarit, Thanom carried on his legacy by maintaining the close alliance with the United States, focusing on development rather than democracy, and leading the fight against the communists in Indochina and at home. In 1973, the Thanom government arrested activists calling for a return to democracy—a move that sparked the mass uprisings of 1973, which resulted in the deaths of 73 people after the military opened fire on the demonstrators. Thanom, his son Colonel Narong, and Narong's father-in-law, Field Marshal Praphat Charusathian, were disgraced and forced into exile, although Thanom and Praphat were later cleared of responsibility for the killings by a police report.[34] Thanom also played a role in the massacre of October 1976: his return as a Buddhist monk sparked the student demonstrations that ended in a bloody massacre at Thammasat University. It was his role in these two massacres that led to the protests over his appointment as a royal guard. Thanom was not involved during the 1980s when, from the military's perspective, it won the victory over communism through its promotion of democracy. Nor was he involved in the 1992 massacre.

The events of 1973 occurred a long time ago. What explains the desire, at this late date, to insist on the honor for Thanom? What explains the depth of the reaction? Lt. Gen. Kittisak Ratprasert, a staff officer attached to the defense minister, has revealed some of the military's motives: it was a sentimental gesture between subordinates and a former commander; it was to honor him as the founder of the 31st Infantry Regiment; and it was to allow him to wear a uniform when he attended the military parade on the king's birthday.[35] For the military, in other words, it was about honor, about dignity, about recognizing the achievements of an officer who, for most of his career, had carried out his mission loyally and faithfully. For the protesters, however, it was an insult to the martyrs of the democracy movement: honoring the former dictator undermined the democracy that had been established.

An examination of the key players in the drama is revealing. The appointment, according to one source, was initiated by Gen. Yutthasak Sasiprapha, defense permanent secretary and son-in-law of Field Marshal Praphat. He then retired before the award was made. The award was approved by the army's commander, General Chettha, reportedly a former aide to Thanom who also retired shortly afterward. The decision was defended by an air force chief adviser, Air Chief Marshal Yutthiphong Kittikachorn, son of Thanom, and by the secretary to the defense minister, Gen. Nareunat Kamphanatsaenyakon, brother-in-law of General Yutthasak.[36] Not only was it a matter of institutional honor, then, but also a matter of family honor. To take another example, eight members of the Nunphakdi family enrolled at the military academy between 1916 and 1961, including the army commander and the regional commander in Bangkok during the 1992 protests, and this does not include relatives with other surnames or loyal subordinates. Nor is the Nunphakdi family the largest or most prominent military family.[37] The history and traditions of the Thai military are deeply entrenched in families such as these and in subordinates loyal to their former commanders, ensuring that honor and history will remain relevant for many. There is considerable hurt, even resentment, that the military's contributions to development and democracy, the victory over the communists, and the other successful missions are overlooked by civilians who remember only the infractions of the military. And there is conflict over how to remove the stain on military honor. Some officers, such as those who sparked the three controversies over history, wish to see it cleansed. Others, such as the current army commander, who called for the release of the investigation report on the May massacre, apparently want to acknowledge past mistakes and look to the future.

For civilian activists, the primary consideration is to ensure that the actions of the military in 1973, 1976, and 1992 are viewed as disgraceful lest they be repeated. For the 1992 massacre, there is also the matter of those relatives and friends still missing. At another level, their identity is closely tied to the democratic uprisings. These events define them as loyal Thai middle-class democrats and define the military as the enemy of democracy (Ockey 1999), an identity that is threatened whenever interpretations of the democratic uprisings are challenged. The interpretation of the history of the 1973 uprising has never been settled. At the time of the recent controversy, it had not even been included in textbooks despite its pivotal role in the development of Thai society and politics. One further element has also focused attention on the interpretation of military history. Since the end of the cold war, the military has had no enemy and no clearly defined mission. As it struggles to find a new mission, to develop a new role, the military also finds itself struggling to defend its role and missions of the past. The struggle over the past is inextricably tied to the struggle over the future.

UNDERSTANDING THE EVENTS OF 1992

Although the events of 1992 may be a watershed in civil-military relations in Thailand, they cannot be fully understood without examining the history, traditions, missions, and military mindset that have developed over the last century. At one level, 1992 can be seen as the culmination of the mission to propagate democracy. After all, the justification for the 1991 coup was to clean up the political system, remove the corrupt politicians, and then return to a purified democracy. We should not forget that in 1991 the coup was acceptable to many for exactly this reason. The protests emerged when the military tried to retain power without removing the corrupt politicians. Not surprisingly, the military attempted to justify the crackdown by raising the communist threat. Unfortunately, with the CPT defunct for some eight years, this proved unconvincing. The military mission of eliminating the communists through democracy, once a great success, now ended in a failure. Having allowed democracy, and in the process eliminated communism it could not now destroy that democracy. This dual legacy, success in defeating communism but failure in propagating democracy, is behind much of the struggle over the meaning of history, and the future role of the Thai military. It is in this light that we must see some of the struggles over history and the military's determination to have the success of earlier missions recognized.

All militaries are mission oriented, few more so than the Thai military. Examining the past missions and traditions of the Thai military reveals the depth of its roles in society and politics. It is a military with professional ethics that have restrained it from entrenching itself at the top of the political system and with a colonial-style focus on internal security reconfirmed during the cold war. It is a military developed as a political force, as a protector of the monarchy, which nevertheless sees itself as democratic. It is a military with factions and certain individuals deeply involved in making money through means licit and illicit. It is a military highly centralized in Bangkok. It is a military that promotes development and propagates democracy as a strategy to defeat its enemies. Its greatest victory was against an internal enemy. It is a military used to making decisions dealing with national security and "internal" matters such as promotion and allocation of its budget. All these things are deeply entrenched and cannot easily be rooted out.

Furthermore, the Thai military is not only mission oriented, it is missionizing. It has spent decades promoting anticommunism, development, and democracy. At present, the military has no enemy and is struggling to find a new mission. Staff officers have discussed a possible military role in narcotics suppression, protection of the forests, disaster relief, and development.[38] All of these proposed roles have a political component. One general proclaimed that by helping to protect the Thai forests, the military would be saving the world from global warming. Although this desire to save the nation and the world is admirable, it is also fraught with risk. Perhaps for this reason, civilians and the military by mutual agreement have given the military a permanent mission by enshrining its role in development in the constitution. Recently it has joined the peacekeeping force in East Timor and has announced the establishment of a peacekeeping training center; it has also been battling the narcotics trade along the northern border, where its efforts have won praise from the queen.[39] Internal Security Operations Command (ISOC), the organization responsible for the suppression of communism, has been converted to narcotics suppression.[40] Whether this will be mission enough remains to be seen. It may prove to be an important transitional mission as the military moves from its past role toward a more professional future. Yet it should be kept in mind that in its own view the military has always come to the nation's rescue in time of crisis. Unless the military's mindset is changed, it may act in similar fashion in the future, even if this involves interference in politics.

Although 1992 may be considered the unsuccessful culmination of a military mission, it marks a watershed in civil-military relations. Here an analogy can be drawn with the 1973 uprising, which had a similarly profound if quite different impact. It may even be argued that civil-military relations were a nonissue in Thailand prior to 1973, because civilians rarely governed for more than a year at a time, whereas the military governed for extensive periods. Since 1973 the military has not governed without an elected parliament for much more than a year at a time. Economic development in the 1960s resulted in the expansion of several social groups, including labor, provincial entrepreneurs, and the middle class. By the 1970s these groups were no longer willing to leave politics to military leaders and were demanding democratic institutions.

Although 1973, like 1992, was a watershed event, liberalization and civilianization did not automatically remove the military from politics. There ensued a period of struggle over the nature of the new relationship. The battle against communism meant that certain unacceptable civilian participants had to be removed from the political process. Most clearly in 1976, but throughout the 1980s and even into the 1990s, Thai democracy has not been receptive to the left or the lower classes in general. Although the counterinsurgency policy of the 1980s led the military to withdraw from many formal political positions, it seems clear that many in the military had every intention of retaining power and indeed developed alternative methods to do so. Only reluctantly did the military retreat from politics, and only when pressured. It may even be argued that military influence at the village level increased during the 1980s. Similarly, when the former army commander, Prime Minister Prem, left office and Prime Minister Chatchai took over, the military's influence actually increased as Chatchai sought to gain military support by turning over even more decision-making power to the army commander than before.

Like that of 1973, the uprising of 1992 can be seen as a watershed event; as in 1973, the transition to a new pattern of civil-military relations was highly contested. Other events, particularly the economic crisis, have helped to shape the new relationship. By the late 1990s, the role of the Thai military in politics and society was clearly on the wane. The most obvious changes have occurred in its political role as retired army officers have largely disappeared from the cabinet and the senate and generals have spoken out less often on political matters. Under a new constitution, civil servants and active-duty military officers are not eligible for cabinet positions or the new senate, which is elected. Retired soldiers won just 18 of the 200 senate seats in the 2000 election.[41] Important changes occurred as well in relation to the budget, promotions, and the military's role in development and the propagation of democracy. The economic crisis meant budget cuts across the board, depicted as a matter of national survival; the military could not refuse the calls for sacrifice. The calls were for large cuts, but also for very specific cuts, as civilians began to tell the military how to spend its budget. Attempts are also being made to increase monitoring of the secret fund and to gain control over military income, especially from its radio and television stations. Continuing globalization, some of it forced on Thailand by international agencies in the wake of the economic crisis, further exposes the role of the military to international scrutiny and serves to limit it. On the other hand, retired generals continue to play powerful roles in all the political parties, and newly retired senior generals are heavily recruited. In this way, retired officers continue to have a major influence on politics.

As for the promotion process, ironically the military itself has ensured the entry of civilians into the process by seeking the promotion of the officer responsible for the killing of demonstrators in 1992. This choice was politically impossible, of course, and objections were raised by various groups in society. When the supreme commander continued to support this candidate, the civilian prime minister had to involve himself in the promotion process. Moreover, another problem with promotion is developing: as members of large military academy classes reach the age when promotion to general is expected, the number of personnel (and positions) is shrinking. The excessive number of generals—many of them without responsibilities—is likely to remain a problem unless attitudes toward promotion change.

The military's role in development and the propagation of democracy has changed as well. Although the military remains involved, the high-profile projects of the late 1980s have ended, and current efforts are local and without publicity. In relations with Thailand's neighbors, top generals continue to pursue personal relationships with their politically powerful counterparts. Although this practice may be externally driven to some degree, the role of the military remains strong. Thus far civilians have been unable to change the basic structure of the military, as well, although the efforts continue.

Finally, it must be mentioned that some things are not yet really contested. The military presence in Bangkok remains high, for example, a legacy from its origins in the 1880s that was reconfirmed each time it staged a coup. In the few cases where facilities have been relocated elsewhere, it was only after significant compensation was paid for the land (and the new facilities were sited near Bangkok). There is no military reason for the excessive number of troops and bases in Bangkok. There are, however, political and economic reasons. It would be much more difficult for the military to exert its influence if its troops were posted in border regions.[42] In addition, there are also better schools, a better lifestyle, and more economic opportunities, not all legitimate, for underpaid soldiers and their families in Bangkok.

Conflict over the military's history and its future role is ongoing. Indeed, the military itself is split over its past and its future. Old military families may be deeply socialized into the traditions, the missions, and the legacies of the past. Other officers, however, have been socialized differently. Officers are socialized not just in the academy but in many of the same ways as society as a whole. Here we must keep in mind that the current army commander in chief was just 30 years old at the time of the 1973 uprising—only a few years older than the students who led the demonstrations. The passing of the large and powerful Class Five from the scene has opened the way for such younger officers. These young officers have spent more of their lives under democracy than under military rule and may find much in common with civilian counterparts in their desire to see an effective democracy and a professional military. Indeed, exit polls indicate that soldiers in Bangkok preferred civilian candidates in the recent senate elections.[43] Differences of opinion in the military appear along other lines as well. Attitudes among staff officers in Bangkok have changed much more than have attitudes of those in the field, for example. At present, the trends are positive. Many said the same thing in 1991, however, just before the coup. The reluctance to withdraw, the desire to rescue the past, perhaps the hope of a return to a greater role in the future—apparently such feelings remain strong among many military officers.[44] Reducing the military's role has been a struggle, and civilian activists feel a need to maintain the pressure. It is fear of a resurgent military that motivates their vigilance and their distrust of the military. Perhaps they are right. It remains to be seen whether the future offers a new era or simply a longing for the past and broken resolutions.

CHAPTER 8

Bangladesh:
An Uneasy Accommodation

Amena Mohsin

> There will never be any coup in Bangladesh.... Everyone [in the army] wants peace and politicians to run the country.
>
> —Maj. Gen. (retired) Mahbubur Rahman, 1996

> Despite the limitation of our resources my government is promise bound to build an efficient, well-equipped, strong, and modern military.
>
> —Sk. Hasina, 1999

ON DECEMBER 6, 1990, PRESIDENT H. M. ERSHAD was forced to resign in the face of a popular upsurge against him. It was a watershed in the political history of Bangladesh, for it terminated fifteen years of military rule. The Bengali nation, otherwise known for its polarized and violent politics, had demonstrated a rare and remarkable unity. The entire civil and political society joined the movement to oust Ershad, the ex-general who had ruled the country for nine years both in and out of uniform. Even the military, the main bastion of Ershad's power, withdrew its support for the regime. Since 1991 Bangladesh has been under democratic rule, and constitutionally the military is under the control of civilian authority. But the military, which zealously guards its corporate interests, is still very much a political force. In several ways, civilian political leaders and the military are dependent on each other and are still struggling to define the relationship between military and state. For the present, there is an uneasy accommodation between the two institutions.[1]

The Bangladesh military is alive to the changed domestic and international political milieu. The demise of the cold war brought in its wake a wave of global democratization. International nongovernmental organizations (NGOs), international human rights organizations, and an international civil society have emerged as political forces that national governments have to reckon with. Military (or military-backed) regimes are no longer acceptable to the comity of nations. At the domestic level, the highly politicized civil society in Bangladesh and its role in the ouster of Ershad demonstrates that military regimes will no longer be tolerated. In fact, Bangladesh has a long tradition of democratic movements. East Bengal's autonomy campaign within the state of Pakistan was in essence a movement to establish the democratic rights of Bengalis. But Bangladesh has yet to evolve a stable democratic system. Political parties have failed to establish themselves as stable democratic institutions. Politics is run on the basis of personalities rather than institutions or ideologies. Political polarization has taken root in civil society as well.

The military has come out of its earlier factionalism, however, and stands today as a coherent, disciplined institution. During its long years in politics, it has through the distortion of the political process gained a dominant position that ensures that its corporate interests will be satisfied irrespective of regime change. The configuration of domestic and international forces makes the possibility of direct military intervention most unlikely. But at the same time the weakness of political institutions and the coherence of the military make the relationship between the civil and the military an uneasy one.

Despite the weaknesses of its political institutions, Bangladesh today is a functioning democracy. Since 1991 two successive civilian governments have assumed power through directly contested elections that have generally been regarded as fair and free. In a bid to democratize the polity, the national parliament in September 1991 adopted a parliamentary system of government through the Twelfth Amendment. The prime minister is the head of government; the president, elected by the parliament, is the constitutional head. The Bangladesh constitution also ensures the supremacy of the civil over the military: it accepts democracy as a cardinal principle of state policy and in principle rules out any role for the military in the political affairs of the state. Article 61, Chapter 4, of the constitution vests the supreme command of the armed forces in the president. Article 62, Clause 1, gives parliament the power to regulate defense matters relating to the raising and maintaining of the armed forces, the granting of commissions, the appointment of chiefs of staff, and disciplinary matters relating to the armed forces. Article 63 provides that the state cannot participate in a war without the assent of parliament (Government of Bangladesh 1996: 46–48).

Institutionally also the military is not autonomous. The armed forces—the army, navy, and air force—are under the Ministry of Defense (MOD). The ministry prepares the defense budget on the basis of requests put forward by the three services. Promotion of senior military officials beyond the rank of colonel is approved by the defense minister, though the recommendations are made by Army Headquarters. The chiefs of the three services are appointed and serve at the discretion of the chief executive of government. The military carries out its functions according to the Army Act. Articles 292 and 293 of the act prohibit military personnel from any involvement in political matters (Government of Bangladesh 1986: 77).

In matters of intelligence gathering and threat assessment, civil institutions have supremacy. The National Security Intelligence (NSI), a civil institution under the control of the chief executive of the government, is in overall charge of national intelligence gathering, both internal and external. The director-general of Forces Intelligence (DGFI) is in charge of all intelligence gathering and is under the Ministry of Defense. Since independence, every chief executive has retained the portfolio of defense minister as well, so the entire military as well as intelligence apparatus has remained under the direct control of the chief executive.

Political analysts have cited extreme poverty, a turbulent socioeconomic milieu, and failure of political parties to evolve as viable institutions as factors leading to military intervention (Ahamed 1998: 116–17). Although the argument has some logic to it, the process is not unidirectional but cyclic. In the Bangladesh context, while the foregoing conditions were in existence, military intervention along with its attendant constitutional and political changes undermined the process of democratization and weakened political institutions. In fact it is no exaggeration to suggest that the military is largely responsible for the polarized state of the Bangladesh polity today. Yet military rule also provided the context for the unity of civil society and political parties. The military recognizes this situation and appears to have accepted civilian supremacy. At the same time, the civilian governments—due partly to their own weaknesses and partly to the past history of military intervention—have come to accept the military's privileged position. Until 1990, all changes in government in Bangladesh had been caused by military action or inaction.

In this chapter I argue that despite the history of military intervention in politics and its high level of politicization, the Bangladesh military is most unlikely to intervene directly in the future. However, despite the military's withdrawal from overt politics, civil-military relations are likely to remain tense. To substantiate this argument, this chapter is divided into four parts. The first explores the military's seizure of political power when civilian governments failed to meet diverse expectations unleashed by the long campaign for independence. The second section examines the militarization of the Bangladesh polity and the military rulers' quest for legitimization. Military rulers adopted a two-pronged strategy: on the one hand, constitutional changes were brought about and a civilianization process was set in place with the military playing a major role in the background; on the other hand, the military was kept satisfied. Consequently the military emerged as a key force in politics, and the Bangladesh polity became polarized. The third section analyzes the post-1990 civilian governments' accommodation of the military amidst the violent polarization of Bangladesh politics. The fourth section examines the May 1996 uprising in the military as a case in point: although the event presented the military with an excuse to intervene in politics, it refrained from doing so. The chapter concludes by exploring the changed international and domestic milieu that has brought about change in the military's attitude. These factors, it is argued, will set the parameters for the future.

MILITARY SEIZURE OF POLITICAL POWER

The assassination of Sheikh Mujibur Rahman (Mujib), the president as well as father of the nation, along with his family members, by a group of young army officers on August 15, 1975, marked the entry of the Bangladesh military into state politics. Yet the Bangladesh military—composed of the erstwhile Bengali members of the Pakistan military as well as the Mukti Bahini (liberation forces)—was already a highly politicized institution when the country was liberated on December 16, 1971. The experience of Bengali military personnel within the state of Pakistan and the nine months of liberation war with Pakistan had politicized this body. This tendency was further exacerbated by the failure of the Mujib regime to involve the military in state-building activities and, more important, its alleged neglect of the military. The regime's failures on the economic and political fronts, as we shall see, had also disenchanted the military.

The Pakistan Legacy

Although they represented the ethnic majority in the multiethnic state of Pakistan, Bengali military personnel within the Pakistan army occupied a marginalized position. The headquarters of the three services were established in western Pakistan. The Bengalis alleged that the Pakistan government continued the colonial policy of recruitment according to the "martial race" thesis.[2] Facts and figures only confirmed their allegations. In 1971, East Bengal's representation in the army was less than 5 percent (Ahamed 1988: 39). In the air force its representation was as follows: officers, 16 percent; warrant officers, 17 percent; other ranks, 30 percent. In the navy: officers, 10 percent; branch officers, 5 percent; chief petty officers, 10 percent; petty officers, 17 percent; leading seamen and below, 29 percent (Ahamed 1980: 69).

Frustrated by discrimination and marginalization, Bengali military officers maintained contact with the Awami League and lent their support to the Bengali autonomy movement. They had also been politicized by their experiences of military rule in Pakistan, where the country was literally administered by an alliance between the civil and military bureaucracy (Jahan 1972). The Bangladesh military, therefore, carried with it a praetorian tradition.

The Liberation War of Bangladesh

The nine-month-long liberation war had thoroughly politicized the forces that were to form the nucleus of the Bangladesh military. The Mukti Bahini liberation force was composed of Bengali troops who had revolted against Pakistan as well as youths who were recruited later. These youths were highly motivated and politically charged. The Bengali troops, a disciplined force, had already become political by the very act of revolt. These troops formed the chain of command of the liberation forces and—as a former part of the Pakistan military edifice—carried an anti-India psychosis with them. The Mukti Bahini therefore wanted to minimize the role of India, which had become a key factor in the liberation war. The Awami League leadership had not only taken refuge in India, but the provisional government of Bangladesh operated from headquarters in western Bengal (Ahmed 1993: 245).

The military leaders resented the reliance of the political leadership on India. Further, though the war strategy was prepared by the high command of Mukti Bahini (Maniruzzaman 1988: 113), the Indian army was involved in training and arming the troops. The Mukti Bahini was further annoyed by the formation of Mujib Bahini—a parallel military force formed by the Indian government consisting of close associates of Mujib—without the knowledge of the Bangladesh political and military leaders. This force remained outside the command of the provisional government and the Mukti Bahini (Mukul 1998).

The Mukti Bahini also alleged that the Indian army stole their thunder by stepping in at the last stage of war; and when the Pakistan forces surrendered to Lt. Gen. Jagjit Singh Aurora of the Indian army, the Mukti Bahini was not represented during the surrender ceremony. These became sore points in civil-military relations in Bangladesh. Thus independent Bangladesh inherited not only a politicized military but also an uneasy civil-military equation.

Mujib and the Military

Perhaps the greatest failure of Mujib lay in his inability to rise above party politics and become a statesman. His government failed to arrest rampant lawlessness and economic decline. Although the military was called out, it was withdrawn once it was discovered that Mujib's own party colleagues and family members were involved in these activities. Moreover, the military as well as the general public resented Mujib's close association with India in economic and military matters (Mohsin 1992).

Most important, perhaps, was the government's failure to build up the military. The cantonments and military institutes destroyed during the war were not rebuilt. The defense budget was not only minimal but was gradually reduced. Mujib rejected a substantial military as a useless extravagance (Ziring 1992: 97). Critics point out that Mujib even tried to create dissension within the army by appointing Safiullah as chief of staff, bypassing his senior, Zia ur Rahman (Zia).[3] Certainly the military also resented the creation of the Jatiyo Rakkhi Bahini (JRB), a paramilitary force, at a time when the military itself was being neglected. In January 1974, a law was passed giving the JRB special powers and legal protection. It was trained with Indian assistance (Hossain 1991: 76). The military regarded the JRB as a parallel institution and a threat to its corporate interests (Ibrahim 1999: 29).

Sheikh Mujib and his family members were assassinated on August 15, 1975, by a group of young majors. Some of them had their own personal scores to settle with Mujib. Although the military high command was not involved in the military coup of August 1975, the coup leaders later alleged that they had informed Zia, the deputy chief of staff, about their plans to bring about a "change" (Sayeed 1994: 218–19). No countercoup in favor of the civilian government took place. Because Mujib, through the Fourth Amendment to the constitution in January 1975, had turned the country into a one-party system—the BAKSAL—there existed no countervailing force that could offer itself as a civilian alternative to the Mujib regime (Kukreja 1991: 142). It is therefore plausible to suggest that the young majors took advantage of the prevailing socioeconomic situation, the political lacunae, and the strained state of civil-military relations.

Though some observers have suggested that the coup leaders had the blessings of the American embassy in Dhaka (Sayeed 1994: 254; Islam 1992: 47–48) and of certain Muslim countries, no conclusive evidence is available. Nonetheless, economic and political changes following the coup do not entirely rule out such a possibility. Of course one can also argue that in view of the general resentment toward the Mujib regime, successive governments deliberately adopted policies that would distance them from their predecessor.

The August 1975 coup not only brought the military into politics, it also changed the nature of politics, the state, and the relationship of the soldier to the state. The coup leaders declared Bangladesh to be an Islamic republic. Though Khondokar Mushtaque Ahmed, installed by the coup leaders as president, later moderated this position, his first speech bore an Islamic tone (Osmany 1992: 128). From then on Bangladesh shook off its secular garb. The state's politics were to become polarized, and the military was to become a factor in them.

THE MILITARY AND THE STATE

Bangladesh experienced a spate of military and quasi-military rule from August 1975 until December 1990. During this period important changes were introduced in the administrative, economic, and political milieus of the state. The primary objective of the military and military-dominated regimes was to keep the military satisfied.

Beefing Up the Military

The two military rulers of Bangladesh, Zia ur Rahman (Zia) and H. M. Ershad, were acutely aware of the military's powerful position. The military had intervened in 1975 when it perceived its corporate interests were being threatened. It should be noted here that though Zia was made the chief of army staff following the August 1975 coup, he did not initiate any coup. Rather he was catapulted into power in November 1975 following a series of coups and countercoups. In 1981 Zia was assassinated by the military when he began building an independent base of his own (Baxter and Rahman 1991a: 53). In 1990 the military withdrew its support from Ershad when it realized that he was becoming a liability. In other words, the military constituted the power behind the governments of the two generals.

At the outset of independence, the army was torn by internal conflict. The freedom fighters were divided along ideological lines: one group wanted a conventional army; the other wanted a revolutionary, production-oriented army based on the Chinese model. There were divisions, too, among the repatriated officers and the freedom fighters: Mujib had given two years seniority to the freedom fighters; the repatriated officers resented the fact that they had to serve under their juniors. Zia tried to redress the situation by promoting H. M. Ershad and Kazi Golam Dastagir, two of the most senior repatriated officers. Zia also appointed Ershad as the deputy chief of staff, a fact much regretted by the freedom fighters. He crushed the soldiers' revolt of November 7, 1977, that had brought him to power and hanged its leader, Colonel Taher. The movement toward a revolutionary army was thus brought to a halt. The JRB—another source of much resentment in the army—was dismantled and incorporated into the army. Zia rapidly expanded the size of the military and raised its salaries, allowances, and other benefits. The military budget increased substantially from $42 million in 1975 to $140 million in 1978 (International Institute for Strategic Studies [IISS] 1985: 172).

The militarization of government began during Zia's rule. At the beginning of 1980, for instance, the number of military officers appointed to top civilian positions was 41; by the end of the year the number had risen to 79 (Riaz 1994: 228). Though Zia's cabinet consisted of civilian and military bureaucrats and technocrats, it was essentially dominated by the military: indeed, it was under the supervision of Zia's principal staff officer (PSO), the most intimate of his confidants from the army (Ali 1994: 30).

The intelligence services, too, were brought under the military's dominance. In 1977 Zia appointed a senior general as director-general of NSI—until then a civilian body and the principal agency for intelligence gathering. This tradition was to continue long after his death. The DGFI, the military organ of intelligence gathering, also gained the upper hand in terms of credibility and reliability.[4] For a society that lacked stable political institutions, such as that in Bangladesh, these developments had far-reaching political implications. In security matters Zia moved away from India and came closer to China. His security perceptions did not come into conflict with the military, whereas the latter had strong reservations about Mujib's security perceptions.

Mujib considered India to be the closest ally of Bangladesh. He had signed the Treaty of Friendship, Cooperation and Peace with India. Article 8 of the treaty forbade Bangladesh to enter into or participate in any military alliance directed against India. Article 9 bound the two parties to refrain from giving any assistance to any third party in armed conflict. With Bangladesh surrounded by India on three sides and pursuing a nonaligned foreign policy, Mujib had felt that the treaty ensured the security of Bangladesh. The military, on the other hand, partly because of its Pakistan legacy and, more importantly, the experience of the liberation war, had an anti-India bias.

Ershad expanded upon Zia's policies. Unlike Zia he did not face any opposition from the military.[5] By 1982, when Ershad took over power in a bloodless coup from the short-lived civilian government of Sattar, the military had been cleansed of its internal factionalism and had begun to claim a constitutional role for itself in the administration of the country.[6] Ershad formalized the entry of military officers into the foreign and civil service on the basis of a quota system. In the foreign service, 25 percent of the posts were allocated to the armed services. The police forces, too, were brought under the military's influence. Indeed, Ershad literally colonized the administration with military personnel. Important bodies such as the National Economic Council, the Committee of Food, Agriculture, and Rural Development, the Energy and Mineral Resources Committee, the Export-Import Committee, the Government Purchase Committee, the Promotion and Service Restructure Committee, and the Pay Fixation and Administrative Reorganization Committee were either led or dominated by military men. They established dominant positions in business circles including the disinvested and private banks, insurance companies, and industrial units. Ershad also offered expensive plots of land and house building loans on easy terms to military officials (Bhattacharyya 1998: 6).

Formal allocations to defense in the annual budget increased on average by 18 percent while the total yearly budget increased by 14 percent. In contrast to the policy followed by previous governments, new pay scales enforced in August 1985 brought parity of salaries between military and civilian employees. Military personnel, it should be noted, enjoy benefits and allowances not shared by their civilian counterparts (Maniruzzaman 1993: 83).

On September 20, 1986, the government issued the Warrant of Preference. Among other things, the warrant gave preference in protocol to the chiefs of the army, navy, and air force over members of parliament. About 40 percent of Ershad's successive Councils of Ministers were drawn from the military.

Militarization of Politics

Both Zia and Ershad realized quite early in their rule that in a highly politicized society such as that in Bangladesh, it was impossible to rule by relying on the military's support or its coercive power alone. Their quest for legitimacy both at home and abroad, therefore, turned them to the path of civilianizing their administration. In the process, however, Bangladesh politics were militarized. This took place in two ways: first, the military became involved in the process of political party building, and retired military personnel were inducted into politics; second, the military became a factor in regime sustenance and regime change.

For Zia, legitimacy was not a problem. He was a popular and valiant freedom fighter whose personal honesty was never in question. More important, he had not come to power by design; rather, as noted earlier, he was catapulted into the political scene by sheer force of events. Zia tried to capitalize on his popularity. In developing his base of support he focused first on rural Bangladesh. He toured the countryside extensively, established direct contacts with people, and undertook popular policies such as canal digging and *gram sarkar* (village government). Zia's popular slogan was "Bangladesh will survive if its 68,000 villages survive."

At the national level the government passed the Political Party Regulations (PPR) in July 1976, which allowed indoor politics with government permission. About 60 political parties applied, and 21 of them, including the Awami League, were allowed to operate. Zia legitimized his own presidency by holding a presidential referendum on May 30, 1977. He resigned from the army and in September 1978 launched his own political party, the Bangladesh Nationalist Party (BNP). During this course of civilianization, however, military intelligence as well as the NSI was used extensively to set up new political organizations, curtail the opposition, undermine their unity, buy support, and buy off opponents. Before long the military had established itself as the most significant political party (Ali 1994: 30–31).

Martial law was ended after the inauguration of the elected parliament in 1979. Zia's civilianization process, however, brought him into conflict with senior military officials—mostly the freedom fighters. They were not only displeased by Zia's leaning toward the rightist forces that in their estimation had undermined the spirit of the liberation war, they were also alarmed because civilianization meant less power for the military in state affairs. Soon it became evident that Zia wanted to keep the military away from politics (Moudud Ahmed 1995: 148). This policy, of course, was unacceptable to the associates who had nurtured him. On May 31, 1981, Zia was assassinated in a military coup led by one his closest associates, General Manzur. On May 20, 1981, at the last conference of General Officer Commanding that Zia attended, Manzur is alleged to have accused Zia of betraying the army and the nationalist cause in his increasingly "civilian political stance" (Ali 1994: 37–38).

After the assassination of Zia, Justice Sattar, the vice president, took charge of the presidency. Under Article 123 of the constitution, the presidential vacancy caused by death was to be filled by an election within 180 days of the vacancy occurring. Elections were subsequently held on November 15, 1981. Sattar won an overwhelming victory and assumed the presidency in his own right. The military elite allowed the BNP's civilian government headed by Sattar to survive for a while owing to Zia's popularity among the soldiers as well as the general public. But soon the army chief General Ershad was pressing for a constitutional role for the military in state affairs. He then forced the Sattar government to form a National Security Council consisting of the chiefs of the three services, the prime minister, the vice president, and the president as its head. The military thus became part of the government's decision-making body. The government, however, was taking time to institutionalize the council, and the military could wait no longer. Finally, on March 24, 1982, Ershad seized power in a bloodless coup and declared martial law.

Ershad ruled for nine long years but could never make himself acceptable to the civil and political society of Bangladesh. He was looked upon as a usurper who had seized power from an elected civilian government. Although this made Ershad more dependent on the military, the need for legitimacy drove him toward civilianization of the government as well. On March 21, 1985, a referendum was held for his continuation in office until the next presidential election. Ershad resigned from the army and in January 1986 floated his own political party, the Jatiyo Party. Once again military intelligence played a crucial role in the formation of this party by buying allegiance and creating splits among the political parties united in the anti-Ershad movement. Thus the Awami League was persuaded to participate in the parliamentary elections of May 1986. Money and arms were issued to trade unions and student leaders.[7] Intelligence officers also played a significant role in devising administrative reforms that would offset Zia's achievements in the rural sector (Ali 1994: 42).

Ershad was sworn in as president on October 23, 1986, and martial law was withdrawn on November 10. All the elections during Ershad's rule were regarded as farcical and managed by the military. Despite the civilianization of government, Ershad, unlike Zia, could not move away from the military because he failed to gain general acceptance by the people. As already pointed out, 40 percent of his Councils of Ministers were drawn from the armed services. His government was often called a "Parliament of Soldiers" (Kukreja 1991: 156).

Polarization of Politics

Both Zia and Ershad introduced divisive elements into Bangladesh politics. Fundamental changes were ushered in with the constitution that changed the nature of the state as well as its politics. During Zia's regime, Islamic ideals were incorporated into the constitution. By the proclamation of Order 1 of 1977, the phrase *"Bismillahir-Rahmanir-Rahim"* ("in the name of Allah, the Beneficent, the Merciful") was inserted at the beginning of the constitution before the preamble. In the same proclamation Article 8, Clause 1, declaring secularism as one of the state's principles, was replaced by the principle of absolute faith in the Almighty Allah (Government of Bangladesh 1994: 10). Article 12, banning communal political parties in Bangladesh, was also dropped. Article 9, stressing the linguistic and cultural unity of Bengali nationalism, was likewise omitted. In place of "Bengalis," the citizens of Bangladesh through Article 6, Clause 2, were now to be known as "Bangladeshis." These changes were given effect through the Fifth Amendment to the constitution on April 5, 1977. These measures helped Zia to consolidate his power base among the general public and the military, for Mujib had been accused of selling out to India (Mohsin 1992: 67). The division between Bengali and Bangladeshi nationalism, however, sowed seeds of discord within the Bangladesh polity, for Bengali nationalism with its emphasis on secularism was the basis of the Bangladesh liberation movement, whereas Bangladeshi nationalism, though territorial and linguistic, had an overtly religious bias. Not only was the Bengali community divided along nationalist lines, but it also distinguished between the dominant Bengali Muslim community and the religious minorities. Communal politics had begun to take shape in Bangladesh.

Ershad accepted the Bangladeshi model of nationhood and gave it a wholly Islamic orientation. He deemphasized the "Bengali-ness" of Bangladeshi nationalism and instead attempted to consolidate its Islamic elements. He based his policy of Islamization on two planks: a mosque-centered society and Islam as the state religion (Sato 1993: 65). This policy was adopted not only to placate the Muslim majority but also to draw the Muslim donor countries closer to Bangladesh. Through the Eighth Amendment to the constitution on June 7, 1988, Islam was declared the state religion of Bangladesh (Article 2, Clause A) with the provision that other religions could be practiced in peace and harmony. Politics not only became polarized as a consequence of military rule but also violent. Long years of resistance against the Ershad government and the use of violence by both sides led political parties to become leader-centric and hoodlum-centric (I. Ahmed 1997).

The two military rulers could not, however, bring about any formal change in the civil-military equation in the constitution. Though Ershad had sought a constitutional role for the military, he could not implement it due to strong opposition from inside and outside the parliament (Kabir 1993: 19). Zia and Ershad were acutely aware of the politicized nature of the Bangladesh polity and realized that any formal change in the equation would be unacceptable

to the people. Although the changes in sensitive issues involving religion have polarized politics, no political party in Bangladesh can even think of reversing them: it would mean political
suicide for the party. As Khaleda Zia, chair of the BNP and a pillar of the anti-Ershad movement, pointed out after her appointment as 'prime minister in 1991: "Ninety-five per cent of
our total population is Muslim. If we attempt to remove Islam as the state religion from the
constitution, then we will be hurting the sentiments of this 95 percent" (MRCB 1991: 16).

In the face of massive agitation against him, Ershad was forced to resign. He had turned to
his own constituency, the military, for support, but by the end of the 1990s the mood in the military had changed. Mid-ranking and junior officers were opposed to any military involvement in
politics (Bhattacharyya 1998: 18). They had witnessed the violent history of coups and countercoups and did not wish to repeat it. The military high command also realized that people would
not accept another imposition of martial law, and the situation might lead to civil war. Moreover,
the political parties were fully aware of the military's critical role. In fact there were slogans calling upon the military to join the antiautocratic movement of the people. But the military realized that its interests would best be served by inaction. Changes had taken place on the international plane as well. A wave of democratization had swept the world following the demise of the
cold war. The donor countries—especially the United States and European nations who form
the "aid club of Bangladesh"—had expressed their displeasure to the government at the state of
affairs (Guhathakurta 1996: 112). It is important to note that 90 percent of the annual budget of
Bangladesh is dependent on foreign aid. The military government realized that it was left without any support base either internally or externally. Ershad resigned on December 6, 1990.

This analysis reveals the complex configuration of Bangladesh politics. Not only have the
military (and military-backed) governments had to accommodate civilian politics through their
civilianization process, but they have not been able to bring about any constitutional change in
civilian control over the military. Nonetheless, the distortions introduced in the political sphere
by those governments allow the military to remain a force in politics and ensure that its corporate interests remain satisfied.

THE MILITARY UNDER CIVILIAN RULE

Bangladesh has been set on a civilianization course since 1991. The two post-1991 civilian governments of the BNP and the Awami League had earlier been dislodged by the military.
Khaleda Zia, the BNP chair and former prime minister, lost her husband, President Zia ur
Rahman, in a military coup in 1981; likewise Sk. Hasina, leader of the Awami League and present prime minister, lost her father Sk. Mujib and other members of her family in the military
coup of 1975. The military factor, therefore, is bound to loom large in the psyche of these two
leaders. On the one hand, there is an element of mistrust; on the other, realizing the mistakes
of their predecessors, they have been cautious not to alienate the military. Hence the military's
corporate interests have been well taken care of by civilian governments.

Institutional Control over the Military

Immediately after assuming power, both Khaleda Zia and Sk. Hasina adopted a hands-on role
in the management of military affairs. They retained the portfolio of defense. They also main-

tained control over the military in their capacity as the chief executive of government as provided by the constitution, in their capacity as ministers of defense, and also through the Armed Forces Division (AFD).

The AFD had its genesis in the Supreme Command Division, which was constituted during military rule as the chief martial law administrator's secretariat. Later, as the military rulers moved to civilian rule, it was incorporated under the President's Office for the efficient management and control over military affairs by the president. Under Khaleda Zia it was renamed the AFD and placed under the Prime Minister's Office, because the country had moved from a presidential to a parliamentary form of government. With the president now the titular head, the prime minister appropriated the powers and functions of supreme commander. It was through the AFD that the prime minister sought to establish her control over the military. The composition of the body and its role, however, framed during the military rule, have the potential of creating tension among the military elite. The AFD has assumed coordinating functions among the three services—army, navy, and air force—and is responsible for formulating defense strategies and policies. It also controls the movement of units, the posting and promotion of senior officers, the procurement of weapons, and the mobilization of troops during national emergencies.

Although the AFD has emerged as the key institution pertaining to military matters, the chiefs of services are not members of this body. It is headed by the PSO, generally of the rank of major general. The PSO advises the prime minister very closely on military affairs—reportedly a source of discomfort for the army chief. (The chief has the rank of lieutenant general whereas the PSO is a major general.) This arrangement also creates tension between the two because the AFD is very significant in terms of role assignment. The navy and air force are reported to be quite uneasy with the AFD as well, because the PSO is traditionally chosen from the army.[8]

The role of the Defense Ministry has been substantially reduced. It now deals primarily with accounts and the civilian aspects of defense. Presumably these changes in the management of military affairs were introduced by Zia and Ershad to keep a check on the military as they moved toward civilianization. The civilian governments of Khaleda and Hasina strengthened the process. They have taken great care in their appointments of chief, PSO, and director-general of the DGFI. Under the civilian governments, these three posts have so far been filled on the basis of their reliability to the government, but they have not been on the best of terms with each other. Under Khaleda, for example, Nasim was director-general of DGFI. Although he had no prior experience in intelligence affairs, he had been a freedom fighter and therefore a close associate of the late Zia ur Rahman. Nasim is alleged to have had cool relations with the army chief, Nooruddin. When Nasim became army chief, Khaleda appointed a director-general of the DGFI with whom Nasim was not on friendly terms (Ibrahim 1999: 83). This was done deliberately, of course, because the chief of intelligence is responsible for keeping an eye on the army chief as well.

Things have not changed under the present Hasina government. The army chief is related to the prime minister, who was refused extension of service by the previous government and had subsequently gone on leave prior to retirement. He was recalled, however, and appointed chief of army staff. The two civilian governments have made strong efforts to make their control over the military visible. Khaleda Zia visited troop exercises and attended military ceremonies. Sk. Hasina is known for her regular attendance of the AFD office and for taking a personal interest in military matters. Like her predecessor, she attends military exercises and ceremonies.

Civilian Control and the Chittagong Hill Tracts

The Chittagong Hill Tracts (CHT) is a critical area that could have proved contentious as the civil side sought to establish its control over the military. The military held control of the CHT due to an insurgency movement that had been going on in the region since the inception of Bangladesh. Under the political leadership of Parbattya Chattagram Janashonghoti Samity (PCJSS), the United People's Party of the CHT, the hill people had started an autonomy movement. The movement acquired a military and regional dimension after the assassination of Sk. Mujib as India began to arm and train the Shanti Bahini, the military wing of the PCJSS (Bhaumik 1996). Consequently in 1977 the area was handed over to the military to curb the insurgency, and since then the CHT has been under the control of the general officer commanding (GOC) of the Chittagong Division (Mohsin 1997: 168).

In the name of counterinsurgency the military controlled the economic, political, and social lives of the people. Gross violations of human rights by the military—including rape, abduction, eviction, torture, forced religious conversion, and eleven major massacres—took place (Mohsin 1997: 177–85). These acts, committed by security personnel in the CHT, enjoyed exemption from criminal prosecution. Indeed, none of the mainstream political parties ever condemned the military atrocities in the region. The military had developed high stakes there. Some of the high military officials were reaping commercial benefits from the plantations and forest resources of the area. The CHT was thus the military's exclusive domain.

But with the arrival of the civilian regime, changes came about in government policy. The GOC Chittagong Division declared that from then on the military would take action only in self-defense. The government was cognizant of international reports of human rights violations in the CHT (Chittagong Hill Tracts Commission 1991, 1992). With democratization, human rights groups within Bangladesh itself became vocal over the issue. As pressure mounted from donor agencies, the CHT issue became an embarrassment for civilian governments. For the first time, investigations took place, and a total of 196 military officials were punished and 96 dismissed.[9] The army's judicial role was curbed, and a parliamentary committee was set up to provide political direction to management of the CHT issue. Peace negotiations with the PCJSS, initially opened during Ershad's rule, were renewed. Although the talks failed earlier because of the intransigent stand of the PCJSS, the Awami League managed to sign a peace accord largely because of India's withdrawal of support from the PCJSS after the Awami League government came to power. Today the CHT is under civilian control, and a regional council, headed by the former PCJSS leader Shantu Larma, is in overall charge of the region's administration. The CHT Development Board, the main body for the region's economic development, is headed by a local person.

The military was actively involved in the peace process and has welcomed the accord. Indeed, military personnel point out that the military itself had impressed upon the Ershad government the need for a political solution. Although they attribute this change to a growing sense of professionalism within the military,[10] it may be argued that by the 1980s the military had acquired a central position in Bangladesh politics and no longer required an insurgency situation to keep its budget high. Besides, the CHT's strategic location ensured that the military would continue to play an important role there. Although this state of affairs has the potential of creating conflict between the two institutions in the future, the government is determined not to antagonize the military. Despite the demand of the PCJSS the region has not been demilitarized, for example, nor has the government compromised on any controversial issue. The government has further declared that the military will be involved in developing the region's infrastructure (Mohsin 1998: 117).

Civilian Accommodation of the Military

Despite the civilian government's efforts to control the military, it has tried to keep the military satisfied. In their party manifestos both the BNP and the Awami League are committed to building a modern military. This is especially a metamorphosis for the Awami League, which had been accused of neglecting the military. More important, the military governments introduced key changes in the constitution that challenged the ideology of the Awami League. A political analyst has therefore called it a tragedy that Sk. Hasina is obliged to woo the same institution that wiped out her family and distorted the ideals of her father (Hannan 1999). But in the context of Bangladesh politics, the civil side will have to accommodate the military until political parties can agree on core values and define the spirit of democracy.

The military's share of the budget has remained consistently high under the two civilian governments. Under the BNP government, on average it took up 16 percent of the total budget. At present, under the Awami League, the military consumes about 19 percent of the budget. The government has increased rations and salaries and provided tiffin allowance and health insurance to the military.[11] New academic and research institutes such as the National Defense College are being set up to provide the military with a broader professional outlook on issues not only military but also civilian. At the National Defense College, for example, senior military officials take academic courses ranging from gender issues to proper civil-military relations. Moreover, Hasina has allowed the 25-year treaty with India to lapse. (The treaty, signed by her father, had caused serious resentment within the military.)

Both parties also have a high induction rate of former military officials. Five ministers of the BNP were ex-officers. The present defense adviser to the BNP chair is a former military chief. Twelve senior military officials—three of them former service chiefs—were nominated by the Awami League in the 1996 general elections. (Five were elected.) The present parliamentary committee on defense is headed by an Awami League member of parliament, General Safiullah, a retired officer who was a former military chief.

Military Acquiescence to Civil Control

The military has come to realize that under the changed domestic and international circumstances its acquiescence to civilian control can best serve its interests. The anti-Ershad movement brought home the power of the people's wrath and the fact that a politicized society such as Bangladesh's cannot be ruled by military power. At the same time, there is an absolute lack of consensus even on fundamental issues such as national identity.[12] Intolerance and the total absence of democratic spirit among the political parties has made politics extremely volatile. This, however, as already pointed out, is a consequence of long military rule. Nonetheless it ensures that the political parties will try to present themselves as credible not only to the people but also to the military in view of the latter's past role in regime change. What is particularly disturbing in this entire matrix is the political opposition's constant attempts to dislodge the government even before its stipulated five-year term is over and draw the military into this game of power—a strategy that has made the military a factor in Bangladesh politics once more while ensuring that civilian governments keep the corporate interests of the military satisfied.

The regime of Khaleda Zia came to an end in February 1996 in the wake of a mass opposition movement led by the Awami League on charges of vote rigging in the Magura by-elections in 1994. The opposition movement soon turned into an oust-the-government movement with the demand that power be handed over and fresh elections be held under a neutral caretaker government. By calling a total of 173 total shutdowns of the country's normal activities, the opposition literally paralyzed the administration. In light of the continued unrest there was wide speculation of military intervention. When the government deployed the navy to keep the Chittagong port operational, the opposition called upon the navy to disobey government orders. In the past the military had intervened under much less chaotic circumstances in the name of law and order. But during the anti-Khaleda movement the military carried out its business as usual and diligently maintained order in the February 1996 parliamentary elections. Military officials wished to avoid walking into a mess again and believed that by charting a neutral course they could protect their interests. They were well aware, too, that the people would not accept military rule.

The Awami League since its inception to power in June 1996 was beset with political and economic problems. Lawlessness became the order of the day. The country reeled under a series of power and water crises. Taking advantage of the situation, the opposition political parties have once again aligned themselves in an oust-the-government movement, this time under BNP leadership. Once again shutdowns and demonstrations have reappeared in the Bangladesh political scene with regular frequency. Again the opposition has tried to wean the military away from the government. The Awami League government at one point involved the military in power and water management and deployed the military police to manage Dhaka's severe traffic congestion. Each time Khaleda Zia has criticized the government's steps as undermining the military's status and position. She has also raised strong objections to the proposed defense purchases of Indian trucks and Russian MiG-29s—questioning the very wisdom of making defense deals with India and questioning the quality of the vehicles also. The opposition has further alleged that the government aims to turn the armed forces into a wing of the Indian army.[13] Such allegations can have profound implications, for the Bangladesh military has a strong anti-India bias. With this in mind, Hasina is reported to have given a go-slow signal on the issue of defense purchases from India. It is widely speculated that the government will not make a move that might place it in conflict with the military.[14] Apparently the opposition is trying to play the anti-India card in order to wrest the military away from the government. The military, however, maintains that these deals were initiated under the BNP government. In fact, the air chief has submitted a report to this effect to the parliamentary defense committee.[15] The opposition has denied the charges. As is often the case in polities such as that

of Bangladesh, the truth of the matter may never surface. But in the process the civilian government has once again exposed its weakness to the military; and this weakness of political
institutions invites the military not only to maintain its influence but also to intervene. The military uprising of May 1996, during the caretaker interlude, substantiates the major arguments
of this chapter.

UPRISING IN THE MILITARY: MAY 18–20, 1996

The regime of Khaleda Zia came to an end in March 1996. Through the passage of the Thirteenth Amendment to the constitution, she made provisions for the formation of a neutral,
nonpartisan, caretaker government. The amendment provides that at the end of the term of
an elected government, after the dissolution of parliament, there will be a nonpartisan caretaker government headed by the chief adviser. This caretaker government is collectively responsible to the president; the chief adviser is to be appointed by the president, and other advisers
are to be appointed on the recommendation of the chief adviser. This government is to carry
out routine duties and is not to make any policy decisions. Its primary objective is to assist the
Election Commission in holding free and fair general elections (Government of Bangladesh
1996: 40–44). The amendment, however, gives the all-important defense portfolio to the president. The AFD also remains with the president. This indeed is inconsistent with a parliamentary form of government—especially when the chief adviser has been given the rank and
status of prime minister. The Thirteenth Amendment was the outcome of the February 1996
elections. But since these elections had been boycotted by all the major political parties, the
BNP was able to pass the bill by a vote of 268 to 0.[16] Quite significantly, the provision relating
to defense was passed secretly and disclosed only after a week (Bhattacharyya 1998: 14).

The major political parties reacted very strongly to this provision and demanded the transfer of defense affairs to the chief adviser. They pointed out that the president, as a party nominee, might use this institution to manipulate elections in favor of the BNP, which would defeat
the very purpose of the caretaker government (Hasanuzzaman 1998: 191). The BNP, however,
maintained that the clause must be inserted to meet national emergency situations when the
military may have to be deployed. As the only elected representative of the people within the
caretaker government, he or she must have the power to execute the decision in such an
eventuality.

Clearly the provision has the power to disrupt the political process through the involvement of the military. The incident of May 1996 was fraught with such a threat. On May 20,
in an unscheduled television speech to the nation, President Abdur Rahman Biswas declared
that he had retired the army chief, Lieutenant General Nasim, along with two other senior military officers: Maj. Gen. G. H. Morshed Khan, the GOC of Bogra Division, and Brig. Miran
Hamidur Rahman, the deputy director-general of the Bangladesh Rifles, a paramilitary force.
In his speech the president announced that the army chief had been dismissed for disobeying
orders given to him on May 18, 1996, to retire two senior military officers and for ordering troop
mobilization toward Dhaka—actions that, according to the president, were tantamount to rebellion. Maj. Gen. Mahbubur Rahman was appointed as the new army chief.[17] The two senior
officers, it was alleged, had been colluding with a certain political party. The president's decision sparked rebellion in a number of cantonments. There were reports of troop mobilizations

both in favor of General Nasim and in favor of President Biswas and the new chief. The 46th Brigade of the Dhaka-based Bangladesh Army is outside the army's regular chain of command. It takes its orders from (and is usually headed by) officers chosen by the president himself—an arrangement instituted by Zia ur Rahman in view of the series of coup attempts during his rule. This brigade, along with the soldiers from Savar cantonment, were mobilized in favor of the president, whereas troops had revolted in Bogra, Mymensingh, Comilla, Jessore, and Jadevpur cantonments (Bhattacharyya 1998: 2). Clashes between troops were also reported. Troops loyal to the president guarded the president's house and the television and radio stations. Appeals were made every 30 minutes from the Bangladesh television station asking the rebel soldiers to return to their barracks. Roads were sealed off to prevent the rebellious forces from marching on the capital.[18]

The retired army chief denied the charges of rebellion. In retiring the two officers, he pointed out, the president had violated the rules by denying them any opportunity of self-defense. Moreover, he said, the army chain of command had not been informed of the decision. So as chief he was only trying to protect the interests of his officers. The government, however, insisted that normal procedures could not be followed because the former chief himself was involved in conspiring with the two officers. The situation was brought under control the very next day after Lieutenant General Nasim handed over power to Maj. Gen. Mahbubur Rahman.

The unfolding of this incident just three weeks before general elections that were to be held on June 12 caught the public by surprise. Hasina denounced the move and demanded public disclosure of the facts and testimony of the accused officers regarding their alleged connections with a political party. She feared that failure to do so could alienate voters. Khaleda Zia, however, welcomed the president's decision and accused the Awami League of colluding with a section of the military in a bid to capture power.[19]

To this day the incident of May 1996 remains a mystery to the general public. One opinion suggests that the president wanted to declare an emergency by dragging the army into politics in order to disrupt the elections and defame the Awami League in the process. Another view is that the Awami League was actually conspiring with a few senior military officers to influence the course of elections in its favor (Ibrahim 1999: 94–95). Whatever the facts, the incident is important for civil-military relations. It exposed the polarized and confrontational nature of Bangladesh politics and the willingness of politicians to involve the military for the sake of party gains without consideration for the democratic process. Ironically, therefore, the political leadership is creating a space for the military to reassert its authority in politics. Nevertheless, despite widespread apprehension, the military chose a neutral course. It lent its full support to the caretaker government for the holding of free and fair elections that brought the Awami League to power. This indeed attested to the military's neutrality during the elections—for not only had the new army chief been appointed by the president himself (a BNP nominee), but the BNP had welcomed the change in the army in May 1996 while Hasina was opposing it.

THE FUTURE

Bangladesh has traversed almost a decade of civilian rule. During this period the divisions between the major political forces have deepened. The same polarization has engulfed the administration and academic institutions. In other words, Bangladesh has failed to evolve a healthy democratic environment that can ensure good governance. On the positive side, the judiciary is asserting its independence. Quite a few of its judgments involving sensitive political issues have gone against the government.[20] The print media, too, have exerted their independence and objectivity to a great extent. Human rights activists, nongovernmental organizations (NGOs), and important segments of the public have continuously aired their concern regarding the state of affairs. Demands for genuine democracy, decentralization of power, and good governance are on the rise among different elements of civil society—all of which indicates the emergence of a third force in Bangladesh politics. Despite the polarization of the mainstream political forces, the process of democracy and democratization may very well gain strength in the future.

The nature of the Bangladesh civil society is the most important factor in this respect. Though there is polarization on critical national questions, on the question of regime there is full consensus that it has to be a civil democratic regime, no matter how imperfect it may be. A military regime is regarded as a step backward. The East Bengalis have a long history of democratic movement against the military regimes of Pakistan because they were the most hard hit by these nondemocratic regimes. After independence, too, the military regimes in Bangladesh could never gain acceptance from the people. Both Zia and Ershad had to shed their uniforms and embark on the path of civilianization. In fact, the long nine years of Ershad's rule had been a battle on his part to gain legitimacy, in which he failed miserably.

The civil society today is most conscious of keeping the military under civilian control. Bangladesh still does not have a national security policy. Members of the civil society—politicians, intellectuals, journalists—are taking an active part in debates initiated by the media to evolve a viable, sustainable national security policy. The parliament subcommittee on defense is being closely scrutinized by the media and public, and questions are being raised on critical issues such as the desirability and necessity of purchase and procurement of expensive offensive weapons. There is a demand for greater transparency and accountability of defense issues. The Pakistan scenario of welcoming military takeovers, as demonstrated by the October 1999 coup of Pakistan, therefore cannot be expected in the context of the political culture in Bangladesh.

The Bangladesh military, too, realizes that the political culture will no longer permit military intervention. It therefore perceives that its wisest course is to remain an apolitical institution. More important, there is a growing recognition among junior and mid-ranking officers about the proper role of the military. The military elite, moreover, is conscious of the damage that was done to its image during the periods of military rule. In its attempt at damage control it has taken care to project the military as a professional institution. Maturity and professionalism are reflected in the current writings of senior military officials, as well, who emphasize the desirability of civil control over the military.[21] Civilian governments, however, must be cognizant of the military and keep its privileges intact if they wish to prevent it from intervening directly in politics. The trajectory for Bangladesh, therefore, is a continuation of the democratic process. Although the civil society is going to be the main force behind this trend, the international environment—especially donor nations and international aid agencies through their agendas of good governance, participation, and empowerment of people—will also play a crucial role in the process.

CHAPTER 9

Indonesia: On a New Course?

Geoffrey Robinson

THE DRAMATIC RESIGNATION OF PRESIDENT SUHARTO in May 1998, and the broader political crisis of which it formed a part, stimulated an unprecedented questioning of the political role of the Indonesian armed forces. Apparently stunned by the vehemence of public criticism, the military leadership announced a series of concessions and promises of reform.[1] The next eighteen months brought dramatic changes in Indonesian political life. The first free elections in more than 40 years were held successfully in June 1999, and in October the new People's Consultative Assembly (Majelis Permusyawartan Rakyat [MPR]) elected a civilian president, Abdurrahmand Wahid, and vice president, Megawati Sukarnoputri. The new MPR also voted to accept East Timor's separation from Indonesia, following a UN-sponsored referendum held in August in which East Timorese had opted overwhelmingly for independence despite powerful military opposition. By late 1999 the Indonesian military's prestige was at a low ebb, and its position as the most powerful political institution in the country after the president was in serious doubt for the first time in more than three decades. In his first six months in office, President Wahid took a number of steps that appeared to weaken the military still further, appointing a civilian as minister of defense, appointing known reformers to senior military posts, and supporting the investigation and prosecution of military officers for alleged human rights abuses. In one of his most daring gambits, in February 2000 Wahid suspended the former armed forces commander General Wiranto from his cabinet post pending investigations into his role in the referendum-related violence in East Timor.[2]

Did these developments mark a major turning point in civil-military relations in Indonesia, or are the skeptics correct in seeing the changes as mere blips in a pattern of military dominance that is destined to continue far into the new millennium? In this chapter I seek to answer these questions by examining recent trends in light of the history of civil-military relations in Indonesia.

Two main propositions are advanced. The first is that relations between Indonesian military and civilian political authorities have indeed been set upon a new course since May 1998, primarily because of the growing confidence of Indonesian civil society, the willingness of President Wahid to use his power to assert civilian supremacy, and a marked shift in the international political and economic context. Domestic protests and international sanctions did not stop with Suharto's resignation. On the contrary, they became more central to Indonesia's political process than at any time since the 1960s. As a result of these pressures, the armed forces leadership was forced to adjust its political strategy and style and to make concessions to civilian authorities and institutions that would have been unimaginable before Suharto's fall. As the speaker of the consultative assembly (MPR), Amien Rais, commented in February 2000, "You couldn't imagine two years ago Mr. Wiranto being sacked by a civilian leader."[3] The emergence of a more confident Indonesian civil society—as well as an international community increasingly willing to intervene in the domestic affairs of sovereign states on issues of human rights and good governance—is likely to continue to place the Indonesian military leadership on the defensive in coming years.

At the same time, and this is the second proposition, adjustments in civil-military relations at the elite level had not yet altered significantly the position of the military vis-à-vis civil society by the end of 1999. Beyond the circle of Jakarta politics, and especially in remote "troubled" (*rawan*) regions such as Aceh and East Timor, the Indonesian armed forces continued to operate according to the old standards, employing violence or the threat of violence against its domestic enemies. The persistence of these old patterns of behavior, as we shall see, stemmed from the fact that the military as an institution had become so deeply embedded in the structure and ideology of the Indonesian state over the previous 50 years. Accordingly, significant change in the relationship between the military and civil society is likely to be more difficult—and take far longer—than shifts in the relationship at the elite level. Nevertheless, in this sphere too, the changes are likely to be driven by demands from below combined with pressures from abroad. These propositions are developed in greater detail in the chapter's three main sections.

The first section surveys the military's involvement in politics since the declaration of Indonesian independence in 1945 and examines the essential doctrinal and institutional bases of military power that developed under the New Order regime of President Suharto (himself a career military officer) after 1965. It shows how military doctrine and institutions have in fact determined the character of the modern Indonesian state and, as well, how that process has affected civil-military relations to the present day. It also suggests that the means by which the military achieved political dominance—in particular its role in the countercoup of 1965 and the subsequent massacre of real and alleged communists—profoundly influenced its ethos and behavior thereafter and shaped the New Order regime. This historical process ensured that the ideology of the state became profoundly anticommunist, obsessed with national unity, and preoccupied by perceived threats of subversion. Above all, it institutionalized what may be called a "culture of violence" within the military and indeed within the state as a whole.

At least since 1965, the military's enormous political power has been legitimized by the "dual function" (*dwifungsi*) doctrine, which stipulates that in addition to its strictly military function, the military is entitled to a direct role in the political life of the country. Both functions have been facilitated, and reinforced, by a cornerstone of national security doctrine: the strategy of "total people's defense" calling for close cooperation between military forces and the civilian population in the defense against threats both external and internal. These aspects of Indonesian military doctrine have helped to justify, in the name of national security, military intervention in all aspects of political, economic, and social life.

Military power has been rooted in a variety of institutional arrangements as well, both legal and illegal. The unique "territorial" structure of the Indonesian army has ensured that the military presence is felt down to the village level in every corner of the country. That presence has been strengthened by the military's near-exclusive control of the most powerful intelligence bodies in the country and, too, by the existence of a number of elite combat units, notably Kopassus and Kostrad, which have been free to operate with little regard for domestic or international legal norms. In keeping with the dual function doctrine, the military has also had privileged access to key positions in the executive branch, the bureaucracy, and the legislature, as well as both formal and informal control of the judicial system. In addition to these legally mandated privileges, the military has been free to engage in illegal or semilegal activities, including a practice euphemistically called "unconventional financing" and the mobilization of thugs into official and semiofficial militias and paramilitary units.

The second section examines the constraints on, and challenges to, military power under the New Order (1965–1998). There were three key constraints. One was the independent power of the president, Suharto, who although a military officer himself occasionally took positions directly at odds with the expressed interests or wishes of the armed forces leadership. The second was the significant limit on the military's political power that stemmed from tensions within the military elite. Third, the political power of the military under the New Order was subject to limits in the form of opposition and criticism from Indonesia's own civil society and from the international community. As important as these constraints eventually became in the final years, for most of the New Order they did not significantly affect the relationship between the military and society at large. International pressure was generally muted, and domestic opposition was easily crushed. The extent of the military's power under the New Order is highlighted by the government's counterinsurgency campaign in the province of Aceh between 1989 and 1998. The study of Aceh during these years shows that the political constraints experienced by the military under the New Order had little, if any, effect on military behavior and norms outside of a small elite at the center. At the local level, the power of the armed forces had become so deeply entrenched that its authority with respect to ordinary civilians was virtually unlimited—and remained that way until Suharto's final days.

Aceh was not unique in this respect. A similar pattern was evident in all areas designated as "troubled"—where there was an armed threat to the state—as in East Timor and West Papua (formerly Irian Jaya). In these areas the military employed counterinsurgency and unconventional warfare strategies that entailed the systematic use of terror and the mobilization of civilians against members of their own community. In such contexts, even the minimal restraints provided by law were removed to permit the military freedom of action. The lack of any effective civilian political or legal control over these operations meant that they frequently resulted in serious and systematic human rights violations. This was also the case in areas that were removed from public scrutiny, domestic and international. Rural areas, even on the island of Java, were especially vulnerable, but so too were poorer communities in the major towns and cities. In such places the military's power in matters of security and sociopolitical affairs was not significantly constrained by civilian authorities. Thus as scholars and pundits of Indonesia's New Order debated—in the manner of the Kremlinologists of old—the meaning of recent shifts in relations between the president and the armed forces leadership in Jakarta, for most ordinary people the relationship with the military did not change: the military remained the institution that governed, and in some cases ended, their lives.

The third section examines changes in civil-military relations that have occurred since the resignation of President Suharto in May 1998 and considers future trajectories. Although domestic protest, presidential intervention, and international pressures have significantly strengthened civilian authority since 1998, as we shall see, the changes have not completely undermined the most fundamental roots of military power. Moreover, the declining prestige of the armed forces after the fall of Suharto—and the possibility that its members may be brought to account for past abuses—may actually increase the prospects for military intervention in coming years. Such a development would be all the more likely if the newly elected civilian government failed to perform satisfactorily, particularly in the sphere of national security. It needs to be stressed, however, that military intervention is more likely to take the form of covert mischief-making or behind-the-scenes maneuvering than an open seizure of power such as occurred in Pakistan in 1999.

President Suharto's resignation in May 1998 unleashed powerful pressures for reform of the armed forces that had been building for some time. Allegations, and in some cases official admissions, of systematic abuse of human rights by armed forces personnel under the New Order accentuated public demands. Domestic protests dovetailed with international pressures and added weight to the arguments of those within the armed forces, both active and retired, who had already begun to push for change. By early 1999, this combination of public protest, international pressure, and soul-searching within the military leadership itself had begun to affect relations between civilian and military authorities in Jakarta. The number of military seats in the legislature was reduced by half (from 75 to 38), military leaders apologized for past human rights abuses, some of the more notorious officers were dismissed, and there was a significant opening of the political system. These developments arguably marked the start of an unprecedented diminution of the military's historical position and a unique opportunity for the assertion of civilian political power. President Wahid seized that opportunity, using his authority to promote officers who appeared committed to military reform, to dismiss or demote those whose loyalty he doubted, and to bring others to account for past human rights violations.

Yet at the same time there were powerful forces pushing in the opposite direction: toward a continuation or reassertion of military dominance. Beyond the glare of public scrutiny, old attitudes, patterns of behavior, and interests persisted within the military. Thus even if some among the military leadership in Jakarta appeared to move in the direction of reform, a great many officers and men seemed inclined to resist, or simply ignore, the changes. The past tendency (and continued capacity) of some units and commanders to engineer social violence, or to mobilize paramilitary forces, posed an especially serious threat to the transition to civilian rule. Also pushing in the direction of a restoration of military power were indications that some military authorities might be prepared to backtrack on reform plans in the face of mounting social violence and threats to national unity. Finally, notwithstanding proposals that it be dismantled, the territorial structure of the armed forces remained unchanged, ensuring a powerful military and intelligence presence in every neighborhood and village in the country.

The chapter concludes with a brief case study of East Timor in the post–New Order period, highlighting many of the trends described earlier. On the one hand, the events of 1999 in East Timor revealed that there were significant elements in the armed forces prepared to defy official government policy—and to do so by resorting to old tricks, such as the use of terror and paramilitary forces. On the other hand, the fact that a popular consultation was successfully held in August—and the consultative assembly (MPR) voted to accept the result in October—testified to the power of a courageous civil society and a new willingness to intervene on the part of the international community. These developments also suggested that in

Indonesia generally, the shift away from military dominance may proceed more vigorously and swiftly than anticipated.

THE ROOTS OF MILITARY POWER

Under the New Order, the Indonesian armed forces (Angkatan Bersenjata Republik Indonesia [ABRI]) became the most powerful political institution in the country next to the president. The political power it attained and the particular manner in which it exercised that power were not rooted primarily in constitutional provisions or legal documents. Rather, they were the product of a historical process of state formation in which the armed forces played a central role. By virtue of the military's close involvement in that process, its ideology and institutions became deeply embedded in the makeup of the state itself, thereby giving the armed forces a uniquely powerful position and making any challenge to the military tantamount to a crime against the state.

History and State Building

Indonesia's military has never been purely professional in the sense of being an apolitical institution that receives and implements orders from a civilian political leadership. Ever since the Indonesian struggle for independence from the Dutch colonial authorities (1945–1949), the Indonesian military—in particular the army—has always played an important role in the political, social, and economic life of the state.[4] This is not to say that the military's road to political dominance has been easy or uncontested. But the experience of political involvement has been there from the outset and has inevitably shaped its outlook, character, and interests. At the same time, the military's involvement in the earliest phases of state formation inevitably shaped the structure and ideology of the state itself.

Although Indonesians served in the Dutch colonial army and in a variety of Japanese military auxiliary bodies (1942–1945), it was only during the revolutionary period (1945–1949) that a national armed force emerged. The experience of fighting for national independence was critical in forming the essential doctrines of that force, and in shaping the worldview of the officers who would implement them over the next 30 to 40 years. By the time independence was achieved in 1949, many military officers had developed a deep contempt for the country's civilian political leaders, whom they viewed as weak for their willingness to negotiate with the Dutch. By contrast, military officers believed that by continuing to fight the Dutch they had saved the nation and had thereby earned a right to play a central role in political life after independence. Their ambitions were temporarily frustrated, however, by the establishment in 1950 of a parliamentary form of government under civilian control.[5]

After a period of relatively strong civilian authority in the early and mid-1950s, the military's political power expanded significantly with the declaration of martial law in 1957 and the imposition of "guided democracy" two years later.[6] Both of these initiatives were supported by the military leadership on the grounds that civilian political authorities were incompetent and corrupt and, moreover, that the parliamentary democracy in place through the early and mid-1950s had proved inappropriate to Indonesia's cultural and political condition. These were debatable claims and may have obscured some less noble motives. But they echoed President Sukarno's

views and hence became the basis for a major shift in the constitutional and normative foundations of the state as well as the relations between civilian and military authorities.[7]

By expanding its political and administrative authority, martial law also gave the military
authority over substantial new economic resources and extended its links with the Indonesian
state. When Dutch and other foreign-owned plantations and properties were expropriated by
the state in the late 1950s and early 1960s, for example, the army used its authority to assume
effective ownership of them. Martial law also increased dramatically the opportunities for
bribery and rent seeking by military authorities entrusted with the granting of licenses, permits, contracts, and so on. Thus by the time martial law was officially ended in 1963, the military had developed a powerful stake in the economic status quo and had strong reasons to cling
to its political and state power.

The system of guided democracy—portrayed by Sukarno as a uniquely Indonesian alternative to parliamentary democracy—deepened still further the political involvement of the
armed forces. By guaranteeing military representation alongside political parties in all major
legislative and executive bodies—and by restoring the 1945 constitution, which enshrined the
principle of appointive representation by "functional group"—guided democracy strengthened
the armed forces' position and stake in political life and set the stage, institutionally and nor-
matively, for its further expansion after 1965. Paradoxically, guided democracy also benefited
the Indonesian Communist Party (Partai Kommunis Indonesia [PKI]), thereby accentuating
simmering tensions between at least some parts of ABRI and political forces on the left.

ABRI's position was further consolidated by the "coup" and countercoup of October 1,
1965, which led to the destruction of the PKI, the massacre of as many as 1 million alleged
communists, and eventually the ouster of President Sukarno. Debate continues over the identity and motives of those ultimately responsible for the initial coup attempt. The official government version claims it was masterminded by the PKI, but many serious scholars contend it
was actually orchestrated by elements in the army as a pretext for a counterattack on the PKI
and Sukarno. Although questions remain about the coup, there is no doubt whatsoever about
the identity of the man who launched the countercoup—or about the consequences of his
actions. The chief architect was Major General Suharto, the man who would eventually remove
his military regalia and serve as president until May 21, 1998. Supported by a range of anticommunist civilian parties and groups, Suharto instigated the destruction of the army's chief
political rival, the PKI, and the establishment of the New Order regime.[8]

Significantly, Suharto's seizure of power was warmly welcomed by the United States and
other anticommunist governments. Indeed, there is substantial evidence that the United States
and its allies actively encouraged army officers to seize power and crush the PKI, and then provided significant material and political support to help them consolidate their victory.[9] Over
the next three decades, the New Order regime continued to benefit from strong support from
governments and financial institutions that saw Suharto's authoritarian rule as a guarantee of
economic opportunity and political stability in the region. The impressive economic growth
achieved during these years was seen by many observers as evidence that authoritarianism
worked—and was often used to justify the heavy restrictions of civil and political rights that
were the hallmark of the New Order regime.

The countercoup of October 1965, and the massacre that followed, tipped the balance
between civilian and military authorities in favor of the military, and further shaped the evolv-

ing Indonesian state. In the first fifteen or twenty years of the New Order regime, the armed forces leadership—in particular the army officers—served as Suharto's loyal partners and played a leading role in virtually every aspect of political and national security decision making and implementation. The New Order also provided unparalleled opportunities for the expansion and entrenchment of ABRI's economic interests in these years (Kristiadi 1999: 104). During the same period, civilian institutions and leaders were pushed to the margins of political life and deprived of meaningful decision-making authority.[10]

The manner in which Suharto and his allies crushed the October 1965 coup and destroyed the PKI prefigured a new style of governance characterized by a near-hysterical anticommunism, an extreme intolerance of dissent, and the intensive use of political surveillance. Perhaps most significantly, the brutal manner in which the New Order came to power set in motion, and helped to institutionalize, what I call a "culture of violence" within the armed forces and within the state as a whole. In using the term "culture of violence" I do not mean to imply that Indonesian peoples are inherently violent. Rather, I use the term to suggest that after 1965, violence—and the threat of violence—became a defining element of the system of norms and patterns of behavior within the Indonesian military and within the New Order state itself. Thus it was not only relations between civilian and military authorities that were affected by the transition of 1965, but the relationship between military authorities and civil society more generally.

Doctrine and Ideology

The military's political power has been buttressed by an array of ideological constructs pertaining to the armed forces' own position within the state, to the definition of national threats, and to national security strategies. The military's central role in state formation has helped to ensure that these constructs have become integral to the ideological infrastructure of the state itself. For this reason, challenges to these doctrines have historically been viewed as acts of subversion against the state—a fact that makes the challenges of recent times all the more noteworthy.

The military's central role in the political life of the country has been justified primarily through the doctrine of "dual function."[11] Originally articulated in 1958 as the doctrine of the "middle way" by the army chief of staff, General Nasution, it was formalized and refined in 1965–1966 and finally enshrined in law in 1982.[12] As outlined in the 1982 law, the dual function doctrine prescribes two related functions for the armed forces: a conventional military role as enforcer of national defense and national security and a second role as arbiter of the country's social and political affairs.

The middle way doctrine stipulated that ABRI would neither abstain from politics nor directly seize political power. However, shortly after it was articulated, and particularly after the 1965 coup, the idea degenerated into a slogan that justified military involvement in the most minute details of political and social life. The dual function doctrine, in other words, was as much the product of an emerging military political dominance as it was the basis for an expanded military role. That is to say, the idea of dual function could scarcely have emerged, or persisted for so long, in the absence of a near-exclusive military jurisdiction in social and political affairs and national security.[13]

Nevertheless, by virtue of its long use as the ideological foundation of extensive military power, the dual function doctrine arguably developed an independent significance during

the New Order. The flood of public protests after May 1998 demanding an end to dual function suggests that it has never been fully embraced by civilians. Yet clearly the doctrine has
affected the self-perception of generations of military officers. Among other things it has
helped them adjust to—and even take pride in performing—functions that military officers
in other countries would consider inappropriate, unprofessional, or both: regulating the internal affairs of social and political organizations, for example, and managing non-defense-
related businesses.

The political power of the Indonesian military has been strengthened by the reality and
the definition of national security threats. Indonesia has not faced a serious external threat for
many years, nor does one appear likely in the future.[14] Accordingly, Indonesian national security doctrine has been dominated by strategies for the detection, prevention, and repression of
internal threats. Paramount among these, in the military's view, have been the threat of subversion by a resurgent communism or an extremist religious movement, and the threat to
national unity posed by ethnic conflicts and regional rebellions, such as those in Aceh, West
Papua, and, until late 1999, East Timor.

Also important in legitimating the military's involvement in political and social affairs and
national security has been the doctrine of "total people's defense."[15] A legacy of the guerrilla
struggle against the Dutch from 1945 to 1949, this doctrine calls for the close cooperation of
regular military forces and the civilian population in defending the country against both external and internal threats.[16] "Total people's defense" is arguably a sensible approach where budgetary and geographical constraints render conventional military forces insufficient to defend
against perceived threats. Nevertheless, this doctrine has helped to blur the distinction between
legitimate defense against external and internal threats, and an ever deeper encroachment of
military authorities into political, social, and economic affairs.

Military Institutions

The penetration of ABRI authority into nonmilitary realms has been facilitated by a variety
of institutional arrangements that have evolved together with—and become integral to—the
Indonesian state.

At the heart of the military's power are certain unique aspects of its command structure.
In accordance with the doctrines of dual function, and total people's defense, the Indonesian
Army is organized primarily along territorial lines.[17] Roughly two-thirds of its forces are dispersed throughout the country in a structure that descends to the village level. Under the current arrangement, the country is divided into ten Regional Military Commands (KODAM).
Each KODAM is further divided into a series of successively smaller geographical command
units: Resort Military Commands (KOREM); District Military Commands (KODIM); and
Subdistrict Military Commands (KORAMIL). At the village level, the armed forces are represented by a noncommissioned officer known as a "*Babinsa.*"

This territorial structure runs parallel to the structures of civilian political authority down
to the village level. In this way it ensures military involvement in and, if necessary, dominance
over the formulation and implementation of policy. It also permits the armed forces to engage
with relative ease in continual surveillance or intelligence gathering and to intervene directly
in all kinds of political, social, and economic matters, including the internal affairs of political

parties, labor disputes, business deals, and so on. "In practice," Crouch writes, "the territorial structure serves as a means of political control."[18]

Military dominance in the realm of national security has also been given effect through a range of centrally commanded institutions with substantial resources and autonomy from control by civilians other than the president. Among the most powerful institutions of the New Order was the Command for the Restoration of Security and Order (Kopkamtib), created by Suharto in the immediate aftermath of the 1965 coup. With virtually unlimited powers of surveillance, arrest, and detention in the name of restoring order, Kopkamtib became a byword for the abuse of military power and the suppression of internal dissent. It was finally dismantled in 1989—just as Suharto was seeking to assert greater control over the military as a whole—and then immediately replaced by the slightly less powerful Bakorstanas.

The preoccupation with internal threats in Indonesian national security doctrine has also permitted the armed forces to claim near-exclusive jurisdiction over the tasks of political surveillance and domestic and foreign intelligence. This power has found expression in a pervasive domestic intelligence network that with only minor exceptions has been controlled by the armed forces.[19] Through its control of these important tasks and institutions, the military has been in a position to exercise a dominating influence in areas of policy that in other contexts might be considered to fall within the realm of civilian authorities.

Finally, mention must be made of the various centrally commanded elite combat units that have been deployed to prevent, control, and crush perceived security threats—particularly in areas considered troubled. The two that stand out in recent times are the elite Special Forces Command (Kopassus) and the Army Strategic Reserve Command (Kostrad).[20] Kopassus is the successor of the Army Para-Commando Regiment (RPKAD), which spearheaded the assault on real and alleged communists in 1965–1966. Like its predecessor, under the New Order Kopassus gained a reputation for professionalism, for its expertise in methods of unconventional warfare, but also for brutality and abuse of authority. The same may be said of Kostrad. Established before the 1965 coup and commanded by Suharto at that time, Kostrad evolved into a formidable mobile strike force, its units deployed in response to perceived major threats to internal security in East Timor, Aceh, Irian Jaya, and elsewhere. Despite its reputation for professionalism and esprit de corps, however, Kostrad units have also been accused of serious human rights violations. With the collapse of the New Order—and revelations about human rights abuse—both Kopassus and Kostrad suffered a serious blow to their prestige, but their ethos and their formidable power remained intact.

Sociopolitical Institutions

The military's pervasive political power has also been rooted in institutional arrangements that extend to all branches of government, including the legislature, the central bureaucracy, the executive branch, and the judiciary, all conventional preserves of civilian authority.

Among the clearest examples of such institutional power has been the allocation to the military of a guaranteed number of seats in the country's main legislative bodies, the DPR and the MPR.[21] The actual number of seats allotted has varied over the years—and was reduced in 1998—but at the end of the New Order ABRI was allocated 75 of the 500 seats in the DPR, and altogether military officers held 2,800 nonelected seats in national, regional, and subregional legislatures.[22] These figures were in addition to the substantial number of seats occupied by retired military officers as representatives of Golkar, the government party.

ABRI's formal legislative power was further enhanced during the New Order by its formal and informal influence in Golkar.[23] This is not to say that ABRI always dominated Golkar or that it did so without opposition from civilians. Indeed, it was forced to share power with civilian politicians and, on occasion, was sidelined by them.[24] Nevertheless, for most of the New Order, Golkar was closely associated with ABRI and was always subject to its influence. In 1998, for example, the vast majority of provincial and district Golkar branches were headed by retired military officers.[25] As Crouch writes, "In the final analysis, ABRI backed Golkar and helped to ensure that it won overwhelming majorities in each election" (Crouch 1998: 20).

The military's potential political power was also evident in its frequent interventions, during the New Order, in the composition and leadership of the token opposition parties, the PDI and the PPP. Although ABRI intervention in the PDI's internal affairs in the mid-1990s was arguably undertaken at the behest of President Suharto, military officials did have the authority to intervene independently in political party affairs if they wished. Outside Jakarta, beyond the watchful eyes of the president, there is little doubt that they did so. ABRI intervention in the affairs of political parties—as well as religious bodies, nongovernmental organizations (NGOs), and other social groups—was coordinated through the highly influential directorates of "sociopolitical affairs" that existed at every level in the ABRI hierarchy. These directorates duplicated the role of the Directorate of Social and Political Affairs within the Ministry of Home Affairs, an ostensibly civilian body whose key posts have historically been occupied largely by military officers.

Military domination of important posts in the Ministry of Home Affairs was just one example of a broad official policy of "*kekaryaan*," under which military officers were appointed to a wide range of civilian positions in the national, regional, and local government apparatus. Originally intended to fill gaps left by the purge of leftists from the civil service after 1965—and also to reward military officers for their loyalty to Suharto—the policy of *kekaryaan* became an independent basis of military power and one of the privileges that the majority of officers have been reluctant to forsake. Under this policy, active-duty and retired military officers were appointed as cabinet ministers, high-level civil servants, diplomats, provincial governors, subprovincial heads, and mayors. Although the number of such appointments began to decline in the mid-1980s, by the late 1990s at least half of the provincial governors and 40 percent of the subprovincial heads were still active or retired military men (Crouch 1998: 18). Altogether, in early 1999 some 4,000 active military officers still occupied such civilian posts, and the number of retired officers in civilian posts was estimated to be at least twice that.[26]

Finally, the military has had the capacity to influence the legal system through formal and informal means.[27] Its formal power has rested mainly in the fact that in dealing with so-called special or political crimes, its officials have been entitled to ignore normal legal procedures. Formal influence has also been facilitated by military domination of Regional Leadership Conferences (Muspida), which bring together representatives from executive, legislative, judicial, and military bodies at the regional and subregional levels. Military authorities have carried significant informal power over the legal system in the sense that whether sanctioned by law or not, they have been free to intervene in virtually any legal case and determine its outcome. Not surprisingly, the armed forces have also maintained exclusive control over the system of military justice—an arrangement ensuring that its officers are seldom brought to justice for serious human rights violations and thereby perpetuating a pattern of impunity and reinforcing the cycle, and the culture, of state violence.[28]

"Unconventional" and Illegal Activities

Apart from its roles in national security management and sociopolitical affairs, the Indonesian military has historically been involved in semilegal or illegal activities ranging from "unconventional financing" to the mobilization of gangs and paramilitary organizations.[29] Both activities have been linked to corruption and to mafia-style crime and have contributed to the entrenchment of military power. But insofar as the abuses stemming from such activities have undermined the prestige of the armed forces, they have also contributed to growing popular opposition.

In absolute terms, and as a percentage of the national budget, state funding for the Indonesian armed forces has been surprisingly modest. In fact, the portion of the national budget allocated to defense and security declined from 27 percent in 1969–1970 to just 6 percent in 1988–1990, after which it remained somewhere between 6 percent and 8 percent until the mid-1990s (Kristiadi 1999: 101). Similarly, unofficial figures suggest that the standard remuneration package for soldiers and officers is very low, leaving a significant number of soldiers below the official poverty line.[30] This apparent underfunding of the most powerful institution in the country is less puzzling when it is understood that budget figures conceal critical sources of military revenue—funds secured through the military's direct involvement in business enterprises and through corruption.

Military reliance on such unconventional financing dates from the revolutionary period and became commonplace during the 1950s, when unit commanders were responsible for routine military expenditures and soldiers' welfare.[31] As noted earlier, the practice intensified with the imposition of martial law in 1957 and with the consolidation of military power after 1965. Military involvement in business took various forms under the New Order. Some officers were appointed as directors of huge public corporations such as the state oil company, Pertamina, and powerful state regulatory bodies such as the National Logistics Board (Bulog). Many others took advantage of their considerable political power—and their influence over the granting of licenses, permits, and bank loans—to establish lucrative enterprises and enter joint ventures with experienced businessmen. Another favored mechanism for generating revenue was the establishment of "foundations" (*yayasan*) that allowed the accumulation and investment of capital on a tax-free basis. The pervasive nature of military power down to the village level also permitted, and perhaps encouraged, officers and soldiers to make money through a variety of corrupt practices including bribery, kickbacks, and protection rackets. Although there is no way of knowing the precise amount of revenue generated from these sources, anecdotal evidence suggests that under the New Order it was substantial.[32]

Closely related but perhaps more worrying from the point of view of ordinary citizens has been the military practice of mobilizing thugs and petty criminals into official and semi-official militias and paramilitary units. Often justified as a means to maintain order, these units have frequently been used to intimidate political opponents, to provoke violence to achieve political ends, and to take part in clandestine military operations aimed at detaining or killing alleged opponents of the government. With only minimal training, such militia forces have been responsible for serious human rights abuses. More generally, the reliance on such groups has arguably contributed to the spread of a culture of violence in society as a whole.

The mobilization of illegal or semilegal violence by military leaders has a long and rich history in Indonesia. Military-sponsored thugs, paramilitary units, and plainclothes officers are known (or believed) to have been involved in many of the most serious instances of political violence, rioting, and social upheaval under the New Order. Military units such as the RPKAD encouraged "civilian" groups to take part in the campaign to annihilate the PKI in 1965–1966 and in many instances provided them with arms and other logistical support to do so, thereby contributing to the vast scale of the killing.[33] Demonstrators and thugs under the influence of high-ranking military officers are thought to have been responsible for igniting the widespread rioting in January 1974 known as the Malari Affair.[34] In an officially sanctioned campaign of mass murder in the mid-1980s, known by the acronym PETRUS, soldiers in plainclothes shot dead as many as 5,000 petty criminals.[35] In East Timor and Aceh, military commanders are known to have mobilized thousands of local youths into paramilitary units over many years and trained them to spy on, terrorize, and kill fellow citizens suspected of antigovernment sympathies. In the final years of the New Order, military authorities habitually mobilized ABRI-affiliated youth organizations and gangs in order to disrupt otherwise peaceful demonstrations.[36] They are widely believed, for example, to have organized thugs to storm the national headquarters of the PDI in July 1996, triggering what was at the time some of the worst rioting in twenty years.

Historically, the resort to such activities—the provocation or engineering of social conflict and violence—has often occurred when struggles for political power emerged within the New Order political and military elite. These methods were also used, and proved to be grimly effective, in preventing or diverting opposition and criticism of the regime by civil society. Whatever the reasons, the military's capacity to employ such tactics was an important source of its political power under the New Order, but at the same time an important reason for its deep unpopularity with ordinary people.

CONSTRAINTS ON MILITARY POWER
UNDER THE NEW ORDER

Even under the New Order, the political power of the military was not unlimited. It was constrained by the constitutional and personal authority of the president, by tensions and conflicts within the military itself, and by opposition and criticism both from abroad and from Indonesia's own civil society. During the late New Order, these forces dovetailed in ways that weakened military authority and ultimately helped to undermine the regime itself. As the case of Aceh clearly demonstrates, however, even in the late New Order these limits did not significantly constrain the military in its relations with the vast majority of the population.

Presidential Power

Under the Indonesian constitution the president, as supreme commander, holds ultimate authority over the armed forces. Although that authority did not significantly impinge on

ABRI's power through the first two decades of the New Order, starting in the mid-1980s the military leadership often found itself in competition with the president for jurisdiction over key areas of state policy, such as senior political and military appointments, decisions over defense procurement, and the definition of the armed forces' appropriate role. In these battles, the military leadership did not always prevail.

In the realm of senior political appointments, President Suharto's vice-presidential choice in 1988, Sudharmono, was selected against the powerful objections of the ABRI leadership.[37] In 1998, Suharto again managed to have his vice-presidential favorite, B.J. Habibie, selected against the wishes of active and retired military officers.[38] Some of the opposition to Habibie's candidacy among military leaders can be traced to yet another policy battle they had lost to civilian authorities. In the early 1990s Habibie, as minister of state for research and technology, had arranged for the procurement of 39 aging naval vessels from the former East German fleet, apparently without consulting the military leadership or at any rate against their objections. This case was symptomatic of a general decline in the military's political influence at the center in the last five years of the New Order. Other signs of that decline were the reduction in the number of cabinet posts and governorships allocated to military men (Kristiadi 1999: 109).

Instances of ABRI's declining authority in relation to the president were evident, too, when it came to senior military appointments. Exercising his ultimate authority over military promotions and assignments, President Suharto succeeded in sidelining a succession of potential challengers while rewarding officers considered personally loyal. Suharto's most conspicuous victory over the military was his sacking of the powerful ABRI commander, General Murdani, in 1993 and the subsequent purge of Murdani loyalists from key command posts.[39] The success of the "de-Benny-ization" campaign was a clear reminder that even the highest military authorities were subject to the authority of the president. Indeed, some observers consider that after Murdani's ouster, ABRI became little more than a "fire brigade" dispatched by the president to smother the fires he had started (Crouch 1998: 2).

The fire brigade metaphor highlights an important aspect of the relationship between the military and the president under the New Order. Although touted as an institution above politics, whose sole duty was to the nation and the state, the armed forces were increasingly used in a regime maintenance function, that is, to keep Suharto in power. That often meant using military force and intelligence capacity to identify, detain, torture, or kill government opponents. Such activities were by no means confined to the notorious trouble spots Aceh and East Timor but took place literally throughout the country. One of the more notorious instances of the pattern, for instance, was the 1997–1998 kidnapping and murder of several student activists by elements of the armed forces near Jakarta.

Civil Society: Domestic and International

In the final years of the New Order, the principal challenges to military power in social and political affairs, as well as national security issues, came from Indonesia's emerging civil society and from the international community.[40] There were at least two related processes stimulating the development of a stronger and more assertive civil society in Indonesia during the late New Order. First, domestic critics emerged with increasing force in response to the actions of the state itself.[41] Through their direct experience as victims of systematic human rights violations, for example, members of different social, class, and ethnic groups began gradually to perceive the military—with its "security approach," its pervasive intelligence network, and its contempt for the law—as the principal and common cause of their problems. Second, a growing impatience with the political status quo developed alongside changes in the class or social structure stemming from rapid economic change. Particularly important in this regard was the significant growth in the late New Order of the professional, educated middle class—lawyers, teachers, journalists, students, artists, NGO workers, and others—who were uniquely capable of articulating the general impatience with the status quo. Not surprisingly, their commitment to political change grew dramatically as the regime began increasingly to target them for repression.

Tensions and conflicts within the military and political elite also enhanced the power of civil society. Observers of Indonesian military politics have noted several different lines of division over the years: conflicts between corrupt "financial officers" and the reputedly cleaner "professional officers"; generational tensions, especially between the "1945 generation" of officers who emerged from the revolution and younger officers trained in military academies; friction between officers considered loyal to the president and his entourage ("the palace") and those seen as critical of it; ideological-cum-religious differences between Islamic-oriented ("Green") officers and those with a more secular-nationalist ("Red and White") orientation; and rivalries of a largely personal nature between high-ranking officers that end up involving their respective followers.

Each of these lines of tension within the elite has had the potential to encourage contending factions to seek civilian allies. And each, therefore, has also had the potential to be exploited by civilians seeking to influence policy or even to challenge the military or the regime itself. In connection with his growing animosity toward the palace in the early 1990s, for example, General Murdani is believed to have encouraged civilian opposition to Suharto. Meanwhile, Suharto took advantage of public protest on certain issues to advance his own agenda against Murdani. The strong domestic and international criticism that followed the November 1991 Santa Cruz massacre in East Timor, for example, provided Suharto with a perfect opportunity to purge a number of Murdani supporters from the military while winning credit by appearing to respond to public concern over human rights violations.[42]

In the final years of the New Order, the challenge to the existing pattern of civil-military relations—and to the regime itself—was also stimulated by conditions outside of Indonesia. For much of the first 30 years of Suharto's rule, strong international support had helped to buttress military dominance and systematic human rights abuse. With the end of the cold war, however, a majority of Western governments began to espouse open concern for human rights and democratization. Although this rhetoric was not always matched by concrete action, it did present an important opportunity for international and domestic groups to advance their concerns. Moreover, in some instances, the rhetoric of Western governments was backed by open criticism and threats of economic sanctions.[43]

Mention should also be made of the impact of international economic developments. Here again it must be recalled that economic interests had encouraged most foreign investors and lenders to remain silent in the face of political abuses and rampant corruption until roughly 1998. Although the economic crisis of 1997–1998 was in significant respects the product of flawed Indonesian government policy and endemic corruption, international economic pressures compounded the problem. Because success in economic development had been the New

Order's main source of legitimacy, the collapse of the economy began very swiftly to undermine the regime's credibility and, with it, the position of the military.

Embedded Power

Yet if, at the center, military authority was to some extent circumscribed or undermined by the president, by friction within the military, by domestic protesters, and by the international community, these constraints did not appreciably diminish ABRI's effective power in relation to the population at large under the New Order. The problem was most pronounced in areas considered troubled, where the military was given even greater than normal autonomy. As already noted, however, military dominance and abusive behavior were by no means confined to these areas. Although a discourse of political reform and concern for human rights gave the impression that things were changing in the early 1990s—an impression largely accepted at face value by Jakarta-based journalists and diplomats—serious investigations found no clear evidence of improvement.[44]

The military's dominance persisted because the task of ensuring national security continued to be regarded, even by civilians, as the legitimate preserve of military authorities and, moreover, because that task had historically been so broadly defined. The military's de facto power at the local level was further strengthened by the fact that some military officials were prepared to use—and rarely were punished for using—violence and other illegal means to pursue their interests and policies. Thus, although the assertion of presidential authority and occasional domestic and international criticism may have begun to limit the political authority of the military in the late New Order, it did not significantly alter the relationship between the military and the vast majority of the population. Given the military's considerable arsenal of doctrinal, structural, and institutional authority, such a state of affairs was hardly surprising.

Case Study: Civil-Military Relations in Aceh, 1989–1998

This characterization of civil-military relations under the New Order is highlighted by events in Aceh between 1989 and 1998. During these years the Indonesian government conducted a counterinsurgency campaign aimed at crushing an armed independence movement known as Aceh Merdeka. In the course of that campaign, an estimated 2,000 civilians were killed and countless others were arbitrarily detained, tortured, and raped.

The events of these years confirm, first, that although ABRI's authority was constrained by the president and by domestic opposition, such limitations did not significantly infringe on the capacity of military commanders to carry out military operations in the name of national security. Indeed, in their relations with civilians in Aceh, military authorities had the ultimate authority. Second, the events in Aceh demonstrate clearly that a culture of violence had become deeply embedded in the Indonesian military by the late 1980s and, too, that the use of terror against civilian populations had become standard practice. Third, they give some sense of the ways in which unrestrained military power was linked to the practice of unconventional financing and how that practice led to further military abuses. Finally, they underline the ways in which the international context encouraged patterns of military abuse and unrestrained power vis-à-vis civilians.

Constraints That Did Not Matter

The government counterinsurgency campaign in Aceh, it now seems clear, was initiated by President Suharto himself. Apart from a genuine concern to put down a rebellion, the president's direct intervention was prompted by a desire to reassert central authority over a regional military command that was perceived to be too autonomous and perhaps even involved in the drug trade and other criminal activities. So in mid-1990, on Suharto's order, the regional military commander was replaced, and some 6,000 additional troops were deployed to the region, bringing the total to about 12,000.[45]

This evidence tends to support the contention that particularly in the late New Order, ABRI did not have ultimate authority. Even in matters of national security, it was subject to the decisions of the president and his immediate circle. Yet, although the president may have been responsible for setting in motion the military operation in Aceh, and perhaps even suggesting which units ought to be deployed, it is clear that once the troops were on the ground, military commanders had ultimate authority to determine and implement strategy and tactics. As Amnesty International wrote, "The political authority of the armed forces, considerable even under normal conditions, now became unchallengeable. In the name of national security, military and police authorities deployed in Aceh were thereafter free to use virtually any means deemed necessary to destroy the [rebel movement]" (Amnesty International 1993: 11).[46]

A Culture of Violence

In deciding how to proceed against the rebels, military commanders applied standard ABRI doctrine and used strategies that had been developed and refined in other theaters of operation during the New Order. By 1989, the regime's counterinsurgency repertoire had expanded considerably, in large part thanks to the experience gained by crushing the PKI and the East Timorese resistance. The strategy employed in Aceh—and the behavior of the troops there—reflected this fact and demonstrated that a culture of violence had become deeply entrenched in ABRI by this time, particularly within Kopassus and other elite combat units. Two distinctive tactics were employed in Aceh that had been tried and refined in other operations, most notably in East Timor: first, the systematic use of terror as a method for dealing with perceived threats to national security; and second, the forced mobilization of civilians to serve as auxiliaries in counterinsurgency operations.[47] ABRI's approach in Aceh ensured that a much broader spectrum of people came to experience the hard edge of the regime, to feel deep bitterness toward it, and to sympathize more completely with the opposition. These methods also encouraged greater violence and disruption in local society and inflicted wounds that would prove exceptionally difficult to heal.

Among the first outside troops to arrive in Aceh in mid-1990 was a Kopassus unit under the command of Col. Prabowo Subianto. Within a few days of their arrival by parachute in Aceh Utara, this unit began to burn down the houses of families suspected of supporting Aceh Merdeka.[48] That was only the start. In subsequent weeks, this unit and others began a systematic campaign to terrorize civilian populations in areas of presumed rebel strength. Their methods included armed nighttime raids, house-to-house searches, arbitrary arrest, routine torture of detainees, the rape of women believed to be associated with the movement, and public execution.[49]

Among the most chilling examples of state-sanctioned terror in Aceh were targeted killings and public executions. For a period of about two years after the start of combat operations, the corpses of Acehnese victims, generally young men, were found strewn in public places—beside main roads, near village security posts, in public markets, in fields and plantations, next to a stream or a river—apparently as a warning to others not to join or support the rebels (Amnesty International 1993: 18). Many victims of summary execution were simply shot and thrown into mass graves, at least one of which reportedly contained as many as 200 bodies (Amnesty International 1993: 18).[50] But if the method of disposal was different, the intent of the mass killings was the same: to sow terror, to create an atmosphere of pervasive fear, and to ensure that witnesses to such crimes remained silent.

Equally important in generating political violence in Aceh was the New Order strategy of "civil-military cooperation"—a euphemism for the policy of compelling civilians to participate in intelligence and security operations against real or alleged government opponents. Like the use of targeted killings, corpse display, and rape, this strategy was not unique to Aceh; it had been developed and refined, for example, in counterinsurgency operations in Irian Jaya and East Timor. Among the most notorious examples of the strategy were the "fence of legs" operations in which "ordinary villagers were compelled to sweep through an area ahead of armed troops, in order both to flush out rebels and to inhibit them from returning fire" (Amnesty International 1993: 12). The military also led campaigns encouraging all civilians to spy upon, turn in, or kill any suspected member of an alleged enemy group. This tactic was an essential element in the dynamic of violence in Aceh. In November 1990, for example, the regional military commander, Maj. Gen. R. Pramono, said, "I have told the community, if you find a terrorist, kill him. There's no need to investigate him. Don't let people be the victims. If they don't do as you order them, shoot them on the spot, or butcher them. I tell members of the community to carry sharp weapons, a machete or whatever. If you meet a terrorist, kill him."[51]

In accordance with standard ABRI practice, military commanders also mobilized local vigilante units and night patrols. Recruits received basic military training and, after being armed with knives, spears, and machetes, were told to hunt down Aceh Merdeka supporters. As they had done during the anticommunist campaign in 1965–1966 and counterinsurgency operations in East Timor, military authorities also organized mass rallies in Aceh at which civilians were exhorted to swear an oath that they would "crush the terrorists until there is nothing left of them" (Amnesty International 1993: 13–14). Failure to participate in such campaigns—and to demonstrate a sufficient commitment to crushing the enemy by identifying, capturing, or killing alleged rebels—often resulted in punishment and sometimes public torture and execution.[52]

Military as Mafia

Aceh's status as a Military Operations Area (which lasted from 1990 to 1998) created unrivaled opportunities for the emergence of a semiofficial mafia with close links to the military and to Kopassus in particular. Members of units stationed in Aceh were able to enrich themselves serving as enforcers, debt collectors, security guards, and extortionists.[53]

Stories of such operations began to abound as Kopassus became firmly established in Aceh in the mid-1990s. In 1997, for example, a local human rights organization reported the case of a man named Abdul Hamid bin Itam, who had been detained by three Kopassus soldiers late at night on September 14, 1996, in the town of Sigli. After being taken to the local Kopassus post, Abdul Hamid had been badly beaten and then shot in the head; his mutilated body was found a few days later about 200 kilometers from Sigli. Although at first this appeared to be a standard summary execution of an Aceh Merdeka suspect, it was later discovered that the dead man had been detained in connection with a private dispute he had had with a local government official in Pidie. The official had evidently hired the Kopassus soldiers to "resolve" the dispute.[54]

Although evidence for the existence of such a military mafia remains largely anecdotal, its existence would be in keeping with patterns in other parts of the country, especially in other areas of long-term military operations. It would also help to account for the extraordinary reluctance of the armed forces to leave Aceh long after Aceh Merdeka had been crushed as a military force.

International Context

The military response to the Aceh Merdeka uprising was also shaped by the international context. The crackdown began more than a year before the November 1991 massacre at Santa Cruz, East Timor, in which as many as 270 people may have died, and the unprecedented criticism at home and abroad that stemmed from it. That criticism, and the unusual decision to reprimand some senior officers, would eventually send shock waves throughout the armed forces, shaking its sense of invulnerability for the first time in decades. But in the years and months before Santa Cruz, leading military figures displayed a remarkable confidence about the success of their terrorist methods.

This was a time, too, when international criticism of the New Order's human rights record had reached a low ebb. Stimulated by a desire to capitalize on the burgeoning economies of the region, Western governments were reluctant to voice concern about or take concrete measures against the violations committed by Indonesian government forces. In these years Western governments routinely argued that the human rights situation in East Timor was improving and that it was pointless, even irresponsible, to question the territory's political status. About human rights violations occurring in Indonesia itself, there was even less concern.

In short, the counterinsurgency campaign in Aceh was set in motion at a time when military authorities felt confident that the brutal methods they had used elsewhere could again be used to good effect and without serious political cost. They were not far wrong. Long after the Santa Cruz massacre had forced recognition of the seriousness of the problem in East Timor and at least some sort of response from the New Order, the widespread violations of human rights in Aceh received scarcely a mention either abroad or within Indonesia. The world's decision to maintain an unseemly silence—to conduct business as usual with the New Order—unquestionably helped to ensure that military operations, and human rights abuses, continued in Aceh for nearly a decade.

AFTER THE NEW ORDER

The public and international clamor for reform that finally triggered President Suharto's resignation in May 1998 accelerated in the weeks and months after his demise and led to wide-

spread criticism of the armed forces, both for its record of human rights abuse and for its association with the New Order. The military leadership responded to the new situation with proposals for reform and with promises of a thorough reconsideration and reorientation of ABRI's
role. Meanwhile, the Indonesian political system lurched unsteadily toward civilian rule. Perhaps the most powerful symbol of that change was the successful, and largely peaceful, national
election of June 1999—the first free and fair election in Indonesia since 1955. Also emblematic
of the change was the election by the new MPR of a civilian president and vice president,
Abdurrahmand Wahid and Megawati Sukarnoputri, respectively, in October 1999.

It is too early to say definitively whether these developments signal a lasting change in civil-
military relations in Indonesia. What follows, therefore, is a modest attempt to detect some of
the more significant trends that have emerged in the post-Suharto period, and on that basis to
make some suggestions about the future trajectory of civil-military relations in Indonesia. This
analysis of current and future trends is followed by a case study of East Timor since the end of
the New Order.

The Trend toward Civilian Power

At least on the surface, the initiatives taken by the Indonesian National Defense Forces (TNI)
after May 1998 appeared to reflect a genuine shift in thinking within the armed forces leadership. By June, a number of high-ranking military officers had prepared detailed proposals for
political, legal, and economic reform.[55] In August 1998, General Prabowo and two of his associates were sacked for their alleged involvement in the kidnapping and murder of prodemocracy activists earlier that year. The same month armed forces commander General Wiranto
issued a public apology for human rights violations committed by ABRI in Aceh and declared
an end to the ten-year-old military operation there. In late 1998 Wiranto announced that the
dual function doctrine would be reconsidered and that the military would henceforth be operating according to a "new paradigm." As a sign of this commitment to change, in November
1998 the name of ABRI's chief of staff for social and political affairs was changed to chief of
staff for territorial affairs. In 1999 the military leadership acquiesced in the reduction of the
number of ABRI seats in the DPR (and MPR) from 75 to 38.[56] In April, the police were separated from ABRI, and the new streamlined armed forces were renamed the TNI. Most surprisingly, perhaps, the military leadership publicly accepted President Habibie's January 1999
proposal to let East Timorese vote on their political future and in October joined other factions
in the MPR in accepting the result, leading to East Timor's independence.

With the selection of Abdurrahmand Wahid as president in October 1999, the shift toward
civilian supremacy appeared to gain further momentum. Wahid immediately asserted his
authority over the military with a series of bold appointments and rotations at the highest levels of the TNI. Breaking with the long tradition of army domination, he immediately appointed
a civilian, Juwono Sudarsono, as minister of defense and a navy officer, Admiral Widodo, as
TNI commander. In January 2000 he dismissed the armed forces spokesperson, Major General Sudrajat, after he made statements questioning the president's authority over the military.[57]
At about the same time, Wahid ordered that in accordance with a 1999 MPR decision on
kekaryaan, the four active military officers in the cabinet would have to retire from the TNI by
the end of March; and all did so without objection.[58] In his most daring move, in February, he

suspended the former armed forces commander General Wiranto from his cabinet position, pending investigations into the general's role in the previous year's violence in East Timor.[59]

Wahid's willingness to face down the military was also evident in his handling of the continuing political crisis in Aceh. As early as November 1999 he resisted strong military demands for a declaration of martial law in the province, saying, "There is no need for that. Martial law will [only] create more problems."[60] Wahid also lent his full support to the prosecution of human rights violators in Aceh, leading to an unprecedented trial that ended in April 2000 with the conviction of 24 soldiers and police and 1 civilian for the July 1999 murder of more than 50 civilians. Although critics noted that the prosecutors had failed to bring charges against commanding officers, the trial nevertheless represented a significant departure from the cycle of military impunity that had prevailed under the New Order.[61]

President Wahid's tough posture seems to have stimulated further serious thinking within the TNI leadership. At a special meeting in April 2000, some 150 top TNI leaders decided that the military should begin to withdraw from its involvement in political affairs and instead focus on its external defense role.[62] That meeting was followed by the news that the Ministry of Defense had begun a review of the national security doctrine and of the 1982 law on dual function.[63] In May some 50 generals took part in a seminar at which the need for serious doctrinal change was debated.[64] At least on paper, then, it seemed that the armed forces were prepared to accept the need for fundamental change and even to consider altering their core doctrine of dual function.

Viewed more systematically, these moves toward greater civilian power have been rooted in four related trends: first, the new confidence of Indonesia's emerging civil society, expressed in vibrant, public political action; second, the willingness of Indonesia's civilian presidents to use the considerable power of their office to face down the military; third, a degree of honest soul-searching within the armed forces leadership itself; and fourth, a recent shift in international norms and practices characterized by a greater willingness to intervene in the internal affairs of sovereign states in support of good governance and human rights. If these trends persist, there is room for optimism that the move toward civilian power in Indonesia will continue. Each of these trends, and their implications for the future, are discussed in greater detail below.

The sudden collapse of the New Order—and the central role of mass public demonstrations in bringing it about—gave a new political confidence to Indonesia's civil society while significantly weakening the military's political position and self-confidence. The relative strength of civil society was discernible not only in the bold demands for change that emerged after May 1998, but in the political breadth of the groups advocating them. NGO activists, spiritual leaders, new political parties, government bureaucrats, and former military officers all spoke out against the very essence of the military's long-standing mission. They called forcefully for an end to the dual function doctrine, the policy of *kekaryaan*, the "security approach," and the allocation of reserved DPR and MPR seats to the military. They also demanded full investigations into past human rights violations, and the punishment of military authorities found responsible.

Before May 1998 these sorts of demands were not only uncommon but would have been grounds for arrest and imprisonment. By the second half of 1998 they had became part of national political discourse, a trend that continued into the new millennium. Moreover, as we have seen, by early 1999 at least some of these popular demands had actually been met, and by 2000 the shift toward civilian supremacy was well underway. Although some critics complained that the reforms had not gone far enough, it was clear that the TNI leadership had been forced to respond to the demands of civil society. That response in itself signaled a profound shift in the balance between military and civilian power. Accordingly, there would appear to be hope that the continued expression of popular dissent might help to promote further genuine reform and shift the balance even further toward civilian authority.

Important as public protests have been, the shift toward civilian supremacy has arguably depended at least as much on the willingness of Presidents Habibie and Wahid to use the considerable power accorded them under the 1945 constitution in the interest of democratization and civilianization. Although commonly characterized as a Suharto crony, Habibie made some decisions that openly challenged military power and military thinking. The most dramatic was his proposal to hold a referendum in East Timor, discussed in more detail below. Wahid's approach has been only slightly less dramatic but, as already noted, in his first year in office he went farther than most imagined possible in establishing the principle and the practice of civilian supremacy.

In short, the political inclinations of the two civilian presidents, and the power afforded them under the current (1945) constitution, have been crucial in recasting the pattern of civil-military relations in the direction of civilian supremacy. The main concern in this regard is that as Suharto so clearly demonstrated, the power that the constitution grants presidents can, and might yet, easily be used to achieve the very opposite objective.

A third encouraging trend for those who favor civilian supremacy is indications that some in the TNI leadership sincerely support that option. Although a measure of skepticism is warranted about the motivation for the TNI reforms after May 1998, the military leadership's claim that these initiatives were genuine cannot be dismissed out of hand. There were, in fact, military officers who had begun to urge a process of reform well before Suharto resigned. The most prominent among this group, sometimes referred to as the military's "intellectuals," was Gen. Bambang Yudhoyono, the author of a comprehensive proposal for reform issued in June 1998.

Suharto's resignation and the torrent of public criticism it unleashed undoubtedly gave added momentum and credence to the views of this group of reformers.[65] So too did the presidency of Abdurrahmand Wahid. Within a few months of his appointment, Wahid had moved a number of known reformers into key positions within the TNI leadership, while simultaneously removing officers thought to be more supportive of the status quo.

One of the most outspoken and controversial of the reformers introduced into the inner circle by Wahid was Maj. Gen. Agus Wirahadikusumah.[66] In late 1999, when he was still a KODAM commander, Major General Agus had gone on record advocating drastic changes in the structure and doctrine of the armed forces, such as the dismantling of the territorial system, and an end to TNI involvement in political affairs. Without such changes, he said, the TNI would go the way of the dinosaur and would be abandoned by the people. At about the same time, Agus openly supported calls for the investigation and prosecution of high-ranking officers for past human rights abuses in Aceh, East Timor, and elsewhere. When Kostrad commander Lt. Gen. Djaja Suparman ominously warned that the trial of generals might anger soldiers, leading to unpredictable consequences, Agus retorted that "TNI soldiers do not serve their generals but the TNI as an institution and the state."[67]

Such attitudes and proposals for reform were shared by a number of other officers whom President Wahid had placed in positions of some power. They included Gen. Tyasno Sudarto (army chief of staff), Admiral Widodo Adisucipto (TNI commander), and Maj. Gen. Ryamizard Riyacudu (Jakarta regional military commander). Their hold on these key posts was by no means guaranteed. It remained a possibility that they would be replaced by officers much less sympathetic to the reform agenda, of whom there were still a great many. Nevertheless, the fact that these reformers occupied key TNI positions at such a critical juncture undoubtedly helped to tip the balance in the direction of civilian supremacy.

Finally, a word about the international context is necessary. In a marked change from the New Order years, international conditions provided a strong push in the direction of greater civilian power after May 1998. The economic crisis continued to leave the regime vulnerable to the demands of foreign creditors, and as of 2000 there was no indication that these creditors favored a return to the corrupt authoritarian system, which many blamed for the crisis. In response to continuing evidence of corruption at the highest levels, such as the Bank Bali scandal of late 1999, and to the disgraceful behavior of the armed forces in East Timor, the International Monetary Fund and the World Bank actually suspended some of their lending programs.

Likewise, the avalanche of evidence of wrongdoing, past and present, left foreign governments and international political institutions such as the UN with little choice but to support the process of reform and civilianization. While expressing some concern about mounting social violence, for example, the U.S. government appeared to give notice that any overt move toward the reassertion of military control over political life would not be welcome. During a visit to Indonesia in early March 1999, for example, U.S. Secretary of State Madeleine Albright voiced strong U.S. support for the June elections and the hope that the process of democratization would ultimately succeed.[68] A similar message of support for civilian supremacy was delivered by the U.S. ambassador to the UN, Richard Holbrooke, in January 2000. Responding to widespread rumors of a military coup, he said pointedly, "We would view with the greatest possible concern any such event. It would do Indonesia immense, perhaps irreparable damage."[69]

As we shall see, the international response to the violence in East Timor after the August 1999 popular consultation was even more resounding. Some governments, including the United States and the European Union, openly blamed the TNI for supporting the militias, and they temporarily suspended military ties and arms transfers. In a rare move, in mid-September 1999, the UN Security Council authorized a multinational armed force to use "all necessary measures" to restore order in the territory.

Military Power Resurgent?

As encouraging as these developments may seem to advocates of civilian rule, there is room for pessimism about the permanence of the shift away from military dominance. Two problems loom especially large. First, the moves toward civilian supremacy, together with other political developments, have begun to produce a backlash within the military, either because they are seen as compromising national security, or because they directly threaten the material and political interests of the TNI itself. Indeed, such concerns have even led to rumors of military coups, first in late 1999 and then again in February 2000.[70] Thus, as is so often the case in the transition to civilian rule, efforts at reform have helped to stimulate the preconditions for further military intervention.

A second problem is that the post-1998 reforms have not completely undermined the key institutional and ideological foundations of military power. Not only does this mean that through much of the country the norms and behavior of the military have not appreciably changed, it also means that military officers who oppose reform or who have some other axe to grind still have the capacity to disrupt political life and to push for a reassertion of military power. These problems and their possible implications for the future are examined in greater detail below.

Notwithstanding sincere efforts by civic leaders to prevent it, after May 1998 the country faced a serious threat of disintegration and descent into widespread social and political violence. Not only did violence erupt in distant places such as Maluku, Aceh, West Papua, and East Timor, it broke out repeatedly right in the capital city, Jakarta, where it resulted in at least a dozen deaths and scores of injuries in 1999 alone. The emergence in 2000 of new armed paramilitary groups—some of them with thousands of members—and their mobilization on behalf of political causes further compounded the danger. The threat and the reality of social violence and regional rebellion raised troubling questions about the course of reform and the future of civil-military relations; and it appeared to open the door to a reassertion of military power in the name of security, order, and national unity.

Was it wise, some began to ask, to weaken the armed forces and to further undermine its morale at a time when it was perhaps the only body capable of maintaining order and guaranteeing national unity? Critics answered that military behavior had always tended to cause or contribute to social and political violence, so that a further weakening of the armed forces could only improve the situation. However, many of those in positions of authority—both civilian and military—took a more cautious view and supported initiatives aimed at enhancing the capacity of the armed forces and limiting the power of civil society.[71]

Two such initiatives were especially ominous. The first was an instruction by TNI commander General Wiranto in February 1999 empowering armed forces personnel to "shoot on sight" rioters and others deemed to be disrupting the peace. The potential dangers of this policy were immediately evident to human rights advocates, and it was not long before several people had been shot dead by security forces. Nevertheless, anxiety about social and political chaos was so widespread that there was remarkably little criticism of the policy.[72] Indeed, key civilian opposition figures—including Abdurrahmand Wahid, who would later be elected president—reportedly spoke out in favor of the shoot on sight order.[73] Civilian support for harsh, even draconian, measures continued in 2000. Responding to an outbreak of rioting in Lombok and to fears that it might spread to neighboring Bali, house speaker Akbar Tanjung urged strong measures against suspected troublemakers: "Find and detain them. If needed, shoot them on sight so they will not repeat the crime."[74]

The second major initiative was a new state security law, submitted to the legislature in September 1999. Although some argued that it was an improvement on the existing regulation of 1959, the new law did give almost unlimited political and judicial power to the TNI in conditions of emergency and crisis. Formulated and fully backed by the TNI, the draft law was vehemently opposed by prodemocracy activists on the grounds that it represented a brazen reassertion of military power. It was opposed by the police, as well, who felt that the law gave the army unacceptably broad authority to take over police functions. Despite these objections, the draft law was passed by the old legislature in September 1999 as one of its last acts before disbanding. Only President Habibie's last-minute decision, in the face of strong popular protest, to postpone signing the bill kept it from being made law. But as social and political violence continued in 2000, pressure again began to mount for the passage of the new emergency law, or some variation of that law, and it seemed only a matter of time before President Wahid would have to sign it.[75]

In addition to concerns over violence and national security, by late 1999 it was clear that some military officers and soldiers saw the reform agenda as a threat to the integrity and autonomy of the TNI as an institution and to the political and material interests of individual officers. First and foremost, many were deeply concerned by the Wahid administration's efforts to investigate and prosecute TNI soldiers and officers for past human rights–related offences. They found the government-backed investigation into the violence in East Timor particularly disturbing because it named six generals, including former TNI commander Wiranto, as probable suspects in serious criminal offences, including crimes against humanity. In the view of many military officers, that investigation established a dangerous legal and political precedent that could ultimately land many of them in the dock. It was perhaps more than coincidence, therefore, that rumors of a military coup began to circulate immediately after the results of the investigation were released in late January 2000.[76]

Second, many lower- and middle-ranking officers were dismayed by a 1999 MPR decision on *kekaryaan* that required TNI officers assuming civilian posts to retire from active duty. Reforming the practice of *kekaryaan* might appeal to a handful of "intellectual" generals whose careers and futures are secure. But for the vast majority of middle- and lower-ranking officers, such reforms threaten to take away everything they expected to be theirs. After all, most joined the military in the expectation that they would enjoy the customary economic benefits of membership, and probably in the hope that they would one day secure a pleasant, and perhaps powerful, civilian post. This group of officers, therefore, has a strong motive to support moves against reform and further civilian control. They may also have an added incentive to engage in various types of unconventional financing—both legal and illegal—a sphere so far untouched by reform efforts.

In addition to questions of motive, certain political habits or tendencies remain from the New Order that have the potential to spark renewed military intervention in politics. One of these is the persistence of conflicts within the highest reaches of the TNI and between military and civilian leaders. The most conspicuous rivalry in the immediate post-Suharto period was between General Wiranto and former Kostrad commander General Prabowo, and their respective supporters.[77] By late 1999, that rivalry had been eclipsed by serious tensions between a group of officers loyal to General Wiranto and another closely linked to President Wahid.[78] And it seemed very likely that new lines of friction would continue to emerge.

The substance of these rivalries was arguably less important than the manner in which they were played out. In both cases, there was concern that they might contribute to a reassertion of military power, either through direct action in the form of a coup or through subterfuge and provocation. Of these two possibilities the latter was the more likely. Most of the protagonists in these affairs controlled—either formally or informally—a sizable body of officers, units, and paramilitary forces and were in a position to provoke social and political violence.[79] So, as political violence began to flare throughout the country in late 1998, there was strong suspicion—though limited concrete evidence—that some of it had been deliberately provoked by Prabowo loyalists in order to undermine General Wiranto and President Habibie, and perhaps to justify a reassertion of military power.[80] Similarly, in late 1999 and early 2000 Wiranto and his group were widely alleged to be provoking unrest and violence—in Maluku, Aceh, and elsewhere—as a way to weaken Wahid's authority and perhaps restore a measure of military power. Indeed, both the minister of defense and the president himself made such allegations, though neither mentioned any TNI officers by name.[81]

In short, there are elements within the military with strong motives—ideological, institutional, and personal—for resisting the trend toward civilian rule. And there are political dynamics at work within the TNI—in particular, intra-elite tensions—that might actually encourage such military intervention in politics. Just as importantly, however, the post-1998 reforms have left largely intact the ideological and institutional foundations of military power already described, so that those who oppose reform and civilian rule still have the capacity to make mischief. It is worth recalling what those foundations consist of, before looking in more detail at how the resilience of TNI power has played out in East Timor.

Arguably the deepest foundations of military power are ideological and doctrinal. Although it is true that the dual function doctrine has been openly challenged by civil society in recent years and that some within the TNI itself have recognized the need for a thorough review of the doctrine, there is a very long way to go before its influence is no longer felt. The reason is that the dual function doctrine is not simply an empty slogan but a principle that has shaped the very structure of the Indonesian state. Simply changing the law regarding dual function will not change habits and practices that have become embedded in that state over five decades.

Just as importantly, real change will require a complete overhaul of long-standing national defense and security doctrines—something that appears to be a long way off. The doctrine of total people's defense, for example, which lies at the heart of the territorial system and justifies military involvement down to the village level, has scarcely been discussed let alone challenged. Likewise, there has been little serious questioning of the role of the military in maintaining internal security and order. To the extent that these issues remain a pressing concern of civilian leaders and society at large—as they seem very likely to do—the military will be able to retain an important element of its authority, notwithstanding reform in other spheres. In short, as long as these basic military doctrines remain as unquestioned elements of the Indonesian state, military withdrawal from political life will never be more than partial.

On the institutional front, a continuing source of military power is the block of seats reserved for the TNI and police in the legislature (DPR) and the consultative assembly (MPR). The number of guaranteed seats was halved in 1998 from 75 to 38, and in 1999 the TNI agreed, under pressure, to withdraw completely from the DPR and MPR by 2004.[82] More recently, however, the military has sought to retain its guaranteed seats in the MPR beyond 2004, claiming that it is still entitled to play a role in shaping state policy.[83] Quite understandably, some observers worry that the military might use its seats in the MPR to influence the outcome of key votes, such as those for the president and vice president, or those on constitutional amendments.

Even less affected by the post-1998 reforms has been TNI control over the country's most powerful and potentially dangerous military institutions. The TNI continues to dominate all of the main domestic and international intelligence bodies. Likewise, its control over the formidable elite combat units, Kopassus and Kostrad, is so far unchallenged, despite Wahid's efforts to bring them for a time under the command of more reformist officers.[84] The size and capability of these units, and the fact that each is commanded by a single officer, makes them a serious potential threat to civilian rule. That danger is further compounded by the fact that these units have long experience in mobilizing semilegal and illegal paramilitary groups and in using them for questionable political purposes.

Perhaps the most important institutional base of military power so far unaffected by the post–New Order reforms is the "territorial" command structure of the TNI, and the vast network of intelligence, combat, and political capacity that it entails. A proposal to dismantle the territorial system, put forward by Maj. Gen. Agus Wirahadikusumah in late 1999, was met with disapproval and seems unlikely to be revived in the near future.[85] With the territorial structure untouched, even middle- and lower-ranking TNI officers retain most of their prereform power, and the military as an institution retains its capacity to intervene—lawfully or otherwise—in all aspects of social, economic, and political life. As Crouch wrote in 1998, "Even if the president were a civilian and the military withdrew from legislatures and bureaucracy, the military will continue to have the capacity to wield enormous political influence as long as the territorial structure remains intact."[86]

Beyond these ideological and institutional foundations, TNI power continues, as in the past, to be conditioned by the international context. Recent changes in that context appear likely to enhance military power and to undermine the incentives to reform. Although the international community remains committed in principle to civilian rule, in early 2000 key governments began to lift sanctions imposed in response to the violence in East Timor. In January, for example, the European Union (EU) ended the embargo on arms sales and military ties with Indonesia it had imposed in September 1999. The U.S. government followed suit in February by quietly resuming educational International Military Education and Training (IMET) programs for Indonesian officers; and in May the U.S. State Department announced that full military-to-military ties had been restored.[87] Both the EU and the U.S. government argued that the lifting of sanctions was done in recognition of the Indonesian government's proven commitment to reform. The danger was, however, that in lifting the sanctions before the reforms had taken root—and before human rights investigations of TNI officers had actually produced tangible results—the international community had removed one of the most important mechanisms for ensuring continued TNI compliance with the reform agenda.

CASE STUDY: EAST TIMOR AFTER THE NEW ORDER

The combination of a confident and fluid civil society and a defensive but still powerful military, and its implications for civil-military relations in Indonesia, are highlighted by the momentous political developments in East Timor since the fall of Suharto.[88]

In a dramatic break with 24 years of New Order and military policy, President Habibie proposed in late January 1999 that the people of East Timor should be given a chance to express their views on the political future of the territory. Specifically, he suggested that East Timorese should be asked whether they accepted or rejected a plan, drawn up under UN auspices in mid-1998, to grant East Timor "special autonomy" within Indonesia. This about-face shocked many Indonesians, in particular the TNI, for which the retention of East Timor and the preservation of national unity at all costs were fundamental articles of faith.

Habibie's proposal led swiftly to an accord between Indonesia, Portugal, and the UN—known as the May 5 Agreements—under which East Timorese would be asked to accept or reject the offer of a special autonomy package. The rejection of special autonomy, the agreements made clear, would set East Timor on the path toward independence. In short, notwithstanding Habibie's perceived weakness vis-à-vis the TNI, he had fundamentally altered a centerpiece of Indonesian government and TNI policy and had opened an unprecedented opportunity for resolution of the East Timor issue. Both his detractors and his supporters suggested that Habibie's proposal was a bid to win the sympathy of the international community, the support of which Indonesia badly needed if it was to rebound from financial crisis.[89] Habibie's initiative was not simply a response to international pressures, however, but was arguably driven equally by his desire to gain legitimacy as a reformer with a domestic constituency. Facing demands for his resignation on the grounds that he was nothing more than a Suharto crony, his dramatic initiative on East Timor could be understood as a bold, though ultimately unsuccessful, political gambit to gain popular legitimacy.

The TNI's Double Game

More puzzling than Habibie's decision to buck 24 years of New Order and military policy on East Timor was the TNI leadership's acquiescence. If ever there were an issue on which one might have expected TNI opposition, perhaps even direct military intervention, this was it. Yet the TNI commander, General Wiranto, assiduously avoided any open challenge to Habibie, citing his constitutional responsibility to support the president. Although serious doubts must be raised about the sincerity of Wiranto's support for the new policy (or for Habibie personally), his reluctance to challenge the president on the issue did provide just enough breathing room for the policy to fly and become the basis for a binding international agreement.

Wiranto's official support for the policy did not mean that all TNI opposition to the policy evaporated, of course, or that he gave it his wholehearted support. On the contrary, by the time the government had agreed to a UN-sponsored popular consultation on the question in early May, military authorities in East Timor had already embarked on a wholesale effort to thwart it. In doing so, they had turned to the trusted repertoire of strategies and practices developed during the New Order and described earlier, including the mobilization of armed paramilitary gangs and the deliberate use of terror against the civilian population. Indeed, as early as January 1999 there were credible reports that militias had killed several supporters of independence, and their acts of terror had forced thousands to flee their homes. After May, when UN personnel began to deploy in East Timor, eyewitness reports and other evidence of such activities continued to mount. By July, some 50,000 people had been forced to flee their homes, dozens had been killed, and the UN headquarters in Dili was consistently reporting that militia terror was the central impediment to the conduct of a free and fair vote.[90]

The extent of TNI complicity in the violence became even clearer after the result of the vote—an overwhelming victory for the independence option—was announced on September 4.[91] Over the next few days, TNI soldiers openly joined militia gangs in a coordinated campaign of violence and destruction that even for East Timor was unprecedented. Facing strong international criticism and the threat of UN military intervention, on September 7 President Habibie declared martial law in the territory. An old East Timor hand, Maj. Gen. Kiki Syahnakri, was appointed martial law commander, and several battalions of elite Kostrad troops were deployed ostensibly to restore order.[92] Far from improving, however, the security situation worsened further in the following days. Dili and other towns, and most villages, were burned to the ground. Warehouses, shops, and homes were looted, their contents loaded onto TNI trucks or ships and taken to West Timor. Real or alleged supporters of independence, including religious leaders, were threatened and others were killed. By the middle of September, an estimated 500,000 people—more than half of East Timor's population—had been forced to flee their homes, and several hundred, at least, had been killed. The destruction was brought to an end with the deployment of a multinational force in late September, and the subsequent withdrawal of TNI forces and their militia allies. Yet even then, the TNI continued its efforts at disruption—allowing, perhaps encouraging, militia men to intimidate the tens of thousands of East Timorese who had been forced to flee to refugee camps in West Timor. In early 2000, moreover, there were credible reports that TNI troops had actually taken part in a series of cross-border attacks against UN peacekeeping soldiers.

In meetings with UN officials and diplomats through 1999, Wiranto steadfastly denied that the TNI was behind the militias or the violence. A series of orders issued by the military commander for East Timor between April and August 1999 likewise suggested an official TNI policy of cooperation with the UN. But Wiranto's denials and the official paper trail were flatly contradicted by the eyewitness accounts of UN officials, by film footage and other documentary evidence, and even by the statements of local military officials and militia leaders themselves.[93] The real question was not whether there was TNI support for the militias—unquestionably there was—but how far up the chain of command that support ran. On this question, an internal UN report prepared in November 1999—based on extensive first-hand accounts and documentation—concluded as follows:

> Evidence gathered by United Nations Mission in East Timor (UNAMET) analysts since May 1999 demonstrates unequivocally that military (TNI) and police (Polri) officers from the village to the district level in East Timor were directly involved in planning and committing acts constituting grave violations of human rights. It also strongly suggests that TNI and Polri officers at the provincial level and above were involved in planning such acts. Senior TNI officers and civilian officials were aware of the pattern of systematic human rights abuse but failed to take adequate measures to stop it.[94]

Very similar conclusions were reached by a UN Commission of Inquiry and by the official Indonesian human rights body, whose findings were released at the end of January 2000.[95]

There was broad consensus among analysts, for example, that one of the key organizers of the militia was Maj. Gen. Zacky Anwar Makarim, who had been sent to East Timor in May 1999 as the TNI's point man for the popular consultation. A career intelligence officer, Zacky had been involved in establishing militia gangs in Aceh during the counterinsurgency campaign of the early 1990s. In January 2000 Zacky admitted that TNI soldiers had committed murder and arson. He denied, however, that these acts had been planned, claiming disingenuously that they were part of Indonesia's "amok culture."[96] Also thought to be involved were the regional military commander for Region IX (containing East Timor), Maj. Gen. Adam Damiri, the subregional commander for East Timor, Lt. Col. Tono Suratman, several of the thirteen district military commanders in East Timor, and a considerable number of lower-ranking officers and retired soldiers.

As of early 2000 there was no concrete evidence directly linking General Wiranto or any other member of the military high command to the militia violence. But the involvement of so many TNI officers in these activities makes it a virtual certainty that General Wiranto and others knew precisely what was going on. If that was indeed the case, the question may fairly be asked: why did Wiranto permit the violence to continue? The most reasonable explanation is that Wiranto, like most TNI officers and men, wished to ensure that East Timor did not become independent but did not want to express his open opposition to government policy. His approach allowed him to appear statesmanlike while, in Jakarta, Habibie could be blamed for a policy that led to chaos and violence and, ultimately, to the "disintegration" of the country.

Civil Society Prevails

The remarkable part of this story is that despite the coordinated and costly effort to derail the popular consultation process, the TNI and its militia allies ultimately failed. The consultation went ahead more or less as planned, achieving something that for more than two decades had been considered impossible: a legitimate act of self-determination for the people of East Timor. Even the TNI-sponsored rampage after the balloting failed to stop the process from running its course. And notwithstanding a good deal of nationalist bluster, when the MPR finally met in October 1999, all the major parties and factions—including the armed forces faction—voted to accept the result of the popular consultation, thereby ending Indonesia's claim to East Timor.[97] The final touch came in February 2000 when President Wahid visited East Timor and offered his apologies for past abuses.

Although it may appear obvious, it is worth stressing that this outcome was largely made possible by the people of East Timor, who showed enormous courage and resolve in the face of militia and TNI violence. It also depended on the emergence of a new set of international norms, or more precisely, on a new willingness on the part of the international community to intervene in the domestic affairs of sovereign states in the interest of human rights and good governance. For the first time in more than three decades and after 24 years of virtual silence on East Timor, the international community openly confronted the government of Indonesia on these issues by threatening economic and military sanctions and even direct military intervention.

In the face of this unparalleled diplomatic and financial pressure, on September 12 the government of Indonesia agreed to accept a multinational force (MNF)—a move that only days before had been considered out of the question by the Indonesian government and most observers. Shortly thereafter, the UN Security Council passed a resolution lending its support to a swift deployment of the MNF. That resolution, moreover, invoked Chapter 7 of the UN Charter and gave the MNF authority to use "all necessary means" to restore security, facilitate humanitarian assistance, and permit UNAMET to carry out its mandate. Notwithstanding earlier suggestions that a force would take months to assemble and deploy, the MNF was on the ground within a week.

Meanwhile, within days of the MNF deployment, UN agencies and private NGOs had set in motion a major humanitarian relief effort. Simultaneously, UN staff in Darwin were meeting East Timorese leaders, including Xanana Gusmao, and plans were being drafted there and in New York for an accelerated transfer from Indonesian to UN authority. At the same time, a rare special session of the UN Human Rights Commission was convened and a resolution passed calling for the formation of an international commission of inquiry to investigate possible crimes against humanity and breaches of international humanitarian law in East Timor.[98] Now there was a chance that East Timor might have an international criminal tribunal, like those established for Rwanda and Yugoslavia, and that men such as Maj. Gen. Zacky Anwar

Makarim and General Wiranto might one day be brought to account. Although the prospects for an international tribunal had seriously faded by early 2000, the threat of international scrutiny had been enough to stimulate the Indonesian government to launch its own inquiry under the auspices of the official human rights commission.[99] It had also been sufficient to compel TNI officers to comply with the demands of the domestic inquiry.[100]

Implications and Conclusions

The case of East Timor serves to highlight many of the general claims made here about civil-military relations in the post–New Order period and provides some clues about their future trajectory.

The evidence from East Timor confirms, first, that civil-military relations have indeed been set on a new course since the fall of Suharto in May 1998, with the military appearing to bow to civilian authority for the first time in decades. Moreover, it neatly highlights the historical forces that have been critical in bringing about that change: the vitality and courage of civil society in Indonesia and East Timor; the emergence of a new set of international norms that condone intervention where there are serious human rights or humanitarian concerns; and the willingness of Indonesia's civilian presidents to use the considerable power of their office to make decisions that run against the interests of the military. Less evident in the case of East Timor, but certainly important in explaining change generally, has been the presence of influential military reformers within the TNI leadership.

To the extent that these four trends hold in the coming months and years, the prospects for further movement toward civilian supremacy are quite good. There are, however, some weak links in the chain. The most obvious, perhaps, is President Wahid, whose skill and courage in facing down the TNI have been instrumental in restoring civilian rule. If for reasons of health or politics Wahid does not last as president—and particularly if he is replaced by Vice President Megawati Sukarnoputri, who is far less enthusiastic about reforming the military—there is a strong likelihood that ground will be lost. Also worrying were moves by the international community in early 2000 to restore normal relations with the Indonesian military before serious reform had really taken root and before domestic human rights investigations had borne fruit. These moves seemed likely to slow the process of reform by removing the strongest incentive the TNI has ever had for acquiescing in it. Such a trend could serve to undermine the still weak civilian authority at a critical stage in its rebirth.

The evidence from East Timor also points to the potential for a serious backlash against civilian authority by the Indonesian military, and for a reassertion of TNI power. It highlights, in particular, how the post-1998 reforms have provided the military with powerful new motives for political intervention, while leaving essentially intact the real bases of its power. In the case of East Timor, the motives for military intervention in 1999 included a concern about order and territorial integrity rooted in national security doctrine; anger at a perceived impingement by civilians and foreigners on the political and operational autonomy of the TNI; and worry over possible financial and material losses by TNI units and individual officers. The threat of prosecution for human rights–related offences, undertaken in the aftermath of the August 30 vote, compounded military anger and added a powerful new motive for further resistance to civilian dominance.

These are, more or less, the same concerns that have been at the heart of military opposition to the process of reform since May 1998, and they are the concerns that may ultimately drive some element of the TNI to seek a reassertion of military power in the coming years. The possibility that a civilian government, backed by the international community, might bring TNI officers to account for past human rights violations or for corruption will provide an especially strong motivation to resist any genuine move toward civilian rule. So too will moves to dismantle the territorial system, to implement the new agreement on *kekaryaan*, to seriously limit TNI control of elite combat units such as Kostrad and Kopassus, or to remove high-ranking officers resistant to reform. In other words, the initiatives that will be most essential in establishing civilian supremacy will inevitably also provide elements within the armed forces with a powerful motive to strike back.

The events in East Timor also serve as a grim reminder of the considerable institutional power that remains at the disposal of the Indonesian military, regardless of policy changes or sentiments articulated by some officers at the center. It is sobering to think that notwithstanding the dire international consequences that were bound to follow, elements of the TNI leadership were prepared to use this power to thwart government policy. Moreover, the manner in which they sought to do so—a perfect example of the culture of violence in motion—demonstrates the dangerous institutional inertia that, outside of a handful of reformist officers, seems to characterize Indonesia's military. As an Achenese human rights activist noted in late 1999, "It will take a long time to change their culture of violence. They are used to thinking they are the only segment of society that is capable of saving the nation. But in fact, the opposite is happening; they are destroying it."[101]

In seeking to undermine central government policy in East Timor, TNI officers made use of a powerful institutional infrastructure that remains essentially untouched by the post-1998 reforms. That infrastructure includes the time-honored territorial system that permits a permanent military presence to be maintained in every village; a pervasive military intelligence apparatus that allows for the surveillance and interdiction of proindependence political activity; and autonomous control of thousands of Kostrad and Kopassus soldiers trained in counterinsurgency warfare. In addition to these legal and institutional foundations, in East Timor the TNI made ample use of the semilegal and illegal strategies and practices developed during the New Order, including the mobilization of armed paramilitary gangs and the deliberate use of terror against civilian populations. All of these institutions and methods remain available for use by elements of the TNI should they wish to intervene in politics at some future date.

In short, although the balance of power appeared to shift toward the civilian side after May 1998, the evidence from East Timor and elsewhere suggested that, outside a small handful of reformers in Jakarta, military authorities continue to behave according to old patterns. Given the TNI's considerable ideological and institutional power, and given the deep historical roots of its culture of violence, the persistence of these old patterns is scarcely surprising. At the same time, the developments in East Timor offer grounds for hope that even the deeply embedded political power of the Indonesian military might still be overcome. For despite their ample resources and their considerable repertoire of dirty tricks, the TNI and its militia allies ultimately failed in their efforts to derail the popular consultation in East Timor. And they failed, it would seem, because of a combination of international and domestic political pressures that in their seriousness were unknown in Indonesia's recent history.

PART V

Ethnic and Dominant Party Civilian Control

CHAPTER 10

Malaysia: A Congruence of Interests

K. S. Nathan and Geetha Govindasamy

CIVIL MILITARY RELATIONS IN MALAYSIA have progressed in a fairly predictable manner from the inception of independence in 1957 until the present time. The role of the armed forces and police in Malaysian society has been sufficiently constitutionalized and politically institutionalized to produce a fair measure of stability, predictability, and certainty.

This study explicates the relationship between a predominantly Malay-led government and an overwhelmingly Malay-dominated armed forces. It is not our purpose to focus too much on historical factors. Rather, our aim is to investigate the development of civil-military relations from colonial rule to the present, with emphasis on how the function of the armed forces has changed from being a subservice-oriented regime under the British to an independent entity by the early 1970s, and under the purview and control of an independent civilian government. Indeed, the Malaysian Armed Forces's character, role, and function have been constitutionalized from the beginning. Our major hypothesis is this: For so long as Malay ethnic security is guaranteed as well as consolidated by the political dominance of the Malays vis-à-vis other ethnic groups, civil-military relations will be stable and characterized by the principle of civilian supremacy. However, if the Malays—both from the ruling United Malays National Organization (UMNO) party and arguably even from the opposition Islamic party—perceive an erosion of their political and economic power in multiethnic Malaysia, the prospect of the military intrusion or intervention in support of maintaining Malay supremacy cannot be ruled out. The Malays have thus far operated as a coherent block where ethnicity is concerned but are divided into splinter groups in pursuing their political, economic, and religious interests. However, the evidence to date still supports the validity of the following fundamental proposition: Malay dominance that is threatened by other groups is more of a concern for the regime than threats arising from intra-Malay power struggles.

The security forces in the Malaysian context include both the regular forces—collectively called the Malaysian Armed Forces (MAF), incorporating the army, navy, and air force—and the Royal Malaysian Police and paramilitary forces such as the Police Field Force, People's Volunteer Corps, and Civil Defense Corps. We substantiate our hypothesis through a discussion of the following:

- The historical evolution of the MAF
- The special role of the police and paramilitary forces

- The organization of the MAF
- Civilian subordination of the MAF (the political economy of the military-civilian relationship)
- The armed forces and nation building

In terms of a theoretical perspective, the concordance theory put forward by Rebecca Schiff (1995) regarding the relationship, mutuality, and interdependence between the military, political elites, and the citizenry provides a useful analytical perspective to view the military-civilian relationship in the Malaysian context.[1] We concur that an integrationist approach is the best way to describe the state of civil-military relations in Malaysia. The four broad categories used in concordance theory to support the integrationist approach, namely, composition of the officer corps, political decision-making process, recruitment method, and military style, are broadly applicable to the Malaysian context and support Schiff's hypothesis that if the military, the political elites, and the citizenry agree on these four indicators, domestic military intervention is less likely to occur. Nevertheless, it must also be emphasized that history, ethnicity, and political economy do much to explain the status of military-civilian relations in Malaysia. Historically, the armed forces originated from the requests of Malay nobility because the British clearly did not have any intention of establishing a Malayan armed forces. The role of ethnicity is evident given that from the beginning the British used the armed forces to pacify and bolster Malay communal pride in the face of an unbalanced economy that clearly favored the immigrant communities. This resulted in shaping the armed forces along the lines of ethnicity so that it became a predominantly Malay establishment that indirectly upholds and promotes the larger interests of Malays as an ethnic group. In terms of political economy, the armed forces have always played a supportive role in the country's political affairs. The communist threat from the 1950s and the withdrawal of the Commonwealth troops shaped the civil-military relations after independence; national security was viewed in the context of development and strengthening nation-building against communist subversion. Through the medium of Keselamatan dan Pembangunan, which is a security and development program, the armed forces were utilized by the government in implementing economic policies and projects to strengthen national security and promote nation-building.

We also concur on a fundamental proposition of concordance theory: "The political decision-making process does not imply a particular form of government—democratic, authoritarian, or any other. Rather it refers to the specific channels that determine the needs and allocations of the military" (Schiff 1995: 7–8). Later we offer some conclusions to explain likely trends in military-civilian relations, including scenarios that might deter as well as encourage military intervention in politics in the twenty-first century.

HISTORICAL EVOLUTION OF THE MAF

Malaysia's 83-year tutelage under British colonial rule has undeniably served as a significant though not crucial factor in structuring the use of military power for civilian purposes. The instrumental role of the armed forces, as evolved from British tradition, was entrenched through policies, procedures, and institutions under colonial rule. The evolving professionalism of the colonial armed forces was virtually adopted by native political elites upon the transfer of sovereignty in the period after World War II.

The earliest form of a civil-military relationship that can be traced in the MAF was that between the colonial administrators and the various military units formed by the British. Before 1933 there was no cohesive local armed unit comparable to the colonial army. The MAF emerged as a result of demands from Malay royals—Sultan Alang Iskandar of Perak, Tuanku Muhammad of Negeri Sembilan, Raja Chulan (Raja Di Hilir Perak), and Datuk Abdullah Haji Dahan (Undang Luak of Jelebu)—who pressured the British to establish an indigenous armed force along the lines of a trained and equipped colonial army.[2]

Thus a Malay Army Experimental Squad comprising 25 men was established under the Malay Regimental Bill on March 1, 1933, and later became known as the Experimental Company in 1934. As the number of soldiers grew, the company was later redesignated as the Malay Regiment. In the 1920s and 1930s, Malaya already consisted of a thriving multiracial population. Because the regiment was exclusively a Malay unit, it bolstered Malay communal pride in an environment of economic imbalance between the Malays and the Chinese and Indian immigrants in Malaya. The creation of the Malay Regiment also reflected British acceptance of the special indigenous status of the Malays (Enloe 1977: 18).[3] Malay traditions and customs were incorporated into the regiment's overall appearance. Their uniforms, for example, reflected the Malay dress, which included the *songkok* and *samping*. Moreover their motto was "Taat Setia" ("loyalty"), which was inscribed in the Arabic script of Jawi (*Malaysia Yearbook* 1998: 503).

At this juncture, the Malay Regiment was subservient toward its colonial master. The unit's orientation to duty was purely British in nature, and political passivity ruled the day. Because civilian supremacy is predicated upon the principle that armed units are responsible for protecting the country and not governing it, the regiment's main political role was to help the colonial authorities maintain internal security.[4] In their first real task, the First and Second battalions of the regiment, which were formed in 1938 and 1941 respectively, fought alongside the Commonwealth forces to defend Malaya and Singapore against the invading Japanese army.

In the immediate aftermath of the Japanese defeat in the mid-1940s, Malaya's national security concerns focused on the threat posed by the Communist Party of Malaya (CPM). In response to this, the British began to expand the local military units. By 1948, the Third Battalion of the Malay Regiment was already in place.[5] Together with the other Commonwealth forces, the local military personnel played a larger role compared to that of the pre–World War II era in conducting operations against these insurgents. During the period of emergency (1948–1960), the army acted as a second line of defense assisting the police and the Commonwealth forces.

Recognizing the need for multiracial military units to reflect the plurality of Malayan society in the 1950s, as well as to integrate non-Malays to combat the predominantly Chinese communists (Enloe 1977: 18), the British administration, with the acceptance of the Malay rulers, established racially mixed units. The Federation Regiment and the Federation Armored Car Squadron, established in 1952, were subsequently merged to form the Federation Reconnaissance Corps on January 1, 1960. The armed forces came under the purview of the federal government once Malaya achieved its independence from the British in 1957. The presence of Commonwealth forces in Malaya until the early 1970s meant that less attention was given to the development of the local armed forces. Apart from the army, the Royal Malaysian Navy was set up on April 27, 1934, under the name of the Straits Settlement Royal Navy Volunteer Reserves, also headed by British officers. Similar to the Malay Regiment, an exclusive Royal Malay Navy Section was established in 1939. The air force was founded much later after Malaya gained its independence in 1957, marking its birth as the Royal Air Force Station, Kuala Lumpur, on June 2, 1958.

In the years after independence, the presence of Commonwealth troops enabled the government led by Tunku Abdul Rahman, Malaysia's first premier until 1970, to prioritize the use of state resources for socioeconomic development. This governmental philosophy attached less importance to the military's professional role in national security: development itself was viewed as security. The government did not see the importance of expanding the local national forces so long as it had confidence in the availability of Commonwealth forces to bolster internal and external security. In 1967, however, the British government announced its intention of withdrawing its military forces east of the Suez Canal. In line with this new policy, the Anglo-Malayan Defense Agreement, signed on October 12, 1957, was replaced by the Five Power Defense Arrangements in 1971 linking Malaysia and Singapore with Britain, Australia, and New Zealand. The withdrawal of British forces from Malaysia, however, left a gap in the country's physical defenses. Suddenly the MAF was catapulted to a position of importance and found itself responsible for the security of nation and state.

In the period of emergency (1948–1960) and until the end of Indonesian confrontation in the mid-1960s, the MAF was for the most part still preoccupied with counterinsurgency operations against the communists and infiltrating Indonesian troops.[6] With the loss of external defense support, the government rigorously sought to emphasize the changing role of the military from an anti-insurgency armed force to a dedicated force capable of fighting a conventional war. Indeed, the fall of Saigon in 1975, the Vietnamese invasion of Cambodia in 1978, and the closure of American bases in Thailand accelerated efforts to develop a military that was more self-reliant and capable of fighting a conventional war against external threats.

Numerous programs based on contemporary training doctrines were designed with a view to upgrading the MAF and improving local training facilities. In an effort to expand the forces, the government created a special program of personnel and firepower, Perkembangan Istimewa Angkatan Tentera (PERISTA), in 1978. By the time the program ended in 1983, a successful homegrown conventional force was in place. The army had expanded from a strength of 52,500 men in 1978 to 80,000 men in 1983 (Yusof 1994: 19). As of 1998 the strength of the MAF was 111,500, comprising about 85,000 troops in the army, 14,000 in the navy, and 12,500 in the air force. Paramilitary forces consisted of the Police Field Force with a strength of 18,500 and the People's Volunteer Corps with a strength of 240,000, of which 15,500 were armed (*Malaysia Yearbook* 1998: 226–27). The government also took steps to increase defense outlays on procurement. Under the PERISTA program, the forces became technologically oriented in that sophisticated modern weaponry—armor, artillery, intelligence, and communications capable of meeting conventional threats—was acquired. The purchases included 450 new armored personnel carriers, Scorpion light tanks and Sibmas armored fighting vehicles, 35 Skyhawk fighter-bombers, and fast attack aircraft.[7] Simultaneously, conventional warfare exercises involving the army, air force, and navy were held regularly to prepare the armed forces to meet any eventuality. In short, the MAF became more modernized in terms of equipment and role, thereby underscoring the link between its earlier evolution as an instrument of British colonial policy and its postindependence development as a professional military force designed to address the changing internal and external security concerns of a young nation-state in Southeast Asia. In this regard, the September 1988 Anglo-Malaysian Memorandum of Understanding (MoU) for Malaysian purchases of sophisticated military hardware from Britain effectively "kick-started" the next phase of military modernization of the MAF for the post–cold war era.

THE SPECIAL ROLE OF THE POLICE
AND PARAMILITARY FORCES

Apart from the MAF, the country's security forces encompass the Royal Malaysian Police and paramilitary forces such as the People's Volunteer Corps and Civil Defense Corps. Although the police and these paramilitary forces fall under the purview of the Ministry of Home Affairs, the tradition of civilian supremacy ensures that both the paramilitary forces and the MAF are seen as complementing each other in the management of security. The relationship between the MAF and the police reflects an alliance for the avowed purpose of contributing stability to the country and the political leadership. The police are seen by the government as the executive arm of the civilian authorities in maintaining public order (Aslie 1990: 52). Although the armed forces play a national role in executing security policies and defense arrangements, the police focus primarily on matters relating to internal security, communist terrorists, and public order.

The Malayan emergency was a critical factor in shaping the role, structure, development, and special position of the police in the government's approach to national security. In that period, the police played a more prominent role than the armed forces in combating insurgents and subversive activities. Indeed, the government views the police force as a vital element that enhances its survival and lends legitimacy via its role in maintaining public order. Consequently, the portfolio of minister of home affairs is usually held directly by the prime minister himself or the deputy prime minister. The current minister of home affairs is the deputy prime minister, Datuk Abdullah Badawi. When the present prime minister, Dr. Mahathir Mohamad, held this portfolio in the 1980s, he demonstrated its value to an incumbent facing rivals intent on taking over the leadership of the country. Indeed, the fate of the breakaway UMNO faction led by Tengku Razaleigh Hamzah in 1987 was partially if not totally sealed by the incumbent prime minister's ability (as home minister) to legally thwart the registration process of political parties that threaten UMNO's political dominance. In such circumstances marked by political turmoil and uncertainty, the police clearly enjoy preeminence in domestic security, and their influence is projected via the security apparatus all the way down to the village level.

Nevertheless, the instrumental use of the police by civilian authorities for partisan political gain could jeopardize their role as custodians of internal peace and public order, especially when the public perceives the police to be indulging in partisan politics in contrast to their professional role as keepers of the peace. Ever since the arrest, detention, and alleged brutalization of the former deputy prime minister, Anwar Ibrahim, in September 1998 by Inspector General of Police Rahim Noor, public confidence in the police has plummeted. The Anwar case has highlighted as well the unsavory tactics used by the police, especially the Special Branch, in the course of obtaining information from detainees. Not only has the act of the highest-ranking police officer badly tainted the image of the force,[8] but also the use of draconian laws such as the Internal Security Act,[9] Sedition Act, and Official Secrets Act by the police in the name of national security has raised questions about freedom of action and speech from non-government organizations and others. In general, then, civilian-police relations have suffered from the high-handed behavior of the police in the events that followed the incarceration of Anwar Ibrahim, although it is arguable that some measure of justice was apparently done following Rahim's resignation and subsequent conviction for the above offense.

From the citizenry itself, voluntary forces such as the People's Volunteer Corps and the Civil Defense Corps act as the third line of defense in the local security network. The two units are composed of trained civilians who can be quickly mobilized to fight side by side with regular units of the police and armed forces in times of need. The civilian authorities view this separation as well as integration of the armed forces, the police, and the volunteer corps as a comprehensive defense strategy that creates a conducive environment for the government's socioeconomic projects. In view of the multifunctional role of the Malaysian Armed Forces—as providers of security and facilitators of socioeconomic development—the MAF's organizational structure underscores its uniquely Malaysian disposition in shifting political, cultural, and strategic contexts.

ORGANIZATION OF THE MAF

When Malaya gained its independence in 1957, most of its top command posts were still held by British officers. The Malayanization process in the 1960s gradually changed the composition of the officer corps, however, as the British component was phased out. In 1964, for the first time, the MAF was led by a Malaysian as chief of armed forces (Crouch 1991: 122). By the time the British withdrew in the early 1970s, the MAF was developing its own mission, organization, and strategy befitting a newborn postcolonial nation. Even with the change of leadership, the MAF has continued the British legacy of maintaining its credentials as a cohesive unit with its own corporate interests by its traditional subordination to the civil authority. For the principle of civilian supremacy asserts that "in a stable democracy, patterns of civil-military relations are established by public law or constitutional tradition, assured control of the military by the civilian government, and are observed by the government and accepted by the armed forces as part of the military ethic" (Zagorski 1988: 407). It is evident that the MAF as a corporate entity is completely loyal to the government of the day and is subordinate to that civil power because of the rule of law, tradition, and its own sense of military professionalism. Most importantly, the model of civil-military relations between the MAF and the civilian authorities has been predetermined by the federal constitution of 1957. The constitution is very clear about the distribution of power between the armed forces and the civilian leadership: Article 132 states that the armed forces are part and parcel of the public service, that is, under civil power.

The MAF consists of the army, the Royal Malaysian Navy (RMN), and the Royal Malaysian Air Force (RMAF). The Ministry of Defense is the main organization responsible for drafting national defense policies, including protection of the nation's strategic military and security interests. The military is ordinarily excluded from making policy by the government based on the principle of civilian supremacy generally adopted by democratic political systems, in other words, the civilians make policy and the armed forces implement it. However, in times of national emergency and crisis such as the May 13, 1969, race riots, the MAF's role in the National Operations Council (1969–1971) could not have been insignificant, even if it was headed by a civilian (Tun Abdul Razak, who later took over as prime minister in September 1970). Here, Bland's theory of shared responsibility regarding civil-military relations is particularly worth noting and tends to complement Schiff's theory of concordance. The theory of shared responsibility rests on two assumptions: (1) the term "civil control" means that the sole legitimate source for the direction and actions of the military is derived from civilians outside the military/defense establishment, and (2) civil control is a dynamic process susceptible to changing ideas, values, circumstances, issues, and personalities and to the stresses of crises and war (Bland 1999: 10). Thus, in the Malaysian context, it can be argued that whereas the MAF's main function is to implement (rather than formulate) national defense and security policies and to be generally responsible for the country's internal and external defense, extraordinary circumstances could upgrade civil-military relations in favor of the military in terms of its role in providing more significant inputs into policymaking for the maintenance of national security. The MAF's three-pronged role may be stated as follows:

- *Primary role.* To defend the nation's sovereignty, territorial integrity, and strategic interests against external threats
- *Secondary role.* To assist civil authorities in combating internal threats, in restoration and maintenance of public order, in flood relief activities and national disasters, and in national development
- *Supporting role.* To complement the nation's foreign policy by participating in UN peacekeeping operations[10]

The basic structure of the Ministry of Defense incorporates both civilian and military divisions. To foster cooperation and understanding, as well as to underscore the distinct functions of the RMN, RMAF, army, and civilians, the headquarters of all three services and the head office of the civilian component are located in the Ministry of Defense complex (Yusof 1994: 43). Civil control of the civilian elites in the military establishment is ensured by the very fact that the secretary-general and deputy secretary-general of defense and various services are civilians. The military component is controlled by the chief of defense forces, whereas the civilian division is headed by the secretary-general, who is the highest-ranking civil servant in the Ministry of Defense. It is generally understood that the secretary-general is more powerful than the chief of defense forces in managing the Ministry of Defense (Figure 10.1).[11]

The defense minister reports directly to the prime minister and the cabinet. He is assisted by the secretary-general and chief of defense forces. All policy decisions relating to national security and defense are determined by the prime minister and the cabinet. These issues are discussed in the National Security Council, chaired by the prime minister. Policies authorized by the National Security Council are then carried out by the MAF under the command of the minister of defense himself.

The defense minister provides the ministry's political leadership. He also acts as chairman of the Armed Forces Council. Although the Armed Forces Council is in charge of command, discipline, and administrative matters relating to the forces, it does not control their operational use. According to Article 137 of the constitution, the Armed Forces Council is the highest

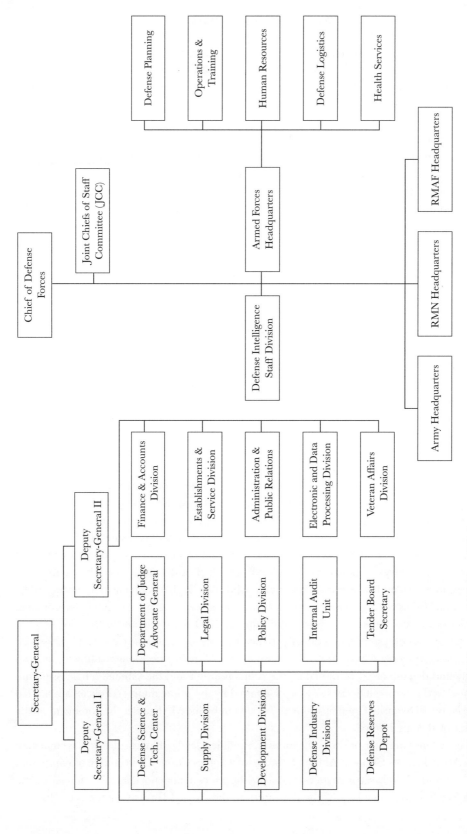

FIGURE 10.1. Organizational Structure of Ministry of Defense.
Source: Yusof 1994, p. 42.

authority responsible for service matters and is under the purview of the king.[12] Article 41 of the constitution states that the Yang Di Pertuan Agong, who is a constitutional monarch, is supreme commander of the armed forces. By law the king is the field marshal of the army, admiral of the fleet of the RMN, and air marshal of the RMAF. Nevertheless His Majesty is to act only on the advice of the cabinet. The king is allowed to sign commissions appointing officers of the service but is not empowered to direct the troops.

If the king is the supreme commander of the forces, then the chief of defense forces is the head of all three services in the MAF. His is a political appointment approved by the prime minister himself (Ahmad 1981: 197). Operating through the Joint Chiefs of Staff Committee, which coordinates and controls military administration, military planning, and operational matters (Yusof 1994: 41), the chief of defense forces provides military leadership and makes decisions for the armed forces in consultation with all three service chiefs. The chief of staff reports directly to the chief of defense forces on all operational and administrative aspects of all three services (Yusof 1994: 43).

The secretary-general heads the civilian organization of the Ministry of Defense. Appointed by the government to provide nonmilitary administrative leadership to the ministry (Yusof 1994: 41), this person advises the minister on nonoperational matters such as finance, policy, defense relations, infrastructure development, defense science, defense industry, and human resource development. At present the secretary-general is responsible for the various divisions such as Defense Science and Technology, Development, Supply, Defense Industry, Defense Reserves Depot, Finance, Establishments and Service, Adminstration and Public Relations, Information Technology, Judge Advocate, Legal, Policy, General Investigation, and Internal Audit. The secretary-general is assisted by two deputies who are in charge of Development and Operations, respectively. Figure 10.1 indicates that Deputy I is in charge of development of the armed forces with respect to defense science, supply, industry, and so forth, whereas Deputy II is in charge of operations, finance, service matters, and so forth. Such an elaborate structure of command and control, undergirded by constitutional authority vested in civilian hands, provides a strong deterrent to military seizure of political power. Undeniably the civilian positions occupied by the minister of defense and secretary-general reduce the space for maneuvering by disgruntled or ambitious military officers keen on acquiring more decision-making power for the MAF. The military elites know that the final say lies with the government of the day.

Although the armed forces have their own sense of corporate leadership and interests, they are nevertheless subjected to the control of the civil leadership. Government policy, as noted, is set by the civilian component of the Ministry of Defense. The military then is empowered to make decisions with regard to how these policies should be implemented. In many respects this is what a civil servant is trained do—to implement policies of the government. Therefore the Malaysian soldier functions like any other member of the civil service. He accepts his directives from the government. The only difference is that he is trained for a particular military role and uses his military expertise in executing the civilian policies.

Civilian Subordination of the MAF

The concept of loyalty to country and king has resulted in a deep-seated belief in subordination of the armed forces to the civilian administration, especially in a country that has acquired a multiracial character with Malay sovereignty as its core principle. Accordingly the military's code of honor emphasizes political neutrality. In theory, the MAF does not participate directly in any kind of political decision making. In reality, however, the military's role in a civilian-controlled decision process is substantial because civilians have no alternative but to rely on the military's expertise on key issues of national security. In the aftermath of the cold war, for instance, signaling the end of ideological threats and the cessation of communist armed struggle in Malaysia, threats to the nation's maritime security have gained in salience and put increasing pressure on the government to upgrade the country's maritime capabilities. According to the current chief of defense forces, Gen. Mohd. Zahidi Zainuddin, the nation's economic survival and its interests in the Exclusive Economic Zone have been given special attention, as have "aspects that contribute to enhancing the quality of life of our soldiers, sailors and airmen."[13] Additionally, the emergence of territorial and resource claims in the South China Sea in the 1990s has invariably strengthened the military's influence on the decision-making process.

In assessing threats and enemies, there is general agreement that in a civilian-controlled military, it is the role of the armed forces to identify the threat posed by a particular enemy and the role of civilians to judge the level of risk and decide whether to respond to it (Feaver 1996: 154). To illustrate the power of civilian control over the military, the former army chief Gen. Zain Hashim once remarked that the MAF's primary concern is to carry out the missions issued by the civilian administration. As far as he was concerned, "it is not even the duty of the armed forces to identify who the external foe is."[14] This statement reflects the military's commitment to noninterference in the political sphere. Clearly the civilian leadership of the Ministry of Defense decides the extent of the military's participation in its given duties. This does not mean, however, that the armed forces have no input whatsoever in matters concerning national security. The prime minister has the authority to declare war, for example, but the prosecution of the war itself is a matter for the armed forces to decide.

It is undeniable that the nation's political stability and economic prosperity depend on the existence of political power wielded by a strong and stable government. The political power is augmented by the military's loyalty to the government of the day and its professed neutrality in politics. The Malaysian government's political legitimacy, which is normally endorsed in periodic general elections, is clearly augmented by the constitutional powers exercised by the police and the military in the name of public order and national security. Through its involvement in nation-building, the MAF more or less shares the same values and aspirations of the civilian elites. Patterned along the lines of the British notion of political neutrality, the MAF will clearly carry out policies that are formulated by the civilian authority for the good of the country. Therefore the MAF has invariably become an instrument of the government to promote its policies. From this perspective, the military is an institution that works hand in hand with the rest of the civil service to promote the development policies of the civilian government.

The MAF has no political or social influence of its own because it does not have a political agenda. Nor does it represent itself as an entity with defined political interests. The armed forces have not portrayed themselves as an independent constituency or an interest group; consequently, their interests are not debated separately within the cabinet or in parliament. Hence the MAF is not closely involved with political institutions even if it might be inclined to display a certain level of political consciousness or indicate its political preferences on issues affecting national welfare. Members of the security elite do not intervene in political activities and are always supportive of the ruling government. Prominent army elites such as the former army chief Gen. Hashim Mohd. Ali firmly believe that the armed forces should be independent of the ruling authorities.[15] Defined as part of the civil service in the constitution, the MAF is not allowed to choose who it wants to support. Thus the armed forces are regarded by the government of the day as a potential weapon to be used against the enemies of the nation's political leadership.

The British and later the federal government always viewed the main internal threat to be the Communist Party of Malaya (CPM) in the peninsula and the North Kalimantan Communist Party (NKCP) in Sarawak. The escalation of the communist threat brought together civil servants, military, and police in the campaign against the CPM and NKCP, which operated through Pasukan Rakyat Kalimantan Utara (PARAKU) and the Pasukan Gerila Rakyat Sarawak (PGRS). In 1972, Malaysia and Indonesia signed the General Border Committee agreement to campaign against PARAKU and the PGRS at the Malaysian-Indonesian border (Yusof 1994: 17–18). With support from the Indonesians and government agencies, the army was able to prevent the CPM and NKCP from seizing power.

In most civilian-controlled governments, especially in the developing countries, the main worry of the ruling elite is the direct confiscation of power by the armed forces (Feaver 1996: 152–53). The most recent example in Asia was the seizure of power by Pakistan's military chief, Gen. Pervaiz Musharaf, and the subsequent dismissal of the civilian government of Nawaz Sharif on October 12, 1999. There have been several opportunities for the MAF to seize political power during unstable periods in the nation's history. Arguably, two such occasions were the confrontation with the communists in the period immediately after independence, and the race riots of May 13, 1969. With so much firepower at its disposal, the MAF could have felt obliged to take over the country ostensibly to defend Malay sovereignty and preserve public order. Instead it preferred to stay out of politics and follow the instructions of the civilian authority, for such a move, if prolonged, would have raised serious doubts about the MAF's legitimacy as an apolitical institution. One reason for this behavior is the close link that exists between the military elite and civilian leadership.[16] More often than not, the posts of chief of armed forces staff and chief of defense forces are occupied by figures who are linked to the prime minister and would naturally pledge allegiance to him. Evidently the MAF did not try to seize power during the period of emergency, because of the nonpolitical attitude of the chief of armed forces staff Gen. Tunku Osman Jewa. As the nephew of Prime Minister Tunku Abdul Rahman, Gen. Tunku Osman would not have toppled his uncle in a political takeover (Ahmad and Crouch 1985: 119).

Indonesia's confrontation (1963–1965) could have provided the MAF an opportunity to assert its power and influence over the civilian authority, but not necessarily to overthrow it. Once again the armed forces were mobilized to defend the country against Indonesian transborder incursions, infiltrations, and subversion. *Konfrontasi* resulted in a number of clashes with Indonesian forces, but these assaults were effectively countered by the army and police. As professional soldiers, the MAF dutifully backed up the government in its first major crisis with an external power. Thus *Konfrontasi* further underscored the military's well-institutionalized role as a provider of security for a civilian government faced with an external crisis.

Nor did the armed forces try to seize political control during the May 1969 race riots. One plausible explanation relates to the fact that when parliament was dissolved, the military's interest was represented in the National Operations Council that ruled the country.[17] Thus the armed forces had an opportunity to take part in policymaking for almost two years. Furthermore, in the aftermath of the riots, the government forged closer links with high-ranking officers in order to obtain the backing of a predominantly Malay military to reestablish Malay political supremacy (Crouch 1991: 123). Following the riots, top-ranking officers were deliberately given more opportunities to participate in "national policy considerations" (Enloe 1977: 19).

Nevertheless, in reality the MAF has always played a secondary role in the country's political affairs. In the aftermath of the race riots of 1969, the National Operations Council was headed by a civilian, Tun Abdul Razak, Malaysia's second prime minister. Even though the army together with the police played a major role in keeping the peace, its participation in the National Operations Council was marginalized by the role assigned to the chief of defense forces, Gen. Ibrahim Ismail—that of a mere council member. Although it can be argued that as a council member in the National Operations Council, the chief of defense forces could take part in national policy deliberations, he still has to take his final directives from a top-ranking politician. Another example of civilian superiority was evident during the signing of the peace treaty between the government and the CPM in 1989. Although the armed forces were very much involved in eliminating communist insurgents, the Ministry of Defense and senior MAF officials were not present at the signing ceremony. Instead, Wan Sidek Abd. Rahman, secretary-general of the Home Ministry, represented the government in the ceremony. Indeed, a strong case can be made that the civilian leadership had wittingly or unwittingly obscured the military's important role in eliminating the communist threat.

THE ARMED FORCES AND NATION-BUILDING

The lingering episodes of communist subversive activities in the 1970s led to a more pronounced link between security and development. Because communist insurgencies were prevalent mostly in poverty-stricken rural areas, security was perceived in terms of developing these areas to promote economic welfare. To counter these insurgencies and revolutionary activities, the government embarked upon social projects in remote areas affected by communist activities, especially at the Malaysia-Thailand and Malaysia-Indonesia borders. Developing these jungle areas, it was anticipated, would also restrict movements of illegal immigrants and insurgents.

Prime Minster Tun Abdul Razak (1970–1976) believed that the MAF's role was to implement the government's development plan in order to stem the resurgence of the communist threat. Defense and development were to be implemented simultaneously (Yusof 1994: 136). As a result, the military gradually started concentrating on its secondary role of assisting the government with policies aimed at nation-building. A new philosophy has been advanced by the government since 1970, following the introduction of the New Economic Policy, with the object of achieving national security *(keselamatan)* while pursuing development *(pembangunan)*, or KESBAN. This security-development nexus therefore, represented the government's emphasis on development as security. According to National Security Council Directive 11, "KESBAN constitutes the sum total of all measures undertaken by the MAF and other government agencies to strengthen and protect society from subversion, lawlessness, and insurgency" (Yusof 1994: 136). And because the thrust of the New Economic Policy was development oriented, with the primary goal of upgrading Malay socioeconomic welfare, this apparently security-based strategy was very much in line with the government's goal of reshaping the political economy to benefit Malay interests. Indeed, KESBAN was a well-designed political strategy to ensure Malay support and loyalty to a regime that was becoming increasingly Malay-dominated. Integrating the security tasks of the armed forces with socioeconomic projects was also a method of building closer links between the armed forces and society, that is, strengthening civil-military relations.

Henceforth the armed forces began to accept a wider role in providing aid and security to these projects. They began assisting various civil agencies in instituting socioeconomic development projects in rural areas. As part of KESBAN, the army played a significant role in providing security for construction projects in isolated areas. The government launched several major KESBAN projects. The Rejang Area Security Command in central Sarawak, for example, was headed by a senior government official. Under his direction, the military together with the other civil agencies undertook small-scale development projects in central Sarawak in order to check the increasing communist threat. Apart from the Rejang Area Security Command, the MAF was also involved in clearing mines and booby traps before construction of the 116-kilometer East-West Highway from Kelantan to Perak. With the highway in place, the communist insurgents were cut off from information and food supplies at the border. Yet another project was the introduction of the KESBAN Belt in 1980: a 550-kilometer-long zone along the Malaysia-Thai border that also covered the northern states of Perlis, Kedah, and Perak. The government started an agricultural revolution that promoted rubber, oil, palm, and paddy cultivation among the rural population with the objective of improving their livelihood. Besides these projects, KESBAN included construction of hydroelectric dams in Temenggor (northern Perak) and Pedu (Kedah) to provide electricity for light industries that would create employment in the rural areas. With the MAF providing security, the success of the KESBAN projects led to a marked decline in the communist threat to the nation, especially near the borders with Thailand and Indonesia.

Today, the MAF continues its assistance in development via a program known as "Jiwa Murni" ("Hearts and Minds"). In one of its many projects, namely, "Tentera Masuk Desa" ("Military Goes Rural"), the MAF constructed a Penan Service Center in Sarawak in 1991. The project involved the construction of basic facilities such as a school, two houses, a boarding house, a dining hall, a kitchen, bathrooms, a shelter for an electric generator, and a playing field—all representing the provision of basic amenities for 700 Penans (Yusof 1994: 144). In the East Malaysian states of Sabah and Sarawak—which are relative newcomers to the Malay-dominated Malaysian Federation, and which have been suspicious of the federal military presence there—KESBAN's ostensible political role in pacification cannot be ignored.

Apart from such civic action programs, the MAF has been widely recognized for its contribution during the monsoon season. In particular, the RMN and the RMAF are always called upon to aid civilian authorities in search and rescue operations at sea and over land. Another contribution of the MAF, especially the RMN, is its involvement in preventing the illegal landing of Vietnamese immigrants on the beaches of Malaysia.

As part of Malaysia's active role in international relations, the forces are also involved in UN peacekeeping activities. Immediately after the end of the emergency period on August 1, 1960, the army sent a peacekeeping contingent to Congo following a request by the UN. Since then the army has been involved in sixteen UN missions all over the world, especially in Namibia, Cambodia, Iran-Iraq, Somalia, Bosnia, and Kosovo. This participation in UN missions over the past 40 years has boosted the image of the MAF and given the officer corps an opportunity to undergo multilevel training in deployment, planning, weapons usage, and different logistics systems, besides contributing a "second track" to the government's foreign relations efforts through its "defense diplomacy" while stationed abroad.[18] So far the MAF has deployed some 14,000 officers to serve in the UN missions, while demonstrating the government's continued commitment to UN peace missions by establishing the Malaysian Peacekeeping Training Centre in January 1996.[19]

With the demise of the cold war by 1991, and in the absence of a clearly defined external or internal threat (since the CMP formally ended its armed struggle against the Malaysian government in December 1989), the military's role has varied from time to time, contingent upon the missions dictated by the civilian authorities. Given that the MAF believes its apolitical stance contributes to the stability of the state, its noninterference in politics has helped the nation to attain a measure of economic and political security (Yusof 1994: 136–38). Clearly, recent evidence concerning the Anwar Ibrahim episode has underscored the ability of the state to use the police and military forces as effective tools in the management of state security—or more correctly, the security of the Mahathir regime—via the Internal Security Act and other restrictive laws pertaining to publication and dissemination of information. Thus, over the past three years since Anwar's incarceration, civil-military relations may have undergone some strain but were sufficiently strong in ensuring the stability and survival of the current political system.

FUTURE TRAJECTORIES

The democratically elected government of the day in Malaysia, as elsewhere, needs the backing of both the police and the military in managing public order and security. In appreciating this imperative for peace and stability, the MAF and the government complement each other under the rubric of national security and nation-building. Former chief of defense forces Gen. Ismail bin Omar once remarked, "There is a co-relation between civilian and military resources and capabilities, because one cannot exist without the other. . . . Ultimately, all components of our society and organs of government have to work in unison to ensure national resilience."[20] This partnership concept has worked well because historically the MAF has always had chiefs of armed forces staff who were conscious about group identification. Usually they have been from the same background and are closely aligned to the leadership of UMNO and especially the prime minister. Allegiance to a particular leader, as well as close alliances, creates easy partnerships and reinforces loyalty to the civilian leadership. Indeed, the role of the police and armed forces has become crucial to the survival of a democratically elected government in the event of a national political crisis or emergency. This would even include intra-UMNO disputes such as the bitter contest for the leadership of UMNO between Tengku Razaleigh and Mahathir in 1987. Evidently, such intra-Malay quarrels did not destabilize civil-military relations in the 1980s.

The military elites and the civilian elites are closely linked, as Crouch has noted, suggesting that insubordination toward the government is very unlikely because both parties share similar interests in the state (Crouch 1991: 129). Because senior military positions are politically appointed, the military elites have continued to defend the present arrangement of power relations. Admittedly, key posts in the force are mostly held by Malays, and the composition of the military is also predominantly Malay, thus implying that the forces will not change a system that supports Malay privileges with respect to initial recruitment, promotion and appointments within the military, professional development through local and overseas study, and career opportunities accruing to ex-military officers upon retirement. The Ministry of Defense, for example, ensures that ex-servicemen who are involved in military-related industries are given defense contracts.[21] Likewise, there have been numerous cases of retired generals being given lucrative jobs in government-related companies and the private sector. In 1997, for example, Gen. Hashim Mohd. Ali, a former chief of armed forces and brother-in-law of Prime Minister Mahathir Mohamad, was appointed chairman and chief executive officer of Sukom 98 Berhad, the company that managed the 1998 Commonwealth Games.[22] Clearly such privileges have the effect of reinforcing the military's loyalty to the ruling elite.

In many developing countries, the budget can be a source of conflict between the military and the government. In Malaysia, however, thus far there has been no friction on matters of defense spending between the MAF and the government. The Sixth Malaysia Plan (1991–1995) saw the government earmark RM6 billion for defense;[23] in the Seventh Malaysia Plan, the government budgeted RM9.1 billion for defense for fiscal years 1996 to 2000 (*Rancangan Malaysia Ketujuh: 1996–2000* 1996). Such allocations have enabled the MAF to modernize in terms of training and weapons. In 1993, for example, such allocations enabled the army to procure trinational FH-70 155-mm guns and Oerlikon 35-mm antiaircraft guns.[24] With respect to training, the air force has had its MiG-29 pilots trained overseas in India, which trained an initial batch of 100 Malaysian pilots, engineers, and technicians in 1993–1994. At the same time its F/A-18D aircrew are being trained by the U.S. Navy locally.[25] Such arrangements ostensibly have the effect of strengthening the civil-military relations component of national security policy formulation, thereby reinforcing the positive linkages between the four main indicators in concordance theory. The Eighth Malaysia Plan (2001–2005) is likely to maintain if not increase the defense allocation, which now stands at about 5 percent of total gross domestic product, given the government's commitment to technologically upgrade defense capabilities to address traditional as well as new security concerns and challenges. Security issues such as illegal immigrants, maritime piracy, congestion over the Straits of Malacca, and competing claims in the Spratlys are likely to be given added emphasis in the new security formulation. In any event, the fundamental pillars of Malaysia's National Defence Policy, namely, self-reliance, regional cooperation, and external assistance, will continue to provide the basis of civil-military engagement and cooperation in the management of internal and external security, and in the realization of Prime Minister Mahathir's Vision 2020.[26] Malaysia's post–cold war security approach envisages diplomacy as a first line of defense with "emphasis on military diplomacy through contacts, exchanges, training, and joint exercises" (Nathan 1998: 535), thus indicating the importance of civilian control in the country's general foreign policy orientation.

The MAF's human resource development is another area that augurs well for recruiting eligible candidates. Emphasis is placed upon upgrading academic qualifications by giving selected officers opportunities to further their studies in local universities such as the National University of Malaysia in Bangi, Selangor, and the University of Malaya in Kuala Lumpur, both of which award postgraduate degrees in strategic studies. Furthermore, some 172 officers graduate from the Malaysian Armed Forces Academy every year. The MAF estimates that by the year 2000, some 30 percent of its officer corps will possess tertiary qualifications, that is, postgraduate diplomas, and masters degrees awarded by local and foreign universities, as well as technology-based educational qualifications from the Malaysian Armed Forces Academy.[27] The government's efforts to upgrade the qualifications of officers not only strengthen that dimension of military professionalism but also ensure that the officer corps remain firmly committed to the constitutional principle of civilian control.

Civilians have always recognized the importance of and promoted professionalism in the military. Military professionalism means that soldiers must be ready to carry out the orders of any civilian government that has legitimate authority in the state (Huntington 1957: 83–84). Although military personnel might in certain circumstances resent taking orders from civilians—and in the wake of the political turmoil following the Anwar episode since September 1998, the prospect of personal rivalry between Malays in the officer corps arising from differences in political and religious orientation cannot be ruled out—the overwhelming majority of the officer corps accept the present arrangement. Without concrete evidence available to the analyst, it is difficult to project the future trajectory of civil-military relations based purely on the circumstances surrounding the former deputy premier's arrest and detention. In any event, given the past record, the Mahathir-Anwar power struggle is unlikely to change the present structure and pattern of civil-military relations in Malaysia as long as it does not threaten the prevailing paradigm of Malay-Muslim dominance of the political system. At least on the surface, the MAF's development has proceeded without political tension between the armed forces and the civilian political and administrative leaders.

Although there is growing evidence of Islamization in the armed forces, in other words, a tendency to link military professionalism through adherence to Islamic strictures such as banning alcohol in military premises (since 1998), it is still unclear how Islam-oriented officers might influence the character of civil-military relations in the future. The government, nevertheless, has been concerned since the early 1990s over the possibly negative effects of Islamization on the MAF's morale and commitment to duty.[28] The then MAF chief, Gen. Yaacob Mohd. Zain, remarked that religious ignorance had created two groups: those who resorted to immoral activities and those who ended up as members of deviationist sects.[29] However, it can be surmised that the progressive diminution (through retirement and nonrecruitment) of non-Malay officers has conduced over time toward the adoption of a so-called Islamic approach to military professionalization (proffered particularly by officers trained in Muslim establishments in the Middle East in the late 1980s), with possible consequences for its traditionally secular character. In any event, even the Islamization of the armed forces is unlikely to threaten Malay dominance because the Malay/Muslim identity would continue to be preserved.

Because the military has always functioned in a subservient capacity to the civilian authority, any attempt at political intervention could translate into a major and possibly irretrievable liability for the armed forces. At any rate, the absence of a prevalent threat and the presence of a stable political environment have removed any temptation to act otherwise. Besides, lack of public support would deter any plausible attempt by the armed forces to overthrow a democratically elected government. In any event, the security and intelligence network is organized in a manner that would give the police advance information about any military plot to seize power from the civilian authorities.

In conclusion, then, a military takeover of the government is conceivable only if the interests of the MAF begin to diverge significantly from those of the ruling elite, or if the civilian government proves itself unable to govern effectively. This view is clearly supported by a body of research suggesting that three major indicators—history, ethnicity, and political economy—have been critical in shaping the origins, evolution, and the character of military-civilian relations in Malaysia. The Malay-dominated political leadership must be seen to be upholding Malay nationalism, welfare, sovereignty, Islam, and all the appurtenances of Malaysian independence. Any direct threat to Malay power and privilege in multiethnic Malaysia could trigger the political consciousness of a predominantly Malay/Muslim armed forces who view their corporate interests, security, and future as closely intertwined with the current regime, that is, the civilian government, which, as presently constituted, is also predominantly Malay/Muslim. Unless these circumstances change, the present scenario of Malaysia's civil-military relations is likely to continue. And the recent victory of the Barisan Nasional in the November 29, 1999, general elections, ensuring more than a comfortable two-thirds parliamentary majority for the UMNO-led BN government, strengthens the confidence of the armed forces who thus far have relied on the civilian authorities to promote the MAF's well-being and professionalism in this multicultural country. For now, therefore, every soldier is a "civilian in uniform" serving a state that is controlled by civilian power.[30]

CHAPTER 11

Singapore: Civil-Military Fusion

Tan Tai Yong

> I will tell you why we do not want professional soldiers. This place must learn to live and work for a living. And if you are only a soldier, you do not contribute to the productivity of the place. So we train.... Every man who is chosen becomes a soldier or sailor.... Then, he goes back to earn a living in a factory, in an office and, for the next ten to fifteen years, he is part of a reservoir of people who understand discipline, who understand the mechanics of self-defense, and who can, in an emergency, help to defend their own country.... In the end, every boy and girl here will understand that what he or she has in Singapore, he or she must be prepared to fight for and defend. Otherwise, it will be lost.
>
> —Lee Kuan Yew, February 21, 1967

WITH A RELATIVELY LARGE CONSCRIPT ARMY, a chronic sense of its own vulnerability, and a constant preoccupation with national defense, Singapore has often been described as a nation-in-arms or garrison state. Although the country may exhibit certain characteristics that are associated with these models of civil-military relations, neither depiction truly explains the Singapore case. The fusion model—in which the military, both in leadership and in structural terms, functions as an integral part of a centralized, bureaucratic state—may more usefully be applied to illuminate civil-military relations in Singapore.

Although the military establishment in Singapore is young and small by Asian standards, it has nonetheless maintained a very visible presence in the country. With a conscript army that draws the overwhelming bulk of its officer corps as well as the rank and file (more than 85 percent) from the citizenry, Singapore, with a present population of nearly 4 million, has one of the highest military participation ratios in the noncommunist world. Since 1967, when compulsory national service was first instituted—requiring every male citizen to serve at least two years in the military upon reaching the age of eighteen, and then to remain in the reserves until at least the age of 40—military service has become part of the national culture, a way of life in Singapore, and "an institution that is all-embracing and all-pervasive."[1] Indeed almost every family in the country has a male member in the armed forces, either as a full-time national serviceman or a member of the reserve, and insofar as Singapore requires all its male citizens to belong to "an armed force that is organized by, or owing allegiance to, the national authorities" (Roberts 1976: 37), the small city-state can arguably be seen as a nation-in-arms.

The impression of an armed state is further reinforced by the vast resources the government consistently allocates to the military, indicating the key importance that defense and security occupy in the national agenda. In 1998 the Singapore government spent $4.3 billion on defense, making the island's defense expenditure per capita not only the highest in the Association of Southeast Asian Nations but in the Asia-Pacific region as well. Based on 1997 figures, Singapore's per capita defense expenditure is more than twice that of Taiwan's, two and a half times that of North Korea and South Korea's combined, and more than six times that of Japan's (International Institute for Strategic Studies [IISS] 1998: 297). This consistently high amount of military spending has allowed the tiny island-republic to embark on an unwavering military buildup over the past three decades, creating in the process one of the best-designed and technologically advanced defense forces in the region. In financial year 1999, defense was allocated 25 percent of the overall budget, amounting to some US$4.5 billion and representing 5.1 percent of Singapore's gross domestic product (up from 4.6 percent in 1998). That the country's defense budget has not been reduced despite the recent economic recession in the region offers a clear indication of the Singapore government's commitment to a steady and long-term buildup of the armed forces. It is little wonder, then, that Singapore has often been regarded by many as a garrison state with a garrison mentality to match.

The military presence in the country is further emphasized through constant media exposure, either in the form of glitzy television commercials for careers in the Singapore Armed Forces (SAF), or as part of the state's ongoing effort to publicize the importance of national service and total defense. Periodically, military code words are flashed on television screens or broadcast through the radio to indicate that a military mobilization exercise is in progress. Recently the government, concerned that a complacent attitude among younger Singaporeans might weaken their resolve to take national service seriously, instituted the observance of an annual Total Defense Day in every school. Total Defense Day falls on February 15 to mark the day in 1942 when Singapore fell to the Japanese. On the leadup to Total Defense Day recently, a photographic exhibit was staged and a film, aptly entitled *On-Guard*, was released showing the state of the armed forces in Singapore as well as paying tribute to the contributions of national servicemen in the defense of the country.

Yet, paradoxically, despite the conspicuous standing of the military in Singapore, and in a region where an apolitical military has been the exception rather than the norm, "the most striking feature of the Singapore scene [vis-à-vis civil-military relations] is the undisputed predominance of the civilian sector over the military" (Chan 1985: 136). Indeed, few would argue with the proposition that from its very inception the SAF has been subjected to tight control at every moment by the country's ruling political elite. Clearly the pattern of civil-military relations in Singapore runs counter to established contentions that a nation-in-arms (if Singapore can be so described) or a high military participation ratio engenders the supremacy of the military, leading inexorably to various forms of militarism. Military considerations are not placed above all else in the state of Singapore, and the SAF, despite its considerable size and resources, has so far remained "one of the least politically-oriented national military forces in Southeast Asia" (Huxley 1993: 1). Neither the nation-in-arms model nor the notion of a garrison state, in which political and military elites conspire to generate conditions where "individual freedom would be sacrificed on the altar of military preparedness" (Lasswell 1941), therefore, captures the essence of the civil-military relations in Singapore.

In reviewing civil-military relations in Singapore, one should perhaps begin with the premise that a clear-cut distinction between a professional armed force and its civilian clientele, a distinction that underlies much of the thinking about civil-military relations elsewhere, may not elucidate the association that exists between the soldier and the state here. It may be more relevant to characterize the Singapore example as a model of civil-military fusion: a case in which the military, rather than functioning as an independent or dysfunctional component outside the civilian polity, is for all intents and purposes an integral part of the administrative structure, playing an essentially complementary role in the social and economic functions of the state. The upshot is a military establishment that does not possess its own independent political or ideological ambitions but instead identifies fully with the values, interests, and national goals set by the civilian government. One does not see, for example, in the case of Singapore, the development of a military elite that has an identity and an agenda separate from those of the administrative and political elites (Khong 1995: 119). The line that has traditionally separated the military from the civil bureaucracy and the political leadership has, consequently, all but disappeared. All this makes the concept of "objective civilian control" (Huntington 1957: 83–84)—where the military is regarded as a separate entity whose political power could be minimized by rendering it more professional—quite inapplicable in the Singapore instance.

Viewed from the fusion perspective, the classic civil-military problematic of the nation-state needing to create an institution of violence to protect it and then fearing that instrument of violence does not occur in Singapore simply because the security and defense of the country remain the collective responsibility of the entire government and nation, not just the armed forces. Seen in such terms, the scenario of a gradual erosion of civilian control over the military—or the emergence of a "confident and aggressive military establishment that does not necessarily subscribe to western notions of an apolitical military"—does not seem quite plausible.[2] In the prevailing context of "strong, complex political structures that continue to enjoy high legitimacy in Singapore" (Chan 1985: 153) and a sustained period of peace and economic growth—as well as a well-entrenched national service ethos and a national security that is based on the concept of total defense—the military in Singapore, both in ideational terms (political beliefs) and material terms (political interests and distribution of power), remains firmly integrated with the overarching institutional framework and political agenda of the civilian government.

THE MAKING OF THE MILITARY

Unlike the armed forces in neighboring Indonesia, Vietnam, and Burma, the SAF did not precede the emergence of Singapore as an independent nation-state. When Singapore gained independence after suddenly separating from Malaysia in August 1965, all that it inherited militarily was a paltry defense force that consisted of two infantry battalions of some 50 officers and about 1,000 men, a navy of two wooden-hulled ships, and no air force. Although local troops were virtually absent, stationed in Singapore were several thousand soldiers from the British and Malaysian armed forces. Indeed, the military had never featured prominently in Singapore's history despite the fact that for a long period the island's value as a colony, other than its position as a trading emporium, lay in its potential as a military base serving British strategic interests east of the Suez. In the 1920s the British decided to build a naval base in Singapore to protect their trade routes and defend their colonies in the East. With its extensive military facilities, including several military airfields and a drydock that could service the largest ships in the world, the colony came to be known as Fortress Singapore.

Although a fairly extensive military edifice had been erected by the British by the early twentieth century, the military remained a colonial superstructure that never sank roots into the local but mainly immigrant society who carried with them the essentially migrant sense of self and communal interest but with little commitment to the state. Attempts at building up a local armed force, mainly for the purpose of performing internal security functions, were sporadic. In 1854, a Singapore Volunteer Rifle Corps was established to assist the police in dealing with communal riots. This unit was later enlarged to include Eurasian, Malay, and Chinese infantry companies and was renamed the Singapore Volunteer Force. Right up to the 1950s, local involvement in the military was extremely limited, and enlistees were mainly from the minority Malay, Indian, and Eurasian communities (Chiang 1990: 28–29). For cultural and other reasons, the Chinese steered clear of the military, and later attempts to conscript them into the army were met with fierce resistance. An attempt by the British colonial government to pass a national service ordinance and introduce the concept of national conscription in Singapore in 1952 was met with strong protests and demonstrations from the Chinese school students (Chan 1985: 140). Although the ordinance managed to enlist 400 young men in its first enlistment exercise, the effort to introduce national service in the 1950s was curtailed because of its unpopularity with the mainly Chinese population of Singapore.

Consequently, outside of a small volunteer force, Singapore, prior to its independence, never had an indigenous military force of any significance. Defense had always been in the hands of an external power: first with the British, when Singapore was a colony, and later, between 1963 and 1965, with Kuala Lumpur when Singapore was part of Malaysia. Although two infantry regiments—the First and Second Singapore Infantry Regiments—had been raised in Singapore in the late 1950s, primarily for internal security purposes, both had a high percentage of Malay personnel from the federation and were joined to the Malaysian Armed Forces when Singapore became part of Malaysia (Mayerchak 1986: 172). Although the modern SAF could in some ways trace its roots to these early military establishments, it was obvious that when Singapore became independent it had little or no local military tradition or military establishment to speak of.

The SAF is without question the creation of the People's Action Party (PAP) government, which has enjoyed uninterrupted power since 1959. Under its preeminent leader, Lee Kuan Yew, who stepped down in 1990 after 30 years as prime minister, the PAP has left its indelible imprimatur on modern Singapore, "its doctrines, ideas, methods and style [dominating] the political climate" in the country (Chan 1985: 137). Lee and his colleagues presided over the constitutional and political developments that brought Singapore into Malaysia in 1963 only to separate two years later under very unhappy circumstances. After being told unceremoniously to leave Malaysia, the PAP government concentrated on building a strong state that would provide the political will and wherewithal to deal with the tasks of economic and social development. With virtually no credible political opposition since the eclipse of the Barisan Socialis in the late 1960s,[3] the PAP's grip on political power in Singapore has been total and absolute. This political dominance has enabled the PAP government to consolidate its control over every aspect of state and society in Singapore and, in the process, mold Singapore very much in line with the vision they had set out to achieve in 1965: political and economic viability through "a nation-building program that emphasized modernization and economic development" (Khong 1995: 113).

Over the years, with its emphasis on political and economic development, Lee and his highly cohesive and effective government moved to depoliticize Singapore by removing political debate from the political arena into the bureaucracy and systematically building what Chan Heng Chee has called an "administrative state" (Chan 1974). Under these conditions, civil servants began playing an increasingly dominant role in managing state and society. Indeed, the integration between political leadership and the civil service was such that the latter became "the principal recruiting ground for political leadership" (Khong 1995: 118). Singapore was consequently managed by a political-administrative elite who then co-opted and tapped the technical expertise of a variety of professionals to help them manage the country. The effectiveness of this administrative state in managing Singapore's development—coupled with the accomplishments of the PAP government in turning the country into a huge economic success with a stable political environment and social cohesion—has generated for the civilian government unchallenged authority and broad-based legitimacy within the country.

The emergence and subsequent development of the SAF, therefore, were largely determined by the state-building preoccupation and strategies of the PAP government in post-1965 Singapore. After its sudden expulsion from Malaysia, the survival of Singapore as an independent state became the dominating concern informing almost all of the government's policies (Chua 1997). Historical memories—mainly its acrimonious breakup with Malaysia—as well as certain geostrategic realities—a tiny, predominantly Chinese, state in a Malay/Muslim sea—heightened the country's sense of vulnerability. The situation was particularly tense in the 1960s when Indonesia was pursuing its policy of confrontation against Malaysia and Singapore. Ultimately the threat of an outright physical attack receded, and Singapore has not faced obvious territorial aggression from any of its neighbors since then. This, however, has not eliminated the government's deep-seated concern over the continued security of the country. In 1982, at a National Day speech, Prime Minister Lee Kuan Yew stated that his greatest concern was to "make the young more conscious of security."[4] Not long after, his defense minister, Goh Chok Tong, voiced similar sentiments that "conflict, confrontation and war is the order of the day and peace and stability is the exception."[5] The public is constantly reminded by the government that order is fragile. References are often made to Sri Lanka, Lebanon, and, more recently, Kuwait as examples of the dangers—and indeed tragedy—that await small states that have gone soft on security. In the national education programs that are constantly being organized for students and civil servants, the "S Cube" phenomenon, emphasizing the interconnectedness of security to survival and success of the country, is invariably invoked. The government has thus proceeded on the principle that Singapore, though small, cannot afford to be pushed around. And because it cannot expect bigger powers to come to its rescue if it should get into trouble, the country must be able to defend itself, especially against the predatory intentions of bigger powers. In other words, in order to survive in an unfriendly world, a small, weak, and exposed Singapore must become "robust, rugged, and self-reliant," particularly in its defense capability (Hanna 1973: 1). This has since remained a cardinal principle of the state where defense is concerned, and it explains why the government has remained so committed to an unrelenting buildup of the SAF.

Self-reliance in defense was sought after not only for self-esteem and regional prestige; it was also regarded as a necessary precondition for Singapore's participation in regional military alliances. Although Singapore had participated in a loose military pact known as the Five Power Defense Arrangement,[6] it nonetheless adopted the attitude that collective security arrangements would work only when there was reciprocity. Singapore had to be prepared to give as much as it received. The need was therefore clear from the beginning: Singapore had to build, as quickly as possible, a credible defense force with the ability to inflict considerable damage on any aggressor, thereby reminding potential enemies that any predatory tendency toward the country would be met with ferocity. To cynics who claim that defense is a waste of resources because whatever armed forces the tiny state could muster would be no match for a large determined power, the Singapore government responds by describing its defense posture as analogous to that of the poison shrimp—the predator who swallows the shrimp will end up paying a high cost for its action. The poison shrimp strategy, which survived into the 1980s, has since been replaced with a "prevail and win" strategy.[7]

It was, however, clear from the outset that defense and security would not be pursued for their own sake. A related but fundamental reason for the emphasis on defense was the concern that unless the government was able to demonstrate its ability to defend itself against potential enemies, it would not be able to inspire the confidence of foreign investors. In the government's perspective, a credible defense force was not merely necessary as a national security force or a status symbol for independent nationhood; in the particular case of Singapore, it was an imperative for the country's economic survival. In the late 1970s, when the communists held sway in Indochina, Dr. Goh Keng Swee, the primary architect of the SAF, observed that the PAP government's decision to build a national armed force had been vindicated: "If that decision [to build a military force] had not been taken, Singapore would be in a weak, unprepared state. The confidence of businessmen and investors would be shaken beyond repair. The prosperity that we have achieved over the decade would crumble overnight" (Josey 1980: 157).

Against such a backdrop, the buildup of a defense force became a truly national concern; alongside the economic and social development of the country, its development was deemed very much a part of the process of state- and nation-building. It was, therefore, considered appropriate that the task of building the SAF be entrusted to no less a figure than Dr. Goh Keng Swee, a politician-bureaucrat widely regarded to be the most brilliant and effective member of the cabinet after Lee Kuan Yew. An economist with a doctorate from the London School of Economics, Goh was then holding the critical finance portfolio in the cabinet. He had little military experience to go by: his only soldiering credential was a stint he had spent as a corporal in the Singapore Volunteer Corps. But under his strong hands the SAF went through its nascent and formative years, its structure, character, and priorities determined by Dr. Goh and the PAP government, very much in accord with the needs and concerns of state formation at that time.

The Ministry of Interior and Defense was quickly set up in 1965, and Goh brought over his permanent secretary, George Bogaars, a history graduate and British-trained professional civil servant, to assist in the task of building up the armed forces. Their first job was to find enough people to fill leadership positions at all levels of the military hierarchy. Because there was a shortage of sufficiently qualified and experienced middle- and senior-level officers who could hold senior military appointments, Goh had to turn to the civil service and the police force for the first batch of army leaders (Peled 1998: 115–16). Consequently, many of the key officers in the newly established military came from nonmilitary backgrounds and had virtually no military experience. Tan Tek Kim, for instance, senior assistant to the police commissioner in 1965, was temporarily transferred to the military to head the General Staff Division, which was given the task of developing the armed forces structure, roles, and operational contingency plans. When the officer training school, the Singapore Armed Forces Training Institute, was set up, a senior civil servant, Kripa Ram Vij, was named its first commandant.[8] Vij, a part-time junior military officer in the Singapore Volunteer Corps, had been given his commission after completing a six-week officer course. To meet the needs of the day, he was rapidly promoted to the rank of colonel in order to head the new military institute (Peled 1998: 116–17). This process of transferring civil servants into the top ranks of the military was continued for a number of years, and several of the younger civil servants who had received training as military officers were later seconded to serve full time in the military.[9]

The seconding of civil servants to the military, it seemed, had a dual purpose. The first aim, necessitated by the severe shortage of military men, was to have a ready group of people with the necessary education to assume command at various levels of the military hierarchy. But by getting ranking civil servants to serve in the military, the government was also preparing for the impending introduction of conscription: by personal example, enlisted civil servants would help future enlistees overcome their aversion to performing national service in the military.[10] The infusion of civilians into the top ranks of the military was not without its implications for the development of the SAF, however. When the SAF started out it was virtually a "civil service in uniform" whose officers functioned not so much as an autonomous set of military professionals but as civil servants who were obediently carrying out the policies of the political leadership. Conceived and raised with the heavy imprint of civilian government's influence, the SAF thus found itself firmly entrenched in the bureaucratic edifice of the state from its birth.

Lacking military experience and expertise, the Singapore government turned to the outside world for advice and help. India and Egypt were approached by Singapore, but both had reservations about assisting an unknown state in a sensitive matter such as defense and declined the invitation (Goh 1973). Finally, Singapore managed to obtain the assistance of the Israelis, whose model of a citizen army was deemed appealing and relevant to the local context. The Israeli methods of fast, intensive, and compact training, coupled with their emphasis on skills and adaptability, were regarded as particularly suitable for Singapore. (Of course, the point was not missed by Singapore's immediate neighbors that the Israelis were perhaps chosen because of the similarity in the security conditions of the two countries.) Serving in an advisory capacity, the Israelis concentrated on building a core of local instructors who would subsequently form the nucleus of trainers for the SAF. They laid the necessary groundwork, stayed a few years, and were progressively phased out; by 1974, the last of the Israelis had left Singapore. The Israelis, although they were the most talked about, were not the only military advisers Singapore had. Since the early years, the SAF has continued to receive considerable assistance from the United States as well as Britain, even after the latter had pulled out its base in Singapore in 1971. The company that the SAF kept had an important bearing on its orientation and outlook: it was perhaps the combination of the inherited British civil-military tradition and the Israeli military model, both of which emphasize the military's complete obedience to civilian authority, that molded and continues to inform the way in which the military remains committed to the civilian government in Singapore.

STRUCTURES OF CIVIL-MILITARY INTEGRATION

The integration of the armed forces into the state structure is facilitated by the setup of the military establishment in Singapore. The SAF forms part of an elaborate defense structure that is tightly integrated for the purpose of unified command and control and to optimize the use of manpower and resources. Together with a number of agencies and institutions that constitute the military establishment, the SAF, as the armed branch, is placed under the firm control of the Ministry of Defense (MINDEF), which is headed by a civilian minister who is responsible for national defense and security.[11] MINDEF gives direction across the entire defense edifice. Through a weekly meeting, chaired by the minister and attended by senior civil servants and the top military brass, MINDEF decides on all matters relating to the military. This is perhaps the ultimate mechanism ensuring control over the military by the administrative elites, because no major decisions concerning the military, including budget allocation for purchase of military hardware, can be made except through the committee.[12] Permanent secretaries who are responsible for overall coordination of defense and security as well as technology and development head the executive arm of MINDEF.

The three main departments in MINDEF that deal directly with the military—manpower, logistics, and intelligence—have until recently been headed by civilians. Today the permanent secretaries are assisted by three functional groups: the Defense Policy Group, which is responsible for formulating and coordinating defense relations, information, and security; the Defense Administration Group, which looks after the manpower, financial, and administration aspects of MINDEF and the SAF; and the Defense Technology Group, which provides the technological wherewithal to support the armed forces (Ministry of Defense, Singapore 1995). All three groups, each headed by a deputy secretary, are dominated by civilians and function as nonuniformed administrative departments outside the armed forces. The general administration of the armed forces comes under the Armed Forces Council, which is presided over by the minister of defense and consists of the minister of state for defense, the permanent secretaries, and the various representatives of the armed forces. The highest decision-making body on security and military matters is the Defense Council, chaired by the prime minister and comprising a small number of senior cabinet members. Military officers do not have a permanent seat in the Defense Council and are represented only in an advisory capacity. Thus all matters relating to national security with political and diplomatic implications are deliberated and decided by the political and administrative elites. The SAF's role is to execute policies made at a higher level.

As an outcome of the fusion of the military into the bureaucracy, the SAF, unlike many armies elsewhere, does not possess its own source of income. Like the other branches of civil service, MINDEF is totally dependent on the government for an annual budget to cover its running costs as well as acquisitions of new weapon systems. Unlike many countries where the military exerts an influence in the political arena and the defense budget is sized by threat perceptions, usually defined by the military establishment, the Singapore government decided early on that defense spending had to be pegged at a fixed proportion of gross domestic product

(GDP). Thus, although the military traditionally consumes a large portion of the national budget, its annual allocation is not allowed to exceed 6 percent of the GDP. By ensuring that defense expenditures are linked to the state of the economy, the government is able to guarantee that they will not expand to the detriment of other areas of national development and, moreover, that defense will not end up as consumption itself but as an ongoing investment for the country's continued well-being. In other words, in Singapore there would never be a need to sacrifice butter for guns.

Pegging the defense expenditure on a fixed percentage of the GDP, while ensuring that the country's military spending will not drain the economy, offers an added advantage: the country does not have to name its enemies to justify the military budget. In a geostrategic environment that is potentially volatile, the aim of Singapore's foreign policy has been to maintain an armed force that can offer enough deterrence and legitimization for diplomacy to work. Although security concerns in Singapore are deeply entrenched in the national agenda, the external threat is rarely made explicit. The government has always insisted that Singapore has no specific enemies: its defense buildup is based not on a particular threat, it says, but on a doctrine to prevent threats from arising (Yeo 1992). Although the government does not name its nemesis outright, it has been pointed out that "Singapore defense policy evinces an overriding concern with the deterrence of Malaysia" (Huxley 1991: 204). Yet, others have pointed out that the case may not be that obvious. Although Singapore-Malaysia relations have had their rocky patches, the defense of the two countries, given their proximity to each other, is indivisible, and indeed, they make "natural defense allies" (Tan 1999: 456). Whatever the threat perception may be, because the SAF is given a fixed budget, it is not tempted to demonize any of its neighbors—removing the need to make the enemy appear more menacing in order to get more money. Likewise, salaries of military officers, like their civil service counterparts, are determined by guidelines imposed by the Ministry of Finance—removing any propensity on the part of the officer corps to organize itself as an interest group in order to lobby for better conditions of service.

Despite consistently generous budget allocations, the Singapore government nonetheless sees its budgetary limits as a sort of disciplining mechanism to drive the military organization to use its allocated resources in a more productive and efficient manner.[13] MINDEF is expected to understand that the resources given to it are not limitless and it is not in a position to bargain for more, thus preventing it from engaging in reckless spending. Similarly, the SAF knows that its annual budget will not exceed a certain percentage of the GDP, and within that constraint it will have to do the best it can with the money available. Careful planning is needed if a service wishes to make a major procurement, for the project may commit its funding for years. It has to be noted, however, that although the civilian government fixes the budget for the military, the SAF exercises considerable influence on the way the money is spent, especially in the purchase of military hardware and weapon systems. Recommendations for such purchases emanate from below according to the roles and functions that each of the services is expected to perform. In this respect, the political leadership leaves the military to work out its professional needs and develop its procurement plans based on its mission. Interservice competition for resources is then regulated by the Joint Staff,[14] which sets the central priorities for the entire SAF. The Joint Staff decides on the allocation of the resources to each of the services, thus preventing interservice rivalry and ensuring that the SAF continues to develop as a balanced and integrated force. The Joint Staff then presents this integrated picture to MINDEF, which makes the final decision on resource allocation.

A prominent feature of the military establishment in Singapore is its impressive defense-industrial capability. Mindful of its limitations in the size of its armed forces, the government has long been convinced of the need to exploit technology as a force multiplier. Defense technology, however, is not controlled or managed by the SAF alone, but in partnership with two other major actors, the MINDEF's Defense Technology Group and the local defense industrial base, headed by the transnational, government-linked Singapore Technologies Group. This defense industrial complex offers perhaps one of the clearest manifestations of civil-military fusion in Singapore. As a local military analyst has pointed out, "The burgeoning defense industrial complex...which supports the SAF's operational readiness...also contributes to the national cause of creating a society with a broad technological base" (Da Cunha 1999: 462). Thus, defense and national development needs are closely integrated and not put at odds against each other. Rather than diverting and draining the country's resources, the defense industry is made to contribute to national economic growth through its nonmilitary business.

THE NOTION OF TOTAL DEFENSE

Whereas structural and budgetary provisions ensure that the SAF functions in accordance with the overall dictates of the administrative and political leadership, the total defense concept, the keystone of Singapore's defense strategy, ensures that the business of defense is not monopolized by the military but remains the shared concern of the entire government. In societies where the military plays a dominant role, the armed forces often regard themselves as guardians of the national interest. In Singapore, national security is not entrusted to the SAF alone. The Singapore government launched its Total Defense concept in 1984. This comprehensive approach to security is premised on the belief that Singapore can survive a war only if the entire society, and not just the military, is prepared and ready for defense. In this respect, total defense encompasses psychological defense, in which the will of the people must be galvanized to resist external threats; economic defense, where the country's business and industry must be bolstered to withstand the pressures and demands of a major crisis or war; civil defense, where the civilian population will be prepared to safeguard themselves and their properties in a conflict; and social defense, which emphasizes the building of cohesion in the country's multiracial society so that the social fabric will not tear asunder in times of crisis. Military defense makes up the fifth pillar of the overall total defense strategy.[15] The SAF constitutes the military arm of the total defense of Singapore, and its role is clearly defined: to deter potential aggressors from attacking Singapore. Total security—the linchpin of Singapore's national security strategy—is envisaged as an integration of three elements: total defense, diplomacy, and internal stability. Total defense is aimed at ensuring that Singapore has the means to deter any would-be aggressors. The government takes pains to explain that Singapore's defense policy is not built on the premise of a specific threat or a known enemy. The country's investment in the military is meant, instead, to enhance its deterrence capability. It is this deterrence that allows diplomacy to work. The operating principle informing this approach is clear: unless a small state like Singapore can demonstrate a deterrence capability, it will not be taken seriously in peaceful discussions with other countries. Nevertheless, the Singapore government recognizes that apart from an adequate defense force, its security depends on an articulate foreign policy and therefore maintains a web of diplomatic links with its neighbors.

Clearly, then, the responsibility and conduct of national security rest firmly in the hands of the civilian government. Although the military's role is embedded in the notion of total defense—in which a well-trained, well-equipped, and technologically advanced armed force serves as a basic deterrence against external aggressors and, at the same time, as a legitimizer to the state's foreign policy (Mayerchak 1986: 182)—it is the incorporation of this force with elements of social defense, economic defense, psychological defense, and civil defense that provides for a truly national defense capability. In other words, the operational philosophy behind total defense, based essentially on the Swedish model, entails the mobilization of the entire population into a comprehensive defense posture. In the event of war, the reasoning goes, all aspects of society will be affected and it is therefore only to be expected that all citizens contribute to the war effort. Thus the defense of Singapore rests ultimately on the entire society, not just the military establishment. And because national security is not the exclusive domain of the armed forces, there is no justification whatever for the military to lay claim to political power and material resources even in the severest of circumstances.

NATIONAL SERVICE

Blurring the clear-cut separation between civilian and military in Singapore is the SAF's existence as a citizen's army. In 1965, as the government of a newly independent Singapore sought to build a self-reliant defense force, it decided on the option of a national service army. Cost was a major consideration. Prime Minister Lee Kuan Yew declared, "We cannot afford a big army, we will go bankrupt. . . . We have 2,000 men in two regiments and they cost $20 million a year. This is not the way for us. We must depend on volunteers . . . weekend soldiers."[16] Two years later, in 1967, national service was implemented and every able-bodied male citizen aged eighteen was required by law to join the army for between two and two and a half years of full-time military training and service. Upon completion of full-time national service, the soldier would be deemed operationally ready and be required to attend training camp for ten to fourteen days a year.[17] By law, every male citizen is obligated to perform national service until he is 40 or 50 years old, depending on his rank. With the implementation of national service, the SAF became a citizen army of conscripts trained and led by a small core of professional soldiers.

At first the decision to introduce national service did not go down well with the people of Singapore, particularly among Chinese parents who believed that "good sons do not become soldiers, just as good iron is not used to make nails." Anxious parents tried desperately to get their sons out of national service, particularly when rumors started circulating in the early 1970s of ill treatment in the army as well as government plans to send enlisted men to Vietnam.[18] These early problems notwithstanding, the Singapore government was convinced that national service suited the country in a number of ways. First, it enabled Singapore to establish a fairly sizable defense force in a short period of time. (The buildup had to be intensified when the British signaled their intention to withdraw military bases from Singapore in 1968.) Second, it was the most economical way of establishing an army, given the new state's limited resources, particularly in manpower. With a conscript army built around reservists who would maintain their civilian jobs, the country could have a sizable defense force without draining the workforce. And third, by not having to build a huge full-time regular army, the state would not have to demobilize a standing force, with all its social and political implications, should the economy be unable to support it.

Apart from serving the country's defense needs, national service could function as an institution integrating disparate ethnic groups through the common experience of military training. Goh Keng Swee was convinced that "nothing creates loyalty and national consciousness more thoroughly than participation in defence... [and] nation-building aspects will be more significant if its participation is spread over all levels of society" (Goh 1973). By having to live, train, and spend time together, the young men of Singapore, at one of the most impressionable times in their lives, would share an experience, it was hoped, that would bridge economic, cultural, religious, ethnic, and language differences and foster acceptance of others (Nair 1994: 15). At this stage it is impossible to assess the full impact of national service on the outlook of young Singaporeans. Nonetheless, there is little doubt that it has given Singapore "an aggregate index of shared experience [that cuts] across barriers of wealth, race, religion and educational level."[19] Thus national service was expected to perform, in addition to a defense function, a nation-building task as well, by creating a national consciousness and ultimately a national identity. It is perhaps in recognition of its nation-building functions that the SAF's mission has a clear external orientation. Citizen armies can easily be galvanized against an external threat but are of questionable utility for suppressing domestic disturbances. Unlike a number of armed forces in Southeast Asia, the SAF has largely been divested of any significant internal security role.

Although the government intended for the SAF to be a key institution for building a multiracial nation, during the first two decades after independence it has had to contend with the conflicting dictates of multiracialism and security, especially concerning the Malay community in Singapore. Although there is no evidence that Singaporean Malays have ever conspired with external forces, the government was nonetheless uncertain where their loyalty would rest in case of a conflict between Singapore and one of its neighboring Muslim states. Fearing a Trojan horse, the government therefore limited intake of Malays into the SAF until the 1970s, and those who were conscripted were sent to serve in fire brigades and civil-defense units (Peled 1994: 121–22). Since 1977, however, as memories of separation recede and the region stabilizes, the government has adopted a phased integration policy: by 1985, the proportion of Malays in the SAF had doubled (Peled 1994: 148–49). Since then it has been widely reported that all eligible Malays have been called up for national service, and many of them have made inroads into the special services, air force, and the officer corps. Today there are many Malay officers holding senior ranks in the SAF and serving in different arms, prompting the SAF to publicly its head on a number of occasions that it does not discriminate on the basis of race or religion. Despite the official pronouncements, the sensitive issue of the Malays in the armed forces rears its head every now and then. In 1987, BG (NS) Lee Hsien Loong created a stir when, speaking at a public forum, he alluded to a possible conflict of interest between nationalism and religion among Singapore's Malay/Muslim soldiers should the SAF be called upon to fight a war in Southeast Asia. More recently, Senior Minister Lee Kuan Yew raised the controversy again when he stated in an off-the-cuff remark that "the SAF had to be cautious when putting Malay/Muslims in sensitive units because of pulls of race and religion and the geographical realities."[20]

National service has not only contributed substantially to the expansion of Singapore's defense capability; it has had an enormous impact as well on the development of the SAF as a military institution. As an overwhelmingly citizen's army the SAF has had to incorporate a decidedly cosmopolitan culture into an institution that by tradition tends to be rigid and hierarchical. Training procedures, for instance, are constantly reviewed with the aim of adapting to the demands of an armed force that draws its strength from civilians. In the past, military training placed emphasis on traditional preoccupations with spit and polish discipline. In dealing with increasingly educated national servicemen with very different attitudes and motivation, however, today's SAF has had to adopt a "people-oriented management" approach. No longer is professionalism among national servicemen identified with strict adherence to military norms and traditions; today it involves possessing the requisite knowledge in tactics and weaponry to function as soldiers.

At the same time, as a predominantly citizen's army, the SAF has had to grapple with the tension between the political demands of mass mobilization and nation-building and the professional demands of a technically sophisticated force that requires constant training. The problem has essentially been resolved in two ways. First, although reservists constitute the bulk of the army, their proportion in the technically specialized navy and air force is significantly lower. Presently the air force and navy maintain a fifty-fifty ratio of reservists to regulars. Second, the SAF, unlike many traditional armies, makes no assumptions about the length of time it takes to train a soldier. Its entire training system is predicated upon the belief that the national serviceman is a thinking soldier who understands what is needed of him and will respond more readily to a focused and compressed course of training. This belief has created an interesting approach to training and motivation.

Motivation is particularly important as the SAF, and indeed the Singapore government, devote a great deal of effort, through education and communication, to emphasizing the "moral cause"—seeking to underscore the importance of having an effective army and the need for tough military training that demands sacrifice and dedication. This emphasis on a moral cause develops in conscript soldiers an attachment not so much to the armed forces as to the nation. In public advertisements and publicity campaigns, the government accents the role of the citizen-soldier in the defense of his home and country. Such campaigns never refer to the military institution or to regimental colors. Although it may be an exaggeration to say that there is now universal enthusiasm for national service, the population generally accepts the need for all male Singaporeans to perform their military obligation to the state.

Just as a national service army makes certain demands of training norms and procedures, it influences rewards and incentives as well. Based on the recommendations of government committees asked to look into the question of recognition and rewards for those who perform national service, reservists today enjoy benefits that range from tax relief and membership in recreational and golf clubs to medical aid and insurance. One of the SAF's main responsibilities is the forging of partnerships with the community—particularly with employers, who are constantly updated on the contents and requirements of in-camp training. Annual awards are presented to employers who support their employees engaged in national service. All this suggests that the SAF is not simply a professional military establishment but a national institution that is highly integrated with society.

The SAF is an organization with strong civilian roots, and the influences imposed by a citizen's army continue to leave a strong imprint on its norms, value system, and doctrines. With more than 80 percent of its troops part-time national servicemen whose interests and inclinations are not closely linked to the military organization, the SAF has never developed a distinct corporate culture. The military is regarded as an institution in which young Singapore men complete their rites of passage and then perform their duty as citizens by spending a couple of weeks each year sharpening their military skills as reservists. Soldiering in Singapore is regarded as a national duty; rarely is it motivated by regimental pride. Loyalty to the unit is often built upon personal ties and comradeship rather than institutional devotion. When a reserve battalion gathers for its annual training camp, it is usually the promise of camaraderie that motivates the men and militates against the disruption and inconveniences they have to put up with when they attend training. This is perhaps the firmest indication that a military coup will never take place in Singapore. Essentially, the SAF is an army of regular "chiefs" without regular soldiers. There is simply no natural military element in Singapore that might constitute a political base for ambitious generals to exploit. Even among the chiefs, constant rotation of duties and short command postings, usually between three and five years, prevent the entrenchment of a power base.

In fast-moving and economy-driven Singapore, even the professional corps have not been spared the civilizing effect. "Occupationalism" has become so prevalent that a military career is regarded more as an occupational option than a vocational calling. More and more the SAF must resort to monetary incentives and generous scholarships to recruit and retain regular servicemen as compensation for the hardship that is associated with military service. To make a career in the armed forces attractive, the SAF portrays itself as a modern, forward-looking institution in which promotions are based on potential, talent, and ability rather than age and seniority. Moreover, salary scales in the armed services have been made largely commensurate with the private sector. Even so, regular officers tend to opt for short-term contracts rather than pensionable service. Although this need not imply that contract servicemen are less professional, it does indicate short-term commitment, which in turn feeds the perception that a career in the military is no more than a transitory occupation offering a decent income. Indeed, there is a correlation between economic growth and recruitment patterns: military service has been regarded as less attractive during times of economic expansion when jobs are plentiful and wages are high, and vice versa.[21] By the 1990s, in fact, the SAF had listed as one of its major concerns the inability to attract and retain the best men as regulars.[22]

In many ways, this dilution of soldiering as a career is in large measure engendered by MINDEF's insistence that the SAF, to remain a young and vigorous organization, must no longer provide lifelong employment: professional soldiers are expected to leave the force by their forties or early fifties. So long as second career options are available for those who must leave the military so young, the SAF regards early retirement as a positive development for the organization. Since the 1980s, the SAF has advertised the military as a short-term career that offers useful training for other sectors of employment. Increasingly, therefore, soldiering in Singapore is regarded as an occupation, not a professional calling, and this has in turn contributed, inadvertently perhaps, to a weakening of a distinctive military ethos in the SAF.

WHAT NEXT?

Over the past 30 years, the SAF has matured into a much larger, highly developed, and sophisticated institution. The scale of the SAF's growth is reflected in the development of army, navy, and air force, each of which is now a full-fledged armed force in its own right. As a mature military organization, the SAF enjoys a high degree of autonomy in its internal and operational matters and, as expected, provides major inputs into the making of national security policy. Nonetheless, ultimate civilian control in budgetary and structural terms remains absolute. And with the administrative and political elites continuing to enjoy legitimacy and approval from the population at large, the conditions that have contributed to ensuring civilian control continue to shape civil-military relations in Singapore.

Of late, however, observers of the Singapore political scene have noted a greater degree of political involvement—if not intervention as such—on the part of the SAF's officer corps. With a growing number of high-ranking "soldier-scholars" making their way into key positions in the civil service and the cabinet from the 1980s, it has been suggested that the military was set to assume significant influence at the center of the policymaking arena. This, goes the argument, is portentous of a development of a "military mindset" into the government decision-making process, giving rise inevitably to an undue emphasis of defense and security considerations or, worse, undue favor towards the military when formulating public policies (Huxley 1995). Moreover, the increasing number of ex-SAF men called upon to serve in politics and the administrative service might lead, it was feared, to the erosion of strong civilian control in the long run. Indeed, the present cabinet has four former senior military officers—including the deputy prime minister, Brig. Gen. (NS) Lee Hsien Loong, elder son of former prime minister Lee Kuan Yew— holding important portfolios.[23] Several top positions in the various ministries, statutory boards, and government-linked companies are also held by former senior officers of the SAF. This growing presence of former military men in key positions in civilian politics has raised concerns over the SAF's growing political influence. Will the expanding role of SAF officers in the political and administrative apparatus erode civilian control over the armed forces? And, as the conventional wisdom suggests, will the crossover of military men necessarily lead to an imposition of their military paradigm into politics and policy formulation, creating in the country a siege mentality and making it more hawkish and assertive in relations with its neighbors?

Although there is no denying that senior ex-SAF officers—scholars as well as nonscholars—continue to fill key positions in government and other civilian organizations, this phenomenon is not a manifestation of the military's increasing role in civilian life or a symptom of creeping praetorianism. This lateral movement of military men to the civilian sector is merely a manifestation of the close nexus that has always existed between the civil and military leadership of the country—a nexus arising from the convergence of interests among the national elites, both inside and outside the military, in Singapore. This recent development can perhaps be regarded as a reversal of the process that took place during the early years of the SAF, when civil servants had to be put in uniforms to set up the military establishment: this time around, it is a case of military men forgoing their uniform to assist in the management of state and society in Singapore. The movement of ex-military men into the civilian polity, therefore, merely represents the government's effort to create a common pool of national elites who can be deployed interchangeably in all institutional fields.

Desperately aware that the survival of a small and resource-scarce Singapore is ultimately dependent on having the most intelligent people in charge, the government has sought to nurture its future leaders by drawing the best and brightest into the administrative and military services via prestigious scholarships. Potential high-fliers, therefore, are lured by generous scholarships to become state scholars who, once they have completed their studies, usually in top foreign universities, go on to form a national elite by filling key positions in the civil and military sectors of government. Given these circumstances, the government has adopted a policy of moving talent around—allowing the most capable to move to the very top of the state hierarchy, putting, in the words of Lee Kuan Yew, "the best minds in charge of the most crucial problems." In a society that has traditionally regarded a military career as unattractive, the SAF has not been viewed as an institution appealing to the young and the bright. Thus various measures had to be put in place to attract them. Setting a personal example, Lee Kuan Yew had both his sons enlist in the military as full-time professionals. Ever since the government introduced the prestigious SAF scholarship scheme in 1971, the military has been able to establish a near monopoly of the country's top scholars. The SAF scholarship scheme was further supplemented by Project Wrangler, introduced in 1974, through which promising young officers below the rank of lieutenant colonel, scholars as well as nonscholars, were groomed for key staff and command appointments in the SAF in order to preempt a brain drain of talented officers from the military (Chan 1985: 147).

Although scholar-soldiers were given rapid promotions in the SAF, few would expect to retire as an army general. Indeed, by the 1980s many of these SAF scholars, still in their thirties, had already risen to the top of the military hierarchy. There was, therefore, a need to move these men into civil appointments in order to free the bottleneck in the top ranks so that others could move up. Consequently, from the 1980s, several of these scholars, many holding the rank of colonel and brigadier, "retired" from the army to assume new appointments in the public service, statutory boards, and government-linked companies.

The movement of senior SAF officers into the civil service was further facilitated by a dual career scheme introduced by the government in 1981. This scheme, introduced to ensure that there would not be a one-way brain drain from the administrative service into the military, allowed scholar-officers from the SAF to join the administrative service permanently, or to return to the military ranks after a two-year civil service posting.[24] Arising from this scheme, a significant number of serving and ex-SAF officers found their way into the upper echelons of the civil sector.

This trend of moving senior SAF officers into politics, the civil service, and government-linked companies will continue. Not only is it part of the government's pragmatic approach to optimizing the country's talent pool, but it is also an inevitable consequence of the SAF's increasing disinclination to offer lifelong employment. Far from suggesting that this influx of military men into the civilian domain will lead to increasing military dominance, the porous boundary between the civilian and military in Singapore may inadvertently dilute the military professional core and prevent the development of a strong institutional identity within the SAF, certainly lessening the likelihood of a militaristic mindset taking root in Singapore.

Although a military mindset is hardly a danger at the moment, the movement of military men into the higher echelons of politics and the public sector could conceivably lead to a military outlook permeating decision making at that level. Because a former military officer would have spent the formative part of his career functioning in a particular paradigm—with its own subculture, jargon, and values—the military experience is bound to impinge on his worldview and value system. Insofar as this worldview is carried into the civilian milieu by an increasing number of military personnel entering senior political and bureaucratic positions, as well as the growing number of reservists in society, one cannot dismiss the argument that there is some degree of militarization of state and society in Singapore.

The fusion model I have posited here is premised on the continuance of the administrative-political structure put together by the PAP government since the 1960s. Although the political dominance of the PAP appears absolute and unchallenged, the question remains: what would happen to the state and its relations with the military should the PAP suffer an unexpected defeat at the polls? Because civil-military relations in Singapore are not of the revolutionary party type, the nexus between the military and the ruling party is by no means established. Although the military now functions as an integral part of an administrative state dominated by PAP government, the armed forces and the party are neither structurally nor ideologically linked. The SAF is clearly a national armed force whose loyalty is pledged to the nation, not to a political party. In Singapore, unlike Taiwan and Vietnam, party symbols are totally absent in the military, and neither the officer corps nor the rank and file is subjected to any form of party indoctrination. Nowhere in the leadership, organization, and doctrine of the SAF is there evidence that the military and the party are wedded in any way. Indeed, since the 1980s the PAP has never been able to garner more than 65 percent of the popular votes in a general election—a share that would certainly have been much higher if all national servicemen were obliged to vote for the ruling party. Thus in the unlikely event that an alternative party should be elected to power, the SAF's relationship with the government would in all probability remain unaffected if the present political system stays intact. In any case, as a conscript force, the SAF would not find it easy to suddenly take on a political role even if opportunities presented themselves. But should an alternative government unravel the political order in Singapore—and in the process alter the military's role vis-à-vis the state—an entirely different scenario might emerge.

CIVILIANIZATION OR MILITARIZATION?

Most assessments of civil-military relations assume that military organizations, as specialized managers of violence, are inclined to seek a position of autonomy that will enable them to maintain a distinction between civilian and military responsibilities. Civil-military relations, therefore, depend on a shifting balance between the strengths of civilian institutions on the one side and the political power of the military on the other.

The SAF is a well organized and, in many ways, a highly professional force. It is large in proportion to the country's size and population, and it remains distinct from the other branches of the state. Yet it exhibits none of the political ambitions that usually come with large, powerful militaries. Rather than chafing at the tight control to which it has been subjected since 1965, the military elite is quite happy to "merge into the administrative framework of the state" (Khong 1995: 119). This is in large measure due to the unique pattern of civil-military relations in Singapore, in which the SAF has systematically been co-opted and fused into the bureaucracy of the state. The form and content of civil-military relations in Singapore is defined largely by a set of ideological and structural norms laid down by a PAP government that has enjoyed uninterrupted power since 1959. Strict structural controls have been imposed on the military from the start, and the armed forces that evolved in the wake of independence were above all a citizen's army whose instincts and interests were more cosmopolitan than puritan. This has precluded the establishment of a military mindset or a clearly defined set of corporate interests on the part of the men and women in uniform. With a security doctrine that depends as much on diplomacy as deterrence, the role of the SAF is clearly subsumed under a broad strategy predicated upon civilian control. Until the country is faced with the unlikely scenario—in the foreseeable future—of grave political decay, leading to a serious loss of legitimacy for the civil institutions, civil-military relations in Singapore will persist in their present state.

In many ways, tight civilian control and national service have civilianized the military in Singapore. An armed force that is so deeply committed to the overall aims of the government—and consists of more than 80 percent part-timers—has little alternative but to develop doctrines, structures, and systems that acknowledge this reality. But at the same time, after more than 30 years of national service, the military has indeed sunk deep roots into society in Singapore. Perhaps a certain militarization of civilian society has also taken place. At one level, with ex-generals occupying key positions in politics and other government agencies, their military experience may conceivably influence the ways in which problems are perceived and policies formulated. At a more basic level, however, with more than 250,000 reservists in the workforce and some 15,000 more joining it every year, it is perhaps inevitable that these reservists, imbued with such military values as patriotism, discipline, loyalty, organizational sense, and teamwork, will be found at every level of state and society in Singapore.

CHAPTER 12

Sri Lanka: Transformation of Legitimate Violence and Civil-Military Relations

Darini Rajasingham-Senanayake

As for the war machine in itself, it seems to be irreducible to the State apparatus, to be outside its sovereignty and prior to its law: it comes from elsewhere. *Indra* the war god is in opposition to *Varuna* no less than to *Mitra*. He can be no more reduced to one or the other than he can constitute a third of their kind.

—Deleuze and Guattari, *A Thousand Plateaus: Capitalism and Schizophrenia*, 1996

AFTER MORE THAN 50 YEARS OF INDEPENDENCE, Sri Lanka, formerly a model democracy, took stock of an armed conflict that has gained a violent and self-sustaining momentum.[1] For seventeen years after it began in 1983, the conflict between the Sri Lankan government's security forces and the Liberation Tigers of Tamil Eelam (LTTE), fighting for a separate state, seemed to have grown beyond its ethnic origins. As in Bosnia and Somalia where internal conflict became a cause for conducting "politics by other means" (Clausewitz 1984)—and a way to acquire otherwise illegitimate profit, protection, and political power—a variety of members of the defense industry, paramilitary groups, and politicians either used or sustained the armed conflict for personal and political gain.

As succeeding governments pursued a military solution to the LTTE's separatist war without entirely ruling out a political settlement with the Tamil-speaking minorities, the armed conflict appeared to develop its own political economy in the war zones and to become an end in itself. The proliferation of paramilitary groups arising from internal dynamics and splits within the two main protagonists—the state and the LTTE—also contributed to the escalation and self-sustaining nature of the armed violence that defeated various attempts at conflict resolution. Simultaneously, the violence had generated war weariness among most of the civilian population and a powerful human rights lobby that sought to transcend the growing regional, political, and ethnic polarization among the island's political elite and civil society.

Sri Lanka's seventeen-year-old armed conflict has also transformed civil-military relations and the texture of democracy throughout the country. Since 1983, emergency regulations promulgated for "national security" reasons have increasingly eclipsed due process and the rule of law in the north and east of the country. The fighting between the LTTE and armed forces has given rise to a de facto partition and resulted in "ethnic cleansing" of historically multicultural and multiethnic communities in the war zones.[2] In the "border areas" (as the war zones have come to be termed in popular culture and the media), civilian administration and law and order had broken down, and competing authority structures emerged in the form of paramilitary security regimes and a political economy driven by violence. Villages on this unofficial partition line are today called "border villages." The unofficial partition splits the island into two— dividing territory controlled by the Sri Lankan government in the south from the no-man's-land run by the LTTE in the north central Vanni regions, a border that the LTTE has attempted to consolidate by intimidating and destroying ethnically mixed villages and urban centers.[3] Simultaneously, in the south of the country where the LTTE had exploded bombs at primary economic targets (the Central Bank and the Central Oil Storage terminal), all major towns were peppered with military checkpoints where civilians are constantly subject to military scrutiny. In the rest of the country, seventeen years of armed conflict had seen the militarization of civil society because of the security situation, the fear of LTTE attack, and the inability of the ruling elite to agree on a political solution to the conflict.

According to official estimates of conflicts between the armed forces of Sri Lanka, paramilitaries, and insurgents, 60,000 had died, 800,000 had been internally displaced, and 26,935 had been killed extrajudicially, by means euphemistically called "disappearances," as of January 1999.[4] The latter number of unaccounted people—overwhelmingly registered in the south of the country between 1989 and 1991, the years of the second Marxist-Maoist Janatha Vimukthi Youth (JVP) uprising, when the Indian Peace Keeping Forces fought the LTTE in the north—alerts us to the fact that the Sri Lankan military had in the space of seventeen years fought two wars against dissenting, armed, and uncivil segments of society, conflicts to which we shall return because they had a decisive impact on civil-military relations in the island.

This chapter traces the transmutation of Sri Lanka—from a model democracy with social welfare indices that were the envy of the developing world in the 1960s and 1970s and with minuscule defense spending—into a dysfunctional democracy plagued by armed conflict. It explores the transformation of state and civil society conflicts into armed confrontation and paramilitary terror, examining the role of political elites and postcolonial nation building in this process and the expansion of the armed forces to more than 110,000 in less than 50 years. In the final analysis I argue that many of the military's shortcomings in the postcolonial period are attributable to the failures of the island's political elite to nurture truly representative democratic institutions, whether in civil society or the military. Moreover, the perversion of democracy and deep social polarization caused by more than seventeen years of armed confrontation between the armed forces and the LTTE will render a solution more complex than merely developing a new constitution to devolve power to the besieged regions in order to assuage the grievances of the Tamil-speaking minority communities.[5]

The chapter reflects, too, on the changing structure of political violence that characterizes postcolonial democratic practice and civil-military relations on the island. It maps how the military confrontations with the JVP in the south and the LTTE in the north have transformed the structure and culture of a once relatively professional military even as it has polarized identities among multicultural communities. Sri Lanka's northern "ethnic" conflict, as we shall see, has been transformed into a dirty war in the border areas. I use the phrase "dirty war" advisedly to describe the post-1983 phase of conflict in the northern, eastern, and north-central provinces of the island, where Latin American–style violence is endemic. In the war zones, terror, torture, extrajudicial killings, rapes, massacres, summary executions, and stop-and-search operations are conducted to generate a culture of terror and enforce law and order among noncombatant populations by armed groups, including the military. Moreover, the violence has spawned a culture of terror (as in some Latin American countries such as Guatemala and El Salvador), and its own structures including hidden economies of terror and taxation.

Because the postcolonial state in Sri Lanka has ceded its monopoly on legitimate violence in the war zones, conventional liberal "state-centric" frames that privilege analysis of command and control structures and jurisdictional boundaries are of little use to explain the intractability of the conflict or the transformation of civil-military relations on the island. Rather, my analysis draws from recent attempts to understand modern wars through analysis of the economic functions of violence (Keen 1998; Kaldor 1999), and the symbolic logic of state institutions and their violence (Foucault 1977; Deleuze and Guattari 1987). Studies of internal wars, such as Keen's and Kaldor's, have critiqued primordial "ethnic" explanations of internal low-scale armed conflicts in Africa, Latin America, and the Balkans and highlighted their political-economic and global dimensions, including the protection rackets that they generate for armed groups, warlords, and politicians. These studies, however, tend to take a primarily instrumentalist approach to modern armed violence and gloss its cultural and social impacts on "civil society," though they might assess humanitarian interventions and structures. While drawing from the political economic approach to armed conflicts, this chapter also attempts to elaborate the symbolic structures and cultures of terror that the long, drawn-out armed conflict has developed in Sri Lanka. It also explores the challenge that the normalization, routinization, and institutionalization of armed violence poses to civil society and democratic practice. I use Deleuze and Guattari's notion of the "war machine" to describe the "rizomatic" (1987: 1–25), or multiple and proliferating, structures that normalize armed conflict in Sri Lanka.[6] For the conflict is increasingly sustained by the continuous mirroring, splitting, and blurring of the agents, causes, and effects of violence, even as the consequences of conflict become its further causes (e.g., population displacement and the building of ethnic enclaves, military reliance on paramilitary groups). The circular process of conflict generating conflict is most evident in the border regions of the country where Latin American–style dirty war violence is endemic, and it takes the form of competing and overlapping (para)military regimes that collectively constitute a violent "security" structure wherein fear generates its own culture and ontology. The notion of the "war machine" captures both the breakdown of systems of meaning that is caused by prolonged exposure to high levels of violence and terror, and the gradual institutionalization of the structure and culture of violence. The processes whereby extreme forms of physical and symbolic violence come to be a naturalized part of everyday life is an aspect of the new and self-sustaining culture and institution of conflict.

In this essay I use the term "border areas" in a double sense: to signify a center-periphery relationship between Colombo and the northern and eastern areas of the island where the war is fought, and as a metaphor or heuristic device to think through the impact of almost two

decades of armed conflict at the borders of the state on its core institutions and practice. My
analysis then derives largely from ethnographic research in the northern and eastern war zones.
Fieldwork was conducted in the northern, eastern, and north-central provinces of the island—
in the areas that stretch across the island from Puttalam in the northwestern province on the
west coast via Vavuniya, to Batticaloa on the east coast—during various stints over a number
of years (1994–1998). These historically multiethnic and culturally hybrid areas of the island
have experienced cycles of war and peace, violent armed conflict including repeated bombing
and shelling of civilian populations by the armed forces, population displacement resulting
from ethnic cleansing by the LTTE and generalized violence, and terror from other paramilitary groups.[7] Hence I rethink civil-military relations at the center through analysis of armed
conflict at the borders of the state—an exercise warranted by the fact that the armed conflict
threatens to undermine the democratic foundations of the island's postcolonial nation-state.

FROM RIOT TO POGROM:
TRANSFORMATION OF LEGITIMATE VIOLENCE

Since the pogrom of 1983, democracy in Sri Lanka has withered as this island of hybrid histories and multicultural communities, which steered a strict course of nonalignment during the
cold war, has been transformed into the stage of one of the world's bloodiest armed conflicts.
Indeed, Sri Lanka has become a spectacularly volatile backwater island that has been outstripped economically by most of its larger Southeast Asian neighbors such as Malaysia and
Thailand. The commonly agreed turning-point in the island's recent history, at least in the liberal imagination, is July 1983. At this time a pogrom in the capital city followed by widespread
"riots" in other major cities consolidated the ethnic enactment of public order and disorder
and transfixed the Sinhala and Tamil communities and diaspora.[8] During the pogrom of 1983,
many lives were lost and homes and businesses burned; the histories and identities of the island's
dominant ethnoreligious communities have been ruptured ever since. Before July 1983, sporadic public disturbances—the religious and ethnic riots of 1915, 1958, and 1977, for example,
and the leftist youth insurrection of 1971—had appeared to be aberrations or spasms in a scenario of overall democratic advance.

There was common agreement among the intelligentsia that segments of the ruling United
National Party (UNP) government were implicated in the violent events of 1983. Minister Cyril
Mathew, well known for his anti-minority rhetoric, was commonly rumored to have been one
of the key figures in the proceedings. Describing the aftereffects of the violence, anthropolo-
gist Serena Tennakoon stated, "The image of Sri Lanka as a tolerant and peaceful society whose
culture is nourished by a 2500-year old Buddhist heritage was rudely shattered when the range
and intensity of violence against Tamils were exposed in the international and, later, local
media" (1988: 295). Flight from Sri Lanka and escalation of the armed struggle in the north
marked the minority response to the pogrom. After the pogrom of July 1983, tensions between
the Sinhala-speaking communities, who constitute approximately 74 percent of the island's
population, and the dominant Tamil minority, which constitutes 18 percent, turned into armed
confrontation.[9] The confrontation took the form of violent conflict between a Sri Lankan state
increasingly dominated by Sinhala chauvinists and the equally chauvinistic Tamil secessionist
LTTE.

The roots of confrontation between the LTTE and the state's military apparatus had been set in the previous three decades, which saw the rise of Sinhala and Tamil nationalisms fueled by a political elite intent on building ethnolinguistic vote banks within a centralized state system. The cost of playing ethnolinguistic politics was the destruction of the island's long history and traditions of multiculturalism, hybridity, and ethnoreligious coexistence. Sinhala-language nationalism was largely a project promoted by the political elite. In its first phase it was aimed at erasing the dominance that the minority Eurasian Burger and Tamil communities had enjoyed during British colonial rule. The high-water mark of this phase of postcolonial nationalism was the Sinhala Only measure of 1956, an act declaring that the Sinhala language spoken by the majority of the island's inhabitants was the only national language—displacing English and simultaneously marginalizing the Tamil-speaking minorities in the north and east of the country.

After the Official Language Act No. 33 in 1956, tensions between an increasingly Sinhala-dominated state and the Sri Lankan Tamil political elites escalated. But it was the pogrom of 1983 that consolidated a common Tamil sense of grievance and identity. It was this event that fueled support for the northern-Jaffna-based LTTE's call for armed struggle and creation of a homeland safe for Tamil people. Since then the conflict has spiraled, displacing between 500,000 and 1 million of the country's 18 million inhabitants and wrecking the story of Sri Lanka's enlightened multiculturalism and democratic advance.[10] As I have argued elsewhere (Rajasingham-Senanayake 1999), in its place has emerged a bipolar ethnic imagination in which Sinhala Buddhists and Ceylon Tamils appear to be perennially locked in combat.[11] In the south and in the capital, Colombo, the crisis signaled by the pogrom and flight is now the tenor of everyday life. This fact dawned slowly and painfully on the country's liberal intelligentsia in the 1980s.

The violent events of July 1983 signified a change in civil-military relations—less because of its unprecedented spread and more because it was a pogrom that fueled other riots in which some segments of society made use of the situation to settle private grievances or enrich themselves. Not only did the police fail to take action against the mob to restore law and order, they appeared to be complicit with anti-Tamil segments of the state. It was common knowledge that rioters and mobs used government electoral lists to identify the houses to be attacked. The organized nature of the attacks during July 1983 was subsequently confirmed by the then inspector general of police. The government's complicity in the violent events also explains why no subsequent commission of inquiry ever took place, unlike on previous occasions such as the riots of 1915, 1958, and 1977. Clearly the government was ceding its monopoly in legitimate violence.

Since 1983 the "ethnic" conflict has evolved into an armed conflict that has gained its own momentum. Increasingly brutal violence by armed groups is enacted under the sign of ethnicity, with little regard for civilian communities. This evolution is indexed in the emergence of new and sinister forms of armed violence such as torture, rape, and massacre whereby organized violence between trained armies of the Sri Lankan government, the LTTE, and other paramilitary groups has eclipsed the civilian riot. The evolving and increasingly autonomous conflict is indexed, too, by the emergent political economy sustained by violence in the border areas. Ethnically motivated civilian riots have been rare and local, and often instigated by local police or military personnel. Otherwise, riots have more often than not been the result of local feuding between the two dominant Sinhala political parties during local and national elections. Feuds between Tamil political parties have been settled by assassinations.

Yet analyses by social scientists—principally political scientists and anthropologists—of the unmaking of the Sri Lankan nation-state have focused on riots as a symptom of the conflict and ethnicity as its cause. Most studies have identified malaise in civil society, which is to say ethnic malaise, as the cause of the conflict. What the ethnic explanations overlook is the fundamentally modern (rather than ancient or primordial) nature of the Sri Lankan armed conflict and the problematic practice of reducing complex modern armed conflicts to "ethnic" explanations and solutions. Moreover, the ethnic explanation elides the changing nature and structure of long-term armed conflicts and the fuzzy distinction between state violence and civil violence. The ethnic explanation tells us little about the changing structures of violence and actors in the conflict in Sri Lanka, where civil conflict has been overtaken by military (and paramilitary) violence. Finally, ethnic explanations have obscured the role of the state and its coercive apparatus in the making of conflict in Sri Lanka, as does the dominant liberal political discourse that views the state as the legitimate wielder of violence.

On the other hand, accounts of civil-military relations have been, by and large, selective and partisan. A systematic analysis of the changing forms of public and political violence—from riots to pogroms against minorities to clandestine violence such as disappearances, torture, rape, massacres of entire villages in remote areas by military and paramilitary personnel indulging in acts classified by the United Nations as "human rights violations"—remains to be written. It has been left to an increasingly vocal human rights lobby, developed in response to state-sponsored terror in the 1980s and 1990s, to document military, LTTE, and other paramilitary violence.

Significantly, although civilian riots have been absent since 1983, the ethnic malaise seems to have been transmuted to the police and armed forces. That is to say, the state apparatus's monopoly on legitimate violence has been transformed into illegitimate and clandestine forms of violence even as the state has ceded its monopoly on violence to various paramilitary groups under the sign of ethnicity. The roots of this transformation lie in civilian political interference in the armed forces and their ethnicization and politicization after independence.

DECOLONIALIZING AND NATIONALIZING MILITARY CULTURE

Several analysts of civil-military relations in Sri Lanka have argued that the lack of a martial tradition accounts for the failure of the state's law and order enforcement machinery to curtail the LTTE threat to national security (Muttukumaru 1987). After all, at independence the Ceylon Defense Force (CDF) lacked the rich tradition of the Indian Army. It had fought no great battles and had accumulated few regimental honors. Nor had the CDF participated in an independence struggle, unlike its Indian counterpart, which had engaged in mutiny against the British Raj at various times. The fact that domestic politics after the crushing of the Kandian revolt against the British in 1848 was relatively nonconfrontational vis-à-vis British rule also meant that the armed forces were not called upon to perform any major feats either in defense of the colonial state or against it. All of this, it is claimed, accounts for the fact that the CDF consisted mainly of volunteers when the professional British component withdrew at independence in 1948.

Much of this is correct, for at independence, when the constitution of Sri Lanka provided for the prime minister to hold the portfolio of defense and external affairs, the army was essentially apolitical and ready to carry out the orders of the government of the day. Moreover it had no great role to perform with regard to external affairs. For the new Ceylonese government had entered into a defense agreement with the British government under which the British retained control of the naval base at Trincomalee and the air base at Katunayake. The ruling elite figured that in the event of an external security threat, the British could come to the island's assistance under the treaty. Hence the need for a military buildup did not arise. During the early postcolonial period, the role of the armed forces, which consisted mainly of ceremonial units, was restricted to helping civilian authority contain disruptive forces if required.

Other analysts have argued that it was the postcolonial politicization of the military that eroded its objectivity (De Silva 1997; Horowitz 1980; Gunasinghe 1989). De Silva, in a selective history of civil-military relations on the island, has suggested that the politicization of the armed forces by successive Sri Lanka Freedom Party (SLFP) governments accounts for partisan elements creeping into the military. What De Silva leaves out is the manner in which the United National Party (UNP) also politicized the forces. During the colonial and early postcolonial phase, the army had maintained a relatively professional performance vis-à-vis internal schisms, even though the Sri Lankan military had a short history and tradition and had not been called upon to deal with any grave external threats or internal dissent. The takeover of the British bases at Trincomalee and Katunayake in 1957 was the first step in the decolonialization and nationalization of the defense establishment. It also implied a limited expansion of the air force and navy.

The politicization and ethnicization of the armed forces that occurred after the takeover of the British bases in 1957, the abortive coup of 1962, and the Marxist-Maoist insurrection of 1971 eroded its professional character. Up to independence in 1948 the defense establishment had not reflected social schisms, nor did it reflect the island's ethnoreligious composition. At independence the officer cadre was dominated by Burgers (descendants of Europeans) and Tamils—both minorities—a pattern that conformed to the colonial policy of "divide et impera." Additionally, the colonial state had monopolized legitimate violence at the prerogative of British rule, and the defense portfolio had been reserved for British control, whereas military organization was designed to meet the regional needs of empire. In the postcolonial period, succeeding governments found it necessary to modernize and expand the armed forces particularly after the 1977 JVP youth uprising in the south. In the process the military was politicized and ethnicized, contributing to the erosion of objectivity.

Previously, officers had come from the highly westernized, hybrid, and English-educated urban elite; with the switch to "swabasha" ("native language") education, however, students from small rural propertied families began to enter the university and subsequently the officer corps. As the composition of the armed forces changed rapidly, the social gap between officer and soldier eroded. The rapid expansion of the military in the postcolonial period meant less hierarchy, less order, and less discipline, as well as the increased ability of civilian political elites to interfere in the recruitment and operation of the armed forces. Because the expansion of the military coincided with an increasingly nationalist orientation, the social composition, context, and organization of the Sri Lankan armed forces turned it into a Sinhala army committed to Sinhala Buddhism. This orientation was reflected in the culture of the military, which began using the new official language after 1956 while mobilizing the symbolism of the Sinhala majority. The creation of the prominent Lion Regiment and the naming of other regiments after Sinhala kings (such as the Gajaba Regiment) marked the increased Sinhala Buddhist orientation of the military. As Newton Gunasinghe has remarked, "This nationalist orientation within the context of Sinhala dominance could not but acquire a chauvinistic tinge" (1989: 245). Thus when the army was called upon to fight the Tamil youth militancy—spearheaded by lower-caste (Kariyar) Tamil youth who felt as disenfranchised from the Sinhala-dominated state as from the upper-caste Tamil political elites who claimed to represent them—the army perceived the war not as a conflict between the government and insurgents but as a clash between Sinhalas and Tamils.

The ethnicization of the military can also be traced to the political elite's efforts to redress imbalances cultivated by the British and to decolonialize military culture. The process of decolonializing military traditions turned into an exercise of politicizing the armed forces, however, which eroded their objectivity as Sinhala nationalism came to dominate the state and its coercive apparatus, effectively marginalizing the minorities. But the ethnicization of the armed forces and police was merely one aspect of the general politicization of state institutions as a result of party political interference, partly to restore imbalances left by the departing colonial power. Ironically the reasons for the erosion of the military's objectivity, as well as its ethnicization and politicization, lie in the strength of civilian leadership and the ease with which leaders of the UNP and SLFP interfered in military affairs (e.g., with appointments and promotions). Thus the process of decolonializing military culture, which coincided with the rise of majoritarian nationalism fueled by political elites during the postcolonial period, was to erode the military's impartiality.

Political interference in the police and military establishments did not, however, go uncontested by the officer cadre. As Horowitz (1980) detailed in his account of the 1962 abortive coup, political interference in the military was one of the main reasons that officers decided to halt what they perceived as a deteriorating law and order situation brought about by the incompetence of the civil leadership. At this time the perception of ethnic discrimination was a minor reason for the attempted coup. Rather, Horowitz has argued that officers were less motivated by personal ambition than by the perception that the civilian leaders were increasingly incompetent and interfering with military affairs. Subsequent events, such as the involvement of segments of the armed forces in the ethnic riots of 1983, seem to confirm the early misgivings of the officers who participated in the 1962 coup.

Though the abortive coup by the military establishment in cohort with some civil servants had very little to do with their ethnic or religious convictions, successive governments tacitly promoted Sinhala dominance within the armed forces. Frequently, promotions of minority officers were denied or delayed. As Newton Gunasinghe has noted, the examples of Gen. Anton Muttukumaru and Cmdr. Rajan Kadirigamar, Tamil officers who headed the army and navy respectively, were not to be repeated. Nor has there been a Tamil inspector general of police since Rudra Rajasingham—who, despite being the most senior eligible officer, was bypassed once before being appointed as head of the police force. Although Rajasingham, who was inspector general of police during the pogrom of 1983, appointed minorities in the armed forces during his term, this presence was eroded after 1983, when many Tamil officers resigned.

Thus, ironically, it was in the postcolonial period—when the police and military services increasingly began to reflect the country's social composition—that the military also came to reflect schisms among the political elite. Beginning with the anti-Tamil riots of 1977, in which

sporadic police neglect and complicity were established by the report of the Sansoni Commission of Inquiry, the succeeding seventeen years of UNP rule saw the transformation of
police and military culture that was to culminate in the country's first pogrom in July 1983. With
the introduction of the UNP constitution in 1978 and the Prevention of Terrorism Act of 1982,
the electoral process had itself been changed: a highly centralized and repressive state structure was being built to counter growing opposition to the regime by educated and unemployed
youth, both Sinhala youth in the south and Tamil youth in the north. Freedom of the press, an
independent judiciary, nonpartisan bureaucracy, and the objectivity of the military establishment were the victims of this process. The politicization and ethnicization of the armed forces,
which occurred during the consolidation of the postcolonial nation-state, and the insurrec-
tionary movements against this process set the stage for the military's slide into partisan politics. The politicization of the police and armed forces, moreover, had implications for the manner in which the JVP insurrections in 1971 and in the late 1980s were dealt with by the military
and their civilian leadership.

THE JVP INSURRECTION
AND THE BEGINNING OF DIRTY WAR TACTICS

The JVP Marxist-Maoist youth insurrection of 1971 was a turning point in the history of the
Sri Lankan armed forces: It was the first time that a Ceylonese (the island was then Ceylon)
soldier felt confident to shoot at a civilian or a suspected insurgent. It was also the first time that
army officers functioned as coordinators of civilian administration, a pattern now well established in the northern war zones. The JVP, or People's Liberation Front, was a group composed
largely of university and school-going urban youth from the dominant Sinhala community from
the south of Sri Lanka, a relatively underdeveloped region of the island. The JVP insurrection
in its first phase shared many parallels with the first phase of the northern Tamil youth insurrection of the LTTE, which it subsequently emulated in the second phase of militancy. After
the JVP's inaugural meeting in May 1965, it grew to prominence in the late 1960s with a revolutionary agenda inspired by Maoism to create a new socialist state and new social order. Starting in April 1971 the first attacks were on police stations until the group was defeated by the
SLFP-led United Front government armed forces by June of that year. During the second phase,
from 1987 to 1989, the JVP took on the UNP government in brutal fashion—this time on a Sinhala nationalist agenda opposed to the Indian-brokered settlement to the conflict in the north,
a settlement that resulted in the Thirteenth Amendment to the Sri Lankan constitution, establishing provincial councils for regional government, and brought the Indian Peacekeeping Forces
(IPKF) to the north of Sri Lanka.

The first phase of the JVP insurrection in the early 1970s exposed the dependence of the
Sri Lankan state on foreign countries for its survival. During that period the port of Colombo
and the airport were guarded by Indian troops, Russia donated some MiG jet planes, and China
donated some light arms. The second phase of the JVP insurrection in the late 1980s and early
1990s—when the group on several occasions brought the capital city to a standstill through terror campaigns—was met with severe counterterrorist measures. The uprising was brutally suppressed by the military, on the instructions of ruling politicians headed by President Rana-
singhe Premadasa, in the absence of foreign assistance. During this second phase of insurrection,

intelligence cells were cultivated within the police to deal with the JVP terrorists. The disappearance of suspected JVP sympathizers as well as human rights workers became commonplace. Segments of the military establishment were involved in illegitimate forms of violence and torture house operations—as the discovery and subsequent inquiry into the mass graves in Suriyakanda in the south indicate. Of course the JVP was itself engaged in killings, disappearances, and murder of government officials, sympathizers, and their family members. The cultivation of intelligence units within the police and military, which carried out terror and torture operations conducted by the special counterterrorist units, was sanctioned by segments of the ruling UNP government. This practice further entrenched party political interference in the armed forces—this time in clandestine and dirty war operations as well as intelligence.

The systematic and institutional nature of politically motivated extrajudicial killings by the military, as well as the extent of party political interference in the police and armed forces, was subsequently highlighted in the final report of the Commission of Inquiry into Involuntary Removal or Disappearances of Persons in the Western, Southern, and Sabaragamuwa Provinces (1997).

> The public perception was that the conspicuous spectacle of impunity could not have existed without the complicity of the political leadership. The various allegations before us of the close participation of the local politicians in the exercise, the various allegations of informers who functioned as the channel of misinformation from the politicians to the Security Forces, the allegations of lists of names of political enemies being supplied to the Security Forces for elimination are all based on this perception.... This perception of the petitioners has found confirmation in the evidence of two Senior officials of that time, one of the Police and the other of the Army, who have given evidence under oath on the role played by politicians of the governing party in the counter-subversion exercise, the practice of the preparation of "lists" by them, and the issue by them of illegal orders, for execution by the Police and Army respectively.

The report of the Commission (p. 55) went on to note the following:

> A feature that struck us most forcefully in our inquiries was the utmost care that had been taken not only by individual perpetrators but also by the system itself to prevent these occurrences being reflected in the official records of the country. Starting with the refusal of the police to record complaints—which was a general feature in all three provinces—through the blatant use of vehicles without number plates, right up to the refusal to allow the bereaved to take possession of corpses identified by them, let alone obtaining death certificates, there is clear evidence of a systematic attempt to keep these death/disappearances from being recorded in the official annals.... They exemplify a generalised practice which in turn warrants the reasonable inference that this practice denotes a generalised direction not to investigate such incidents.

The process of political interference that led to the transmutation of the police and military's legitimate role became systematic during the 1989–1990 JVP uprising. Succeeding promulgations, of which the most pernicious is Emergency Regulation 55 (ER 55), which permits burial without inquest, institutionalized a culture of brutality and immunity in certain parts of the military engaged in counterterrorist operations. ER 55 applied to war-torn situations when conduct of a formal inquest was not feasible, and a police officer of the rank of an assistant superintendent of police could issue a certificate for the disposal of the body and report the matter to the High Court of Colombo for further inquiry. However, the security forces did not seem restrained by the nuances in the application and invoked its operation in other areas too. The dirty war violence of the antiterrorist campaign against the JVP in turn left a legacy in the northern theater of operations. Several military personnel who were involved in counterinsurgency operations against the JVP were subsequently posted to the northern LTTE theater. More mass graves have been recently exposed at Chemmani and the Duraiyappa Stadium in Jaffna—revealed by an army soldier convicted after a civil trial for the gang rape and murder of a fifteen-year-old schoolgirl and other members of her family in 1998 following an international campaign by human rights groups.

A culture of impunity—propagated, enabled, and fostered by political interference in the police and armed forces—has since been evident in the military operations in the north where noncombatants have often born the brunt of LTTE attacks on the armed forces. The legacies of dirty war violence practiced in the JVP insurrection also resonate in the way party political interference hindered the police and armed forces from carrying out their duties impartially in local government elections in the southwest of the country in January 1999. Election monitors have reported that the police and armed forces stood by unwilling to intervene in the violence. Much of the violence was enacted by thugs who doubled as election organizers for the governing People's Alliance Party (PA) and to a lesser extent the UNP opposition.

From the long view of postcolonial politics, then, it is arguable that the 1983 pogrom in Colombo and the anti-JVP campaign of the late 1980s and early 1990s marked the emergence of a new pattern of civil-military relations, that is, the blurring of civil and military violence on the island. The forms of violence practiced in the second phase of JVP insurrection during the late 1980s had much in common with the confrontation with the LTTE. Both confrontations took the form of dirty war violence. But whereas the LTTE conflict resulted in the development of a war machine, the JVP conflict was brutally crushed in the absence of international support for a class struggle and with the indirect assistance of the IPKF, which had been invited to consolidate an Indian-brokered peace accord between the Sri Lankan government and the LTTE. The presence of the IPKF in the north enabled the military to concentrate on antiterrorist operations against the JVP in the south. Both the JVP and LTTE conflicts fundamentally altered the size and role of the armed forces and civil-military relations in Sri Lanka. Taken together these two violent encounters between the military and armed youth from the majority Sinhala and minority Tamil communities configured the direction and development of the Sri Lankan war machine in the northern LTTE sphere of operations.

DIRTY WAR IN THE NORTH: PROLIFERATION
OF PARAMILITARY ORGANIZATIONS

As the armed conflict between the LTTE and the military escalated in the north and east after July 1983, a number of Tamil paramilitary groups began to proliferate, further blurring the boundaries between civil and military violence. Alongside the LTTE's and the government's military regimes of passes and checkpoints exist the subregimes of other armed groups: the Eelam People's Revolutionary Front (east coast), the People's Liberation Organization of Tamil Eelam (PLOTE, Vanni), the Eelam People's Democratic Party (Jaffna), the Rafik Group, and the Tamil Eelam Liberation Organization. All these groups, comprising mainly youth and teenagers, carry guns. Some of them are bankrolled by the Sri Lankan government and collaborate with the army to fight the LTTE, thus blurring and splitting the ethnic lines of the conflict. Frequently their local law and order functions spill into disorder, torture, and illegal taxation of local populations. Since the late 1980s the LTTE has sought to eliminate other Tamil armed groups that initially worked with it. A well-known case involved the killing of Uma Maheswaran, the leader of PLOTE. The paramilitary cadre remains outside the authority and discipline structure of the armed forces, which are marginally better trained and better aware of human rights and humanitarian law—the laws of war pertaining to the protection of civilian life and property. At the national level, their leaders have joined the Sinhala political elite and are installed as members of parliament, again blurring the ethnic factor. Today they support the ruling PA government headed by President Chandrika Bandaranaiake-Kumaratunge.

Paramilitary groups have developed various systems of taxing traders and civilians through control of the main transport routes (and the movement of persons and goods) and through an economy of terror, scarcity, and fear. They have benefited from the uncertain security in the border areas and found new ways to fund themselves. In Vavuniya, the largest town in the border zones, PLOTE has a monopoly on the fish and coconut industry through its control of transport into the town. Fish traders returning from the coast must pass paramilitary checkpoints where they are heavily taxed in cash or kind. The LTTE pioneered the system of terror and taxation on the movement of people and goods. Since then the army, too, has resorted to curtailing the freedom of movement and goods, more often than not in the name of security and military operations. Often, when the army issues passes and identification papers, there is a degree of corruption. Residents of high-security areas frequently complain of being asked to pay money to army personnel before they are issued identification papers and passes to cross the border. Additionally, a number of poorly trained and armed Home Guard units have been set up in the border areas by the army and the Special Task Force. As the Sri Lankan government attempts to clean up the image of the armed forces, largely as a result of international pressure from human rights groups, they depend on Tamil paramilitary groups that have gained greater visibility and power to conduct and run protection rackets and a clandestine economy.

Civilians become tools in such a scenario, and the displacement or confinement of people in camps constitutes a profitable exercise for armed groups. Displaced and nondisplaced civilians in the border zones have learned to live amidst overlapping regimes of terrifying security and punitive taxation perpetuated by the paramilitaries. For those in the conflict regions, the right to set up residence in an area of one's choice and the right to move is seriously restricted by the LTTE and the government's security regimes. Whereas the Sri Lankan Army restricts the movement of Tamils displaced southward, the LTTE prevents Sinhalas from moving or settling in the north. In fact, both the LTTE and the Sri Lankan government have used displaced persons as shields or buffers during military campaigns. Police and army personnel in the north and the border areas have been increasingly involved in protection rackets and profiteering from the ban on the movement of goods and persons from south to north and vice versa.

The authority that paramilitary armed youth and Home Guard members have gained though wielding guns has begun to resonate in their communities. Incidents of paramilitary cadres and military deserters using their weapons to commit crimes or settle personal vendettas have risen dramatically. The same is true of a large number of military deserters in the south. Incidents of checkpoint rape, as well as restrictions on mobility and the pass system, par-

ticularly affect young women who are body-searched. In this context, militant groups who infiltrate camps have little difficulty recruiting new cadres from deeply frustrated and resentful
youth: men and women, girls and boys. At the same time recruitment to the military and paramilitaries has spiraled up. The LTTE in a desperate bid for reinforcements now boasts a "baby
brigade" of child soldiers. Increasingly, those who wield guns in the armed conflict tend to be
very young, teenagers and children, some of whom have been involuntarily inducted into the
conflict. Youngsters with guns, of course, have little knowledge of humanitarian law.

A precedent for the pattern of paramilitary groups carrying out dirty war operations in
coordination with the Sri Lankan military was set by the IPKF and Indian intelligence, otherwise known as the Research and Analysis Wing, when the IPKF controlled the border zones in
Sri Lanka from 1987 to 1990 after the signing of a "peace accord" between the Indian and Sri
Lankan governments. Subsequently, in the early 1990s the Sri Lankan president Premadasa,
who was opposed to the presence of Indian forces in the country, provided clandestine funds
and arms to the LTTE to fight the IPKF, thus again blurring the lines between the military and
paramilitary groups. The armed forces (and indirectly some of the paramilitary groups) have
benefited at different times and places from training in violence under various foreign experts
including the IPKF and military experts from Israel and the United States. Human rights violations have been conducted by all the groups—a fact that alerts us to the exogenous and global
dimensions of the armed conflict.

By the mid-1990s there were various informal agreements between the local military commanders and paramilitary groups operating in the border areas for mutual protection against
the LTTE. It is not uncommon to see paramilitaries and army or Special Task Force personnel manning checkpoints together to detect LTTE infiltrators in the border areas. Indeed, the
other paramilitary cadres often know and can identify LTTE members. Such informal agreements mean that the paramilitary has a freer reign than do government forces to terrorize people, torture them, and extort money at gunpoint. Armed groups (including state military personnel), as we have seen, have gained increasing control over civilian life and the movement of
persons and goods by controlling major transport routes and creating new security structures
and protection rackets. These new structures of the border political economy constitute an
obstacle to peace, for the militants have every reason to prolong the conflict in order to profit
from their activities.

Cumulatively, it is evident that because the armed conflict escalated in 1983, segments of
the state's military apparatus have been involved in illegitimate forms of violence—even as the
state has ceded its monopoly on violence to a number of paramilitary groups. At the same time,
the distinction between civilian and military, between unarmed and combatant, has become
increasingly blurred in the context of widespread militarization of civil society stemming from
the large numbers of deserters from the armed forces, the proliferation of paramilitaries, and
generalized violence. The deputy minister of defense has provided the most recent official estimates of deserters: in August 1994 there were 28,000 deserters. Seven amnesties were offered
to the deserters from June 1, 1995, to February 25, 1998. During this period 22,825 returned.
Some of them deserted the army again, however, and on May 5, 1998, there were 15,000 deserters. Of this number, 13,051 had returned as of May 24, 1998. The cycles of recruitment and
desertion spiral upward.[12]

THE WAR MACHINE:
TRANSFORMATION OF LEGITIMATE VIOLENCE

The emergence of the modern war machine, which reconstitutes the state's monopoly on legitimate violence, forces us to rethink Max Weber's classic reading of the modern nation-state and its coercive apparatus. Weber's formulation tells us little about how the state actually legitimized its monopoly of force through the deployment of particular forms of violence, thus making violence a routine and natural part of its operations and some forms of violence more legitimate than others. In his deconstructive history of the relationship between government and violence, in *Discipline and Punish* (1977), Michel Foucault traces how modern forms of governmentality constitute regimes of power imposed on the consciousness of citizens as well as new regimes of legitimate violence. In Foucault's reading, corporeal forms of punishment increasingly are delegitimized in the operation of the modern state vis-à-vis its citizenry. Thus the seditionist (against the modern state rather than the medieval king) is no longer rewarded with the triple punishment of being hung, drawn, and quartered in exemplary fashion. Rather, in modern times the legal-bureaucratic nature of the state requires procedures of "due process." More often than not the seditionist ends up dead in battle or in the privacy of a prison cell, rather than at the public guillotine. This, then, is the legitimate violence of the modern liberal nation-state against dissenting subjects and citizens. A number of UN conventions specify illegitimate violence: torture, cruel and inhumane treatment, and extrajudicial killings.

Yet modern states have repeatedly demonstrated a tendency to stray from the use of what has been determined by the international consensus as legitimate violence in order to maintain acquiescence among its populations or against enemy states. Postcolonial Sri Lanka in the war years (since 1983) is one such case in which the government strayed in order to control civil unrest by increasingly violent segments of society. The result has been the dirty war, spiraling in force—with state violence mirroring terrorist violence—leading up to the dirty war in the border areas. The forms of violence practiced by the state apparatus as well as by armed segments of civil society turned paramilitaries have blurred the boundaries between legitimate and illegitimate forms of violence and conflated the difference between state violence and civil violence. This blurring of the forms and agents of violence evident in many internal armed conflicts today is encapsulated in Deleuze and Guattari's reading of the war machine—which once set in motion is irreducible to the state, beyond its sovereignty, and prior to its law (1987: 352).

Carolyn Nordstrom, one of the few social scientists who has studied the Sri Lankan armed conflict from the perspective of the border, characterized the conflict as a "dirty war." I am largely in agreement with Nordstrom, because the forms of violence practiced in the border areas were commonly used in Latin American contexts where the concept was developed. In El Salvador and Guatemala, the notion of the dirty war described the practice of illegitimate violence by the state against its own populations. These wars were characterized by the use of torture, disappearances, and rape to intimidate and eliminate civilians suspected of sympathizing with the militant groups. Yet unlike in Latin American countries, where state violence was unleashed against poorly organized peasants, in Sri Lanka the militants (due to the LTTE's global operations) have frequently matched the state's firepower and violence. Moreover, in the

Sri Lankan conflict noncombatant populations in the border areas have been targeted in order to control the nation's political process through the construction of a culture of terror.

Clearly the conflict since 1983 has been transformed into a dirty war that blurs ethnic lines and "original causes." Increasingly the conflict in the border areas is being waged between various armed groups trained in dirty war tactics across the Sinhala-Tamil ethnic divides, because many of the Tamil paramilitary work with the armed forces to combat the Tamil nationalist LTTE. Civilian violence along ethnic lines is practically nonexistent. The transformation of political violence from riots to torture and extrajudicial killings and massacres by the military forces and paramilitaries alike in the border areas marks the evolution of the conflict and the development of a dirty war machine supported by a hidden economy. This transformation of the Sri Lankan conflict is indexed also by the proliferation of paramilitaries who have blurred the lines between civilian and military groups and the forms of civil and military violence. This blurring of the forms of violence was first evident in the pogrom and riots of 1983 when factions of the police stood by and watched the violence.

The problem with Nordstrom's analysis is that it makes no attempt to place Sri Lanka's regional dirty war in the wider political landscape. By failing to distinguish between the center and the border zones, it oversimplifies the complexities and regional differences in the Sri Lankan conflict. Nordstrom's analysis, which also draws from African conflicts, dovetails with the analyses of political scientists who emphasize that armed conflicts generate a culture and economy that benefits the armed players—whether these players are the military industry and elite or local warlords (Stanley 1996; Reno 1998). But many of these analyses take a purely instrumentalist approach to the violence and focus on the benefits that the war brings to the military establishments, warlords, or political elites. That armed conflicts benefit the military industry and arms dealers, local and foreign, is well known in Sri Lanka. What is less clearly understood is how these modern internal conflicts between state armies and paramilitaries might generate their own self-perpetuating political-economic structures and culture. Owing to censorship regarding the security forces, it is impossible to present figures about the huge profits accruing to high officials in the military. There is no doubt that military and related families at the highest echelons of power have made large fortunes. Some of the corruption has been chronicled by Iqbal Athas, a leading defense analyst and journalist at the *Sunday Times* whose life has been threatened on more than one occasion because of such exposés. Although a systematic and no doubt dangerous inquiry into the "winners" at the peak of the arms trade remains to be conducted, my study explores the second part of the political economy: the winners in the border areas who also sustain the conflict.

The armed conflict in Sri Lanka has not only generated a culture of terror. It has slowly eroded a deep tradition of multiculturalism, cultural hybridity, and multifaith coexistence in a region where four of the world's great religions—Buddhism, Hinduism, Christianity, and Islam—have coexisted for centuries. This is not to suggest that there were no clashes between communities and groups in the prewar period: clearly there were religious, community, and caste conflicts. The point is that conflict was not inevitably based on ethnolinguistic causes but on a multiplicity of local factors. As the war has escalated, however, older modes of ethnoreligious coexistence, accommodation, and integration among bilingual Sinhala, Tamil, and Muslim communities have been destroyed in various parts of the island. This process has in turn polarized collective identities in civil society. Significantly, though, ethnically motivated civilian violence has by and large been absent since the pogrom of July 1983, despite grave provocation such as the attack by the LTTE on the sacred Buddhist temple, the Dalada Maligawa, on January 25, 1998. This fact augurs well for a peace process in the long run.

It is in this context that ethnic explanations of the Sri Lankan armed conflict since 1983 hide more than they reveal. Not only do ethnic explanations echo nationalist rhetoric, but they reinstate a sneaking ethnic primordialism (sometimes via an instrumentalist logic) to explain armed violence and mask the fundamentally modern character of armed conflict. That is, ethnicity is presumed to be somewhere present as a root cause and mobilized for particular interests. Here I have sought to show how conflict generates a new culture—polarization among multiethnic communities—as well as a new political economy. Indeed, the armed conflict appears to have achieved a self-perpetuating structure and agency.

Ethnic explanations of armed conflict mask the fact that conflicts generate culture and hard ethnonationalist identities, and moreover, that increasingly the process that perpetuates armed conflict in Sri Lanka is related to a transforming global political economy. The war economy exists in concordance with politically motivated violence. Though the armed conflict has given rise to a hidden economy—not only in the highest echelons of the military where weapons purchase decisions are made, but at the grassroots level where a few rupees are made each time the paramilitary taxes a catch of fish or a police officer issues identification papers for a small fee—in the Sri Lankan case it is only a by-product of the political stalemate. The war has also resulted in the creation of a new elite: the armed forces personnel and their families. Although thousands of soldiers and paramilitary cadres have died, others have grown rich through corruption maintained by the so-called security situation and necessitated by arms and services purchases. Likewise, the LTTE sustains itself more from funds raised outside Sri Lanka than from funds raised among the people it purports to be defending. The process of globalization has therefore tempered the old formulation that a guerrilla movement needs the support of the people "as fish need water" to sustain it—for the LTTE is also alleged to be sustained by international trafficking in persons and goods and the Tamil diaspora. This is another feature of the modern war machine. Many noncombatant civilians living in the border areas have become increasingly skeptical of ethnonationalist rhetoric and violence used by the armed groups to sustain themselves and the war machine. Many of them view the war as autonomous from and counterproductive to their concerns. Increasingly it is a politics of desperation and deprivation that leads youth to join the armed groups for want of anything better to do, and the economy collapses.

Paradoxically, as the military apparatus has ceded its monopoly on violence to paramilitary groups, it has increased its sphere of control over traditionally civilian posts and administrative duties in the war zones. Currently, in the northern Jaffna peninsula as well as in the border areas where the conflict is being waged, the military leaders (local army brigadiers) perform many civil administration functions. Assistance to displaced civilian populations in the border areas—provided by such international humanitarian agencies as the United Nations High Commissioner for Refugees, Red Cross, Médecins sans Frontières, and a number of international and local nongovernmental organizations—must first pass the scrutiny of the military command in the area. The military also gives clearance for settlement of displaced persons in the border areas. Thus has the war machine proliferated in the border areas—problematizing the conventional distinction between civil violence and state violence and blurring and splitting the ethnic logic of conflict. Reining in the paramilitaries, which in other places such as East Timor and Aceh in Indonesia have demonstrated their violence, remains one of the great challenges of peace building in Sri Lanka.

CIVIL-MILITARY RELATIONS
IN A DYSFUNCTIONAL DEMOCRACY

Despite the growth of the military complex and its spheres of influence in everyday civilian life in the north and east of Sri Lanka, civilian government remains in control of the military apparatus and chain of command in Colombo, the country's capital and seat of political power. After more than fifteen years of armed conflict, the portfolio of defense remains in the hands of the elected government. The current president of the country is a woman—the daughter of two former prime ministers—who came to power on a platform for peace and a negotiated settlement with the LTTE. She remains minister of defense. Yet the military establishment, whose everyday operations are overseen by the deputy minister of defense, has gained increasing prominence in national life since the breakdown of peace talks with the LTTE and the reimposition of extended emergency rule. The Sri Lankan government has also shown a commitment to the care and protection of civilians in the war zones controlled by the LTTE and indeed has been commended by several human rights and humanitarian agencies for its continued supply of relief aid to LTTE-controlled areas. On the other hand the military, like the LTTE, has used civilians as human shields in operations in the northeast and has banned the transport of a number of goods such as fuel and batteries and even fertilizer to the north and east, on security grounds, also enabling the hidden war economy. Additionally there are restrictions on the transport of a number of goods including soap and food items that might be transported into the war zones—a fact that causes much grief and resentment among civilians and local authorities living in those areas. The contradictions and paradoxes of the Sri Lankan case raise several challenges for our understanding of modern internal armed conflicts and their implications for democratic practice and governance.

Until recently, several commentators on civil-military relations linked Sri Lanka's exemplary social welfare policies and high social indicators to its lack of militarization in the early postcolonial period (see Table 12.1 for defense spending increases). Thus historian K. M. De Silva in an account of the "Police and Armed Services" (1997: 347) noted that "Sri Lanka traditionally has taken pride in its welfare state developed since the mid 1930s. The price it paid for this was the neglect of the security services." Other observers have similarly read the absence of a military tradition and militarization in Sri Lanka (especially in comparison to India and Pakistan) as a direct reason for "the island's brilliant record of achievement in improving the living conditions of the impoverished masses" (Deger 1986: 232). In a study of the economic effects of military expenditure, Deger noted that Sri Lanka's "reticence in the military domain seems to be more than compensated for by its performance elsewhere.... Lack of militarization must have helped considerably in achieving the desired standards, particularly since resources have not been diverted into the defence sector from more desirable ends."

Implicit in such an analysis is the idea that civil-military relations are a zero-sum game— that if the military expands its role, civil society loses both economically and politically. In Sri Lanka, however, while the armed conflict has created a war machine, economic growth has

TABLE 12.1   Military Spending in Sri Lanka.

Year	Actual Expenditure on Defense in Sri Lankan Rupees (billion)
1976	.334
1977	.402
1978	.540
1979	.652
1980	.827
1981	.908
1982	.955
1983	1.512
1984	1.870
1985	2.770
1986	5.300
1987	8.000
1988	6.500
1989	5.800
1990	9.340
1991	14.130
1992	17.400
1993	18.270
1994	22.400
	(Imposition of 4% Defense Levy on all goods and services)
1995	33.200
1996	39.200

Source. Consortium of Humanitarian Agencies 1998 from Accounts of the Government of Sri Lanka.

continued apace. In 1998 growth was estimated at 4.8 percent. At the same time, figures of defense spending encapsulate the growing importance of the war machine and attest to the significant impact of armed conflict in the border areas on the national economy. In 1978, the annual expenditure on defense was only 1.5 percent of the gross national product (GNP) at $40 million. By 1985, expenditure on the armed services had risen to $215 million, or 3.5 percent of the GNP. In 2000 armed services spending stood at 5.3 percent of the gross domestic product (GDP) and 40 percent of total government expenditure. One reason for the continued economic growth despite the armed conflict is the regional nature of the conflict, which has been offset by economic growth in the south of the country as well as the burgeoning war economy and humanitarian industry in the north. The conflict has also spawned a powerful human rights element in civil society and within a tiny segment of the military that is attempting to clean up its image. Of course, pressure from the international community on a government that is responsive to such concerns has also helped in this process. Clearly, then, the armed conflict has split civil society and the military establishment even as it has blurred civil-military lines—a sign that civil-military relations are not (and perhaps never were) a zero-sum game.

Over the years of armed conflict, command and control structures have been transformed and retransformed, but the civilian president of the country has always remained the head of the armed forces. A recent change to the command structure was the decree signed by President Chandrika Bandaranaiake-Kumaratunge to set up a National Security Council (NSC) under the Public Security Ordinance, promulgating Emergency Regulation 1 of 1999, through a gazette notification on May 27, 1999. Setting up the NSC in no way altered the accountability of the defense services to the political establishment. The defense establishment remains under the authority of the president, who is also the chair of the NSC. As one of the island's leading defense analysts, journalist Iqbal Athas, has pointed out, the NSC "replaces what was an ad hoc system of operation which was exercised by the Deputy Minister of Defence through his ex-officio position in the Ministry of Defence. The NSC overrides the six months old Joint Operations Bureau."[13] A few weeks, later another gazette notification amended the NSC notification and reasserted the primacy of the deputy minister of defense.

This repeated restructuring of the line of command signals the absence of a satisfactory arrangement that balances the competing interests of a divided governing elite with military considerations. In fact, several ex-servicemen have recently argued that civilian control of the military has been excessive to the point that party political interference in the armed forces has countermanded not only the military chain of command but discipline within the armed forces at large in the war against the LTTE. Former air vice-marshal Harry Goonetillake has repeatedly and publicly argued that military campaigns have been undertaken for political expediency rather than with military goals in mind. Thus military operations against the LTTE have been undertaken less on the basis of sound strategic calculations and more according to the need for battlefield successes to bolster the election campaign of the ruling party. The manner in which Jaffna was captured by the armed forces and used to boost the political power of the deputy minister of defense seems to confirm this assertion. Perhaps the most glaring example of political expediency undermining military operations against the LTTE arose when the UNP government under President Premadasa actively funded and armed the LTTE to fight the IPKF in the early 1990s. The LTTE's armaments were soon used against the Sri Lankan military, however, when the third Eelam war commenced after the withdrawal of the IPKF.

These revelations of how political interests have affected the military's conduct of the war against the LTTE support the argument I have sought to make here. The objectivity of the armed forces in postcolonial Sri Lanka has been consistently undermined by powerful interests within successive ruling governments, be they UNP, SLFP, or PA. The ethnicization of the military is only one aspect of its overall politicization as a result of politically motivated nationalist politicians interfering in the military's structure and conduct of operations.

Yet as the armed conflict in the north and east of the country has brought little military success, the military has increasingly lost legitimacy in the eyes of large segments of civil society because of exposés of corruption pertaining to arms purchases at the highest level in the armed forces, unprecedented military spending, and high-profile cases brought against the military for the rape and harassment of women in the conflict zones.[14] The failure of the police and armed forces to curb election violence in the south—coupled with the memory of the brutal military suppression of the JVP in 1971 and subsequently in 1989–1991—has resulted in a scenario in which many civilians fear the police and armed forces as much as they do the para-military groups. But given the general subservience of the military establishment to civilian political interference and the absence of a history of military rule in Sri Lanka, it is difficult to envisage the emergence of a military state despite the proliferation of the war machine. Rather, the disturbing scenario is one of a political elite increasingly captive to the war machine.

The challenge of restoring peace, law, and order remains in the hands of the civilian political elite of Sri Lanka and the LTTE. Both have cooperated to foster the war machine, at various stages of the county's postcolonial modernization process, through competitive and lately bloody politics for personal power and profit in the guise of ethnic liberation. Simultaneously, the prolongation of the armed conflict has brought a significant shift in perceptions of large segments of the military and civil society that the ethnic conflict cannot be resolved by military means: a political solution is imperative. This desire for peace was reflected in the landslide victory of the PA, headed by Chandrika Bandaranaiake-Kumaratunge, who ran on a platform for peace at the national election in 1994. The devolution package for power sharing with the minorities was stalled by the UNP opposition, however, because a two-thirds majority in parliament is necessary for the new constitution to become effective. Thus the growing consensus among large segments of the Sri Lankan state, military, and civil society can be summed up in the words of the final report of the Commission of Inquiry into Involuntary Removal or Disappearances of Persons in the Western, Southern, and Sabaragamuwa Provinces (1997: 49): "Whatever may be said in support of the identification and punishment of a few military leaders in the situation where the state is in the control of a military regime, such a limited exercise can never suffice or be condoned in the situation of a state which is under the control of a civil government."

In the final analysis, many of the military's shortcomings in the postcolonial period can be traced to the failures of the political elite to nurture truly representative democratic institutions both in civil administration and in the military. The self-same processes of political competition along ethnolinguistic lines that resulted in Sri Lanka's ethnic conflict, now transmuted into a war machine, have also ensured that no government will be able to bring forward a peace package without the party in opposition seeking to destroy it. Ironically, the strength of the dual-party system and adherence to democratic rituals in amending the constitution to devolve power to the besieged regions as a means of solving the conflict also ensures that a political solution remains distant. In short, too much regard for legal procedure on the one hand and too little regard for ethics on the other have stymied the proper work of democracy.

The challenge thus remains for the political elite to formulate a political solution to an armed conflict that seems to have gained momentum and bred an economy of its own because of the dysfunction of Sri Lanka's democratic process—which is to say, the schisms among the political elite. Constructive attempts to resolve this conflict must move beyond legal and constitutional matters—principally the devolution of power to the regions dominated by the minority Tamil community—and focus on the new structures of violence that have arisen in the course of more than fifteen years of armed conflict and the demilitarization process. Although the devolution package is a fundamental part of a political settlement, it is not a panacea for conflict resolution because devolution could also solidify ethnic thinking and ethnic absolutism if not properly designed to protect local minorities. In fact, if devolution of power to the regions does not go hand in hand with the restoration of multicultural communities, the return of displaced people, and the dismantling of the culture of terror generated through the war machine, devolution could become a blueprint for the creation of ethnic enclaves and even more conflict. The de-ethnicization and depoliticization of the military must be prioritized if the armed forces are to regain their moral authority as the legitimate wielder of violence and perform their role independently of party political interference and ethnic and cultural bias. In this context—given the often provocative nature of LTTE activities that have invoked military violence on noncombatant civilian populations—it is worth quoting from the special commission on the need for a disciplined, nonpartisan, and multiethnic armed force: "Although the recognition that all crimes are to be condemned should never be lost, it is most important to emphasize the special character of the crimes committed by the state which uses its power to violate the law rather than to uphold it" (Commission of Inquiry into Involuntary Removal or Disappearances of Persons in the Western, Southern, and Sabaragamuwa Provinces 1997: 49).

The Sri Lankan case demonstrates that the study of civil-military relations in situations of modern internal armed conflict must go beyond ethnic explanations of violence and analyses of command and control structures and jurisdictional boundaries at the national level. If creative solutions to these seemingly intractable armed conflicts are to be found, one must recognize regional disjunctures and the complex political economy and culture generated by modern armed violence.

PART VI

Communist and
Totalitarian Civilian Control

CHAPTER 13

China: Conditional Compliance

James Mulvenon

ON JUNE 3–4, 1989, THE CHINESE PEOPLE'S LIBERATION ARMY (PLA) forcibly suppressed the protest movement that had occupied the center of Beijing. Among its other instructive lessons, the events of 1989 dramatically highlighted the extent to which the military continues to be a central force in Chinese politics, despite the nation's remarkable economic and social modernization since 1978 (Joffe 1996: 299). Traditionally the military's power derived from the paramountcy of its external and internal security roles. More important, the military's influence resulted from the essential value of its support for the policies of the civilian elite (Jencks 1991). As Ellis Joffe has written, "[The military] will remain indispensable backers of the new leadership. This is because they command the forces that may be used to determine the outcome of an elite power struggle, displace rebellious local figures, put down a mass uprising or even carry out a coup" (1991: 299). Recent years have witnessed significant new developments, however, both within the PLA and in the Chinese milieu writ large. The death of Deng Xiaoping and the rise of a postrevolutionary leadership in both the party and military, combined with the increasing professionalization of the military officer corps and the deideologization of Chinese society as a whole, potentially herald a new era of party-military relations.

This chapter explores the origins and major features of the new, emerging dynamic between party and military. I argue that the best term to describe the emerging civil-military arrangement, more accurately known as "party-military relations," in China is Ellis Joffe's notion of "conditional compliance."[1] The Chinese military is compliant with civilian wishes in two critical respects. First, it actively supports the legitimacy of Jiang Zemin as paramount leader and the single-party rule of the Chinese Communist Party (CCP) with the full political and coercive weight of the military institution itself. Second, the PLA has accepted a more circumscribed role within the Chinese system, largely staying out of nonmilitary policymaking areas, such as the economy, and focusing on professional development instead of factional conflict. In areas of corporate identity, such as military modernization or defense planning, the military seems to retain virtual autonomy unfettered by civilian control. In areas of foreign and security policy, such as Sino-U.S. relations, Sino-Japan relations, Sino-Taiwan relations, South Asian issues, Sino-Russian relations, South China Sea issues, and arms control, the military seeks to influence policymaking. In other nondefense, nonsecurity areas, the PLA appears to have ceded or lost the ability to influence policy.

The reasons for this compliance are complex. Viewed in terms of the last 70-plus years, the major continuity is party domination of the military, manifested in the lack of a historical legacy of praetorianism or coup d'états by the PLA. In the past, this relative quiescence could be explained largely in terms of personal, historical, and institutional variables. For decades the Chinese military was subordinated in a system dominated by powerful leaders with personal connections to the senior military leadership. To enforce that subordination, the military was penetrated from top to bottom by a political work system intent on maintaining the military's loyalty to the party (Shambaugh 1991). In recent years, however, there has been significant change in both of these areas. As Joffe has pointed out, Jiang Zemin does not enjoy the same relationship with the PLA as did Mao Zedong or Deng Xiaoping—giving the military a degree of leverage over Jiang that it did not have with previous leaders. As a result, military acceptance and validation of Jiang's leadership require a complicated mix of formal institutional authority, patronage, and bureaucratic bargaining over resources and influence. Swaine wrote, "Senior party leaders undoubtedly play a complex and nuanced game in their policy interactions with the military leadership, seeking to retain the initiative and maintain overall flexibility by alternately placating, resisting, or diluting military views and pressures through a complex mixture of personal persuasion, balancing of bureaucratic interests, and direct control over formal organs and policy channels" (1996: x). For his part, Jiang has spent a substantial amount of his time cultivating a relationship with the PLA and catering to its interests. He regularly pays his respects to military elders, visits units, extols military heroes, supports budget and procurement increases, honors PLA traditions, and listens to their concerns about internal and external affairs. Jiang remains critically dependent on the military's political support.

At the same time, however, two important trends—the professionalization of the officer corps and an unprecedented generational shift that has led to an effective separation of military and civilian elites—have constrained the extent to which the PLA can exploit this leverage (Mulvenon 1997b; Swaine 1992). The generational shift is particularly important. China has witnessed a tectonic transformation of the civilian and military leaderships from a symbiotic revolutionary guerrilla generation to a technocratic pairing of bifurcated military and civilian elites. The deaths of the revolutionary military generation and changes in the political setting, especially the passing of Deng Xiaoping and the ascension of a collective leadership under Jiang Zemin, mean that the current generation of military leaders does not possess the same level of political capital as its predecessors and, therefore, is less able to act as power brokers within the system. As a result, the institutional and individual opportunities and capacities for the military to intervene in the policy process have been reduced, thereby strengthening civilian control of critical realms. Moreover, the military's intervention in politics in general and the policy process in particular has both narrowed and deepened, depending on the issue or the people involved. The relative weakness of the collective civilian leadership means that bureaucratic wrangling is still required on key policy and resource distribution issues, but this bargaining should not be described as occurring between "equal" parties. Thus it could be argued that the PLA's conditional compliance is as much a function of transitional trends in the Chinese system itself as it is a result of the changing dynamic between the paramount leader and the military. Together the interaction of these two structural changes produces the dynamic we see in party-military relations.

The chapter is divided into five principal sections. The first section reviews the literature on party-military relations in China between the formation of the PLA in the revolutionary period (1927–1936) and the end of the Dengist era in 1997. The second and third sections analyze the jurisdictional boundaries between the state and military in control of political power and national security decision making. These arguments are then explored in greater detail in the fourth section through two empirical case studies. The first case study illustrates the distribution of political power in China by examining recent attempts by the civilian leadership to divest the PLA of its business empire. The second outlines the PLA's role in policymaking related to national security, in particular, military participation and influence during the 1995–1996 missile exercises near Taiwan. The final section discusses possible trajectories for Chinese party-military relations and offers suggestions for future research.

LITERATURE REVIEW

The literature on Chinese party-military relations is extensive and rich in quality (see Bickford 2000; Swaine 1992; Joffe 1987; Jencks 1982; Bullard 1984; Godwin 1988; Cheng 1990a; Shambaugh 1991; Whitson and Huang 1973; Paltiel 1995). Indeed, party-military relations were the subject of choice for PLA specialists for many years, given the general lack of information about other aspects of the military system. To a certain extent, the evolution of the literature on civil-military relations in China has been profoundly shaped by Samuel Huntington's classic *The Soldier and the State*, which outlined a compelling though controversial taxonomy of civil-military relations. The author began by positing a Weberian ideal type: a professional and apolitical military subject to unquestioned civilian control. Huntington described this arrangement as "objective civilian control" as opposed to "subjective civilian control," which was characterized by the less reliable maximization of civilian power at the expense of military power (Huntington 1957).

Huntington believed that objective civilian control is predicated upon a certain level of military professionalism in the officer corps. In his formulation, the modern warrior, evolved from the aristocratic dilettante, is committed to three distinguishing characteristics of the military profession as a special vocation: expertise, responsibility, and corporateness (1957: 8). Expertise is defined as the functional knowledge gained through education and training that separates the professional from the layman. Responsibility is the duty to apply these martial skills selflessly on behalf of the state (p. 9). Corporateness is the officers' "sense of organic unity and consciousness" that they are a group set apart from laymen; it is achieved through group discipline and training (p. 10).

These categories and the belief in the divisibility of political and military spheres, however, led students of Leninist party-military relations over the years to reject Huntington's theories as inappropriate. In the Chinese case, for instance, the overlap of military and party elites during the pre-liberation and early liberation period (1927–1953) precluded a clean separation of political and military roles. This led Perlmutter to create the new analytical category of "revolutionary soldier" as opposed to the professional soldier of Prussia, for example, and the "praetorian soldier" of postcolonial countries in the postwar era (Perlmutter 1977). This revolutionary soldier, a unique product of the national liberation movements, exists in symbiosis with the political revolutionary in the pursuit of state power (Shambaugh 1991: 530; Jencks 1982: chaps. 1–3). In Shambaugh's words, "The politicization of the military and the militarization of the party...were mutually reinforcing" (1991: 530). The net result was an organic party-military relationship in which neither half of the equation could be credibly isolated from the other.

After liberation in 1949, the relationship between the PLA and the CCP continued to confound Huntingtonian ideal types. The pre-1949 military-party elite divided into distinct "military" and "political" leaderships during the mid-1950s, but the ties forged in combat before 1949 maintained what Bullard has called the "interlocking directorate" at the highest levels (Bullard 1984; Whitson and Huang 1973). Additional "separations" of military and political elites were attempted by Marshall Peng Dehuai in the 1950s, after Lin Biao's failed coup in 1971, and in the reforms of the 1980s, but they were unsuccessful. The reasons for these failures are twofold. First, professional bifurcation was impeded by a number of highly effective organizational devices—including the political commissar system, the discipline inspection system, and the party committee system—used to facilitate political penetration and control of the military apparatus (Shambaugh 1991: 546). Second, the military continued to be a key political actor in the system, both as a factional player and as the guarantor of internal stability. An excellent example is the Cultural Revolution, which resulted in such high levels of administrative chaos that an ambivalent PLA was forced to assume a greater role, and Tiananmen in 1989, where the PLA was ordered to restore control to the capital at the behest of a reconsolidated central authority. Indeed, these interventions should not even be seen as praetorian behavior. As Perlmutter and LeoGrande asserted, "To speak of military 'intervention' is a misnomer; the military is a normal participant in politics in Communist systems" (Perlmutter and LeoGrande 1976). Thus Shambaugh correctly insists that Huntington's professional/political dichotomy is false in the Chinese case in the pre-Deng period, because the "CCP and PLA were intertwined and sustained each other's power for more than 60 years" (1991: 533).

But times have begun to change. The death of Deng Xiaoping in 1997 and the ascent of Jiang Zemin have finally ushered in the postrevolutionary political leadership with no experience of military service. A similar generational change, along with a deep process of professionalization, is occurring in the officer corps and highlights a growing divide between the respective military and civilian elites (Swaine 1992: ix–x). At the same time, it must be recognized that the PLA's increasing expertise is a double-edged sword. Military proficiency can be used for nonprofessional purposes, and the professional military education system can be used for building networks. As Abrahamsson (1972) contended, a professional army may simply be a more unified and capable intervening force in domestic politics. Given the PLA's importance in the post-Deng environment and the increasing separation of military and political elites, this strengthened unity of the PLA makes it a potentially powerful determinant of Chinese domestic politics.

JURISDICTION IN THE POLITICAL ARENA

To ascertain how the PLA's conditional compliance translates into jurisdictional boundaries in the control of political power, six critical elements of the system must be analyzed:

- The structure of the political system at the national and regional levels
- The military's roles and missions in this system
- The arrangements for command and control of the armed forces, including authority for unit movements and internal ideological and security mechanisms
- The methods of appointment and rotation of senior military personnel

- The leadership base and the process for selecting political leadership
- The institutional structure for crafting political, social, and economic objectives and policies, in particular the extent to which the military has responsibility for or veto power over specific issues

Overall, the evidence suggests that the civilians attempt with varying degrees of success to use structure to shape and enforce compliance, but they also cede to the military levels of autonomy in critical internal and extrabureaucratic areas. Areas in which the civilian party leaders attempt to shape and enforce compliance include the structure of the political system, the roles and missions of the military, the command and control system, party penetration of the military, senior personnel decisions, rotation of military personnel, and selection of the political leadership. At the same time, the civilian party leaders "purchase" compliance by permitting the PLA to act autonomously within certain carefully zoned areas, such as defense policy and military personnel decisions below a certain level, and shape senior personnel decisions and certain aspects of Chinese external security policy. In return for this relative autonomy, the military refrains from intervention in other policy arenas and does not challenge the principle of civilian control of the military.

The Structure of the Political System

The Chinese political system is dominated by the CCP, an authoritarian political organization dedicated to single-party rule (Lieberthal 1995). Although there is a separate governmental apparatus, this structure is penetrated at all levels by the CCP, either through the party membership of government officials or through external party controls (Schurmann 1966). There is a similar dichotomy in the civilian control of the military. In principle, there are two equal governing bodies: the State Central Military Commission and the Party Central Military Commission (Paltiel 1995). In reality, however, these two organizations are one and the same with identical memberships (known in Chinese as *"yige danwei, liangge paizi,"* "one work unit, two nameboards"). Because the CCP is the real power in China and exercises its influence through the Party Central Military Commission (as well as the political commissar system, the discipline inspection system, and the party committee system), it is more accurate to describe civil-military relations in China as party-military relations. Although the importance of the party's penetration of the military and personal connections between senior party and military members has declined, the Chinese military remains compliant to this political structure for at least two reasons: a proud tradition of subordination to party control, even during chaotic periods; and an institutional fear of the potential foreign and domestic costs of any instability associated with regime dislocation. The PLA would likely fare worse bureaucratically and enjoy fewer privileges under nearly any other type of system.

Roles and Missions of the Military

Within the system outlined here, the PLA has a number of dedicated roles. First and foremost, it is charged with maintaining the single-party rule of the CCP. As outlined in the literature review section, the PLA has been forced to perform this task on more than one occasion in the past; the Tiananmen suppression in 1989 is only the most recent example. Continued compliance with this onerous function is clearly conditional to civilian attention to PLA institutional interests. It is widely believed, for example, that the PLA was rewarded for its loyalty in 1989 with substantial budget increases. Second, it is responsible for defense of the nation, which includes defense of China's borders and its claimed territories. It also has responsibility for protecting China's "sovereignty," which is a code word for the eventual reunification with Taiwan, as well as defense of Chinese claims in the South China Sea and Senkaku/Diaoyutai area. Third, the PLA is still clearly saddled with an internal security role, though its renewed operational control of the paramilitary People's Armed Police is meant to preclude the PLA from ever having to participate in another operation like Tiananmen. Fourth, the Chinese military continues to be involved in nonmilitary activities, ranging from economic development missions to flood control, though the number of active-duty units tasked with these missions has declined.[2] In terms of party-military relations, the net result of these varied missions is a military with both "professional" and "political" mandates, blurring Huntington's clean distinctions and legitimating continued military involvement in political affairs.

Command and Control

Befitting a system in which the top political leaders are actively concerned with the military's potential for independent behavior, the Chinese command and control system is "highly centralized, vertically structured, and very personalized" (Swaine 1992). Through a series of interlocking and carefully guarded organizational and procedural mechanisms, the top civilian leadership, embodied in the personal authority of the paramount leader, maintains strict operational control over China's military units. With proper authorization, authorities in Beijing can either activate units through the well-established chain of command or bypass the intervening units and issue direct orders to units. PLA commanders on the ground, by contrast, can only move small units without prior authorization from Beijing.

This command and control system was sorely tested in Tiananmen in 1989. Although the civilian government and party apparatus effectively collapsed, Deng and a group of retired elders were able to maintain reasonably stable control of Chinese military and paramilitary forces, successfully restoring order with minimal dissension in the ranks.[3] At the same time, the Tiananmen operation exposed some of the structural weaknesses of a system that seems geared toward allowing "the supreme leader to wield virtually absolute control over the PLA as his personal instrument of power, largely unhindered by legal or institutional constraints or the objections of less authoritative individuals" (Swaine 1992: 133). Tiananmen exposed the extent to which the cohesion and effectiveness of this system depends on a leader's ability to ensure his personal access to the command center in Beijing and to maintain his personal authority within the party and military hierarchies. For Deng, this authority was not in question. But as Joffe (1999) has persuasively argued, Jiang Zemin does not enjoy the same unquestioned stature, despite his persistent efforts to shape and cultivate stronger relations with the military leadership. A future internal crisis could expose this faultline, undermining the basis for the PLA's conditional compliance with civilian authority.

In addition to the command and control system governing units, the civilian leadership also employs three different organizational mechanisms to ensure the party leadership's influence vis-à-vis the military: budgets, personnel, and ideology. Budgets are addressed later in the chapter. In terms of personnel and ideology, there are three critical organs that theoretically enforce PLA compliance with party authority: the political commissar system, party committee system, and discipline inspection system.[4] The evidence suggests that the importance and effectiveness of these organs appear to have declined. Political officers are now tasked with far more nonideological work, ranging from issues involving morale and daily life of the rank-and-file to the more important work of personnel management (promotion lists, maintenance of internal military dossiers, and the like). In terms of content, political work within the military is less frequently focused on ideology. Instead it concentrates on the instrumental ethos of party control of the military, in particular, loyalty to the CCP under the leadership of Jiang Zemin as the "core." In other words, the PLA is told to support the "absolute leadership of the party," whatever Jiang and the party may happen to believe.

For the Chinese military, this development suggests that future PLA compliance with party authority will not be based, as in the past, on the party's ability to interpret the "truth" but on the military's satisfaction with the job performance of the top leadership, as well as the extent to which the preferences of military and civilian leaders remain congruent. One critical variable that will affect both of these assessments is the economic health of the country, and, by extension, the level of internal stability. As the organization ultimately charged with the maintenance of stability, either directly (à la Tiananmen) or through operational control of the People's Armed Police, the PLA could find itself in a situation where it needed to assume de facto control of certain areas of the country. With a weak, collective leadership in power and governed by a nonideological, instrumental ethos, the PLA might be less likely to relinquish control in a future crisis, particularly if the military leadership thought the crisis had in fact been precipitated by misguided civilian policy decisions.

Appointment and Rotation of Personnel

The Chinese military's personnel policy has two critical features that affect party-military relations. First, the paramount civilian leader is charged with the direct appointment of high-level officers, presumably ensuring the loyalty of large-unit commanders during times of political and social upheaval. There is a general consensus that Jiang selects the PLA's top officers, including the members of the Central Military Commission (CMC) and the military region commands, many of whom he meets during his frequent inspection tours of PLA facilities.[5] Although the criterion for promotion in this environment is probably personal loyalty to Jiang, he must also select men who are capable of managing an enormous bureaucratic machine at his behest. Overall, therefore, the military leadership appointment system in the PLA still suggests a personalized relationship between the top civilian leadership and the military, with PLA compliance conditional on civilian policies and the latter's attention to military institutional concerns. Promotions at levels below the central military leadership, by contrast, appear increasingly institutionalized and reflect "professional" criteria.

The second personnel policy critical to party-military relations is similar in content to the Chinese imperial policy of the "law of avoidance" (Fairbank et al. 1965), which was designed to prevent the rise of regional power bases or what Mao called "independent kingdoms" *("duli wangguo")* or "mountaintopism" *("shantouzhuyi").*[6] The current governing principle is colloquially known by the Chinese aphorism *"wu hu si hai"* ("five lakes and four seas"), meaning that military officers must be drawn from all corners of the country (Lam 1996). Chinese officers at the level of military region commander and above are not permitted to stay in a slot for more than a set number of years. This rotation system has been methodically successful in preventing the creation of regional power centers, giving the central civilian leadership a high measure of confidence that warlords or coup cliques cannot rise from outlying commands.

Selection of the Political Leadership

The actual process of selecting the political leadership is one of the most opaque features of the Chinese system. The role of the military is even more difficult to discern. In discussing party-military relations, the critical question of selection is whether the military plays an active or passive role in this process of selecting and validating the top political leadership. The evidence suggests that the military does not play an autonomous kingmaker role—defined as the ability to independently nominate or reject candidates for top positions. This is not to say, however, that the PLA is powerless in this area. For example, the military clearly rejected attempts by Deng Xiaoping to place Hu Yaobang and Zhao Ziyang on the Central Military Commission.[7] The PLA's ability in the past to prevent civilians other than the paramount leader from joining the CMC was largely a function of the personalistic authority of PLA elders such as Yang Shangkun. As the revolutionary generation is replaced by separate civilian and military elites, however, the PLA enjoys fewer sources of leverage to force the selection or nonselection of particular leaders, and fewer institutionalized channels of preference articulation in this regard, limiting the extent to which it can be the determining factor in a promotion or dismissal. This change is clearly highlighted by the recent appointment of an additional civilian, Hu Jintao (Jiang Zemin's "chosen successor"), to the CMC over the reported objections of certain military leaders who nonetheless complied with the directive because of Jiang Zemin's attention to their concerns in other areas such as budgets. This is a classic example of the new conditional compliance in party-military relations.

The PLA and National Policy

As Harding (1987) has persuasively argued, the PLA's historical involvement in elite policy-making circles has been an important mechanism to advance the military's programmatic interests while also playing an arbiter role between competing civilian groups. Although incidents of overt PLA intervention in politics have declined overall in recent years, the current conditional compliance arrangement permits the PLA to intervene in carefully circumscribed areas of "corporate identity" and "corporate interest," provided that it refrains from intervening in areas outside of these parameters. Put crudely, the PLA's interests have gone from being "a mile wide and an inch deep" to "an inch wide and a mile deep." Areas of corporate identity, vested in authority of the senior military officials on the CMC, focus primarily on the autonomy of personnel decisions but also deal with other military resource allocation issues. Areas of corporate interest, by contrast, are represented by direct PLA participation in key foreign policy-making forums—especially those that focus on relations with Taiwan, Japan, the United States, or arms control—as well as dominance in defense and internal security policymaking.[8] All other arenas, with the exception of defense-related economic policy, seem to have been ceded by the military leadership to the civilian leadership.

The manner in which the PLA expresses its preferences has undergone an important transformation as well. The passing of the revolutionary military generation has significantly reduced the salience of informal, personalistic channels to the political leadership. At the same time, the loss of a military representative on the Politburo Standing Committee means there are now fewer institutionalized channels for articulation of military policy preferences on nondefense issues. Two important exceptions are the Foreign Affairs Leading Small Group and the Taiwan Affairs Leading Small Group—the critical loci for interagency deliberation on foreign policy questions (Lieberthal 1995: 192–234). PLA participation in these forums is discussed in greater detail in the next section.

JURISDICTION OVER NATIONAL SECURITY

As we have seen, a critical feature of the PLA's conditional compliance with party authority is augmented military involvement in narrowly circumscribed policy areas. One of the most important of these areas is national security policymaking, where the military is an increasingly important, though by no means dominant, participant (Shambaugh 1987). To ascertain how the PLA's conditional compliance translates into jurisdictional boundaries in national security, we must examine four elements of the system:

- The institutional arrangements for defining the national security problematic, including intelligence collection and threat assessment
- The institutional arrangements for formulating and implementing national security doctrine and strategy
- The management of specific domestic and international security problems
- The process for allocating and controlling the defense budget, including development of force posture and defense procurement

Recent research has revealed that "military involvement is evident in all four security policy subarenas [national strategic objectives, foreign policy, defense policy, and strategic research, analysis, and intelligence], albeit to widely varying degrees, ranging from near-total control over defense policy to limited but significant influence over foreign policy" (Swaine 1996: x). The military is an important actor in all phases of national security policymaking, as well, including assessment, planning, and implementation. The net effect of this military involvement is admittedly more indirect than direct: primarily the military performs a critical "shaping" role in national security policymaking with episodic attempts at intervention. At the same time, however, the relative success or failure of Chinese leaders in dealing with some of the country's most challenging foreign policy problems, such as Taiwan, will have profound implications for party-military relations. A dramatic international humiliation, for example, particularly a loss of Chinese sovereign territory through perceived civilian mistakes, is one of the circumstances that might end the PLA's conditional compliance to the authority of a civilian leader.

Defining the National Security Problematic

In 1987, David Shambaugh first highlighted the extent to which research organs within the military bureaucracy assessed the external threats faced by China (Shambaugh 1987). Ten years later, interviews led Michael Swaine to assert that "the military's role in shaping national strategic objectives and in providing strategic analysis and intelligence to civilian leaders is significant and apparently increasing" (1996: x). The key military institutions involved in producing strategic research, analysis, and intelligence are the Second (Intelligence), Third (Signals Intelligence), and Fourth (Electronic Warfare) subdepartments of the General Staff Department, as well as the Academy of Military Sciences' Department of Strategic Studies and the National Defense University's Institute for Strategic Studies. Of these, the Second Subdepartment (Er Bu) is the most important source of security- and military-related strategic analysis for the senior Chinese leadership. It compiles information from a wide variety of open and classified sources, including China's attachés abroad. Under the leadership of Gen. Xiong Guangkai, one of Jiang Zemin's close advisers, the General Staff Department "Watch Center" (staffed primarily by members of the Er Bu and related research institutes such as the Chinese Institute for International Strategic Studies and the Foundation for International Strategic Studies) produce the daily intelligence summary for the Politburo and the CMC, as well as reports analyzing China's external threat environment, including the capabilities of foreign military powers in Asia (Shambaugh 2000b). Thus the military's view of China's security situation is one of the principal sources for the civilian national security policymaking elite.

Formulating and Implementing National Security

The PLA's role in the formulation of national security doctrine and strategy is hard to ascertain. The PLA's institutional importance clearly suggests a significant participatory role. Among the reasons for this involvement, Swaine argued, are "the centrality of the military to defense policy, the military's overall concern with national security issues, and the high prestige and party status of the top PLA elite" (1996: 11). Under Deng's leadership, this influence was exercised primarily through civilian interaction with individual military leaders, including military elders and senior PLA officers holding high party posts. Under Jiang, on the other hand, the military's influence on the formulation of national security strategy is probably more diffuse. The elders are mostly gone, and Jiang could not have enjoyed the same relationship with them anyway. Instead, the principal military leaders with whom Jiang interacts are professional military bureaucrats who work more within the boundaries of the institutions than did the elder generation. For this reason, perhaps the military-originated intelligence and analysis he receives has a much greater influence on the formulation of China's national security strategy than the advice of individual military leaders.

Managing Domestic and International Security Problems

One of the principal features of the conditional compliance arrangement is PLA involvement in narrowly circumscribed policy areas of corporate interest to the military. The most important of these concern national security. Although the PLA does not directly "manage" international security problems, there are at least seven respects in which the PLA is an active participant through its membership on critical foreign policy decision-making bodies: China-Taiwan relations, Sino-U.S. relations, South Asia issues, Sino-Japan relations, Sino-Russian relations, South China Sea issues, and arms control. As the body charged with "defense of Chinese sovereignty," which includes claimed territories that are not yet "reunified" with China, the PLA leadership believes it must be involved in policymaking regarding Taiwan (Shambaugh 1996). Similarly, given the important role of the United States (and by extension Japan) in any potential Taiwan scenario as well as the wider security issues that concern both Beijing and Washington, the PLA also believes it must have a say in decisions regarding relations with the American and Japanese governments. There is evidence to suggest that the PLA's influence in these areas, particularly since the death of Deng Xiaoping, has increased. One exception to this trend appears to be arms control, which was previously dominated by the military but now seems driven by a newly energized, pluralized, and increasingly civilianized arms control process (Swaine and Johnston 1999).

Allocating and Controlling the Defense Budget

From internal Chinese sources it is possible to outline the process by which the Chinese defense budget is created, though the actual budget figures are the subject of intense debate (see Shambaugh 2000b; Bitzinger 1995; Bitzinger and Lin 1994; Wang 1996).[9] Briefly, the military's central allocation is determined by a "down-up-down" process. First the CMC, Ministry of Finance, and other relevant ministries decide total expenditures for the year according to the "general principles for overall military expenditure" established by the highest echelons of the CCP (Shambaugh 2000b: chap. 5). Afterward, successive layers of the military hierarchy estimate their funding needs and report these to the top, which reviews the estimates and transmits the final budget breakdowns to the PLA.

For party-military relations, however, the first step of the process is the most important, because "general principles for overall military expenditure" is a bureaucratic way of discussing the relative priority of the PLA's budget compared with the budgets of other state ministries and institutions. This priority is a function of both the PLA's real military priorities and the civilian leadership's calculation of the military's perceived political value. For example, the PLA began receiving double-digit percentage budget increases after 1989. Although one justification for higher allocations was the gross underfunding of the PLA during the 1980s, the real motivation for the increases was to reward the military for its loyalty during the Tiananmen operation. In a similar way, the expected additional budget increases in 1999 are meant to be compensation for lost enterprise revenue. In both cases, the party leadership has sought to reinforce the military's compliance with central authority through financial remuneration.

Defense procurement is also partly top-down, particularly in the case of expensive foreign weapons purchases from the Russians, such as the Su-27s, *Kilo*-class submarines, *Sovremenny*-class destroyers, Il-76 transport aircraft, and S-300 SAM batteries (Gill 1999; Yan 1998). In each instance, the money for these arms purchases did not come from the official defense budget. Instead, the State Council opened special hard-currency capital accounts for the amount of the specific sale. During the 1990s, experts have estimated that the PLA had between $1 billion and $1.5 billion per year in such accounts for foreign purchases, though there has been fluctuating barter as well. Although the PLA could make a clear case for the military uses of every system and platform, civilian control over these off-budget funds highlights the extent to which budget authorizations are mechanisms for continued civilian domination of the military. At the same time, however, the renewed tensions over Taiwan and Jiang Zemin's need to maintain military support for his policy of negotiation with the island suggest that the increases in procurement allocations are in fact an additional means of ensuring the PLA's conditional compliance with civilian authority.

CASE STUDIES

Two case studies illustrate the changing dynamic of party-military relations in the post-Deng era. The first case study deals with the party-military implications of the decision in mid-1998 to divest the Chinese military of its internal business empire. The second case study addresses the PLA's jurisdiction in national security affairs, especially the influence of the Chinese military in Taiwan policymaking during the crisis of 1995–1996.

Case Study 1: Commercialization and Divestiture of the Military Economy, 1978–1998

Between 1978 and 1998, the PLA underwent a dramatic transformation. Faced with the contradictory forces of a declining military budget and pressures to modernize at the end of the Maoist era, the army reluctantly agreed to join the Chinese economic reform drive by converting its long-standing internal military economy of farms and factories to market-oriented civilian production.[10] Its hope was that the resulting profits could replace lost expenditures and help finance the army's long-needed modernization of weaponry and forces. In the two decades since these decisions were taken, the PLA became one of the principal actors in the Chinese economy, controlling a multibillion-dollar international business empire that ran the gamut from large farms to world-class hotels and transnational corporations. This amalgam of military and commercial interests, known colloquially as "PLA, Inc.," resulted in an entirely new organizational form for a Leninist system: the "military-business complex."[11]

China's party-military dynamic played a key role in shaping this decision to permit the PLA to commercialize its internal economic production assets. Given the importance of the PLA in Chinese domestic politics, Deng Xiaoping could not unilaterally slash the military's budget without some form of side payment. To make up for lost budget funds and thus retain the military's political support, Deng allowed the PLA to expand its "zones of authority" to include commercial activity. In time the center's ability to supplement the PLA with additional budget funds declined further, making the military increasingly dependent on the revenues from its growing business empire. Even when corruption and profiteering in the ranks became endemic, this fiscal catch-22 meant that the military and political leaderships could not consider removing the PLA from business. Jiang Zemin reportedly found the situation unpalatable. But in the absence of replacement funds he recognized that the military-business complex was necessary to maintain the PLA's conditional compliance to his authority. As the PLA approached the twenty-first century, most observers seemed convinced that the civilian leadership and the PLA would be forced to maintain this uncomfortable arrangement for some time to come.

On July 22, 1998, at an enlarged session of the CMC, however, CMC chairman Jiang Zemin publicly called for the dissolution of the military-business complex. Although the divestiture was immediately touted by Western and Chinese media as a dramatic reversal of policy, it should instead be seen as the logical culmination of more than six years of rectification and consolidation campaigns in the military enterprise system. Indeed, it was not even the first divestiture announcement. A decision to divest had actually been made a year earlier, in May 1997, though the major transfers were not set to begin until three years later in May 2000. The reasons behind the acceleration of the divestiture timetable are not entirely known. There are at least two competing stories. One claims that divestiture was initiated by an angry Jiang Zemin upon receiving an account of the unbridled corruption of six PLA and People's Armed Police companies, the most egregious of which involved oil smuggling that was bankrupting the country's two geographically based oil monopolies.[12] The second story actually begins with Zhu Rongji (Lawrence 1999). Reportedly, Zhu angered the PLA at the July 17, 1998, meeting of the antismuggling conference by accusing the General Political Department's Tiancheng Group of rampant corruption. In particular, he singled out a case in which the company had avoided paying RMB50 million in import and sales taxes after purchasing a shipment of partially processed iron ore from Australia. "Every time our customs officials tried to snare these bastards, some powerful military person appeared to speak on their behalf," Zhu allegedly charged at the closed-door meeting. As anger and resentment spread through the PLA leadership, Jiang Zemin appeared at the conference four days later to lend his support to Zhu, confirming that "some units and individuals" in the PLA were involved in smuggling. According to this account, Jiang thereupon announced the divestiture order.

These accounts of the decision to divest the PLA of its enterprises raise a fundamental analytical question: how did the PLA and the CCP work their way out of what could only be described as the fiscal and political catch-22 of military commercialism? The answer would speak volumes about the PLA as a military organization, in particular its relationship to the civilian apparatus. Since the announcement, two major schools of thought have emerged.

The first view asserts that the decision to divest the PLA of its businesses reflects an attempt at reassertion of civilian authority over the PLA by Jiang Zemin. For evidence, some point to Gen. Zhang Wannian's use of the phrase "supreme leader" for Jiang Zemin as a new effort by the party leader and his supporters to cultivate a Mao-like cult of power within the PLA (Sun and Jia 1998). Advocates of this position also point to the fact that only a few top military leaders were informed of the announcement ahead of time, effectively presenting the PLA with an unpopular fait accompli. Some have even questioned the logic of upsetting the PLA at a time of economic downturn and potential social upheaval in China; they concluded that Jiang felt he had to expend precious political capital to rein in the PLA no matter what the costs. Finally, analysts have noted the high-profile investigation in late July 1998 of a company with strong ties to the military, Hong Kong–based J&A Securities, which seemed to signal that Jiang was willing to confront even the most protected military enterprises (Chan 1998a, 1998b, 1998c; Peng 1998).

A second school of thought argues that the divestiture was largely supported by a corruption-weary, senior military leadership—provided that they received a sufficiently generous compensation package.[13] If this assertion is true, the heart of the bargain between the PLA and the civilian leadership would center on financial compensation—in this case two separate payoffs.

The first was the one-time transfer of the PLA's divested enterprises. Reportedly, the financial burden for these enterprises, including their weighty social welfare costs and debts, was to be placed upon local and provincial governments rather than the central government, though no money was to change hands. The second negotiation focused on the annual budget increases to make up for lost enterprise revenues. Before the divestiture was completed, Hong Kong sources reported that the PLA would receive between RMB15 and 30 billion per year, with the exact time frame subject to negotiation (Lam 1998a). Two months later, the same author reported that the PLA would receive RMB50 billion as compensation for its lost enterprises (Kuang 1998; Lam 1998b). The *Wall Street Journal* quoted U.S. diplomats as saying the government offered about $1.2 billion but the military demanded $24 billion. Sources at the GLD claimed in December 1998 that the PLA would receive between RMB4 and 5 billion in additional annual compensation, complementing continued double-digit budget increases.[14]

As the divestiture entered 1999, however, serious bureaucratic and political conflicts began to surface. In particular, it became increasingly clear that the compensation package for the enterprises was going to be far less than the military expected. In March 1999, Minister of Finance Xiang Huaicheng announced that the military budget for the new fiscal year would be RMB104.65 billion (Xiang 1999). Outside observers immediately noticed how meager the figure was both in relative and absolute terms. In relative terms, the 12.7 percent increase was not significantly higher than the 12 percent increase of the previous year—calling into question the notion that the PLA's fiscal priority had been augmented. Even in absolute terms, the increase of RMB13.65 billion between 1998 and 1999 was not that much larger than the RMB10.43 billion increase between 1997 and 1998 (and reportedly included only an RMB3 billion compensation for the loss of business income). Where was the additional RMB15 to 50 billion reported in the Hong Kong media? Why did the military receive only RMB3 billion extra when even the official *China Daily* newspaper pegged the estimated annual profits and taxes of the enterprises at RMB5 billion ($602 million)?[15]

There are several plausible explanations for this budgeting outcome. The first, and most difficult to prove, is that that PLA was sufficiently compensated with off-budget funds that are not calculated into the official budget. Given the byzantine nature of the Chinese budgeting process, we may never have a definite estimate of any off-budget compensation. The second explanation is that the PLA did not have as much leverage in the divestiture process as outsiders thought, thus allowing the civilian leadership to get the military out of business on the cheap. The third possibility, supported by a loud chorus of PLA grumbling and complaining, is that the military was duped by the civilian leadership and its implicit promises of a higher level of compensation. Indeed, there is evidence to suggest that the RMB3 billion of compensation is based on the conservative profit estimate of RMB3.5 billion (on total revenue of RMB150 billion) that the PLA gave to Zhu Rongji before the divestiture announcement in July. This low estimate was very much in line with previous PLA estimates by the General Logistics Department, which consistently undervalued the profit of the military enterprise system in order to lessen the central tax burden of the commercial units. If this story is true, then the major source of the PLA's animus may be that it was hoist by its own petard. It is difficult to judge which of these three explanations is correct. But the fact remains that vocal elements within the PLA appear to be significantly dissatisfied with the compensation package above and beyond the usual bureaucratic appetite for ever greater resources.[16]

These disputes between the military and the civilian leadership highlight the enormous difficulties inherent in the effort to decommercialize the PLA. The appearance of alleged divisions, however, does not necessarily mean that the decision to divest was rammed down the throats of the PLA leadership—the latter, after all, could have agreed with the general thrust of the campaign but felt dissatisfied with the results. Instead, the current evidence suggests that although the PLA and political leaderships both agreed in principle with the goals of divestiture, the PLA now feels slighted by the meager compensation and the aggressiveness of anti-corruption campaigns within its ranks. Given that divestiture is still a work in progress, the long-term implications of these developments for Chinese party-military relations are not entirely clear. But they certainly highlight the extent to which the political and military leaderships play a complex and nuanced game in their policy interactions with one another. On the one hand, the relatively weak political leadership could not simply order the PLA out of business without a series of side payments. On the other hand, the civilian leadership seemed willing to incur the costs of not fully meeting the compensatory demands of the military and thereby risking future party-military confrontation on this issue. Indeed, the whole issue might actually have exploded into conflict had the U.S. Air Force not dropped precision-guided munitions on the Chinese Embassy in Serbia in May 1999. As a result of that attack and the increase in Sino-Taiwan tensions, most analysts feel confident that the PLA will receive substantial annual budget increases in the tenth Five-Year Plan (2000–2005), ensuring the fiscal basis for the PLA's conditional compliance to civilian authority.

Case Study 2: The PLA and the 1995–1996 Missile Tests near Taiwan

In October 1995 and March 1996, China conducted a series of missile tests in the waters surrounding Taiwan—first as a response to Lee Teng-hui's visit to Cornell University in June 1995 and later as an attempt to affect Taiwan's impending presidential election in March 1996. The United States reacted to the March tests by dispatching two carrier battle groups to the Philippine Sea, marking perhaps one of the most tense confrontations between Beijing and Washington in recent memory. Since the spring of 1996, the PLA's role in the internal Chinese decision-making process surrounding the tests and the military's assessment of their success or failure has been the subject of an intense and unresolved debate. Based on the available evidence, it appears that the PLA did not "dictate" policy toward Taiwan during the 1995–1996 crises (Swaine 2000). Instead, the PLA consulted and interacted with a wide variety of players in the policy arena, which was largely though not completely dominated by Jiang Zemin.

From a party-military perspective, this turn of events marks an important shift in the relationship between the senior party leader and the military on Taiwan policymaking and highlights the explanatory power of the conditional compliance framework. Previously Taiwan policy was clearly dominated by both Mao Zedong and Deng Xiaoping; military views on major foreign policy issues were channeled almost exclusively through the paramount leader (Joffe 1999). Under Jiang's leadership, by contrast, the number of additional party, state, and military actors involved in Taiwan affairs has increased significantly, and the policymaking process has become increasingly "bureaucratic in structure and procedure, pragmatic in approach, and consensus-oriented in deliberation and decision-making" (Swaine 2000: 64). No longer can a single dominant leader dictate to the military on foreign policy issues. Instead, the military's preferences must be factored into any decision lest its compliance with the decision be undermined.

Building on one of the themes of this chapter, the change to a more inclusive style of foreign-policy decision making can also be explained by the generational change from Deng and his revolutionary cohort to the weaker, collective leadership of Jiang Zemin ("first among equals") and a new generation of pragmatic technocrats whose authority depends less on personal connections than "policy successes, substantive policy expertise, organizational controls, and the ability to persuade rather than dictate" (Swaine 2000: 28). This transition was further accelerated by the creation of a variety of interagency Taiwan policy organs charged with reacting to the "rapid expansion of cross-strait...interactions, the initiation of a quasi-governmental, bilateral set of political negotiations, and the challenges posed to Beijing by Taiwan's expanding economic capabilities and diplomatic activities" (Swaine 2000: 27). The net result is an intricate Taiwan policymaking system marked by extensive horizontal and vertical consultation, deliberation, and coordination between various military and nonmilitary actors—a system designed to involve the military in policymaking that falls within its perceived corporate interest and ultimately co-opt the military's compliance with civilian-directed policies.

Although the military and the top political leadership share many common interests in Taiwan affairs, they must increasingly cope with new policy differences over how to deal with Taipei. As we have seen, the military pays close attention to Taiwan policy because of its larger role as defender of the motherland and Chinese sovereignty. As Joffe wrote, "The military see themselves as chief protectors of China's territorial interests and national honor" (1999: 37). Pride and patriotism, of course, are universal hallmarks of a military officer corps (Huntington 1957: 79). In the PLA, however, this nationalism has a "particularly sharp quality" because Chinese officers function in an "intense patriotic milieu, which continuously inculcates them with a sense of mission as protectors of these values" (Joffe 1999: 37). This patriotism is often translated into bureaucratic imperatives: "Certain 'litmus test' sovereignty issues, notably Taiwan and the South China Sea, can become arenas for contending élites to prove their mettle and hence are prone to exaggerated nationalist impulses and rash actions" (Shambaugh 1996: 272). Until the Taiwan issue is resolved, it will continue to be the focal point of this nationalist fervor.

Overall the PLA's view is largely congruent with the political leadership's desire to reunify Taiwan with the mainland or at the very least prevent the Taiwanese leadership from explicitly declaring independence from Beijing. This convergence of views on the basic premises of policy is one of the strongest pillars of the PLA's compliance with civilian leadership on this issue. The military and civilians often diverge, however, in the bureaucratic planning and implementation of Taiwan policy (Swaine 2000). Before the events of 1996, there were frequent reports of conflict between the military and the Foreign Ministry over Taiwan affairs, with the PLA exhorting the foreign minister, Qian Qichen, and Jiang Zemin to "hold firm" on sovereignty issues (Shambaugh 2000c).

Yet the PLA faces a paradox that prevents it from simply pressuring the civilians to rash action. Certainly the PLA wants to keep pressure on Jiang Zemin to resolve the Taiwan issue for both normative (nationalism) and material (budgets) reasons. As we have seen, the PLA enjoys a normative self-image as the sword and shield of Chinese nationalism, and its officer corps is even more socialized than the general populace to believe that Taiwan should be rejoined to the mainland. Materially the PLA leadership increasingly views the China-Taiwan situation as its central force-planning scenario—an opportunity to justify the acquisition of new equipment and weapons systems. Thus Taiwan is an issue in which "core questions of China's territorial integrity, national honor, and international stature come together in an explosive mix [and] catapult the military straight to the center of the policymaking arena" (Joffe 1999: 38).

Despite these normative and bureaucratic incentives, however, the PLA is confronted with countervailing forces that are perhaps formidable enough to temper the military's hawkish leanings. First, the historical record makes it clear that the Chinese military, viewed in historical terms, sent troops into battle only when they calculated that success was assured and there was minimal risk of escalation—two critical elements that are absent in the Taiwan situation (Joffe 1997). As Jencks and other analysts have shown, the PLA currently does not have sufficient amphibious, heliborne, or airborne lift to successfully invade Taiwan in a quick operation (Jencks 1997). Further, a blockade or economic warfare would be difficult to implement with the PLA's limited logistics capability and in any case would not achieve the goal of bringing the Taiwanese government to heel before the arrival of the U.S. Seventh Fleet. Indeed, the only credible weapons in the PLA's arsenal for use against Taiwan are short-range ballistic missiles, cruise missiles, and "fifth column" sabotage, which together are not enough to conquer a determined Taiwanese population but could instead have the unintended consequence of destroying Taiwan and thus causing incalculable damage to China's "global stature, regional relations, and economic development" (Joffe 1999: 39). Thus the PLA faces an operational environment in which the probability of failure and unacceptable escalation with the United States is too high for comfort—with the added disincentive that a failed invasion of Taiwan is equivalent to de facto independence for the island and thus the death knell for the legitimacy of the regime on the mainland. The military leadership is understandably wary of placing too much pressure on the political leadership, lest Jiang Zemin "write a check" that the undermodernized PLA cannot cash.

Despite this mixture of common and divergent interests between the military and the top political leadership, the importance of the Taiwan issue in the Chinese political system makes it essential for the civilians to dominate policymaking. Why did Mao, Deng, and now Jiang feel the need to control Taiwan policy? Jiang must retain control over Taiwan policy for both symbolic and substantive reasons (Swaine 1998). First, the paramount leader, beginning with Mao and continuing with Deng, has always controlled Taiwan policy, so any change in this arrangement would be an implicit threat to Jiang's supreme authority. Second, noted Swaine, the "proper handling of the Taiwan issue is critical to the maintenance of regime legitimacy and political stability, given the close linkage between Mainland-Taiwan reunification and Chinese nationalism" (p. 4). Third, Taiwan policy is a critical determinant of the paramount leader's historical legacy. Whereas Mao and Deng were content to let reunification wait for 50 or even 100 years, developments on Taiwan may not give Jiang Zemin a similar luxury, forcing him to accelerate the process of territorial consolidation. More important, the loss of Taiwan would be an enormous blow to the personal reputation of Jiang, who would doubtless be vilified as one of Chinese history's greatest traitors.

Given the importance of controlling Taiwan policy for the paramount leader, the military can either change or alter the policy from without (intervention) or within (collaboration and consultation). Broadly speaking, the military has consistently chosen the latter option. One reason was offered by Swaine (2000: 65):

> Those who seek to explain the evolution of China's grand strategy toward Taiwan in terms of various struggles between sharply opposed personal or bureaucratic factions (e.g., Jiang Zemin versus Qiao Shi or the PLA versus Jiang and the Foreign Ministry) greatly exaggerate the level of contention at work, overlook the basic, longstanding consensus that exists among Chinese élites regarding grand strategy toward Taiwan, and neglect the preponderant influence exerted by Jiang Zemin after 1994.

Indeed, other members of the Politburo Standing Committee and CMC exert significant influence over basic decisions only when there is disagreement among the civilian elites or the leadership is confronted with a crisis. The evidence suggests that this divergence was not present during the 1995–1996 tensions: Jiang never wavered from a hardline position after Lee's visit to Cornell and therefore never found himself in contention with the PLA over the basic line. This is not to say there were no serious conflicts between the military and the top political leadership on Taiwan policy during this period. But the evidence suggests that these differences were limited to issues of timing, operations, and levels of coercive violence. In fact, it was precisely because of their agreement over the basic policy that the military complied with civilian leadership on the issue, though Jiang's hawkish posturing should also be interpreted as a calculated concession to military preferences. In this way, the party-military dynamic during the Sino-Taiwan crisis in 1995–1996 is an instructive microcosm of the conditional compliance arrangement between the PLA and Jiang in the foreign policy arena.

FUTURE TRAJECTORIES AND IMPLICATIONS

In this chapter I have argued that Chinese party-military relations are now characterized by the military's conditional compliance with civilian control. The current harmony of this arrangement is premised on the largely congruent interests of the military and the party elite, though the strains exposed by the divestiture process and the Belgrade Embassy bombing might portend a new, growing division between the military and top political leadership. For the future, the question that must be asked is this: under what circumstances could the PLA's compliance end?

This question is particularly appropriate in light of growing concerns about the downturn in the Chinese economy. With the abandonment of Communist ideology, the basis of CCP legitimacy has shifted to the continued deliverance of economic prosperity to the population. As the drop in growth rates continues to undermine the already shaky foundation of China's banking and state-owned enterprise system, however, one must expect protests in rural and industrial areas to increase, threatening the stability of the regime. These events will mobilize the interests of the PLA, which still considers internal security and the maintenance of stability two of its basic concerns. What is unclear, however, is whether the PLA would again seek to stabilize the situation by seizing de facto control of the country à la Tiananmen or the Cultural Revolution, particularly if the military leadership felt that the crisis had been precipitated by civilian policy decisions. In such a conflict, the separation of military and civilian elites might in fact lead to a praetorian PLA bearing closer resemblance to the "patriotic" juntas of Latin America and Southeast Asia than the Leninist military of the past.

Other circumstances might lead to a similar outcome: a major foreign policy disaster (such as the "loss" of Taiwan) that is directly linked to mistakes by the civilian leadership, for example, or egregiously intrusive or embarrassing meddling in PLA internal affairs (such as continued high-profile corruption investigations in the postdivestiture period). Over the longer term, it is not even clear that the PLA would stay on the sidelines during a period of domestic political reform, especially if the reform movement was in any way predicated on harsh judgments against the military's actions in the 1989 Tiananmen Square massacre. Instead, any political reform movement that hoped for success would likely require the participatory support of the PLA. Attempts to codify mechanisms of state (as opposed to party) control of the military, as discussed by Shambaugh, might serve as a useful transition to this outcome (Shambaugh 2000b).

By contrast, the prospects for continued PLA compliance, at least in the short term, could be bolstered by a new period of sustained economic development. Economic recovery, even if the trajectory was lower than previous bumper years, would likely forestall the impending state-owned enterprise crisis and give the bureaucracy an opportunity to restart badly needed reforms. Affluence would likely buy off some civil society groups, while emboldening others to push the envelope. The legitimacy of the CCP would be bolstered in the short-term, especially if the party continues to reshape itself as a professional manager class, though long-term developmental trends would still suggest the rise of an assertive middle class and gradual democratization à la South Korea or Taiwan. For the PLA, this prosperity would therefore soften the zero-sum nature of the civilian leadership's choices between military modernization and continued economic reform. Double-digit budget increases would be a smaller strain on the central budget, especially if meaningful tax reform were implemented. Thus, prosperity would assuage the PLA's institutional desire for greater resources and its institutional concerns over social stability, removing two primary obstacles to continued conditional compliance.

Future study in this area should focus closely on the relations between the supreme leader and the top military leadership. Observers should watch especially for evidence of fissures on policy or personal grounds. At the same time, analysts should pay attention to long-term trends in the PLA itself and strive to discover new data sources that might illuminate the extent of professionalism in the officer corps. Both of these factors will be important signs of the PLA's willingness to support or even defend the leadership of Jiang and his successors.

CHAPTER 14

Vietnam: From Revolutionary Heroes to Red Entrepreneurs

Thaveeporn Vasavakul

> Time will pass, but the victory of our people in the anti-U.S. war of resistance for national salvation will forever be recorded as one of the most brilliant chapters in our national history and as a shining symbol of the total triumph of revolutionary heroism and human intellect. It will go down in world history as a great exploit of the 20th century and an event of enormous international importance marked by a profound epochal character.
>
> —Resolution of the Fourth National Congress
> of the Vietnamese Communist Party

THE VIETNAM PEOPLE'S ARMY (VPA) was founded in December 1944 as the People's Liberation Armed Force. In the decades that followed, it has expanded and developed into a quasi-conventional army consisting of three types of forces. The main force included the army, navy, and air force; the regional or local force comprised infantry companies organized geographically and with limited mobility; and the militia/self-defense force was organized along administrative lines (village and precinct) or economic lines (commune, factory, work site). Its size grew as well, from a mere 34 members in 1944 to encompass a regular standing army of 1.26 million, reserves numbering 2.5 million, a border defense force of 60,000, and various paramilitary groups totaling an additional 1.5 million in 1987 at the peak (Thayer 1994: 2). A wide range of troops comprise these three forces: regular soldiers, sailors, and airmen in the main force; provincial, regional, district, and commune-level troops in the local force; and militia troops, mobile militia troops, assault youth troops, self-defense patrols, and village troops in the self-defense force. Currently, there are seven military regions and three military zones.

Over the decades, the VPA structure has been extended to include a comprehensive educational and cultural apparatus. It has developed a system of schools and research institutes with separate sets of textbooks and research periodicals for its own establishment. It has set up its own publishing house and runs a series of daily and weekly newspapers as well as literary periodicals. To publicize its mission, the VPA runs museums, produces television and radio programs, and owns film studios, dancing troops, artistic companies, and sports clubs. All these institutions, although they mainly serve the VPA circle, also target the Vietnamese public at large (Bo Quoc Phong 1995a).

As in other socialist countries, the VPA structure is fully integrated into two systems of control: the state and the communist party. At the head of the state are the Ministry of Defense, the National Defense Council, the office of the commander in chief, and five military directorates (Political, Technical, Economic and Defense Industry, Rear Services, and Intelligence). At the head of the Vietnamese Communist Party (VCP) are the Political Bureau, the Party Central Committee, and the Central Military Party Committee (CMPC) (Pike 1987a; Tong Cuc Chinh Tri 1997).

Compared with other modern armies, the VPA meets many of the criteria of a "professional" army. Historically it has concentrated on the main function of all armies—national defense—as illustrated by the war against France (1946–1954), subsequent wars with the Republic of Vietnam and the United States (1959–1975), and military conflicts with Cambodia and China (1977–1989). Moreover, it has remained under civilian control since its inception in 1944. Following the revolution there has been no Bonapartism—no rise of a military strongman—that has characterized many postrevolutionary regimes, including France in 1789 and Thailand in 1932. Its success during the Franco-Vietnam and American wars did not immediately give rise to a general-turned–political leader such as Charles de Gaulle or Dwight Eisenhower. The VPA has so far remained one of the few armies in Southeast Asia that has not engaged in bloody suppression of domestic political forces to buttress incumbent governments, as was the case in Indonesia, Thailand, and Burma. On this score, its record has been far better than its Chinese counterpart.

Several developments in the 1980s and 1990s, however, have cast doubt on its professionalism. During the 1990s, the VPA has repeatedly entered the political, economic, and social spheres. Military political representation that had declined after the end of the Vietnam War began to rise. At the Seventh National Party Congress of the VCP in 1991, fifteen members of the VPA were elected to the 146-member Central Committee, comprising some 10 percent of the total committee membership, up from only 7 percent at the Sixth National Party Congress in 1986. Gen. Le Duc Anh was voted in as president in 1992. At the Fourth Plenum of the Eighth National Congress that met in December 1997, Lt. Gen. Le Kha Phieu, chief of the General Political Directorate, was elected secretary-general. Although he was replaced by Nong Duc Manh (a civilian party member) at the Ninth National Party Congress that met from April 19 to 22, 2001, military representation in top decision-making bodies (the Politburo, Central Committee, and the revived Secretariat) continues. The 1992 constitution recognized the VPA as the backbone of Vietnam's "all people's national defense force and public security system." The Fourth to the Eighth Congresses (1976–1996) endorsed the VPA's economic role, and at the Seventh Congress there was a shift in military representation away from the Ministry of National Defense toward the military services and the military's own corporate interests. By 1993, some 70,000 soldiers, 12 percent of the entire standing army, were reportedly employed full-time in various commercial enterprises. Local militia units had also set up more than 160 enterprises, and the VPA main force had approximately 60 of its organizations engaged in economic activities (Elliott 1992; Thayer 1994). Its newly acquired economic jurisdictional authority has subsequently been legalized. Has Vietnam repeated the pattern of Thailand in the 1930s and Burma and Indonesia in the 1960s—when civilian control of the military was eroded by expansion of the military's jurisdiction into nonmilitary realms?

This chapter examines the VPA's role and its relationship to the party and state institutions in the context of state building—especially in the era of *doi moi* (renewal) officially endorsed in

1986. State building in Vietnam since independence in 1945 has unfolded in roughly three waves. The first occurred in the 1950s when the leadership of the Vietnamese communist movement applied socialist principles to craft a new independent state. The second took place after reunification of the Democratic Republic of Vietnam (DRV) and the Republic of Vietnam in 1975 when the DRV model was imposed on former South Vietnam. The third unfolded in the 1980s following the official endorsement of the policy of *doi moi* by the Sixth National Party Congress of the VCP in 1986 and the final abolition of the central planning system in 1989.

To explain the VPA's state-building role in the era of *doi moi*, the chapter begins by outlining its role in state building during the first and second waves, when the objectives of national reunification and national defense were paramount. We then turn to the position of the VPA in the one-party state, focusing on its relationship with the VCP and addressing the absence of Bonapartism. The chapter then discusses why the VPA has come to play a larger economic, social, and political role in the era of *doi moi* and how its jurisdictional expansion was manifest.

Essentially, I argue that the VPA's contribution to state building has shifted from national reunification and defense to maintaining domestic stability and promoting "socialist-oriented" market economic development. Its rising internal security role was precipitated by perceived threats to the one-party state following the collapse of the socialist bloc, and the expansion of its economic role was largely a response to the need to finance the military establishment in the fact of the country's fiscal crisis. Both of these expanded responsibilities were legalized and institutionalized. As we shall see, these roles have enabled the VPA to become more vocal in initiating, endorsing, and shaping certain policy agendas. This can be seen in its active engagement in policy debate both before and after the party congresses of the 1990s as well as its increasing role in non-defense-related realms. Despite its increasing role in agenda setting, however, the VPA has by no means become the most influential political actor in the system. It has had to share power with other state organizations in the process of putting forth and implementing its policy preferences and indeed, as we shall see, continues to remain under the control of the VCP. Public criticism of both the Ministry of Defense and the general chief of staff by the Central Committe prior to the Ninth Congress, and the departure of the incumbent general secretary Lt. Gen. Le Kha Phieu, suggests not only a process of defining power sharing but also continued party control of the army.

THE FORCE OF THE NATION-STATE: 1944–1989

Most Western studies of the VPA have focused on military doctrines and combat capabilities—predilections driven by military and strategic concerns during wartime. These themes, however, fail to explain why the People's Army gained a popularity that enabled it to expand its size and strength over the decades. From the perspective of state building, the VPA's contribution was not only military but also cultural and political. From its inception in 1944, the very existence of the VPA helped give a concrete meaning to the concept of a modern Vietnamese nation. As Lockhart (1989) argues, the origins of the VPA cannot be separated from the birth of the modern Vietnamese nation. From the very beginning, the notion "army" was closely linked, if not isomorphic, to that of "people," "nation," and "citizen" (*dan-dan toc-quoc dan*).

The link between soldiers and people was further consolidated when the Indochinese Communist Party adopted the Maoist strategy of people's war in the late 1930s and applied it in the

1940s and 1950s during the war with France. In the decades that followed, the VPA became bound to the society in a complex web of political, social, and economic relationships, and experience over the years taught the VPA that it could not function let alone expand unless it was capable of exerting a significant influence in the society.

The liberation army was the main force that contributed to the success of the August Revolution of 1945. With guerrilla tactics and armed propaganda, the Vietnam Independence League, known as Viet Minh and founded in 1941 under the leadership of Ho Chi Minh, mobilized public support against the colonial powers, first in the remote northern provinces of Viet Bac during the international upheavals of 1939 and March 1945. Between March 1945, when the Japanese deposed the French, and August 1945, when Japan surrendered, the Viet Minh, using armed propaganda tactics, was able to expand the army's regular main force in the Viet Bac area from 500 to 5,000 members. It also rapidly multiplied irregular armed propaganda units, national salvation units, self-defense forces, and guerrilla units to include around 200,000 people (Lockhart 1989: 104). Exploiting the situation of famine in the north, a very weak central government in Hue, and general discontent in all major centers beyond its base in Viet Bac, the Viet Minh launched open attacks and ambushes on the French and Japanese and their symbols of domination.

After the August Revolution, the People's Army continued to be a driving force in consolidating the power of Ho Chi Minh's Democratic Republic of Vietnam. The DRV's central administration collapsed after the war with France broke out, but with armed propaganda units the Ho Chi Minh government was gradually able to make its authority felt at the local level. Despite the revolutionary rhetoric since August 1945, the Vietnamese revolution remained superficial—closer to a coup d'état, really, than a transformation of society. There was no fundamental political, social, and economic change at the local level. There was no new means of linking particular interests or creating regional and local unity. There was little redistribution of wealth and virtually no land reform. The majority of the Vietnamese remained indifferent to the anti-French struggle. The People's Army sustained the newly independent state by mobilizing popular enthusiasm through armed propaganda. Regular units were broken down into armed propaganda detachments in order to reorganize political-military affairs in the provinces. Armed propaganda units in the region also played a prominent role in preparing the local defense by organizing meetings and demonstrations to prepare various lines of defense as well as to put pressure on those who might be reluctant to carry them out (Lockhart 1989: 201–5).

The government, with its limited budget, encouraged self-sufficiency among armed units—a policy that encouraged armed units and the population in each region to develop a reciprocal economic relationship. Self-Sufficient Committees consisting of economic cadres were set up to explain the government's policy, plan production, allot fields to the regional forces through negotiations with people in the village, and generally implement what came to be known as the system of "small-scale economic activity." It was carried out by independent regiments at an interprovincial level when peasant units were given the task of clearing land and other long-term economic tasks. In its land-clearing projects, irrigation projects, and raising livestock and poultry, the army had to coordinate its activities with the local population. In areas close to the battlefront, party publications emphasized the need for armed units at all levels to protect and help harvest the rice crop. These economic arrangements were reinforced through political work among the local people because not every Vietnamese citizen wanted to give a bowl of rice to the army (Lockhart 1989: 211). Following the strategy of a people's war, by 1954 mobilized peasants had formed village guerrillas that in turn formed quasi-regular regional units of regimental strength and ultimately the main-force divisions that brought about a major victory at Dien Bien Phu in 1954.

The VPA continued its role as the primary force for state building during the Vietnam War. The main objective now was national reunification. During this period, it expanded to include the National Liberation Front of South Vietnam. Aid from the socialist bloc enabled the armed forces of the DRV to begin to modernize and develop into a modern, conventional army under the leadership of professional officers. The armed units south of the seventeenth parallel, however, developed very much in accord with the guerrilla model.

In the second wave of state building, after 1975, North and South Vietnam were reunified, and the system developed in the DRV was imposed on the newly liberated South. During the first years after reunification, the VPA was in charge of administering the South, demobilizing the Saigon army, running reeducation camps, and wiping out armed resistance in the Mekong Delta and the lowland area of Central Vietnam. The VPA also fought the United Front for the Liberation of Oppressed Races (FULRO) before declaring its victory in the early 1990s. After 1975, Vietnam came into military conflict with Cambodia and clashed militarily with China for the first time since 1789. War with China both reinforced the doctrine of the people's war and the call for force modernization. During this time, the VPA was drawn into training local self-defense forces and supervised the construction of new economic zones in mountainous, coastal, and island areas. It also assumed new educational duties at both university and school levels. Its involvement in the Cambodian conflict lasted until 1989.

The VPA placed its revolutionary fighting mission in the context of Vietnam's tradition of resistance to foreign invasion. It evoked personalities such as Tran Quoc Tuan, Le Loi, and Quang Trung—patriots who defeated the Mongol invasion in the thirteenth century, the Ming invasion in the fifteenth century, and the Qing invasion in the eighteenth century. From the very beginning, a link with tradition is seen in the names given to war zones. The Second War Zone (covering the provinces of Hoa Binh, Ninh Binh, and Thanh Hoa) was called Quang Trung, the regal name adopted by Nguyen Hue, who defeated the Qing troops in 1789. The Third War Zone (encompassing Phu Tho and Yen Bai provinces) was called Hoang Hoa Tham, the name of a Vietnamese local leader who led resistance against French colonialism at the turn of the twentieth century (Lockhart 1989: 126). These practices were retained during the decades that followed.

The VPA's legitimacy resided in the fact that it was a manifestation of a new national consciousness stimulated by colonial rule, national reunification struggle, and national defense. Its growth in size and popularity during the war years followed its success in entrenching itself as cultural symbol and a popular political force. It continued to be a strong political and cultural force within the Vietnamese society that had sustained it despite the end of the war. Its historical legacy, moreover, served as a solid springboard for its venture into new missions in the postwar era.

PATTERNS OF PARTY-MILITARY RELATIONS

The absence of Bonapartism in Vietnam, despite the VPA's major contributions during the August Revolution of 1945 and the wars with France, the United States, Cambodia, and China, stemmed from a number of doctrinal, historical, and organizational factors.

Because the VPA has been a people's army in cultural, political, and military terms, no single person could claim credit for its victories. Historically, as William Turley (1988) points out, the absence of party-military friction owned much to the circumstances in which the Vietnamese communists came to power. It was the party that created the VPA, and those who joined the army were loyal to the party's principle of national liberation. Organizationally, the absence of Bonapartism can also be attributed to the mechanisms designed by the Vietnamese Communist Party over the years to institutionalize party control of the military. Apart from being under the legal jurisdiction of the Ministry of Defense, the entire VPA structure was also placed under the party leadership.

The system of party control applied to all state agencies. The VCP has relied on various mechanisms to oversee the operation of the state apparatus: high-ranking party members have assumed senior positions within the state; party congresses and central committee plenums issue resolutions to direct the implementation of state policy; party committees work with ministries in implementing policies. The party has also set up organizations within the state apparatus that serve as a link to political institutions: party grouping (*dang doan*) in the National Assembly and mass organizations; party affairs sections (*ban can su*) in state agencies; and party committees in the security forces (Dang Phong and Beresford 1997).

These general mechanisms have been grafted onto the armed forces as well. The term "party control" may not entirely capture party-military relations, however, because at the apex and upper middle levels an interwoven, interlocking "dual role elite" has characterized the authority structure (Perlmutter and LeoGrande 1982). In examining the VPA, Turley (1977) and Thayer (1994) emphasize the inextricably intertwined nature of the higher echelons of the party-military leadership. All of the party's political leaders were generals and political commissars in military units; the military was their second career. Gen. Vo Nguyen Giap, for example, was an organizer of the Indochinese Communist Party's Democratic Front in 1936–1939 and coauthored with Truong Chinh a report on the peasantry in 1938. Song Hao, head of the General Political Directorate and vice-minister of defense in the 1960s; Nguyen Chi Thanh, head of the General Political Directorate; and Hoang Van Thai all assumed political positions before entering the VPA (Turley 1977). Conversely, several top civilian party leaders were authoritative in military-related matters. Ho Chi Minh produced a number of writings on the military, and Le Duan, general secretary from 1960 to 1986, wrote on the military situation in southern Vietnam and designed military strategies during the American war. In the 1990s, about 70 percent of all VPA officers concurrently held party membership, and almost all the officers in the VPA from company level upward were party members (Thayer 1994: 3).

In addition to this overlapping elite structure, the VCP has established a system of party committees to oversee the VPA. At the top is the CMPC. Founded in 1946, it was known as the General Political Committee (Tong Chinh Uy) between 1948 and 1952, the General Military Committee (Tong Quan Uy) from 1953 to 1961, and the Military Party Committee (Quan Uy Trung Uong) from 1961 to 1982. Although it was replaced by the Military Council in 1982, it was restored in 1985 under the name Central Military Party Committee (Dang Uy Quan Su Trung Uong). It is considered to be the leading party agency responsible for implementing party directives in the VPA (Tong Cuc Chinh Tri 1997). The VCP also relied on the General Political Directorate to carry out party and ideological work with the VPA and oversee an increasing number of military commanders who were not party members. Set up in 1946, the directorate included departments dealing with organization, agitprop, culture, publications, and personnel. Although it was considered an organization within the Ministry of Defense, it was also placed under the leadership of the Secretariat of the VCP and the CMPC. Later, when the Secretariat was abolished, the directorate was placed under the Political Bureau and the CMPC. The Ninth Congress of the VCP that met in April 2001 revived the Secretariat, and it is likely the old command structure will be put in place again.[1]

Despite the absence of Bonapartism, party-military relations were not altogether free of tension. As many observers have pointed out, the rise of professional officers and the need for technological modernization could encourage tendencies to challenge ideological control. In Vietnam, signs of tension between "red" and "expert" surfaced in the 1950s and 1960s. In some ways, the tension was fostered by the structural and doctrinal transformation of the VPA itself. During the American War, the People's Army grew into a modern conventional army under professional officers. It was also influenced by the Soviet military doctrine that emphasized conventional war waged by the main force (Turley 1988).

A review of documents on the system of party control of the VPA shows that after 1975 two patterns of contending authority relations emerged: one granted supremacy to the system of party committees and the other to the unit commander. The later was put in place during the period from 1979 to 1985.

The 1976 party statute and Politburo Resolution 11 endorsed the supreme authority of the party committee system.[2] The hierarchy was headed by the Military Party Committee (MPC) and the Ministry of Defense Party Committee (MDPC)—the highest-level party "action" arm within the Ministry of Defense. Beneath the MDPC administratively were the party committees descending from military region down to corps, division, regiment, and battalion levels. According to the 1976 party statute, members of the MPC were appointed by the Central Committee and consisted of Central Committee and Politburo members responsible for military affairs; the general secretary of the party assumed the position of secretary. At the military region level, both military officers and provincial party chiefs were included in the authority structure because military regions spanned several provinces. At the division level and above, members of party committees in the VPA were appointed by the Central Committee and the Politburo, and committees at lower levels were elected and ratified by the upper echelon. The MPC received and refined directives and resolutions of the Politburo and the Central Committee. At the local level, the military zone and provincial and municipal party committees made joint decisions on military affairs. If they disagreed, they were required to report to the upper echelon for deliberation. Provincial and municipal party committees provided leadership to all military units within their territory. These units, however, managed troops and technical infrastructure in consultation with both the military region and provincial and municipal party committees. The MPC also supervised the General Political Directorate, which was responsible for party and political work in the armed forces, and the party committee at each level guided the political commissar.[3]

The party committee system was superseded by the one-command system (*che do thu tuong/che do mot nguoi chi huy*), which was endorsed by the Fourth National Party Congress of the VCP in 1976 but not implemented until May 1979.[4] The one-command system represented a different pattern of party-military authority relations. Under this system the unit commander retained ultimate authority and was responsible for all tasks: military, political, logistic, technical, and economic.[5] Although the unit commander had to follow collective decisions and answer to the party

committee at his level as well as the upper echelon, he was allowed to initiate action under special circumstances. If there was disagreement between the unit commander and the party committee, the former had higher authority but had to report the disagreement to the upper echelon
(Dang Vu Hiep 1983). The unit commander was also superior to the political officer: he was considered the highest commander of the unit *(nguoi chi huy cao nhat don vi)* while the political commissar was an assistant on political affairs *(nguoi giup viec ve cong tac chinh tri)*.[6] Supporters of the one-
command system, pointing to the Soviet Union as a model, emphasized the need for quick and
timely responses in carrying out modern warfare (A. I. Bu-Cop 1981a, 1981b; Nhu Phong 1983).

The Fifth Congress resolution of 1982 continued to endorse the one-command system.
Politburo Resolution 7, which followed, abolished the system of party committees and assigned
the functions of the party committee to the unit commander. It also created the military councils—consisting of the commander, deputy commanders, political commissar, and members—
and the commander of each level headed the appropriate military council. At the ministerial
level, the council implemented resolutions of the party and the state and advised the defense
minister on strategic matters. Lower-level councils implemented resolutions of the party and
the Ministry of Defense. Although military councils could not initiate action or assign military
party work, they might deal with cadre work within the jurisdiction assigned.[7]

Resolution 7 also clarified the relationship between regional commanders, regional political directorates, and provincial party committees: the highest authority resided in the hands
of the regional military commander. The provincial and municipal party committee oversaw
the commanders of units within their boundaries to ensure they followed the directives of the
regional military commander. Disagreements between the provincial and municipal party committee and the regional commander had to be reported to the Politburo, Secretariat, or Ministry of Defense, although the former still had to follow the latter's orders while waiting for
deliberation. The Political Department of the military region would coordinate (*phoi hop*) party
work issues with relevant departments of the provincial and municipal party committee.

In August 1983, a directive issued by the Secretariat placed the political commissar under
the direction of the unit commander but above other military officers.[8] The political and party
work offices followed the guidance of the upper echelons, military councils, and unit command
of each level. The General Political Directorate was mainly in charge of nonprofessional military matters; its officers were granted comprehensive responsibility for cultural, ideological,
political, and personnel tasks, combining the role of the party committee secretary and the
political officers in the previous system.[9] They supervised the operations of the VPA newspaper *Quan Doi Nhan Dan* (People's Army), the Army Museum, the army's cultural clubs, artistic
troops, the cultural periodical *Van Nghe Quan Doi* (Arts and Army), film studios, and political
training schools. They were also involved in implementing the party's foreign policy—particularly in the relationship between Vietnam, Cambodia, and Laos and relations between Vietnam and other socialist countries. Finally, they were responsible for coordinating with other
agencies to formulate military policy and provided guidance for the financial management of
the party in the military (Dang Vu Hiep 1983; Chu Huy Man 1984).

The one-command system was in place only for a short period of time. In 1985, the party
committee system returned.[10] At the central level the MPC was restored. Assuming the new
name Central Military Party Committee, it was the main party organization within the army
responsible for helping the Politburo, the Central Committee, the Party's Defense Commission,

and the Secretariat with military and defense tasks. The commander was answerable to both its party committee and the upper-level commander, whereas the political officer was placed under the higher echelon of the party committee and its own party committee. This change was endorsed by the Sixth National Party Congress of the VCP, which met in December 1986 and passed a resolution revising the party statute. Clause 38 of the statute endorsed collective leadership of the party committee system.[11]

This clause was elaborated in a policy pronouncement on party organization issued by the Secretariat in July 1987. According to the document, the unit commander had to be under the leadership of the party committee (*phuc tung su lanh dao tap the cua dang uy*), reporting to the committee on the situation within the unit and implementing assignments under the supervision of the committee. However, in case of military action, the commander would report to the committee on the tasks assigned by the upper military echelon, measures to initiate war, and other contingencies. The committee would discuss and pass resolutions. Also in an emergency, the unit commander had the power to act first and report later.[12] The supremacy of the party committee and the principle of collective leadership were reconfirmed by the 1991 and 1996 party statutes.[13]

Overall, what emerged in the late 1980s and 1990s shows signs of a compromise that gave the VPA more internal autonomy. It was clear that the VCP reasserted its control over the VPA through the party committee system. Prior to 1985, the political commissar was subordinate to the unit commander but senior to other military officers, but by 1987, the commissar and political and party work offices were placed under party committee and upper-echelon control.[14] However, the VCP also continued to grant the VPA some internal autonomy in the area of professional military matters. The unit commander was allowed to act if necessary and report later. Equally important, the responsibilities of the General Political Directorate and its party committees dealt mainly with nonprofessional military matters. This combination of collective leadership and internal autonomy remains the case in the late 1990s (Pham Van 1998).

It is also pertinent to note that the emphasis on bureaucratic hierarchy did not mean that the role of personalities would be completely neutralized. Personalities remained relevant in at least three areas of party-military relations: the relationship between the Ministry of Defense and the general secretary; the relationship between the unit commander and the political commissar; and the relationship between the commander of the military region and the provincial or municipal party chief (Bo Quoc Phong 1995a).[15] According to party statutes, for example, the head of the CMPC was the general secretary whereas the deputy head was the minister of defense. But until 1978, Gen. Vo Nguyen Giap, minister of defense, also assumed the position of the CMPC secretary. After he left office, only the general secretary (Le Duan, Truong Chinh, Nguyen Van Linh, Do Muoi) served as head of the CMPC. In the 1980s, the unit commander was often the political officer and the secretary of the party committee, as well—in other words, a complete monopoly of power. As Thayer's study of the 1992 National Assembly elections has pointed out, the results showed that candidates from the military establishment were more popular than those from the provincial and municipal civilian sector (Marr and Thayer 1993). The popularity of certain military leaders or local military establishments undoubtedly undermined the bureaucratic line of authority, which in turn could foster internal tension, especially when different policy preferences emerged.

REVOLUTIONARY HEROES AT A TURNING POINT: 1989–1991

From the perspective of state building, the 1980s and 1990s represented a turning point. Two clusters of factors, all interrelated, catalyzed the process. One was the VCP's official endorsement of the policy of *doi moi* at the Sixth National Party Congress in 1986, following chronic economic crisis and foreign policy difficulties after the imposition of the socialist model on South Vietnam and military conflict in Cambodia. The other was the changing direction of Soviet foreign policy after the rise of Mikhail Gorbachev in 1985 and the political crisis that developed in the socialist bloc between 1989 and 1991 that culminated in the collapse of communist rule in the Soviet Union and Eastern Europe. These forces shaped the development of the Vietnamese state structure in general and the VPA structure in particular. Indeed, these developments justified a shift in the VPA's role from external defense to internal security and a transition from revolutionary fighters to red entrepreneurs.

From National Defense to Internal Security

The endorsement of *doi moi*, with its emphasis on an open-door foreign policy and economic renewal, marked the beginning of the end of Vietnam's almost five decades of continuing war and military conflict. Following the *doi moi* spirit, in 1987, the Politburo issued Resolution 2 calling for the withdrawal of forces from Cambodia and Laos and a reduction of the VPA's size by half through demobilization (Thayer 1994: 14–17). In 1989, Vietnam announced the complete withdrawal of troops from Cambodia, ending more than ten years of military conflict with its Southeast Asian neighboring countries and China. The Vietnamese leadership began to approach China for normalization of relations in the late 1980s. Following the Seventh Congress's proclamation that Vietnam would befriend all countries in 1991, a peace agreement was signed with China. In the years that followed, with the exception of minor clashes along the northern border and encounters with Chinese patrol boats in the South China Sea, the VPA, for the first time since its inception, experienced peace. Between 1988 and 1993, the size of the armed forces was indeed cut in half: from around 1 million to 500,000.[16] Defense expenditure was reduced considerably, as well, owing to manpower cuts and transition from war to peace. The defense budget dropped from $2.54 billion in 1988 to $720 million in 1992.

Unlike neighboring countries in Southeast Asia, in Vietnam a substantial reduction of external threat and a more open international environment did not completely undermine the VPA's position in the political system. In Thailand, for example, the military coup in 1992 to counter "the spread of communism" was met with skepticism and outright popular resistance. In Vietnam, the VPA's position in the domestic realm was strengthened in the wake of the crisis in the socialist bloc that culminated in the collapse of socialism as state ideology in Eastern Europe and the Soviet Union between 1989 and 1991. During that political crisis, VPA leaders rendered support to the VCP by endorsing the resolution of the Sixth Plenum of the Central Committee in March 1989 that asserted the supremacy of one-party rule,[17] as well as the resolution of the Seventh Plenum in August 1989 condemning the intervention of imperialist forces in the internal affairs of socialist countries.

Around this period, the concept of "peaceful evolution" (*dien bien hoa binh*), a term used to refer to political instability triggered by an external enemy, became a constant theme in speeches given by military officers. VPA leaders argued that the collapse of the Soviet Union and Eastern Europe was not only precipitated by problems inherent in socialism but also from the fact that imperialist forces, especially the United States, had capitalized on domestic difficulties to topple the regimes. Peaceful evolution was a war without gunfire. It relied on political, ideological, psychological, economic, technical, foreign policy, and cultural measures to develop conditions that would undercut socialism within the homeland of socialism itself.

To counter these advances, the armed forces argued that it had to cultivate a close relationship with different social groups. To prevent the VPA itself from being "infected" (*mien dich*), the armed forces had to strengthen themselves on both the ideological and the cultural fronts. This task would be the responsibility of writers, artists, journalists, performers, publishing houses, and artistic troops within the VPA establishment itself (Dang Vu Hiep 1996). The VPA also designed a general plan to cope with internal threat, should it appear, by assigning its regular forces to defend vital areas including offshore islands, oil and gas exploration zones, and border regions (such as the central highlands, the Plains of Reeds, and Long Xuyen quadrangle). As Thayer details in his study, each military region, province, and district would have its own strategic areas treated as special defense zones. In Military Region IV, for example, three separate defense areas were identified: the sea, cities along National Highway 1, and the mountain and forest area. Military Region V considered the Paracel and Spratly islands and the territory where Vietnam joined Laos and Cambodia as sensitive zones. Military Region IX identified the sea area and the southwest border with Cambodia as special defense zones (Thayer 1994: 46).

In 1994, the midterm party conference officially recognized "peaceful evolution" as one of the major threats to the nation-state. The concept, further clarified and expanded, became entrenched in the new political vocabulary of Vietnam in the era of *doi moi*.

From Warriors to Entrepreneurs

The rise of Mikhail Gorbachev and his new thinking in foreign policy had a major impact on the development of Vietnam's military establishment. At the beginning, during the war with France, the VPA received assistance from China to develop a regular infantry force supported by heavy artillery. After the partition of Vietnam in 1954, it received military assistance from both China and the Soviet Union that allowed specialized corps, especially naval and air forces, to develop. In 1968, aid from the Soviet Union surpassed China's in modernizing the Vietnamese naval and air forces and continued to do so after the signing of the 1978 Treaty of Friendship and Cooperation (Thayer 1997). Gorbachev's new foreign policy advocated a cutback in warship deployments to the Indian Ocean and in foreign military assistance. Moscow subsequently withdrew all its military forces from Cam Ranh Bay and did not renew the Vietnam-Soviet military agreements that expired in 1990. In 1991, Soviet military assistance to Vietnam was cut by one-third (Thayer 1997).[18]

These changes in Soviet policy had an impact on the central Vietnamese government budget in general and the defense budget in particular. Vietnam's fiscal crisis, which had developed during the transitional period from central planning to a market economy, did not allow further increases in the military budget. In the 1990s, all three armed services were lacking in military equipment, spare parts, training, and technical advice. Procurement to replace and upgrade equipment has been minimal and no modernization program has been presented. It was in this context that the VPA moved into the role of entrepreneur—a move justified by the central government's fiscal crisis. The VPA's economic role in the era of *doi moi* was legalized by government decisions in 1989.

The VPA's involvement in the economy was not, however, altogether new. The history of military-run production units dates back to the period before the August Revolution, when VPA units began producing weapons, and defense industries continued to expand after the end of the Franco-Vietnam war in 1954 (Bo Quoc Phong 1995b). In 1958, the Fourteenth Plenum of the Central Committee, for the first time, officially emphasized the need to link economic development with defense (Hoang Minh Thao 1998). In the 1960s, during the American war, VPA units carried out production activities around military encampments by growing vegetables or raising livestock. A larger economic undertaking, however, directly linked with state plans, began in the early 1970s (Dang Kinh 1976).[19] By 1975, a number of units under the control of the Ministry of Defense, military regions, military corps and services, and provincial military units were engaged in agriculture, industry, transportation, basic construction, the opening of new economic zones, railroad construction, forestry, irrigation, airport construction, and construction supplies (Xa Luan 1976). After the war, in 1974 and 1975, the 24th Plenum of the Central Committee allowed all VPA units to remain involved in economic development—emphasizing that this engagement was both a "strategic and long-term task" (Nguyen Anh Bac 1976; "Nghi quyet" 1976). In 1976, Gen. Vo Nguyen Giap announced that economic development was a political mission of a socialist army endorsed by both Marx and Lenin. Moreover, economic gains, especially in construction, transportation, agriculture, and defense industries, would strengthen the postwar national economy (Vo Nguyen Giap 1976). Apparently, Giap was rebutting opponents who cast doubt on the expansion of the VPA economic role. In another speech given in July 1977, Giap divided VPA units into regular fighting units and those specializing in economic production: the former undertook economic activities to improve the living conditions of unit members and their families; the latter, like other state-owned enterprises, worked to fulfill production targets assigned by state plans. These two types of units could be placed under different jurisdictions ranging from ministry to military zone to local self-defense forces. There was no unified organizational structure for units specializing in economic production; their organization would depend on the tasks and the level of technology available (Vo Nguyen Giap 1977a, 1977b).

In the late 1980s, official publications from the VPA circle generally supported the VPA's involvement in economic activities. At the beginning, these activities were viewed as a way of enabling VPA units to cover the additional costs of providing retirement benefits, housing, and other amenities to demobilized soldiers. Later they were considered a means of making up for the lost Soviet aid and the fiscal crisis of the Vietnamese state in general. Proponents of the VPA's economic role highlighted the fact that military production units had so far been successful: they not only improved the lives of unit members or reduced the military's burden on the budget but also contributed revenue (*nop ngan sach*) to the state budget.

The VPA's role in the economy in the late 1980s differed from that of the past, however. Above all, the VPA had to operate in a market-oriented economy. Although there were indications that the central planning and subsidization mentality survived among military-owned production units, the general tendency was to move toward business accounting. The documents issued by the CMPC and the Council of Ministers in March 1989 were aimed at easing the transition of military production units to market mechanisms. The CMPC directive of 1989 confirmed the VPA's involvement in economic production to improve the livelihood of the units and to contribute to the state budget.[20] Though the Ministry of Defense would serve as "line ministry," the main agency responsible for economic activities would be the General Economic and Defense Industry (Tong cuc Cong nghiep quoc phong va kinh te)—a merger of the Economic General Directorate and agencies responsible for defense industries. The State Planning Commission, the Ministry of Finance, and related branches would help the Council of Ministers formulate financial and technical plans for these enterprises. Military-owned enterprises (MOEs) had to follow party policies and state laws regarding remittances to the state budget.[21] MOEs would be placed under the jurisdiction of the authorities of the areas in which they were located. Those located in the provinces, for example, would be under the management of the local people's councils and had to contribute to the local budget. The province's responsibility to MOEs was the same as toward centrally owned enterprises operating in the locality.[22]

In terms of organization, units specializing in production and defense industries were advised to reorganize themselves as enterprises, unions of enterprises, or state corporations (following Council Minister Decision 217 and Circulars 716 and 1640 of the Ministry of Defense). They had legal status, could operate accounts (including foreign accounts), and could form joint ventures with domestic and, in some cases, foreign companies. MOEs with sufficient qualifications would be allowed to cooperate with foreigners, especially with Laos, and Cambodia.[23] Units repairing weapons would be categorized as large-scale enterprises that could apply business accounting procedures immediately; small-scale enterprises would undergo gradual reform.

This CMPC directive was legalized by Council of Ministers Directive 46/CT on defense and economic production of the army and Government Decree 22/HDBT to set up the General Department of Defense Industry and Economy (Tong Cuc Cong Nghiep Quoc Phong va Kinh Te).[24] Both party and state documents issued in 1989 facilitated the transition from central planning to a market economy. They also had the effect of legalizing the relationship between the Ministry of Defense and MOEs and the latter's position in the economic system.[25]

RED ENTREPRENEURS AND STATE BUILDING IN THE 1990S

The continuing integration of the VPA and its increased influence in the political system in the 1990s could be traced to its role in supporting the VCP during the crisis in the socialist bloc and its expanding economic base in the 1980s. In the 1990s, VPA leaders voiced their opinions on issues related to their own corporate interests as well as the building of a new economic and political order.

The Vietnamese political system offered various channels for political sectors to voice their concerns. First, the party circulated draft documents for comment and general discussion before endorsing the final version. The period leading up to congresses or Central Committee plenums, therefore, was an occasion for different sectors to express their opinions. Second, party committees within different state sectors or mass organizations regularly held meetings and congresses to discuss the party's draft policies. Third, different sectors were granted bloc representation in the party apparatus and the National Assembly. Finally, each political and social institution had its own infrastructure with separate sources of finance, research institutes, publishing houses, journals, and newspapers. It relied on these resources to put forth its policy preferences.

Differences between VPA leaders and other party leaders could be detected before the Eighth National Party Congress in 1996. In August 1995, in an unprecedented manner, Prime Minister Vo Van Kiet circulated a memo to the Politburo discussing some of the issues related to future development. Kiet focused on four areas: the international system, socialist orientation, the role of the administrative state in economic development, and party reform.[26] Kiet argued that international relations were no longer characterized by confrontation between socialism and imperialism but reflected a situation of multipolarity. He also downplayed the power of imperialism, contending that the United States could no longer use anticommunist rhetoric to mobilize public opinion against Vietnam. Kiet identified socialist orientations with a prosperous people, a strong nation, and an equitable and civilized society. The degree of development of the state economic sector and the agricultural cooperative model, he said, was not indicative of a socialist orientation. He also suggested that the state economic sector be thoroughly reformed. Regarding party reform, Kiet criticized the party leadership style: autonomy must be granted to executive and juridical agencies, he maintained, and to elected representative bodies. He also suggested that the principle of democratic centralism be replaced with democracy within the party.

In early 1996, *Thong Tin Chuyen De* (News in Focus), a journal reserved specifically for the VPA circle, published a series of opinions on general directions for the building of the new socioeconomic and political order that argued against Kiet's interpretation of the new situation. One article, for example, attacked certain political, economic, and ideological positions as the "rightist opportunist tendency" found within the party rank and file, listing four major features of this tendency. First was the denial of contradictions between socialism and capitalism, between imperialism and suppressed nationalities, and between the exploiters and the exploited. Second was the rejection of the concept of democratic centralism and the separation of the concept of a state governed by law from the concept of class. Third was the rejection of the proletariat class character of the party and party leadership through the system of party committees. Fourth was the selective use of the party's slogan, "Rich People, Strong Country, Civilized Society," while ignoring the socialist elements underlying it. VPA publications argued that all four features were compatible with what the United States and antagonistic forces had advocated (Nguyen Nam Khanh 1996).

Some VPA leaders addressed only certain aspects of Kiet's speech. Senior Lt. Gen. Le Kha Phieu, then a member of the Politburo and secretary of the Party Central Committee (and later general secretary of the VCP), admitted that the collapse of socialism had created a major psychological shock (*soc*) among socialist leaders. He placed this development in a historical context, however, arguing that Marxism had moved from being merely an ideological current in the latter nineteenth century to the status of state ideology and, moreover, had gone through ups and downs in its confrontation with capitalism (Le Kha Phieu 1996). Doan Khue, then defense minister, emphasized both national independence and international cooperation, domestic and foreign sources of capital, international integration and exports as well as replacement of imports with domestic products, and a multisectoral economy with the state sector as the leading force. Economic development had to go hand in hand with the development of human resources and the improvement of living conditions, culture, education, and social equality (Doan Khue 1996).

Discussions prior to the Eighth National Congress, however, dealt only with general political orientation. In practice, throughout the 1990s, the VPA continued to consolidate its internal security and economic development tasks. Yet this did not mean it could monopolize the political stage. Despite its stronger bargaining position based on its newly consolidated role, the

VPA had to interact with other state agencies within the sectoral political framework of the *doi moi* era (Vasavakul 1997). As a state institution, it had to share power with other state organizations in the process of articulating and implementing its policy preferences. To shed further light on these points, let us take a closer look at the issues related to national defense and internal security and the jurisdiction of the VPA's economic role.

Modernization, Diplomacy, and Internal Security

After the Seventh National Party Congress in 1991, which saw the VPA's rise to political prominence in major political bodies, the VPA seemed to have a stronger bargaining position. As Thayer observed, in 1992 the defense budget increased for the first time since 1975, and in 1993 Deputy Prime Minister Phan Van Khai reported an increase in state revenues and emphasized the need to allocate state funds to meet the needs of national defense and security—specifically in the South China Sea (Thayer 1997). The 1990s, however, saw no major change in Vietnam's foreign and security policies. The VPA carried out only limited force modernization, and the Vietnamese leadership continued to emphasize diplomatic means to ensure external security.

Within the VPA establishment, there have long been two views on how to modernize the military. The first view, based on traditional and contemporary experience, holds that it is not necessary to have modern weapons and technical equipment to counter a modern enemy. Moreover, proponents of this view acknowledge, the current budget does not allow for a full program of force modernization. A second view, however, emphasizes the modernization of the Vietnamese forces and urges the purchase of weapons to make up for technological deficiencies. Proponents of this view cite the Gulf War in 1991 and NATO's bombing of Kosovo as lessons.

The first view has been adopted as the official line. The essence of this path, as summed up by Doan Khue, the late minister of defense, was to combine "'modernizing' soldiers' and citizens' standard of using weapons and technical equipment with the selective modernization of the weapons and means themselves" (Thayer 1997). In the 1990s, there was no sign of a major move toward military modernization. At best, there was a restructuring program in combination with ad hoc purchases to fill gaps for short-term needs. The restructuring included the amalgamation of the activities of the General Department of Administration, Economy, and Technology and the Defense Industry department to form a new department in the early 1990s. Apart from a reduction in strength by 50 percent, the VPA is currently amalgamating the air defense corps into the air force, a move that will result in a reduction of manpower by 40 or 50 percent, that is, by 12,500 personnel.

In terms of procurement of equipment, the main objective was to cope with the situation in the Spratly Islands. The VPA purchased Sukhoi-27 aircraft with the ability to pass over the archipelago from Bien Hoa Air Base in Ho Chi Minh City. It purchased eight helicopters to assist the U.S. Joint Task Force in missing-in-action operations. It also purchased six old MiG-21s from Russia at reduced prices. (Due to poor overhauling of equipment, practically 80 percent of the aircraft were not serviceable.) It procured naval equipment, including two Tarantul II missile corvettes (Type 1241) and two North Korean midget submarines to operate in Cam Ranh Bay. These naval acquisitions increased Vietnam's defense potential; the VPA's South Sea Fleet was estimated to possess 25 submarines, 5 destroyers, 10 frigates, and about 200 amphibious vessels.[27]

Overall, the VPA has remained quantitatively and qualitatively incapable of containing the Chinese naval threat. It is possible that the dilution of its pre-1989 military power has encouraged Hanoi to focus on diplomacy and expand its range of external relationships. Senior Vietnamese intelligence officials privately concede, for example, that security considerations were the key factor behind Hanoi's joining the Association of Southeast Asian Nations (ASEAN) in 1995 (and its ASEAN Regional Forum). Diplomatic efforts were being launched since it was impossible to rely on Russian warships at Cam Ranh Bay in light of the Kosovo crisis. Since the Hanoi ASEAN summit in December 1998, Vietnam has stopped protesting to China over the Spratlys. In early 1999, General Secretary Le Kha Phieu signed an agreement with China; its military aspects were aimed at solving the land border issue by the end of 1999, solving the Gulf of Tonkin issue by the year 2000, and holding bilateral talks to resolve the Spratlys question in the immediate future. Reports from military circles, however, indicate that clashes still occurred despite the goodwill expressed by the two parties in the agreement.

The VPA's internal security role was further emphasized in the 1990s. The 1992 constitution regarded the VPA as the backbone of Vietnam's national defense and public security system. However, its public security role was not absolute. The VPA has adopted a collective and nonviolent strategy to deal with "riots" (*bao loan*). In 1997, *Khoa Hoc Quan Su*, a limited circulation journal published by the Center for Scientific, Technological, and Environmental Information of the Ministry of Defense, published a series of articles on "riot" management. The authors identified sources of riots as coming from reactionaries or external enemies who exploited local resentment over issues related to land, ethnicity, taxation, and religion. They also outlined certain principles in dealing with riots. First, the main person in charge would not come from the military establishment, but from the civilian sector, either deputy head of the provincial party committee or deputy head of the People's Committee. This person would form a committee consisting of representatives from the local police force, the army, and other local party and government agencies. These articles argue that the main strategy was to understand the situation and identify participants and ringleaders in order to deal with them appropriately. It was necessary not to treat participants as monolithic and separate those considered to be reactionary ringleaders from the general population as soon as possible. Emphasis was given to the principle of "skillful" (*khon kheo*) and "supple" (*mem deo*) management. Force should be avoided, and if it had to be used, it should be limited in scale (Tran Minh Thiet 1997; Nguyen Kim Ton 1997; Dinh Tu Linh 1997).

The role of the VPA during the Buddhist demonstration in Hue in 1993 and the Thai Binh debacle in 1997 corresponded with the principles outlined in these writings. The VPA was silent during the Buddhist demonstration, and it did not resort to the use of force during the rural unrest in Thai Binh.[28] Its role during the Thai Binh debacle was mainly political. Troops were sent in to stabilize the chaotic areas in conjunction with other local agencies. The main strategy adopted by the party and the government was "negotiation" to identify ringleaders and "persuasion" to deter further unrest. After the expulsion of more than 200 local party and government leaders in the province of Thai Binh, a substantial number of vacant positions were reportedly assumed by army officials. The VPA's role during ethnic unrest in the central highlands in late January and early February of 2001 was also restrained. This unrest was reportedly precipitated by religious tension as well as the ethnic minority's resentment of the Viet's seizure of land in the area. Army units were reportedly sent to oversee the situation, but the VPA's subsequent reaction to the unrest was mainly political. In early February, *Quan Doi Nhan Dan* (People's Army) published an article discussing the communist authorities' warning to religious leaders to maintain solidarity and avoid allowing religion to be used as a divisive factor.

In the following months, the VPA-run mass media contributed substantially to the general campaign against the United States for its role in instigating the unrest. The campaign intensified in the weeks leading to the Ninth Congress of the VCP in April 2001.

Military-Owned Enterprises and the Market Economy

By the early 1990s, the VPA's economic role had shifted from simply engaging in economic tasks to improving efficiency and performance. To justify this economic role, advocates of the military's economic role have pointed to historical precedents, the traditional role of the Vietnamese people in defending and building the country, the compatibility between military infrastructure and economic organizations, and material gains to both VPA units and the state budget. In 1995, the position of the MOEs in the Vietnamese economy was confirmed, and military-run production units were again classified into different categories that played different roles in the Vietnamese economy and the process of state building.

Economic Jurisdiction.   In 1995, the Ministry of Defense issued a decision to clarify the position of military-run economic enterprises. It grouped military units engaged in economic production into two classes: regular units involved in the economy and military-owned enterprises (*doanh nghiep trong quan doi*).

Regular units involved in production were forces within the military that spent time outside of military training to engage in productive labor in three categories. One included military units to increase production. The other included science and technical agencies, research institutes, and schools, capitalizing on their specialized knowledge and infrastructure to provide technical services or carry out experimental productions.[29] The third included operating hotels, repair stations, and military hospitals that had not been registered as business enterprises but were allowed to operate for business purposes.

Military-owned enterprises, following Decision 388/ HDBT, could be set up by decision of the prime minister or the minister of defense. Businesses were divided into defense industries (*doanh nghiep quoc phong*), defense-related economic enterprises (*doanh nghiep kinh te quoc phong*), and exclusively commercial enterprises (*doanh nghiep chuyen lam kinh te*). Defense industries were firms producing or repairing weapons and other military equipment; these firms were part of the VPA structure. Defense-related economic enterprises coordinated economic development with defense needs by producing goods and providing material and welfare for civilians or for the areas along the border or on islands of strategic importance. Exclusively commercial enterprises were firms within the military that produced goods for civilian use similar to other state-owned enterprises (SOEs). MOEs were granted autonomy in managing and developing capital. For defense enterprises, capital came from the state budget (that is, from the Ministry of Defense). Capital for commercial purposes could be mobilized from different sources according to state law and the guidelines from the Ministry of Finance.

The 1995 document had the effect of consolidating the role of the Ministry of Defense as the line ministry. It also endorsed the legal status of MOEs and placed their development in the context of the development of state-owned enterprises following rules and regulations imposed by the central government. Different MOE enterprises functioned differently and had different implications for the creation of a new economic order.

Exclusively Commercial Enterprises.   Exclusively commercial enterprises, owned by different components of the Ministry of Defense, were governed by state laws and regulations governing SOEs. In terms of quantity, they formed only a small fraction of SOEs: just 300 out of more than 6,000 in the mid-1990s. But in terms of quality, they reportedly performed well compared with other SOEs.

In the 1990s, the VPA embarked on several undertakings to improve the performance of businesses in a market economy. In 1993, it established a joint-stock commercial bank to mobilize capital for its businesses. In 1995, it reportedly operated at least 335 companies, 10 percent of which were joint ventures with foreign partners. About 100,000 personnel of an estimated 600,000 were employed by these joint-venture companies, whose combined sales revenue was more than $360 million (up from $220 million in 1994 and $170 million in 1993). Between 1995 and 1997, small and medium-sized enterprises in the same line of business were merged to strengthen their competitiveness with local, joint-venture, and foreign companies. This move reduced the number of enterprises to about 200 in 1997. Some 56 percent of these enterprises were joint ventures.[30]

It has been difficult to assess how well MOEs have performed compared with other SOEs, but the general impression is that they have been doing well. According to Deputy Defense Minister Nguyen Van Rinh, for example, although the Vietnamese economy was severely affected by the economic crisis in Asia, MOEs could continue to develop. Income in 1998 increased 7.6 percent over 1997. The average worker's salary within MOEs in 1998 was around 780,000 dong per month ($55), which was higher than the monthly remuneration stipulated in the labor law.[31] MOEs also entered competition with other SOEs. *Quan Doi Nhan Dan*, for example, recounted in detail a military-run garment company (under jurisdiction of the rear services) that decided to buy a machine from a Korean factory in Vinh Phu and began to produce its own material. It turned out that it was more efficient and could produce higher-quality textiles than that supplied by the Nam Dinh textile enterprise.[32]

Combining Development with Defense.   In reacting to China's policy of divesting military-owned enterprises in 1998, VPA leaders reportedly emphasized that its MOEs did not concentrate merely on commercial gains but served social and security functions as well. They referred specifically to defense-related economic enterprises located in remote areas deemed to be security-sensitive. The concept of "combining economic development with defense," repeatedly evoked by VPA leaders in the 1990s, has so far been instrumental in its domestic economic and security role. Security-sensitive areas include remote border areas, islands, and mountainous territory inhabited by minorities. Rural Vietnam, moreover, has not yet received benefits accruing from direct foreign investment.

Defense-related economic zones were developed in the central highlands, where VPA units concentrated mainly on planting rubber and coffee. A series of articles in the army newspaper *Quan Doi Nhan Dan* discussed how Corps 15 (Binh Doan 15) and its state farm unit, known as Enterprise 75, developed a defense-related zone in the province of Gia Lai. Corps 15 and Enterprise 75 mobilized capital from various sources, including short-term and long-term loans as well as contributions from enterprise workers. The enterprise offered regular training sessions for workers regarding the party's minority policy and the customs of the area's Gia Rai ethnic group. It maintained a good relationship with local government officials, especially at the district and commune levels, a policy that stabilized the area politically. The enterprise

subcontracted agricultural production to minority families, although the policy met with difficulty at first since the minorities were only familiar with slash-and-burn cultivation.[33]

In 1998, the government assigned VPA units to carry out additional socioeconomic development plans in the central highlands and Central Vietnam. One plan concentrated on the
southern part of Dac Lac, another on the northern part of Binh Phuoc, and a third on the Bac
Hai Son area—all of which were considered defense-related economic zones. The long-term
plans for Dac Lac and Binh Phuoc covered the period from 1999 to 2007: the goals were to
plant rubber, coffee, industrial plants, and forest trees. The plan for the Bac Hai Son and Dong
Van areas in Quang Binh, covering the period from 1999 to 2003, focused on rice growing, fruit
trees, animal husbandry, and reforestation. Deputy Defense Minister Nguyen Van Rinh called
for different government agencies to facilitate the implementation of these projects. One measure dealt with the legal transfer of land to the VPA for management until it was satisfactorily
developed. Another allocated funding to build infrastructure in these areas: roads, hospitals,
and schools for army units as well as the local population. A final measure dealt with tax exemptions to alleviate financial burdens during the first years of investment.

Apart from economic activities, military units also helped implement social policies assigned
by the central government—such as literacy campaigns, universalization of education, primary
health care, improvement of cultural and educational information, and poverty alleviation. In
1992, the border patrol signed an agreement with the Ministry of Education and Training to
implement educational programs in each province; since then, border military units have been
directly involved in anti-illiteracy campaigns and popularization of primary education.[34]

Concerns over internal security and the process of peaceful evolution further legitimized
the concept of combining economic development with defense—allowing the VPA to become
involved in decision making regarding investment or development plans. At the time of the
Eighth National Party Congress in 1996, an article in the army's special journal *Thong Tin Chuyen
De* (News in Focus) lamented that politicians (*nha chinh tri*) did not pay attention to the economic
strategy of peaceful evolution. The author added that the military's involvement in economy
was not only justified by tradition but was essential since it also served defense purposes (Dang
Vu Hiep 1996). At different administrative levels, civilian officials were compelled to consult
military officials when security issues were involved. At the provincial level, the province of
Khanh Hoa was a case in point, owing to the importance of Cam Ranh Bay. At the national
level, the VPA circle more or less contributed to the process of trade negotiation with the United
States.[35] In this case, many VPA leaders supported a closer relationship with the United States
as a means to counter the perceived threat from China.

FUTURE TRAJECTORY AND IMPLICATIONS

Developments at the turn of the century continue to confirm power sharing between the VPA
and other state institutions. Prior to the Ninth National Congress of the VCP, the Central Committee issued a statement criticizing both Pham Van Tra, defense minister, and Le Van Dung,
general chief of staff. When he was interviewed during the Party Congress, Defense Minister
Pham Van Tra admitted that he had been criticized but clarified that it was for a security breakdown during the November visit of the then U.S. president Bill Clinton. During the historic
visit, a Vietnamese-American dissident, Ly Tong, succeeded in flying a small aircraft from Thai-

land to Ho Chi Minh City and dropped leaflets calling for an end to communist rule. In the last few months the army and the security services put all their weight into the "war" of succession between conservative and reformist forces for the top VCP leadership positions. It is likely that the top generals were victims of the power struggle betweeen the embattled general secretary and those who sought to replace him.

At the Ninth Congress of the VCP that met in April 2001, General Secretary Lt. Gen. Le Kha Phieu was replaced by Nong Duc Manh, chairman of the National Assembly since 1992. Phieu was criticized on at least four accounts by different sections of the Central Committee of the Eighth Congress. The first dealt with favoritism—the appointment of supporters from his home province to major positions in the party and the government. The second involved his attempt to monopolize power by merging the positions of the general secretary and the president. Third, he was considered to have made inappropriate use of the security services to investigate the personal lifestyle and property holdings of top-ranking party members. Fourth, he was criticized for his overly pro-China foreign policy, exemplified by his concessions to China in negotiating border issues, as well as his conservative outlook during President Clinton's visit to Vietnam in November 2000. The charges against Phieu reflected the general thinking among the top party leaders who favored maintaining regional balances when it came to personnel management, avoiding any concentration of power, and pursuing a well-rounded foreign policy in dealing with major powers including China, Russia, and the United States. The criticisms were undoubtedly driven by both personal and sectoral interests.

Despite Phieu's departure, the VPA continues to have representation in the major decision-making bodies. The new Politburo consists of one member from the VPA (Minister of Defense Pham Van Tra), whereas the newly elected Central Committee has fifteen members from the VPA. The Ninth Congress abolished the Political Bureau Standing Board and revived the Secretariat. Of its nine members, the Secretariat has one from the army (Lt. Gen. Le Van Dung, general chief of staff). The security police have one representative in the Politburo and three in the Central Committee. The overall representation of the VPA in major decision-making bodies has been reduced only slightly.

These developments continue to confirm the communist party's control over the army. Although military representation in major political bodies, especially the Central Committee, has risen since the Seventh National Party Congress in 1992, it has not yet reached the levels of the 1960s and 1970s. Top military leaders have remained "political generals" who are not likely to become spokespersons for professional officers. Furthermore, civilian party members have been allotted seats on the CMPC. Despite the continuation of party control, however, the 1980s and 1990s also show signs of some restructuring in party-military relations. While perpetuating party control, the VCP has granted more internal autonomy to the VPA, especially in making decisions on professional military matters. The General Political Directorate is mainly responsible for nonprofessional military areas.

As this chapter has argued, there has been a shift in emphasis in the VPA's role from reunification and external defense to guaranteeing regime security and domestic stability as well as promoting a market economy with socialist features. Perceived threats to the regime following the collapse of the socialist bloc between 1989 and 1991 legitimized the VPA's internal security role, and Vietnam's fiscal crisis following the termination of Soviet aid and the move from centrally planned to market economy legitimized its expanding economic role. Although the VPA has a key role in internal security, this role is also shared with other agencies, including the security police, mass organizations, and the civilian government offices. Available evidence suggests that riot management has emphasized negotiation and persuasion, not force. There is no sign, at least for the moment, that the violent use of force, as in neighboring countries, will replace political intimidation and suppression.

On the economic front, the VPA is not the only army in Southeast Asia to become involved in the economy. In Thailand and Indonesia, too, the military has assumed an economic role at one time or another. Their forms of economic involvement have differed in several ways, however. In Thailand and Indonesia, military officers tend to promote individual rather than corporate interests. They have served on boards of directors in private enterprises, become shareholders, or set up their own private companies, for example, thereby benefiting individually from economic involvement. In these countries, the number of enterprises directly owned and run by the military, as well as their scope, has been modest. The VPA's involvement in the economy is collective, however, growing from a small-scale effort to make the armed forces self-sufficient with respect to its food to a large-scale undertaking with both commercially oriented and defense-related purposes. Moreover, the VPA's involvement, at least officially, strengthened the state economic sector. Before *doi moi*, VPA units operated under the centrally planned system like other socialist production units: they received input from the state and delivered a quota. In the *doi moi* era, certain VPA production units have been categorized as state-owned enterprises. Unlike in the other Southeast Asian countries, there is a close connection between the VPA's economic role and the development of the state economic sector as a whole.

It is likely that regular combat unit MOEs will continue to engage in economic activity, but with the legalization of MOEs, exclusively commercial enterprises owned by the VPA have been governed by the same state laws and regulations governing state-owned enterprises. Integration into the system of state-owned enterprises means that these military enterprises will be closely linked with the fate of the state sector in general. Currently, pressure on SOEs comes from the policy of corporatization and Vietnam's need to reduce the size of the state sector in order to comply with the requirements for membership in the World Trade Organization.

What distinguishes the VPA's economic role from the rest of the SOEs, however, is the role of defense-related enterprises and the concept of "linking the economy with national defense" that underlines it. "Red" is combined with "entrepreneurial." However, the armed forces' newly legalized roles have not given it absolute political power; the VPA has to, within the framework of sectoral politics, interact with other state agencies in developing policy agendas and policy solutions. The budget increase in the early 1990s, although indicative of the VPA's stronger bargaining position, allowed only limited modernization of the armed forces in response to Chinese advances on the Spratly Islands. Vietnam has continued to rely on regional cooperation and diplomacy in defending its international security interests.

The VPA has been vocal in charting the country's future course. It has emphasized socialist orientation and criticized deviations. At the same time, it sees the necessity of *doi moi* and the country's involvement in a market economy. It is within this framework of combining defense with economic development—combining red and entrepreneur—that the VPA is likely to play an important role in shaping the new political, economic, and social order. Party control of the military is likely to continue for the foreseeable future. Any future change in party-military relations will tend to come from factors outside the party-military institutionalized relationship. Such factors include instability of the political system in times of succession struggles or large-scale mass revolts.

CHAPTER 15

North Korea: Institutionalized Military Intervention

Chung-in Moon and Hideshi Takesada

"THE MILITARY IS THE PARTY, THE STATE, AND THE PEOPLE." This statement appeared in a long editorial on Kim Jong Il's political leadership by the Central News Agency of North Korea on October 20, 1998. The editorial characterized his mode of political governance as *"sunkun jungchi"* ("primacy of the military in politics") and defined it in terms of three elements: the military's centrality in North Korean politics, strengthening the military with utmost priority, and the military's leadership in the pursuit of socialist goals.[1] *Sunkun jungchi* epitomizes the political changes in North Korea since Kim Jong Il's assumption of political power following the death of his father, Kim Il Sung. The military's primacy in politics contradicts the previous configuration of North Korean politics where the Korean Workers' Party (KWP) prevailed as the dominant political machinery and the military was simply an instrument of party domination.[2] The pronounced centrality of the military under the Kim Jong Il regime has precipitated an array of intriguing puzzles. How should we interpret the ascension of military power? Who is in control of North Korean politics? Is it Kim Jong Il, the KWP, or the military? What are the implications for civil-military relations in general and national security policy in particular?

In this chapter we explore these questions within a broad framework of civil-military relations in North Korea. The first section presents a brief overview of contending analytical perspectives. The second describes the genesis of North Korea's military and traces the historical and jurisdictional evolution of civil-military relations. The third examines change and continuity in three components of civil-military relations in North Korea: political domination, national security policymaking, and socioeconomic roles of the military. The fourth section addresses the determinants of change by focusing on the security environment and external threats, regime dynamics, and institutional arrangements and inertia. Finally, the chapter suggests several analytical, empirical, and policy implications.

In elucidating the dynamics of civil-military relations in North Korea, however, two major caveats are in order. One is the data problem. North Korea is the most closed country in the world, and it is virtually impossible to conduct field surveys there. Access to information on its military is all the more difficult to obtain. Thus we have relied here on official documents released by the North Korean government and on secondary resources in Japan and South Korea. Apart from the data constraint, there is a conceptual problem. Organized civil society is not developed in North Korea, strictly speaking, and thus it seems misleading to study civil-military relations. We have overcome the dilemma by operationalizing civil society in terms of political society, that is, political party (Stepan 1978). Therefore, what we analyze here involves primarily party-military relations.

As we shall see, the chapter illustrates several interesting aspects of civil-military relations in North Korea. There is, for example, an interesting evolutionary pattern beginning with state and party dominance over the military, progressing to military dominance over the state and party, and culminating in a constitutional guarantee of institutionalized military intervention in civil politics in 1998. Despite its growing power and influence, however, North Korea's military appears to be a tool of political domination by Kim Jong Il and an institutionalized guardian of Kim's regime security, at least for the time being. Furthermore, in a society where national security and regime security are identical, the military can exercise a preponderant influence in national security policymaking. And as the largest and best-organized force, the military plays a paramount role in the country's socioeconomic life. So long as the Kim Jong Il regime stays in power, the triumvirate of leader, military, and party is likely to continue, and the military will remain the dominant force in politics.

CONTENDING PERSPECTIVES

Three contending models may be deployed to account for civil-military relations in North Korea. The first is the institutional conflict perspective, which is predicated on constant conflicts between party and military (Kolkowicz 1967). Under the socialist system, the military is an instrument of party and state domination. In reality, however, the military attempts to maximize its institutional interests such as the defense budget and professional autonomy. These efforts often undercut the party's control over the military, resulting in a conflictual relationship with the party and posing a threat to party dominance and political stability. It is for this reason that the Communist Party regards the military as a potential challenge and therefore reinforces strict controls over the military through political commissars, constant political indoctrination, and surveillance by security and police apparatus. Several scholars have applied this conflict model to the study of civil-military relations in North Korea (Kwon 1989a; Kee 1963). Kwon argued that the KWP and the military have shown cycles of confrontation and conflict over red versus expert, regular versus irregular military forces, and guns versus butter (Kwon 1989a: 203–7). The purge of Defense Minister Kim Chang-bong and the chief of covert operations in South Korea, Hur Bong-hak, in the late 1960s exemplifies the intense conflict over red versus expert as well as regular versus irregular army. Kim and Hur were purged because of their insistence that the regular army should be the mainstay of North Korea's military strategy and that the military must be independent of party control if it is to carry out a professional military strategy. A dispute between party officials and military officials over the issue of military modernization and economic development in 1967 is another example confirming the conflict model. When the Soviet Union resumed its economic assistance to the North in 1967, party officials such as Pak Kum-chol and Li Hyo-sun advocated the allocation of this aid to economic development. But military hard-liners such as Kim Chang-bong, Choe Kwang, and Choe Hyon opposed it and called for greater allocation of economic resources to the military instead. The dispute resulted in the victory of the military; more than a hundred party officials including Pak and Li were purged. In light of such evidence, party-military relations in North Korea can be characterized as conflictual.

The second perspective is the participation model (Colton 1978). Unlike the institutional conflict model, the participation perspective argues that the party and the military cannot be artificially demarcated but are linked through institutional arrangements. The Communist Party prevails over the military in overall power sharing, but the military participates in decision making, especially in matters of national security and military affairs. The People's Liberation Army (PLA) of China presents a classical example in this regard. The military's political influence arises from its functional and historical prerequisites in national security affairs. Thus institutional arrangements that facilitate or inhibit military participation in decision making become an important variable in accounting for civil-military relations (Perlmutter 1982: 780–81). According to this view, it is misleading to characterize North Korea's party-military relations as conflictual. In the earlier period of state formation in North Korea, the KWP attempted to impose tight control over the military, resulting in precarious party-military relations. But Kim Il Sung's consolidation of political power through the 1960s and 1970s encouraged and institutionalized participation of the military in party politics through its incorporation into the party structure. Thus the party and the military have not been confrontational but interlinked through a functional division of labor (Chung 1995: 74). The military's active role in the process of Kim Jong Il's succession politics confirms the participation model (Shin and Jun 1994: 11–76). In other words, although the military in the North is a subset of broadly defined party and state structure, it is an active participant rather than a submissive agent in party politics and national security policymaking.

The third perspective transcends the dichotomy between party and military by suggesting an interest congruence between the two (Odom 1978). Its proponents argue that the party and the military under the communist system enjoy shared norms and values and converge in interests in the pursuit of state ideals and objectives. It is natural for them to engage in harmonious and cooperative relationships. Refuting the institutional conflict model, this camp argues that the military's professional autonomy does not necessarily contradict its subordination to party ideology. Because the military is by and large an integral part of state and party, it is inconceivable to regard them as separate entities. Disputes over national security reflect the intra-party debate process, not competition between the two institutions or their separation. In accord with this view, the military's institutionalized participation in party politics is a reflection of the organic unity of party and military.

In our view, the interest congruence model accounts best for contemporary civil-military or party-military relations in North Korea, where the supreme leader, first Kim Il Sung and then Kim Jong Il, runs both the party and the military. The two institutions are the most pronounced instruments of domination available to the supreme leader. Their interests converge in sustaining the supreme leader's regime security. Traditionally North Korea was governed by a trinity of party, state, and people, but the military was added as a further element. On the fifty-fifth birthday of Kim Jong Il (February 16, 1997), the KWP convened a central report session and announced that "Comrade Kim Jong Il has invented a new idea of favoring the military in which the military is the people, the state, and the party." The report stated further that the North Korean People's Armed Forces (KPA) is the military of *suryong* (the supreme leader), the party, and the people.[3] Given that the party, the military, and the people are integral parts of the supreme leader, they cannot be disaggregated into components. The extreme form of organic corporatism (or personality cult) framed around the supreme leader Kim Il Sung and his successor Kim Jong Il does not allow any artificial separation of party, state, and military (Cumings 1993; Suh 1999; Yang 1994). Indeed, a congruence of interests between party and military is built into the governance structure of North Korea's political system.

Although the third perspective depicts recent developments in party-military relations adequately, it cannot be used as an encompassing analytical framework. As we shall see, North Korea has experienced different stages of party-military relations since its founding. In the early stage (1948–1961), the KWP and the military often engaged in conflict over institutional interests. But in the 1960s the military was allowed to participate in party politics by being incorporated into the institutional structure of the KWP, and it became more influential in national security decision making. Since 1970, the party and the military have been fused into the governing structure of the supreme leader, making it virtually impossible to separate the two in institutional and functional terms. Kim Jong Il's inauguration as supreme leader has further integrated the party and the military into a single entity in which the military enjoys a position of unprecedented preeminence. Now we turn to an analysis of party-military relations in North Korea since 1948 with these three contending perspectives in mind.

CHANGE AND CONTINUITY
IN JURISDICTIONAL BOUNDARIES

Party-military relations in North Korea have shown interesting patterns of change and continuity in jurisdictional boundaries since 1948. Although the party prevailed over the military in the 1950s, the military began to exert a great influence over the party throughout the 1960s. Since the early 1970s, however, the supreme leader has been able to place both the party and the military under his control with obscure jurisdictional boundaries. This section traces the shifting jurisdictional boundaries of party-military relations in North Korea.

Genesis of the North Korean Military: 1948–1950

The genesis of the military in North Korea followed a pattern similar to that in South Korea. Withdrawal of the Japanese imperial army after its defeat in World War II left a political vacuum in the North. To cope with this vacuum and social instability, voluntary paramilitary units such as the Red Guard were organized as domestic security forces. But the Soviet occupation forces disbanded all voluntary paramilitary units and organized a domestic security unit composed of 2,000 personnel in November 1945. On January 11, 1946, a railroad security unit was organized, and soon a training camp was established in Kaechun with local branches in Sinuiju, Jeongjoo, and Kanggye. Inauguration of a formal military institution in North Korea coincided with the launching of the Security Cadre Training Regiment in Pyongyang in September 1946. The regiment was composed of its headquarters, a guard unit, the Pyongyang Academy, an aviation school, and three training units in Kaechon, Nanam, and Pyongyang. The regiment was reorganized into the People's Collective Army Corps on May 17, 1947. Along with this, the two training branches were also reorganized into the First and Second Divisions while the third training unit in Pyongyang became the Third Independent Combined Brigade. Soviet assistance had facilitated the birth of a modern military institution. On February 8, 1948, even before the formal inauguration of the Democratic People's Republic of Korea, North Korea declared the founding of its armed forces (Choi 1991: 151–54; Chang 1991: 44–88; Park 1996: 688–98).

As in South Korea, the armed forces in North Korea were composed of several factions.[4] The most pronounced faction was the anti-Japanese guerrilla forces led by Kim Il Sung. Prior to national independence, these forces had engaged in an extensive struggle against Japanese colonial rule in Manchuria, a struggle that had taught them an important lesson: building a strong military is as important as building the state and the party (Kim 1945 [1979]). The anti-Japanese guerrilla forces constituted the mainstay of the newfound North Korean military for two reasons: one is that faction's strategic importance in state building; the other is closely related to the origins of its members. Most anti-Japanese guerrilla forces came from the peasant class, and it was difficult for them to join the KWP as leaders because they lacked formal education and organizational expertise (Suh 1988: 105; Wada 1992: 303). The domestic and Soviet factions, by contrast, were deeply involved in domestic political activities such as the founding of the KWP. The guerrilla faction could easily seize hegemony in the process of building the North Korean military because of its sheer size and its contribution to national independence. Its members continued to enjoy prominent status even after the founding of the KPA. The minister of defense (Choe Yong-gun), chief of staff (Kang Gun), commander of the Second Army Corps (Kim Kwang-hyop), and commander of the Front Command during the Korean War (Kim Chaek) all came from the anti-Japanese guerrilla faction (Suh 1988: 101–2; Wada 1992: 294–314).

The second major faction of the newfound KPA was the Chosun Volunteer Forces (CVF), a component of the Yanan faction (returnees from China). The CVF worked closely with Mao's PLA, and it attempted to return to North Korea immediately after national liberation in August 1945. But the Soviet occupation forces blocked its return, and only a few leaders were allowed back into North Korea. Those who remained in China participated in the Chinese civil war by taking sides with Mao's PLA. During this time the CVF grew into a formidable military body, with three divisions of 50,000 combat forces, by absorbing Koreans in China's northeastern provinces. After the war was over, the entire CVF was allowed to enter North Korea. The Yanan faction constituted one-third of the KPA in size, and most of the KPA's mid-ranking officials came from the Yanan faction. The commander of the Artillery Command (Mu Chong), commander of the First Corps (Kim Ung), commander of the Sixth Division (Bang Ho-san), commander of the Fourth Division (Lee Kwon-mu), and many other commanding posts were occupied by members of the CVF. The Yanan faction was the only force to challenge the hegemonic position of the guerrilla faction in terms of size and capability. But checks and balances designed by Kim Il Sung and the Soviet occupation forces, as well as internal fragmentation, prevented it from emerging a major challenger in North Korea's military and politics (Park 1996: 703–5; Choi 1991: 157; Chang 1991: 466–68).

Two other factions participated in the founding of the KPA: the Soviet faction and the domestic faction. The Soviet faction was modest in size, and its members were assigned mostly as political commissars and technical and logistic support. With the exception of Nam Il, who was promoted to chief of general staff of the KPA, no other members enjoyed prominent positions. Furthermore, there was a weak horizontal link among members of the Soviet faction (Suh 1996: 163–64). The domestic faction, by contrast, led by Pak Hon-yong, engaged heavily in party politics rather than in the construction of the military. Thus neither the Soviet nor the domestic faction played a significant role in the genesis of the North Korean military.

During the KPA's genesis, the link between the KWP and the military was rather weak. Although the KWP was the dominant party, it was unable to penetrate and control the KPA. At that time, the KPA was composed of two wings: the general chief of staff and the department of cultural affairs. Whereas the general chief of staff was in charge of overall military operations, the department of cultural affairs was responsible for ideological and political guidance. Nevertheless, both wings were placed under the jurisdiction of the Ministry of National Defense. Moreover, Choe Yong-gun, who was minister of national defense, was chairman of the Korean Democratic Party, not the KWP, and thus there was no institutional link between the KPA and KWP.

Several factors explain the lack of KWP control over the KPA. First, although he was both chairman of the KWP and head of the cabinet, Kim Il Sung was unable to consolidate his power in the KWP. Thus, placing the KPA under the control of the KWP could bring about factionalization of the KPA through penetration of rival factions in the military. Second, there was a concern that excessive politicization of the military through a tight linkage with the KWP could undercut recruitment of young volunteer forces. Third, the KPA was in the formative stage, and loss of professional autonomy could lead to inefficiency and demoralization of military organizations. Finally, unlike in the Soviet Union, here there were no ideological struggles among leaders, and North Korea could build the KPA without the KWP's engagement and guidance (Lee 1988: 161; Choi 1991: 174–75). Thus party-military relations in the early period (1948–1950) were shaped by personal connections of the anti-Japanese guerrilla faction in the KWP and KPA.

Institutionalizing Party-Military Relations: 1950–1962

A major change in party-military relations came in the wake of the Korean War (1950–1953). A surprise attack by North Korea jeopardized the whole of South Korea with the exception of the southeastern part of the peninsula. But a dramatic reversal came with Gen. Douglas MacArthur's landing at Inchon in September 1950, and the KPA began to retreat. The army's retreat was so chaotic and disorderly, however, that Kim Il Sung changed the department of cultural affairs to the General Political Bureau, placed it under the KWP's control, and appointed Pak Hon-yong, vice-chairman of the KWP, as its head. Along with this institutional change, Kim began to tighten the party's control over the military.

Several factors were responsible for the shift. First, Kim realized that personal links between party and military leaders, based on their ties with the guerrilla faction, were not enough to warrant control over the KPA: not only had several key military leaders perished during the Korean War, but there he had a feud with Choe Yong-gun over the issue of invasion.[5] Second, Kim was concerned that the Yanan faction was gaining influence within the military—evidenced by the appointment of Yanan faction members as vice-commander (Kim Ung) and vice–political commissar (Pak Il-u) of the newly formed China–DPRK Allied Forces Command (AFC), which commanded the Chinese volunteer forces as well as the KPA. The rise of the Yanan faction can be ascribed to its impressive performance during the Korean War and the new patronage that came with China's official engagement in the war. And third, North Korea had transferred its operational command and control to China with the formation of the AFC. Thus, technically speaking, the KPA was under the command and control of Gen. Peng Dehuai, commander of the PLA in Korea as well as the AFC. No longer able to prevail over the KPA, Kim Il Sung was desperate to institutionalize the KWP's political control over the KPA (J.-S. Lee 1995: 240; Park 1996: 287–304; Chang 1991: 152–56).

Kim undertook three steps to ensure party control over the military. His first step was to consolidate his power within the KWP by eliminating key members of the rival domestic faction, the Namrodang (the KWP of southern Korea), starting with Pak Hon-yong, vice-chairman of the KWP and vice-premier in 1951. But with the Yanan and Soviet factions still intact, Kim could not ensure the consolidation of his power over the KWP. In fact, on the occasion of the twentieth plenary session of the Soviet Communist Party in February 1956, in which Khrushchev defamed Stalin, both Yanan and Soviet faction members began to criticize the personal worship of Kim Il Sung and called for the primacy of the party over individual leadership. Their challenge failed, however, and Kim purged them. Kim consolidated his power in the KWP by making an official declaration of the end of factional politics within the party at the first KWP deputies meeting on March 6, 1958 (J.-S. Lee 1995: 270–284).

Along with his newfound power over the KWP, Kim undertook measures to remove rival factions within the KPA. Kim purged Gen. Mu Chong, the leader of the Yanan faction and his most trusted Chinese ally, as early as 1951 in the middle of the Korean War.[6] Mu Chong represented one of the few potential rivals to Kim Il Sung. Purges of the Yanan faction continued through 1956: Pak Il-u and Bang Ho-san, leading members of the faction as well as heroes of the Korean War, were purged one by one. The factional struggle in the KWP in August 1956 provided Kim Il Sung with a decisive moment to eliminate potential challengers in the military. In 1958–1959, there was a systematic move to purge members of the Yanan and Soviet factions. Kim Ung, vice–national defense minister, and Lee Kwon-mu, chief of general staff, both members of the Yanan faction, were removed from their positions. And leading members of the Soviet faction such as Choi Chong-hak, chief of the General Political Bureau, and Yu Song-chul, chief of operations, were also dismissed (Yeo 1991; Suh 1996: 168–70). As a result, the guerrilla faction virtually monopolized the party and the military: this faction accounted for 30 of the 85 full members of the KWP Central Committee and 8 of the 50 alternate members. Only three Yanan faction members and one Soviet faction member were included in the Central Committee (Bukhanyonguso 1983: 1019–57). And the KPA's representatives to the KWP Central Committee were all staffed by the Kim Il Sung faction (Choi 1991).

This consolidation of power in the party and the military by Kim and his faction led to major institutional changes regarding the KPA. First of all, the KPA's historical origin was reaffirmed as stemming from the anti-Japanese guerrilla forces. Its legitimacy, therefore, was based on the tradition of anti-Japanese guerrilla warfare (Yoon 1990: 60). At the fourth party congress, convened in September 1961, the preamble to the KWP's bylaws stipulated that "the Korea Workers' Party is the direct successor of an honorable revolutionary tradition which Korean communists bred in the process of anti-Japanese armed struggle" (Bukhanyonguso 1983: 672). The revolutionary tradition of anti-Japanese armed struggle became the foundation of the KPA as well. Officially the KPA was defined as the armed forces of the KWP, and it was required to set up a party committee that was placed under the KWP's Central Committee (Bukhanyonguso 1978a: 231; Suh 1996: 172). The installation of party committees within the KPA was completed by 1961. Moreover, Article 67 of the KWP bylaws defined the General Political Bureau as an executive organ of the party. Such institutional arrangements ensured the party's complete control over the military. Thus even though the KPA was formally under the jurisdiction of the Ministry of National Defense, its political wing, namely the General Political Bureau, overlapped with the KWP through the party military committees.

Ascent of the Military: 1962–1970

Factional struggles within the party and the military, therefore, led to greater institutionalized control over the military by the party. But the incorporation of the military within the party structure brought about new sources of discord between party cadres and military officials over military policy. Though the military was controlled by the party, it was allowed to participate in the formulation of military policy. The 1960s were marked by fierce competition in the party between military hard-liners and civilian soft-liners.

The KWP's Central Committee plenary session, held December 10–14, 1962, issued a statement about strengthening North Korea's self-defense. The statement not only emphasized strengthening national defense, even at the expense of economic development, but also called for arming the entire North Korean population and fortifying the entire country. At the same time, the defense forces were to be modernized and the KPA was to become the elite force. These four elements have constituted the mainstay of North Korea's military doctrine ever since (Bukhanyonguso 1978a: 280).

Adoption of this doctrine was closely associated with a changing security environment. Increasing American threats in the wake of the Cuban missile crisis, the rise of revisionism in the Soviet Union, and emerging erosion of the solidarity of the socialist bloc (evidenced through the Sino-Soviet rivalry) heightened North Korea's perception of threat (Chung 1978: 62–79; K.-S. Chung 1997a: 103–12). Above all, the soured relationship with the Soviet Union played a critical role in altering North Korea's military policy. North Korea tilted toward China in the Sino-Soviet rivalry by supporting China in its border conflict with India while criticizing the Soviet appeasement policy in the Cuban missile crisis (Chung 1978: 75). The Soviet Union retaliated by terminating economic and technical assistance to the North, recalling its technical advisers in 1960, and cutting off military assistance. North Korea attempted to reverse the trend by dispatching a military delegation led by the defense minister, Kim Kwang-hyop, to the Soviet Union in November 1962, but the delegation got a cold reception and returned to North Korea three days later with nothing to show. It is this change in the external environment that precipitated the adoption of a new military doctrine resembling a traditional socialist strategy of "people's war" (Hamm 1998: 166–68).

Such a shift significantly strengthened the military's position within the party. At the second deputies conference of the KWP, held in October 1966, four of the fifteen full politburo members and four out of eleven alternate members were KPA representatives. This growth of military power, coupled with newly emerging factional struggles, triggered conflicts with civilian party cadres. Leading party officials such as Pak Kum-chol and Yi Hyo-sun, members of the Kapsan Operation Committee, not only were critical of the new party line favoring Kim Il Sung's monolithic leadership, but also advocated the importance of economic development over a defense buildup; the military hard-liners such as Choe Hyon and Choe Kwang, however, favored the priority of defense buildup in resource allocation. In this confrontation the military hard-liners won, and leading civilian soft-liners were purged (Choi, Sung 1997: 166).

The hard-liners' victory was a result partly of Kim Il Sung's tactical maneuver to remove those who challenged his leadership and partly of his emphasis on military modernization and strengthening (Kim 1966 [1988]: 456).

But the doctrine of strengthening military power soon clashed with the doctrine of the KWP's control over the KPA. Military modernization was predicated on the military's greater autonomy and professionalization. Military leaders such as the defense minister, Kim Chang-bong, the chief of staff, Choe Kwang, and the head of covert operations in South Korea, Hur Bong-hak, argued for the primacy of regular war as opposed to people's war and the autonomy and professionalization of the military free from the party's political control. As a way of demonstrating their hard-line position, they engineered major military provocations such as the seizure of the U.S. naval ship *Pueblo* and the commando raid on the Blue House, South Korea's presidential mansion, in 1968 (Kwon 1989a: 205; Chung 1996: 100).

Alarmed by the rise of the military's influence and its hard-line position, Kim Il Sung began to purge military leaders.[7] The official reasons for the purge were noncompliance with the party line of people's war as well as military factionalism. While the defense minister, Kim Chang-bong, and the head of covert operations in South Korea, Hur Bong-hak, were executed on charges of antiparty and antirevolutionary treason, others including the chief of staff, Choe Kwang, were dismissed from active service. The purge was politically motivated to restrain and discipline the military's dogmatic position (J.-S. Lee 1995: 317–18). As a result, aggressive military acts by the North were sharply reduced. Its military provocation in the demilitarized zone fell from 829 cases in 1967 to 58 cases in 1971 and 7 cases in 1973.

There was no major jurisdictional change during this period: the Ministry of National Defense continued to be placed under the control of the cabinet. But the purge of military leaders further strengthened the party's control over the KPA through effective utilization of political commissars. The KWP decided to dispatch its political commissars to the division and regiment levels. Military officers were placed under the direct control of the KWP's secretariat bureau, whereas political commissars were under the control of KWP Central Committee's department of organization and guidance. This purge of the military paved the way to Kim Il Sung's monolithic rule over party and military. A constitutional amendment in 1972 institutionalized Kim's monolithic rule by not only establishing the *suryong* system and *juche* thought as the main tenets of its governing structure but also changing the cabinet system into a presidential system that allowed the concentration of political power in the presidency (Choi 1996: 194).

Changing Civil-Military Relations: 1970–2000

As Kim Il Sung consolidated his power in the party and the military, he began to deliberate on his successor. At first his brother, Kim Yong-ju, emerged as the most formidable candidate. Elected as party secretary in November 1970, he was elevated to the position of sixth in party rank. In 1972 he became cochairman of the North-South Coordination Committee, as well, indicating his ascent to power. At the end of 1972, however, Kim Yong-ju began to disappear from the political scene. He was removed from the politburo and even from the 248-member KWP Central Committee in October 1980. If Kim Yong-ju was on the decline, however, Kim Il Sung's son, Kim Jong Il, was on the rise. Kim Jong Il, who began his party career in 1964 as an official of the department of organization and guidance, came to the political forefront on the occasion of his election as party secretary in September 1974 and member of the politburo of the KWP Central Committee in February 1974 (Kim and Kim 1996: 65–66).

Kim Jong Il gradually consolidated his position as successor to his father by initiating the "three revolutionary teams" movement in 1973, which was instrumental for recruiting second-generation elite, and then occupying strategic party posts in 1980. The sixth KWP congress, held in 1980, made Kim Jong Il's succession official by promoting him to the fourth rank in the politburo, the second rank in the party secretariat, and the third rank in the party's military committee. Given his new status in the three bureaus of the KWP, he ranked right next to his father, Kim Il Sung. A year later, in October 1981, the junior Kim was promoted to the second rank in the politburo next to Kim Il Sung (Choi 1996: 238). Thus the 1970s and 1980s can be called the period of consolidating succession politics in North Korea.

Kim Jong Il was also developing a steadfast grip over the military. His official affiliation with the military started with his appointment to the KWP's military committee in 1980. In September 1989, he was promoted to the second rank in the military committee—surpassing Vice-Marshal Oh Jin-woo, the most trusted comrade of Kim Il Sung since the days of armed struggle against the Japanese. In May 1990, the Supreme People's Assembly, the highest legislative body in North Korea, appointed Kim as first vice-chairman of the National Defense Commission (NDC). In December 1991, Kim was promoted to the position of commander in chief of the KPA and, along with Oh Jin-u, was given the title of marshal on April 20, 1992. In the same month, the Democratic People's Republic of Korea (DPRK) constitution was amended so that the NDC chairman assumed supreme command of the entire people's armed forces. Kim Jong Il then became NDC chairman. Moreover, there was an overall reshuffling of military posts along with extensive promotions to the rank of general.

These changes reflected the process of Kim Jong Il's power consolidation in the military. Kim ensured his control over the military in three significant ways. First, he used the "three revolutionary teams" in penetrating and controlling the military.[8] The teams, which belonged to the KWP's Central Committee, were originally designed to eradicate bureaucratic excesses and promote productivity, but they soon turned into Kim's personal guards to eliminate opposition to his political succession. Devoted to their original mission of doubling the KPA's combat capability through strengthened physical training and spiritual indoctrination, they were also instrumental for detecting military officials who opposed Kim's succession. (See Lee 1988: 344–49; for details on this operation see Kwon 1989b: 191 and Shin and Jun 1994: 62–64.)

Second, Kim made extensive use of party machinery in controlling the military. In 1973, Kim was assigned to the post of party secretary in charge of the department of organization and guidance as well as the department of propaganda. As secretary of organization and guidance he now had an institutionalized way of monitoring and controlling the military. Since 1969 political commissars of the military had all been appointed by the department of organization and guidance. And all security and intelligence agencies such as the Department of National Security (DNS), the Ministry of Public Security, and various military and civilian inspection agencies were placed under its control. The DNS penetrated into every level of the KPA. Thus Kim, as head of the department, could integrate all the lines of intelligence from party organizations, general staff, and DNS units in the military and monitor every detail of military moves as well as cross-check intelligence reports from different agencies (Jun 1994: 49).

Third, Kim Jong Il relied on selective co-optation of military officers in consolidating his power and control over the military. In the beginning, Kim sought support from the first-generation military leaders who had participated in the anti-Japanese guerrilla warfare along with Kim Il Sung. Oh Jin-u, Lim Chun-chu, and Choe Hyon were behind the rise of Kim Jong Il. But Kim also began to form his own support base from second-generation military leaders. Oh Geuk-ryol, forerunner of the second-generation leaders, rose with Kim Jong Il by becoming chief of staff in 1979. But Oh sought the military's modernization and professionalization and even deliberated on the elimination of political commissars from the military (Chung 1996: 89; H.-K. Lee 1995: 205–8). As his military line contradicted Kim Il Sung's emphasis on the primacy of red over expert, Oh was removed from his position in 1988. Choe Kwang, who had been purged in 1967, replaced Oh and expressed his strong support for the military's revolutionary role and Kim Jong Il's succession politics (Lee 1992: 57–58). In addition, immediately after his inauguration as supreme commander of the KPA, Kim promoted eight first-generation military leaders including Oh Jin-u and Choe Kwang to the rank of marshal and vice-marshal and another sixteen leaders including Cho Myong-rok to the rank of full general. Of 664 generals who were promoted, 524 were second-generation military leaders (Ahn 1992: 191–92). These men became the vanguards of Kim Jong Il within the military.

Ironically, Kim's consolidation of power over the military coincided with the sudden death of Kim Il Sung in July 1994. Since the senior Kim's death, the military has become more visible in the political arena. At the hundredth-day memorial of Kim Il Sung's death, military leaders such as Vice-Marshal Paek Hak-rim, Kim Bong-yul, and Kim Ik-hyon were ahead of the party secretary, Kim Ki-nam, in power ranking. After October 1995 Marshal Li Ul-sul, Vice-Marshal Cho Myong-rok, and Vice-Marshal Kim Young-chun continued to ascend in power ranking—culminating in sixth to eighth position only after Kim Jong Il, Li Jong-ok, Pak Song-chol, Kim Yong-ju, and Kim Yong-nam. They had reached the apex of power (Chung 1998: 68). In addition, Kim began to adopt the concept of "a strong and prosperous nation" *(kang-sung daekuk)* as a new political slogan.[9] With this catchphrase Kim justified "the primacy of the military in politics" *(sungun jungchi).*[10] As an overt expression of his support of the military, Kim frequently visited military bases and attended events. He also incorporated police functions of the Ministry of Public Security into the military. More important, the presidency of the DPRK was abolished and as chairman of the NDC Kim was empowered to rule not only the military but the entire country. With this development, military intervention in party and civil politics was institutionalized (Suh 1999: 95–96). The military's power and influence, then, had become much stronger than it was in the late 1960s (K.-S. Chung 1997b: 43; Suh 1999: 96).

This does not mean, however, that the military is in full control of party politics and the state. While enhancing its status, Kim has simultaneously strengthened his grip over the military: "Grasping ideology and the military is tantamount to grasping the foundation of the construction of the strong and prosperous nation under the *juche* banner."[11] This statement underscores Kim's governing philosophy. Along with it, Kim has strengthened ideological indoctrination of the military as well as unified his control over it (Chung 1998: 73). Such a trend is evidenced by the dramatic elevation of the position of chief of the General Political Bureau, which is in charge of political education, guidance, and organization in the military. Vice-Marshal Cho Myong-rok, chief of the General Political Bureau, has become vice-chairman of the NDC—even surpassing the defense minister and the KPA chief of general staff in power ranking. Clearly, then, Kim is directly controlling the military through the General Political Bureau (Choi 1998: 46–47).

In tandem with the consolidation of Kim Jong Il's political power within the military, the relationship between party and military has undergone profound changes. In December 1972, the amended socialist constitution renamed the Ministry of National Defense as the Ministry of People's Armed Forces (MPAF) but continued to place it under the State Administrative Council that replaced the cabinet. Nonetheless, the MPAF was taken away from the State Administrative Council in 1982 and was placed under the jurisdiction of the party secretariat along with the Department of National Security and the Ministry of Public Security until 1986. Between December 1986 and May 1990 the MPAF was again relocated under the Central People's Committee. A major change came in May 1990: the MPAF was placed under the direct control of the NDC, which was also detached from the Central People's Committee. The amended socialist constitution in September 1999 elevated the NDC as the supreme commanding authority with a full command and control of the KPA and MPAF. In view of this, two salient jurisdictional aspects can be delineated. One is that the cabinet does not have any institutional claim over the military. The other is that the military's jurisdictional location has changed rather arbitrarily along with Kim Jong Il's power position. Thus its jurisdictional boundary has followed Kim's power trajectory, strongly implying personalization of the military institution.

PARTY-MILITARY RELATIONS: THREE DOMAINS

Apart from the shifting jurisdictional boundary, party-military relations can be approached from functional perspectives. The most pronounced functional domains through which we can meaningfully elucidate the changing nature of party-military relations are the degree of political domination and subjugation of the military, the relative power and influence of the military in national security policymaking, and the impacts of the military in social and economic life.

Political Domination

The historical trajectory of party-state-military relations in North Korea reveals an interesting trend. Whereas in South Korea the politicized military has become more civilianized, North Korea reveals a reverse pattern. As in most countries, the military in the North was originally under the control of the state, namely the Ministry of National Defense. But gradually it has become politicized by means of deep and extensive penetration of the KWP, eventually resulting in an institutional intervention into civil and party politics through the NDC and the KWP's Central Military Committee. As Tables 15.1 and 15.2 illustrate, the two organizations are staffed mostly by senior military officers, and civilians are underrepresented. Does this imply military control over party politics? Since Kim Jong Il's succession and constitutional amendment in 1998, speculation has abounded on who is in charge of North Korean politics. Is Kim Jong Il really in control of the military? Or could it be that the KPA is in control of the DPRK, and Kim Jong Il is only its puppet? Some even argue that the KPA, which has become all the more powerful, does not give Kim Jong Il a chance to speak his mind and is using his authority to expand its power (Takesada 1998; National Institute of Defense Studies [NIDS] 1997; Suh 1999).

TABLE 15.1   Members of the National Defense Commission: March 5, 1999.

Position and Name	Other Responsibility	Rank
Chairman		
Kim Jong Il	General Secretary	Marshal
First Vice-Chairman		
Cho Myong-rok	Head of General Political Bureau	Vice-marshal
Vice Chairman		
Kim Il-chol	Minister of KPA	Vice-marshal
Member		
Lee Young-mu		Vice-marshal
Kim Young-chun	Chief of General Staff of KPA	Vice-marshal
Yon Hyong-muk	Member of Politburo	
Li Ul-sul	Commanding General of Guard Corps	Marshal
Paek Hak-rim	Minister of Public Security	Vice-marshal
Chon Byong-ho	Party Secretary	
Kim Chol-man	Chairman of Second Economic Committee	General

Source. The Republic of Korea (ROK), Ministry of Unification (2000: 151–52); Republic of Korea National Intelligence Services (*www.nis.go.kr*).

TABLE 15.2   Members of the Party Central Military Committee: March 5, 1999.

Position and Name	Other Responsibility	Rank
Chairman		
Kim Jong Il	General Secretary	Marshal
Member		
Paek Hak-rim	Minister of Public Security	Vice-marshal
Li Ul-sul	Commanding General of Guard Corps	Marshal
Li Du-ik		Vice-marshal
Cho Myong-rok	Head of General Political Bureau	Vice-marshal
Kim Il-chol	Minister of KPA	Vice-marshal
Oh Ryong-bang	Vice-minister of KPA	Vice-marshal
Li Ha-il	Chief of Military Department of KWP	Vice-marshal
Kim Ik-hyon	Chief of Civil Defense Department of KWP	Vice-marshal
Kim Myong-kuk	Commanding General of 108th Mechanized Corps	General
Pak Ki-so	Commanding General of Capital Garrison Command	Vice-marshal
Li Yong-chol		Vice-marshal
Kim Young-chun	Chief of General Staff of KPA	Vice-marshal
Kim Du-am	Director of Kumsusan Memorial Palace	General

Source. The Republic of Korea (ROK), Ministry of Unification (2000: 151–52); Republic of Korea National Intelligence Services (*www.nis.go.kr*).

We think this line of reasoning is faulty. If Kim Jong Il is the KPA's puppet, there are some striking contradictions. Those who hold power in the military are Kim Jong Il's right-hand men. Oh Jin-u, former minister of the People's Armed Forces, was asked by Kim Il Sung to support Kim Jong Il. And Supreme People's Assembly delegates and those promoted to important party positions were appointed by Kim Il Sung's authority. If they had come to any disagreement with Kim Jong Il, they would have been the first to be pushed out of the power circle. Furthermore, they are not in disagreement with one another. Any serious disagreement between the two could lead to mutual collapse. Insomuch as Kim Jong Il needs military support, the military also needs Kim's personal blessing. Or if Kim Jong Il is on the losing side vis-à-vis the military, he may turn to the KWP as an alternative power base. Because there are no signs of such developments, it is more reasonable to conclude that Kim Jong Il is sitting at the apex of the military and party structures.

We draw this conclusion after having looked into Kim's penetrating and extensive control mechanisms over the military. The North Korean military is composed of both KPA and paramilitary forces. The KPA includes regular forces, the Guard Corps, and the Capital Garrison Command; the paramilitary forces comprise the Korean People's Guard, Workers and Farmers Red Guard, and Red Youth Guard. At the same time, there are several military administrative organizations such as the KWP's Central Military Committee, the National Defense Commission, the KWP's Department of Military Affairs and Department of Civil Defense, the General Bureau of Logistic Mobilization, and the Ministry of People's Armed Forces. Whereas the Central Military Committee oversees political and policy aspects of the military, the NDC is in charge of military and administrative control of the KPA. Along with this dual control structure, the North Korean military is an integrated force in which the chief of staff commands the army, the navy, and the air force. Kim Jong Il and the KWP prevail over the military through control and co-optation.

As Figure 15.1 demonstrates, control over the military is undertaken through diverse channels. Article 46 of the KWP's bylaws defines the KPA as the KWP's revolutionary armed forces. Article 27 stipulates that the KWP's Central Military Committee oversees organization and strategy of the military, overall military buildup, and the defense industry. The Central Military Committee (until 1984 it was the military committee under the KWP's Central Committee) can be viewed as an umbrella organization for the military. But actual control of the military is undertaken through the General Political Bureau and the party committees in various units of the military. Following the Soviet example, in February 1948 North Korea established a cultural bureau within the military to carry out its political education. But it was placed under the Ministry of National Defense without any institutional links with the party. Although it was renamed the General Political Bureau during the Korean War, it was still under the influence of the cabinet rather than the party. When Kim Il Sung was able to eliminate rival factions in October 1958, however, the General Political Bureau was placed under the direct control of the party. At the same time, party committees were established at the battalion level and up, and party squads and cells were installed at the company and platoon levels, respectively. The General Political Bureau as an executive wing of the party's military committee reports directly to the Central Committee of the KWP. Thus the party center can monitor the military at every level.

Central to this monitoring and control are the political commissars. Since January 1969 the KWP's secretariat has selected and assigned political commissars from the MPAF and all

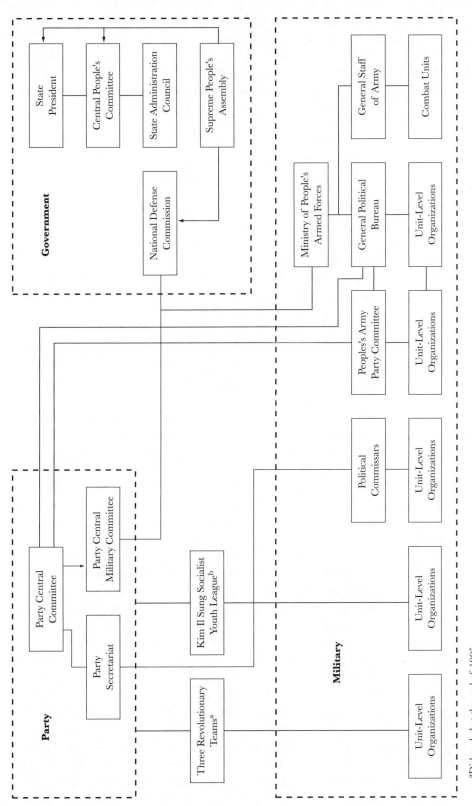

Government

State President

Central People's Committee

State Administration Council

Supreme People's Assembly

National Defense Commission

Ministry of People's Armed Forces

General Staff of Army

Combat Units

General Political Bureau

Unit-Level Organizations

Peoples's Army Party Committee

Unit-Level Organizations

Party

Party Central Committee

Party Central Military Committee

Party Secretariat

Kim Il Sung Socialist Youth League[b]

Three Revolutionary Teams[a]

Political Commissars

Unit-Level Organizations

Military

Unit-Level Organizations

Unit-Level Organizations

[a]Disbanded at the end of 1995.
[b]Formerly the League of Socialist Working Youth.

FIGURE 15.1. Party-Military Relations: 1992–1998

the way down to the regiment level. Their role is to monitor, supervise, and coordinate military affairs. Political commissars are also assigned to the battalion level and below under the title of supervisor. Military education plans and even operational commands do not become effective without the political commissars' approval—a system that often results in conflict between commanding officers and political commissars. In most cases, the political commissars prevail. Commanding officers who do not cooperate with political commissars are bound to encounter setbacks in promotion and assignments. Thus it is through an extensive network of political commissars that the party monitors, supervises, and controls the military.

The KWP also has a grip over the military through its department of organization and guidance. This department oversees the military through two primary functions: one is the appointment of political commissars; the other is the supervision of security and intelligence, apparatus such as the Department of National Security (DNS), the Ministry of Public Security, and the Department of Military Inspection. The appointment of political commissars gives the party direct control over the military, and its supervision of security and intelligence facilitates its indirect control through information collection on movements within the military. The department of organization and guidance, as we have seen, gets intelligence reports from three sources: intramilitary party organizations, the chief of staff line, and DNS units in the military. In this way the KWP can cross-check intelligence reports from different sources and consolidate its control over the military.

But one must not forget that Kim Jong Il is in full control of the party. And the KWP's control over the military is tantamount to Kim's control over the military. Several factors support this thesis. First, Kim has consolidated his power over the KWP. He is the head of two key organizations, the politburo and the secretariat, undergirding his institutional control over the party. Second, apart from the institutional control, the KWP has become Kim's personalized instrument of domination. The party has not performed effectively since the early 1980s. Despite its mandate to hold a party congress every five years, it has not held one since the sixth congress in 1980. A plenary session of the KWP's Central Committee has not been held since December 1993. The two most critical organizations of the party, the politburo and secretariat, have not held regular meetings. Clearly the KWP's weakened position is related to the appointment of Kim Jong Il as its general secretary in October 1997. The position was supposed to be filled by an election of the Central Committee. But there was no election and Kim was appointed by a joint recommendation of the Central Committee and the Central Military Committee. Equally critical is the increasing number of empty seats in the party. Since the death of Kim Il Sung, the Supreme People's Assembly announced a major cabinet reshuffle in October 1998, but no personnel changes can be seen in the party. Several key positions, such as chairman of the Central Military Committee, chairman of the Central Inspection Committee, and secretary of international affairs, have not been filled (Choi 1998: 49). All this indicates functional and institutional deformities implying Kim's greater control over the party. On this basis the KWP can be seen as a sort of dummy organization that simply legitimizes Kim's personal control over the North Korean polity, society, and military.

The tightened control has been supplemented, however, with extensive co-optation. While Kim has been reinforcing control over the military, he has co-opted the military by extending an array of benefits and incentives. First, there was an ideological realignment framed around *sunkun jungchi*, the tenet emphasizing the military's centrality in politics. According to this ideology, the military has been transformed into the vanguard of North Korean politics, society, and national security. Second, the institutional foundation of civil-military relations was shifted in favor of the military by turning the NDC and the Central Military Committee into the primary governing organizations and staffing them mostly with military generals (see Tables 15.1 and 15.2). Such an arrangement allowed the military's institutionalized intervention into civil and party politics. Third, Kim introduced a wave of military promotions unprecedented in North Korean history. No country in the world has as many marshals, vice-marshals, and full generals as North Korea—an explicit token of co-optation of the military through reward. Finally, Kim has been using a subtle form of political symbolism: not only has Kim turned himself into a military man by becoming a marshal, but he has been championing military causes by frequenting military barracks and attending military events. Since he has succeeded Kim Il Sung, his visibility has been pronounced only in the military arena: of his 48 public appearances in 1996, for example, 34 were related to military events (K.-S. Chung 1997b: 44).

In sum, then, party-state-military relations in North Korea have changed. State control has been replaced by party control. At present, the KWP still retains institutional mechanisms through which it controls the military. But since the death of Kim Il Sung and ascension of Kim Jong Il, the military has penetrated party and state and transformed itself into the most significant political actor. The crisis-management-oriented and military-led DPRK seems to be under martial law with an institutionalized intervention of the military. Nevertheless, the military's ascension is limited in the sense that it serves as an instrument of political domination by Kim Jong Il. Thus the ultimate political hegemony appears to belong to Kim Jong Il alone.

National Security Policymaking

The dynamics of national security policymaking are obscure, making it quite difficult to trace the role of civil-military relations in formulating national security policy. From the limited sources available, it appears that North Korea's national security policymaking has a dual structure. There is a formal structure comprising the KWP's Central Military Committee, the NDC, the Ministry of People's Armed Forces, and the supreme command of the KPA. But it is also known that Kim Jong Il relies on an informal group composed of his personal advisors in national security policymaking (J.-M. Kim 1998). Because it is difficult to collect and verify data on the informal structure, here we focus primarily on the formal structure.

Ever since the constitutional amendment in 1998, the NDC has been the primary security decision-making body in North Korea. The amended constitution stipulates that the NDC is the supreme guiding organization of the military (Article 100) and that its chairman commands the entire armed forces (Article 102). Article 103, however, limits the scope of the NDC's activities to the guidance of the armed forces and defense buildups, the activities of central organizations related to defense matters, and the appointment and dismissal of senior military officials. Thus the amended constitution institutionally allows its chairman to enjoy unlimited power. It is noteworthy that the amended constitution abolished the position of the head of the state, whereas the NDC chairman was described as the head of state by Kim Yong-nam, chairman of the standing committee of the Supreme People's Assembly, without any constitutional provision. Kim Yong-nam described the NDC chair as "the highest position in the DPRK in charge of protecting the socialist state system and people's destiny as well as developing and strengthening the nation's strength and defense capability by controlling the totality of political, military, and economic power" (J.-M. Kim 1998: 71). Likewise, the NDC can be regarded as the ultimate decision-making body of national security policy in North Korea during peacetime.

The Central Military Committee, which began as the military committee under the party Central Committee in December 1962, plays a leading role in national security policymaking (Republic of Korea, Ministry of Unification 1996: 497). Its importance was renewed when it became one of two organizations, along with the party Central Committee, to recommend Kim Jong Il as secretary general of the KWP, bypassing the committee's plenary session. Article 27 of the KWP bylaws stipulates that the party's Central Military Committee commands the armed forces by deciding on the nature and methods of military policy as well as organizing and guiding defense buildups and military development. Although the four military lines adopted in 1962 and other key policy decisions have been initiated by the Central Military Committee, activation of the NDC limited its functional and jurisdictional boundary (Chang 1999: 192; Chung 1995: 81). Despite its weakened position, the committee still ensures the party's involvement in national security policymaking. An interesting aspect is that although the NDC and the Central Military Committee are institutionally separate, with the goal of ensuring mutual checks and balances, they overlap in personnel composition. As Tables 15.1 and 15.2 illustrate, Kim Jong Il, Cho Myong-rok (chief of the General Political Bureau), Kim Il-chol (minister of the People's Armed Forces), Kim Young-chun (chief of staff), Li Ul-sul (commanding general of the Guard Corps), and Paek Hak-rim (minister of public security)—all of whom are essential military figures in the North—serve in both organizations. Thus despite differences in jurisdictional boundaries, they can be treated as identical organizations.

In contrast with many other countries, it appears that the MPAF does not engage in actual policymaking. As an executive wing of both organizations, it commands the general staff under the direction of the NDC. Operational control of the army, the navy, and the air force belongs to the general chief of staff. Because its minister serves in both organizations, channels of communication and feedback between the two and the ministry can be easily facilitated (Chang 1999: 79–80). The Supreme Command does not have any role in national security policymaking during peacetime. In wartime, however, it assumes command of the KPA. Given that Kim Jong Il is the supreme commander and Oh Jin-u, then minister of the People's Armed Forces, is the vice–supreme commander, the Supreme Command must be superior to the ministry. During wartime, the supreme commander can command the KPA directly without going through the ministry. Moreover, it commands paramilitary forces that do not belong to the KPA, such as the People's Guard (under the Ministry of Public Security), Red Youth Guard (under the party secretariat), and Workers' Red Guard (under the department of civil defense of the party secretariat) (D.-Hoon Lee 1993: 136; Chung 1995: 45–46).

This organizational structure indicates that national security policymaking in the North is rather straightforward. Kim Jong Il and the military exercise great power and influence, whereas the party and the state have a limited role. But North Korea's national security policy has shown shifting patterns over the years. During the Korean War and the 1950s, state and party maintained the upper hand over the military in formulating national security policy. But the 1960s can be characterized as a period during which the military penetrated party and state and monopolized decision making in national security and military affairs. The rise of military influence led to an aggressive, hard-line national security policy. Apart from the adoption of the four military lines, North Korea undertook an offensive and provocative policy during the 1960s. The commando raid on the Blue House, the capture of the U.S. naval ship *Pueblo*, and the active military buildup underscore this trend.

Since the advent of Kim's monolithic rule in the 1970s, however, North Korea has shown a contradictory posture by seeking both hard-line and soft-line policies simultaneously. The conciliatory gesture shown through the North-South joint communiqué of July 4, 1972, was soon followed by military provocation on the west coast in 1974. In 1987, the DPRK shot down a South Korean airliner while talks on cosponsoring the Seoul Olympics were in progress. In September 1996, a North Korean submarine infiltrated South Korean territorial waters at a time when North Korea was hosting a major international investment fair in the Rajin-Sonbong area to which South Korean firms were invited. More dramatic was the launching of the Taepodong I missile on August 31, 1998, while the Geneva framework of October 1994 was being implemented. Recently North Korea has revealed a nearly surrealistic security posture. While it allowed South Korean tourists to visit Mount Keumkang via an east coast route, it undertook a major naval provocation on the west coast in June 1999. The aggression on the west coast made a stark contrast with the tranquility on the east coast.

Thus one cannot account for the patterns of national security policy solely by looking into variations in party-military relations. The military's superiority over the party has not always led to a hard-line posture. As the North-South interactions illustrate, the DPRK has displayed both hard-line and soft-line elements. It has endorsed North-South dialogues, for instance, and then instantly negated them. Although these two opposite attitudes may appear contradictory, in reality they are not. The DPRK has always been combining hard lines and soft lines. Two interpretations are feasible in this context. One is North Korea's political-military strategy, which is formulated by skillfully blending peaceful negotiations and a hard-line military gesture in order to maximize its national and regime interests. In this way, North Korea has attempted to put South Korea under military pressure while dividing the United States and the Republic of Korea or dividing the United States and Japan. Viewed from the outside, the DPRK appears to behave irrationally, but in fact its behavior is rational.

The other interpretation is closely related to bureaucratic compartmentalization. In North Korea, which is characterized by an excessive concentration of decision making in the supreme leader, horizontal consultation and consensus among party, state, and military are rarely achieved. On the contrary, vertical command and control, compartmentalized functional division of labor, and fierce loyalty competition among different units have become essential features of decision making in the North. In this circumstance, it is virtually impossible to envisage a sharp dichotomy between hard-liners and soft-liners in which the military takes the hard-line role while the party and bureaucracy take the soft-line position. They simply follow the functional mandates dictated by the supreme leader: the military is bound to take a hard-line posture; bureaucrats and party officials in charge of international cooperation are bound to show a conciliatory gesture. Thus the contradictory behavior is built into the structure of monolithic decision making under Kim Jong Il's one-man rule.[12] Regardless of the interpretation, strategic or bureaucratic, national security policy in North Korea under Kim Jong Il has become increasingly bifrontal despite a high degree of centralization in decision making.

In sum, then, shifting patterns of party-military relations have influenced national security policymaking in three distinct ways. First, when state and the party prevailed over the military, as in the 1950s, North Korea's national security policy appeared to be conciliatory and inward-looking. Second, when the military was superior to state and party during the 1960s, North Korea undertook a more provocative stance. Third, consolidation of party, state, and military under Kim's one-man rule has led to a contradictory posture of combining hard-line and soft-line policies simultaneously. As long as Kim Jong Il maintains his regime, these erratic patterns of national security policymaking are likely to continue.

The Case of the Second Economy

Since the end of the Korean War, the military has had an enormous impact on North Korea's society and economy. It is no exaggeration to state that North Korean society has been to a great extent incorporated into the military. Out of a population of 22 million, more than 8 million are involved in military or paramilitary organizations in one way or another (Republic of Korea, Ministry of National Defense 1999: 44). In a sense, North Korea can be seen as a huge garrison state, and the military has become the ideological and organizational backbone of its society. Even more critical is the role of the military in the North Korean economy. North Korea's military has been a primary source of economic development and decay. It was instrumental in rebuilding North Korea from the ruins of the Korean War and fostering rapid industrialization in the 1960s. In fact, the North Korean economy was superior to that of South Korea until the early 1970s. North Korea's superiority stemmed from its rapid heavy industrialization, which was designed to promote the defense industrial sector. Since North Korea adopted the four military lines in 1962, it has allocated more than 20 percent of its gross national product to the defense sector annually. During the First Seven-Year Economic Plan (1961–1970), for example, North Korea allocated 75 percent of manufacturing investments into heavy industry with greater forward and backward linkages. During the Six-Year Economic Plan (1971–1976), investment in heavy industry rose to 83 percent (Choi 1992: 128–29). The big push served as an engine of growth in North Korea.

But the skewed pattern of industrial development began to reach the point of diminishing returns in the mid-1970s. Excessive investment in heavy industry and defense industries under the closed economy critically undermined the foundation of its productive capacity. While export earnings were dwindling and foreign investments were virtually nil, the need for hard currency was rising fast because of the two waves of oil shocks in the 1970s, successive crop failures, and extensive demands for replacement of old capital goods and components. Furthermore, structural rigidity embedded in North Korea's planned economy severely retarded economic efficiency. The DPRK economy entered a disastrous state in the late 1980s. Throughout the 1990s, its growth was negative, exports declined, and foreign debts accumulated. Energy shortages became particularly serious. Blackouts began to affect both industrial activities and people's daily life. A vicious circle of energy shortage, underutilization of production, and economic stagnation has virtually paralyzed the North Korean economy. Chronic food crises stemming from both structural and climatological factors have further undermined the possibility of economic recovery. It was at this point that outside observers began to predict the collapse of the North Korean economy and the end of the Kim Jong Il regime. No one doubts that North Korea's current plight can be traced to classical substitution effects between gun and butter. Reckless heavy industrialization in the 1960s and the 1970s victimized the entire national economy.

Moreover, there are no signs of altering North Korea's current economic path. Apart from its controversial nuclear development project, North Korea's research and development as well as test launching of medium-range and long-range missiles including Taepodong I are eloquent testimony in this regard. While suffering from severe shortages even of basic consumer goods, North Korea has been able to develop cutting-edge weapons. How is this possible? To solve this riddle, it is necessary to understand the peculiar nature of the North Korean economy, which is composed of a civilian economy and a second, or defense, economy. The role of this second economy has been especially detrimental to the shaping of the overall North Korean economy (Paik 1996; Y.-J. Chung 1997; J.-H. Choi 1997; Federation of American Scientists [FAS] 1998). The second economy refers to economic activities related to the production, distribution, and consumption of all the materials in the military sector. Thus it includes everything from weapons production at military factories to the rice reserved for the military and the manufacturing of military uniforms (Radiopress 1998). In contrast to the West, where the second economy is a subset of the civilian economy and the defense industry is by and large defined as weapons production, the DPRK has a broader definition that includes guns, cannons, ammunition, military vehicles, military aircraft, military vessels, communications facilities, missiles, uniforms, shoes, and raw materials for military production (Bukhanyonguso 1978b: 451–58). As a result, the second economy has far outstripped the civilian economy.

The second economy is the result of an aggressive defense-industry policy undertaken since the early 1960s. Within the broad framework of this policy, all factories in the North are obliged to allocate materials to the defense sector first. Otherwise, managers of state enterprises are subject to court martial. At the same time, all civilian manufacturing firms are also obliged to allocate a certain portion of their production capacity for the defense sector, and the military directly supervises this production. Along with this, the Central Military Committee holds regular meetings on the promotion of the defense industry, attended by committee members, standing members of the politburo, party secretaries of the relevant provinces, and party secretaries and managers of state enterprises. These meetings evaluate the overall performance of defense-industry production, and enterprises that do not meet their targets are subject to immediate punishment.[13] Finally, the second economy gets top priority in the allocation of strategic materials, research and development funds, and manpower (Chung 1998: 84). It is with this policy that North Korea has managed to demonstrate such an unusual capability in defense-industry production, as evidenced by the launching of the Taepodong I missile.

The second economy's privileged position is closely associated with a unique institutional arrangement: it is controlled by the Second Economy Commission (SEC), which was originally placed under the Central People's Committee of the Supreme People's Assembly but was relocated to the NDC in 1993. The relocation seems natural given that one of the NDC's main functions is overall promotion of the defense buildup. Both Chun Byong-ho, party secretary in charge of defense industry, and Kim Chol-man, chairman of the SEC, are NDC members (Chang 1999: 188). The SEC is a vast organization composed of eight bureaus including the General Bureau of Foreign Economic Relations, which is in charge of foreign acquisition and sales of defense products and services (Y.-J. Chung 1997: 99). The Second National Academy of Science is also under SEC control. Apart from the SEC, the MPAF is engaged in defense-industry activities, though its role is very much confined to manufacturing essential military goods and repairing broken equipment.

Military equipment is produced by the SEC, procured by the KPA, and then exported overseas through either the SEC or the KPA. Annual exports are estimated to bring in US$200 million to $1 billion in foreign currency (IISS 1997: 262). Because the largest export item is weapons, the military weighs heavy in the North Korean economy.[14] And as civilian exports have dwindled, the relative weight of weapons exports has become more important than ever before. North Korea's efforts to export missiles can be understood in this context. Regardless of the cost-benefit calculation, however, overemphasis on the second economy has brought about severe negative externalities such as misallocation of resources, depression of the consumer goods sector, and uneven industrial development, all of which are undermining the overall health of the North Korean economy. Moreover, the military's share of the national budget makes the situation worse. According to figures in 1996, the military spent US$5.4 billion, whereas the gross national product was $20 billion. This indicates that the role of the second economy is increasing. Additionally, the military constitutes the largest group of consumers in the DPRK, including one million active-service military members and their families. All this adds up to the fact that the stronger the second economy, the weaker the civilian economy.

The second economy has been a mixed blessing for North Korea. On the one hand, it is a competitive sector through which North Korea can maximize hard currency earnings by exporting weapons. On the other hand, it has become the primary source of distorted resource allocation and economic downturn. Nevertheless, for all its negative effects, North Korea is still committed to promoting the second economy. This commitment has resulted from the military's rise and Kim Jong Il's pursuit of national and regime security by strengthening North Korea's defense.

PATTERNS OF CONTINUITY AND CHANGE

Civil-military relations in the DPRK are unique. Not only is the notion of "civil" as used in Western nations absent, but North Korea's civil-military relations are remarkably different from those of other countries. As we noted in our introduction, the North has party-military relations, not civil-military relations. A close examination of the North Korean case reveals an interesting historical trajectory of party-military relations: party dominance over the military has evolved into military dominance over the party, eventually culminating in Kim Jong Il's personal dominance over the party and the military. Such a pattern of evolution can be ascribed to the consolidation of the two Kims' personal power and their preoccupation with regime security. Thus North Korea's civil-military relations should therefore be understood in terms of personal dictatorship and one-man rule. Furthermore, party-military relations in the DPRK are different from those in the former Soviet Union in the sense that North Korea's party-military relations are based on people's loyalty to Kim Il Sung and Kim Jong Il and their belief in them as flawless leaders. In this regard, party-military relations in the North have a religious aspect: the essential elements are a cult of personality, one-man rule, excessive centralization of power in the Kim family, dictatorship, and loyalty to the Kim family. The pentagon doctrine—supreme leader, party, state, people, and military—exemplifies this aspect clearly.

Likewise, regime dynamics based on one-man dictatorship and his consolidation of power have been responsible for shaping the evolutionary dynamics of party-military relations in North Korea. Regime dynamics have not only shaped the terrain of political domination in party-military relations but have also had a profound impact on the formation of national security policy and the military's socioeconomic role. On the surface, the North's national security policy appears to be an outcome of dynamic interactions between party and military in which the shifting balance of power between the two dictates its nature and direction. In reality, however, the balance is ultimately determined by the preference of the supreme leader, Kim Il Sung and later Kim Jong Il. In the 1950s, when North Korea desperately needed economic reconstruction following the Korean War, Kim Il Sung sided with the party and restrained the military in the pursuit of national security goals. During the 1960s, Kim consolidated power in the party and the military, but a precarious security environment forced him to seek self-reliance in defense, which in turn enhanced the status of the military, resulting in a hard-line national security posture. North Korea's contradictory security policy since the 1980s can be explained by looking into the political calculus of the supreme leader. Kim Il Sung and Kim Jong Il both needed a strong army in order to ensure national security from external threats. But they were equally desperate to secure their regime's survival by reactivating the country's economic vitality through limited openings. Mandates of national and regime security under monolithic rule have often been responsible for the North's contradictory national security policy. Promotion of the second economy can be understood in a similar vein. For the two Kims, heavy industrialization was the key to national and regime security—not only because it would accelerate forces of production in socialist construction but also because it could strengthen the defense-industry sector, which is vital to self-reliance in defense. Such a political calculus has led to continuity in the pursuit of the second economy.

External threat is the other factor accounting for change and continuity in party-military relations. If the Sino-Soviet rivalry, the rise of revisionism in the Soviet Union, and an assertive U.S. containment policy induced the military's superiority over the party in the 1960s, improved North-South relations and the advent of détente paved the way to party dominance over the military in the 1970s. Consolidation of the party and the military under Kim Jong Il's one-man rule cannot be separated from external threats. The demise of the Soviet Union, the dissolution of the Eastern European bloc, and Seoul's diplomatic normalization with the Soviet Union and China have bred an acute sense of isolation and insecurity in the minds of North Korean leaders. The U.S. military presence in the South, increasing diplomatic pressures on the North by the United States and its allies in the wake of the nuclear crisis and the ballistic missile fiasco, growing diplomatic isolation—all have furthered the sense of insecurity in the North. It is with this threat perception that Kim Jong Il's one-man dictatorship has been legitimized and new political slogans of *"kangsungdaekuk"* ("strong and prosperous nation") and *"sungun jungchi"* ("the primacy of the military in politics") have been emphasized. A North Korean official has made it clear that as long as the external threat prevails, North Korea will continue its military-centered policy line.[15] As Lewis Coser (1956) has hypothesized, external threats have strengthened internal unity around the supreme leader and the military as his instrument of political domination.

As long as the external threats continue, the military is likely to exercise a profound influence on national security policy. The same can be said of the second economy as reaffirmed through the amended constitution in 1998, which emphasizes the continuation of the four military lines. But external threats are not the only variable that might affect national security policy and defense industrialization. Bureaucratic compartmentalization under Kim's monolithic rule can certainly influence the direction of national security policy. Vertical command and control and fierce loyalty competition could lead to more erratic policy behavior than ever before. As contending bureaucratic interpretations of broadly defined national and regime interests confront one another, North Korea is likely to show conflictual and cooperative behavior simultaneously.

Thus party-military relations in general—and political domination, national security policy, and the military's socioeconomic role in particular—have been deeply influenced by the political regime in the North, which can be characterized as a monolithic organic corporatism (J.-S. Lee 1995; Cumings 1993). The doctrine of the trinity—supreme leader, party, and military—and the pentagon principle—the unity of the supreme leader, the party, the state, the people, and the military—all underscore the unique corporatist arrangement in North Korea. Thus it becomes essential for us to understand its evolving nature. Beneath the North Korean version of organic corporatism lie strong domestic cultural and historical conditions and foreign influences. The DPRK modeled party-military relations on those of the Soviet Union; the cult of personality came from China. Even before 1945, DPRK leaders carried out partisan activities with the support of the Soviet Union. These experiences were translated into party-military relations at the time of the establishment of DPRK in 1948, and they had a decisive impact on the operational modes of political and military organizations. Political officers were given critical roles owing to the Soviet influence. The cult of personality, which prevailed in China during the Mao Zedong era, was influential as well. In the 1970s, the DPRK led by Kim Il Sung strengthened its *juche* (self-reliant) line and his deification. This too was influenced mostly by Maoist China.

Apart from emulating China and the Soviet Union, the DPRK appeared to have appropriated elements of Japanese prewar political culture as well as those of the Confucian tradition. The primacy of the military and emphasis on "a strong and prosperous nation" have a striking resemblance to prewar Japanese militarism, which was framed around the idea of *"fukok kyohei"* ("rich nation, strong army") and the mentality of crisis management through national mobilization, superiority of the military, and strengthening of leadership. Equally important is the role of Confucianism, for the rise of monolithic organic corporatism in which the supreme leader is equated with people, state, party, and military. In Confucianism, the father is absolute. And in North Korea the word *"oboi"* ("father") has an absolute semantic connotation: Kim Il Sung gained people's respect by telling them he was their father, and his son had the legitimacy to succeed his power and authority. It is through this political culture of the Confucian tradition that people accepted a one-man-centered power structure and succession of power and charisma from father to son (Takesada 1998: 99–105). In view of this political culture and subsequent formation of the monolithic organic corporatism, it is hardly feasible to imagine any viable social and political opposition to Kim's leadership. The military is not an exception to this.

PATTERNS AND IMPLICATIONS

The study of civil-military relations in North Korea suggests several implications. First is the uniqueness of those relations. There is no civil society in a strict sense, and political society (the KWP) has incorporated civil society into its own organizational structure. Thus it would be more accurate to call them party-military relations. North Korea has seen an evolving pattern of party-military relations: a sequential phase of institutional conflict between the party and the military in the 1950s, the military's participation in the party in the 1960s, and a leadership-driven congruence of interests between the party and the military since the 1970s. In the process, North Korea has become one of few countries in the world where the military's political intervention is officially institutionalized. However, it should be noted that such an institutionalized military intervention through the NDC cannot be construed as a sign of military dominance over the party politics. On the contrary, such arrangement can be seen as a tactical move to facilitate and consolidate political domination by the supreme leader, Kim Jong Il.

Second, this unique pattern is by and large a result of regime dynamics peculiar to North Korea. The regime under Kim Jong Il can be characterized as a monolithic organic corporatism in which party, state, people, and military constitute the integral parts of the supreme leader. The organic unity has facilitated a leadership-driven congruence of interests in national and regime security. The regime's durability in North Korea can be ascribed to this unique organic arrangement among its component parts. Thus it seems quite inconceivable to disaggregate the party and the military into two separate entities. Nevertheless, it is plausible for them to engage in bureaucratic and functional conflicts as part of loyalty competition to the supreme leader. No country in the world, not even Cuba, Libya, or Iraq, shows such an extreme form of organic corporatism blurring the relationship between political society and the military. Such regime arrangement has facilitated Kim's firm grip over party and military.

Third, external threats have shaped the evolution of regime dynamics and party-military relations in North Korea. External threats have not only enhanced internal unity around the supreme leader; they have also encouraged a convergence of power into the military as anointed by the leader. For the military is the only organized means that can ensure the nation's and the regime's security simultaneously. The military's primacy in politics, its institutionalized intervention in party and state, and the emphasis on the second economy—all of which have become more pronounced in the wake of the 1994 nuclear crisis—confirm the convergence thesis. And this observation bears an important policy implication: a hard-line or containment policy toward North Korea will only strengthen the military's position and lead to a vicious cycle of containment and confrontation.

Finally, path dependence matters. Kim Jong Il's consolidation of power has entailed institutional realignments that have in turn created new vested interests. The military and members of Kim's inner circle are the primary beneficiaries of these new institutional arrangements. Insofar as they stay in power by supporting Kim Jong Il, the current pattern of military centralism in civil-military relations is likely to persist. The impact of this path dependence is noticeable, too, in national security policymaking and the second economy. Consequently, the military will continue to be influential in national security policymaking and the socioeconomic arenas.

However, one caveat is in order. Power and influence of the military are likely to be delimited by political calculus of supreme leadership. In the process of consolidating political power after the death of Kim Il Sung, the military has been the vital asset to Kim Jong Il. But the primacy of the military in politics and the hard-line position in national security policy alone cannot assure Kim of his popular support and political legitimacy. Kim needs to resolve negative consequences of the hard-line position, such as international isolation, economic crisis and stagnation, agricultural failures and famines, and the deteriorating quality of life of the North

Korean people. To correct these failures and to improve people's quality of life, both of which are critical to his legitimacy, Kim Jong Il might be forced to realign his policy on the economy, national security, and the military. The June 14 summit talk of 2000 with president Kim Dae-jung of South Korea appears to be an eloquent token of Kim's impending changes in the direction of opening, reform, and peaceful coexistence with the South. Such changes could strain relationships among the leader, party, and military. Thus, it might be premature to conclude the military's dominance over party. After all, relationships between party and military are likely to be variable, ultimately being determined by Kim's leadership choices.

PART VII

Military Control of the State

CHAPTER 16

Pakistan: Return to Praetorianism

Babar Sattar

THE MILITARY IN PAKISTAN IS PRONE TO INTERVENTION whenever its institutional interests are threatened by a civilian government and cannot be secured otherwise. This was made abundantly clear on October 12, 1999, when the army chief, Gen. Pervaiz Musharaf, overthrew the democratically elected government of Nawaz Sharif. The poor performance of the Sharif government had eroded its support base and thus mitigated any possibility of civilian resistance to military rule in the immediate term. And although General Musharaf repeated the customary charges of corruption and incompetence that had induced the military to take over—as military rulers had done in the past—these were not the primary causes leading to the events of October 12.

In his address to the nation on October 17, General Musharaf made no bones of the fact that one of the paramount factors instigating the military to intervene, demolish the civilian government, dismiss the parliament, suspend the constitution, and muzzle the political process was the threat Sharif's government posed to the military as an institution. "It is unbelievable and indeed unfortunate," he said, "that the few at the helm of affairs in the last government were intriguing to destroy the last institution of stability in Pakistan by creating dissension in the ranks of the armed forces of Pakistan."[1]

The coup of October 12 was an act of reactive militarism whereby the military took charge of the country, without a national agenda, essentially to safeguard its institutional and corporate interests. Direct engagement of the military in politics had been decreasing ever since the restoration of democracy in 1988. And a point had arrived at which the armed forces had largely come to be seen as a junior partner of the civilian government, especially after the forced retirement of General Musharaf's predecessor, Gen. Jehangir Karamat. Although management of national security is viewed by the military as one of its exclusive functions, there is evidence that Sharif was interfering with operational and policymaking issues the military had traditionally considered its own domain. If this trend was allowed to continue, the military feared that the status quo in terms of civil-military relations would tilt decisively against it as an institution.

Moreover, domestic political events in the 1990s had undermined the military's ability to exert decisive control over the exercise of state political power—a bone of contention between successive civilian governments and the military—from behind a curtain. Although the military almost seemed prepared, albeit grudgingly, to reconcile itself to a loss of veto power vis-à-vis domestic political decisions, it was not prepared to dispense with absolute control over institutional matters as well as national security management, even if that meant thwarting the democratic process by a show of brute force.

Pakistan has had a checkered political history. Its system of governance has been oscillating between democracy and martial law for the last 52 years. For nearly half the country's history, Pakistan has been administered directly by military generals with the assistance of a civilian bureaucracy. During the remaining period, the military has exerted its influence over civilian governments from behind the scenes. But the exact nature of this influence, the channels and procedures used for its exercise, its impact on policy and decisions of national importance, and, more important, the source of the military's extraconstitutional authority have remained subjects of intense debate.

All governments in Pakistan have offered unequivocal commitment to maintaining a strong military for protecting the country's security interests. This commitment has promoted the military's growth. Civilian institutions, however, have not experienced a simultaneous strengthening. Pakistan's failure to evolve mature democratic institutions, to institutionalize the acquisition and exercise of state power, and to inoculate democratic norms and values among the masses has rendered its civilian governments vulnerable to military intervention in politics. The "establishment," a term used in Pakistan to describe the civil-military bureaucratic nexus, has projected the armed forces as a messiah ensuring the very existence of Pakistan and appointed to umpire and guide the country to a better future. Although external security threats and the continuing state of belligerence with India have afforded the military a large role in Pakistan, the civilian elite's administrative incompetence and the sluggish and lopsided development of political institutions provide the raison d'être for the military's domestic political role.

The counterargument, however, is that repeated military interventions have been instrumental in undermining the authority of civilian governments. The engagement of the military in politics in the formative years might have been by invitation of nonrepresentative politicians, but the coups that followed were acts of reactive militarism inspired by the desire to protect and promote the military's institutional and corporate interests that have also been growing over time. Repeated military interference disrupted the political process and prevented the evolution of institutional norms and conventions, thus keeping vital state institutions weak and in a state of perpetual dependence on the military.

The question then is what drives the military into politics? Do altruistic objectives explain repeated military intervention? Is it nostalgia for lost power? Or is it the mere consequence of confrontations between civilian political elite and the military? The constant tension in civil-military relations can be explained by the huge discrepancy between the role of the armed forces as defined by the constitution of 1973, and their self-perceived role. According to all the constitutions Pakistan has had, the federal government is supposed to exercise control over the armed forces. But in practice, even during democratic rule, there has been only a semblance of civilian supremacy.

Because of the preponderant role that the military has played in the history of Pakistan and its monopoly over the ultimate means of coercion, the military has arrogated to itself the right to define Pakistan's supreme national interest, gauge the civilian government's performance, and take appropriate action, which has ranged from admonition to removal of the government. The military views itself as the guardian of Pakistan's ideological frontiers and is therefore required to inject stability and continuity into the polity and deliver the country to a better future, and its definition of military professionalism stems from such a self-image.

In this chapter I investigate continuity and change in civil-military relations in Pakistan. Such an analysis would not be possible, however, without surveying this relationship in a historical context. Because it is not my purpose here to document the history of civil-military relations in detail, the survey simply traces the causes of military intervention in politics and highlights sources of continuity and change that explain the dynamics of evolving civil-military relations. The formal provisions of civil-military relations have been traced, as well, to explicate the discrepancy between the constitutional role and the military's self-perceived role. The ethnic composition of the armed forces and the role of intelligence agencies have been considered, too, to see if these factors have had an impact on civil-military relations.

In order to study continuity and change in civil-military relations after 1988, we draw a distinction between the military's role in managing national security and its role in the exercise of state political power. The final section reflects on the future course of civil-military relations. As we shall see, the management of national security has been a military preserve in the past and is likely to remain so. Shared or divided jurisdiction has been characteristic in the exercise of state political power. The military has remained skeptical of the unfettered exercise of state power by elected politicians even in democratic times. The chapter concludes with an observation: Although the military's overt political role declined between 1988 and 1999, it remained the most powerful and organized institution of the state. And despite a decade of civilian rule, the concept of civilian political control over the military was never established. Thus on the eve of the twenty-first century, when democracy was being viewed globally as a fundamental human right, the military in Pakistan was able to pull off a coup d'état and assume direct control of the state. But the main question is whether Pakistan can get out of the vicious cycle in which it is caught up between military dictatorships and nonperforming autocratic civilian governments. Civil-military relations in Pakistan, by all means, constitute an unfinished agenda.

DYNAMICS OF CIVIL-MILITARY RELATIONS

It takes a combination of factors—Pakistan's colonial heritage, a leadership vacuum in the immediate postindependence period, weak political institutions and lack of continuity in political processes, the politics of migratory leadership, economic forces, the postcolonial state and overdeveloped state theses, the Indian threat and lingering territorial disputes, Pakistan's geostrategic environment, and direct institutional links of Pakistan's army with the United States—to explain the steady transformation of the military's role in politics between 1947 and 1958: from influence and blackmail in the late 1940s and early 1950s to the displacement of governments in the mid-1950s to the supplanting of civilian government by military rule in 1958. (See Rizvi 1987: 12–20; Waseem 1994: 102–31; Jalal 1991: 26–135; Alvi 1983: 40–53; Hashmi 1983: 102–14; Tahir-Kheli 1980: 643.) But it was the character of the postcolonial state in Pakistan—highly centralized, unitary, and authoritarian—that made the military's intervention in politics possible in the first place. Certainly the geopolitical location of Pakistan, the tense security environment in which it was born, and the shamefully pragmatic U.S. foreign policy during the cold war provided a congenial external environment for military takeover in Pakistan. But these external factors alone could not have instigated a coup in Pakistan and ensured its success. Indeed, we must look to the authoritarian style of governance that had plagued the country much before the military imposed its first martial law in 1958.

The military played no role in Pakistan's independence movement. In fact, the military's reorganization took place after Pakistan had already appeared on the globe as a nation-state (Rizvi 1987: 21–36). Before independence the officers of the British Indian Army, a fairly efficient military machine, were obliged to choose between the Indian and the Pakistani military establishment. Military hardware was divided between India and Pakistan, as well, which became another source of bitter controversy (Jalal 1991: 37–44). At the time of its evolution there was no confusion regarding the military's role in the state. It was established as a professional body responsible for managing the security of the state and directly subservient to the executive civilian authorities of Pakistan (Government of Pakistan 1989: 264–65).[2]

Pakistan was born with an insecurity syndrome. It was widely believed that India was out to undo Pakistan's sovereign existence, and therefore, survival was viewed as a challenge (Ali 1967: 276–315). The issue of the accession of princely states to either India or Pakistan formed the unfinished agenda of the subcontinent's partition. The use of force in deciding the fate of princely states transformed the mutual animosity between India and Pakistan on the eve of independence into an unrelenting state of belligerence. But more important, it made the military relevant in shaping the Pakistan-India relationship and in turn reinforced the imperative for Pakistan, as the smaller and weaker of the two, to possess a strong military machine. The external threat from India (and to some extent from Afghanistan) made the establishment of a strong military organization a priority for Pakistan in its early years. The First Kashmir War between India and Pakistan in 1948 only heightened the security concerns of the government of the day.

It was also believed widely in Pakistan that the Radcliff Award was unfair and that gross irregularities and injustices had been perpetrated against Pakistan while British India's assets were being divided among the successor states (Ali 1967: 203–22; Hussain 1998: 111). The inequitable division of military hardware was seen as a design to weaken Pakistan's defenses against external aggression. In order to secure the country's territorial boundaries, the cash-starved government of Pakistan allocated a huge proportion of its meager resources to bolster defense and create an efficient fighting machine. This policy provided for the steady growth of the military at a time when the other institutions of the state were in utter disarray.

The direction of institutional evolution in postindependence Pakistan led to the centralization of state authority in the federal executive body. Innumerable factors explain the lopsided institutional development in Pakistan's early years, a development that weakened the democratic institutions of the country to a level where political and electoral processes stood discredited altogether (Waseem 1994: 6–164). Power-wielders in the immediate post-1947 period defined the ideology and national interest of Pakistan in a manner that led to the imposition of a monolithic culture upon a multiethnic society. The postcolonial state in Pakistan was not flexible enough to accommodate regional groups in the policymaking and power-sharing mechanisms.

It was the Muslim minority provinces in prepartition India that led the independence movement. This leadership, which ran a successful campaign for Pakistan and saw itself as a legitimate claimant of power after its creation, did not have a permanent constituency in the country and thus stood to lose command if the distribution of political power was to be decided by the electorate. Moreover, democracy promised the Bengalis of East Pakistan a permanent advantage in the new state because of their overall numerical majority in Pakistan, which they could use in parliament "to dominate the central government" (Jalal 1995a: 53). But again, the Punjabi and the migrant elite were not prepared to allow control of the country to slip into Bengali hands.

Very early after independence Pakistan witnessed two types of conflict: one was between the center and the provinces; the other was between representative and nonrepresentative institutions of the state. The outcome of the second conflict became apparent "as bureaucrats and generals called the shots [and] politicians willing to do their bidding were shunted in and out of office" (Jalal 1995a: 72). An extreme manifestation of the first type—which continues to haunt Pakistan—was the creation of Bangladesh in 1971. In short, the center and the nonrepresentative institutions, in concert with each other, emerged victorious and subsequently chipped away the administrative, political, and financial autonomy of provinces while disenfranchising the people of Pakistan.

Because the Muslim League as a political party was not sufficiently organized to serve as a platform to administer state authority in the areas comprising Pakistan, the postindependence power elite chose to rely on nonelected institutions to perpetuate its control over the polity. State authority was monopolized and centralized in the administrative institutions of the state, which was developed at the expense of representative political institutions at the national, provincial, and local levels. While Pakistan was undergoing transition to a bureaucratic polity due to the disproportionate growth of the civilian bureaucracy and the military, the armed forces were called upon time and again either to enforce the writ of the civilian authorities or to address social problems that fell exclusively within the domain of civilian institutions.

In the immediate postindependence period, the military dealt with refugee rehabilitation. Later it was called out in aid of civilian agencies to address law and order—a product of language riots and many other factors—in East Pakistan between 1952 and 1958. Even in West Pakistan a limited martial law was enforced in Lahore by the civilian authorities themselves during the anti-Qadiani movement in 1953. The military was also used extensively in flood relief operations. In addition, the armed forces were undertaking social activities simultaneously—in education, in establishing small industries, and more. Such activities helped the military to develop a nationalistic identity (Tahir-Kheli 1980: 643).

All the important moves on Pakistan's national chessboard in the early 1950s were made by the civil and military bureaucrats who represented the nonelected institutions of the state (Waseem 1994: 137–44). Governor Gen. Ghulam Mohammed made Gen. Ayub Khan, the commander in chief of Pakistan's armed forces, the defense minister in 1954. Veena Kukreja (1991: 70) pointed out, "The induction of Ayub Khan in the new cabinet as defense minister and also as C-in-C was not only unprecedented but also unprincipled and wholly opposed to the ideas of civilian supremacy over the military establishment. In his capacity as the defense minister the army chief became his own boss." Further, Gen. Ayub Khan was invited to present "a short appreciation of the present and future problems of Pakistan," which he did on October 4, 1954. The general not only provided administrative, legal, political, and economic guidelines to the government on how to run the country but also devised the parity scheme that divided Pakistan into two administrative units.

The need to augment its defense compelled Pakistan to tap all possible sources of support. With meager indigenous capability to counter the superior Indian military machine, Pakistan's defense managers began to rely on external financial and military support to meet the country's defense needs and on cold war alliances to enhance its security. In the face of U.S. developmental orientation vis-à-vis the Third World—especially the notion that authoritarian regimes might be effective agents of modernization and change—the military was encouraged to develop direct institutional links with Washington and London. Ayesha Jalal (1995a: 54) argued, "It was the interplay of domestic, regional and international factors during the late forties and fifties—in particular, the links forged with the USA—that served to erode the position of parties and politicians within the evolving structure of the Pakistani state by tipping the institutional balance towards the civil bureaucracy and the military."

President Iskander Mirza removed the civilian government in October 1958 and appointed Ayub Khan as the chief martial law administrator in the country. As reasons for such drastic action Mirza cited "the ruthless struggle for power, corruption, the shameful exploitation of simple, honest, patriotic and industrious masses, the lack of decorum, and the prostitution of Islam for political ends" (Rizvi 1987: 271). Yet martial law was justified, not by calling democracy an inappropriate system of governance for Pakistan or by denying the concept of civilian supremacy over the armed forces, but rather on the basis of expediency and public welfare (Rizvi 1987: 271–78).[3]

Ayub Khan removed President Mirza from office the same month, assumed overall charge, and ruled the country for more than a decade. He introduced the 1962 constitution, which promised a return to democracy. Until his exit in 1969, however, Pakistan experienced a one-man rule in which the bureaucracy conducted the affairs of the country under the military's supervision. In March 1969, Ayub Khan saw his way out after he found himself isolated in face of a mass national movement that wiped away even the military support for his regime. He handed over power to the commander in chief of the Pakistan army, Gen. Yahya Khan. Once again the military had ridiculed the constitution and the rule of law, which provided that the speaker of the assembly was to assume the president's powers in case the latter resigned. But this extraconstitutional move, too, was justified on the basis of necessity (Rizvi 1987: 279–81).[4] Yahya's martial law was transitional, however, swept aside by the turbulence that culminated in the East Pakistan debacle.

Ayub Khan ruled Pakistan for more than a decade that saw significant economic growth. Yahya Khan on the other hand stayed in power for a much shorter period and presided over Pakistan's disintegration. But a common lesson learned from both regimes was that although the military faces little difficulty taking over the levers of political power, it finds it exceedingly difficult to solve basic social, political, and economic problems facing the country.

A factor that constantly provided for the augmentation of the military as an institution was Pakistan's external threat perception, especially the continuing state of belligerence with India. The Pakistan-India wars of 1965 and 1971 and repeated border skirmishes multiplied the country's security sensitivities. Lingering territorial disputes committed Pakistan to strengthening its armed forces and allocating a lion's share of its meager national budget to defense expenditure, which has seen a steady increase over the years. And a hostile regional security environment not only helped to polish the charismatic appeal of the armed forces, but also afforded them more flexibility in defining Pakistan's national security interests in a manner that strengthened their position vis-à-vis civilian institutions.

After Pakistan's army lost the war of 1971 that led to the creation of Bangladesh, Yahya Khan handed over power to Zulfiqar Ali Bhutto's Pakistan People's Party (PPP)—the majority party in West Pakistan. Zulfiqar Bhutto took over at a time when the military's prestige was at its nadir. As an elected representative he reinforced the concept of absolute civilian supremacy over the military in Pakistan (Rizvi 1987: 287–88).[5] Moreover, he drafted the constitution of 1973, which endorsed a parliamentary form of democracy for Pakistan. Civil-military relations experienced a substantial change under Bhutto, who took political, administrative, and legal steps to disengage the military from politics (Tahir-Kheli 1980: 644–48).

Shirin Tahir-Kheli called General Zia-ul-Haq's coup of 1977—which dismissed Bhutto's government along with the assemblies and held the constitution in abeyance—a case of reactive militarism (Tahir Kheli 1980: 644–48). True to its self-appointed role as savior of the country, the military once again assumed direct control of Pakistan after declaring that the government stood discredited, because of widespread allegations of rigging the March 1977 elections, and no longer possessed the ability to run the affairs of the country (Rizvi 1987: 289–93).[6]

Zia's martial law differed from that of his predecessors—primarily because of increased problems of legitimacy and the military's politicization. This period witnessed major changes in the pattern of civil-military relations. Although Zia did follow the erstwhile practice of co-opting the civilian bureaucracy as a junior partner in the martial law government, he reduced his reliance on it by engaging the military more directly to manage the political affairs of the country. Earlier military rulers had restricted the military to the task of supervising the system of governance managed primarily by the civilian bureaucracy. Zia was the first dictator to offer the military officer corps a mammoth opportunity to advance personal careers and seek lucrative jobs in the civilian sector.

In the formative years of Zia's regime, the chief martial law administrator and the corps commanders constituted the state oligarchy. The corps commanders were made the regional martial law administrators and later the governors of all four provinces: Lieutenant General Fazal-e-Haq (1978–1985), General Rahim-ud-din (1978–1984), Lt. Gen. S. M. Abbasi (1978–1984), and Lt. Gen. Ghulam Gilani Khan (1980–1985) served as governors of the NWFP, Baluchistan, Sindh, and Punjab respectively. By conducting the corps commanders conference as a cabinet meeting, Zia contrived new decision-making channels and engaged the military in day-to-day administrative affairs, thus getting the institution used to asserting its will and authority in all affairs of the state. The practice of appointing retired military officers to high civilian posts—as provincial governors, federal secretaries, ambassadors, and heads of important national corporations (such as Water and Power Development Authority and Pakistan International Airline)—in praise of the "special services" they had rendered during active service still continues as a legacy of the Zia rule.

Later Zia repromulgated the constitution of 1973—with due modifications to perpetuate his control—and called for nonparty national elections in 1985. The transition back to democracy did not take effect until the elections of 1988, however, which had been called by Zia himself but took place after his demise. The transition was by no means smooth. After the PPP's election into office in 1988, Pakistan saw three more general elections. None of the elected governments completed its scheduled tenure in office.

The civilian governments of Benazir Bhutto and Nawaz Sharif developed differences with the military leadership. Indeed, differences with the military were seen as the principal cause for the dismissal of Benazir Bhutto's first government (1989–1990). Moreover, the dissolution of Nawaz Sharif's government (1990–1993) and Benazir Bhutto's second government

(1993–1996) would probably have been impossible without the military's connivance and consent. And the overthrow of the Sharif government in 1999 was exclusively a military affair.

Apart from the military's alleged role in making and breaking civilian governments in the post-1988 period, this institution is believed to have had a prominent role in the formulation of policies on all issues of national importance. During civilian rule the military emerged as an arbiter of the last resort with overriding authority in all political and institutional conflicts of significance in the country. The right to democracy has not yet come to be recognized as an inalienable right in Pakistan. Vital state institutions remain dysfunctional or languish in a state of transition wherein their norms and procedures are not firmly entrenched. During the last decade of failed democratic rule the common citizen did not attain the promised blessings of self-governance, and this accounts for the lack of public attachment to democracy and its institutions in Pakistan.

CIVIL-MILITARY RELATIONS IN THEORY AND PRACTICE

In theory there is no confusion regarding the command and function of the armed forces. In Article 243, the 1973 constitution lays down in unequivocal terms that "the Federal Government shall have control and command of the Armed Forces." The function of the armed forces is clearly spelled out by Article 245(1) of the constitution, which says, "The Armed Forces shall, under the direction of the Federal Government, defend Pakistan against external aggression or threat of war, and, subject to law, act in aid of civil power when called upon to do so" (Khosa 1996: 131).

Clearly, then, the constitution establishes civilian control over the armed forces in absolute terms. The armed forces are primarily the defenders of Pakistan's frontiers but can also be called upon to enforce the authority of the civilian government and can be charged with internal security duties that the civilian government deems fit. Thus the armed forces are in service of the state and the society, and have no sanction to act on their own discretion or pass judgment on the functioning of the civilian government. Under Article 244 of the constitution, every member of the military takes an oath to uphold the constitution and refrain from engaging in any political activities whatsoever.

To perpetuate the rule of law and provide an additional deterrent against military adventurism and intervention in politics, the constitution holds in Article 6 that "any person who abrogates or attempts or conspires to abrogate, subverts or attempts or conspires to subvert, the Constitution by use of force or show of force or by other unconstitutional means shall be guilty of high treason" (Khosa 1996: 4).

These provisions have been in force since 1973. Even the earlier constitutions in force between 1947 and 1973 did not provide for the military's role in politics. The desire to establish effective civilian supremacy over the armed forces guided the composition of Pakistan's Higher Defense Organization (HDO) in late 1975 and instituted civilian control over the defense forces (Government of Pakistan, Ministry of Defense 1976).[7] The Defense Committee of the Cabinet is the supreme decision-making authority in all defense matters. This committee is responsible for defining the task of the armed forces, reviewing the organization of defense and preparedness for war, coordinating the plans and actions of all ministries in defense matters, and supervising the conduct of war.[8] The Defense Council is second in the defense decision-making hierarchy and is entrusted with the translation of defense policy into military policy.[9] Under the present structure of the HDO, the chiefs of staff of the army, navy, and air force are to exercise the command functions over their respective services, along with being "military advisors to the Prime Minister, the Cabinet, and the Defense Minister" (Rizvi 1987: 302). Despite the Zia interlude, the structure of the HDO laid down by Zulfiqar Bhutto, which vested the representative government with supreme authority over the armed forces, was not formally discarded. Yet even when elected representatives of the people were running Pakistan's parliamentary democracy, one found only a semblance of civilian supremacy, especially in defense matters. The HDO has proved a sham, because the Defense Committee of the Cabinet and the Defense Council never made substantial defense-related decisions. Although both these bodies remained de jure power-wielders in all defense matters during democratic times, real authority resided elsewhere. How Pakistan's defense policy is actually formulated is anyone's guess. But it is abundantly clear that very little civilian input goes into this policy.

That there is no disagreement in principle regarding the system of governance is apparent from the proclamations made by military dictators while imposing martial law in Pakistan. It is not difficult to discern a pattern in military takeovers. The exploitation of the country and its people by ruling politicians, along with political crises threatening the sovereignty and integrity of Pakistan, are always cited as causes for the military's intervention in politics. That the military might have political ambitions is strictly denied: the objective of military rule is stated to be the establishment of conditions congenial for the revival of democracy and constitutional government. The military's flagrant disregard for the constitution and the rule of law is justified on the grounds of expediency—not only by the military itself but also by the judiciary.[10]

In theory, then, there is no scope for misconstruing the military's job description. The constraints of the constitution have not prevented the military from threatening the use of brute force to dislodge a civilian government. A segment of the civilian populace does, however, mistrust the capability and intentions of civilian governments. These detractors of civilian governments view the military as a de facto watchdog of the political system and the performance of civilians in office. And there has been continuing talk of transforming the military's de facto role in politics into a de jure one initiated by the military itself. General Zia-ul-Haq first launched the proposal of legitimizing this role in 1979, but he desisted from translating it into reality (Tahir-Kheli 1980: 649–50). The debate over the creation of a National Security Council has continued in the post-1988 period, though the proposal has failed to muster overwhelming support from all quarters in Pakistan. An ordinance issued by President Farooq Leghari did constitute a Council for Defense and National Security for a brief period after the dismissal of Benazir Bhutto's government in 1996, but the ordinance was not renewed and the council thus stood dissolved. Gen. Jehangir Karamat, a former chief of army staff, provided fresh impetus to the debate when, addressing the Pakistan Navy War College on October 5, 1998, he suggested the formation of a "national security council or committee at the apex" that would "institutionalize decision making."[11]

Due to the mistrust and frustration created by a decade of civilian rule, proposals to amend the law of the land in order to formally incorporate the military in the decision-making process are finding greater support among various segments of the society, including prominent members of mainstream political parties. Adherents of the "controlled democracy" concept argue that creation of a permanent National Security Council will not only stabilize civil-military relations but will be a useful addition to the current system of checks and balances over the exercise of executive authority. Letting the service chiefs sit on National Security Council that is sanctioned to guide the cabinet, it is argued, will simply remove the discrepancy between the military's role in theory and in practice. The present military regime has already created a National Security Council and will, in all probability, endeavor to make this arrangement permanent before heading back to the barracks.

THE MILITARY'S ETHNIC COMPOSITION

Pakistan's ethnic communities are not represented in the armed forces in proportion to their overall share in the population. A disproportionate ethnic composition was something the Pakistan military inherited from the British Indian Army, even if not quite its recruitment policy based on the martial race concept. The British believed that "certain races furnished fine fighting men and certain races exhibited little or no aptitude for military service" (Rizvi 1987: 135). As a consequence, the bulk of the army was recruited from the Punjab, the NWFP, and the kingdom of Nepal.

Although the Ayub Khan government seemed anxious to do away with the biased recruitment policy of the British, the general recruitment pattern prevailed even after independence. The Punjab and the NWFP—especially Kohat, Peshawar, Attock, Rawalpindi, Jhelum, and Gujrat—emerged as the prime areas for military recruitment in Pakistan. Although the government was not oblivious to the underrepresentation of certain ethnic groups in the armed forces, its efforts to harmonize this demographic imbalance brought no significant change. Consequently the military and ruling elite have remained targets of scathing criticism for not making the military representative of the federation of Pakistan in order to give it a truly national character.

Before the birth of an independent Bangladesh, many in East Pakistan shared the feeling that "the military, unlike the civil service, did not adopt a conscious policy to counteract the [ethnic] imbalance" (Jahan 1972a: 25). Likewise regional and nationalist political parties in the provinces of Baluchistan and Sindh, which are underrepresented in the armed forces, have at times exhibited their skepticism by calling the military an instrument of the Punjabi-Pakhtoon ruling elite, not the federation of Pakistan. Such fears, though not wholly unfounded, do not spring from the military's recruitment policies. They are rooted instead in the failure of the polity to forge a federation of autonomous provincial units and the inability of elites in majority provinces to address the concerns of smaller provinces. Despite allegations that the military was indifferent to East Pakistan's underrepresentation, steps were taken to boost the induction of Bengalis in the armed forces—"lowering of the height requirement from 5 ft 6 inches to 5 ft 4 inches to allow for the shorter stature of Bengalis," for example (Hussain 1979: 128–29). Similarly in the post-1971 period, the military has adopted other measures—raising Baluch and Sindh regiments, for example, and establishing the Pannu Aaqil army base in Sindh—to address recruitment disparities.

But in view of its professional limitations and the demographic features of Pakistan, the military can make only a limited effort to balance its ethnic composition. According to Rizvi (1987: 145), "The importance of fair representation of different regions in the armed forces cannot be denied, especially in a country where the military exercises political power. This has to be harmonized with the imperatives of military discipline, cohesion and efficiency. If pure and simple principles of democracy are applied to the military, it would cease to be an efficient fighting machine." As a voluntary fighting force, Pakistan's army cannot adopt a quota-based recruitment policy to accommodate a larger number of Sindhis and Baluch. The military profession has neither caught the fancy of Bengalis in the pre-1971 period nor has it attracted the Sindhi and Baluch mind to the extent that it has in the Punjab and the NWFP. History, culture, and sociology explain this phenomenon to some extent. Traditionally the Baluch and Sindhi communities have been reluctant to subject themselves to the discipline, hierarchy, and rigors of military life. As in the case of East Pakistan, the scanty number of initial applicants from Baluchistan and Sindh reveals that ethnic groups in these provinces are underrepresented, not because they do not qualify for the armed forces, but because they do not wish to join (Rizvi 1987: 140).

As an institution the military does not have an ethnic mindset. The regional and ethnic fault lines fragmenting Pakistani society have not manifested themselves within the armed forces. The credit for this goes to the basic training in military academies, which largely deconstructs the personalities of fresh recruits and remolds them in accordance with military requirements, inculcating a predominantly Pakistani identity. Moreover, secondary identities do not help upward social mobility in the armed forces because the promotion criteria are fixed and generally believed to be based on merit. This undermines the need to highlight regional or ethnic identities.

Nevertheless, as long as the military is perceived as a key political actor in the state and is used to quell regional movements and agitation against the center, its ethnic composition will continue to be projected by regional ethnic parties as part of a larger design of majority provinces to perpetuate their hegemony over smaller units of the federation. And, whatever the true causes of ethnic imbalance, underrepresentation of Sindhis, Baluch, and Mohajirs in the military breeds skepticism within these communities, especially when the military assumes internal security duties such as those undertaken in Baluchistan in the 1970s and Sindh in the 1990s. During martial law regimes, when political processes are stifled and democratic institutions are excluded from decision making, the smaller provinces believe they have been deprived of their voice. The latest military takeover is a case in point. Although the ruling junta claims to stand for the rights of smaller provinces, the Pakistan Oppressed Nations Movement—an alliance of nationalist parties from minority provinces—has been the most vociferous opponent of military rule from day one and has demanded an immediate return to democracy.

THE INTELLIGENCE MACHINERY

The military in Pakistan monopolizes the intelligence machinery. Although the elite intelligence agencies, Inter Services Intelligence (ISI) and Military Intelligence, are headed by active-duty generals, the practice of appointing retired officers to command the civilian intelligence agencies, the Intelligence Bureau and the Federal Investigation Agency, is a familiar one.

Military Intelligence, as its name suggests, is a purely military agency with counterparts in the air force and the navy as well. In the past, however, it has been asked to undertake operations within the country outside its usual scope of activity and to make presentations on domestic political issues. The ISI was created immediately after independence and draws its staff from the three services as well as the civilian sector. It was directly responsible to the three services through the Joint Chiefs of Staff Committee (JCSC) until 1975, when Prime Minister Zulfiqar Ali Bhutto issued an executive order creating a political cell within the ISI. Ever since, the ISI has been under the direct control of the chief executive, at least in theory, and has continued to report to the JCSC on matters related to the armed forces. General Zia-ul-Haq refurbished the ISI and came to rely on it. Assignment of the Afghanistan operation augmented the role of the ISI, which is still believed to be controlling foreign policy initiatives vis-à-vis Afghanistan.

The ISI's influence over Pakistan's foreign office aside, its political wing is deemed to have played a controversial role in the domestic political arena. The ISI is believed to have disbursed Rs140 million—acknowledged by the ISI's director-general, Lt. Gen. Asad Durrani, in an affidavit filed in the supreme court—to influence the results of national elections in 1990. According to Durrani, in September 1990 as director-general of ISI he received instructions from the chief of army staff, Gen. Mirza Aslam Beg, to provide logistic support for the disbursement of donations made by Karachi businessmen to the Islamic Jamhoori Itihaad (IJI) election campaign.[12] The ISI then opened up accounts in Karachi, Quetta, and Rawalpindi and distributed Rs6 million to IJI candidates in all four provinces of Pakistan in order to influence the 1990 general elections. The IJI did succeed in mustering a majority in the parliament, leading to the formation of the first Nawaz Sharif government. General Beg, however, has denied the allegation. When the money was donated by Younas Habib in 1990, Beg is reported to have said, the ISI was working under the direction of higher authorities; as chief of army staff, his concern was merely to ensure that the money received by the ISI was utilized properly and could be accounted for. In this regard Air Marshal (ret.) Asghar Khan filed a petition (HRC 19/96) urging the supreme court of Pakistan to inquire into the misuse of funds by the ISI. The case is still pending before the court.

Another issue mired in confusion is the question of control over the ISI. Although the ISI is supposed to report to the prime minister, in practice it is far from clear who actually controls this agency. Only once has a person other than a serving general of the Pakistan army headed the ISI—when Benazir Bhutto appointed Lt. Gen. (ret.) Shamsur Rehman Kallu as its director-general during her first tenure as prime minister. And that too created an unbridgeable schism between the prime minister and the chief of army staff. Although this agency is responsible to the JCSC for defense matters, never has an officer of the navy or the air force been appointed to head the ISI.

That three former director-generals of the ISI—Lt. Gen. Hameed Gul, Javed Nasir, and Asad Durrani—were unexpectedly retired from active duty reflects the influence of this office and the associated sensitivity. In a setup where the chief of army staff is in charge of all military appointments, postings, and promotions, it is highly unlikely that a senior serving general would attempt to form an independent communication channel with the prime minister—even if as director-general of the ISI he is required to do so in theory—without the express consent of the army chief. Should a director-general wish to establish closer ties with the prime minister or the civilian government, he can only do so at the peril of losing his military career.

Because of the nature of the job, of course, secrecy and ambiguity shroud the functioning of all intelligence agencies around the globe. But the internal duties of the ISI, its influence within the Foreign Office, and the functioning of its political wing have the potential to further complicate civil-military relations unless this agency is monitored closely. According to the report of a commission constituted to review the working of security and intelligence agencies in Pakistan (Government of Pakistan 1989),

> Meant originally for purely military use, [ISI] now combines many of the functions which in the USA are dealt with by the CIA and FBI, and is handling functions much beyond its scope. For example it took over foreign policy direction on the question of Afghanistan from the foreign office, for which it was neither qualified nor answerable to any higher authority.... Likewise it should in no case handle internal political matters, which should be the responsibility of IB [Intelligence Bureau]. Similarly vetting of service personnel which ISI handles should be the responsibility of the respective service intelligence organization.... We also feel very strongly that a blanket authority to ISI or for that matter to any other agency to monitor telephones of our own nationals is totally unjustified and no civilian government should authorize this.

Although this report was produced more than a decade ago in 1989, there is little evidence to suggest that either the military or the civilian governments have heeded its recommendations. The ISI is still believed to be performing duties it was assigned by the Zia regime. Thus it remains a powerful tool in the hands of the army to influence domestic political events.

MILITARY'S EXPANDING SOCIOECONOMIC ROLE

The military's socioeconomic role in Pakistan has become pervasive. Even while the search for a new balance between civilian and military institutions in a democratic dispensation continued, civilian reliance on the military had not declined. The army's growing functions "in aid of civil power" led to the propagation of the creeping-coup theory: "What the army is looking at now is an internal threat—the one that arises from a combination of bad governance, financial mismanagement, endemic corruption and externally sponsored covert internal warfare."[13] Independent analysts were cynical about the army's theory of "changing threat perception" and the military's new role, for it appeared to be a rationalization for a large standing army at a time of grave national financial crisis.

The new role of the armed forces in aid of civil power, contrived under the Sharif government, has attracted public scrutiny and criticism. But the extensive social functions being performed by the military in almost all realms of public life in an institutionalized manner—and the influence this confers on the armed forces—have gone almost unnoticed. The armed forces, for example, have established a huge educational network spread across Pakistan. The institutions operated, managed, or supported by the military include schools and colleges in military cantonments, residential public schools, federal institutions in cantonments, special education and teacher training institutes, service book clubs, the Army Education Press, the National Institute of Modern Languages, the National University of Science and Technology, cadet colleges, and Fauji Foundation institutes (Government of Pakistan, Independent Bureau for Humanitarian Issues 1999: 3).

The Army Medical Corps (AMC), one of the largest branches of Pakistan's army, sustains a broad network of medical facilities for the benefit of armed forces personnel as well as civilians. The AMC runs two specialized institutes to train its own pool of doctors, nurses, and paramedics. In addition to the base hospitals—combined military hospitals—the AMC operates specialized institutions that provide the best health facilities in the country, in terms of technology and expertise, to soldiers as well as civilians. These facilities include the Armed Forces Institutes of Pathology, Dentistry, Blood Transfusion, Cardiology, and Urology. The military's contribution to the health sector alone can be gauged from the fact that it is almost exclusively running the medical establishments available to civilians in the federally administered northern areas, as well as Azad Jammu and Kashmir.

Disaster management, too, is viewed as an exclusive responsibility of the armed forces. Starting from the management of refugees after the country's independence, the military has undertaken relief operations dealing with floods, earthquakes, major road and railway accidents, mercy missions in the mountains, and antiboar and antilocust operations, almost to the exclusion of civilian disaster management agencies.

The armed forces have also made a significant contribution to the development of Pakistan's logistics, transportation, and communication infrastructure. Two principal organizations—the National Logistics Cell (NLC) and Frontier Works Organization (FWO)—have acquired a semicommercial character over the years. Converted into a self-financing organization in 1982, the FWO alone has executed projects worth Rs35 billion in terms of structures, architecture, computer applications, roads, airfields, town planning, field investigations, engineering, and geotechnical surveys (Government of Pakistan, Independent Bureau for Humanitarian Issues 1999: 109). The NLC, for its part, is engaged in managing warehouses, building and refurbishing national highways, bridges, culverts, and bypasses, operating a transport fleet also used in relief operations, and shipping of liquid cargo and oil across the country. Notwithstanding their performance, the NLC and the FWO have retarded the development and growth of the private sector as well as civilian agencies that should bear responsibility for the work being performed by these two organizations. According to the Independent Bureau of Humanitarian Issues (IBHI) study of the military's role in Pakistan's socioeconomic development, "In fact, FWO and NLC have started bidding against each other for the award of construction contracts, which is definitely undesirable" (Government of Pakistan, Independent Bureau for Humanitarian Issues 1999: 136).

The commercial interests of the armed forces have grown considerably over the years. Apart from the military's role in the establishment, development, and maintenance of public-sector enterprises, it has developed noteworthy private industrial and commercial stakes in the country. Besides the activities of the military's welfare foundations and trusts—the Fauji Foundation, Army Welfare Trust (AWT), Shaheen Foundation, and Bahria Foundation—the business concerns of these organizations are mushrooming. Today the Fauji Foundation and AWT are among the biggest commercial/industrial complexes of Pakistan. The IBHI report reveals, "Besides assets of Rs9 billion in its fully owned enterprises, Fauji Foundation is a major shareholder in the assets of several other reputable companies—Fauji Fertilizer (Rs15 billion: share 43%); Fauji Jordan Fertilizer (Rs17.2 billion: share 22%); Fauji Cement (Rs6.8 billion: share 46%); Fauji Kabir Power Company (Rs8.5 billion: share 45.33%). Of these, Fauji Fertilizer alone has an annual turnover of Rs12–15 billion.... Similarly AWT, besides its own assets of Rs18 billion, is a major shareholder in Askari Commercial Bank Ltd. (26 branches, total assets Rs28.7 billion), Askari Leasing (Rs5 billion), Askari Cement (Rs9 billion) and other enterprises (Rs1 billion)" (Government of Pakistan, Independent Bureau for Humanitarian Issues 1999: 175–76).

Thus leaving aside the military's coercive power, its role in education and training, health and medical services, disaster management, logistics, construction, transportation, and the industrial sector alone makes it more influential and resourceful than any other civilian institution of the state.

CIVIL-MILITARY RELATIONS AFTER 1988

General Zia-ul-Haq first floated the idea of a National Security Council to legitimize and institutionalize the military's role in politics. Although the idea failed to muster the required support, Zia deftly traded off this proposal with getting the Eighth Amendment to the constitution endorsed by the parliament. This amendment afforded President Zia the discretionary authority to oust an elected government from office as well as make key executive appointments, including provincial governors, the chief justices of Pakistan and the four provinces, the chief election commissioner, and the service chiefs. In this manner General Zia established constitutional control over the executive and the legislature. Prime Minister Mohammed Khan Junejo was the first victim of Zia's overarching constitutional authority: his government was dismissed when it started to assert itself on foreign policy issues (apart from having alienated the military by attempting to reduce the perks of senior officers).

Controlled Transition to Democracy

The Bahawalpur air crash that claimed the life of President Zia along with other senior military officers in 1988 ended the Zia regime abruptly, but the hangover of army rule continued to haunt the country. Although Pakistan was still being governed under the constitution of 1973, the system of checks and balances introduced by the original document had been rendered dysfunctional. The character of the supreme law of the land was transformed considerably during eleven years of military rule. All power was now in the hands of the president. The arbitrary use of martial law and presidential orders during Zia's regime had left Pakistan with weak civilian institutions. Another legacy was the absence of institutional norms and conventions and, as well, highly fluid concepts of the rule of law.

President Zia had continued to hold the post of chief of army staff. Thus his exit created a sudden power vacuum in the anomalous system that could be filled only by the military in the immediate term because of the absence of performing democratic institutions: organized political parties, an empowered civilian executive, a vocal parliament. Little wonder that immediately after Zia's demise the seniormost officer in the army, Gen. Mirza Aslam Beg, proclaimed himself chief of army staff, called the chairman of the senate, Ghulam Ishaq Khan, to the GHQ, and invited him to take over as president of Pakistan (rather than the chairman of the senate taking over as president under the constitution and then appointing a chief of army staff).

In the immediate aftermath of the Bahawalpur crash, General Beg could probably have imposed another martial law on Pakistan. But apart from the political and legal considerations, a major factor constraining direct military involvement in politics might have been a view, shared by senior military officers, that direct political control of the country did little good for the country or for the military. It was far preferable to assert one's influence and control the democratic process from behind the scenes. Despite the return of democracy to Pakistan, the late 1980s were a time when the military had the power to make and break governments.

President Ishaq Khan dismissed the government of Benazir Bhutto in 1990 at the behest of the military. After emerging victorious in the general elections of 1988, the PPP sent its first emissary to the chief of army staff. Even before forming a government, a four-point agreement was reached between the PPP and the military: the former would support Ghulam Ishaq Khan as president, retain Yaqub Khan as foreign minister, honor the deal already made with the International Monetary Fund, and refrain from meddling in the military's "internal affairs."[14] The army soon felt alienated, however, because it found certain policies and decisions of the elected civilian government in breach of the understanding reached before the PPP took office. Benazir Bhutto, for instance, appointed Lt. Gen. (ret.) Shamsur Rehman Kallu as director-general of ISI instead of asking the chief of army staff for a list of suitable candidates from among the serving officers and then picking one of them as is currently the practice.[15] And during the army operations in Sindh during her first tenure she refused to give the military sweeping powers under Article 245 of the constitution. To make matters worse, in the midst of this army operation, civilian law-enforcement agencies undertook an operation to capture alleged Mohajir terrorists from an old settlement in Hyderabad city called Pucca Qila without taking the military into confidence, while there was disagreement between the government and the military over the manner and timing of this operation (Shafqat 1997: 229–30).

The Muttahida Qaumi Movement of the Mohajirs (MQM) and the PPP, which started off as coalition partners after the 1988 elections, had fallen apart by September 1989. As a Mohajir himself, General Beg did not approve of the PPP's policy vis-à-vis the MQM. But more important, the military thought the elected civilian government was meddling in areas the army considered its bailiwick. Lt. Gen. Alam Jan Masud revealed after his retirement that the decision to use the presidency to dislodge the PPP government was reportedly made during a corps commanders conference in Murree between July 21 and 23, 1990.[16] There is little doubt that the army and the presidency became platforms to harness the "pro-Zia forces" and assemble the IJI to confront the PPP in the 1990 elections. Not only is the military believed to have led the MQM into the IJI fold and to have devised the electoral strategy for the political coalition, but secret ISI funds were also funneled in to support the IJI's election campaign and clinch victory for desirable candidates (Inayatullah 1997: 223–75).

Thus even after the restoration of democracy in 1988, the military remained a powerful actor exercising its influence to form political alliances, make and break civilian governments, and dismiss elected parliaments. Another endowment of the Zia era was the military's clout with the judiciary. After his retirement as chief of army staff, General Beg "conceded that he did try to influence the Supreme Court of Pakistan in 1988 not to give a verdict for the restoration of Mohammed Khan Junejo's dismissed government or the dissolved National Assembly."[17] As a consequence of making this statement, General Beg had to face contempt charges in the supreme court. In a letter to the apex court during the contempt trial, General Beg clarified that he had informed the supreme court about his commitment to holding national elections according to the announced schedule and that it would therefore be in the best interest of the nation to let the elections be held.[18] This revelation merely confirms that in the post-1988 period the military had assigned to itself the task of guiding the budding democratic process in Pakistan. And the weakness of civilian institutions vis-à-vis the military enabled the armed forces to dominate all other institutions of the state and advise them on how best to secure the national interest.

The Military: Political Ombudsman

As Pakistan's transition from a military-controlled state to a democratic polity continued, the pattern of civil-military relations underwent changes as well. By 1993 the democratic process had attained a momentum of its own, and the PPP and the Muslim League had established themselves as the country's two main political parties. Under the leadership of Gen. Asif Nawaz and later Gen. Waheed Kakar, the military was also making deliberate efforts to project an image of political neutrality by dissociating itself from alliance making and other political scuffles.

The informal decision-making mechanisms earlier dominated by the military had by 1993 come to be controlled by a troika comprising the president, the prime minister, and the chief of army staff. The Eighth Amendment had ushered in a new era in which executive authority was divided between the president and the prime minister. In the face of a developing political culture and lack of institutional conventions, the system of checks and balances instituted by the Eighth Amendment afforded the military a bigger role in the political arena. Within the troika the chief of army staff came to be seen as the arbiter of last resort in all conflicts between the president and the prime minister and thus the first among equals.

The president and prime minister both sought the support of the chief of army staff to improve their bargaining position vis-à-vis each other. The unflinching desire of elected political officers—the president and the prime minister—to acquire control of the military and the determination of all political groups—mainstream political parties, religious parties, and ethnic parties—to gain the sympathy and support of the military augmented the clout the chief of army staff already enjoyed. The chief of army staff office, in turn, became a bone of contention between the president and the prime minister, because it determined the balance of power between these two.

An extreme manifestation of this situation was the dismissal of Nawaz Sharif's government in 1993. Prime Minister Nawaz Sharif enjoyed amicable relations with neither President Ishaq Khan nor chief of army staff Gen. Asif Nawaz, and splits were apparent within the troika by mid-1992.[19] With the presidential election approaching, all three members of the troika were uneasy with each other. Differences between the president and the prime minister came to a head, however, with the sudden death of the chief of army staff and the issue of appointing a new army chief. Ishaq Khan's decision to appoint Gen. Waheed Kakar—sixth on the seniority list—as chief of army staff, without taking the prime minister into his confidence, pushed the prevailing mistrust between the president and the prime minister to a point where reconciliation became hopeless.

Thus Nawaz Sharif was dismissed in 1993, not because he had fallen out with the army, but because he had antagonized a president who refused to put up with him any longer. That the president might have taken the military into his confidence before exercising his discretionary authority under the Eighth Amendment is likely. But the fact that this time the president was acting predominantly in his own interest rather than on behalf of the military made this dismissal different from that of Benazir Bhutto's government in terms of the military's involvement in the ouster of an elected civilian government.

During the political crisis of 1993, Gen. Waheed Kakar began counseling the president and the prime minister in an attempt to normalize relations between the two, especially after the supreme court restored Nawaz Sharif's government by declaring the president's dissolution order illegal. But when the deadlock could not be overcome, a bargain was struck: both the president and the prime minister agreed to tender their resignations in order to pave the way for fresh elections to be held by a neutral caretaker regime. In acting as interlocutor and guarantor of the arrangement, the chief of army staff made his bid as an informal political ombudsman acting as an honest broker in case of differences between other state institutions or their heads (rather than a partisan head of the army participating in palace intrigues). But supervision of the agreement itself—which obliged the chief executive of an elected government and the president, who was also supreme commander of the armed forces, to resign from office—highlighted the envious standing of the chief of army staff in the troika.

Such a role was once again apparent during the executive-judiciary showdown in 1997, which caused an institutional crisis and paralyzed the state machinery. Gen. Jehangir Karamat, the chief of army staff, was on a foreign tour when the tussle between the chief justice and the prime minister grew ugly. He had to cut this tour short, therefore, because his physical presence in Pakistan was deemed essential in times of grave institutional crisis. Once again the chief of army staff was seen holding meetings with the president, the prime minister, and the chief justice to ease tensions and resolve the conflict. On at least one occasion the president reportedly asked the chief of army staff to use his influence and urge the chief justice not to move further on this collision course.[20] It was only after the chief of army staff had refused to pressure the prime minister into submission that the drama reached its climax: a full bench of the supreme court held the chief justice "in abeyance," and the president, having refused earlier to take action against the chief justice and threatened with likely impeachment proceedings, resigned from office.

Toward Greater Civilian Control

The general elections of 1997 led to another major transformation in the pattern of civil-military relations. These elections were a consequence of the dismissal of the PPP's second government by President Farooq Leghari. A minister in Benazir Bhutto's cabinet during her first government, Leghari was sponsored by Bhutto to the presidency as a colleague and close confidant. The government's dismissal in 1997 resembled that of 1993 in the sense that this time, too, the government was not sent packing merely because the military wanted it to go. Essentially the government was deposed because the president and the prime minister failed to share power under the formula devised by the Eighth Amendment and the military was not opposed to the government's disappearance.

After dismissing Benazir Bhutto's government, President Leghari established an advisory Council for Defense and National Security (CDNS) through an ordinance. Headed by the prime minister, this body was to comprise important cabinet members and the service chiefs. The CDNS was devised by President Leghari to accommodate the military in the decision-making process, at the highest level, on a permanent basis. After the elections of 1997, however, the ordinance was allowed to lapse and along with it the CDNS, because it was not a creation of the constitution. The overwhelming victory of the Muslim League in the elections of 1997 came as a surprise to the whole nation, including the president and the army. Nawaz Sharif's two-thirds majority in the national assembly strengthened the prime minister's office and reduced the role of the president and the armed forces in supervising the exercise of state political power, as was the practice earlier when weak civilian governments remained in office.

Then came the Thirteenth Amendment, which sounded the death knell of the Eighth Amendment, removed the powers the presidency had gathered during Zia's days, and buried the concept of troika. In terms of civil-military relations, the impact of this development has been consequential. The erstwhile system of checks and balances on executive authority afforded the military a platform from which it could pressure the prime minister. Aware that there existed a legitimate means of shunting an elected government out of office before the completion of its term, the prime minister also took kindly to the counseling of the military and the presidency. The Thirteenth Amendment, however, shrunk the military's coercive ability to control and guide the political policies of a civilian government. The elected political leadership knew it could be ousted from office only through extraconstitutional means, and this certainly limited the military's bargaining power. Further, the Fourteenth Amendment made it illegal for members of parliament representing any political party to shift loyalties. This diminished the chances of in-house changes, especially when the government in power enjoys a comfortable majority in parliament.

In the 1990s Pakistan witnessed a trend of judicial activism. The supreme court passed authoritative judgments to guard its own independence and nullify acts of the legislature and the executive that were considered ultra vires of the constitution. The government invoked Article 245 of the constitution in 1998 to deal with the chaotic law and order situation in Sindh, for example, and called upon the military to act "in aid of civil power." An ordinance was promulgated that obliged the army to form military trial courts (MTCs) in Sindh and act as prosecutor, judge, and executioner to mete out speedy justice to the masses. Free of the administrative, financial, and judicial control of a superior judiciary, the MTCs constituted a parallel judicial system that was dismantled by the supreme court. While declaring the MTCs illegal, the supreme court rejected the "doctrine of necessity"—which earlier had been used to justify events such as the imposition of martial law by Zia-ul-Haq—as a legitimate argument to validate the MTCs. Although greater judicial independence could not deter the military from overthrowing an elected civilian government on October 12 and suspending the constitution, constitutional and legal questions have acquired far more significance today than in 1977 when General Zia dismissed the Bhutto government.

These are some of the political and legal developments that explain why a civilian prime minister, whose tenure in office less than a decade back depended on relations with the military high command, succeeded in forcing the chief of army staff, Gen. Jehangir Karamat, into premature retirement for making a public statement critical of the civilian government's performance. In addressing the Naval War College, General Karamat was only giving vent to the frustration caused by the dismal state of national affairs and Pakistan's socioeconomic downslide—a frustration he shared with his compatriots. But as a functionary of the state and prime minister's security adviser, he was unwise to make such remarks while in service and irresponsible to make them public through an Inter Services Public Relations press release. This was not the first time an army chief had castigated the performance of a civilian government. A few years earlier, however, such a statement would have disconcerted the prime minister, and he would have thought more in terms of appeasing the army chief rather than taking disciplinary action against him.

Back to Praetorianism

Karamat's forced retirement did not go down well with the military as an institution, even though Musharaf took over without any apparent hesitation. The successful execution of disciplinary action against an army chief of staff strengthened the Sharif government's mistaken belief that it was possible to establish personalized control over the armed forces by appointing loyalists to key military positions. In its gloating, however, the Sharif government failed to comprehend that during his speech at the Naval War College Karamat was giving vent to the disaffection shared by the military, rather than making a statement of personal ambition. Because of the swift change of guard at the GHQ, the ouster of Karamat did not cause a public commotion. But it did create a feeling of indignation within the military.

Early in 1999 the Sharif government initiated the Lahore process, which aimed at improving relations with India. Traditionally Pakistan's defense policy has dictated its foreign policy, especially on India, Afghanistan, Iran, and nuclear issues. And because defense policymaking falls within the domain of national security management, the military views it as its preserve and does not trust politicians with the handling of national security or related issues. At first the military probably did appreciate the value of the Lahore process amid international pressure to reduce tension between the nuclear rivals in South Asia. Nevertheless, there developed a general feeling that it was not being kept fully informed on all aspects of the Lahore process and, moreover, that the Sharif family's business interests were determining Pakistan's policy vis-à-vis India.

The Kargil episode gave another deadly blow to civil-military relations. When in a secret military operation Pakistan's armed forces and freedom fighters occupied strategic peaks in Kashmir on the Indian side of the Line of Control early in 1999, a limited war flared up between Pakistan and India. Although Pakistan denied direct occupation of the peaks, it had to withdraw its forces and freedom fighters from the Indian side under international pressure—a retreat that cost Pakistan the lives of over 400 soldiers as well as tremendous national humiliation. Although the operation was planned and executed by the military and approved by the prime minister, neither was prepared to shoulder their share of the blame for this disaster. Nawaz Sharif and his colleagues tried to create an impression that the prime minister was not really consulted before the operation was launched. The chief of army staff, however, responded publicly that the prime minister had indeed consented. Further, his trips to army garrisons after the Kargil debacle, aimed at revitalizing the morale of the troops, created the impression that the operation had been bungled by an unreliable and weak political leadership.

Kargil was not the only cause of deteriorating civil-military relations, but it exacerbated these differences to a point where any chance of their amicable resolution appeared bleak. The contradiction between the Lahore process—a major foreign policy initiative aimed at resolving outstanding disputes through diplomacy—and Kargil—a reflection of Pakistan's defense policy aimed at pushing the military solution—exposed the deep-rooted differences between the Sharif government and the military. Controversial press reports regarding backdoor diplomacy between India and Pakistan during the Kargil operation—stories that the Sharif government's special envoy Niaz A. Niak had reached an agreement with his Indian counterpart Brajesh Mishra over the fate of Kashmir—did little to improve estranged relations between Sharif and the army. Further reports that Sharif's personal business concerns continued exporting to India sugar worth millions at the height of Kargil only strengthened the general perception that the prime minister had made even national security interests subservient to family business interests.

The chief of army staff, General Musharaf, took even more seriously Sharif's attempts to interfere with the postings and promotions of senior military officers. Not only do service chiefs in Pakistan fiercely guard their autonomy to deal with operational matters, but the chief of army staff derives his strength from his corps commanders and senior staff officers. There was evidence that Sharif was trying to create dissent within the military high command—dissent that would inevitably impair the chief of army staff's bargaining power vis-à-vis the civilian government as well as make his removal easier. Little wonder that the chief of army staff decided to retire Lt. Gen. Tariq Pervaiz, who was related to a minister of the Sharif cabinet, after the general held a private meeting with Sharif that was against military norms and regulations.

Sharif sacked General Musharaf on October 12, while he was representing Pakistan in Sri Lanka, and appointed Lt. Gen. Khwaja Ziauddin as the new chief of army staff. Ziauddin was refused admission into the GHQ, however, and told to await the return of Musharaf. The government then gave instructions that the plane carrying Musharaf was not to be allowed to land in Karachi. Meanwhile, the military took over the country and Musharaf returned to Pakistan and sacked the prime minister and his government. The sloppy manner in which the Sharif government tried to remove General Musharaf—and the fact that his replacement was a relatively junior lieutenant general from the Engineers Corps—proved to be the immediate cause of the Sharif government's doom.

The military did not merely overthrow the civilian government because it was bad at governance, or corrupt, or a bad economic manager, or had politicized the bureaucracy and attacked the supreme court. It was overthrown because it had repeatedly interfered with both operational and policymaking issues that the military viewed as its exclusive business. The replacement of General Musharaf with Lieutenant General Ziauddin would have signaled a decisive change in civil-military relations in favor of the former—and the military was unwilling to let that happen.

Although the Thirteenth Amendment took away the president's discretionary authority to dismiss an elected government, and the Fourteenth Amendment reduced the chances of an in-house change, these developments also limited the army's ability to exercise control over civilian governments from behind the scenes. Thus the only option available to the military to secure its perceived institutional interests on the eve of October 12 was by overthrowing the civilian government. And that is what it did.

CONSTRAINTS ON THE MILITARY'S ROLE IN POLITICS

Soldiers are exempted from the public resentment that crystallizes against nonperforming civilian governments. This in turn cultivates goodwill for the armed forces and makes it possible for them to assume direct control of the polity and initiate a reform process. But experience of the past has proven that the military finds it exceedingly difficult to retain control because of international impediments, domestic political considerations, and professional concerns. Disengagement from politics poses an even bigger challenge, and the military ends up becoming a part of the problem rather than the solution.

International Impediments

Democracy is the predominant political system in the world, and the right to democracy has come to be viewed as a basic human right by the international community. The Western powers have committed themselves staunchly—especially before their domestic audiences—to promoting democratic values as a global norm. And this prevents them from supporting autocratic systems of governance even if political expediency might demand it.

In the post–cold war period, the politics of economics has acquired primary importance in international relations and has tarnished the absolutist concept of state sovereignty. Growing global interdependence is making it extremely hard for countries to defy the will of the international community, especially those ranking low in the international hierarchy of states. The armed forces in Pakistan are also aware that direct military intervention in politics causes the international community to frown. And with the country's extensive reliance on international monetary institutions and direct foreign funding, just to keep itself afloat, the military will be kept under constant international pressure to restore democracy as soon as possible.

Domestic Considerations

Ideas of self-governance, once provoked, are hard to quell. Even though the brand of democracy practiced in Pakistan during the last decade was not truly representative and did not empower the common citizen, the country was being governed under a constitution that established a trichotomy of powers—executive, legislative, and judicial—and, moreover, had a developing civil society, outspoken nongovernmental organizations and human rights groups, and a vocal press that fiercely guarded its independence. Little wonder that immediately after the takeover General Musharaf proclaimed that "this is not martial law, only another path towards democracy" and promised that the military would not stay any longer than was necessary to "pave the way for true democracy to flourish in Pakistan."[21] The question of legitimacy will pose a bigger problem to the present military regime than it did to earlier martial law governments, and the armed forces will find it increasingly hard to retain direct control of the country for an extended period of time.

At the dawn of the twenty-first century Pakistan is confronted with an array of problems. A leadership vacuum, institutional crisis, economic debility, ethnic strife, religious and sectarian conflict, illiteracy, poverty, and corruption have created a vicious circle that, in turn, engenders a crisis of the state. Martial law is no panacea for these multifarious troubles. Even the military is aware of this. Indeed, by annexing political power the military might end up shouldering the blame for the impending anarchy. Exercising influence from behind the scenes, therefore, remains the best option for the military.

At a time when huge debt, external and internal, is pushing Pakistan to the brink of bankruptcy and the polity seems headed toward sociopolitical chaos, the military sees itself as a savior and the only prospective agent of change. Its self-assumed role as guardian of the state encourages the military to contemplate a fire-brigade operation to put the process back on track and reinvigorate the institutions of the state.

A society is different from a regiment. It cannot be managed with a stick. Although democracy provides a long-term basis for managing competing ethnic, religious, cultural, and economic interests in a country, the military is not designed to embrace diversity and administer chaos. And the longer the military is involved in politics, the more its political weaknesses come to the fore.

Pakistan's military is very conscious of public opinion and makes special efforts to project itself as an apolitical institution—an instrument of national integration. Sustained engagement with political processes, however, makes the armed forces a target of public criticism and threatens to blemish the image that the military guards so fiercely. Overt involvement in politics brings the very integrity of military high command into question, which in turn depresses the morale of troops. Thus prolonged control of the government will either compromise the military's image or endanger free speech—or, worse still, both.

Professional Concerns

The military's direct intervention in politics adversely affects its sense of professionalism. Indeed, the military's politicization and continuous interaction with civilians can create disaffection within its ranks and compromise its security duties by undermining the core attributes of a soldier: discipline, esprit de corps, and the like. This is a lesson that Pakistan's army should have learned from its earlier martial law experiences.

Although the specific form of democracy and decision-making processes can be questioned, there is little disagreement, even within the military, that democracy is the only acceptable form of government for Pakistan. This consensual view is a product of the fact that military leaders have come to see the threat to Pakistan's security in a wider perspective. The global security, political, and economic environments have undergone a change that has important ramifications for Pakistan as well. Economics as an element of security did not figure so prominently during the cold war and the days of uninterrupted flow of resources to Pakistan.

Although sociopolitical order was of paramount concern for all state institutions in the past, the focus has now shifted to socioeconomic order. People have begun to realize that many political problems are bred by economic distortions. Although the military can probably bring sanity and harmony to sociopolitical disorder in the short term, it must not view itself as the best manager of the national economy in today's international economic order.

WHY INTERVENTION?

The military has a near monopoly over brute force in almost all modern nation-states, and Pakistan is no different. The military is aware that it takes only one armed unit to assume direct control of the state. And in Pakistan's case the legacy of the past also nurtures the desire of ambitious military commanders to play an active role in politics: military dictators have administered the country for almost half its independent life.

One instigating factor is that the military enjoys de facto immunity against the laws administered by civilian authorities of the state. Its training and socialization have induced a superiority complex among members of the military corps, who see their civilian counterparts as inefficient, disorganized, and corrupt. Armed forces personnel do not generally believe themselves to be answerable to civilian law enforcement agencies. Senior military officers have also, at times, tried to protect their subordinates in crimes ranging from traffic violations to murder.

All military personnel are subject to the Pakistan Army Code without discrimination. The military's immunity from civilian law enforcement agencies and legal codes is justified as being essential for the morale of troops. But this protection engenders an impression within the military that it is above the law of the land administered by civilian institutions—another source of conflict between civil and military institutions.

The constitution endows the armed forces with the responsibility to guard Pakistan against external threats and act "in aid of civil power" when called upon by the federal government to do so. But the military also views itself as the guardian of Pakistan's ideological frontiers and an institution that is needed to inject continuity and stability in the polity. Thus the military seems to assume the task of continuously monitoring the system of governance and removing, in its self-defined supreme national interest of Pakistan, any snags that might erupt from time to time. It is this self-perceived job assignment that introduces a contradiction between the theoretical and practical role of the military in Pakistan and entices the armed forces to pass judgment on the government's performance. In the worst-case scenario the military does not rule out the possibility of jumping in to actuate the political processes. Although the military is conscious of its constitutional obligation to serve the federal government, it justifies its interventionist role as serving the ultimate interests of Pakistan: sociopolitical disorder caused by inept civilian leadership is seen as a situation justifying intervention, morally if not legally.

The civilian leadership, too, encourages military adventurism. The role that political parties expect the military to play has varied considerably. When in office, politicians want the armed forces to serve as an instrument of the ruling party or coalition, rather than an arm of the state, and strictly desist from making political statements. But when in opposition they expect the military to confront the government of the day, act as a pressure group, and serve as an instrument of change by facilitating midterm elections. Lt. Gen. (ret.) Asad Durrani summed up this duplicity in a personal interview with the author in 1998 by stating, "The second choice of every political party in Pakistan is the military. The first is obvious."

Even after the restoration of democracy in the post-Zia period, Pakistan's system of governance, although different in form, was no less autocratic in character than that introduced by dictatorial regimes. The state in Pakistan itself is confronted with a crisis of legitimacy. Indeed, people refuse to pay taxes or even their utility bills. Because the elected representatives have inspired so little confidence among the masses, the military emerges as an institution that enjoys more credibility. It is the want of strong civilian institutions firmly rooted among the masses and the political leadership's doubtful commitment to democracy that makes the political arena susceptible to military intervention.

REFLECTIONS ON THE FUTURE

The relationship of civilian institutions with the military constitutes an unfinished agenda. The configuration of power within the parliament after the 1997 elections suspended the military's role as referee for some time but did not forfeit it altogether. The history of civil-military relations in Pakistan suggests that an absolute majority in parliament, strong constitutional guarantees, a compliant president, and a hand-picked chief of army staff are not enough to establish effective civilian control over the military.

It is the weakness of civilian institutions and the political leaders' lack of unequivocal commitment to democracy that endanger the continuity of political processes in Pakistan. The legitimacy acquired by the elected representatives at the polls is usually lost in the postelection period as a result of nonperformance. As long as civilian governments fail to deliver when in office and people fail to reap any tangible benefits of democracy, the public's attachment to democratic institutions will not grow, concepts of legitimacy will remain fluid, and the system of governance will remain vulnerable to military interference.

Although direct military control over the state's political power declined over the 1990s, its monopoly over the management of national security continued unabated. The military has always viewed national security as falling within its exclusive jurisdiction. The handling of nuclear policy is a case in point. Even in democratic times the army has remained the de facto watchdog of Pakistan's nuclear establishment comprising the Pakistan Atomic Energy Commission and the Khan Research Laboratories, both autonomous bodies. Apart from managing Pakistan's nuclear program, the military has also dominated policymaking in nuclear matters. For five years an Arms Control Cell has been functioning in the army general headquarters. This cell—which has been performing the role of a think tank for Pakistan's policy vis-à-vis the nonproliferation regime—has now been separated from the Combat Division and placed under the Strategic Planning Division. There is an Arms Control and Disarmament Cell within the Foreign Office as well, which maintains close liaison with army general headquarters. And although the former prime minister Nawaz Sharif was believed to have made the final decision to detonate nuclear devices in May 1998, he could hardly have challenged the advice prepared by the army headquarters and the Foreign Office, in tandem, and approved by the chief of army staff.

Although the military is also believed to dominate Pakistan's foreign policy in matters that overlap with Pakistan's security policy—India, Afghanistan, Iran, nuclear issues—its input is taken very seriously before formulating policies vis-à-vis major Western powers, especially the United States. The military's influence over foreign policy is understandable, for it holds the reins of the ISI, which is solely responsible for external intelligence. Moreover, the military conducts comprehensive research and analysis in its areas of interest. The notes and briefings prepared at army headquarters are then scrutinized at the highest military level, giving them the required institutional backing. Thus during briefings of any kind under civilian rule—before cabinet committees, parliamentary committees, or the Foreign Office—military representatives are far better prepared than their civilian counterparts and can easily outmaneuver them.

Even strong civilian governments have failed to reduce their reliance on the military in dealing with mundane administrative matters and law and order problems. Indeed, the Sharif government—one of the strongest that Pakistan has ever had—called in the military to act "in aid of civil power" and run a parallel judicial system and rescue the Water and Power Development Authority and prepare it for privatization, among other things. These actions amounted to an open confession by the elected civilian government that it could not deliver without the military's support. The military agreed to play the role of junior partner of the Sharif government for two reasons. First, it saw itself acting in the national interest. Second, there appeared to be no other option in those circumstances: the government in office enjoyed an absolute majority in parliament; the opposition was the weakest the country had had in a long time (and was thoroughly discredited too); the president was a confidant of the ruling family; and after the Thirteenth Amendment there was no legitimate way to oust the government.

Yet sources of tension were inherent in the military's new role. In the past, the military had been able to distinguish between power and responsibility and decouple the two. Power had traditionally been viewed as "a resource to be prized and firmly retained"; responsibility, by contrast, was "not only a burden, but by making the holder of responsibility the target of popular discontent it [undermines] power" (Alvi 1990: 52). It suited the military that civilians should shoulder the responsibility (and blame) for allocation and utilization of resources as long as defense and security matters fell within the exclusive domain of the military and its operational autonomy and corporate interests were not challenged. But the military's new role has confronted it with a dilemma: while the military had the burden of responsibility for undertaking complicated civilian tasks, the civilian political leadership made the decisions and would have bagged the credit in case the military's new role turned out to be a success. The military was unlikely to remain comfortable with an arrangement that required it to do the dirty work of a political government.

Moreover the political leadership, while relying upon the military and engaging it in civilian functions, did not undertake the political reforms needed to back up the supposedly short-term firefighting operation with lasting institutional arrangements. The government seemed to have fallen prey to the illusion that if there was no legal way to remove the government, it could establish personalized civilian control over the military. The events of October 12, 1999, exposed the flaws in the Sharif government's understanding of civil-military relations. Instead of taking measures to strengthen the constitutional machinery and work in concert with other institutions, the government tried to use the military as a lever to prevail over them. It failed to recognize, apparently, that weakening civilian institutions was tantamount to undercutting its own legitimacy and support base.

With another military government in power that shows no intention of returning to the barracks anytime soon, the situation in Pakistan seems to have come full circle yet again. On October 14, 1999, General Musharaf proclaimed emergency throughout Pakistan, assumed the office of the chief executive, brought the country under the control of the armed forces, and simultaneously promulgated a Provisional Constitutional Order. The general insisted that this did not amount to imposition of martial law, but was another path to "true" democracy. But the military government needed time to revive the country's economy, complete the accountability process, recover plundered national wealth including bank loans running into billions, prepare fresh electoral rolls, and ensure harmonious functioning of vital state organs. Thus, although the restoration of representative democracy could be a while, people should suspend disbelief, ignore the dismal performance of past military regimes, and support the Musharaf government.

After two and a half years of direct control, General Musharaf's government has little to its credit, and public mood seems to have shifted from optimism to despair for good reason. Accountability antics cannot be expected to take public focus off real problems for long. The process has proved to be both flawed and overambitious. It left the military and judiciary out of the accountability net and did not even have the desired deterrent effect. It has not provided a huge boost to the economy as envisaged, because the government has been unable to recover the millions stashed away by corrupt politicians, bureaucrats, and generals in foreign accounts.

The coup of 1999 has further aggravated the institutional imbalance between vital state institutions, which has been a major cause of Pakistan's afflictions. Whatever little checks were applicable to the exercise of executive authority even during the autocratic government of Nawaz Sharif have now been demolished. The military government's claims of strengthening state institutions ring hollow in the aftermath of the promulgation of the Oath of Office (Judges) Order 1999 on December 13, 1999. This order obliged all judges of the superior courts to be bound by the Proclamation of Emergency and the Provisional Constitutional Order, which, inter alia, barred all courts from making any order against the chief executive. This was done immediately before the supreme court was to hear petitions challenging the legal effect and validity of the army takeover.

The chief justice of Pakistan and five other judges of the supreme court refused to take the oath and were removed from office. Seven other judges from provincial high courts were not invited to take the oath and were discharged arbitrarily. It was hardly surprising that the new supreme court bench justified the military takeover on grounds of state necessity. This doctrine was propounded by the supreme court in 1977 in the case against General Zia's martial law (Nusrat Bhutto case) but has been extensively criticized ever since in legal circles and was rejected by the supreme court in the Shiekh Liaqat Hussain case in 1999, where it was held to be buried forever. It was ironic that the apex court had to dig state necessity out of its grave in less than a year's time.

More disconcerting was the authority granted by the supreme court to the chief executive to promulgate legislative measures and the power to amend the constitution of 1973. This made a mockery of the celebrated constitutional concept of separation of powers by leaving Pakistan with a chief executive who was the embodiment of all executive and legislative powers and a judiciary that showed little sign of independence. The supreme court legitimized military rule for three years starting October 12, 1999. It also directed the chief executive to appoint a date for holding national elections 90 days before the expiry of this period. But this does not mean that he is obliged to hold elections within the next three years, only that he is required to announce a date.

The military government is planning to bring about comprehensive devolution of power to local bodies. But this plan does not address the central issue of concentration of excessive power in the center. The devolution plan further undermines the concept of provincial autonomy by aiming to establish semiautonomous local units and does not identify ways to restructure the center-province relationship and build an effective federation. Rather than placing the local bodies within the provincial structure of governance, the government has stated in no uncertain terms that even the elected local bodies will continue to be monitored by military teams.

Pakistan's economic revival depends upon cultivating a socioeconomic environment that helps regain the trust of the nation and stops the flight of capital, builds local investor confidence, and attracts foreign private investment. What is inimical for such a goal is lack of public faith in the institutions of justice, absence of transparent decision-making processes, and general uncertainty regarding the future. These are all factors that a military government is incapable of dealing with. The present arrangement is certainly not permanent. Even if the military can control the law and order situation and ensure stable economic policies for the next three years, there is nothing to guarantee that the transition back to democracy will not fail as before, and that military will not intervene. Such uncertainty can hardly be the breeding ground for investor confidence.

The military's repeated assertions to put Pakistan back on the democratic path should not be construed to mean that it will abandon interest in politics in future. Past experience shows that while evolving a political framework for the future, the military finds it imperative to cultivate political groups that continue its policies and protect its corporate and personal interests (Rizvi 1987: 259). Even after returning to the barracks, the military is likely to assume the task of guiding and controlling democracy from behind the curtain, thereby undermining the authority of civilian governments and representative democratic institutions. Any country where the soldiers feel obliged to monitor and control the political processes can only remain a sham democracy.

With the military administering Pakistan since October 1999, civil-military relations are once again in a state of flux. Military rule is no solution to Pakistan's multifaceted problems, and its honeymoon period is unlikely to last very long. Democracy will have to be restored sooner rather than later. But the military's future role in a democratic dispensation will depend on how long it decides to stay in direct control and how it performs during this period. If the armed forces voluntarily return to the barracks at an early stage, they are likely to carve out for themselves a permanent supervisory role over politics from within the National Security Council, as in Turkey. But if they stay long enough to discredit themselves in politics, such a bargain would be harder to strike. On the whole, then, the future of civil-military relations could not be more uncertain.

CHAPTER 17

Burma: Soldiers as State Builders

Mary P. Callahan

FOUR DECADES AFTER SEIZING POWER, the Burmese Tatmadaw (armed forces) has created a chokehold on political power unrivaled in the world. A decade after establishing the latest incarnation of junta rule in a bloody crackdown on a nationwide prodemocracy movement, today's generals have barely been touched by the suspension of international economic assistance, the imposition of an arms embargo, and bans on new investment in Burma by U.S. and European firms. Throughout the four decades of military rule, rumors of intramilitary splits among officer factions, elite infighting (hard-liners versus soft-liners), infantry mutinies and foot soldiers' desertions, and the inevitable demise of the regime have been notable for their frequency and their inaccuracy. All around them, Burma's generals witness the crumbling of authoritarian regimes. But in Burma, military rule endures.

Why did Burma end up with this exceptionally authoritarian, military-dominated, political system? In the 1950s Burma was widely considered one of the more successful postcolonial experiments in parliamentary democracy. In the late 1980s a nationwide "people power" movement brought millions of Burmese into the streets to call for democratic reform. But at these two critical points in history—just when the development of a more responsive style of governance seemed absolutely inevitable—relations between the military and the state were transformed in such a way as to eliminate any serious civilian, reformist contenders for political power. In this chapter I explain how these transformations brought about the institutionalization of the most durable military rule in the postwar world.

During these two eras of increasing citizen participation in national affairs, two national security crises prompted a substantial reorganization of military forces as well as state institutions: the first Kuomintang crisis (1950–1953) and the 1988 uprising in major urban areas throughout the country. In each of these crises, the central government based in Rangoon faced a threat to the regime's stability. In the Kuomintang (KMT) crisis, elected civilian leaders implored the United Nations to rid Burma of Kuomintang troops and their American advisers, who hoped to recapture China from the communists. When two appeals to the United Nations failed, elected political leaders asked the Burmese army to retool so that it could handle the job itself. They also assigned the Tatmadaw governing responsibilities in the region where the KMT threat existed—pressing army battalion commanders into administrative and political roles they never fully relinquished in the postwar era. The government's response in the KMT crisis saved the Rangoon regime for the short term but did so at the cost of any civilian control over army affairs for decades to come. In 1988, the long-overdue collapse of the iso-lated socialist economy and severe mishandling by the police of a series of apolitical distur-bances led to an outpouring of antigovernment demonstrations. As in the KMT case, this cri-sis represented a real threat to the regime's stability and national security. In this case, however, the regime crumbled from within. At the party congress held in July 1988, party chairman and longtime dictator Ne Win ended single-party rule and promised to hold multiparty elections. Popular demonstrations continued, however, and the tensions built, particularly in Rangoon and Mandalay. Finally, on September 18, 1988, army units deployed throughout most of the major urban areas and replaced Ne Win's presidential appointee with a new junta: the State Law and Order Restoration Council (SLORC). In the decade to follow, the SLORC not only took charge of the political system but embarked on the most ambitious army transformation program in Burma's history.

In both of these cases, a reorganization of the military led to new forms of state building and rebuilding with the military—and not a political party, bureaucracy, or civilian organiza-tion—at the helm. By "state building" I mean the process in which state actors and managers organize resources and personnel to extend the geographic and functional "reach of the state" (Shue 1988). The geographic extension of the state occurs when policies adopted in the national administrative center are implemented by centrally designated, locally based organizations in territory beyond that center. The functional extension of the state occurs when state actors take on and successfully carry out new tasks not previously undertaken or implemented.

In the years surrounding the KMT crisis in the 1950s and the 1988 uprising, various state institutions competed for scarce material resources, human capital, and political power. In both of these instances, the Tatmadaw eliminated other contenders for power and resources, although in each case the army's aggrandizement of national power followed a different logic. In the 1950s, the institutional innovations that transformed the army into a powerful force emerged from the ad hoc decisions, whims, and fantasies of field and staff officers who attempted to fight off insurgent threats to Rangoon as well as the more menacing KMT threat. Although civilian political and bureaucratic leaders initially played a role in formulating secu-rity policy, the army used its access to international resources unavailable to civilian contenders to end civilian oversight of army affairs and brought all state-building activities under one mil-itary department or another. In the 1988 crisis, the only nonmilitary contender for national power was the Burma Socialist Program Party (BSPP). Weakened at the local level by two decades of corruption and mismanagement, the party was destroyed with finality by senior party leadership at its party congress in July 1988. Although the army, too, had suffered from organizational weaknesses during this period, its three decades of counterinsurgency warfare had built institutions with far more staying power than those of the BSPP.

THE EARLY YEARS

From 1948 until 1962, the Burmese political system looked on paper like a model of democratic governance. The 1947 constitution provided, for example, that sovereignty resided "in the peo-ple." All citizens were guaranteed equality of rights and opportunity; citizens also were guar-anteed freedom of expression, assembly, and association, so long as the exercise of these rights did not interfere with public order. Moreover, the constitution established a judiciary independent of the executive branch of government. This included a supreme court that would "issue directions in the nature of habeas corpus." Civilian control over military spending, defense policy, senior officer promotion, and other affairs was ensured through the office of the permanent parliamentary secretary for defense, who served under the minister of defense.

The 1947 constitution also established a federal framework to provide for minority rights in a majority-rule parliamentary system.[1] A bicameral national legislature was inaugurated guaranteeing representation to minority ethnic groups in the Chamber of Nationalities. The constitution set forth a variety of solutions to the problem of local and regional authority in minority-dominated areas. In the eastern regions where the KMT crisis would unfold and where the Shan peoples (10 percent of the national population) lived, all the traditional Shan principalities were amalgamated into one state, which was constitutionally guaranteed a right of secession after ten years. The elected 50-member State Council constituted legislative authority in the Shan State, while in local affairs the hereditary Shan aristocracy—the *sawbwas*—was allowed to retain its traditional powers and authority.

In the early years of independence, these constitutional arrangements appeared to be establishing strong democratic roots in society. National parliamentary elections were held in 1947, 1951, 1956, and 1960. The Anti-Fascist People's Freedom League (AFPFL)—the former wartime resistance organization–turned–political party—was victorious in the first three elections and accordingly formed AFPFL-dominated governments. In the 1960 election, former prime minister U Nu led his new Pyidaungsu (Union) Party to a decisive victory over the military-supported Stable faction of the collapsed AFPFL. Turnouts in these elections were often high. And in accordance with Western expectations of electoral systems, electoral losers vacated their offices and winners took over.

Furthermore, by the early 1950s another crucial element of democratic rule had emerged in the form of a "loyal opposition." Growing out of a faction that broke off from the AFPFL in 1950, the National United Front (NUF) developed into a viable opposition party that gained 47 seats in the 1956 Chamber of Deputies election, including numerous seats previously considered safe by the AFPFL. In that election, the NUF vote polled more than 30 percent of the popular vote compared to 48 percent for the AFPFL (Tinker 1967: 90). Beyond its electoral strength, the NUF also commanded extensive media attention and succeeded in organizing trade union and peasant organizations outside the AFPFL's umbrella structure. Later, the two successor parties to the AFPFL that competed in the 1960 elections continued the tradition of a loyal opposition as they worked within the provisions of the 1947 constitution. In many ways, the NUF's success in the 1956 election and the election of U Nu over the military-backed candidate in 1960 represented major steps toward institutionalizing a truly competitive parliamentary system.

These developments were extremely promising—particularly given the precarious security conditions of the entire first decade after World War II. The postwar period began in chaos. In 1945, General Aung San and his nationalist forces turned against their Japanese allies by forming a shaky alliance with communists and the British Special Operations Executive. The result was a tenuous coalition of mostly ethnic-majority Burman nationalists fighting alongside the same Anglo-Burman and Karen troops they had fought against in 1942 and considered "mercenaries."[2] Upon defeating the Japanese, these British-led forces were reorganized despite considerable divisions among British officials, indigenous loyalists, Burmese socialists, com-

munists, and rightists. Tension was rife, and within two months of independence in 1948 the
Burma Communist Party revolted; the Karen National Defense Organization rebelled in 1949.
By this time, half of the government troops had mutinied and nearly that proportion of the
army's equipment was gone; important cities such as Mandalay, Maymyo, Prome, and even
Insein (a suburb of the capital, Rangoon) fell to insurgent control. At the same time, private
"pocket armies" were rallying under competing politicians all around the country. Hence by
the time Ne Win assumed the position of commander in chief in 1949, he commanded only
2,000 remaining troops.

That the Burmese army emerged from this chaos as a powerful force that would dominate
state and society for more than 30 years is indeed remarkable. In the throes of this chaos, there
were few signs that the military leadership (or anyone else) could even envision such a future.
The Tatmadaw was but one of numerous armies that emerged at independence in 1948; many
were illegal, antistate armies, but there were also quasi-legal paramilitary squads maintained
by cabinet members and other politicians in the Socialist Party, which dominated the ruling
AFPFL.[3] The period was replete with challenges both to and within the Tatmadaw and the
state—challenges often backed by arms and violence. In the first decade of independence, for
example, the Tatmadaw faced a civil war waged by former classmates and comrades, a foreign
aggressor (the KMT) backed by a superpower, and an ex-colonizer and later the U.S. Central
Intelligence Agency (CIA) trying to shape the army in its own fashion and for its own purposes.
There was a lack of training facilities, a void of military doctrine, and a War Office administrative system ill suited to the exigencies of internal security functions and counterinsurgency
operations. At independence, the government was nearly bankrupt. And to make matters worse,
the ammunition and other equipment supplied by foreign aid had strings attached that further
threatened Burma's borders and sovereignty.

Moreover, the Burman nationalist officers who had stayed in the postwar Tatmadaw found
themselves shut out of control over the armed forces in the years between the end of World
War II and independence in January 1948. During this time, the returned British regime reorganized the Tatmadaw from a massive, unwieldy, guerrilla-style resistance force into a small,
almost skeletal, standing army. Not surprisingly, by 1948 the leadership roles in this army were
monopolized by officers sympathetic to the British—mainly Karens and Anglo-Burmans.[4] By
contrast, the ethnic Burman nationalists who had served in the wartime Patriotic Burmese
Forces (PBF) had very little institutional clout within the Tatmadaw and spent much of the
1945–1949 period consulting with AFPFL politicians on ways to redress their institutional weakness within the armed forces and create "a Burma Army worthwhile having" (Maung Maung
1947: May 25 entry). Their goal was attained in January 1949 when the Karen insurgency rendered the loyalty of the army's Karen leadership suspect; this gave the former PBF contingent
in the Tatmadaw a legal basis for placing most of the Karen leaders on indefinite leave. None
of them ever returned to prominence as active-duty officers in the army.

This purge did not end the difficulties of the Tatmadaw, however. In overseeing anti-
insurgent operations in the early years of independence, the post–Karen War Office had little
in the way of the resources or skills necessary to take the helm of the highly centralized, British-
designed, military bureaucracy. Furthermore, the continued presence of a civilian permanent
secretary (U Ba Tint) and his staff duty officer (Lt. Col. Hla Aung)—both perceived as sympathetic to expanded British influence in the army—led former PBF field commanders and Gen.

Ne Win to simply disregard the British-inherited bureaucracy in the conduct of all these operations. In fact, a former field commander noted that Ne Win told him to ignore the military chain of command and instead come straight to him when he needed anything.[5]

THE KMT CRISIS

This setup was workable when the Tatmadaw was fighting weaker, disunited internal rebels. The U.S.-backed KMT buildup in Burma, however, presented a far more formidable threat.[6] This threat was not the KMT itself but the consolidating Chinese communist regime. Throughout the early 1950s, Burmese national leaders worried that the communists, in the course of trying to stabilize their position in mainland China, would find it necessary to eliminate the remaining KMT troops located on the fringes of China—in particular in Burma. When diplomatic initiatives to end the KMT buildup and to appease Peking failed, the Burmese government sent the army to the troubled region in the hopes of showing Peking that Burma intended to wipe out the KMT. At the behest of Prime Minister U Nu, the army established a military administration in this region and soon embarked on a massive transformation of the armed forces. This process entailed a program of institution building in the mid-1950s to impose a "modern," bureaucratized, European-style standing-army structure onto the array of personal networks that constituted the Burma Army. As weak civilian institutions fell apart under the domestic and global pressures of the 1950s, the Tatmadaw was busy with what can only be seen in hindsight as state-building activities. It must be noted, however, that there is no evidence that Ne Win or any other army leaders conspired from the outset to build an army capable of running the Burmese polity over the next several decades. That this happened was simply an unintended consequence of the turbulent 1950s.

This transformation did not suddenly materialize upon the arrival in the Shan State of the first 2,000 KMT stragglers from Yunnan province in 1949. At that point they did not pose much of a threat, particularly in comparison with the communist and Karen rebel groups threatening the Rangoon government. But as more disciplined, better-organized, and better-armed KMT units began entering Kengtung in 1950 and receiving airdrops of U.S.-supplied arms and other supplies over the next few years, the 12,000-strong force became the major concern of Burmese political and army leaders (Taylor 1973).

Despite the numbers and the U.S. backing, KMT general Li Mi's two offensives into Yunnan in 1951 failed miserably. Soon thereafter the KMT began putting down roots inside Burma and preparing for a longer stay. Many of the rank-and-file and leaders of the KMT in Burma delved into opium smuggling; this lucrative business not only financed weapons purchases for future anti–People's Republic of China offensives but also made KMT leaders very wealthy. Gradually, by 1953, the KMT had come to control the Kengtung, Manglun, and Kokang subdivisions of the Shan State. For all practical purposes, the KMT constituted a foreign occupying force in these regions—a force supported, trained, and financed by the United States.[7] As Taylor wrote (1973: 15–16), the KMT "had forced the [civilian] administration of the government of Burma to flee the area and had themselves assumed the functions of de facto government, including tax collection. They built over one hundred miles of road, seventy in Burma and thirty in Thailand. The KMT, according to the government of Burma, even issued calls for the Burmese to overthrow the central government."

Military Administration

From the union government's perspective, the Shan State grew increasingly dangerous in the early 1950s with a perplexing array of anti-Rangoon forces—Burmese communists, Karen rebels, and the KMT—traversing this territory, forming ad hoc alliances, fighting one another, and competing with each other and the Rangoon government for resources and opium.

The real threat the KMT posed to the Union of Burma, however, was from the Chinese communist regime. The Nu government, which notably was the first foreign noncommunist regime to recognize the People's Republic of China in 1949, feared that the continuation of U.S.-backed preparations for a KMT invasion of China from Burmese soil would provoke the Chinese communists into simply annexing the entire country. Furthermore, Burmese observers worried that the United States might be setting up a second front of the Korean War in northeastern Burma (Lintner 1994). When reports filtered back to Rangoon that Chinese communist troops were amassing along the Yunnan border, the government proclaimed martial law on June 24, 1950, in the Shweli River valley area of the North Hsenwi subdivision of the Shan State. Within two years, military administration had gradually spread to 22 of the 33 Shan subdivisions.

Many observers at the time saw a political motive behind the prime minister's decision to send the army to the Shan State. At the time, Nu was negotiating with the Shan traditional leaders, the *sawbwas*, to bring greater central control to the region and weaken the *sawbwas*. As one British embassy official noted after his 1953 trip to the Shan State, "The Burmese claim that this [military administration] was made necessary by the KMT situation, but in fact the areas worst affected by the Chinese [KMT] insurgency—Kengtung for example—have not been declared under martial law." He concluded that there seemed to be good evidence to suggest that the *sawbwas* were right in their suspicions that martial law was imposed because of "their resistance to the re-shaping of administrative boundaries...by which they lose ancient feudal rights" (British Embassy 1953). In 1953, the *sawbwas* and the government arrived at a compromise by which the chiefs would retain their titles and receive compensation from the Union Government in return for giving up their administrative authority beginning in 1956 (Silverstein 1958: 54).

Whatever the motive for imposing martial law, battalion commanders suddenly found themselves acting as administrators and not as the guerrilla or field commanders they had been in the past. Their prior experience of administering territory by allying with local socialist politicians and former Thakin pocket army leaders in the early insurrection period was nothing like the experience of running local government in the Shan State. In the latter case, there were no old student-union ties or links of any kind with local populations (Maung Maung 1953).[8] At the same time, Shan leaders and their subjects found their lives being run by Burman and Kachin army officers and their soldiers. During the more than two years of martial law throughout most of the Shan State, the Tatmadaw grew increasingly unpopular among local inhabitants. The embittered wife of a Shan *sawbwa* wrote later of the "unscrupulous treatment of the hill people" by the army, which "behaved like ruthless occupation forces rather than protectors of the land" (Sargent 1994: 143).

The imposition of martial law in the Shan State beginning in 1950 meant that the army was seriously overcommitted. It was fighting the Karen National Defense Organization, the

Communist Party, and other insurgents in central Burma and many of the frontier areas. More-over, it was facing a possible showdown with the U.S.-backed KMT in extremely difficult ter-rain—all the while wondering when China would lose patience with Burma's inability to con-trol the KMT. The addition of military administration duties, which required greater logistical support from the War Office in Rangoon, severely tested the abilities of field commanders. For the first time in postcolonial counterinsurgency operations, this was not a case where field com-manders could tap into networks of old friends, former student union colleagues, or other acquaintances to arrange for local militia, politicos, and kingpins to support ad hoc counter-insurgency campaigns. In most cases, Tatmadaw officers and soldiers did not even speak the language of the Burmese citizens they were ordered to administer and protect.

On the battlefield, early Tatmadaw operations against the KMT were disorganized and easily defeated. In 1953, the military waged its first-ever full-scale, combined-forces, coun-teroffensive against the KMT. It was repulsed within three weeks by superior KMT firepower. According to one Burmese air force pilot who flew air support during the operation, "It was a complete disaster."[9]

Army Transformation

These operational failures against a potentially formidable foreign threat provoked a complete overhaul of the armed forces. Field commanders, staff officers, and civilian government lead-ers alike quickly became aware of the need to transform the Tatmadaw from a fragmented, postresistance, decentralized, guerrilla force to one capable of defending the sovereignty of the union. For the first time, all these self-sustaining, isolated, independent battalions had to com-bine forces to fight what could become a major war. The KMT crisis forced the already inward-focusing Tatmadaw leadership to begin a course of experimentation and reorganization that would persist through the end of the decade. Although in its initial stages—the 1950–1953 period—the planning process brought few of these plans to fruition, the process nonetheless laid the foundation for an institutional development of the military that expanded army roles over the next decade. Additionally, the process of planning brought about significant realign-ments of influence, loyalties, and resources within the Tatmadaw.

Operational disasters led to calls for reform from field commanders and staff officers alike. In the first step toward reform, Lt. Col. Aung Gyi—a senior staff officer based in Rangoon—formed the Military Planning Staff (MPS) to provide immediate advice in "charting a clear-cut course of military activities and in advising the Government to map the road to peace within the State and readiness for national emergency covering all aspects, military, political, social, economic, etc." (Union of Burma, War Office, General Staff Department 1951a). According to the August 1951 memorandum of authorization from the same office, the rationale for the planning staff's formation was this: "We have been working mostly on an ad hoc or impromptu basis without giving much thought to coordination and correlation of different Departments of State.... We are virtually at war and what is worse a more devastating one as any civil war is [*sic*].... I cannot afford to wait for changes in organization and I am immediately in need of a nucleus Planning Staff."

Once established under Lt. Col. Aung Gyi and Lt. Col. Maung Maung, the MPS sent study missions to Britain, the United States, Australia, and the Soviet Union. In their view, what separated the early postcolonial Tatmadaw from these "progressive" armies around the world was the Tatmadaw's organizational weakness at the center and the lack of institutional clout and autonomy for army leadership to plan, evaluate, and carry out strategy and tactics (Union of Burma, War Office, General Staff Department 1951b). At that point the Burma Army was still a disorganized collection of guerrillas. What it needed was to become an army capable of standing up to the KMT and potentially the CIA and the People's Republic of China. To do so, the MPS completely restructured the division of labor between civilian and military leaders over defense policy—notably shrinking the civilian secretary's sphere of control over internal army affairs (Callahan 1996: 423–25). Furthermore, the MPS terminated the contract for British advisers to the Tatmadaw, wrote Burma's first draft of military doctrine, and undertook the creation of educational and training institutions (such as the Defense Services Academy at Maymyo) that remain in place to today. Finally, the MPS unified the army, navy, and air force into a single structure under the command of the most senior army officer. Although the MPS argued that the unification was done in order to bring the Tatmadaw into line with the practices of "all progressive countries," former PBF officers and Gen. Ne Win also sought to weaken the power of the pro-British officers who ran the navy and air force.

The MPS also created a series of organizations that embarked on ostensibly strategic programs that in fact turned out to be major state-building endeavors. Most significant over the next decade were the Defense Services Institute and the Psychological Warfare (Psywar) Directorate. In 1951, Aung Gyi set up a commissariat to replace inefficient and unworkable unit-run canteens. Called the Defense Services Institute, this operation expanded quickly into the sale of bulk and consumer goods to soldiers; by 1960 Aung Gyi and his colleagues at the Defense Services Institute were running banks, an international shipping line, and the largest import-export operation in the country (Kyaw Soe n.d.).[10] The Psywar Directorate was established in 1952 when Prime Minister U Nu criticized the army for an excessive budget allocation for its reorganization plans. Nu objected that the large amounts of money requested to finance an army that could protect the border for just a few months were a waste compared to the social and economic problems that needed to be addressed. The solution, according to former brigadier Maung Maung, was to promise Prime Minister Nu to modify the plans to take into account a pet project of Nu's: psychological warfare.[11] Thus emerged the Psywar Directorate with Aung Gyi unofficially at its helm and Lt. Col. Ba Than as director.[12]

Once the Psywar Directorate was established, Aung Gyi reports that he gave Lt. Col. Ba Than a great deal of latitude to win over the hearts and minds of the Burmese population, domestic insurgents, and soldiers inside the Tatmadaw. Over the next decade, Psywar initiatives included establishing the army archives (the Defense Services Historical Research Institute) and sponsoring performances, radio shows, and pamphlet publication and distribution.[13] Furthermore, Ba Than and Aung Gyi moved quickly into the commercial magazine market by launching their *Myawaddy* magazine in 1952 to "provide balance" to a market dominated by antigovernment publications. Four years later, *Myawaddy*'s circulation was 18,000, the largest of any popular magazine.[14]

The Psywar Directorate also sponsored projects aimed at convincing Tatmadaw officers and soldiers that they were part of a national army fighting for a just cause.[15] It was toward this goal that Aung Gyi, Maung Maung, and Ba Than organized preliminary meetings in 1956 to prepare an ideology for the armed forces. They invited former communists and socialists to write an ideology synthesizing communism and socialism within the context of a Buddhist society. U Saw Oo (editor of the socialist *Mandaing* newspaper) and U Chit Hlaing (former communist follower of Thakin Soe) worked with Lt. Col. Ba Than to prepare the draft, which was then submitted to the annual Commanding Officers conference in 1956. The discussion of ideology ran four hours at the conference. Over the next two years, at succeeding conferences, Psywar leaders Aung Gyi and Ba Than presented new drafts of this ideological statement that ultimately became the basis for the post-1962 socialist regime's core ideology: "The Burmese Way to Socialism." Moreover, the Psywar Directorate developed ambitious proposals for Philippine-style civic-action programs and planned to open a Psywar School at Mingaladon with its first class to graduate in 1958.[16]

Warriors as State Builders

By the late 1950s, the Tatmadaw had completed its most significant structural transformation and had become a war-fighting machine. In 1962, this new Tatmadaw boasted 57 infantry battalions, five regional commands, and more than 100,000 soldiers—a considerable expansion from the paltry three or four battalions and 2,000 soldiers wearing Tatmadaw uniforms just after independence in 1948 (Union of Burma, Chief of Staff [Army] 1962; see also British Embassy 1962).[17] Moreover, although the growth of supporting arms and services lagged behind the infantry's expansion, other institutional innovations signaled remarkably fast progress toward the MPS's goals. By 1962, for example, the third class of the Defense Services Academy had graduated, and the army's other educational and training institutions had developed a wide range of sophisticated specialty courses rivaling those found in developed countries. Meanwhile, combined air force, army, and navy operations—coordinated from Rangoon and from field headquarters—began to make headway against entrenched insurgent groups. The number of antigovernment insurgents dropped from 25,000 in 1953 to around 10,000 in 1962. These remnants roved mainly in small bands and no longer posed an immediate threat to the union government. Furthermore, the threat from the KMT was much reduced by the success of the army's Operation Mekong in 1961.

As was the case in early modern Europe, the strengthening of Burma's coercive institutions not only made the army stronger vis-à-vis external enemies but also rendered it more capable of exerting power in the domain of the ruler (Tilly 1990; Giddens 1987; Rasler and Thompson 1989; Burke 1997). Importantly, improvements in civilian bureaucratic capacities did not keep pace with the transformation of the army. Over the next decade this uneven development across sites of power within the national state led to military aggrandizement of resources, responsibilities, and powers in traditionally nonmilitary realms.

Given the turbulent political conditions and the difficult economic times of the 1950s, how did warriors become successful state builders in Burma's postcolonial period? Drawing on the experiences of absolutist states in Western Europe, Cohen et al. (1981) suggested that the Tatmadaw's victory in the 1948–1950 civil war might have laid the foundations for greater centralization by establishing the sovereignty of the center once and for all. But the world had changed by the mid-1950s, and the resources that army leadership deployed to effect this institutional transformation did not come from domestic sources newly linked to the center as a result of victory in a civil war. Instead, the Tatmadaw looked overseas for the funding and tools for state formation. Given the insecurity of Burma's geographic position in the cold war, army leaders began wooing arms manufacturers and superpower rivals, the enthusiastic suitors who pursued most new nations in the early postwar period. Purchasing missions composed of the Burmese War Office, field command, and navy and air force staff traveled around the world and brought back fighter-bombers from the Israelis, Italian advisers to establish the first ammunition factory, and U.S. counterintelligence trainers from the CIA.

Although this pattern of seeking vendors and assistance from wide-ranging overseas sources mimicked the Nu government's foreign policy of balanced neutralism, there was a significant difference in the military's external relations vis-à-vis those of civilian leaders. Although key Tatmadaw leaders had influence over Nu's foreign policy, these same army leaders acted independently when buying arms in the world market and negotiating programs of military assistance. There was virtually no oversight by civilian politicians. Moreover, during this period army leaders—and not civilian home ministers or permanent secretaries—were much courted by British, Yugoslav, Czech, and U.S. arms manufacturers and dealers who paid for many of the purchasing and study missions that inspired army leaders to expand the military's influence in the domestic realm.

In response to the threat of total warfare posed by the KMT crisis, the Tatmadaw initially took charge of managing all aspects of the cold war's impact on its own affairs in the 1950s via these overseas treasure hunts. By the end of the 1950s, however, the army's vista had broadened, and it soon was displacing weaker state agencies and financial interests in regulating the impact of the world economy on Burma's national economy. This occurred when the army's commissariat, the Defense Services Institute, expanded to take over most major import-export operations for the whole country. The Tatmadaw's effectiveness and administrative autonomy in these activities contrasted sharply with the failures of the government bureaucracy and the ruling political party (the AFPFL), suggesting yet another early source of the army's growing strength vis-à-vis other institutions within the postcolonial state in Burma.

THE SOCIALIST PERIOD

The state-building activities of the Tatmadaw in the 1950s made possible the two coups of 1958 and 1962, which brought army leaders to national political power and eliminated their civilian competitors once and for all. Under the leadership of the commander in chief, Gen. Ne Win, the 1962 coup group formed a Revolutionary Council of military officers to replace the cabinet and parliament. The council suspended the 1947 constitution, established the Leninist-style Burma Socialist Program Party (BSPP), and outlawed all other political parties. Under its ideological banner, the Burmese Way to Socialism, the BSPP attempted to impose a central command economy and eliminate foreign control over business in Burma. The army-dominated BSPP restructured state and society and ruled unchallenged for 25 years. Aside from one brief outbreak of antigovernment protest in 1974, army and party leaders managed to contain all serious conflict to the frontier regions where mainly minority peoples lived. No group threatened the continuity of the regime.

Civil-military relations during the socialist period continued to be characterized by a number of intraelite tensions. Most important, after 1971, when the army-dominated BSPP decided to transform itself into a mass party, control over political outcomes shifted from the army high command to the party secretariat. Although most of the party leaders were former military officers and many cadres were military officers in mufti, military leaders became disenchanted with the increasing power of party leaders in Rangoon and in local arenas by the early 1980s. In particular, many infantry officers complained in interviews conducted throughout the 1990s that the BSPP was too busy dispensing patronage to its followers throughout the countryside to recognize the dangers in Burma's frontier regions. In fact, most observers think that the Tatmadaw could have unified Burma and ended the civil wars twenty years ago had the BSPP committed the resources to the objective (Selth 1996).

THE 1988 UPRISING:
REASSERTION OF ARMY PREROGATIVES

The collapse of the Socialist Party in 1988 cleared the way for correcting the BSPP's neglect of counterinsurgency imperatives. Although the BSPP's apparatus had been coming apart for more than a decade, it was not until 1987 that it was dealt the final blow. At that time, following a series of unexpected demonetization measures that devastated the economy and wiped out the savings of most Burmese people, student demonstrations erupted in Rangoon and continued sporadically into the following year. The police used harsh tactics to put down the demonstrations, including one incident in March 1988 that led to the suffocation of 41 students in a police van. Public outcry over this incident led to further demonstrations, some of which began attracting participants from beyond the Rangoon university campuses. BSPP officials tried to restore order throughout the country, but to no avail. As antigovernment forces expanded their following, the BSPP convened an extraordinary party congress in July 1988 during which Party Chairman Ne Win and President San Yu resigned from the party leadership. For many Burmese, it appeared that the government had collapsed. Democratic reform seemed not only possible but inevitable.

Nationwide demonstrations continued throughout August and into the first half of September. During this time, millions of Burmese took to city, township, and even village streets to support political and economic reform. In the months of protests that built to this crescendo, rumors were rife regarding the Tatmadaw's role in what was shaping up as Burma's democratic revolution. Unlike the police, who were responsible for the deaths of the 41 protesters locked in a van, the military's reputation was untarnished in the early months of the uprising. Anecdotes circulated of military units and individual soldiers even supporting the antigovernment forces—pointing perhaps to a fissure in the regime that might lead to a democratic opening. But there were also popular theories that Ne Win and the military were orchestrating the public protests so they could use the instability as a reason to crack down and reassert power through the barrel of a gun. Ultimately, army leaders deployed strike forces to crush street protests in Rangoon in August 1988. One month later, Gen. Saw Maung installed himself as the chairman of a new military-led regime: the State Law and Order Restoration Council (SLORC) (Lintner 1989).

The SLORC suspended the 1974 constitution and abolished all the national governing institutions of the former single-party state. Under the SLORC's orders, the crack troops of the armed forces put an abrupt end to the prodemocracy demonstrations, killing thousands of unarmed civilians in the process. The SLORC distributed cabinet portfolios to senior military officers, and Gen. Saw Maung assumed the responsibility of prime minister and defense minister. Martial law was declared. Gatherings of more than three people were banned. Organized public participation in protests and other political events ended overnight. Although the SLORC enacted economic reforms aimed at opening the market and correcting the financial weakness that had sparked the 1988 uprising, the regime refused to make any serious structural or currency reforms for fear of generating politically explosive hardship. In an effort to control public opinion, political opposition has been systematically intimidated and all media have been censored.

Despite these tactics, as well as attempts by the military regime to hamper party-building and campaign activities, opposition led by Aung San Suu Kyi (daughter of independence hero Aung San) swept the 1990 parliamentary elections. The junta's subsequent refusal to honor the election results, the arrests and flight of many successful opposition candidates, the five-year house arrest of Suu Kyi herself, and the numerous restrictions on party activities over the last decade have all but decimated Aung San Suu Kyi's loosely organized populist party, the National League for Democracy.

Remaking the Tatmadaw

As in the case of the KMT crisis, this national security crisis spawned not only an army transformation but also the initiation of a wide range of state-building programs, once again emanating from the Tatmadaw. With the BSPP gone, the SLORC had to begin almost from scratch to rebuild the collapsed state. It did so with the only tools it considered reliable: its military personnel. In asserting central control over political, economic, and administrative power throughout the country, the junta constructed a government that took stability and order as its highest priority. This entailed a massive expansion of the armed forces. In the first eight years of junta rule, the Tatmadaw grew from 186,000 to more than 370,000 soldiers. The junta spent more than $1 billion on 140 new combat aircraft, 30 naval vessels, 170 tanks, 250 armored personnel carriers, as well as rocket launch systems, antiaircraft artillery, infantry weapons, telecommunications surveillance equipment, and other hardware (Brooke 1998; Davis and Hawke 1998).

In addition to improving the weaponry available to combat forces, the regime also undertook extensive reforms of the Tatmadaw's command and control structure to increase the high command's authority throughout the country. The Ministry of Defense was reorganized in 1990, and most combat units were placed under the central Bureau of Special Operations. New army units have proliferated, including two mobile light infantry divisions, specialized engineer battalions, and armor and artillery units. New army garrisons have been set up in towns and villages throughout the country, as well, while the number of naval bases and air stations has also increased (Selth 1999: 11). The military's industrial base has expanded, too, as the regime has launched an import substitution program in the critical area of arms manufacturing (Hawke 1998).

This expansion and modernization of the military has been accompanied by the establishment of an array of welfare, health, and educational facilities that seem to be creating an "exclusive social order" of privilege for active-duty and retired soldiers (Selth 1999). Modern hospitals and clinics have been built to serve military families. Private businesses are co-opted to make regular "donations" to army welfare organizations that appear to be evolving along the lines of the *yayasan* foundations in Indonesia (Lowry 1996: 139–41). Cheap—but high-quality—rice and access to scarce cooking oil are available to most soldiers and officers. Finally, the regime has greatly expanded the military's higher education facilities while closing civilian universities for most of the decade following the 1988 coup.[18]

State Rebuilding in the 1990s

As in the 1950s, the remaking of the military led to the concentration of state-rebuilding initiatives and resources under one military department or another. The most prominent state builders have been the Office of Strategic Studies (OSS) and the regional commanders. Founded in 1994 under the Directorate of Defense Services Intelligence, the OSS has evolved into an organization attributed with near omnipotence in Burma's political realm (Lintner 1998). Like the Military Planning Staff in the 1950s, OSS departments appear to have taken on responsibilities for coordinating and perhaps even initiating policies in areas as significant as the drug trade, the economy, ethnic minority affairs, and foreign relations.[19] With "strategy" broadly defined, OSS also has overseen research projects aimed at rewriting Burma's national history, a campaign initiated by the SLORC in the early 1990s. Specifically, the OSS has attempted to historicize the modern nation and place Burma at the origin of all human progress. Toward that end, the OSS took charge of the Pondaung Primate Fossil Exploration project. With little or no archaeological expertise, the dig has produced specious claims that fossils found in the Pondaung region prove that "human civilization began in our motherland" (May May Aung 1997) and that ethnic groups lived harmoniously in Burma all the way back to the Neolithic period.[20]

While the OSS appears to have taken responsibility for formulating and coordinating policy on everything from fossils to foreign affairs, the junta delegated the day-to-day responsibilities for state rebuilding throughout the countryside to its regional commanders.[21] As a result, political authority throughout the country came to rest not in the junta, but in the hands of the regional commanders. Three new regional commands were established (bringing the total to twelve), and regional commanders were given de facto authority over all political and economic affairs in their area of operation. Although there was variation from one region to another, the junta asked regional commanders to eliminate political dissent, dismantle the old socialist state and party, and negotiate new administrative and economic arrangements. Accordingly, regional commanders have built roads, housing, suburbs, and markets. They have rearranged urban and rural populations to accommodate tourism and other industries. And they have expanded their surveillance and crowd control capabilities. Along the way, these regional commanders have amassed enormous wealth and power.

How has the extension of the geographic and functional reach of the state been financed? In the 1950s, military expansion and state-building activities were financed almost entirely by external sources. In the 1990s, the funding was more complicated. Some of the military modernization program was paid for by government revenues. Most observers think that annual spending on the military during the 1990s ran between 40 and 60 percent of the national budget. Although it is impossible to know precisely how much of the government's revenue comes from the "whitening tax" on foreign exchange profits from the opium and methamphetamine trade, there is no doubt this off-budget source of revenue provides some degree of capital for arms purchases (U.S. Department of State 1998). Additionally, early purchases of arms and ammunition were financed by soft loans from China. Other weapons suppliers include Pakistan (until 1991), Singapore, Israel, Poland, North Korea, and a number of European private arms dealers. Payments come out of the regime's dwindling foreign reserves (Selth 1996: 22–26).

Beyond the weapon modernization program, the explosion of army-led institution building throughout the country has been financed by a range of other off-budget revenue sources besides the tax on drug profits. The most significant of these sources is Union of Myanmar Economic Holdings, Ltd. (UMEH). Founded in 1990, UMEH has grown into the largest indigenous firm and has a registered capital of 10 billion kyat ($1.4 billion at the official exchange rate). UMEH is owned jointly by the Directorate of Defense Procurement (40 percent) and retired and active-duty military personnel (60 percent). UMEH controls the lucrative gem trade in Burma, and all major foreign investors must enter the Burma market via a joint venture with UMEH. Given that there is no public reporting of UMEH finances, in essence the company operates an immense off-budget slush fund on behalf of the military leadership, who probably have channeled profits into arms acquisitions programs and the dozens of initiatives aimed at constructing the Tatmadaw's new privileged social order and reordering the civilian population throughout the countryside (Houtman 1999; IRRC 1997).

The Limits of Military Modernization and State Rebuilding

As in the 1950s, state building in the 1990s has been neither smooth nor without setbacks. Military initiatives to extend the geographic and functional reach of the state have produced at least four outcomes that run fully counter to these objectives.

First, this junta has built a rickety yet enduring state apparatus that is at least for now beholden to the whims of regional commanders.[22] On several occasions throughout the 1990s, the Rangoon-based junta has tried to curb the incipient warlordism of the regional commanders. Anyone who travels outside Rangoon witnesses the mansions, luxury cars, and regal treatment of these officers. Another example of these center-periphery tensions came in the reorganization of the junta into the State Peace and Development Council (SPDC) in November 1997. The reshuffle allowed the junta's top four leaders to purge the most corrupt cabinet ministers (several of whom had launched their illicit empires while serving as regional commanders), to demote most of the regional commanders by assigning them ministerial portfolios in Rangoon, and to place junior general officers in regional commands and on the junta itself for the first time in a decade. In the future, the ongoing tensions between the junta and the upcountry commanders may not be so easily resolved by cabinet and command reshuffles. If the center demands greater control over upcountry resources and the commanders balk, the Rangoon regime—whether it is this junta or a democratic government—will have to find some kind of compensation to induce field commanders to give up their power and wealth. To date, the Rangoon-based junta has tried different mechanisms to entice regional commanders to toe the regime's line, but none has seriously changed the organizational setup that devolves power to regional military commanders.

The second unforeseen consequence of this military-led state-building process is that in establishing the army's extraordinary dominance of national affairs, it has also created unprecedented discipline problems in all ranks. In its efforts to add nearly 200,000 soldiers to the ranks of the Tatmadaw, the regime ordered village and town leaders to furnish quotas of recruits. But local leaders have not sent their most promising youths off to the army. Instead, the massive recruitment has brought young hoodlums, ruffians, and criminals into the ranks in large numbers. Discipline and morale appear to be at an all-time low.

Third, this redirection of military objectives to state-building programs rather than combat has created an unprecedented gap in experience between army leaders and young soldiers. This results directly from the SLORC's successful campaign to obtain cease-fire agreements with minority insurgents between 1989 and 1996. (Some seventeen pacts were signed during this period.) For the first time in this army's history, therefore, the "military" experiences of officers commissioned over the last ten or fifteen years are unlikely to include extensive combat. In fact, officers as high ranking as majors and in some cases lieutenant colonels today probably have less war-fighting than road-building experience. This is not to suggest that road building is a new job for the Tatmadaw. Today's senior officers were indeed involved in infrastructure and civic projects in the 1970s, but these projects were part of the counterinsurgency effort—projects aimed at keeping themselves and their academy classmates alive in hard-fought battles. Today's junior officers build roads that many admit are likely to wash away with the next rains and are unlikely to contribute much to Burma's economic development.

The cessation of hostilities in the cease-fire territory produced the fourth unanticipated consequence of the state-rebuilding process in the 1990s. Although the cease-fire agreements resulted in a temporary cessation of hostilities, they also allowed some of the ethnic insurgent groups to hold onto their arms, to police their own territory, and to use their former rebel armies as private security forces to protect both legal and illegal business operations. Tatmadaw units are often disarmed upon entering territory patrolled by these ethnic armies; upon exiting the territory, they receive their weapons again. Even in Rangoon, Wa and Kokang leaders move freely about the capital with armed guards wearing the uniforms of drug baron armies and paying little attention to the law enforcement officers they inevitably run up against. This clearly represents a crack in the edifice of army rule that stretches from Rangoon through regional command headquarters to the frontier areas of the country.

These four unintended consequences of the SLORC/SPDC state-rebuilding process in the 1990s suggest that the armed forces are not the omnipotent, fully unified organization that contemporary political debate imputes to them. Significant internal military dilemmas—the most serious of which are the new intergenerational gap in the officer corps and the center-periphery tensions between the junta and regional commanders—command at least as much of the attention of Tatmadaw leaders as do concerns about Aung San Suu Kyi and the opposition. This is not to argue that these internal military problems will cause the downfall of the SLORC/SPDC regime; I simply wish to suggest the complexity of the current political deadlock. Much of the debate about Burmese politics today assumes that the regime's intransigence on liberalization measures comes from a position of strength and arrogance. In fact, this analysis of the state-rebuilding project undertaken in the 1990s has revealed sources of weakness that probably account as much for the regime's unyielding behavior as do the strengths that have resulted from running the country.

As in the 1950s, this state-rebuilding process in the 1990s was carried out in a largely ad hoc fashion. Many observers argue that the Burmese junta adopted Indonesia's New Order as a model for reorganizing the polity. The main evidence for this claim is that in 1995, the SLORC initiated a national convention charged with drafting a new constitution that would ensure the Tatmadaw a "leading role" in national affairs similar to the *dwifungsi* (dual function) doctrine in the New Order. Although members of the junta have read Indonesia's 1945 constitution as well as the constitutions of other nations,[23] it seems very unlikely that the Indonesia model would hold great appeal for Burmese leaders given the marginalization of Indonesia's armed forces from the inner circle of decision making in the 1980s and 1990s.[24] Moreover, the national convention stopped meeting in 1997—apparently because of irresolvable debates over which of the 135 national races would qualify for statehood in the new constitution. Like most of the junta's initiatives, the national convention was kicked off with great fanfare and abandoned when it engendered unmanageable outcomes. The Tatmadaw's experiments in state building in the 1950s seem fully replicated in the makeshift pronouncements that pass for policy in the 1990s.

PATTERNS AND EXPLANATIONS

It was the two threats to regimes in postcolonial Burma that created the conditions in which state institutions came to be defined, articulated, and dominated by the Tatmadaw. In response to the KMT crisis in the early 1950s and the popular uprising of 1988, the armed forces of Burma crafted ad hoc combat campaigns to defeat these threats. Neither threat could be blamed on easily identifiable, geographically containable populations, however, which led battalion commanders and military planners almost inevitably into broader programs aimed at reordering, reeducating, and redefining the population throughout the entire country. Soldiers became state builders. This is not to suggest, of course, that security crises inevitably lead to military domination of politics. In fact, most of the postcolonial nations of South Asia and Southeast Asia were engulfed in regime-threatening civil warfare for a decade or more following independence. Yet only a few of these states—such as Burma and Indonesia—came to be dominated by the armed forces. In other regimes under fire—Malaya and the Philippines—state armies fought against quite serious threats but remained largely under civilian control. What explains this variation in outcome?

One possible answer lies in variations in counterinsurgency combat strategies pursued by governments in the years surrounding transitions to independence. Nearly all South Asian and Southeast Asian states faced serious internal insurgencies in the 1950s. Most governments responded initially with purely military approaches to eliminating antiregime forces. But in Malaya (later Malaysia) and the Philippines, the governments quickly abandoned the coercive, military approach and opted for accommodation strategies to incorporate and co-opt the opposition—attempting to win over the "hearts and minds" of regime opponents and the population. As in the development of parliamentary institutions in early modern Europe, citizens of newly independent (or soon-to-be independent) Asian states as well as critics of ruling elites had to be offered incentives to cooperate, which often entailed some kind of power-sharing arrangements or institutional reforms that allowed for more inclusive politics. This political strategy required the concurrent bureaucratization, centralization, articulation, and empowerment of both nonmilitary and military institutions of governance.

In Indonesia and Burma, by contrast, the states experimented with accommodationist strategies but never really budged from the purely military approach. This led to the development of powerful centralizing militaries and the concurrent withering of civil services and political parties that provided direct channels of input from the populace. Moreover, in both of these cases it was the armies—not civilian bureaucracies—that experimented with political counterinsurgency strategies (such as Burma's Psywar operations in the 1950s and OSS programs in the 1990s) to co-opt internal populations that otherwise might support insurgents. In Burma and Indonesia, this state-making process created parallel structures of governance that regulated the country's political, social, and economic life. One limp structure lay in the civilian realm; the other structure, more robust, lay in the military bureaucracy. In neither Burma nor Indonesia did civilian groups or institutions ever establish the dynamism or influence of civilian governance in Malaysia or the Philippines.

This comparative insight should not be taken to suggest that political counterinsurgency strategies inevitably produce the kinds of governing institutions that might be called "democratic"; out of Malaysia's counterinsurgency experience evolved a political system that is hardly representative or open in any sense of the term, and the civic action campaigns of the 1950s in the Philippines laid the groundwork for the emergence of Marcos's most undemocratic revolution. However, the comparison does suggest one more limited, nonetheless significant, finding. States that pursue coercion-intensive, military solutions to internal security and political crises will likely see their militaries take on a range of functions—law enforcement, economic regulation, tax collection, census taking, magazine publishing, political party registration, food aid distribution, etc.—that have little to with traditional defense responsibilities. In Stepan's terms, this involves a transformation of the "military-as-institution" into the "military-as-government" (Stepan 1988). In independent Burma's two most serious internal crises (in the 1950s and 1988), this transformation went even further. Because each crisis coincided with and was exacerbated by the utter breakdown of the state machinery, the movement of military-as-institution into nonmilitary affairs could take place only with an extensive overhaul first of the military itself, and then of the state as well. Internal military reform in the 1950s and after 1988 involved resource mobilization, administrative centralization, and territorial expansion, all of which became benchmarks of the subsequent military-led, state rebuilding process. In a sense, the military solution to internal crises crowded out other potential state reformers, turning officers into state-builders and the military-as-institution into the military-as-state itself.

PART VIII

Conclusion

Asian Civil-Military Relations: Key Developments, Explanations, and Trajectories

Muthiah Alagappa

IT IS EVIDENT FROM THE PRECEDING COUNTRY STUDIES that the relationship of the soldier to the state in Asia has undergone substantial change over the past five decades, but there have been significant continuities as well. As reflected in Figure 18.1, at the founding moment, civilian supremacy characterized civil military relations in every country investigated in this study except Thailand. Beginning in 1958 and through the 1960s and 1970s there was a surge in military and military-backed regimes. Since the mid-1980s, however, the trend in Asia has been toward a reduction in the political power, influence, and role of the military, and a corresponding increase in civilian supremacy. Reversals in a few countries, as in Pakistan in 1999, are possible, but a repeat of the 1960s and 1970s appears rather unlikely. For reasons explored in this chapter, the declining political influence of the military appears quite firmly rooted and set to continue into the foreseeable future. However, advance in effective civilian control over the military in postauthoritarian states is likely to be gradual and subject to protracted struggle and negotiation and, at times, setbacks. Limited military role expansion is also possible, especially at the local level, in countries that have experienced civilian control for a considerable period. Further, the content of state-soldier relations is likely to vary across countries even when they have similar political systems. Civil-military relations in Asia in the foreseeable future will continue to be complex and dynamic and will be characterized by multiple patterns, although democratic civilian control is likely to become the dominant mode.

Taking a regional perspective, in this final chapter I identify and explain the key changes and continuities in Asian civil-military relations as well as anticipate future trajectories. The key argument is that the initial surge and subsequent decline in the political influence of the military in Asia are best explained by the changing significance of coercion—rise then decline—in governance as posited by the propositions advanced in the Introduction and amplified in Chapter 1. In Asia, as elsewhere, postcolonial and postrevolutionary governments faced enormous challenges in state and nation building as well as in constructing legitimate political systems. Although experiences varied, in many countries power and authority were not concentrated in the state, state institutions were unable to dominate the entire country, minorities

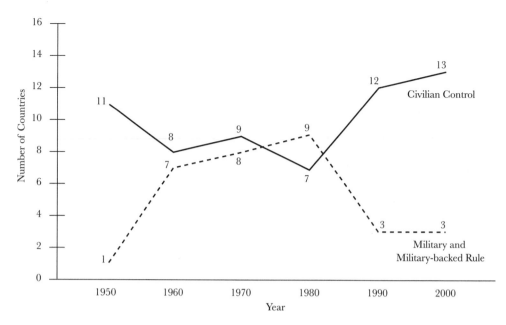

FIGURE 18.1.   Civilian versus Military Control in Asia: 1950–2000.

resisted integration into national communities, political systems were challenged by groups espousing rival organizing ideologies, legitimacy of governments was contested by the competing elite, and in several cases the new states were confronted with severe international threats to their very existence. Internal and international security were prime concerns of a large number of Asian countries. State coercion played a dominant role in most if not all these processes in a large number of countries, leading to role expansion and a dramatic increase in the organizational and political power and influence of the military. Although Asian countries still continue to face major challenges, over the last five decades or so several have made substantial progress in the internal and international consolidation of nation and state, and in the development of widely accepted systems and institutions for political domination. In these countries the resort to coercion, especially the private, partisan, and repressive use of force in governance, has declined, and so has the political power and influence of the military.

Many Asian countries, particularly those in East Asia and Southeast Asia, also experienced high rates of economic growth for well over two decades. The highly successful export-led growth strategies of these countries integrated their national economies into the global capitalist economy, instituting new rules and procedures for their management, with spillover social and political effects. Sustained economic development in the capitalist mode made for a more complex economy that demanded sophisticated management that was well beyond what can be provided by the military. It also set in train the development of new domestic forces—an independent private sector, growth of middle and working classes, strong and vibrant civil societies among them—making for much more complex states and societies, with the latter demanding greater welfare, accountability, and participation in governance. Such development also strengthened other state institutions, tilting the distribution of power against the military and altering the norms and rules of governance.

Concurrently, and especially since the mid- to late 1980s, the international context altered decidedly in favor of democracy, human rights, and the market economy. International organizations and key external actors condemned military coups and ostracized military governments. Not only have these developments altered the normative structure and distribution of power in favor of civilian institutions, with a corresponding decline in the political influence of the military in several countries, they have also generated close domestic and international scrutiny of military institutions and their activities. The interplay of coercion, political legitimacy, and economic development in the context of change in the international system, I argue, explains long-term change or lack thereof in Asian civil-military relations.

Organized in six sections, the chapter begins with a brief overview of the key changes and continuities in Asian civil-military relations over the last five decades. This is followed by explanation of four key features in the history of Asian civil-military relations in the post–World War II era: uninterrupted civilian control in Japan, India, Malaysia, Singapore, Sri Lanka, China, and Vietnam; the surge of military or military-backed regimes in Thailand, Pakistan, Burma, South Korea, Indonesia, Bangladesh, the Philippines, and North Korea; the subsequent trend toward democratic civilian control in the Philippines, South Korea, Taiwan, Bangladesh, Thailand, and Indonesia; and the continuation of military rule in Burma and Pakistan. The final section anticipates future civil-military trajectories in Asia.

CONTINUITY AND CHANGE: AN OVERVIEW

Change and continuity, as noted in Chapter 1, can be investigated only with respect to a specific baseline, which in this study is the founding moments (independence or liberation from colonial rule or occupation, victory in revolution, defeat in war, secession, or separation) of the contemporary Asian states. Though there were variations and overlaps, essentially three patterns characterized Asian civil-military relations at the founding moments. Versions of democratic civilian control characterized state-soldier relations in eleven of the sixteen Asian countries investigated in this study—the Philippines, India, Pakistan, Sri Lanka, Burma, Indonesia, South Korea, Japan, Malaysia, Singapore, and Bangladesh. The second pattern—Leninist party control of the military—characterized civil-military relations in Vietnam, the Republic of China on Taiwan (ROC), and the People's Republic of China (PRC). To a lesser degree, it also characterized civil-military relations in North Korea. Military rule—the third pattern—characterized civil-military relations only in Thailand. Despite the differences in the nature of political, administrative, and economic systems, the military was subordinate to civilian authority in all but one of the sixteen countries investigated in this study. Thailand was the sole exception. Even there, despite the key role played by military officers in the 1932 overthrow of the absolute monarchy, civilians dominated the first constitutional government. The military viewed itself as a democratic force in a supporting role until the 1933 coup. Thus a remarkable but often unacknowledged fact was the dominance of civilian supremacy or control at the founding moments throughout Asia.

But this was not to last. Countries that adopted the democratic pattern at their founding moments followed three different trajectories. India and Japan continued democratic civilian control. Countries following the second trajectory—Malaysia, Sri Lanka, and to a lesser degree

Singapore—continued to exhibit features of democratic civilian control, but over time ethnic considerations dominated the composition of the military as well as the basis for civilian control, moving civil-military relations firmly in the direction of subjective civilian control. Military or military-backed rule constituted the third trajectory, followed by Pakistan (1958), South Korea (1961), Burma (1958, 1962), Indonesia (1965), and Bangladesh (1975). The Philippine military was co-opted in support of authoritarian rule during the presidency of Ferdinand Marcos.

Of the countries that came under military or military-backed rule, the Philippines (1986), South Korea (1987), Taiwan (1987), Thailand (1973, 1992), Bangladesh (1991), and most recently Indonesia (1998) have moved toward the democratic pattern of civil-military relations. In this pattern, the military is subordinate to and takes its direction from the duly elected government of the day. The military's role, in large measure if not exclusively, is in the security realm. At the time of writing, democratic civilian control appears to be consolidating in Taiwan and South Korea, whereas the transition is still ongoing in the other countries. Thailand and Pakistan alternated between military control and weak or pseudo versions of democratic civilian control, with Thailand appearing to have escaped this pattern in the early 1990s. Thailand now appears set on the path of democratic civilian control, whereas Pakistan is still caught in the vicious circle. The transition to democratic civilian control in Bangladesh and Indonesia is still in an early phase. These two countries could well follow an alternation trajectory. Finally, Burma has continued to experience military rule since military reintervention in 1962.

Of the four countries that adopted the Leninist pattern, Communist Party control of the military continues to characterize civil-military relations in China and Vietnam. In Taiwan the Leninist pattern has been replaced by democratic civilian control, whereas civil-military relations in North Korea increasingly resemble those of a garrison state, with the Korean People's Army (KPA) dominating the state under the leadership of Kim Jong Il. A striking feature of these four countries is that although the military has been involved in politics, sometimes deeply in crushing political uprising or in intraparty factional struggles, there has not been a military coup d'état. The institutionalized military dominance in North Korea appears to be the closest to military intervention in politics in an Asian Leninist party state.

As shown in Figure 18.2, the number of countries adopting the democratic pattern of civil-military relations dropped from a high of eight in the early 1950s to two in the late 1970s and has since risen to eight at the time of writing. This number includes four countries—the Philippines, Thailand, Bangladesh, and Indonesia—that are still in the transition stage but excludes the three quasi-democracies—Sri Lanka, Malaysia, and Singapore—in which ethnic considerations form a key pillar of civilian control of the military. Military intervention and domination of politics reached a peak in Asia in the mid- to late 1970s and early 1980s when nine countries were under military or military-backed rule. During this period, the military played key roles even in countries such as China and North Korea that were not under military rule. At the time of writing only Burma and Pakistan are under military rule, and the KPA is playing a dominant role in North Korea. Leninist party control of the military has also declined from four countries in the 1950s to three in the 1990s if North Korea is still included in this category. Clearly, democratic civilian control of the military, after having reached a nadir in the 1970s and early 1980s, is now on the rise in Asia, and this trend appears likely to continue, although there could be temporary reversals.

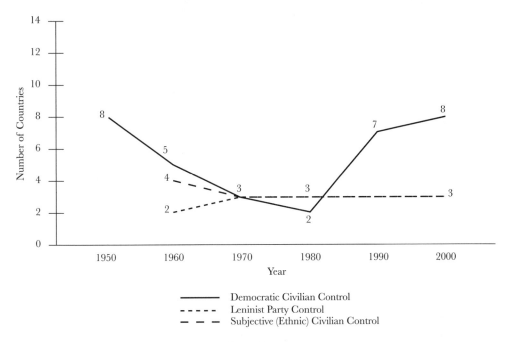

FIGURE 18.2.   Breakdown of Type of Civilian Control: 1950–2000.

EXPLAINING UNINTERRUPTED CIVILIAN CONTROL

Of the sixteen countries investigated in this study, uninterrupted civilian supremacy has characterized civil-military relations in seven countries: Japan, India, Malaysia, Singapore, Sri Lanka, China, and Vietnam. It is possible to argue that civilian control also characterized civil-military relations in the Philippines, Taiwan, and North Korea because none of them has been under military rule. In each case the military was under the control of a civilian dictator—Chiang Kai-shek and later Chiang Ching-kuo in Taiwan, Kim Il Sung and later Kim Jong Il in North Korea, and Ferdinand Marcos in the Philippines. However, with the possible exception of Kim Il Sung, military backing was essential for the survival of each one of these dictators, and the militaries were active participants in the political process, experiencing dramatic role expansion in the nonsecurity realm. As such they have been excluded from this group. Of the seven countries that have experienced uninterrupted civilian control, democratic civilian control has characterized civil-military relations in two, subjective (ethnic) control in three, and Leninist party control in the remaining two countries. Although the pattern of civil-military relations has not altered in these countries, the actual content has. In this section I detail and explain these changes, as well as the continuity in the pattern of civil-military relations.

Democratic Civilian Control: Japan and India

Japan and India have experienced dramatic political changes in the last decade. In both countries, dominant political parties—the Liberal Democratic Party (LDP) and the Indian National Congress (INC)—that controlled state power for much of the period until 1990 have weakened considerably, especially in India, where the Nehru-Gandhi dynasty that dominated the INC and ruled India with a firm hand for much of the first four decades appears to have collapsed. Dominant party governments in both countries have been replaced by frequently changing coalition governments. Notwithstanding these and other major political changes and challenges, democracy and democratic civilian control of the military have endured in both countries. The militaries remain subordinate to and take direction from the incumbent government, and their role has been confined to the security arena. The Indian military has internal and international security roles, but the Japanese military's security role is strictly international. Even there, its tasks and capacity are deliberately circumscribed. The security roles in both countries are carried out under the strict oversight of civilian authorities. There has been no role expansion. The two militaries have not participated in politics even during a national emergency such as that in India from 1975 to 1977, and they have not been engaged in socioeconomic roles or in organized illegal activities. Strict civilian oversight has been exercised over promotions, assignments, arms procurements, role and mission definition, and large-scale deployment.

Although the pattern of civil-military relations has remained unaltered, the basis for civilian control has changed over time, especially in Japan. In the 1950s the rationale for civilian control of the military in Japan was rooted in distrust of the military and fear of militarism, and the purpose of civilian control was to suppress or contain the military and prevent the revival of militarism. Civilian control then did not constitute democratic civilian control in the true meaning of the term. As a state institution, the Self-Defense Forces (SDF) lacked legitimacy, and its role was limited and kept unclear by design. The military was excluded from security policymaking, which was then dominated by the Gaimusho (Ministry of Foreign Affairs). Because political leaders refused to be associated with the military, civilian control translated into civilian bureaucratic domination.

From the mid-1970s, the rationale for civilian control began to shift from fear and antipathy toward the military to a relationship based on democratic principles. Though apprehension is still strong in some quarters, there is now much greater public support for the Japanese state and for the military as a legitimate state institution. The culture of pacifism and antimilitarism is still strong in Japan, but it is much less equated with antimilitary sentiments. The SDF's internal and international roles have been clarified and expanded, and the standing of the Defense Agency vis-à-vis other ministries and agencies has been elevated. There is now discussion of upgrading the Defense Agency to the level of a ministry. And civilian control has shifted from bureaucratic domination to control by elected political leaders who now set the security agenda and manage the policymaking process. The input of the SDF in security policymaking has grown and is beginning to resemble that in other democratic countries. The Gaimusho now interacts on more equal terms with the Defense Agency civilian officials and the military. With experience and greater confidence in the democratic system and process on the part of Japanese political leaders and the public, the mainstream view of the civil-military problem in Japan has shifted from containment of the military and prevention of the revival of militarism to definition of the proper role for the military in the context of the peace constitution (the revision of which is under discussion in Japan) and finding the right balance in reconciling democratic civilian control with military expertise.

In India too, the negative view of the "collaborationist" military and the discomfort with and neglect of the military in the early postindependence years have been transformed. It is useful to recall here that the Indian military, a British colonial institution, played no role in the long, nonviolent political struggle for independence that was led by highly legitimate and charismatic civilian leaders who were committed to a democratic system of government.[1] Uncomfortable with the military's colonial heritage and generally uneasy about powerful military establishments, the Indian political leadership took several measures immediately after independence to curtail the power and influence of the army and enhance civilian control of the military. These measures included abolishing the powerful position of commander in chief (traditionally held by the army chief) and strengthening the role of the civilian bureaucracy in the defense decision-making process. With a few exceptions, the INC leadership had little interest in and knowledge of military affairs. Hence civilian control of the military in India became increasingly dominated by the civilian bureaucracy.

Tainted by its colonial heritage and imbued with the British apolitical ethos, and in the context of powerful and charismatic political leadership and strong bureaucratic institutions, the Indian military not only willingly acknowledged civilian authority but in fact accepted a reduction in prestige and position vis-à-vis other state institutions. Over time, especially after several successful wars with Pakistan and despite and in some ways because of the devastating defeat in the 1962 war with China, the Indian military has emerged as a strong and respected national institution. However, as in Japan, the rehabilitation of the Indian military has not contributed to an increase in its political power and influence at the national level. This is all the more remarkable in light of the weakening of the political institutions at the center, the rise of violence in Indian domestic politics, and the consequent increase in the internal security role of the military and paramilitary forces.

Several analysts (Cohen 1990a; Ganguly 1991a; Dasgupta Chapter 3 this volume) have argued that the Indian political leadership and society have become militarized. They posit the prominent role of unelected civilian officials and the increasing internal security role of the military as troubling developments with potential to undermine democratic civilian control. Except for the internal security argument, we do not find the other claims persuasive. To begin with, major decisions of war and peace, and, more generally, security policy have always been made by Indian political leaders with input from civilian and military officials. Civilian bureaucrats and scientists may play a key role in influencing policy, as for example in the development of a nuclear capability, but ultimate jurisdiction lies with the political leadership. The cabinet and the parliament retain budgetary authority. The claim that the political leadership has become militarized also does not bear scrutiny.

Increasing reliance on the threat and use of force in the pursuit of national security, the acquisition of nuclear capability, and a substantial increase in defense spending may reflect growing realist behavior on the part of Indian political leaders. However, this does not constitute militarism or the erosion of democratic civilian control. It is pertinent to note here that concern with the growth of the military-industrial complex in the 1950s and 1960s led several observers to predict the development of a garrison state in the United States. This prediction did not materialize. There are many wrinkles in any democratic system, and the balance among political, civilian bureaucratic, and military institutions and leaders is likely to alter periodically. The key test, however, is whether the system has the flexibility, mechanisms, and procedures to check and correct the imbalances over time. This appears to be the case in India.

However, there is little doubt that the rise of political violence and the massive deployment of the military and paramilitary forces in the internal security role have eroded democracy and democratic civilian control of the military at the state and local levels in certain parts of India. Approximately 40 million people live under martial law, and appointed officials including retired military and police officers have at various times governed Kashmir, Punjab, Mizora, Manipur, and Assam. Emergency laws enacted in the name of national security have become numerous and permanent, eroding due process and the rule of law as well as other democratic rights of citizens. The blurring of the civil-military distinction and the abuse of state power by military and paramilitary personnel in carrying out their duties not only compromise democratic civilian control but also create tensions within the military, as well as between the military and paramilitary forces and with civilian bureaucrats. However, unlike the Sri Lankan military, which is waging a war against a Tamil secessionist movement, the Indian military operates under the tight control of the elected government and close scrutiny of civilian bureaucrats. Despite the growing internal security role and the many weaknesses of Indian political institutions and leaders, and the enhanced standing of the military as a national institution, democratic civilian control has in large measure endured in India.

Why has democratic civilian control endured in India and Japan while it collapsed in many other Asian countries? Explanations that focus exclusively or even primarily on the characteristics and interests of the military institution such as professionalism (a professional military is apolitical) and corporate interests (the military will intervene if its corporate interests are negatively affected) are of little help in explaining the persistence of democratic civilian control in these two countries. In the Indian case, the professionalism thesis has to reconcile strict democratic civilian control at the national level with erosion of the civil-military distinction at the local level. In the Japanese case the Imperial Army was highly professional but also political, whereas the post–World War II Japanese military is highly professional and apolitical. Professionalism has little to do with the apolitical nature of the postwar military in Japan, which is a function of the negative experiences and consequences of its earlier political role. Further, the change that is occurring in the basis for democratic civilian control in Japan cannot be explained by professionalism because the degree of professionalism of the post–World War II Japanese military has remained unaltered. Similarly, military nonintervention cannot be explained by the corporate interest thesis. Both militaries, especially the Indian military, believe strongly that their interests have been neglected by the civilian bureaucrats and successive elected governments. According to the corporate interest thesis, the Indian military should have intervened to advance its interests. But it has not.

Explanations that focus on the legitimacy of the nation-state and the political system, and the role of coercion in governance can better explain not only the continuation of democratic civilian control in both countries but also the changes that have occurred within this pattern. In postwar Japan, the legitimacy of the state and especially the military was suspect. Hence a series of political, constitutional, legal, and institutional measures were instituted to contain the military. Over time, the changes in the post–cold war international security environment as well as changes in domestic politics eroded the fear and antipathy toward the state and the military and altered the content of civil-military relations. Gradually a consensus has developed in Japan over the need for the SDF and the U.S.-Japan security arrangements. The consensus on defense and security matters became stronger in the 1990s in the wake of the demise of the LDP's political dominance and the emergence of a coalition government comprising the LDP, the Socialist Party, and a couple of centrist parties. The advent of coalition governments initially increased the power of the civilian bureaucrats, but in the mid-1990s the civilian bureaucracy became the object of much criticism for policy failures, scandals, and cover-ups, paving the way for greater political control of defense and security matters.

Concurrently, international developments—especially the Gulf War and the demand that Japan contribute "blood as well as treasure" in meeting its international obligations, the revision of the U.S.-Japan defense guidelines, which required substantial input from the SDF and Defense Agency officials, and the growing uncertainty in Japan's post–cold war security environment—demanded a wider security role for the SDF. Successful performance in its various international undertakings as well as its role in internal disaster relief operations further enhanced the standing of the SDF. Taken together these domestic and international developments elevated the standing of and confidence in the SDF, clarified its role, and increased political control over security matters and in the management of the SDF.

The democratic system of government has widespread legitimacy in Japan. Coercion plays no role in the acquisition and exercise of state power. Further, unlike in India, the Japanese nation-state, which has been in the making for a much longer period, is not the object of internal or international contestation. Because coercion plays no role in internal governance, the SDF's role is limited to the international realm in the context of the U.S.-Japan Security Treaty. The dramatic post–World War II economic development of democratic Japan, culminating in it becoming an economic superpower, has also contributed to the consolidation of democracy in that country. Although some frustration has emerged from the inability of governments to address the economic stagnation of the 1990s, there is little discontent with democracy itself. If anything, attempts have been made to correct the "imperfections" of Japanese democracy. Most certainly the military and coercion have not been viewed as legitimate means for overcoming the economic stagnation or the other challenges confronting the country. The net effect of the changes noted earlier and the widespread support for the democratic system of government has been movement toward a more normal democratic pattern of civil-military relations.

In the Indian case, state coercion has been deployed routinely and at times on a massive scale, but at base the Indian nation-state and the democratic political system, though relatively new, enjoy a high degree of legitimacy. Predictions of the collapse of the Indian nation-state have not materialized. On the contrary, a large segment of the population has come to identify with the Indian nation-state. The ideas underpinning the Indian nation-state have been challenged from time to time both at the center and in the periphery. Over time many of these challenges have been managed, though some acute challenges still remain. State coercion plays an important role in the management of such conflicts. Unlike the cases of Pakistan, Burma, and Indonesia, deployment of the military in the internal security role has not resulted in role expansion of the Indian military because it has been carried out under the control of a legitimate government that has the authority to amend or rescind that role. Further, although important, coercion is often accompanied by political negotiations and economic measures.

Equally important and in some ways even more fundamental is the widely held belief among the political elite, civil society, and the military leadership that despite its many drawbacks, democracy is the best form of government for a large, diverse, and complex country such as India. Despite the high level of political violence, the acquisition and exercise of state power in India is carried out in large measure through the ballot box and democratic institutions. The repeated acquisition of state power at the national and state levels over the past five decades through democratic elections, and its exercise primarily though not exclusively through noncoercive political and bureaucratic institutions has delegitimated other forms of government including autocratic and military rule. The ongoing devolution of power to regional states and to lower castes, while making for tensions and conflict over "who gets what," has strengthened identification with the Indian nation-state and the democratic system. Governing India at the best of times is extremely difficult, and independent India cannot be governed through coercion alone—as the military knows well from its involvement in the internal security role. The negative experiences of neighboring Pakistan and Bangladesh reinforce this view. Liberalization of the Indian economy that began in earnest in 1991, its more rapid growth since then, and its increasing integration into the global capitalist economy are likely to further consolidate the democratic system in that country and further tilt the distribution of power against the military and, also, away from the state. The normative structure and the balance of power in Japan and India clearly favor civilian supremacy. Thus the civil-military problem in both countries is not one of preventing military intervention but of reconciling civilian political and bureaucratic control with military expertise and interests at the national level. In the case of India the problem extends to managing the deployment of military and paramilitary forces in the internal security role without the abuse of state power and erosion of the principles associated with democratic civilian control.

Subjective Civilian Control: Malaysia, Singapore, and Sri Lanka

The militaries in Malaysia and Singapore continue to be subordinate to civilian authority, and their role in governance is limited to the security realm. With the termination of the communist insurgencies, external security has been their primary concern, although they also continue to have an internal security role to assist in the preservation of public order in situations beyond the control of the police force. Security policymaking including threat assessment in both countries is firmly under the control of civilian authorities. The military role is limited to providing professional advice. The militaries have no explicit socioeconomic role, and they do not engage in illegal activities. In Malaysia, the military has provided security for development (KESBAN) in remote areas. With the ongoing change in the structure of the Malaysian economy, even this development-related role has declined. In both countries promotions, assignments, budget allocation, arms procurement, and nonroutine troop deployment are all subject to civilian jurisdiction and oversight by the political executive and the civil service branches of government. The legislature and judiciary are only marginally involved. Military law in Malaysia and Singapore is embedded in and subordinate to the national legal system. Much of the foregoing also applies to Sri Lanka at the national level. However, in the north and east of the country, where the government is engaged in a war with the Liberation Tigers of Tamil Eelam (LTTE), the Sri Lankan military is barely subject to civilian political, legal, or administrative control. For the most part, the military is the government and the law unto itself in the areas under its control in the conflict zones. And in conjunction with some paramilitary forces that the government supports in the war against the LTTE, local military commanders have engaged in illegal activities to enrich themselves. An underground war economy and a culture of violence perpetrated by all sides in the conflict have grown up around the war. Civilian control has little or no meaning in the conflict zones.

Civilian control of the military in Malaysia, Singapore, and Sri Lanka (at the national level) is of the subjective genre. Ethnic considerations are paramount in the social composition of the military and in its subordination to civilian authority, especially in Malaysia and Sri Lanka. From its inception as a colonial force in 1933, the military in Malaysia has always been identified with the Malay community. In the postindependence period, the Malay character of the military along with other provisions—such as the special position of the Malay rulers (sultans), Islam, and the Malay language; Malay political dominance; and affirmative action for the Malays—came to be viewed by the Malay community as an entitlement and reflection of its special indigenous status and privileged position in the country. However, force did not have to be deployed to assert the special position of the Malay community until May 1969, when the election outcome and the events it precipitated were perceived by that community as threatening its privileged position. The military was deployed in the context of a national emergency declared to deal with the race riots that followed the election. For two years the country was governed by a National Operations Council with emergency powers vested in a chief executive—a Malay bureaucrat turned politician who at the time of the crisis was the deputy prime minister and later became the prime minister.

In the immediate aftermath of the May 1969 riots, the Malay community and political leadership came to view the military and the police force as a crucial though not sufficient basis on which to maintain Malay political dominance. The importance attached to the military and police forces was evident in the dramatic expansion of these two institutions and in their more pronounced Malay composition. Malays had always constituted a high percentage and held most key command positions in the police and especially the armed forces. This became even more pronounced in the post-1969 period. Since May 1969 the military and the police force have had an unstated role to uphold a Malay-dominated political system. However, since then it has not been necessary to resort to the threat or use of armed force to sustain Malay political dominance. That has become well entrenched through political and economic means.

In Singapore the subjective content in civil-military relations derives from the hegemonic position of the People's Action Party (PAP), which has dominated Singapore in terms of ideology as well as organizational, economic, and coercive power since 1959. The fusion of the party, state, and government complicates civil-military relations in that island city-state, raising questions about the purpose and basis for military loyalty to civilian authority. Is the military loyal to the PAP or to the incumbent government? In light of the dominant position of the PAP and the absence of credible alternatives, this question may appear esoteric. Nevertheless it is important. If the loyalty is to the PAP or to the Singaporean state as defined by the PAP, then the military can be expected to support and defend the dominant position of the PAP, as was the case in Taiwan where the military was loyal to the Kuomintang (KMT) well into the 1990s and opposed political parties that advocated Taiwan independence. However, unlike in Taiwan, there is no institutional connection between party and military in Singapore, and the military is not involved in political penetration and socialization of society. Further, the PAP itself has altered dramatically from its early days when it was led by "real" politicians with grassroots support. Today it is dominated by technobureaucratic elite in a political role, and the party has transformed itself into an election-winning machine. Nevertheless, the PAP is still the governing party, and the military, formed and shaped under the firm guidance of the early PAP leaders, is an integral part of the PAP-dominated political order. It is quite possible for the military to shift loyalty should there be a change in government, and such a shift may be less problematic than that which is occurring in Taiwan. For the moment, however, a change in government appears unthinkable (although no hegemonic party has remained in power forever). It is in this context that it is possible to argue that there is a strong subjective dimension to civil-military relations in Singapore.

Despite the subjective nature of civilian control, the militaries in Malaysia and Singapore have not been involved in the politics or the administration of their respective countries. Why has this been the case? Though not irrelevant, purely institutional and congruence of interest explanations obscure the more important political and ideational considerations that have shaped civil-military relations in these two countries.

Though there is some dissatisfaction, especially in minority communities, the nation-state and the political system as presently constituted are not objects of violent challenge in either country. The last violent resistance ended with the termination of the communist insurgency threat. Based on the principle of Malay dominance, Malaysia has a widely accepted system and institutions for the acquisition and exercise of state power. Since independence, governments in Malaysia have had a high degree of legitimacy, and they have been effective in delivering public goods and raising the living standards of the people (Case 1995). In Singapore too, despite misgivings, the political system and government enjoy a high degree of legitimacy (Khong 1995). The PAP has performed well. The high degree of legitimacy bolstered by sustained high rates of economic growth have also strengthened the noncoercive institutions of the state, allowing governments in the two countries to limit and deploy coercion in a selective manner to intimidate and suppress dissidents and the opposition.

State coercion is an important feature of governance in both countries. The police force and its intelligence apparatus have been deployed by incumbents to buttress their positions and to emasculate opposition leaders and dissidents. However, the application of state coercion is rooted in legal provisions such as the internal security act, with enforcement undertaken by the legal arm of government and the Special Branch of the police force. The military has been excluded from the exercise of internal political coercion. Further, while important and visible, coercion is not the mainstay of governance in these two countries.

Although keen to ensure the Malay-ness and loyalty of the armed forces, the United Malays National Organization (UMNO) leadership has been careful to keep the military out of politics and counterbalance the brute power of the armed forces with a relatively strong police field force. The military's internal role has been limited to fighting (along with the police field force) insurgencies under civilian direction, providing security for development, and assisting the police in preserving public order. Even these limited roles, as noted earlier, have declined in salience. In Singapore too, while the PAP government has actively developed an effective war machine to ensure the survival of that country in a Malay sea, government policies have effectively marginalized the military. A new challenge for civil-military relations in Malaysia could arise from intra-Malay political struggle—a relatively recent development. A key basis for military subordination to civilian authority is rooted in the principle of Malay dominance. It could well be that the intra-Malay struggle does not matter as long as the incumbent government is legitimate and Malay dominated. The military will take its direction from that government. However, the situation can alter dramatically if the military is drawn into the struggle and begins to take sides. Thus far this has not been the case.

In contrast to Malaysia, civil-military relations in Sri Lanka at the outset of independence were not rooted in ethnic considerations. Over time, however, with the growth of Sinhala-Buddhist nationalism and ethnicization of politics, and political interference by the Sri Lanka Freedom Party (SLFP) and the United Nationalist Party (UNP) to correct the ethnic imbalance in the military as well as to use the military for partisan politics, the Sri Lankan military has been transformed into an institution committed to constructing and upholding a Sinhala-dominated nation-state and political system. The ethnicization of Sri Lankan politics and government resulted in discrimination against the minority Tamil community that escalated over time to the level of a pogrom. Eventually this led to an armed insurrection, with the LTTE fighting for a separate homeland for the Tamil community. Instead of seeking a political solution, successive governments sought a military victory. Military force and other means of coercion became the mainstay of the government approach to the conflict in the north and east of the island-state. The military became deeply engaged in internal security, prosecuting an "ethnic" war against the LTTE.

The change in the basis for civilian control and the increasing prominence of coercion in governance in certain regions of the country had little effect on civil-military relations at the national level, where the leading political parties and successive governments were and are all Sinhala dominated. The military continues to be subordinate and accountable to the democratically elected government of the day. However, even at the national level, civilian perception of the military is not uncontroversial. Though the military has been lionized by some Sinhala groups, its image has been tarnished in the eyes of civil society through the exposure of corruption in high ranks, the high profile trials for rape and harassment of women in the conflict zones, its brutal suppressions of the Janatha Vimukthi Youth in the late 1980s, and its inability to bring the war against the LTTE to a successful conclusion.

In the conflict zones, however, civilian authority barely exists. Coercion has become the primary means of governance and resistance. Government reliance on coercion, its lack of effective control over the military in the persecution of the conflict, and its virtual abdication of responsibility has increased the power and influence of the military, which is the de facto government in the conflict zones. To complicate matters, the military, which does not have a monopoly of violence in the conflict zones, has condoned and supported the proliferation of nongovernment paramilitary groups that support the war against the LTTE. Further, along with paramilitary groups and the LTTE, it engages in illegitimate violence against the civilian population and profits from the political economy that has developed along with the war. The emphasis on military means and the ruthless behavior of the armed forces have further alienated the Tamil community, increasing its disenchantment with the Sinhala-dominated state.

To summarize, in Malaysia and Singapore the nation-state and the quasi-democratic dominant party political systems enjoy a relatively high degree of legitimacy, although they may not be to the complete satisfaction of all groups. State coercion is deployed in both countries to enforce authority in certain situations, but such coercion is selectively employed and is not the mainstay of governance. Governments have repeatedly acquired power by conforming to the rules of the political system. Their legitimacy has been bolstered by sustained high levels of economic development, which have further strengthened the noncoercive capacity of the state in dealing with internal problems. Consequently the military's primary role is in external security, and here too, policymaking is firmly in the hands of civilian authority. In contrast, the legitimacy of the nation-state and the political system in Sri Lanka, although accepted by the majority Sinhala community, is rejected by a large segment of the discriminated-against minority Tamil community and violently contested by an active and militant segment of that community. Coercion has become the mainstay of government policy in dealing with the political problem in the north and east of the country, contributing to military role expansion and domination in the conflict zones.

Communist Party Control: China and Vietnam

The militaries in China and Vietnam continue to submit to and protect the hegemonic position of their respective communist parties. The role of the People's Liberation Army (PLA) in crushing the 1989 Tiananmen protest and consolidating the position of the Chinese Communist Party (CCP), and the continuing support of the Vietnam People's Army (VPA) for the hegemonic position of the Vietnamese Communist Party (VCP) in the context of *doi moi* and the perceived threat of "peaceful evolution" demonstrate the loyalty of the PLA and the VCP to their respective communist parties. However, the basis for and nature of party control, as well as the scope of military participation in governance, have altered substantially over time.

Liberation armies played a crucial role in the success of the revolutions in both countries. The PLA was the linchpin of the military-rural strategy that ultimately led to CCP victory over Japan and the KMT in the battlefields, and the establishment of the PRC in 1949 (Ting 1982; Dreyer 1982; Shambaugh 1997). Enjoying enormous authority and power in the immediate aftermath of its victory over the Nationalist forces, the PLA controlled local government in large parts of China. Because the CCP had not yet developed the capacity and mechanisms for administering the country, the PLA undertook not only the management of political and civil affairs but also socioeconomic functions. Contrary to popular belief at the time that the PLA would not relinquish its regional levers of power and that China would revert to some form of regional warlordism, power was smoothly transferred from military to civilian (CCP) organs by 1954, demonstrating that the PLA was an integral part of the CCP and subordinate to its political leadership (Joffe 1982).

Three key reasons accounted for the PLA acceptance of the supremacy of the party. First, the PLA was a creation of the party and it shared with the CCP the same personnel pool. In the early years there was little role differentiation between top civilian and military leaders, making for what has been termed the "dual role elite" (Perlmutter and LeoGrande 1982). Second, the dual role elite firmly believed in the principle of central party control—a commitment born out of nationalism that had animated all Chinese communist leaders and was buttressed by their indoctrination, training, and experience (Joffe 1982). As argued by Ting (1982) and Shambaugh (1997), an essential symbiosis existed between party and military in the pursuit of state power. Third, the highly legitimate CCP under the leadership of the charismatic Mao Zedong as well as other long-march veterans relatively quickly developed the organizational capacity to enforce its control over the PLA through an elaborate system of party committees, political commissars, and political departments that ran parallel to the military chain of command (Cheng 1990a).

It is possible to argue that although the PLA had a commissar system and a system of party organization to control the military, under Mao and later also under Deng, it was not the party but the supreme leader who had effective control over the military. The military reported only to the Military Affairs Commission, which in turn reported only to Mao. In situations of political crisis the military was the power base that Mao relied on to consolidate his position, as for example during the Cultural Revolution. Hence Mao's regime was in fact a quasi-military regime (Nathan 1997). Under Deng too, the PLA remained largely independent, reporting only to the Military Affairs Commission chaired by him. Retaining control over the commission even after he gave up his positions in the party and the state, Deng deployed the military to crush the prodemocracy forces that almost toppled his regime in 1989.

Military conflict and victory were also central to the success of the Vietnamese liberation struggles against the Japanese, the French, and later the Americans. As in China, Vietnamese political agitation against French colonial rule preceded the military struggle that began during the turmoil engendered by Japanese occupation. Like its Chinese counterpart, the Vietnamese military was a creation of and firmly wedded to the political objectives and strategies of the VCP (Pike 1987b; Turley 1982, 1988; Thayer 1985). VPA leaders at the founding moment and through the first and second wars of national liberation were senior party officials who wore two hats and had no difficulty integrating political and military objectives. Politicomilitary doctrines such as *drau tranh* (armed struggle), people's war, and united front—developed by senior party leaders such as Ho Chi Minh, Le Duan, and Vo Ngyuen Giap, who had no formal military training—blurred the distinction between civilian and military leadership and responsibilities and legitimized the army's political, economic, and security roles (Pike 1987b; Turley 1982).

There was considerable overlap between the top posts in the party political bureau and the army high command. The political generals did not subscribe to the civil-military dichotomy or an apolitical military. As the most cohesive and well-organized institution, the VPA, after its 1954 victory, was assigned economic construction and production tasks. With the onset of the second Indochina war, it was assigned the mission of liberating South Vietnam and unifying the country. The VCP leadership wanted a professional army but also a political one under the control of the party. From the outset, the VPA had a political orientation and role. However, because the VPA was founded by the VCP, with high-ranking party officials as its first general officers, the military was not a separate institution with a distinctive political outlook. Instead it was fused with the party and assigned a position subordinate to the political leadership.

Thus from the outset, an organic approach that views the military as an integral component designed to ensure the hegemonic position of the party dominated communist Chinese and Vietnamese thinking about civil-military relations. Military subordination to the Communist Party in both countries rested on ideological and nationalist foundations. Marxism-Leninism provided the ideological justification for the party-state system and the hegemonic position of the party in that system; Chinese and Vietnamese nationalism provided the unify-

ing purpose and rationale for the liberation struggle against foreign aggression and the feu-
dalistic KMT in the case of China. These foundations were reinforced by several other considerations: a charismatic political leadership that had successfully prosecuted the liberation
struggle; the political prominence of the dual role elite who occupied senior positions in the
party and the military, and their belief in the supremacy of the party; and the dual control system that enabled party control of the military through penetration of the military chain of
command. Over time, however, the basis for party control of the military and the content of
military participation in governance have altered substantially, particularly in China.

The idiosyncratic and ideational foundations that underscored party-military relations in
that country have become diluted or irrelevant. Of consequence for the hegemonic position of
the party and by extension party-military relations is generation change in both party and military leadership. Charismatic leaders such as Mao Zedong and Deng Xiaoping who commanded enormous personal authority emerged from a unique set of circumstances. Despite
efforts to cultivate the aura of supreme leader, it appears unlikely that party leaders, now and
in the foreseeable future, can achieve a standing comparable to that of Mao and Deng. Exercise of authority increasingly is contingent on positions held in the party or the state, and the
material rewards the leaders can dispense. The dual role elite that was central to symbiosis of
the party and the military also has passed from the scene. Contemporary Chinese political and
military leaders have become more specialized in their vocation, and in the absence of shared
experiences, the military has emerged as a distinct institution, quite separate from the party.

On the ideological front, Marxism-Leninism has been challenged and eroded by several
developments: the transition to a market economy and integration of the Chinese economy
into the global capitalist economy, the political and economic transformations in the Soviet
Union and Eastern European socialist bloc that accompanied their domino-like collapse, the
near hegemonic status of democracy and capitalism in the international normative structure,
and the growing prominence of these values in U.S. and European foreign and economic policies. In addition to invalidating a key characteristic of the party-state system, the transformation of the Chinese economy and its integration into the global capitalist economy require specialized knowledge and a complex set of institutions, policies, and personnel that are
increasingly beyond the capacity of the CCP. They require the development of specialized state
institutions and their separation from the party, undermining the CCP's claim to moral and
intellectual leadership.

The successes of economic liberalization and the stability that has characterized China in
the post-Tiananmen period in stark contrast to the turmoil in Russia have in some ways
strengthened the CCP. However, the inequity and abuses, especially by party members, that
accompanied economic liberalization have also tainted it. The claim to legitimacy for the party-
state system and the hegemonic position of the CCP have shifted to political stability, economic
development, and nationalism (preventing "splittism," unifying China, standing up to the West
and the United States in particular, and raising the international power and position of the
PRC). Material and instrumental considerations, not moral and intellectual leadership, have
become the mainstay for maintaining party dominance.

These developments have eroded but not transformed the dominant position of the party
in the party-state system, and party control of the military. However, instrumental loyalty is less
reliable than that rooted in a strong ideological commitment. Party leaders cannot take mili-

tary subordination and political support on their behalf for granted. They have to build support within the military as well as cater to its needs, while simultaneously seeking to control it. To enhance party control, especially in the wake of the Tiananmen protest, the party leadership has attempted to reinvigorate the political work system in the military (Shambaugh 1991). The relationship and interaction between party and military, and more generally political decision making in China, have become less personalized and more bureaucratic, with the military making its input through the committees in which it is represented.

In terms of the scope of participation in governance, the PLA continues to be a force in political domination, although its profile in high-level party committees has declined (presently the military has no representation in the Politburo Standing Committee) and its nonsecurity role has become more circumscribed. The military has played and is likely to continue to play a critical role in leadership change as long as the process is not institutionalized. This role will be more crucial in situations in which succession is characterized by factional struggle. The PLA may also rally behind the party to crush dissidents and protests as it did in 1989. However, when compared to earlier periods, like the Cultural Revolution, the military has been much less visible in the political arena in the 1990s. The PLA has no major role in social or economic policymaking, which would appear to be increasingly beyond the expertise of the PLA. The exception is the commercial sphere where, by design, its participation escalated quite dramatically in the 1980s and 1990s. Even in this area a serious effort is now underway to divest the military of its business enterprises. The manner in which the divestiture was initiated, the wrangling over "proper" compensation, the relatively slow progress in decommercializing the military, and the tension this effort has created are reflective of the new, more instrumental and bureaucratic character of Chinese civil-military interaction.

Security policymaking is one area where military influence in decision making appears to have increased, although this is difficult to establish. The apparent increase in military influence could well be genuine, forcing civilian leaders to take a more hard-line position than they otherwise would. Alternatively, the assertive Chinese position may reflect the common hard-line position of the civilian and military leaders, in which case the claim of increased influence would not hold. Nevertheless, ultimate jurisdiction on key security issues such as Taiwan appears to lie with the senior party leader (Swaine 2000). On the issue of institutional autonomy, unlike in earlier periods, military leaders have not been able to resist civilian membership (other than the supreme leader) in the Central Military Commission. Overall, in the last decade or so, there would appear to have been a decrease in the political power and influence of the military and a reduction of its nonsecurity role in governance.

In Vietnam, however, the VPA's political profile appears to have become more prominent in the 1990s. The VCP has been relatively more successful than the CCP in renewing its legitimacy at the leadership and societal levels (Vasavakul 1995). When faced with a chronic economic crisis arising from the failure of its socialist model in the mid-1980s—exacerbated by its entanglement in Cambodia and change in Soviet policy—the VCP, invoking the ideology of Ho Chi Minh in support of its policy of renovation *(doi moi)* that it launched in 1986, redefined socialism. Concurrently, an effort was made to strengthen the state apparatus and the National Assembly and also to co-opt intellectuals and moderate opposition members. However, the VCP resisted political reform, especially multiparty competition for state power. Seeking to continue its monopoly of power in the wake of the crisis and collapse in the socialist bloc and facing the threat of "peaceful evolution" from the West, the VCP cracked down on opposition.

The VPA rallied behind the VCP, strongly endorsing and seeking to perpetuate one-party rule. In contrast to earlier periods when its focus was almost exclusively on liberation, unification, and external defense, beginning in the early to mid-1990s the domestic arena has commanded more attention. The VPA was in the forefront in developing a plan to counter the perceived threat of peaceful evolution. Earlier the VPA also took a lead role in implementing *doi moi* and in the process substantially expanded its economic base and role. Through its support for the VCP during the political crisis in the socialist bloc and expanding its economic role under *doi moi* in the name of defense and development, the VPA, which has always been central to state building in that county, appears to have strengthened its position in the Vietnamese political system. It has become a key force in shaping the contemporary political and economic order in Vietnam.

With the ideological and idiosyncratic foundations for party control of the military undermined, the continuation of party control in China and Vietnam can now be explained only in material-institutional terms. Despite the erosion of legitimacy, there is no alternative to the communist parties, which continue to be the most powerful political organizations in both countries. The significance of state institutions is growing, especially in China, but those institutions are still dominated at the higher echelons by party leaders. Although the militaries are politically important, they also have been tarnished. They do not have the moral high ground, power, or interest to undermine the dominant position of the communist parties. Further, the militaries are incapable of managing the increasingly complex economies that face huge challenges of change. The Western international community, which actively promotes democracy and human rights, will react negatively to a military takeover. More importantly there is no compelling reason—political or corporate—for military intervention. Institutional channels exist for the PLA and the VPA to participate in politics and policymaking as well as to pursue their corporate interests. Continuation of the present arrangements is thus in the best interests of the party and the military. Not only do both stand to lose from a rupture of these arrangements, there is also the prospect of instability that could plunge their countries into chaos. Control on the basis of congruence of interests, however, is less durable and more prone to change.

Summary

Discussion in this section of the continuation of civilian control supports the main proposition that in countries in which coercion is not the mainstay of governance, the influence and role of the military will be limited and civilian supremacy will prevail. Even in situations where state coercion is deployed on a massive scale, military role expansion will be limited if the incumbent government enjoys a high degree of legitimacy and the use of coercion is limited to specific purposes, controlled by civilian agencies, and accompanied by political and socioeconomic policies to address the problem or issue of concern. Coercion is not a factor in governance in Japan. It has, in varying degrees, been more prominent in the other countries—in suppressing challenges to the incumbent rulers as, for example, during the Cultural Revolution and in the Tiananmen uprising in China, and in the quelling of the May 1969 race riots in Malaysia. Coercion has also been prominent in dealing with separatist movements in India, Sri Lanka, and China. However, except for the situations in China during the Cultural Revolution and the 1989 popular protest, in every other case state coercion has been deployed by governments not to consolidate their position but in the pursuit of public goals and interests. Even in such situations, if civilian authority is absent at the local level or if the exercise of state coercion is not overseen by civilian authority, then it can lead to an increase in the power and influence of the military at the local level, as has been the case in Sri Lanka and, to a lesser degree, in India. The keys are legitimacy of the nation-state and the political system, the capacity of the state to manage the challenges confronting it through political and socioeconomic measures, and limitation of the recourse to coercion. The type of political system itself does not matter. Civilian control has endured (and failed) not only in democracies but also in quasi-democracies and Leninist political systems. In countries where coercion becomes the mainstay of governance, the political power and influence of the military rises, leading to the erosion and loss of civilian control.

SURGE OF MILITARY REGIMES

In the remaining nine countries investigated in this study, the political power and influence of the military increased substantially. All these countries came under military rule or military-backed authoritarian or totalitarian rule. In Thailand, Pakistan, Burma, Indonesia, South Korea, and Bangladesh the military seized political power. In the remaining three countries—Taiwan, the Philippines, and North Korea—the militaries did not seize political power, but they were an integral part and a key pillar of the authoritarian and totalitarian governments. In every case, the scope and jurisdiction of military participation in governance experienced dramatic expansion.

Why was there a surge of military and military-backed regimes in these countries? The explanation of the professionalism thesis would be that these militaries intervened because they were not professional or became less professional. There is no evidence of declining professionalism. The fact was that some militaries such as those in Burma, Indonesia, and Bangladesh, given their guerrilla and revolutionary origins, were not professional in the Huntingtonian sense. Other militaries such as those in Pakistan, South Korea, and Taiwan were relatively more professional, with combat experience in major international and/or internal wars. On the counts of expertise and corporateness, they ranked equal or even higher than the militaries of countries such as Malaysia and Singapore where civilian supremacy has been the norm. However, a high level of professionalism did not prevent the Pakistani, South Korean, and Taiwanese militaries from becoming politicized. As argued in the Pakistan, Bangladesh, and Thailand chapters in this volume, the corporate interest argument may be relevant in some situations. However, corporate interest is a supplementary or reinforcing factor, not the fundamental driving force for initial military intervention. If it were, the Indian military, as noted earlier, should have intervened. Similarly, the Japanese military, which until quite recently could have perceived itself as unfairly treated, did not intervene. Corporate interests may become more salient once military role expansion has occurred and the military has a privileged position, as for example in Pakistan after the mid-1950s, Indonesia after 1958, and Burma after 1962. Attempts to rein in the military in such situations can produce a negative reaction from the military and provide the rationale for military reintervention.

The institutional imbalance argument would appear to have greater merit in explaining the surge of military regimes. According to this thesis, the weak political and administrative institutions of the new states could not cope with the political, social, and economic mobilization and demands unleashed by independence and a democratic system of government. The mismatch between demand and delivery created political instability, undermining the legitimacy of civilian political leaders and institutions and leading to role expansion and intervention by the military. In these countries the military was by far the most organized and cohesive state institution that was also committed to national modernization and development.

However, the institutional imbalance explanation suffers two critical weaknesses. First, at the outset of independence the military was not a strong institution in many countries. Compared to the civilian leaders who waged the political struggle against colonial rule and who succeeded to state power upon independence, the military leaders had little or no national or international standing. Further, in several countries the military was a weak, disunited, faction-ridden, regionally organized guerrilla organization. The question then is how did the military subsequently become a strong institution able to overpower civilian institutions? The answer to this question is rooted in the growing reliance of political leaders on state coercion to maintain their hold on state power. The second shortcoming is that institutional explanations obscure the political origins and nature of many militaries, the factional struggles within the political and military elite, the cross-institutional linkages, and the role of international actors, all of which contributed to military role expansion and intervention. Not infrequently, military role expansion and intervention was a consequence of the congruent interests and alignment of conservative political leaders with politicized and ambitious military leaders, both of whom had little or no interest in the development of democratic institutions of government. In other words, it was not simply that one set of institutions (civilian) was weak and failed, and another set (military) was strong and development oriented. An array of internal and international factors that over time strengthened certain sections of the military and political elite while weakening others paved the way for military role expansion and eventual domination of politics or military-backed authoritarian rule. But even this fails to explain why the military and not some other institution, for example the civilian bureaucracy, became stronger and played the lead role in the seizure of political power.

The military developed into a strong institution because of the increasing centrality of its key asset—coercion—in the governance of these countries in the early years. Coercion became predominant for a number of reasons: the concern of incumbent rulers with regime security and their effort to suppress competing elite; suppression of domestic—regional and ideological—threats to the unity of the country from groups that resorted to organized violence to achieve their political ends; and coping with international military threats to state survival. The key point is that the incumbent rulers came to view and rely on state coercion as crucial for their own survival as well as for the internal and international security of their states. Consequently they allocated a large portion of state resources to the armed forces and increased its scope and jurisdiction in governance—not just in the security realm but in others as well. The military grew in size and effectiveness. In the process it became more unified and efficient, reaching into all parts of the country. Gradually it took on administrative and developmental tasks, creating an image of the military within the armed forces and in the public at large as having the potential to build the new state and to act as the guardian of the nation-state. The role expansion of the military crowded out civilian institutions, which progressively became weaker. Concurrently the military ventured into business activities—often rent-seeking in nature—for corporate reasons (to supplement the military budget) as well as for personal enrichment. The military developed a vested interest in preserving the status quo that privileged it. This story or versions of it based on the centrality of coercion in governance, I believe, best explains the surge of military regimes in Asia from the mid-1950s through the mid-1970s.

Military Control of State Power

The above story holds up well in explaining military intervention and subsequent domination of politics in Pakistan, Burma, Indonesia, Bangladesh, South Korea, and, to a lesser degree, in Thailand. In this section, I first provide empirical support for the claim regarding the military seizure of power. This is followed by a discussion of how the military, once in power, sought to eliminate all opposition and perpetuate its hold on power.

Military Intervention.   Pakistan, Burma, Indonesia, Bangladesh, and South Korea were all born with acute internal and/or international security problems. Thailand, too, was confronted with international threats to its survival in the mid- to late nineteenth century. In nearly every case coercion became crucial for preserving the unity of the state and protecting it from internal and external threats, leading to a rapid expansion of the military and paramilitary forces. However, such expansion by itself did not lead to military intervention. It was the declining legitimacy of incumbent rulers and their increasing reliance on state coercion that increased the political and administrative power and influence of the armed forces, culminating in military intervention.

Pakistan was born with an acute insecurity syndrome that has only gotten worse over the years. Concerned with a serious threat to national identity and integrity from India and Afghanistan, the early Pakistani governments allocated a very high percentage of national revenues to the military, leading to a rapid expansion of the armed forces, which, contrary to popular belief, was not a strong institution at independence (Shafqat 1997). The expansion in the size and capability of the armed forces was considerably boosted by Pakistan's alliance with the United States through its membership in the Southeast Asia Treaty Organization (SEATO) and Central Treaty Organization (CENTO). Yet, rapid expansion to cope with internal and international security threats by itself would not have led to an increase in the political power and influence of the military.

Military role expansion and intervention in Pakistan came about because of the deliberate actions of a civilian-military elite that sought to exclude elected political leaders from power and hinder the development of democratic institutions (Rizvi 1985; Shafqat 1997). After the early death of the charismatic Mohd Ali Jinnah in 1949 and the assassination of his deputy Liaquat Ali Khan in 1951, Pakistan was confronted with a serious leadership crisis (Rizvi 1991). And the Muslim League, unlike the National Congress Party in India, was not mass based and was unable to transform itself into a governing party. The party splintered after the death of Jinnah. Under Ghulam Mohammad and Iskandar Mizra, who dominated the political scene after the death of Liaquat, the civil bureaucratic–military elite came to form the core of Pakistan's power structure. The rapidly expanding military colluded with the civilian bureaucratic elite and conservative politicians to deliberately undermine democratic norms and processes with intent to secure a hegemonic position in the country (Shafqat 1997). From the early 1950s, the military was drawn into political and economic planning and decision making. Faced with the prospect of an election that could undermine his position, President Mizra declared martial law in 1958 and appointed Gen. Ayub Khan as the Chief Martial Law Administrator. Since then, Pakistan has been under military rule from 1958 though 1971, 1977 through 1988, and 1999 through the time of writing.

Burma, too, was confronted with acute security problems at independence—more internal than international. It was plunged into a civil war immediately after independence. It also had to cope with the threat posed by the KMT presence in that country, the ideological cum military threat posed by the Communist Party of Burma, and the threat of disintegration arising from the autonomy demands of its numerous minority communities. As in Pakistan, coercion gradually became the mainstay of government, contributing to an increase in the political power and influence of the military. Unlike in Pakistan, where a professional military became politicized, in Burma the military was politicized from the outset because of its role in the independence struggle. It did, however, accept civilian control at independence out of conviction as well as expediency.

At independence the Tatmadaw (Burmese military) was a weak and faction-ridden force. However, because of its law and order responsibilities in central Burma, its role in fighting minorities, insurgents, and the KMT force in the periphery, and the large budget allocation for defense, by the late 1950s the Tatmadaw had become a relatively cohesive and strong institution reaching into all parts of the country (Taylor 1985). Role expansion occurred steadily in the 1950s as the military took administrative control of many districts after the 1948–1952 civil war. The military engaged in a variety of "civic action" projects in direct competition with civilian authorities, and by the mid-1950s it became quite independent of them. The civilian authorities, on the other hand, because of the civil war and conflict with the minorities as well as the ideological and personality splits among themselves, relied increasingly on the military to sustain their power. With the final split of the Anti-Fascist People's Freedom League in 1958, which also threatened to split the army and plunge the country into another civil war, the military convinced Prime Minister U Nu to hand power to a military caretaker government under Gen. Ne Win; that arrangement lasted for eighteen months.

Military role expansion in the political and security sectors became well entrenched during this period. The Defense Service Institute expanded rapidly, becoming the "most powerful business organization in the country," adding an economic dimension to military role expansion (Walinsky quoted in Taylor 1985). The Tatmadaw increasingly came to see itself as the guardian of the Burmese nation-state and as the key institution with responsibility to maintain the unity and integrity of Burma. This belief and related concerns were the primary motivating factors of the 1962 bloodless coup against the U Nu government. The military perceived U Nu's policies to make Buddhism the official state religion and to increase the number and powers of minority states as threatening the unity and integrity of the country, which they had forged with much blood in the preceding decade.

Like the Burmese military, the Indonesian military, which has its origins in the revolutionary struggle against Dutch colonial rule, had a political orientation from the outset. The revolutionary struggle in Indonesia was as much military as political, and the military units played a key role in the success of the revolution.[2] Despite its key role and its distrust of the political leadership, the Tentera Nasional Indonesia (TNI) submitted to civilian control at the time of independence in 1949.[3] But the military soon became disenchanted with the democratic model of civil-military relations and sought an expanded role embodied in the doctrine of the Middle Way. However, the military did not seek to dominate politics. This was never its goal until a series of unanticipated developments propelled it into the political helm in 1965. Military intrusion, role expansion, and eventual domination of politics were a function of the coercion-intensive nature of nation building in the 1949–1963 period, the declining legitimacy of the parliamentary system adopted at independence, Sukarno's personal ambitions, Sukarno's initial reliance on the military to abrogate the parliamentary system of government and to replace it with the system of Guided Democracy under which the military emerged as a key political force, and the subsequent attempt by Sukarno to outmaneuver the army by creating divisions with it and by establishing an alliance with the Partai Kommunis Indonesia (PKI).

Indonesia, like so many of the postcolonial Asian states, was an artificial construction.[4] The military played a key role in preserving the unitary character of Indonesia that was challenged almost immediately after the formal transfer of sovereignty in 1949. Although most leaders and peoples subscribed to the idea of a unitary Indonesia, there was resistance in some regions, especially in Eastern Indonesia, where in April 1950 an independent Republic of South Moluccas was proclaimed. This and other such resistance were crushed by the Indonesian army, which also conducted military operations against the Darul Islam revolt in Western Java. More regional rebellions broke out in the mid-1950s.[5] The regional crisis grew more serious in March 1957 with the proclamation of martial law by the regional military commander for East Indonesia. The situation was further aggravated by the setting up of a rebel government in Sumatra by the so-called revolutionaries under the name Pemerintah Revolusioner Republik Indonesia. The latter was supported by the Permesta rebels, and it also had the clandestine support of the United States. The whole nation was falling apart. At the urging of the military, President Sukarno declared nationwide martial law, placing the military in charge of dealing with the regional rebellions. The military acted decisively, and by mid-1958 the situation was brought under control. The military also played a key role in the liberation of West Irian,[6] the one territory that the Dutch did not transfer in 1949.

The key role of the military in crushing these resistances and preserving the unitary character of Indonesia had several consequences. First, the military became a more unified and stronger institution. The dismissal of rebellious regional military commanders in 1958 facilitated the development of a more unified armed forces with an integrated command structure that reached into all parts of the country. The military, however, was still far from a well-organized, disciplined, and cohesive body. Second, the experience reinforced the TNI's contempt for democratic civilian control and its belief in a broader role that would later become codified and legalized in the doctrine of *dwifungsi*. Third, it reinforced the military's self-image and role as the guardian of the nation-state it helped to create—an image that was forged during the revolution.

Concurrent with and, in part, precipitating the regional challenges to the unitary character of the Indonesian state was the political struggle in Jakarta. The frequent collapse of cabinets (seven cabinets in as many years) and their inability to satisfy political, status, and material expectations undermined the credibility of the parliamentary democratic system among a large segment of the Indonesian elite. Dissatisfied with his figurehead position in the 1950 constitution, President Sukarno did not subscribe to the parliamentary system. With the legitimacy of the liberal democratic system in decline and the growing atmosphere of crisis in the country, Sukarno's advocacy of national solidarity and *konsepsi* (democracy with leadership) had wide appeal, including in the military. Although it had initially supported the democratic governments, for a number of reasons, including its diminished position after 1952, the military became hostile to the civilian politicians. The alliance of Sukarno and the army proved to be formidable, leading to the replacement of the democratic system based on the 1950 constitution, with Guided Democracy under the leadership of a powerful president as provided for in the 1945 constitution.

The military's political and economic role expanded considerably in the Guided Democracy era (1959–1965), during much of which a nationwide martial law was in effect. As observed by Harold Crouch (1985: 56–59), military officers unambiguously entered the political elite, with the armed forces playing direct roles in the government and administration of the country. In addition to making up the bulk of Sukarno's supreme decision-making body, military officers filled many key positions at the national and provincial levels. They were also appointed as members of the national and regional legislatures. Military officers entered the economic elite as well. Military involvement in business increased sharply under martial law, with a major expansion occurring with the nationalization of Dutch enterprises in 1957. Such involvement was in support of the military as an institution (securing additional funds for the military) as well as for personal enrichment. The net effect of military participation in governance during the Guided Democracy era was to make it a strong institution and a key political and economic force.

The marriage of convenience between Sukarno and the military quickly came to an end as Sukarno sought to counterbalance the growing power of the military by creating his own support base within the military and relying more on the PKI. Although still keen to preserve good relations with the president, the military opposed Sukarno's effort to create his own support base in the armed forces and to foster the rise of the PKI, which it perceived as presenting an ideological threat to the nation as well as a threat to its own position. Occurring in the context of rapidly deteriorating economic conditions and political chaos, the Sukarno-TNI-PKI rivalry led to an abortive coup and countercoup in 1965, the bloody elimination of the PKI, the eventual resignation and death of Sukarno, the political ascendance of Major General Suharto, and military domination of the political helm.

As in Burma and Indonesia, the Mukti Bahini (freedom fighters), which comprised several disparate and competing groups, played a key role in the nine-month civil war that led to the liberation of East Pakistan and the formation of Bangladesh on December 16, 1971. Despite its key role and highly politicized character, the Bangladesh military submitted to civilian authority. The military was disunited and weak in comparison with the political leadership—Mujibur Rahman and the Awami League—which was highly popular. Committed to civilian supremacy, Mujibur developed a constitution that provided for a parliamentary system that subordinated the military to the incumbent government (Kukreja 1991). Within four years, however, Mujibur was assassinated and the military assumed political power.

The 1975 coup has been explained in terms of the overdeveloped state thesis as well as the corporate interest argument (Alavi 1972; Chapter 8 this volume). Neither explanation is satisfactory. To begin with, the Bangladesh military was a small and fractured organization without a unified command structure. It was deeply divided between freedom fighters and returnees (those who were repatriated from West Pakistan after the war), as well as along personality and ideological lines. There were radical differences among these groups over the organization and role of the army in the newly independent state. The small, poorly trained, and ill-equipped military was hardly a coherent institution, let alone an overdeveloped one. By contrast, the Awami League and its associated organizations were far better developed and had many more resources. With respect to the corporate interest argument, admittedly military leaders were dissatisfied with Mujibur and the Awami League on several counts—neglect of the military and its budgetary needs; lack of recognition of the role played by the military units in the liberation struggle; the perceived excessive reliance of Mujibur on India; the creation of the Jatiyo Rakkhi Bahini, which the military perceived as a "palace guard" and rival; Awami League interference in military affairs; and the abuse of power and venal corruption by the family of Mujibur and senior members of the Awami League. Despite these and other grievances, for the reasons noted earlier the military was not in a position to intervene. And, the fact is that the military did not intervene as an institution (Ahamed 1998: 109). There was no plan to seize political power. Rather, as in Indonesia, the Bangladesh military came to dominate politics quite unexpectedly. As documented by several studies (Ahamed 1998; Hossain 1991), personal grudges and rivalry between a small group of midlevel military officers and some family members and close associates of Mujibur were the immediate cause that led to the assassination on August 15, 1975, of Mujibur and all his family members except two daughters. A countercoup to prevent the radicals from assuming power was foiled by another coup that catapulted Maj. Gen. Zia ur Rahman, a popular freedom fighter, to power. He assumed power by default, not by design.

Despite the unexpected turn of events, military rule was not opposed by the body politic. It was even welcomed by a public that was tired of mismanagement and instability. Though Mujibur enjoyed unprecedented popularity in the early years, his legitimacy and that of his Awami League party declined quickly. Mujibur and his party were unable to rise to the challenge of rebuilding a poor, war-torn country. Soon, the many problems confronting the new and turbulent state, as well as Mujibur's governing style, plunged Bangladesh into political and economic turmoil. Mujibur sought to transform the multiparty political system into a one-party authoritarian state, banning all other political parties and closing down newspapers except those belonging to his associates. While millions of people suffered starvation and death, Mujibur's family members and close aides were enriching themselves through corrupt and illegal practices. With its legitimacy in rapid decline, the government increasingly resorted to repressive measures to hold on to power. It declared a state of national emergency in December 1974 and suspended for an indefinite period fundamental human rights that were guaranteed by the constitution (Ahamed 1998: 105). In January 1975, at the urging of Mujibur, the constitution was amended to provide for a presidential form of government with power vested in Mujibur to declare Bangladesh a one-party state.

With the deteriorating law and order situation, the military was increasingly deployed in aid of civil power. Participation and success in these operations enhanced the unity and cohesion of the armed services, which came to believe that their services were indispensable. As internal threats mounted and the army became more deeply involved in operations against cross-border smuggling, dealing with "extremists," and maintaining law and order, the military officers "began to believe that only the Bangladesh military can save the country" (Ahamed 1998: 109). Military participation in governance exposed the shortcomings of the incumbent government and enhanced the confidence of military officers in their ability to manage state power and administer the country. The interaction of declining legitimacy of the civilian government, rise of coercion in governance, and military grievances better explain the emergence of military rule in Bangladesh than the arguments cited earlier.

Explanations of military intervention in South Korea also have often been based on the overdeveloped state thesis (Kim 1997; Chapter 4 this volume). As noted earlier, such explanations have to answer two questions: (1) why and how did the military develop into the most powerful institution of the state, and (2) must the development of a strong military necessarily lead to political intervention? As in the countries already discussed, at the outset the South Korean military was not a strong and cohesive institution. It comprised several competing factions that had fought against Japanese colonial rule and the Korean elements of the Japanese colonial army. This changed when the military was expanded rapidly to cope with acute internal and external security problems. Political turmoil, violence, and sabotage characterized the early years of the newly proclaimed Republic of Korea. The confrontation between left- and right-wing parties made for social and political chaos, leading to a ban on leftist political parties on the ground that they were conspiring to overthrow the government. To cope with internal instability, the American occupation government (1945–1948) and subsequently the Syngman Rhee government (1948–1960) strengthened the civilian bureaucracy, the police force, and the military apparatuses of the state. Concurrent with the domestic political turmoil, the Republic of Korea was soon plunged into a major war with North Korea and its allies that lasted until the armistice in 1953. In the context of the war and with massive assistance from the United States, the South Korean military expanded from 100,000 in 1950 to 700,000 in 1956. Although it was subsequently scaled back, by then it had become a well-organized, modern armed force. However, such development alone need not have led to the seizure of political power by the military in 1961.

Military involvement in politics can be traced to the declining legitimacy of the Rhee government and its increasing reliance on state coercion to stay in power. Political support for Rhee had declined substantially since his election in 1958. Instead of addressing the massive political, social, and economic challenges confronting the country after the disastrous war, much of Rhee's effort was directed toward political maneuvering and engineering constitutional amendments to enable him to hold on to power. He rigged elections and declared martial law. Along with the civil police force, the military—controlled and manipulated by Rhee—began to function as a political arm of his increasingly authoritarian and repressive government (Graham 1991). Rhee was forced to resign in the face of massive student protest and civil unrest that followed the fraudulent elections of March 1960. Withdrawal of military support for Rhee was a crucial factor in his decision to resign, indicating that the military by then had become a key force with veto power in the governance of the country.

The turmoil that accompanied the resignation of Rhee and the massive challenges still confronting the country did not lead immediately to military intervention. In fact the National Assembly adopted a major political reform bill with a view to creating the institutions for a parliamentary democracy. Elections were held in 1960, and a new civilian government acceded to power. But this government was immediately confronted with massive student protests, labor unrest, party factionalism, and continuing deterioration of the economy. The resulting political instability and the civilian government's failure to act on corruption in the army provided the impetus for a group of young officers under the leadership of Gen. Park Chung-hee to seize political power in May 1961. It was the increasing role of coercion in governance that resulted in the buildup of the military as well as the rise of its power and influence in the state. The interaction of declining legitimacy of the political leadership (not so much the weakness of civilian institutions), political instability, and factional struggle within the military led a segment of the military to seize power. Park relied even more on state coercion to sustain his power. Under him the military became a deeply politicized and powerful institution (Han and Park 1993). Senior officers came to believe that as "defenders and protectors of a society under constant threat from external invasion," they had an obligation and claim to be involved in politics. Further, by the early 1980s, the military had become a more cohesive institution, the core of which comprised graduates from the South Korean Military Academy.

In Pakistan, Burma, Indonesia, Bangladesh, and South Korea, the prominence of state coercion in the internal and international consolidation of the new nation-state, as well as the declining legitimacy of civilian governments and the increasing reliance of incumbent rulers on coercion to sustain their power, led to the strengthening of the state coercive apparatus and role expansion of the military. Military intervention in Thailand, one of the few Asian states that was not colonized, was also rooted in the construction of the modern Thai nation-state and the declining legitimacy of its absolute rulers. However, unlike the countries already discussed, it was not the increasing reliance of the absolute monarchs on coercion that led to military role expansion and intervention, but the dissatisfaction of a new quasi-traditional elite with the royal monopoly of power in the bureaucracy and the military.

Confronted with the threat of British and French colonialism and seeking to avoid the fate of many other Asian states including their Thai cousins, the Shan and Lao kingdoms that came under British and French domination, respectively—King Mongkut (Rama IV, 1851–1868) and especially King Chulalongkorn (Rama V, 1868–1910)—initiated a comprehensive set of reforms to "civilize" and modernize the Siamese state (Wyat 1984: 181–222). The goal was internal and international consolidation of the kingdom and its territories. A professional army and an interior civil service were developed as part of this reform. Until then there was no separation between political, administrative, and military functions, especially at the top levels. The king was the ruler, administrator, and military commander, and armies were raised from subjects and foreigners in times of war. Development of a distinct and professional military force continued apace through the reign of King Vajiravudh (Rama VI, 1910–1925), a graduate of Sandhurst and a soldier at heart. By 1920, as observed by David Wilson (1962: 255), "the distinction between military and civilian had become fully functional." The Thai military was characterized by "centralization, professionalism, infusion of a spirit of nationalism and also of institutional pride, and, finally, a high degree of organization."

The primary function of the army, its senior ranks staffed mostly by royalty and noblemen, was protection of the king and the internal consolidation of the kingdom. Internationally, the modern Thai army was a key marker of sovereignty. Along with the interior service, the military became a key pillar of the absolute rule. Military interests and values were exalted and linked to the idea of the Thai nation that was articulated and vigorously promoted by Rama VI.

However, the modernization of Thailand and the development of nationalism did not mix well with the continued monopolization of political power by the absolute monarchs who resisted political change. Chulalongkorn opposed constitutionalism, and Vajiravudh rejected calls for political reform as "selfishly motivated, disloyal and certain to bring ruin to Siam" (Wyat 1984: 232). Disenchantment with absolute rule grew and became quite intense in the 1920s and early 1930s among segments of a new elite that had been growing since the rule of Chulalongkorn. Beginning in 1912 there were many rumors of coup and a number of abortive coups. Finally, in 1932 a small group of middle-level civilian and military officials carried out a lightning coup d'état.

This was a not a military coup against civilian authority, but a coup by a small group of quasi-traditional, midlevel, civil-military bureaucratic elite against the royal monopoly of political power. The midlevel military officers who took part in the coup did not have command over most of the troops in Bangkok let alone the nation. Further, the military participants in the coup did not envisage a lead role for themselves. They viewed themselves in a supporting role of a civilian-led democratic government. Only after the 1933 coup did the military come to dominate Thai politics. Also, though labeled as such, the 1932 overthrow of the monarchy was not a democratic revolution.

The immediate causes of the 1932 coup included dissatisfaction with the limited opportunities for promotion to higher ranks and senior positions that were filled almost entirely by royal appointees, and the drastic cut in the defense budget occasioned by the great world depression. The longer-term structural cause lay in the tension between modernization and absolute rule, the declining legitimacy of absolute rule among the Bangkok elite, the growing force of nationalism, and the demand by a growing counterelite to share in the exercise of state power. The institutional imbalance thesis that has often been deployed to explain military intervention and domination of Thai politics is relevant in explaining subsequent military domination of politics for an extended period of time, but not the initial intervention.

Military Domination of Politics.   Once in power, the military in all these countries dominated the political helm for extended periods. Except for a few brief intervals, the military dominated Thai politics from 1933 to 1973 and thereafter continued to play a key political role until 1991. Again, except for a very brief period, the Bangladeshi military controlled political power from 1975 to 1991, and elements of the South Korean military dominated the political helm from 1961 to 1987. The military ruled Pakistan from 1958 to 1971 and from 1977 to 1988, and seized power again in 1999. Even when the Pakistan military did not occupy the top political office, it was a key political player with power to make and break governments. The Indonesian military was at the political helm from 1965 to 1998, initially in its own right and subsequently as a crucial pillar of the Suharto regime. In Burma, the military has ruled continuously since 1962. What explains such long periods of military domination of politics?

The key is the preponderant if not overwhelming power commanded by the military relative not only to other state institutions but to the society as a whole. Once in power the military constructs a political and legal order in which it is the primary or only center of power. Alternative centers of power are severely curtailed, destroyed, or mobilized in support of the military government. Viewing itself as the central state institution, the military structures its command system and deployment and constructs extensive surveillance and control mechanisms to extend its reach throughout the country. Also, arrogating to itself the state-building role, the military penetrates, controls, and directs all other state agencies. In the extreme case the military virtually colonizes the state and its institutions. The state becomes an extension of the military. The military also seeks to create a state that is autonomous from and overpowers society. In this connection it seeks to depoliticize politics and inhibit if not prevent altogether the development of political and civil society—especially the development of strong, independent political parties and interest groups. Political parties are often banned or allowed to operate only within narrowly defined parameters. The press is controlled and freedom of association is severely restricted or not permitted. A subservient rent-seeking business class that enriches the military is fostered. The net effect is that with enormous political, organizational, economic, and coercive power, the military is able to continue dominating the political helm unchallenged.

This preponderant power explanation has considerable force in explaining military domination of Thai politics from 1933 to 1973. By 1932 the civilian and especially the military bureaucracies that were developed as part of the modernization of the Kingdom of Siam had become highly organized and powerful institutions (Samudavanija 1982: 7). With increased budget allocation in the post-1933 era, massive moral and material support from the United States in the 1950s and 1960s to fight internal and international communist threats, extensive involvement of the military in commerce mostly in partnership with Chinese businessmen, and control over the mass media (newspapers and radio and television networks), the military became an even stronger institution (Bunbongkarn 1998; Girling 1981).

While strengthening itself, the military eliminated or retarded the development of alternative power centers. Though accorded a constitutional position and still revered by the Thai public, the monarchy, which in the pre-1932 era exercised absolute power, became virtually a nonentity in the first twenty years of military rule. It would not reemerge as a power center in its own right until the late 1960s. Even then, the reemergence was due to the personal motive of Gen. Sarit Thanarat, who sought to revive and deploy the prestige of the monarchy to enhance his own position. The democratic system and institutions, for their part, commanded little elite attachment and almost no public support. Thai society viewed politicians with disdain while it highly respected civil servants, including the military. Lacking mass base and resources, political parties continued to be weak into the 1960s and could not develop into an independent alternative to the military. And military rulers took a series of measures in the name of security and development that severely constrained the development of political society. The balance of power was clearly in favor of the military. During the 1933–1973 period, clubs were trumps. The acquisition and exercise of state power in Thailand in this period had little regard for the formal democratic rules in place that were honored more by their breach than by their observance (Chantornvong and Chenvidyakarn 1991). Political disorder, economic crisis, and social unrest provided the public rationale for the military interventions in 1947, 1957, and 1971. This, however, was not the whole story.

It is pertinent to recall here that the 1932 coup that laid the foundation for the military-bureaucratic political domination was driven not by concern with political disorder and social unrest but primarily by nonroyal bureaucratic discontent with royal monopoly of political power. Since then, struggle for power among competing individuals and factions within and across the military, civilian bureaucracy, political parties, and the monarchy has been a key factor driving the "vicious cycle of Thai politics." A coup was followed by the promulgation of a constitution, revival of political parties, elections, convening of parliament, a honeymoon period, and then a crisis leading to another coup (Samudavanija 1982). Personal and factional struggle for power (not always confined to the military) was a key subtext of civil-military relations. Coups were the means through which factional struggles within the military and sometimes between civilian leaders were played out, and leaders alternated in power. It was not always a military leader replacing a civilian leader but quite often one military leader replacing another. In some instances, sections of the military and civilian elite acted in concert against incumbents—civilian or military. It is important to note that the factional struggles and coups during the 1932–1973 period occurred in a context where the military was the dominant institution.

Thai military rule has been described as akin to Perlmutter's (1977: 107–8) "reluctant ruler army syndrome" (Samudavanija 1982). Except for Sarit (1957–1961), Thai military rulers were reluctant to assume active and direct political roles. They preferred to leave political and socio-economic governance to civilian bureaucrats and co-opted political leaders. Their primary focus was consolidation of their position within the army, personal wealth accumulation, and national security. On occasions they did attempt to create political parties, but these were not mass based, and the purpose was to secure a degree of constitutional legitimation. Thus Thai military rule, for the most part, was military-civilian rule.

Military rule in South Korea was distinct in that the military as an institution was deliberately excluded from political involvement (Kim 1997). The country was governed by Gen. Park Chung-hee (1961–1979) and Gen. Chun Doo-hwan (1981–1987), who resigned from the military to head quasi-civilian governments in which the key appointments were filled by serving and retired military officers from their loyal factions. Factionalism, which was and continues to be pervasive in the South Korean military, appears to account for the exclusion of the military as an institution from politics and the reliance on key personalities from the loyal faction.

Notwithstanding this distinctiveness, the military faction in power has followed the same route of monopolizing political power and controlling all levers of state power to perpetuate its dominance. Park took a series of measures designed to weaken opposition to his rule within the military as well as within the political arena. Taken over a period of several years, these measures included military purification ostensibly to purge corrupt and incompetent officers, the creation of two powerful institutions—the Korean Central Intelligence Agency (KCIA) and the Supreme Council for National Reconstruction—both of which were filled by loyal military officers, the circumvention of constitutional constraints on the president, the declaration of national emergency in 1971, the institution of the Garrison Act to deal with student demonstrations in Seoul, the declaration of martial law in 1972, and the adoption of the Yushin constitution. The Yushin constitution allowed Park to succeed himself indefinitely and enabled him to issue emergency decrees, which he did from time to time to limit the political activities of opposition and dissident groups.

Like Park, Chun promulgated a new constitution under which he was elected president without competition for a seven-year term. He disbanded all political parties of the previous regime and banned hundreds of political leaders and activists while permitting the formation of several new parties that would not effectively challenge his hold on power. He strengthened the KCIA (renamed the National Security Planning Agency) and Military Security Command and deployed them to control the military and keep political opposition in check. The new

National Assembly enacted legislation that allowed the government to effectively control the press and labor movement (Han and Park 1993). Military domination of South Korean politics from 1961 through 1987 with a brief respite in 1979–1980 had the net effect of curtailing the development of other state institutions, especially in the legislative and judiciary branches of government, preventing the development of political society and curtailing civil rights.

As in Thailand and South Korea, the Indonesian military also became an overwhelming force dominating state and society. However, unlike in South Korea, the Indonesian military as an institution was deeply involved in the governance of the country. Claiming the right to rule on the basis of restoring political stability and promoting economic development, the TNI, renamed Angkatan Bersenjata Republik Indonesia (ABRI), under the direction of Suharto created a strong and autonomous state with a military-dominated political order based on its interpretation of *pancasila*—the national ideology (Pabottingi 1995: 246–53; Crouch 1985: 60–70). To strengthen its hold on power, the military created a subservient legislature that was dominated by the Golkar (the military's electoral machine) and a simplified and emasculated party system that had to operate within very narrow boundaries. Through a system of functional representation at the national and provincial levels, the military controlled the House of Representatives (DPR) and the People's Consultative Assembly (MPR), which elected the president and the vice president. The military severely restricted political mobilization and competition on the ground that unbridled competition would lead to instability. In line with this and to give the appearance of democracy, the military permitted the operation of two amalgamated political parties whose composition, constitution, and leadership were controlled in large part by the military. Moreover, these two parties were not allowed to establish party organizations below the district level. The military-supported Golkar, on the other hand, was allowed to organize down to the village level. These and several other measures were instituted to ensure that Golkar would win the elections and have a majority in the DPR.

The military also dominated the executive branch of government. The president and most vice presidents were retired military officers, and key noneconomic portfolios in the cabinet were held by serving and retired military officers. The military also created a pliant judiciary and a supportive bureaucracy that was heavily penetrated at the national and provincial levels by military personnel in the name of *kekaryaan* (secondment of expert personnel). The press was controlled and freedom of association was limited. The military itself became more integrated and unified, with politically loyal officers holding key positions. Its territorial structure and deployment enabled the military to maintain a firm grip on the country. A key feature of the New Order was a powerful presidency that eventually came to manipulate and deploy the military as a personal arm. Except for the regularly scheduled elections that were certain to be won by Golkar, politics was absent under the New Order. In the name of security and development, the military crushed all opposition, including public protests. Force was used freely and often in a punitive manner to coerce the public and secure obedience. The military became so pervasive and dominant that it became impossible to think of a post-Suharto scenario in which the military was not a key player.

In Pakistan too, the military became the most powerful institution in the country. Ayub Khan, who ruled Pakistan from 1958 to 1969, engineered a constitution that instituted a system of basic democracy that would guarantee his election as president. He acted ruthlessly against political leaders, barring them from public life, and banned political parties. Ayub generously rewarded the military and the civil service, which were his power base, although he also kept a close watch over the military. Under Ayub there was still some distinction between military as government and military as an institution.

This changed under Zia-ul-Haq. During his tenure Pakistan was totally dominated by the military. Zia engineered a constitution that established not only his supreme position but also the dominant position of the military. Penetrating almost every sector of the state, the military colonized all state institutions at the national and provincial levels, including the federal civil service (Rizvi 1991). Zia co-opted a section of the civilian elite (bureaucracy, businessmen, and conservative Islamic leaders) but deliberately excluded from the system (through carefully controlled nonparty elections) political leaders who did not share his vision. Those who were popular and could pose a challenge to his authority such as Zulfiqar Bhutto were eliminated. Seeking to prevent opposition political groups from joining together to launch a national movement, Zia enacted policies that impeded political interaction and alignment and fragmented the opposition. There is little doubt that development of political and civil society was severely retarded under Ayub and Zia. This was made worse by lack of agreement among civilian leaders on the basis for political community as well as the principles, norms, and institutions for the acquisition and exercise of state power. Military political dominance in Pakistan was boosted considerably by American political and diplomatic support and economic and military assistance, initially in the context of the anticommunist SEATO and CENTO alliances and later in the context of opposition to the Soviet invasion and occupation of Afghanistan.

It is pertinent to note here that the military handover of power to civilian leaders in 1971 and 1988 occurred not because the distribution of power had shifted against the military, but because of the humiliating defeat in the war with India, which led to the dismemberment of the country in 1971, and the death of Zia in an air crash in 1988. In both cases the military, still the most powerful institution in the country, envisioned a guardian political role for itself. Also, from the time of Ayub, the army has resisted civilian involvement in security policymaking and in the management of military institutional matters. Elected civilian leaders had to negotiate with the military and could accede to power only on the understanding that they would refrain from intruding into these two areas. Any intrusion brought a sharp reaction, including dismissal of the government or a military coup, as happened during the rule of every elected government. Deeply resenting the attempt by Zulfiqar Bhutto (the first elected prime minister since 1947) to establish civilian control over the military, then–army chief Zia, at the urging of the Pakistan National Alliance that was soundly beaten by Bhutto's Pakistan People's Party in the 1977 elections, engineered a well-orchestrated disturbance throughout the country and seized power (Rizvi 1985). In the eleven years of civilian rule that followed the death of Zia, the military retained firm control over national security and institutional matters. It also exercised veto power over the civilian governments headed by Benazir Bhutto and Nawaz Sharif. In 1999 it acted against Prime Minister Sharif very much along the same lines as Zia had against Zulfiqar Bhutto in 1977.

Unlike in Pakistan where there have been periods of quasi-civilian rule, in Burma the military has been at the political helm continuously since 1962. Since assuming power, the military has completely dominated the political helm and has not allowed even token political participation and competition. Claiming the right to rule on the basis of the Tatmadaw's historic role as savior of the Burmese nation and projecting themselves as the true heir of the Burmese independence hero Aung San, military leaders monopolized political and economic power and governed first through a Revolutionary Council (1962 to 1974) that combined all the powers of the state, then through the Burmese Socialist Programme Party (1974 to 1988) in a one-party state system. After refusing to transfer power to the National League for Democracy (NLD), which won a landslide victory in the 1990 multiparty elections organized by the military, the Tatmadaw has continued to rule Burma first through the State Law and Order Restoration Council and since 1997 through the State Peace and Development Council. Ne Win dominated military rule from 1962. Since 1988 and especially after 1997, leadership has passed on to a new generation of officers who appear to be equally if not even more committed to holding on to political power. The military has acted ruthlessly against any alternative power center on the pretext that it will divide the country and bring it under foreign domination. The most recent victim of the military's obsession with total domination is the NLD under the leadership of Aung San Suu Kyi. She herself has been under house arrest from July 1989 to July 1995 and again since February 2000, while thousands of members and supporters of the NLD including elected members of parliament have been killed or jailed.

From the foregoing discussion it is clear that once the military assumes control of the political helm, it monopolizes political power, curtails or destroys alternative power centers, severely restricts the space for politics and dissent, and dominates the state and society. However, except in Burma, such total domination has not been sustainable over the long term. A fundamental weakness of military regimes has been their inability to convert preponderant power into authority and their continued reliance on coercion to sustain power. Policies instituted by the military to consolidate its power have in the long run undermined the legitimacy of military rule, reduced the relevance of coercion in governance, and altered the distribution of power increasingly against the military. Before moving on to discuss the resurgence of democratic civilian control in Asia, I review and explain civil-military relations in a group of countries in which the military did not seize political power but nevertheless was a key political player and experienced considerable role expansion.

Military-Backed Regimes

In Taiwan, North Korea, and the Philippines (1972–1985), the militaries were an integral part and a crucial pillar of the Leninist and authoritarian regimes. They played a key role not only in the security realm but also in the political and economic realms. Documenting the military role expansion in these three countries, this section addresses two questions: why role expansion occurred and why the militaries did not seize political power.

Civil-military relations in Taiwan until 1987 and in North Korea until the demise of Kim Il Sung were in the mold of the Leninist pattern, but the political system in each country was distinct. Although the structure of the Kuomintang (KMT) Party and its relationship to the state and its institutions, including the military, were unmistakably Leninist, state-society relations in Taiwan were authoritarian, and the KMT regime was embedded in a capitalist economy (Cheng 1993: 195–97).

The centrality of state coercion in consolidating KMT control over Taiwan, defending Taiwan against communist Chinese invasion, and the goal of liberating the mainland from communist rule and unifying China underscored the broad scope of military participation in governance. Having lost the mainland and under real threat of military invasion and political penetration by the victorious CCP, Chiang Kai-shek, a political-military leader, was convinced that authoritarian rule with a strong military was crucial to ensure the security of the ROC on Taiwan and achieve the purpose of national unification (Bullard 1997). Confronted with social fragmentation on the island of Taiwan and believing that internal unity was critical for KMT survival, Chiang also used the military as a major instrument for penetration and political socialization of Taiwanese society through indoctrination, propaganda, and education. Throughout the martial law period from 1949 through 1987 the military played key roles in internal security, political socialization, nation building, and economic development (Bullard 1997). In discharging these roles, the military deeply penetrated and controlled society. Chiang's concerns with regime survival, national security, and unification had a major impact on the pattern and content of civil-military relations in Taiwan.

A key factor influencing civil-military relations in Taiwan was the massive campaign initiated by Chiang for political learning from the devastating defeat on the mainland. Chiang identified the corrupt nature of the ROC army as a fundamental reason for the KMT defeat in the civil war. According to him the army had lost its "soul." Military officers were concerned only with their own position and wealth, not unlike the warlords during the 1916–1928 period. The relationship between the army and the party, the civil administration, and the people had therefore been turned upside down (Cheng 1990a: 24–25). Attributing these defects to unsound party political work in the army, and believing that strong political control contributed to the earlier Nationalist Revolutionary Army success in the Northern Expedition and later to the success of the PLA in the civil war, Chiang enunciated the cardinal principle that "the party leads the military." He tasked his eldest son, Chiang Ching-kuo, to rebuild the political control system and revitalize the ROC army on the basis of this principle.

Military role expansion in Taiwan was significant, but it took place not in competition with the KMT but in support of and under the direction of the party. Unlike in North Korea, where the military eclipsed the party, the military in Taiwan, which by the early 1970s had been transformed from a corrupt and demoralized army into a relatively clean and strong institution, was an extension of and controlled by the KMT (Cheng 1990a; Ross 1986). Though powerful, the ROC army exercised its influence primarily through established channels in the party and government where it was well represented. In this and several other respects, the KMT-ROC military relationship mirrored that between the CCP and the PLA. However, unlike the CCP, intraparty struggle was much less a feature of the KMT, and political succession was not an issue in Taiwan until the 1980s. Gen. Chiang Kai-shek dominated the political scene until his death in 1975, and he was succeeded by his son and heir apparent, Chiang Ching-kuo. The 1977–1980 period was an exception when Gen. Wang Sheng, perceived in some quarters as the likely successor to Chiang Ching-kuo, attempted to expand the influence of the General Political Warfare Department (GPWD) that he headed to make it a strong political force in the KMT power structure (Cheng 1990a). The growing influence of the GPWD was reflected in the strengthening of the "revolutionary line" within the KMT. This development, however, was curtailed with the dismissal of Wang Sheng by Chiang Ching-kuo, who valued highly the unity of command in the military as well as the unity of party and military.

The object of the military's loyalty was the KMT, which was synonymous with the state and country, and the military's political, economic and social roles were not unlike those in communist states. The loyalty of the ROC army to the KMT was rooted in several related considerations. As in the PRC the higher echelon of the political leadership and that of the military leadership were fused. They were all from the mainland, closely connected, and shared the same values and goals—anticommunism, defense against communist Chinese penetration and invasion, recovery of the mainland, unity on Taiwan that was deemed to require political socialization of the native Taiwanese and suppression of dissident forces, economic development, and alliance and subsequent alignment with the United States. Further, the ROC army was rebuilt after 1949 under the leadership of Chiang Ching-kuo. Together with the KMT, the army was the mainstay of the party-state system that operated in Taiwan until 1987.

In North Korea, the Korean Worker's Party (KWP) did not have institutional control over the military in the formative years. This changed in the late 1950s and 1960s. Seeking to rid the army of factionalism and to limit the growing power of the Yonan faction as well as to build up the KPA in the wake of the reversals suffered in the later stages of the Korean War, Kim Il Sung sought to exert greater control over the army. As he consolidated his position in the KWP through a series of purges, Kim brought the KPA under party control, instituting a dual control system that was common in communist states.

In the 1970s, party dominance of the state and the military was transformed into the personal dominance of Kim Il Sung. Loyalty to party was replaced by loyalty to the supreme leader. However, under the dictatorship of Kim senior, the party still controlled the military. Under Kim Jong Il, the political profile of the military has become much more pronounced. Penetrating the party and the state, the KPA has emerged as the most significant political actor and base for the dictatorship of Kim junior. Instead of submitting to the control of the party, the military now dominates it and the state. The loyalty of the KPA is to Kim Jong Il. It is pertinent to observe here that Kim Jong Il assumed the position of president in his capacity as chairman of the National Defense Commission, and the military has been officially described as the "party, state, and people."[7] It may not be an exaggeration to state that the military has become the ideological and organizational backbone of North Korea. However, despite its growing power and influence, the military still appears subordinate to the reclusive Kim Jong Il, who also appears to dominate the party. The change in North Korea—from state control to Leninist party control to dictatorship to a garrison state pattern—would appear to be fundamental, possibly constituting a pattern change rather than a within-pattern change.

Eclipsing the party, the KPA has become the dominant institution in the country. In addition to its crucial roles in political domination and in security policymaking, the military also plays a critical role in the economic arena, the origins of which can be traced to its key role in economic reconstruction after the Korean War. With increasing emphasis on self-reliance, especially in matters of defense, considerable resources were directed to the defense sector, contributing to the growth of a strong second economy under control of the military. The KPA is presently North Korea's largest employer, purchaser, and consumer. The military has become the key lifeline of the regime and the state.

Personal loyalty, the revolutionary credentials of Kim senior, and the dual control system he instituted explain military subordination to Kim Il Sung and the KWP.[8] Increasing concern with national and regime security, as well as with reunification, led to the "military first" policy in the 1980s that increased the power and influence of the KPA. The military first policy has become even more prominent under Kim Jong Il. Lacking his father's revolutionary credentials, Kim junior relies on the military as his power base and to maintain the totalitarian system of government. However, he does not appear to be the captive of the military. His command over the KPA was demonstrated during the North-South Korea summit in June 2000 as well as the major military reshuffle he initiated in October 2000 to promote younger officers to fill key senior positions. The basis for the close relationship between Kim junior and the KPA is unclear. Most likely it could be pragmatic—mutual interest—rather than charismatic or ideological as was the case with the senior Kim's control of the party and military.

The Philippine military, which played only a subordinate role in the liberation of the country from Japanese occupation and played no role in the winning of independence from American colonial rule, was subordinate to democratic civilian authority from 1936 to 1972. Civilian supremacy, enshrined in the 1935 constitution and the National Defense Act enacted in the same year, was institutionalized under American rule and continued in the postindependence period. In the absence of major international security threats and in the context of a defense treaty with the United States, during the 1936–1972 period the Armed Forces of the Philippines (AFP) was primarily engaged in internal security operations against the Huks (in the 1950s) and against the Communist Party of the Philippines and its military arm, the New People's Army (in the 1960s). Military involvement in the internal security role blurred the distinction between civilian and military functions and organizations and also involved the military in political disputes. Toward the end of the 1960s, the military began to view itself as having two roles: national security and nation building. In 1969 the AFP chief of staff stated that "the traditional perspective of the AFP as a war organization was too narrow.... [T]he proper role ... should include external security, internal security, peace and order, and socioeconomic development" (quoted in Hernandez 1985: 171–72).

Until 1972 the role expansion of the military was gradual and under civilian control. Thereafter, under martial law (1972–1981), the scope and jurisdiction of military participation in governance increased dramatically. Marcos, who co-opted the military to bolster his autocratic rule, assigned the military the tasks of maintaining law and order, preventing all kinds of lawlessness, insurrection, and rebellion, and enforcement of the laws and decrees promulgated by the president (Hernandez 1985: 184). To carry out the expanded security role, police forces throughout the country were integrated into a national constabulary force that came under the control of a military officer. Military tribunals (later replaced by military commissions), which had jurisdiction over a wide range of issues, were set up throughout the country. The military implemented several economic development programs of its own and became involved in the control, management, and operation of all utilities, and a large number of active duty officers filled executive positions in government at the national and provincial levels. The role expansion of the AFP was accompanied by increases in its size from about 55,000 in 1972 to 250,000 in the mid-1980s and in the defense budget from $136 million in 1972 to $420 million in 1977. Under Marcos, the military became a participant, junior partner, and key pillar of the constitutional-authoritarian regime. Increasingly the AFP was transformed from a national to a private army in the service of Marcos and his cronies (Selochan 1998: 65). The AFP, dominated by Marcos's cronies who in many ways replaced the traditional politicians as the dispensers of patronage, was implicated in the murder of Senator Benigno Aquino in 1983 (Berry 1986).

Military role expansion in the Philippines was civilian initiated. It can be explained by the increasing reliance of Marcos on state coercion to stay in power beyond the two-term limit imposed by the constitution. On the pretext of combating subversion and preventing lawlessness, as well as ridding the Philippines of corruption and inefficiency and constructing a "New Society," Marcos declared martial law in September 1972, about a year before the expiration of his second term. Courting the military from the time he was a senator, Marcos elevated the standing of the AFP and gave it wide powers under martial law. To ensure the loyalty of the military, however, Marcos appointed loyalists and cronies to senior positions in the AFP. The meteoric rise of Gen. Fabian Ver and the phenomenon of overstaying generals demonstrate this point well. With ample opportunities to enrich themselves, the top echelon of the AFP had a key stake in preserving the system.

Marcos's control over the military was also facilitated by the considerable legitimacy he enjoyed in the early period of martial law. His emphasis on constitutional authoritarianism, the organization of plebiscites, and *barangay* democracy, his commitment to socioeconomic reform, and his shift to an export-led economic development strategy appealed to the urban middle class, to the technocrats in the bureaucracy, to the entrepreneurs in the private sector, and to ordinary Filipinos (whose welfare Marcos claimed was being addressed for the first time), generating considerable public support. Over time, for reasons discussed in the next section, his legitimacy eroded. Marcos relied even more on coercion to sustain power, but this only exacerbated his legitimacy problem. Further, the new mission of the AFP to defend the Marcos regime and its involvement in the assassination of Benigno Aquino divided the military. By 1985 two distinct factions had formed: one under General Ver that was loyal to Marcos and the second under General Ramos, who was then head of the Philippine Constabulary (Berry 1986; Mackenzie 1987). Dissatisfied with the conditions in the regular army that was fighting the communist and Muslim insurgencies and resenting the political generals, a key segment of the military from the second faction plotted a coup in the lead-up to the 1986 snap election. Following the inconclusive result of that election, it played a key role in the eventual ouster of Marcos.

Although the militaries in the three countries did not seize political power, a segment of the AFP came close, demonstrating the risk of involving the military in political struggles. In North Korea, the military eclipsed the KWP, and Kim Jong Il's future is closely tied to the KPA. Only in Taiwan has the military continued to be subordinate to civilian authority—the KMT—whose legitimacy was not challenged in any fundamental manner until the mid-1980s.

RESURGENCE OF DEMOCRATIC CIVILIAN CONTROL

Though they were able to amass preponderant power and dominate the political helm for extended periods, with the exception of Burma, military and military-backed governments were not able to sustain power indefinitely. They were replaced in the Philippines (1986), South Korea (1987), Thailand (1973, 1992), Bangladesh (1991), and Indonesia (1998). In Taiwan, democratic transition began formally in 1987 with the lifting of martial law. Without exception the new pattern of civil-military relations in all these countries is in the democratic mode. In this section I explain the collapse of military regimes and the resurgence of democratic civilian control of the military, the nature of the civil-military problem in postauthoritarian Asian states, and the incremental progress made in promoting and consolidating democratic civilian supremacy.

Collapse of Military Regimes

In explaining uninterrupted civilian control, I argued that the political power and role of the military was and continues to be limited in countries where coercion is not the mainstay of gov-

ernance. In these countries, the system for political domination and the nation-state as constructed, though challenged in some quarters, are widely accepted. Although it may be important, coercion is not the primary or even a key basis for the acquisition and exercise of state
power. Even in countries where coercion is deployed on a massive scale, the power and influence
of the military is still limited because such deployment is controlled by a legitimate civilian
authority. Military intervention and domination occurred in countries where the legitimacy of
the nation-state and the system of political domination was weak and contested, and where
civilian leaders relied on state coercion to sustain their power. In these countries the power and
influence of the military increased, usually to the detriment of civilian leaders and institutions.
In this section I argue that the legitimacy deficit of military governments and the decreasing
relevance and effectiveness as well as the counterproductive nature of coercion in addressing
many (though not all) of the challenges confronting the military government and the country
explain military exit from politics.

The legitimacy deficit of military and military-backed governments flows from a fundamental weakness: their unwillingness and inability to share power and construct a widely acceptable competitive political framework for the acquisition and exercise of state power. Often military and autocratic rulers seek to construct pseudoparticipatory systems to perpetuate their
own hold on state power through the emasculation of political parties and restriction of political competition. Their emphasis on stability, order, and efficiency, and more broadly the techno-
administrative approach to governance, as well as the belief that they know what is best for the
people, invariably cuts military governments off from the societies they govern. Oblivious to
and unwilling to accommodate changes in the society under its domination, especially on matters affecting political governance, the military, even if its initial intervention had public support, loses touch with and alienates the political and civil societies. Further, without check and
balance, military governments become the captive of a small group that increasingly fails to
differentiate between private, corporate, and public interest. Massive corruption sets in. Opposition to the military government mounts. Labeling any and all opposition as subversive and
detrimental to stability and development, the military seeks to crush it through coercive means.
The net effect is that government becomes even more coercion intensive. Increasing reliance
on coercion, however, further undermines the military's title to rule, setting in train a down-
ward spiral. This has been the experience in South Korea, the Philippines, Thailand,
Bangladesh, and Indonesia.

Unlike the 1961 coup that was accepted as almost inevitable by the South Korean public,
the several Park-led governments under the Yushin constitution in the 1970s and especially
Chun Doo-hwan's seizure of power in 1980 were not accepted widely. From the outset, Chun's
government faced a grave and persistent legitimacy problem rooted in significant part in the
brutal suppression of the democratic movement in Kwangju (Kim 1997). To consolidate his
position, Chun promulgated a new constitution that had several features similar to that of the
Yushin constitution. It severely curtailed political competition and guaranteed Chun's election
as president. He also deployed military and intelligence agencies to intimidate and control opposition groups in political and civil societies and within the military. Such a system was widely
contested by the banned opposition parties that with the lifting of the ban on former politicians in 1985, coalesced into a single party. Challenging the legitimacy of the Chun government and the constitution that they claimed unfairly advantaged his party, the opposition

demanded constitutional reform before the next election, which was due in 1988 (Han and Park 1993).

Because the government had a clear majority in the National Assembly, the battle for constitutional reform was waged in the streets and on campus grounds. Faced with mounting pressure from the political opposition and civil society, as well as from the United States, in February 1986 the Chun government decided that the constitution would be revised. However, the ruling and opposition parties were deadlocked over the nature and extent of revision. With continuing deadlock and the split in the opposition (between Kim Young-sam and Kim Dae-jung), in April 1987 Chun decided to suspend constitutional revision and announced that the next presidential election would be held under the highly unpopular 1981 constitution. This decision was met with universal disapproval precipitating massive antigovernment protests and violence that further escalated after June 10 when Chun formally nominated Roh Tae-woo as the ruling party's presidential candidate. One student died and hundreds were injured in the ensuing clashes. Although initially Chun considered imposing martial law, fearing the risk of a civil war with a highly mobilized civil society, he indicated his willingness to resume negotiations on constitutional reform. The situation was defused only when Roh Tae-woo accepted all of the opposition demands and agreed to a speedy review of the constitution.

As in South Korea, military and military-backed governments in Indonesia, Bangladesh, and the Philippines were unwilling to construct inclusive political frameworks that would allow genuine competition for political power. Suharto, Zia, Ershad, and Marcos all concentrated power in their own hands. As elaborated in the previous section, they all devised political systems such as *pancasila* democracy in Indonesia and *barangay* democracy in the Philippines that severely restricted and even decimated political opposition with the purpose of perpetuating their own hold on power. Ultimately these efforts failed to gain public acceptance. In Thailand, the military and political parties shared power in a quasi-democratic framework from 1980 through 1988. However, such power sharing became increasingly untenable in light of the growing tension between the public demand for an elected prime minister and more broadly for greater democracy, and the military's unwillingness to accept a reduction in its power and prerogatives enshrined in the quasi-democratic framework. In nearly every country discussed in this section, there was mounting public opposition to military and military-backed autocratic rule. Governments invariably responded by becoming more repressive. Increased reliance on coercion, however, only served to further discredit governments and bolstered the political opposition. The key asset of the military—coercion—increasingly became less relevant and quite frequently counterproductive in political and other areas of governance.

Military governments often seek to justify the restrictive political framework as well as compensate for their political shortcomings by emphasizing economic development, security, and stability. But these have not been durable pillars of support. In so far as economic development is concerned, both success and failure undermined military governments. In the case of South Korea, the Park governments in the 1960s and the Chun government in the 1980s performed remarkably well on economic development. Park successfully reoriented the South Korean economy away from import substitution to export-led industrialization, and in the 1970s he instituted policies to shift the economy from low-value-added labor-intensive manufacturing to high-value-added capital-intensive production for export. The Chun government for its part instituted economic liberalization and stabilization policies that in combination with a favorable international economic environment promoted rapid growth of the Korean economy. Between 1967 and 1987 the South Korean economy grew at an annual average rate of 7 percent, transforming an underdeveloped low-income economy to a newly industrializing economy with a per capita income of $3,000. Although it initially bolstered the legitimacy of autocratic rule, over time, sustained rapid economic development and increasing dependence on the world market also generated sociopolitical changes and new sociopolitical groups in South Korea, as well as international pressure that empowered the society at large and altered the distribution of power between the state and society. Both the old political opposition and the new social forces challenged the monopolization of power by the ex-military presidents and their factions in the military.

Successful economic development had similar consequences in Thailand. Sustained rapid economic growth under the Sarit and Thanom-Praphat governments in the late 1950s and through the 1960s generated new social groups (students, industrial labor movements, and farmers associations among them) that protested against political stagnation and the increasing socioeconomic gap between the urban rich and rural poor (Morell and Samudavanija 1981). The extraordinary mobilization of the new social groups in 1973 and the violent response of the military eventually led to the collapse of the military government. The Indonesian economy also experienced sustained high growth rates. From 1965 to 1980, it grew at an annual average of 7 percent and from 1980 to 1990 at 5.5 percent, with beneficial consequences for poverty alleviation, education, and infrastructure development (Bresnan 1993: 284–88). Such growth initially bolstered the authority of Suharto. Over time, however, the growing disparity in income distribution and the massive corruption on the part of his family undermined the legitimacy of the Suharto government (Pabottingi 1995). The gap between growth and equity and that between monopolization of power by Suharto and the military and the growing public demand for political participation, combined with increased military repression to contain and punish opposition forces that were frequently labeled as subversive, further discredited the government. The final stroke that led to the collapse of the Suharto government was delivered by the 1997 financial crisis that took a very heavy toll on Indonesia. A similar story but one rooted more in failure than success in economic development can be told with regard to the Marcos government in the Philippines. Initial success in economic development bolstered his legitimacy. Over time, however, the gap between promise and delivery widened, exposing the emptiness of his development rhetoric and undermining the legitimacy of his government. His rhetoric was in fact seized by the opposition to challenge the monopolization of power by Marcos and his cronies.

As with economic development, both success and failure in advancing security and stability worked against military governments. As the security situation improved, the rationale lost its relevance. The public became cynical with the continued deployment of security to justify the repressive politics and policies of military governments. In the case of South Korea, for example, although there was acknowledgment of the threat from North Korea, beginning in the late 1970s it was clear that South Korea had become the stronger party in the conflict, that the international situation was in its favor, and that the overall security situation in the Korean peninsula had stabilized. Continued deployment of the security rationale in this altered context was viewed skeptically by the Korean public, which increasingly was convinced that the threat was being manipulated to serve the interests of the incumbent government. In the case of Thailand (until the early 1980s) and the Philippines under Marcos, the internal security situation actually worsened. The failure of the military to deal with the communist and ethnic insurgencies as well as the manipulation of the security rationale to serve regime interests had a negative impact on the legitimacy of these governments. In post-1965 Indonesia, the military commitment to restore stability and order was welcomed by large segments of the public. However, continued harsh and punitive action in the name of security and stability alienated the public in Java and the outer islands, especially in the outlying regions of Aceh, East Timor, and West Papua, increasing resentment toward the Suharto government and the military.

Apart from their inability to accommodate political change that led to tension and conflict with political and civil societies, military governments also confronted problems with the military as an institution. To consolidate their positions and to prevent countercoups, Thanom, Suharto, Marcos, Zia, and Ershad all held on to or appointed loyalists, cronies, or politically inconsequential officers to key senior positions. They also developed counterbalancing factions, patronage networks, and extensive surveillance and intimidation mechanisms. Despite these measures, they were not always able to unify and command the loyalty of the armed forces. As elaborated in Chapter 1, division within the military and withdrawal of military support were key factors in the collapse of military governments in Thailand (1973), the Philippines (1986), Bangladesh (1990), and Indonesia (1998).

Concurrent with the foregoing domestic cleavages, challenges, and struggles, the international context underwent dramatic change as well. *Perestroika* under Gorbachev and the subsequent collapse of the Soviet Union and its Eastern European satellites, as well as the success of the export-led market economies of East and Southeast Asia and the rebound of the American economy, highlighted the bankruptcy of the political and economic models of socialism and the ascendance of capitalism and democracy. The emergence of the United States as the sole global power and its promotion, with European backing, of democracy, human rights, and capitalism dramatically altered the material and normative structures of the international system. These structures and the policies of the Western powers were inimical and hostile to military coups and governments. Through incentives and sanctions, the Western powers advocated democratic development, which bolstered domestic prodemocratic forces and groups. Because of its crucial economic and security connections, the United States had an important impact on developments in the Philippines, South Korea, and, to a lesser degree, in Thailand. Even though Bangladesh has no such strong connection to the United States or Europe, global political trends such as the spread of the Third Wave of democracy were not without consequence for political development in that country.

The combination of domestic and international developments discussed above culminated in major confrontations and public uprisings that delegitimated military and military-backed rulers in Thailand, South Korea, the Philippines, Bangladesh, and Indonesia, compelling them to initiate reforms or hand over power to civilian leaders. In Taiwan too, there was a transition from a military-backed authoritarian regime to a democratic one. But unlike that in the Philippines, South Korea, Bangladesh, and Indonesia, the transition in Taiwan was less traumatic and less violent. After an initial confrontation in 1979, the transition followed a "transactional" path with negotiations between the ruling KMT party and the opposition forces (Cheng 1993). The reasons for this different path have been discussed at length elsewhere (Cheng 1993; Nathan 1990). Here it suffices to note that despite the difference in path and the salience of other factors (such as the role of Chiang Ching-kuo and the international isolation of Taiwan), some of the factors that applied to regime change in other countries—for example, the sociopolitical consequences of a sustained high rate of economic development, alteration and improvement in the security situation, public cynicism with the deployment of security to serve the parochial interests of the KMT, massive corruption, and change in the international context—also were of consequence in Taiwan.

The preceding analysis of military regime collapse suggests an important refinement of my key proposition, which states that as the weight of coercion in governance increases so does the power and influence of the military. This contention holds only in situations where the military does not control the political helm. If the military holds the reins of power, then, rather than enhance its power and influence, increasing reliance on coercion has the opposite effect. As with civilian governments, increase in the weight of coercion in governance is a reflection of the weakness or lack of legitimacy of military governments. The enormous brute power commanded by the military becomes less relevant in addressing the political and socioeconomic challenges confronting the military government. The requirement is for moral power, and here the military suffers a deficit that it is unable to rectify.

Legitimacy deficit and the declining salience of coercion—the key asset of the military—combined with mounting demand for political participation and a competitive political system are the key variables that explain the reduction in the power and influence of the military government and its eventual ouster from power. The changing distribution of power brought about, in part, by economic development and the altered normative structure is important, but this must be distinguished from the institutional imbalance thesis. The latter cannot explain the military exit from power in South Korea, Thailand, the Philippines, Bangladesh, and Indonesia. Although sustained economic development did strengthen the noncoercive management capacity of the affected states, it was not strong civilian political institutions that dislodged the military from power. It was the coalition of political and civil society forces operating outside the system and their massive protests and uprisings that delegitimated and morally overpowered the military rulers.

The military professionalism thesis is even less relevant in explaining military exit from politics in these countries. However, as noted earlier, the conflicting demands of the military as government and the military as institution did make for tension and division within the military. Reformist elements within the military played a key role in the ouster of government in the Philippines and in defusing the situation in South Korea by accepting the political demands of the opposition. Withdrawal of military support contributed to the ouster of the military government in Thailand (1973), the Zia and Ershad governments in Bangladesh, and the Suharto government in Indonesia. The corporate interest thesis explains, in part, why military governments were reluctant to give up power. It also defines, again in part, the nature of the posttransition civil-military problem and the military's approach to civil-military relations, as well as the progress made in consolidating civilian control.

The Posttransition Civil-Military Problem
and Consolidation of Democratic Civilian Control

Often, perception of the civil-military problem in the posttransition era is laden with emotion and rooted in a negative view of the military. The goal frequently is to ostracize the military—

considered a problematic (even an evil) institution—and render it powerless, punish those responsible for past abuses, reduce resource allocation to the military, and bring it under strict civilian control. Although understandable, such an approach suffers three shortcomings. First, the military is a key institution of the state. It is not in the long-term interest of the state and it is also not conducive to healthy democratic civilian control to view the military as an enemy of the state that has to be suppressed or contained. Second, this approach skews the issues to be addressed and their priorities. Although past abuses should be dealt with and the broad scope and jurisdiction of the military should be curtailed, these should be addressed in a more objective manner. It is crucial to begin with a determination of the proper place and role of the military in the state. Only then can the real nature and extent of the problem be ascertained and a decision made on when and how the other roles should be terminated. It is also crucial to determine who or what institutions have the authority to define the mission and role of the military and who the military should be accountable to in carrying out its duties and how. On the bases of these determinations, decisions can be made on role and jurisdiction adjustment, military reform, civilian oversight, resource allocation, measures to deal with past abuses and prevention of recurrences, and other related matters.

Third, even this more objective and forward-looking approach focuses only on the military dimension of the problem. The equally important civilian component of the problem is often ignored or taken for granted. It is useful here to recall that it was the increasing reliance of civilian leaders on the state coercive apparatus to sustain their hold on power that strengthened the military in the first place and broadened its scope and jurisdiction. Development of a legitimate and durable political system for the acquisition and exercise of state power as well as the development of noncoercive state capacity for managing the problems confronting the country are thus an important part of the problem. Ultimately, success in democratic civilian control will hinge as much if not even more on the consolidation of democracy and development of state capacity than on the specific measures instituted to control the military. A broader conception of the civil-military problem that focuses on both the controlled and the controller is required; and progress in ameliorating the civil-military problem should be measured on both counts. Unfortunately, writings on the civil-military problem focus largely if not exclusively on the military dimension of the problem. Issues relating to consolidation of the democratic system and development of state capacity are addressed by different groups of scholars, usually those working on political system change and the role of the state in development. There is a need to draw on all these different literatures to better understand the nature of the civil-military problem and the progress made in ameliorating it.

The nature, scope, and intensity of the civil-military problem in the posttransition states under consideration in this section vary quite widely. The type of military participation in governance in the previous regime and the manner in which democratic transition occurred are key variables in defining the posttransition civil-military problem. In Taiwan, the military was subordinate to the ruling KMT, which dominated state and society for over five decades. Democratic change, which occurred in an incremental manner, was the outcome of a demand-supply strategic interaction between the reformers within the ruling party and the opposition (Cheng 1993; Tien 1997). In this context, the military dimension of the civil-military problem included shifting the loyalty of the military from the KMT to the democratically elected government, ensuring accountability of the military to the elected executive and legislative branches of government, disengaging the military from its internal political-security role, divesting the commercial enterprises owned by the military, and developing civilian capacity to exercise effective oversight.

Considerable progress has been made on these issues since 1987, but there are still remaining challenges. On the acid test as to whether the military will be loyal and accountable to any democratically elected government, the acquiescence of the military to the election of Chen Shui-bian, leader of the proindependence Democratic Progressive Party (DPP), is an important milestone—especially in light of the "conditional loyalty" expressed by retired and serving military officers in the lead-up to the election. However, the issue is not fully resolved and will continue to be a key test of civilian supremacy for as long as the political status of Taiwan remains unsettled. On the issue of accountability, progress has been made in increasing transparency of defense matters, streamlining the command structure, and filling senior positions in the military. However, the military still resists the appointment of a genuine civilian defense minister, military officers still hold the key positions in the National Security Bureau, and the military inhibits oversight by the Legislative Yuan by withholding information and using procedural delay tactics. Considering the security arena as its turf, the military has yet to fully accept civilian control in this domain. A related key problem is the lack of civilian expertise and capacity in the state executive and legislative bodies to oversee defense matters.

Military exit is more complete in other areas of governance. In the political arena, with the resignation of General Hau as premier in 1993, the military has become a separate and distinct institution that is no longer answerable to the KMT. Active duty military officers can no longer hold office in KMT decision-making organs, and political parties have been barred from operating within the military. However, active service personnel can be members of political parties in their individual capacity. With the dissolution of the Taiwan Garrison Command in 1992, the military's penetration and political socialization role in society has also ended. Internal security is now the responsibility of the police force, which has since become a separate state institution. With regard to the issue of commercial enterprises, including media units owned by the military, a gradual process is underway to divest them.

The changeover from party to government control, and adjustment in the scope and jurisdiction of the military role in governance have been accompanied and enhanced by the strengthening of democratic forces and institutions in Taiwan. Several key transitions have occurred since the lifting of martial law in 1987 (Tien 1997): the emergence and acceptance of opposition parties (especially the DPP), the passage of political power from the mainlanders to the native Taiwanese elite both within the ruling KMT and the state signified in the transition from Chiang Ching-kuo to Lee Teng-hui in 1988, legitimization and institutionalization of the ideas of accountability and open competition for political power, the free election of the Legislative Yuan in 1995, the direct election of Lee to the presidency in 1996, the city and county elections of 1997 that brought about alternation of power at the local level, and most recently the partial alternation of power at the national level through the election of Chen Shui-bian as president in March 2000.

With the election of Chen, an important threshold has been crossed both in the consolidation of democracy and in democratic civilian control of the military in Taiwan (Diamond 2001). Further progress in democratic civilian control of the military hinges on continued deepening of democratic reform. Here there are still many challenges, including constitutional weaknesses, an underdeveloped competitive party system, the still dominant position of the

KMT, money and mafia-like politics, and the unresolved question of national identity (Chu 2001). Having obtained only 39.3 percent of the votes cast, and with the Legislative Yuan still under the control of the KMT, Chen faces an enormous challenge of governance. The challenge is exacerbated by the critical stand of Beijing and its tightening of the use of force condition, and a lack of experience and talent within the DPP to form an effective administration. The economy, especially the stock market, has nose-dived. At the time of writing, confidence in the Chen administration is very low. It remains to be seen whether Chen can govern let alone deepen democracy. Some have argued that democratic development may stagnate or even suffer dilution under Chen (Chu 2001). Although the challenges confronting Chen are indeed formidable, it is highly unlikely that future acquisition of state power in Taiwan can be through means other than the ballot box or that politics will revert to the era when the KMT dominated state and society. The competitive party system, though not fully developed, provides checks and balances as well as alternatives for the electorate. The large middle class and civil society will also vigorously oppose any reversion from democracy.

In South Korea, military intervention in politics under Chun Doo-hwan was limited to the Hana faction that secured control of the military and the political helm. The military as an institution was not involved in political governance. In fact Chun excluded it from politics and deployed the national defense and security agency to monitor and control the military. State intelligence agencies also penetrated nearly every segment of society: student movements, churches, labor movements, and even the military. Thus the key posttransition civil-military concerns in South Korea were the elimination of the political influence of the Hana faction, reforming the military and ridding it of factions, restructuring and reforming the security and intelligence agencies, and establishing civilian control over security policymaking.

A start was made under Roh Tae-woo, who was responsible for the democratic opening and the first president elected under the 1987 constitution, to address these issues. However, because Roh himself was a member of the Hana faction, he had little interest in substantially reducing the political influence of that faction. Only under President Kim Young-sam did the civil-military problem become a high priority. Kim purged members of the Hana faction in political positions as well as in the military. More than twenty generals were discharged or transferred, and four were tried for mutiny, which was defined to include couplike actions. Former presidents Chun and Roh were tried, convicted, and imprisoned for treason and corruption. This has been perceived as a severe deterrent against future coups. Kim also targeted corruption in the military procurement program and revamped the personnel promotion and appointments system to rid the military of factions. Under Kim Young-sam and later under Kim Dae-jung, the restructured and reoriented security and intelligence agencies were brought under civilian control. They no longer have domestic political intelligence and regime security functions. The link between these agencies and the military has also been severed. Active duty military officers can no longer serve in them.

Progress also has been made in enhancing civilian control over the making of security policy. In terms of ideology and threat assessment, the civilian political leadership has prevailed over the military. This was dramatically illustrated by the adoption of Kim Dae-jung's sunshine policy despite reservations in the conservative military hierarchy, and the holding of the first North-South Korean summit in June 2000. At the more routine level of security policy, however, although civilians along with retired military officers now staff the National Security Council and like agencies, the military still prevails in decision making on issues such as doctrine, arms procurement, and personnel management. Continued improvement in North-South Korean relations, should this occur, and increased civilian expertise and capacity on defense matters are likely to further erode military dominance in this area.

As in Taiwan, progress in civilian control of the military in South Korea has been accompanied and enhanced by deepening democratic development in that country. Here too, several important transitions have occurred: the direct election of Roh Tae-woo to the presidency in 1987; the election of the first civilian president, Kim Young-sam, in 1992; and the election of long-time dissident and opposition politician Kim Dae-jung to the presidency in 1997. The election of Kim Dae-jung is all the more significant because it occurred despite an alleged veto by the military and in the midst of a severe economic crisis, which in an earlier era would have brought the military into play. None of the political parties consider involving the military in politics; and the highly mobilized civil society including a vigorous press in South Korea is a key barrier to any increase in the military's political influence.

However, political parties and legislatures are still weak, factionalism is still strong in politics and in the military, and political power in South Korea is still personalized and concentrated in the office of the president. Powerful presidents with no checks and balances can abuse state power. It has, for example, been alleged that in light of the poor performance of his party in the 1995 local elections, Kim Young-sam reempowered the security and intelligence agencies to ensure a more favorable outcome in the upcoming national elections. Kim Dae-jung reportedly is favoring politicians and generals from his Cholla region. Despite these and other weaknesses, the balance of power in South Korea has tilted decisively against the military, and the norm of democratic civilian control appears to have been internalized by the political and civil societies and increasingly also by a growing number of military officers who see rewards in staying apolitical. It is becoming unthinkable for the military to play a political role in the foreseeable future.

In the Philippines, martial law augmented the power of President Ferdinand Marcos rather than enhancing the autonomy of the military. Co-opted by Marcos, the military in essence was a praetorian guard. Marcos's extraconstitutional method for sustaining political power politicized the military and over time created divisions within the AFP. The key problems in the post-Marcos era were the reinstitution of a constitutional method for acquiring and exercising state power, including presidential succession, and reversion of the control of the military from exclusive control by the president to shared or joint control by the different branches of government as provided for in the new constitution that was adopted in a public referendum in 1987. Other concerns included depoliticizing the military, redefining its role, and terminating its jurisdiction in nonsecurity areas.

Since 1986 considerable advances have been made on all these issues, including that of presidential succession. Throughout her six years in office, Corazon Aquino confronted extraconstitutional challenges from pro-Marcos forces as well as from rebels within the AFP whose purpose was not military government but replacement of Aquino with a civilian leadership of their own choosing. With massive popular support as well as the support of the AFP chief Fidel Ramos and the United States, and through a reshuffle of the Defense Department, Aquino outlasted these attempts. Ramos succeeded her through the 1992 elections, and Estrada was elected president in 1998. Fourteen years after the people power revolution and with two presidential successions though the ballot box, it appeared that the transfer of power through constitutional methods had become established. Such appearance was punctured by the extra-constitutional ouster of President Joseph Estrada in January 2001. Democracy in the Philippines is still a weak reed, and the Philippines's political system is only thinly institutionalized. Personalities matter more than issues and parties, and economic development has stalled. Personalization of power, corruption, and cronyism are still rampant. Norms of democracy have not been fully internalized. Political leaders still behave capriciously, and there is public impatience with the democratic method as demonstrated by the manner in which the Estrada controversy was handled. His trial in the Senate was brought to an abrupt halt by his loyal senators who opposed the consideration of new evidence. For its part, rather than follow the constitution and the law, the opposition organized a massive "people power II" rally and encouraged the defection of the military leadership. These developments, particularly the defection of the military leadership, compelled Estrada to step down. The manner in which Estrada quit office and Gloria Macapagal Arroyo was inaugurated as the new president raises serious doubts about the robustness of democratic succession in the Philippines. Although reversion from democracy is unlikely and will be vigorously opposed by civil society, manipulation of the constitutional method and extraconstitutional challenges still cannot be completely ruled out.

On the issue of civilian control, the national legislature has reasserted its authority. Through the commission on appointments and other congressional committees, it now exercises oversight of appointments, the military budget, and other defense matters. Together with provincial and city officials, it also exercises oversight of the Philippine National Police (PNP)—formerly the Philippine Constabulary. The military role in governance has been considerably narrowed. It no longer has responsibility for law and order. That is now the responsibility of the PNP, which has been removed from the AFP chain of command and placed under the Department of the Interior and Local Government. The AFP still has responsibility to fight the remnants of the communist and Muslim insurgencies; however, its primary role is in external defense. The internal security role and the political influence of local military commanders did intensify/increase under Aquino in her "total war" against the insurgencies that emphasized military and police action. But this is much less the case now. When the military engages in internal security operations, as for example in the actions against the Moro National Liberation Front and the Abu Sayyaf group in the southern Philippines, it operates under the close supervision of civilian authority. Resubordination of the military and the police to elected authority now appears almost complete. The continuation of democratic civilian control, however, hinges on the continued commitment of civilian leaders to play by democratic rules and not involve the military and the police in pursuit of their personal and political interests.

The civil-military problem in Thailand has a long history and has altered over time. The contemporary problem is captured by two conflicting developments in the early 1990s: the military ouster with public endorsement of the corrupt civilian government in 1991, and the massive public opposition to the subsequent military attempt to regain its political power and influence that have been steadily on the wane since 1973. Culminating in the bloody event of 1992, the latter development was resolved by the intervention of the widely respected king and the military's exit from power. Development of clean, stable, democratic government, excluding the military from the structure of political governance, redefining the role of the military and reducing its scope and jurisdiction in the nonsecurity areas of governance, and enhancing civilian oversight of the military as an institution and its security function are the key concerns that inform the contemporary Thai civil-military problem.

Substantive progress has been made in removing the military from the formal structures of political domination. The new constitution promulgated in 1997 bars civil servants and active duty military officers from cabinet positions and the senate, which now is elected. Military personnel wishing to participate in politics have to retire from active service and enter the system through the competitive political process. Many ex-generals occupy top positions in the major political parties, and more than 30 former senior military officers ran for office in the January 2001 election. Although it has no formal standing, informally the military is still an important political player engaging in behind-the-scenes roles. It has also spoken out on political issues and on foreign and security policies, although ultimately it has abided by the decisions of the cabinet. Despite its informal power and role, the military appears to have accepted that military domination of politics is now an anachronism in Thailand and the world and that it has to operate within a democratic framework and be subordinate to civilian authority. It has begun to redefine its place and role in Thai society in this altered context.

Substantial role redefinition has occurred since 1992. The trend has been toward narrowing the scope and jurisdiction of military participation in governance, but the military still has broad roles, some of which could be deployed in a future crisis situation to reempower the military. In the political arena, for example, the military envisages a role in defending democracy with the king as the head of the nation. On the surface it appears uncontroversial, but the nature of this role and how it will be operationalized are unclear, and the role could become problematic as it was in earlier years. It is pertinent to observe here that although it supported the passage of a new constitution that prohibited active duty officers from participating in politics, the military also worked hard to exclude a provision that would have made coups illegal. Similarly, although military jurisdiction in foreign policy and economic development has narrowed, the military still has key roles. In foreign policy, it is still the lead institution in dealing with Burma, Cambodia, and Laos—a role that has been sanctioned by the Senate Military Affairs Committee.

In the economic arena, the new constitution confers a developmental role on the military. However, unlike in earlier eras when the military engaged in major economic projects and enriched itself in the process, the current development role has a larger social dimension covering issues such as environmental protection, countering drug trafficking, protection of natural resources, and disaster relief. With democratization and the termination of the communist insurgency, the internal security role of the military also has undergone major change. Immediately after 1992 the laws that empowered the military to act in crisis situations—such as the 1952 Government Administration in a Crisis Situation Act, the 1954 Martial Law Act, the 1976 Internal Security Act, and procedures for deployment of the military in riot control—were all amended or rescinded. Deployment of the military for riot control, for example, now requires cabinet approval (Bambrungsuk 2001). Maintenance of law and order including riot control is now the responsibility of the police force. The Capital Peace-Keeping Command, a key organization for security in Bangkok since 1976, has been abolished. The primary military role now is external defense, and the military has been reorienting itself in this direction, although with the withdrawal of Vietnam from Cambodia and the end of the cold war, there is no real external threat to the country.

Unlike role redefinition, civilian oversight of the military as an institution has been much more controversial, and the record here is mixed. Although the minister of defense in the Chuan cabinet (1997–2000) was a civilian, and the military accepted this, several key features of the reform effort to streamline and restructure the command system, including the requirement that the supreme commander and service chiefs report to the civilian permanent secretary in the Ministry of Defense, and the proposed reduction in the size of the Defense Council, have been shelved because of military objection. The new command structure adopted in January 2000 makes for a more integrated armed forces and increases the power of the supreme military commander, but the service commanders still retain considerable power and autonomy vis-à-vis civilian officials. Similarly, not much headway has been made in the effort to alter the basis for promotion from entitlement to institutional need and merit. This and the accompanying effort to reduce the number of generals in the army have stalled because of military objection. Despite these difficulties, some progress has been made in enhancing civilian oversight of the military budget, arms procurement, auditing of secret funds, taxing the military's off-budget revenues, and reducing its legal and illegal business activities. On the issue of the budget, for example, along with other agencies and programs, the military had to accept a cut and defer its modernization program in the context of the severe financial crisis that hit Thailand in 1997. It has been a struggle, and the military still retains considerable autonomy in these areas. Reduction of military autonomy could be further hampered by the conservative nature of the Thaksin Shintawara government, which took office after the January 2001 election. Shintawara's cabinet has several ex-generals including Chavalit Yongchaiyuth, who is the defense minister. Chavalit had previously opposed civilian interference in "purely defense matters" such as arms procurement. Nevertheless, the situation today is a far cry from the 1970s and 1980s, when the military was almost completely autonomous.

Further consolidation of democratic civilian control in Thailand is likely to be much more than just a function of the military's willingness to submit to civilian supremacy. Consolidation of democracy and development of expertise and capacity on the part of civilian institutions to exercise oversight are critical as well. Consolidation of democracy in Thailand faces two major challenges. One is the development of strong political parties and stable democratic government that can deliver public goods devoid of corruption. The second is the willingness of civil society to use democratic methods and avoid resorting to street politics and extraconstitutional methods to express dissatisfaction and bring about change in government. Political parties are still weak, corruption is endemic, civil society is impatient, and Thailand still faces major challenges of governance. Democratic consolidation in Thailand is likely to be slow and incremental as in the past, but the process appears irreversible. The balance of power has shifted substantially against the military since 1992. Also, coercion—the key asset of the military—is much less relevant in addressing the many challenges facing contemporary Thailand.

In Bangladesh, massive demonstration by political and civil society in a rare and remarkable show of unity combined with inaction by the military brought about the ouster of President (formerly General) Ershad in December 1990. Because the country had been under military rule for fifteen years and because the military had developed into a powerful organization during this period, the key civil-military problem was to keep the military at bay and prevent another coup. Bangladesh has been under democratic rule since 1991. The two main political parties have alternated in power. Civilians hold the position of defense minister, and the military has for the most part remained politically neutral. It is possible to conclude from these statements that the civil-military problem has been resolved, but the reality is different. Bangladesh politics remains intolerant, vengeful, polarized, and volatile. Political and civil society leaders have little commitment to democratic methods. Opposition parties constantly attempt to oust the incumbent government through street politics and extraconstitutional methods. Both the ruling and opposition parties are based on personalities rather than ideology or issues. And appointments to senior positions in the armed forces are based on personal connection. Civilian control of the military in reality is control by the prime minister, who invariably is also the defense minister. The cabinet and the legislature play almost no role. The incumbent government and opposition both seek to draw the military into politics for their immediate political gain without consideration of the long-term consequences, thus creating space for the military to reassert itself in politics.

That the military has not intervened in politics for a decade is not a result of the development of strong democratic institutions or acceptance and internalization by the military of the principle of civilian supremacy. The reasons are more pragmatic. One is the recognition by the military that intervention will be vigorously opposed by the civil society (print media, human rights organizations, students) that is emerging as a strong third force in Bangladesh politics, as well as by the international community. Though polarized on a number of issues, civil society appears united in the support for democracy. Equally important is the recognition by the military, at least for now, that its corporate interests can be protected by staying a politically neutral course. The military's share of the national budget has remained high, it is well represented in politics by retired military officers who have been inducted into the major parties, and governments have taken the military's anti-India proclivity into account in managing relations with India. Thus civilian accommodation of the military's interests and the opposition of a vigorous civil society rather than democratic political development appears to account for civilian control of the military since 1991, which by any account is still shallow and reversible.

In Indonesia the civil-military problem is rooted in the replacement of autocratic rule by a democratic system of government, the redefinition of the military's sociopolitical role and institution of change in the related structures of governance, and development of civilian control of the military. The decimation of political society and the entrenchment of the military in almost every sphere and level of government under Suharto makes the civil-military problem in Indonesia an acute one. In addition to the longer-term goals of instituting and consolidating a democratic framework and redefining the relationship between the state, society, and the military, an immediate concern has been to prevent a military coup.

Rumors and warnings of a military coup were widespread, particularly during the tussle leading to the forced resignation of General Wiranto from the cabinet in February 2000. However, a coup is an unlikely prospect in the immediate future because the military emerged from the 1998 crisis and the 1999 referendum in East Timor as a thoroughly discredited institution. The political balance of power is arrayed against the military. The politically active public that continues to be in the forefront demanding the termination of the sociopolitical role of the military will vociferously oppose a return to military or military-backed rule under the present circumstances. But for reasons discussed later, greater military involvement in politics, including a return to military or military-backed rule, is a distinct possibility in the medium term that cannot as yet be ruled out.

Nevertheless, more than anticipated headway was made in the first year of postautocratic rule in removing the military from the structure of political domination, redefining the military role, and increasing civilian oversight of the military as an institution. On political domination, the passage of new laws and regulations has effectively terminated the military's stranglehold on the political system (Anwar 2001). The political and electoral laws passed in February 1999 ushered in a competitive political process leading to the first free and fair elections since 1955 and the formation of a democratically elected government under President Abdurrahmand Wahid. The seats allocated to the military and the police force in the DPR have been reduced from 75 in 1997 to 38 and at the regional level from 20 percent to 10 percent. It is anticipated that the military will have no seats in the DPR after the 2004 elections. Similarly, the military was expected to lose its functional group representation in the MPR after the next general elections. However, with the backing of the two large political parties—the Partai Demokrasi Indonesia-Perjuangan (PDI-P) and Golkar—the military has been allowed to retain its functional representation in the MPR until 2009. Despite this victory, the military is no longer the key force in the legislature. The military's position in the executive branch of government at the national and provincial levels has also weakened considerably, although not to the same degree as in the legislature. Several military officers (all of whom had to retire from active duty) were appointed to cabinet positions, and the rising star in the present cabinet is former Gen. Bambang Yudhoyono. He is the coordinating minister for security affairs and has been described by President Wahid as the type of person who should succeed him.[9] Many New Order governors and regents at the provincial level and below have been impeached. Others have had to resign from the military and compete through elections. Military domination of key administrative positions in government through *kekaryaan* (secondment) has also ended.

Considerable headway has also been made in the formal redefinition of the role of the military; and the military itself took the initial step in October 1998. In response to the changing conditions, the TNI attempted to redefine and reposition itself through a new paradigm that deemphasized its previous security approach and stressed power sharing and an indirect and less influential role for the military in national decision making. Though considered a major shift by the TNI, the new paradigm did not go far enough in meeting the strong public demand for termination of the sociopolitical role altogether. A more substantial change occurred in April 2000, when, after a meeting of military leaders, the TNI commander declared that as a national defense force the military's primary duty is in national defense and that the TNI will not be responsible for internal security. The latter now is the responsibility of the police force, which has been removed from the TNI chain of command. Initially placed under the coordinating minister of defense, command and control of the police force have since been shifted to the office of president pending a decision on its final location.

In practice, the police force has been unable to deal with internal security, especially in places such as Ambon, Maluku, and Kalimantan, which are experiencing intense ethnic and religious conflicts, and in regions such as Aceh and West Papua, where there are demands for secession. The key force in dealing with these situations continues to be the military, and even the military has been unable or unwilling to bring these situations under control. It is pertinent to observe here that the territorial deployment and command structure that still exists provides the TNI with enormous influence on matters pertaining to internal security. Thus although the military states that its primary role is in national defense, it is unclear what national defense means and includes. Is it limited to defense against external threats or does it also extend to internal threats to the unity and integrity of Indonesia such as secession? Also, to be durable, change in role definition has to be accompanied by alteration in force posture, command structure, and deployment. For budgetary and other reasons, these have not occurred.

Similarly, progress in civilian oversight of the military as an institution is mixed. For the first time civilians have been appointed to the position of defense minister, but the minister's authority over the TNI is unclear and appears limited. Moreover the senior coordinating minister for security affairs in the cabinet has thus far been a retired general. In terms of senior promotions and appointments, President Wahid moved swiftly to appoint reform-minded officers to command the TNI and the three services and to fill other key senior positions. Wahid also removed officers who were critical of his handling of the Wiranto affair. Subsequently, however, he was not able to get his way, for example, in the October 2000 reshuffle, when the conservative wing of the military, with the backing of the major political parties, especially that led by Megawati Sukarnoputri, was able to block his proposed appointments. Wahid has also been accused of following Suharto's path in appointing loyalists to senior positions with a view to using the military as a personal power base. It has been argued by civilian and military leaders that the president should have no say in the appointments below the level of chief of staff, which should be based on objective criteria, including merit. In the absence of a widely accepted system for promotion and appointments to senior positions, such difficulties will be difficult to overcome.

Thus, although initial progress in democratic civilian control of the military exceeded expectations, the process has stalled and many challenges still remain. Instituting a system for military promotions and appointments and avoiding political interference in these matters, providing adequate funds for reorganizing the military and reorienting it toward the external defense function, terminating the military's business involvement, strengthening civilian police and limiting the military's role in internal security, replacing the military's territorial command structure, creating civilian institutions with the necessary expertise and capacity to oversee the military and defense matters, determining the areas in which the military should be allowed autonomy, deciding on future military representation in the MPR, handling the past abuses committed by ABRI, and more generally redefining the role of the TNI and restructuring its relations with other state institutions are among the issues that still have to be addressed (Anwar 2001).

Equally if not even more important is the need to develop a general public consensus on democracy and to strengthen and eventually consolidate the fledgling democratic system. This entails broadening and deepening the commitment to democratic values that is still narrow and shallow in Indonesia. For the vast majority of the people, improvement in their living conditions is the primary concern. This places a greater burden on political society and the politically active civil society groups. A consensus must be developed among them to refrain from involving the military in politics. They must also commit themselves to the democratic methods for acquiring and exercising state power. Constitutional changes are required to provide for separation of powers between the executive, legislature, and judiciary and to institute checks and balances among them. The proper place, role, and control of the military must be defined. The goal should be a decisive and enduring shift in the political and institutional balance in favor of democratic civilian authority and the internalization by civilian and military leadership of the norm of democratic civilian control.

Further progress in democratic civilian control depends on the cohesiveness of civilian political leadership and the ability of the government to address the multitude of political, economic, and social challenges confronting that country. In this regard the situation has become less encouraging. After a promising start, the civilian political leadership has fragmented. Erratic behavior as well as signs of corruption and new cronyism in his administration have dissipated President Wahid's moral authority. Vice President Megawati has yet to demonstrate her potential as a national leader. Jockeying for power, the other leaders have begun to challenge Wahid and position themselves to succeed him. The threat of impeachment and political backing for conservative generals, especially from Megawati's party and Golkar, has enabled the military to hang on to its 38 seats in the MPR and has also forced Wahid to backtrack on his proposed reshuffle of senior military officers. With growing political instability, deteriorating economic conditions, and a worsening law and order situation, there is growing impatience among the public, who increasingly are taking the law into their own hands. Some military commanders have begun to voice concern over the infighting among political leaders and their inability to preserve the unity and integrity of the state.

Beginning in late 2000, Armed Forces commander Admiral Widodo Adisucipto and territorial affairs chief Lt. Gen. Agus Widjoyo have called for a reassessment of the government's policy on security affairs. In March 2001, Army Comdr. Gen. Endriartono Sutarto and Defense Minister Mohammad Mahfud suggested reconsideration and revision of the security and defense affairs bill before parliament that would formally assign responsibility for internal security to the police force. The revision proposed by the military would leave it in charge of internal security for a specific period until the police force develops the capacity to deal with unrest like that in central Kalimantan. That the police force is not up to the task is not in question. But the military may have a deeper motive as well. Continuation of the internal security role would allow the military to retain its territorial command structure, which is an important source of off-budget revenue. The key point is that military commanders at the national and regional levels are becoming more outspoken in asserting that civil-military reform depends as much on the controller as on the controlled. Further reform in their view hinges on the commitment and ability of civilian political leaders to maintain the unity and integrity of the country as well as to govern effectively.

Thus despite the not inconsequential achievements, effective civilian control of the military appears unlikely at least in the short to medium term. Even under favorable circumstances, substantive change in the "culture of violence" that has become ingrained in the state and the military for more than 30 years as well as in the TNI's long-standing self-conception as the national guardian would require persistent effort over a prolonged period of time (see Chapter 10). As observed by ex-general and current coordinating minister for security affairs Susilo Bambang Yudhoyono, "We cannot change overnight the practice, the mindset, the beliefs, and behavior of the military [that has been developed] over 35 years."[10] And although it may appear rather unlikely right now, return to military rule or military-backed civilian rule is a possibility. Over time the stigma of military-backed rule may abate, and the Indonesian public may become positively disposed to a promise of "strong government" to cure the ills of the nation. Already large segments of the Indonesian political society, military, and public at large are warming to the prospect of a strong nationalist government under the conservative Megawati Sukarnoputri. In light of her nationalist and conservative credentials and her sympathy for several former senior military officers, including General Wiranto, who were forced to quit over alleged human rights abuses, it appears unlikely that a government headed by her would actively pursue civil-military reform. For the present and in the foreseeable future, however, it is important to note that any effort to reinstate the sociopolitical role of the military is likely to be vociferously opposed by the growing Indonesian civil society as well as the international community. In light of the ongoing turbulent political and economic changes and the accompanying uncertainty, civil-military relations in Indonesia are likely to remain fluid.

Explaining Incremental Advance

From the foregoing discussion, it is clear that although democratically elected governments have replaced military and autocratic ones in South Korea, Taiwan, the Philippines, Thailand, Bangladesh, and Indonesia, and there have been alternations in power in the first five countries, democratic civilian control of the military has advanced only in an incremental fashion and is still far from complete. It is most advanced in South Korea and Taiwan, less so in the Philippines and Thailand, and least advanced in Bangladesh and Indonesia. All these countries still face a number of challenges. Those confronting Bangladesh and Indonesia are the most extensive and acute, with the prospect of stagnation and possibly even reversal of the fledgling democratic pattern of civilian control.

In explaining progress (or the lack of it) in enhancing democratic civilian control, my argument runs as follows. A decisive shift in the distribution of power in favor of democratic forces and against antidemocratic forces in the society at large that includes but is not limited to the military is the crucial variable in explaining the onset of democratic transition and initiation of democratic civilian control. In the immediate aftermath of the collapse of the military regime, when the military is on the defensive, the new civilian leadership has considerable moral authority and leverage in shaping national policy, including civil-military reform. Such a window of opportunity is usually short. Further enhancement of democratic civilian control hinges on the continuation and strengthening of the distribution of power in favor of democratic forces and their translation into strong democratic institutions. As the democratic framework and institutions become stronger and deep rooted, and as state capacity develops noncoercive means to address the challenges confronting the country, the salience of coercion in governance and the power of the military further declines, tilting the balance of power even more durably against the coercive institutions of the state. Sustained functioning of the military within a democratic framework enhances the legitimacy of the political system and inculcates and internalizes the norm of democratic civilian control in the military and the society at large.

In all six countries considered in this section, the advantage in brute power lay with military or military-backed governments. However, with the exception of the government in Taiwan, all lost their moral authority to govern. The application of coercion to sustain themselves in office further undermined rather than enhanced their political authority. The shift in the balance of moral power combined with the inaction or withdrawal of the support by segments of coercive institutions led to the ouster of the military and autocratic governments. In nearly every case, the military or the military faction that controlled the political helm in its own right or backed an authoritarian ruler emerged from the crisis as a thoroughly discredited institution and on the defensive. The balance of power was clearly in favor of the forces advocating regime change. Those forces usually comprised a wide array of organizations, groups, and movements: opposition political parties from different parts of the political spectrum, students, churches and religious groups, organized labor, business associations, the press, human rights organizations, other nongovernmental organizations, and in some cases such as the Philippines, reformist elements within the military. Often these groups were united only in their opposition to the incumbent military or military-backed government. Nevertheless, the unity of these groups, however opportunistic and temporary, was critical in bringing about the change in government and regime.

The continuation of a favorable balance of power is crucial for strengthening and deepening democracy and developing strong institutions for democratic governance. However, coalitions forged to oppose an autocratic ruler often break down soon after the ouster of the incumbent government. In their quest for political power, opposition parties splinter, and competing interests dominate their political interaction. This allows conservative forces, including the military, to regroup and limit damage. The pace of democratic reform, including civilian control of the military, slows. In South Korea for example, the split between Kim Young-sam and Kim Dae-jung in 1987 contributed to the victory of Roh Tae-woo, a member of the Hana faction. For him, reducing the power of that faction and reforming civil-military relations were not high priorities. These had to wait until the presidency of Kim Young-sam, the first genuine civilian president in the post-1987 period. Similarly, the collapse of the anti-Marcos coalition in the Philippines exposed Aquino to challenges from the right and left, increasing her reliance on the core of the AFP under the leadership of Ramos. Reliance on the very institution that had to be reformed tempered the content and pace of civil-military reform. The appointment of a large number of retired military officers, including those from the Reform the Armed Forces Movement, to key government positions under the succeeding Ramos administration further tempered civil-military reform in the Philippines. Coalition breakdowns occurred in Bangladesh and Indonesia as well.

Apart from increasing the leverage of the military and slowing civil-military reform, polarization and maneuvering among political parties can lead to political penetration and involvement of the military in politics for personal and party gain, as has been the case in Bangladesh. In Indonesia, Abdurrahmand Wahid has been accused of such motives, and in South Korea Kim Young-sam's empowerment of the intelligence agencies in 1995 could be and has been interpreted as trying to improve the prospects for his party in the 1997 elections. A strong understanding among political parties not to involve the military in politics and a deep commitment on the part of civil society to act as a watchdog in keeping the military out of politics are crucial for the continuation of civil-military reform. The power and commitment of civil societies are particularly important in countries such as Bangladesh, where the political parties are deeply polarized and democratic institutions are still weak. It is crucial for reform-oriented leaders to cultivate and mobilize like-minded groups to keep the balance of power in favor of reform.

However, this alone is not enough. To be durable, the favorable balance of power should be deployed to create and empower strong democratic institutions, which are crucial for the next stage of civil-military reform. As the medium through which power is translated into policy, institutions can strengthen democratic civilian control in several ways (Pion-Berlin 1997). By compelling political, bureaucratic, and military actors to interact in accordance with specified rules and procedures in the development of policy, institutions condition all actors to operate under a democratic framework and reduce (though not eliminate) the salience of power in their interaction. The cross-cutting alliances and cleavages made possible by the interaction through institutions also contribute to the development of understanding and respect for different perspectives, leading to moderation and compromise. These developments enhance the legitimacy of the democratic system. Accustomed to operating in a democratic framework, the military in the long run internalizes the norm of civilian control. Further, institutional design—in terms of issues, jurisdiction, and actors—can affect policy outcome, which is the substance of civil-military relations. By being able to influence the substance of policy as well as the power and interests of competing actors, institutions can also affect the civil-military balance in favor of civilian authority.

However, strong democratic institutional development has not been a key feature of the countries under consideration—at least not thus far. Institutional development is perhaps most advanced in Taiwan, where increasingly the military has to interact with political and civilian bureaucratic officials in the making of security policy and in matters pertaining to the management of the military as an institution. Even in Taiwan, as pointed out in Chapter 5, there are several institutional gaps and weaknesses that have to be rectified. Institutions such as the Legislative Yuan and the Control Yuan, with responsibility for oversight of the military budget and arms procurement, for example, have been inhibited in discharging their functions effectively because of a lack of expertise and institutional capacity as well as legal provisions and procedures that limit access to information in a timely fashion. Democratic institutions with oversight responsibilities in the areas of security policymaking and management of the military as an institution are also in various stages of construction in South Korea, the Philippines, and Thailand. However, because of limited resources and competing priorities as well as military evasion and intransigence, they have not been high priorities. Poor institutional development explains in part the tentative nature of civilian supremacy in the Philippines and Thailand, and even more so in Bangladesh and Indonesia. Institutions for making and implementing policy on a wide range of issues have yet to be constructed in the latter two countries.

In terms of priority, the focus of civil-military reform has been on removing the military from the structure of political domination. Considerable progress has been made in this area in nearly all countries, although the durability of change in some is open to question. Progress in other areas (redefining the military role and reorienting the military toward the external defense function, terminating off-budget revenues from military-owned business enterprises and illegal activities, and civilian oversight of security policy as well as the management of the military as a state institution) is more varied and has been influenced by considerations of resource availability, the presence or absence of security threats, and the corporate interests of the military.

Resource availability is a key consideration in reorienting the military away from internal security toward its external defense function. In Taiwan and South Korea, resource availability has not been a major obstacle. Further, because of the grave external threats confronting these two states, external defense has always been a key focus of their militaries. Termination of a military role in internal security and intelligence in Taiwan and South Korea has been a function of political will and availability of civilian expertise. However, resource constraint has been a key factor in Thailand, the Philippines, and especially Indonesia. The military modernization programs in Thailand and the Philippines, which are an integral part of reorienting the militaries to the external defense function, have been delayed because of a lack of resources—especially in the Philippines, which has since attempted to provide, in part, for its external security needs by reinvigorating its security relationship with the United States. Indonesia has made the least progress in reorientation of the military to the external defense function because of the continuing grave internal security threats, a weak police force, absence of clear external threats, and lack of resources. Lack of adequate government funding for the military has also made it difficult to terminate the off-budget revenues of the militaries in Thailand and Indonesia. It is estimated that government funding accounts for less than 30 percent of the military budget needs in Indonesia (Crouch 2000). Lack of adequate funding has also contributed to the erosion if not breakdown of the TNI command and control system, making central control of regional and local forces—especially in the outlying regions—difficult, with negative consequences for implementation of military reform and accountability of military commanders.

Civilian oversight of security policy and the management of the military are two areas in which progress has been more limited even in Taiwan and South Korea. Limited progress in these areas may be explained by the presence of acute security threats, the shortage of qualified civilian personnel, and military resistance to civilian encroachment in areas that it considers its turf. For fear of provoking the military, civilian political leaders have trod lightly in these two areas. However, substantive and durable democratic civilian control requires the civilian authority to have ultimate jurisdiction in these areas as well, although it may delegate specific powers to the military establishment. Continued military jurisdiction in these areas provides the military with power not only to limit civilian authority but also to overturn it when its interests are negatively affected, as has been the case in Pakistan.

To summarize, the deepening of democratic civilian control hinges on the continuation and strengthening of the prodemocracy forces and deploying such power to construct strong democratic institutions, including those necessary to exercise oversight of the military. Concurrent development of the state's noncoercive capacity to address the many internal and international challenges confronting these countries is essential so that reliance on state coercion can be reduced.

EXPLAINING PERSISTENCE OF MILITARY RULE

Pakistan and especially Burma appear to be defying the current trend toward democratic civilian control in Asia. Pakistan has oscillated between civilian and military rule, whereas Burma has been under continuous military rule since 1962. This section explores two questions. First, why has Pakistan continued to persist in the oscillation mode while other countries such as Thailand appear to have escaped the vicious cycle? Second, why has the Burmese military been able to hold on to political power for nearly four decades while its counterparts in South Korea, Thailand, Bangladesh, and Indonesia have been compelled to exit politics and subordinate themselves to civilian authority?

Pakistan: A Failed State?

Since independence in 1947, Pakistan has experienced three periods of civilian rule (1947–1958, 1971–1977, 1988–1999) and three periods of military rule (1958–1971, 1977–1988, 1999–present).

The unelected civilian governments of the postindependence era were replaced by the martial law government of Ayub Khan, who ruled from 1958 to 1969. Following the humiliating military defeat by India and the secession of East Pakistan, Zulfiqar Ali Bhutto, a civilian political leader from Sind, dominated the political helm from 1971 until 1977, when the military reintervened. Gen. Zia-ul-Haq controlled political power from 1977 until his death in 1988. This was followed by a quasi-democratic period during which Benazir Bhutto and Nawaz Sharif, both civilian political leaders, alternated in power until 1999, when the elected Sharif government was ousted in a military coup by Gen. Pervaiz Musharaf, the current ruler of Pakistan. Although they were at the political helm for relatively long periods—Ayub Khan from 1958 to 1969, Zulfiqar Bhutto from 1971 to 1977, Zia-ul-Haq from 1977 to 1988, and Benazir Bhutto and Nawaz Sharif during the 1988–1999 period—both civilian and military leaders failed to develop a widely accepted political system and play by its rules. Their unwillingness to share political power and develop a broad-based political system resulted in political polarization and confrontation, and the frequent resort to extraconstitutional methods to acquire and sustain state power.

Zulfiqar Bhutto came to power with two enormous advantages (Rizvi 1985). He was the first elected prime minister since independence in 1947, and he had a strong support base in the two politically critical provinces of Punjab and Sind. Also, following the humiliating defeat by India and the loss of East Pakistan, the military was a discredited and demoralized institution. These advantages were compromised to a degree by the fact that power was transferred to Bhutto not after the 1970 elections in which his party emerged dominant in West Pakistan, but after the 1971 defeat and dismemberment of Pakistan, and also because Bhutto's critics held him responsible for the disintegration of Pakistan (Shafqat 1997). Despite these constraints and the dire circumstances of postwar Pakistan, Bhutto had unprecedented power and opportunity to develop a democratic framework in that country. But this opportunity was soon lost because of the autocratic tendencies of Bhutto as well as the polarized nature of politics in Pakistan and the massive political, administrative, and economic problems facing the country.

Instead of building his party and a democratic political system, Bhutto personalized and concentrated power in his hands and increasingly became an autocrat. The changes in the command structure and the constitutional and legal measures instituted by Bhutto to establish civilian supremacy alienated the military (Shafqat 1997). The military also felt threatened by the new paramilitary Federal Security Force created by Bhutto to deal with the deteriorating law and order situation and to reduce his reliance on the military and thus diminish its influence deriving from its monopoly on coercive power. Bhutto's land reform, nationalization, and other socioeconomic policies with a socialist cast alienated the previously privileged groups as well as some of his supporters in government and in the society at large. His secular tendency was opposed by Islamic parties, and his centralization policies were opposed by regional parties. Soon, an anti-Bhutto alliance emerged with the sole purpose of ousting him from power. Although Bhutto's party won a landslide victory in the 1977 elections, the opposition alliance, refusing to accept the outcome and fearing that they would not be able to defeat him through democratic means, appealed to the military on the ground that the election had been rigged. For the military, which was alienated by Bhutto but unable to confront him because of the still fresh memory of 1971 and because of Bhutto's huge popularity among the masses, the opposition appeal provided a good rationale for intervention. The military intervened to restore law and order in the context of a nationwide disturbance that it orchestrated.

A similar opportunity to build an inclusive democratic system was lost during the 1988–1999 period, especially after the 1997 election in which the Muslim League led by Nawaz Sharif won an overwhelming victory; and the military appeared to be conceding political power in exchange for control over security policy and management of its institutional affairs. However, Sharif and Benazir Bhutto before him engaged in policies and actions designed to entrench their personal political dominance and enrich themselves. They penetrated and deployed state institutions including the judiciary to serve their own political purposes. In the process they severely damaged state institutions and their capacity to govern. Law and order broke down, and public services were unable to deliver even the basic necessities such as water, electricity, and transport services. The economy had all but collapsed. Concurrently ethnic and religious strife and center-regional tensions escalated. Public confidence in democracy, which was never high, was severely undermined. The Sharif government increasingly relied on the military to provide basic services, restore law and order, and administer troubled areas. The opposition, on the other hand, sought to ally with the military to oust the incumbent government.

Sharif's approach to the military was informed by two objectives. One was to personalize control over the military and deploy it in support of his government. This he attempted through control of promotion and postings. His second goal was to diminish the power and influence of the military through constitutional and legal changes. The pursuit of these objectives, his intrusion into security policymaking (for example, the Lahore process) and the institutional affairs of the military, both of which the military considered its preserve, and his apportionment of blame on the military for the negative outcome of the Kargil war with India increased tension between the military and Sharif. His attempt to sack General Musharaf and replace him with a loyalist was the final straw that brought about the latest round of military intervention in October 1999.

The military record in forging political consensus and constructing a viable political system is no better. Every military government in Pakistan suffered a legitimacy crisis (Rizvi 1991). The effort of Ayub Khan to construct a pseudodemocratic framework, characterized as basic democracy, that would entrench his power failed. In the face of a severe crisis precipitated by Zulfiqar Bhutto's newly formed Pakistan People's Party (PPP) and the loss of the support of the military, Ayub, at the urging of military commanders, transferred power to Gen. Yahya Khan, who declared martial law to consolidate his power and restore law and order. Yahya's effort to shepherd the country toward democracy through the March 1970 elections had the ulterior motive of preserving military influence. However, the outcome of the elections created a political impasse between the pragmatic alliance of the military and the PPP, which secured a majority in West Pakistan, and the East Pakistan–based Awami League, which won a majority in Pakistan as a whole. The refusal of the military-PPP alliance to transfer power to the Awami League ultimately led to the mass uprising in East Pakistan, brutal suppression, plunder, and rape by the Pakistani military, a massive refugee exodus to India, Indian military intervention, the humiliating defeat of the Pakistani military, and the eventual dismemberment of Pakistan. In this situation, the military had no choice but to hand over power to the PPP led by Bhutto.

Similarly, the attempt by Zia, who ruled from 1977 till his death in an air crash in 1988, to create a party-less democracy that would entrench his dominance and that of the military failed. Through an alliance with Islamic parties and careful cultivation of the judiciary (as well as punishment of those judges who would not go along), Zia legalized his unconstitutional ascendance to power and developed a political constituency in support of his military regime. At the same time, through political, legal, and economic means as well as terror, he attempted to destroy political opposition to his regime—especially the Bhutto family. Zulfiqar was tried for murder and hanged in 1979. Under Zia, the military penetrated and dominated every level and sector of government. The political, military, and economic support provided by the United States in the context of opposing the Soviet occupation of Afghanistan and the remittances from Pakistani nationals working in the Middle East were a boon to the Zia regime. Zia's divide and rule policy and the deep penetration of the military into politics polarized political society and led to the creation of the Movement for the Restoration of Democracy (MRD).

Under pressure from the MRD and the United States, Zia allowed limited political participation through the party-less elections in 1985, which initiated a phase of guided democracy under military tutelage and a strong president. The experiment failed because, from Zia's perspective, the government led by Mohammad Khan Junejo became too independent. In a preemptive strike in May 1988, he dismissed the prime minister, dissolved the assemblies, and destroyed the fragile pseudodemocratic structure he had created. Not only did Zia fail to promote political consensus and build a viable political system, he left behind a socially and politically polarized Pakistan that was torn apart by ethnic and religious strife. Under his regime, political parties and more generally political development were severely retarded. The military, however, had grown to become the most powerful national institution—with power to make and break governments in the ensuing quasi-democratic period from 1988 through 1999.

With neither the political nor the military elite capable of constructing a viable political framework, and the contending political parties and the military bent on ousting the incumbent government by any and all means, Pakistan has swung between civilian and military governments and, during the 1988–1999 period, between radically opposed political parties with autocratic leaders that had no commitment to democratic principles. Every leader, whether he or she was civilian or military, has attempted to monopolize political power, dominate and plunder the state, and deploy state power for private gain with little regard for the public good. Decades of misrule by civilian and military leaders alike have deeply polarized political and civil society, creating deep cleavages over the identity of the state and system of government as well as over the relationship between Islamabad and the provinces. Institutions of governance have been decimated, and the economy is near collapse. Pakistan is not far from the conditions of a failed state. There is no third force like the king in Thailand who can moderate and adjudicate between contending forces. Also, with little or no economic development, there has been no comparable development of the Pakistani state and society. Over the years the nature of the state and political forces at work have not altered much except for the fact that the Islamic parties have become stronger and the military has become the most powerful institution in the country. And coercion—the key asset of the military—continues to be crucial in internal politics and ensuring the international security of the country. However, it is also clear that the military cannot rule by itself. Some form of accommodation and power sharing among the competing political forces, including the military, is required to break the vicious cycle, as was the case in Thailand during the 1978–1988 period. A prolonged period of power sharing and stable government during which the focus is on economic development, building state capacity, and addressing the many grave challenges confronting the country appears to be necessary for the incubation of democracy in Pakistan and military exit from politics.

Burma: Domination through Force and Terror

With the onset of democracy in the Philippines in 1986, in South Korea in 1987, and the lifting of martial law in Taiwan in 1987 followed by the transfer of power to Lee Teng-hui in January 1988, it seemed almost certain to the Burmese public and the international community that the 1988 "people power" revolution in Burma would succeed as well. Transfer of power from the military-dominated Burma Socialist Program Party (BSPP) to the charismatic Aung San Suu Kyi, daughter of Burmese hero Aung San and leader of the popular opposition, and a democratic form of government were widely anticipated. The resignation of strongman, party chairman, and former Gen. Ne Win and the former general President San Yu in the extraordinary BSPP congress convened in July that year and Ne Win's promise of a multiparty system were interpreted as indication that a democratic transition was indeed in the offing. The military, however, was not about to relinquish power. In August that year, it launched a coup against the BSPP government, crushed the prodemocracy demonstrations, and created the new military-led State Law and Order Restoration Council (SLORC), which imposed martial law.

To refurbish its domestic and international legitimacy, which had been severely tarnished by the 1988 massacres, the SLORC organized national elections in 1990 that it hoped the military-backed National Unity Party would win. The election was viewed by the military and the opposition as a test of political legitimacy (Yawnghwe 1995). Despite the heavy odds against it and much to the surprise and dismay of the military, the opposition National League for Democracy led by Aung San Suu Kyi, who was under house arrest during the election, won an overwhelming victory. Refusing to accept the outcome, the SLORC redefined the purpose of the election and rejected the anticipated transfer of power. The military-led government, though clearly illegitimate from the perspective of the bulk of the Burmese people, has managed to hold on to power now for well over a decade and shows no sign of sharing power let alone relinquishing control of the political helm. How is this to be explained? Why has the Burmese military been able to hold on to power while the militaries in Pakistan and Indonesia, two other countries in Asia that have experienced extensive military penetration of the state, have been compelled to exit politics, even if only temporarily?

The explanation lies in the total domination by the military of the Burmese state leaving no space for political and civil society, its annihilation of contending political forces, and its extensive surveillance and intimidation networks that penetrate and control society through fear and coercion. As observed by Mary Callahan in Chapter 17, the state in Burma especially after 1988 has been based on and built by the military to the exclusion of all other forces. In fact the military is the only institution in town. Eschewing coalitions and ruthlessly suppressing and eliminating opposition, the military has concentrated all political, economic, and coercive power in itself. It does not permit any alternative rallying point. Although military domination of the state was extensive in Pakistan under Zia, he did co-opt like-minded politicians and technocrats and also permitted (or could not prevent) the continued operation of political parties, though under severe restriction. These opposition parties formed the Movement for the Restoration of Democracy that mobilized the political opposition focused on the demand for political participation. In Indonesia, although they could never aspire to power and their functioning was closely monitored and regulated by the military, two nongovernment political parties whose composition, constitution, and leadership were determined by the military were allowed to function during the Suharto era. Their activities and participation in the regularly scheduled elections, despite the undemocratic methods and purposes, provided some semblance of competition and an avenue for expressing dissatisfaction with the government, if only indirectly. Most important, the limited political space in Pakistan and Indonesia threw up leaders around whom the public could rally in times of crisis. This was not the case in Burma. Apart from Aung San Suu Kyi, who by chance happened to be in Burma during the crisis and emerged as the leader of the popular movement, there is no other opposition political leader of any standing. The military has jailed, killed, or forced into exile anyone showing signs of independence from the government. In the absence of political organization and leadership that can channel and sustain political demands, the periodic popular protests in Burma have not had lasting consequences.

The Pakistani, Indonesian, and Burmese militaries all have used coercion extensively and have shown no hesitation in exterminating "subversives." But the Burmese military has been most ruthless. It has been willing to incur much higher costs—both domestically and internationally—than its Pakistani and Indonesian counterparts to sustain itself in power. Since the 1990 experience, the Burmese military government has not been concerned with public legitimation. Its only concern has been maintaining the unity and loyalty of the military units that it has by providing for their welfare. The Burmese military has emerged as a special privileged class. Further, in Burma there is no distinction between military as institution and military as government, especially under the SLORC and the State Peace and Development Council. Regional military commanders are also the political commanders, and they have as much stake in preserving the system as the commanders in Rangoon. Despite rumors, there has been no serious internal division or conflict. To a considerable extent this also was the case in Pakistan under Zia. However, in Indonesia a distinction gradually emerged between the government of Suharto and the military, which increasingly became his political tool. Suharto manipulated and rewarded the military to retain its loyalty. He also counterbalanced it with other constituencies. Although still loyal to Suharto, the separation allowed the military to indicate to Suharto at a crucial moment in May 1998 that it was best for him to step down.

Through sheer force and terror the Burmese military has dominated and continues to dominate the country. The only local groups that can challenge the military through force are the minority resistance movements. The military has dealt with them in two ways: cooperation with Thailand to restrict the flexibility of the minority movements, and cutting (tactical) deals with the minority resistance movements, allowing them to keep their arms and control their respective territories.[11] The cease-fire agreements have freed up resources enabling the military to focus on its primary goal of sustaining its hold on state power.

Because of the subsistence nature of the economy and its limited international exposure as well as the neutral and then isolationist foreign policies followed by Burma over the last five decades, international pressure from the United States, the European Union, and other international agencies has not had much impact on the military regime. Chinese political and diplomatic backing, Chinese military assistance, the constuctive engagement policy of the Association of Southeast Asian Nations (ASEAN), and Burma's admission to ASEAN have ameliorated the economic and diplomatic isolation of the regime. In light of the support of the PRC and the Southeast Asian countries for the regime, and because Burma is not of strategic or economic importance, the Western countries have not gone and appear unlikely to go beyond exhorting political change through political, diplomatic, moral, and economic pressure. Because self-preservation is at issue, the military regime has been willing to bear considerable cost.

The regime can be dislodged only by domestic countervailing forces or cracks within the military. For now there is no sign of either. The military also does not appear likely to voluntarily share power with other forces or oversee political change in the manner of the Turkish model. Thus, despite its illegitimacy, the military regime looks set to continue its domination of Burma through coercion in the foreseeable future. It is galling to think, let alone accept, that in modern times a country can be dominated for such an extended period through sheer force and terror. But the Burmese military rulers seem to be operating in a warped world of their own creation.

FUTURE TRAJECTORIES: GROWING DOMINANCE OF DEMOCRATIC CIVILIAN CONTROL

Except for Burma, civil-military relations in all Asian countries investigated in this study are in the midst of change—more dramatic in some than in others—and further change is a prospect especially in the socialist states and in the states undergoing democratic transition. Although the "ultimate" patterns are unlikely to become clear for quite some time to come, the trend in Asia is toward a reduction in the political salience and role of the military with a corresponding increase in civilian control.

Reduction in the political role of the military can in large part be traced to the internal and international consolidation of Asian states and the decreasing weight of coercion in governance. International security still continues to be a key concern of several Asian countries. However, except for Taiwan and the two Koreas, no country is in danger of disappearing from the political map. Internally too, although the political construction of several Asian nation-states is still contested, such contestation is increasingly a feature of the periphery. State coercion has been deployed, sometimes massively, to deal with regional demands for autonomy and secession, but it has not affected the civil-military balance in the political heartland. Even at the local level, the increase in the power and influence of the military has not been significant where coercion has been deployed for a specific purpose of the state and carefully controlled by a legitimate and accountable political authority.

Equally if not even more important, the systems for acquisition and exercise of state power in the political heartland have or are becoming more established in many Asian countries—Japan, India, Malaysia, Singapore, Sri Lanka, Taiwan, South Korea, and to a lesser degree the Philippines and Thailand. The political systems in Bangladesh and Indonesia are still fragile and subject to reversal. The Leninist political systems in China and Vietnam are still the only game in town, although it is likely that will alter in due course. As political systems have become more established, coercion has become less central to governance. The acquisition and exercise of state power increasingly hinge on conformity with accepted principles, norms, and rules, performance, and consent of the governed. Attempt by the military to subvert or nullify the system, especially in the democratic and democratizing states, will be opposed by political and civil societies. In addition to the growing normative barrier, sustained economic development in countries such as Taiwan, South Korea, and Thailand has made for complex states, societies, and economies that are no longer susceptible to control and management by the state coercive apparatus. There has been a dramatic increase in the noncoercive capacity of many Asian states.

The net effect of sustained economic development, integration of Asian economies into the global capitalist system, growth of strong civil societies, development of stronger national identities and more legitimate political systems, a less threatening international security environment, and a changed international material and normative structure has been to fundamentally alter the civil-military balance as well as ideas about governance. These are now quite decisively tilted against the military. At the same time, it is important to acknowledge that state formation and construction of political systems are long and difficult processes with potential for setbacks and even reversals. There are still many issues of contention, and coercion will continue to feature in the internal and international governance of Asian states, as witnessed by the dramatic increase in security legislation, growth in paramilitary forces, and continued high defense spending (Collier 1999). However, coercion is not the mainstay of government. Relative to earlier periods, the role of coercion in the acquisition and, to a lesser degree, in the exercise of state power has reduced quite substantially. This has translated into a decline in the political power of the military and narrowing of its scope and jurisdiction in governance. However, not every country is strong in all the developments noted above. Some are weak on one or more counts, whereas Bangladesh, Indonesia, Pakistan, and Burma are weak on many counts. In these countries, coercion and the military still play a central role in governance.

The rise of civilian control does not equal one pattern of civil-military relations. Asia has in the past and will continue in the foreseeable future to be characterized by multiple patterns. The subjective type of civil-military relations grounded in ethnic considerations in Malaysia, Singapore, and Sri Lanka (at the national level) is durable and likely to continue. Similarly, the Leninist pattern of civil-military relations in the Asian socialist states is likely to continue in the short to medium term; in the longer term, it appears untenable and likely to change. With the growing irrelevance of the communist ideology and greater integration of the Chinese economy into the global capitalist economy, the party-state regime in the PRC begins to resemble in important ways that of the pre-1987 KMT regime in Taiwan. However, there are significant differences as well, and it is not foreordained that the PRC would follow in the path of Taiwan (Dickson 1997, 2000). At the same time, the vanguard role of the CCP and its monopolization of power will also be increasingly difficult to sustain.

Although the "ultimate" form of government in the PRC is difficult to predict, it will almost certainly have to be more participatory with greater differentiation between the party, the state, and the military. In this context, the already weakened symbiotic relationship between the CCP and the PLA is likely to further alter. Of crucial significance would be the pace and manner in which political change occurs in the PRC. If it occurs gradually and relatively peacefully under the leadership of reform elements within the party, the PLA is unlikely to be a key player in the process. However, if change is demand driven with the CCP resisting it, then the military may become more consequential with a corresponding increase in its power and influence relative to the political leadership.

Vietnam confronts a similar scenario except that the VCP and the VPA are still fused to a greater extent and enjoy a higher degree of legitimacy than their counterparts in China. Further, the Vietnamese state, society, and economy are still relatively underdeveloped, making it easier for an authoritarian government to continue dominating the country. However, here too changes are likely, although at a slower pace. Although the process of political change may provide opportunities for their respective militaries to increase their political influence, it appears highly unlikely that either China or Vietnam will come under military political domination. On the other hand, military intervention in North Korean politics is high and institutionalized. Easing of the international security situation (assuming the North-South Korea detente proves durable) and opening up of the North Korean economy should temper the military's international security and economic development roles. However, because it will still continue to be Kim's crucial power base, the political centrality of the military in North Korea appears unlikely to alter any time soon. Dispute between Kim and the military or factional struggles within the military over key issues including the pace and direction of the North-South detente and opening of the economy could well alter this situation, but this moves us into the realm of speculation.

Although Asia will continue to be characterized by multiple patterns, democratic civilian control is becoming the dominant mode of civil-military interaction. This has been the pattern in postwar Japan and in India and is likely to continue. Although civil-military relations in Malaysia, Singapore, and Sri Lanka are of the subjective type, they do exhibit certain features of democratic civilian control. Democratic civilian control is being consolidated in Taiwan, South Korea, and to a lesser degree in the Philippines and Thailand as well. Bangladesh and especially Indonesia are still in an early stage of their democratic transition. Military exit from politics is almost total in Taiwan and South Korea. In the Philippines, Thailand, Bangladesh, and Indonesia there has been a formal exit, but the militaries still wield informal political influence. In these countries, the militaries have attempted to retain as much autonomy and control as possible over institutional matters, off-budget revenues, and security policymaking. However, civilian authorities have also made major advances in restricting military jurisdiction in these areas. Right now it is a mixed picture.

Democratic civilian control is still relatively weak in the Philippines and Thailand and fragile in Bangladesh and Indonesia. These countries could experience limited military role expansion with the distinct possibility for reversal in Bangladesh and Indonesia. Alternation between civilian and military rule may characterize civil-military relations in these two countries as has been the case in Pakistan. However, as exemplified by the case of Pakistan, indefinite military rule is not tenable. In such countries, it is possible to envisage the emergence of some form of power sharing among civilian and military leadership in an interim stage that could eventually lead to civilian control.

The experiences of the last several decades suggest that enhancement of civilian control entails strengthening the legitimacy, capacity, and roles of civilian institutions, sustained economic development, and reducing the salience of coercion in governance. These hinge on forging political agreement on the basis of the nation-state and the system for political domination, making economic growth and development a key priority, as well as developing political and socioeconomic policies and processes to address political and social problems. This does not imply that coercion is irrelevant for governance. Only that its role should be limited and indirect and be viewed as the ultimate sanction, not the first recourse.

In this connection, it is important to observe that although the role of coercion in the international consolidation of the nation-state—safeguarding international security—is salient, the significance and role of coercion in domestic governance in enforcing the writ of the government and in maintaining internal order and security—because of its more direct connection to political legitimacy and capacity—is the more crucial determinant of the relationship between the state and the soldier. The prominence of coercion in securing loyalty and obedience from citizens of the state is a direct reflection of the weakness of the political legitimacy of the nation-state and the government. There is no such corresponding relationship between the international deployment of state coercion and political legitimacy. The impact could be positive or negative depending on the circumstances. Further, there is much greater prospect of translating the internal security role and deployment into political power and influence. It is therefore imperative to limit the role of coercion in internal governance. When necessary, deployment of coercion and the military in the internal security role should be limited to legitimate state purposes and carefully controlled to prevent abuse of state power and to ensure oversight by civilian authority that is itself legitimate and accountable to the citizens of the state.

NOTES

INTRODUCTION

1. The chief justice of Pakistan and five other judges of the supreme court refused to take the new oath of office as required by the order of December 13, 1999, which among other provisions barred all courts from making judgments against the chief executive. They along with seven other judges from provincial high courts were discharged. The reconstituted supreme court validated the Musharaf coup on grounds of state necessity—a rationale that was rejected earlier in that year by the supreme court in the Sheikh Liaqat Hussain case.

2. During Suharto's New Order era, the Indonesian military was known as Angkatan Bersenjata Republik Indonesia (ABRI). To reflect the "new paradigm" and to distance the military from the Suharto era, its designation was changed in 1999 to Tentera Nasional Indonesia (TNI). This was the designation of the Indonesian military before 1965.

3. These three arenas of polity are identified by Stepan (1988).

4. Characterizing the interpretations of Durkheim, Weber, and Marx as evolutionary, Giddens (1987: 31–34) argues the case for a "discontinuist interpretation" of the emergence of the modern state.

5. The others are heightened surveillance, capitalistic enterprise, and industrial production.

6. Liberal and neo-Marxist perspectives are two other common perspectives on the state.

7. The distinction between military as government and military as an institution is made by Stepan (1986: 72–78).

8. During the early years of the cold war, some scholars like Lasswell (1941, 1962) and Mills (1956) raised concerns about the growing civilian-military-business nexus and the rise of the garrison state in the United States. Recently, journalists and scholars (Ricks 1997; Holsti 1998–99) have argued that the gap between civilian and military authorities in the United States has been growing and that military influence in security policymaking has been on the rise (Desch 1996; Dunlap 1996). For a rebuttal, see Collins (1999). On the growing cultural divide, see Stout (1998). For an overview of the recent studies about the health and direction of civil-military relations in the United States, see Feaver (1999: 230–33).

9. Quoted in Richard C. Paddock, "Constitutional Coup ended Estrada's Rule," *Los Angeles Times,* January 22, 2001.

10. Arturo Bariuad, "Arroyo courts the military," *The Straits Times,* February 20, 2001.

11. Andrew Nathan (1997) characterizes the Mao regime as a quasi-military regime because Mao's power to an important degree was based on his exclusive control of the Chinese military through his chairmanship of the CMC.

12. On the military participation ratio, see Andreski (1971: 33).

13. For a recent survey of PLA studies, see Shambaugh (1999).

CHAPTER 1

1. This discussion draws its inspiration from Colton (1978), but it is substantially different in content. In some ways the framework developed here is similar to but still distinct from that advanced by Pion-Berlin (1992), Pion-Berlin and Arceneaux (2000), and Trinkunas (2000). Pion-Berlin distinguishes institu-

tional autonomy from political autonomy and emphasizes decision-making power. Trinkunas, too, emphasizes jurisdiction as the crucial factor in measuring progress made in crafting civilian control in emerging
democracies.

2. An issue is a separate item, whereas an issue area is a recognized cluster of concerns that are interdepen-
dent. See Haas (1980).

3. Many typologies of military participation in politics have been advanced. The scheme proposed here is
based on Nordlinger (1977) and Perlmutter (1977).

4. On military prerogatives, see Stepan (1988: 92–127) and Luckham (1996a).

5. For a more detailed discussion of military professionalism and its causal connection to the political orientation of the military, see "Introduction" in Alagappa (2001).

CHAPTER 2

1. Some of the restraints on the SDF—such as the exclusively defense-oriented policy and the denial of the
right of collective self-defense—come from the government's interpretation of the constitution. Japan's exclusively defense-oriented policy means that the SDF can be mobilized only when Japan is under attack by another
country; moreover, forces must be kept to the minimum level necessary for defense. It also prohibits Japan from
acquiring such offensive capabilities as intercontinental ballistic missiles, long-range bombers, or offensive aircraft carriers. The right of collective self-defense refers to "the right to use force to stop armed attacks on a foreign country with which it has close relations, even when the state itself in not under direct attack." See Japan
Defense Agency (1997: 101–3). The three nonnuclear principles and the ban on arms exports are government
policies. The 1 percent of gross national product limit on defense spending was adopted by the Miki government in 1976 but abolished by the Nakasone government in 1986.

2. The links between defense authorities and the civil economy, including problems of weapons procurement, are beyond the scope of this study. For these issues, see Samuels (1994), Green (1995), and Chinworth
(1992). In the postwar Japanese political context, the police are not considered an instrument of coercion and
hence are not dealt with here. For an analysis of Japan's policy of internal security focusing on the Japanese
police, see Katzenstein and Tsujinaka (1991).

3. Book-length research on Japan's civil-military relations in Japanese can be found in Hirose (1989) and
Nishioka (1988). In English, see Welfield (1988), Berger (1998), and Katzenstein and Okawara (1993).

4. The independence of the supreme command was initially intended to insulate the military from politics,
but ironically it was used to legitimize the military's involvement in politics. See, for example, Tobe (1998).

5. The principle of civilian control was incorporated into the command structure of the Police Reserve Force
under strong American influence. See Tanaka (1997: 74–78).

6. There have been many court cases disputing the constitutionality of the SDF (as well as the Japan-U.S.
Security Treaty). The lower tribunals have tended to rule against the constitutionality of the SDF, but such rul-
ings have been overturned by the supreme court on the grounds that matters of defense and national security
are beyond the scope of judicial review.

7. The SDF law, however, has no provisions enabling the prime minister to receive professional advice directly
from the chiefs of staff, the highest military advisers, or even from the chairman of the Joint Staff Council, the
highest-ranking officer of the SDF. See Yamaguchi (1991: 158–70).

8. The National Defense Council, established within the cabinet in 1956, had long served as a certifying
body for important issues affecting Japan's security.

9. Uniformed officers of the SDF are sometimes seconded to internal bureau posts, but no SDF officer has
ever been appointed a division chief or higher. See Hirose (1989: 66, 70–71).

10. Laws subject to study are classified into three categories: laws under the jurisdiction of the Defense Agency
(classification 1), laws under the jurisdiction of other ministries and agencies (classification 2), and laws relating
to matters not clearly falling under the jurisdiction of any ministry or agency (classification 3). The April 1981
report outlines the problems associated with classification 1, whereas the October 1984 report specifies issues
associated with classification 2. In view of the nature of studies on classification 3, the Cabinet Security Affairs
Office has been coordinating with other ministries and agencies to determine the jurisdictional boundaries so

that further studies can be carried out. For the progress of studies on emergency legislation, see Japan Defense Agency (1997: 355–65).

11. For opinion poll data, see Asagumo Shimbunsha (1976: 276; 1998: 691).

12. The post of chief of the Finance Division of the Defense Agency's Bureau of Finance, for example, is occupied by an official seconded from the Ministry of Finance. A Foreign Ministry official takes up one of the Defense Agency's four councillor posts to advise on international affairs. The post of director of the Equipment Bureau is normally held by an official seconded from the Ministry of International Trade and Industry.

13. In July 1984, the Research and Planning Department of the MOFA was upgraded to the Information Analysis, Research, and Planning Bureau in order to enhance intelligence gathering and analysis.

14. Japan Defense Agency (1986: 67–69). The establishment of the Security Council of Japan originates from policy recommendations made by an ad hoc Subcommittee on the Functions of the Cabinet chaired by Ryuzo Sejima, an adviser to Prime Minister Nakasone. See Angel (1988–89).

15. See Angel (1988–89: 595). Initially, the MOFA resisted the proposed reorganization of the Cabinet Secretariat, because it feared that the new apparatus might undermine the principle of single-track diplomacy. Eventually, the MOFA supported the reorganization on the condition that the External Affairs Coordination Office be headed by a MOFA official. See *Yomiuri Shimbun*, June 25, 1986, and January 24, 1988.

16. See Ueda (1983, 1997). For the perspective of the Maritime SDF, see Uchida (1980). On the U.S. Navy's "swing strategy," see Evans and Novak (1979).

17. See also *Sangiin yosan iinkai kaigiroku* (House of Councillors, Budget Committee Proceedings), no. 5, 75th Diet, March 8, 1975, pp. 31–32.

18. For details of the Sakata-Schlesinger talk, see *Boei antena* 183, October 1975, pp. 12–49.

19. Ibid., pp. 35–36.

20. On the Japanese side, its membership included the director of the North American Affairs Bureau of the MOFA, the director of the Defense Policy Bureau of the Defense Agency, and the Chief Secretary of the Joint Staff Council; on the American side, it included the minister at the U.S. Embassy and the chief of staff of U.S. forces, Japan.

21. *Asahi Shimbun*, November 28–29, 1978.

22. Boeicho (1977: 132).

23. Article 100 of the SDF Law was amended in November 1994 to enable SDF aircraft to be used for evacuating Japanese nationals in the event of an emergency in a foreign country.

24. The reorganization of the SDC in June 1996 had a similar effect on the power relationship between the Defense Agency and the MOFA. In the reconstituted SDC, the Japanese side is represented by the director-general of the North American Affairs Bureau of the MOFA, the director-general of the Defense Policy Bureau of the Defense Agency, and the representative of the SDF Joint Staff Council; the U.S. side is represented by the assistant secretary of state, the assistant secretary of defense, and representatives of the Joint Chiefs of Staff, the U.S. Pacific Command (CINCPAC), and the U.S. Forces, Japan (USFJ) (Japan Defense Agency 1997: 167).

25. In July 1997, the Bureau of Operations was established within the Defense Agency as an upgrade of the Operations Division of the Bureau of Defense Policy (Funabashi 1999: 110–17).

26. The idea of upgrading the Defense Agency to a ministry, strongly proposed by the LDP's three defense-related committees, was withdrawn from the administrative reform agenda.

27. In June 1998, the National Diet approved an amendment to the international peace cooperation law clarifying problems associated with the use of weapons and somewhat expanding the scope of Japan's participation in peacekeeping operations. The question of the use of weapons, which had been left to the judgment of individual personnel, was now left in principle to the discretion of the field commanding officer. The amended law enabled Japan not only to participate in monitoring elections in foreign countries but also to take part in humanitarian relief operations such as those under the UN High Commissioner for Refugees, even when there is no agreement on a cease-fire. The Japanese government sent personnel to monitor elections, under UN coordination and support, in Cambodia in July 1998 and in Bosnia-Herzegovina in September 1998.

28. Five areas where efforts should be made to promote cooperation are set out in the Japan-U.S. Joint Declaration on Security: continued close consultation and exchange of information and views on the international situation; a review of the 1978 Guidelines for Japan-U.S. Defense Cooperation; promotion of the bilateral cooperative relationship through the Acquisition and Cross-Servicing Agreement (ACSA) signed on April 15, 1996;

enhancing mutual exchange of technology and equipment; and prevention of the proliferation of weapons of mass destruction and their means of delivery, as well as cooperation in the study of ballistic missile defense (Japan Defense Agency 1997: 286–89). A revised ACSA, signed by Tokyo and Washington in April 1996, provides a framework for reciprocal provision of logistic support, supplies, and services between the SDF and the U.S. forces in joint military exercises, UN peacekeeping operations, and international humanitarian activities.

29. The three bills related to the guidelines were the "surrounding situations bill," concerning measures to ensure the nation's peace and security in areas surrounding Japan; a revised SDF law that allows SDF warships and other vessels to be used to rescue Japanese nationals; and a revised ACSA signed by Tokyo and Washington in April 1998, which enables the SDF to provide rear support to U.S. forces in "surrounding situations."

30. The account in this section is drawn from numerous sources including Kunimasa (1997–98), Armacost (1996), Asahi Shimbun Wangankiki Shuzaihan (1991), Boei Nenkan Kankokai (1992), Tanaka (1995), Purrington (1992), and Purrington and A.K. (1991).

31. See *Asahi Shimbun*, September 13, 1990.

32. See *Asahi Shimbun*, August 23 and November 16, 1990.

33. See *Asahi Shimbun*, November 6, 1990.

34. According to a *Yomiuri Shimbun* survey issued on April 26, three of four Japanese supported the dispatch of minesweepers to the Persian Gulf, whereas 18 percent opposed it. See, for example, Delfs (1991).

CHAPTER 3

1. *Militarism, militarist,* and *militarization* are used in this chapter in their common meaning. "Militarism" is "the military spirit...the glorification or prevalence of such a spirit, attitudes, etc. in a nation...the policy of maintaining a strong military organization in aggressive preparedness of war" (*Webster's New World* 1984: 901). "Militarist" is the support of militarism. "Militarization" is "to make military; equip and prepare for war...to fill with warlike spirit" (*Webster's New World* 1984: 901). "Militarism" and "militarist" are larger concepts than "militarization." "Civilian militarism" specifically refers to the prevalence of the military spirit and attitudes among civilian authorities. This "civilian militarism" percolates into civil society through a discourse that conflates internal and external security. "Civilian militarization" refers to the warlike mobilization of civilian institutions and civil society. In India, civilian authorities are "militarist," so there is "civilian militarism." "Civilian militarization" is the result of "civilian militarism." Because civilian authorities and institutions lead India's militarism and militarization, the formal civil-military balance remains in place. If, however, we value civilian control not just for its own sake, but because civilians display nonmilitarist attitudes, then our final purpose is defeated. It becomes doubly dangerous when civilians with militarist attitudes gain control of the decision-making process. For further discussion, see the section on civilian militarism in this chapter.

2. For an excellent though slightly out-of-date analysis of the concepts of military role expansion as they apply to India, see Elkin and Ritezel (1985: 489–502).

3. This chapter focuses mainly on the Indian Army because it dominates the civil-military arena. Not only is it the biggest service in terms of budget and personnel, but it is the most frequently used. Both of India's external threats are over land in the west and the north. The army contributes to the fight against insurgency as well. According to *The Military Balance* (IISS 2000), the strength of the Indian Army is 980,000, the Indian Air Force (IAF) strength is 140,000, and that of the Indian Navy is 55,000. A thirteen-year average shows that 47.9 percent of the defense spending went to the army, 24.3 percent to the air force, 11.7 percent to the navy, and 16.1 percent to other departments of the Ministry of Defense (Jaswant Singh 1999: 227). Though the army clearly leads in revenue expenditure, that is, pay and maintenance, the IAF is the biggest spender on the capital account. Until 1986, the Indian Army had suffered 40,000 war casualties, whereas the IAF had 227 and the navy 398 (Chibber 1986: 40). The army continues to wield greater influence despite its relative equalization with the other services over the past 50 years. The nuclear tests present the first real possibility of a reduction in the army's relative importance.

4. Another set of studies has looked at civil-military relations, broadly defined, and India's ability to project military power. Here there have been two approaches. One, offered by Indian writers, points to the deficiencies in the Indian national security planning system and how they might be fixed—usually with greater

centralization (see, for instance, Jaswant Singh 1999). The other, offered mostly by outsiders, identifies the cultural and social incapacity that prevents India from becoming a great power (see, for instance, Rosen 1996 and Tanham 1992). Both these approaches extrapolate the desire of a select national security elite to project power as the will of the country. The positions taken by the national security elite reflect "centralizing power" that allows the elite to monopolize decision making. However, the elite lack "developmental power," the broad support required to successfully implement policies (for more on the concepts of power and how they apply to India generally, see Kohli 1994: 91–98). We see this in the inability of the elite to transform India's national security program from one of internal security to power projection. Despite the best efforts of the national security elite, for instance, most Indians care little about projecting power—even though the public generally ratifies post facto elite actions such as the nuclear tests that seem to make India more powerful militarily. The majority of Indians, however, are more militaristic because of what is happening within the region rather than outside it (and here, it might be useful to see Pakistan-related problems as "riot control with armor").

5. This is not to suggest that the Indian Army entered the counterinsurgency business in the mid-1980s. Starting with the Naga insurgency in 1954, the Indian Army has suppressed rebellions in the states of Mizoram, Manipur, and Tripura. By the 1980s, however, the insurgency in the Northeast became more urgent. The Brahmaputra Valley in Assam and then the Assam Hills were engulfed by rebellion. For analyses of the rebellions themselves see Ganguly (1997), Widmalm (1997), Marwah (1995), Baruah (1994), George (1994), Hazarika (1994), and Hardgrave (1983). For an overall view of the increasing role of coercion see Mathur (1992: 337–48).

6. Despite the growth in paramilitary numbers, the army has not been able to avoid internal security duties or manpower increases. Concurrent deployments in three major regions forced the army to raise its own internal security group, the Rashtriya Rifles, in the early 1990s. Between 1994 and 1996, the number of annual recruits (normally 40,000 to 50,000) more than doubled (Ghosh 1996: 229). The army was even compelled to mobilize and quadruple its reserve corps, the Territorial Army (IISS 1985–97).

7. For the 1986 figures, see Gupta (1988: 82–83). In 1965, the BSF was raised with a strength of 25,000. Other paramilitary units such as the Assam Rifles and the Indo-Tibetan Border Police more than doubled. The Central Industrial Security Force has added 40 to 50 percent strength.

8. That India's overall military participation ratio, the number of men-at-arms as a percentage of the total population, is still low, around 0.2 percent, is more the consequence of a high population rather than low level of militarization. This percentage rises slightly to about 0.6 percent if, instead of total population, we use the male population in the age group 15–54 as the denominator (for figures of sex and age breakup of India's population see United Nations 1998: 238). If we included nongovernment armed groups in the numerator, the percentage would increase further. There are no ready working estimates of total strength of all armed groups in India.

9. The situation is somewhat analogous to the period before the British pacification of India in 1740–1817. See Rosen (1996: chap. 5), which deals with the initial phase of the British conquest of India. Moreover, Third World state building necessarily involves the internal and external elements of security in a dynamic mix; see Ayoob (1995). For official details of weapon recovery in Kashmir, see the Indian Army's Kashmir deployment Web site, http://www.armyinkashmir.org/weapons.html; see also http://www.armedforces.nic.in.

10. See Pathak (1992). The report claims a police counteroffensive against gangs in Delhi and western Uttar Pradesh and quotes a police officer as saying: "We have managed to kill 30 gangsters over the past one year." The rest of the story is replete with the exploits of the gang leaders as well as the police. See also Mannan (1992) and Ahmad (1992). For scholarly treatment of the underlying issues, see Saha (1994) and Rajgopal (1987). For the representation and impact of collective violence, see Brass (1997). See also the thirteen case studies of communal violence in Ghosh (1987: chap. 10).

11. See Dasgupta (1999). See also complaints about the excessive coverage of Kargil on government-owned media in "Capturing Heights," *Economic and Political Weekly,* July 10, 1999, p. 1861.

12. Robert L. Hardgrave Jr. observes, for instance, that the "tribal regions of the Northeast remain under a form of quasi-martial law, reflecting both the continuing danger of the unrest and the strategically vulnerable nature of the region" (Hardgrave 1983: 1173–74).

13. For details of deployments in Kashmir, for instance, see Pachauri and Meraj (1990: 8–13) and Gupta (1990a: 30–37). See also "Kashmir: Echoes of War," *Economist,* January 27, 1990, p. 33; "Kashmir: Fighting Words," *Economist,* February 3, 1990, p. 32.

14. See, for instance, the description of the Kashmir Valley in Badhwar (1990b: 10–16). See also Badhwar (1990a: 31).

15. Roughly 100 people were killed in the two weeks following New Delhi's imposition of direct rule over the state.

16. The government—not just aware of international pressure on this issue but also concerned about its own legitimacy—responded to the human rights problem by setting up the National Human Rights Commission in 1993. The commission investigates excesses committed by police and paramilitary forces all over India. The army, which has been off limits to the commission and the courts, submitted itself to a fairly intrusive investigation by the Press Council of India, an independent body (Karan 1997: 126–27). Recently the Punjab High Court has reopened cases of "missing persons" from the period of counterinsurgency campaigns.

17. For details of the tactics used by security forces see Sandhu (1992: 28–33). Though this news report is about the Punjab police, it is a good description of the extrajudicial methods employed in fighting insurgencies. The paramilitary forces are known to use all these methods. Where the army is deployed over substantial periods of time, it too is reported to resort to similar methods (although with far fewer instances of gross human rights violations).

18. While army personnel cannot be sued in civilian courts for human rights violations, paramilitary and police officers are vulnerable to judicial action—recently the Punjab High Court reopened a number of "missing persons" cases.

19. There are other laws—such as the Unlawful Activities (Prevention) Act of 1967, sections of the Criminal Procedure Code of 1973 (which generally applies to all crimes), the Arms Act of 1959, and the Prevention of Damage to Public Property Act of 1984—that bestow special powers for security forces. For details see Sinha (1995: 120–80).

20. TADA can only be imposed two years at a time. It is renewable as a new law at the discretion of the parliament. In Punjab, for instance, TADA remained in force for more than ten years.

21. Vinayak (1992: 92). The reason for the low rate of conviction, according to the news report, was mainly the continued intimidation of witnesses by Sikh militants—despite the extensive witness protection offered by the act. Poor investigation work and lapses in procedure were also cited as reasons for the law's ineffectiveness.

22. In Punjab, for instance, the army patrolled the border with Pakistan on the west and sealed up the marshes that were being used to supply guns and coordinate militant efforts. The paramilitary forces and the Punjab Police were given the task of fighting the militants in the villages, towns, and cities.

23. Officers of the CRP jokingly (but not without some truth) say that "CRP" stands for "Chalte raho pyare" (Keep on the move, my dear). For an account of overdeployment see Gupta (1988: 82–83). The news report quotes a paramilitary officer whose unit was moved 33 times in 1987 and 31 times each in 1986 and 1985. A riot control deployment of central paramilitary forces in the town of Moradabad, in Uttar Pradesh, lasted from 1980 to 1984.

24. A variety of reasons are cited to explain post-1947 civilian control and distrust of the military. See Cohen (1990), Ganguly (1991b), Kukreja (1991), Bhimaya (1997), and Kundu (1998).

25. *Harijan*, April 21, 1946; reprinted in Gandhi (1960: 242).

26. This is true of most parliamentary systems. Further, the parliament exercises indirect control over the military through the Lok Sabha's (lower house of the parliament) Standing Committee on Defense and the Estimates Committee, which exercises certain oversight powers. In 1992–1993, the parliament commissioned and received the Nineteenth Report to its Estimate Committee (chaired by former defense minister K. C. Pant), which included sections on defense policymaking. Earlier in the 1990s, the Ministry of Defense appointed a high-level Committee on Defense Expenditure, headed by a former minister of state for defense, Arun Singh. The Arun Singh Committee, as it came to be known, recommended a plethora of changes not just in defense expenditure but in manpower and strategic planning as well. The report has not been made public as yet and certainly has not been implemented.

27. With the benefit of hindsight we can say that some of the Singh-Sundarji efforts proved counterproductive. Since the reorganization, the Indian Army has been primarily involved in domestic duties. An alleged opaque deterrence between India and Pakistan since 1990—which came out in the open in 1998—significantly reduced the possibility of a general war with Pakistan. Consequently, the Brasstacks model has been of little practical use. Moreover, the wear and tear of equipment during Brasstacks and related exercises exacerbated

disruptions in the supply of spares after the disintegration of the Soviet Union. Moreover, significant civil-military relations issues emerged. Was there communication between the Indian Army, the Ministry of Defence, and the Prime Minister's Office? Had the balance of power caused the military during the late 1980s to reflect a more powerful army (Bajpai et al. 1995: 103–4)? For details of future problems, see Gupta et al. (1993: 22–41).

28. Other reasons offered for the arms buildup are ad hoc reactions to the Pakistani rearmament, Washington's munificence for supporting the *mujahedin* in Afghanistan, Moscow's willingness to sell arms (in exchange for support on Afghanistan), and the windfall of an economy beginning to turn around (Smith 1994: 79–80; Amit Gupta 1995: 448).

29. Though the army considers the primary lesson of the mutiny to be a failure of command, the incident gave pause on two counts. First, if a community so inextricably tied to the army could rebel, what was next? Second, how far could the army go in its internal security duties without alienating its base of support? Though figures vary, purely Sikh units (rank and file) constitute 2 percent of the army, another 4 to 8 percent are believed to be scattered in non-Sikh units, and the officer corps is believed to be even more overrepresented (Rosen 1996: 212; Cohen 1988: 131; *Economist*, June 16, 1984; *New York Times*, June 14, 1984). It is believed that a "quarter" of IAF pilots and "substantial numbers" of navy personnel are also Sikhs, though these services have never adopted a "martial races" policy (Cohen 1988: 132). Sikhs comprise only 2 percent of the country's population (http://www.cia.gov/cia/publications/factbook/geos/in.html#People). Ironically, the army commander in charge of the assault on the temple was a Sikh and the man who organized the Sikh militant defense, a Sikh, was a highly decorated retired army officer. (See Gupta 1984a: 64; 1984b: 26.)

30. Paramilitary organizations have been accused of responding ethnically in Ayodhya—where paramilitary units did not move against Hindu fanatics destroying an ancient mosque—and in numerous Hindu-Muslim riots the police and the paramilitary have been charged with siding with the Hindu community.

31. See Bhagwat's interview on *Rediff on the Net*, February 25, 1999, http://216.32.165.71/news/1999/feb/25vb.htm.

32. For details of the various projects and the elements of corruption see Pillai (1999) and Chawla and Joshi (1999: 19–24).

33. Malik called Bhagwat's charges against him baseless. See *Rediff on the Net*, March 10, 1999, http://216.32.165.71/news/1999/mar/10malik.htm.

34. In the mid-1980s, chief of army staff General Sundarji was accused of validating the Rajiv Gandhi administration's decision to purchase Swedish self-propelled howitzers—the ensuing corruption scandal lost Gandhi the election in 1989. Sundarji later rebutted the allegation in an interview, saying that he had been willing to cancel the howitzer contract but Gandhi insisted on it. For details see Pathak and Mitra (1992: 23).

35. The Indian defense establishment continued the highly secretive practices of the British period. Stephen Rosen (1996: 200) notes: "The army forbids units competing against each other in sporting events from posting their unit designations on the scoreboards for fear of giving away secrets." In this environment it is especially useful when such a controversy occurs in full public glare. Accusations of corruption, treason, ineptitude, conspiracy, politicization, and even communalism in the military flooded the Indian press for a few months in early 1999. India's top two news magazines took opposite sides in the controversy. As the Bhagwat affair unfolded in public, the news stories provided a unique opportunity to appraise civil-military relations in an unusually secretive defense establishment. *Frontline* was supportive of Bhagwat; *India Today* came out on the side of Defense Minister Fernandes, the man who sacked the admiral. For typical treatments by the two magazines, see the stories in *Frontline* by Muralidharan (1999a, 1999b); in *India Today* see Chawla and Joshi (1999: 19–24) and Chawla (1999).

36. For two impassioned opinions, see Ramdas (1999) and Nalapat (1999: 10).

37. A description of India's top leadership being conveyed news of the success of the nuclear tests includes the senior members of the BJP government: "[Prime Minister] Vajpayee, in an emotion-choked voice, thanked the two scientists who made it happen." The news report adds that on April 8, 1998, "anxiously-waiting" Kalam and Chidambaram were finally given the go-ahead by Prime Minister Vajpayee. See Joshi (1998a: 12–13).

38. There are always doubts about aircraft as a nuclear weapons delivery system. See Chari (1999).

39. The estimated cost of a nuclear deterrent is Rs 25,620 crore, or about $6 billion at 1999 exchange rates. Spread over ten years, this is not expected to have a deleterious effect on development. The figure is about half the annual defense budget; over ten years, about 5 percent of the budget. For budget figures see *The Military*

Balance (IISS 1985–97). For cost estimates of the nuclear program, see Joshi 1998b: 22–23). These estimates make numerous presumptions. They presume, for instance, that the Indian Army's manpower requirement and conventional capability can be scaled down to release money for a nuclear program. (See, for instance, Manavendra Singh 1999a: 59–63. Singh suggests a scaling down of conventional capability across the board.) At a time when insurgency deployments account for the major commitment of Indian troops, cutting back on manpower seems impractical. It also presumes the easy development of a nuclear submarine. This is hardly a small problem. Although India can build medium-sized submarines with 1970s German technology, it does not have the capability to build the larger submarines required for a nuclear core. The choice would be one of two: build a smaller nuclear core to fit the current capability or design a whole new platform. After all, smaller submarines stay underwater for shorter periods. The larger point, in terms of civil-military relations, is that the Indian nuclear program is not only controlled by civilian authorities, but its future is determined by civilian scientists, the civilian economy, and the general level of technology in the country. The scientific and technological inputs are politically significant as well. Abraham (1998), for instance, argues that science has been one of the pillars of Indian nation building. Perkovich (1999) has identified scientific fervor as one of the key contributors to India's nuclear weapons program. For the political will of scientists in India, see Kalam (1998).

40. For details of weapon platforms under consideration for purchase see Joshi (1999).

41. A curious but visually striking picture that conveys the idea of civil society's militarization is the many photographs showing defense and atomic scientists in military camouflage. The camouflage, apparently part of the secrecy surrounding the tests, constitutes a powerful image. See, for example, the cover photograph of *India Today International,* June 22, 1998.

42. Assertive civilian control over nuclear weapons indicates a deeper mistrust between civil and military institutions. Peter Feaver has suggested that states where the military has not historically intervened in politics are more likely to delegate control of nuclear weapons to the armed forces. Conversely, then, states that do not delegate control of nuclear weapons—even when they do not have a history of military intervention—betray their fear of such an eventuality. Feaver found that early periods of nuclear arsenal building in the United States, Britain, and Israel were attended by irrational fears and assertive control over nuclear weapons (Feaver 1992: 175–77).

43. See "PM Approves Formation of National Security Council," *The Hindu,* November 20, 1998, p. 1.

44. For a list of members of the NSC Advisory Board, see "22 Member Security Advisory Board Formed," *Hindustan Times* (New Delhi), November 29, 1998, p. 1.

45. After the nuclear tests, there has been preliminary discussion of establishing a nuclear triad of land-based intermediate-range ballistic missiles, roaming nuclear-powered and nuclear-armed submarines, and fighter-bombers. See Chengappa and Joshi (1998). Erecting such a triad will come down to commitments of money and relative importance of the forces, however, and could cause interservice tensions. On the issue of a chief of defense staff, the two smaller services, the navy and the air force, have strongly resisted the move. The fear is that the army will gain effective control over the entire military. The civilian leadership—both politicians and the bureaucracy—has opposed the proposal because control over the entire military would become concentrated in a single person, creating a potential threat to civilian institutions.

46. The equalization of the services has come at a cost. In the 1965 war, there was no interservice coordination either. P. C. Lal, who was air vice-marshal in 1965, writes: "We thought of fighting an air war against the PAF [Pakistan Air Force] and what we considered to be strategic targets, assigning relatively low priority to support [of] the Army. Separate plans were hastily drawn up by each Service with no joint consultation worth the name" (Ganguly 1991: 18–19). Interservice coordination did not improve much in the 1971 war either. Except for the Indian Navy's (some say fortuitous) blockade of the Karachi port, the main battles were fought by the army.

47. See "India Considers Budget Increase," *Defense News,* November 1, 1999, p. 26. Predictably, the story also suggested that Kalam, the head of India's defense research organizations, was in favor of accelerating indigenous production rather than foreign acquisition. The 20 percent increase demanded by the services would reverse the downtrend in defense expenditure in the 1990s.

48. "Two-thirds of all tanks in the Army (including those in the frontline armoured formations) are mothballed or underused. In a regiment of about 45 tanks, only 15 are allowed to participate in routine training exercises, with each tank being restricted to 200 km of running" (Jaswant Singh 1999: 260–61). Aircraft serviceability is down to about 40 to 50 percent in the air force, and navy vessels spend most of their time in dry docks (Jaswant Singh 1999: 260). For a comparative military balance between India and Pakistan, see Arun Singh

(1997). A report of the Comptroller and Auditor General of India in 1993 found that 50 percent of the army's training facilities were being utilized (Gupta et al. 1993: 23).

CHAPTER 4

1. Both the *munban* and *muban* classes were included in *"yangban,"* which later became the term for the scholar-gentry class.

2. Moreover, the Taejun Treaty during the Korean War specified that U.S. military advisers would have considerable influence over military appointments and promotions.

3. This is why he preferred young officers from the Manchurian army over old Japanese military academy graduates: young officers were easier to control.

4. The "Pusan Scandal" was a clear example of this. Rhee declared martial law in Pusan in order to amend the constitution for his presidential election.

5. This can be seen in the background of his first cabinet members: eight were former ministers and five came from the military.

6. *Chosun Ilbo*, February 22, 1994.

7. To gain political power, apparently he had to get rid of the Hana faction and its support of the old military-oriented elite.

8. *Donga Ilbo*, July 13, 1998.

9. *Donga Ilbo*, July 6, 1998.

10. *Chosun Ilbo*, October 23, 1998.

11. *Chosun Ilbo*, October 25, 1999.

12. *Donga Ilbo*, April 25, 2000.

13. Security was not part of Kim Young-sam's agenda. This position, however, was attacked by conservative circles after the North Korean submarine crisis. See Seon-ho Lee (1996).

14. *Donga Ilbo*, June 15, 2000.

15. *Minjoo Ilbo*, October 6, 1990.

16. *Minjoo Ilbo*, May 8, 1990.

17. In April 1973, Yoon was charged with corruption along with several close associates including three generals. They received maximum sentences of fifteen years in prison. Furthermore, a related investigation forced some 200 officers to resign, although this was considered a political scandal. Park is said to have realized that Yoon's power had become a threat and decided to get rid of him. See the interview in *Sindong-a*, December 1989.

18. *Hangook Ilbo*, October 8, 1990.

19. Direct meetings between the president and the NDSC commander became customary and had been practiced during Chun and Roh's presidencies. The KCIA director reported in the same fashion.

20. *Juganchosun*, September 1996.

21. *Chosun Ilbo*, May 14, 1998.

22. From the Supreme Council for National Reconstruction Law (Article 17).

23. *News Plus*, May 13, 1997.

CHAPTER 5

1. The first chief of general staff to appear in the Legislative Yuan to answer questions was General Tang Fei on September 30, 1998.

2. *China Times* (Taipei), March 25, 1999.

3. *China Times*, March 23, 1999.

4. *Legislative Gazette*, December 16, 1993, p. 23.

5. China News Agency (http://www.cna.com.tw), September 30, 1998.

6. The historical accounts of this section come mainly from the following books and related news reports or analyses: Chang (1992, 1993) and Lo (1995).

7. This phenomenon has been called the "Lee Teng-hui Complex."

8. For the ROC's arms procurement process, see Lo (1999).

9. *China Times,* March 21, 1998, p. 4.

CHAPTER 6

1. Regarding this source (Davide et al. 1990): Upon the issue of Administrative Order No. 146 by President Corazon C. Aquino on December 6, 1989, the Philippine Congress approved, on January 3, 1990, Act No. 6832, which effectively created the so-called Fact-Finding Commission that authored *The Final Report.*

2. Citation from President Aquino's commencement speech at the Philippine Military Academy (PMA), March 23, 1987, cited in Bello (1987).

3. Some of the themes discussed here are also treated in Hedman (2000: 39–40, 43–50).

4. Citation from Hernandez (1985: 163); figures from International Institute for Strategic Studies (IISS) (1973: 30).

5. Since the Commonwealth, several (former) PC chiefs have been appointed AFP chief of staff, including Maj. Gen. Mariano N. Castañeda (1947–1951), Lt. Gen. Manuel F. Cabal (1959–1961), Lt. Gen. Pelagio A. Cruz (1961–1962), Gen. Segundo P. Velasco (1967–1968), Gen. Manuel T. Yan (1968–1972), Fidel V. Ramos (1986–1989), and Renato S. de Villa (1989–1991).

6. For a discussion of the PC during the early American period see, for example, Yarrington-Coats (1968).

7. See, for example, Villamor (1958). See further Republic Act 557, enacted on July 17, 1950.

8. For an early and influential discussion of the role of Congress in military promotions see Hernandez (1979: 87–89).

9. *Pembela Tanah Air* refers to the buildup of a military force of some 65,000 troops, with Indonesian officers up to the level of battalion, under the Japanese occupation of the Netherlands Indies.

10. See, for example, Lansdale (1959: 1–4).

11. The USAID-sponsored Public Safety Program excerpt from the classified report "Survey of Philippine Law Enforcement" outlines the following recommendations: "the upgrading, consolidation, and centralization of the activities of the various law enforcement agencies of the Philippine government"; cited in Shalom (1986: 113).

12. Executive Order 120, February 16, 1968, expanded Metrocom. After the joint survey referred to in note 8, USAID police assistance to the Philippines reportedly increased from "$62,000 in 1962 . . . to $618,000 in 1968 [and] $608,000 in 1969"; cited in Gillego (1972: 12).

13. According to Donald Berlin, this reshuffle included "the forced retirement of fourteen of the military's twenty-five flag officers, including the Chief and the Vice Chief of Staff, the Army Commanding General, the Chief of Constabulary, and all four Constabulary zone commanders. In addition, over one-third of all Constabulary provincial commanders were relieved." See Berlin (1982: 187).

14. Though already inaugurated under President Diosdado Macapagal, the National Defense College did not start offering regular courses until Marcos's first year in Malacañang. In its capacity as a finishing school of sorts for commanding officers, it subsequently turned out almost 100 graduates between 1966 and 1973.

15. In the realm of intelligence gathering and dissemination, a new and enlarged security apparatus—the National Intelligence Security Agency (NISA)—emerged under the leadership of Fabian C. Ver. Initially designed merely to facilitate the coordination of intelligence matters between the different services of the AFP (a function the Intelligence Service of the AFP, also headed by Ver, inherited), under martial law NISA was transformed into an executive office of the president and, in fact, became the most powerful arm of the government. "When he became the AFP Chief of Staff . . . Ver relinquished formal command of the PSC to Brig. Gen. Santiago Barangan. In reality, however, Ver and his sons exercised *de facto* control over PSC. Col. Irwin Ver was the PSC's Chief of Staff and Lt. Col. Rexor Ver was [the] Commander." See Tesoro (1986: 94–95).

16. Reportedly Marcos had first appointed Melchor undersecretary of defense on the basis of the Melchor's proposal for a military role expansion into management, engineering, transportation, and communication. In a curious echo of Huntington's thesis, Melchor thus argued that because "military men are trained as managers" they possess expert knowledge as well as social responsibility. See Melchor, "Project Compass," cited in De Quiros (1997: 367). See also "The Ascendancy of the Military," *Philippines Free Press,* April 25, 1970, pp. 5 and 62.

17. Benigno Aquino in Nick Joaquin, *The Aquinos of Tarlac,* cited in De Quiros (1997: 81).Of course, Enrile was reappointed as secretary of defense after failing to capture a senatorial seat in the November 1971 elections.

18. Berlin (1982: 196) notes the following change of command: "the retirement of eighteen Philippine flag officers and the appointment of new commanders of all the military services, Constabulary zones, Army divisions, and separate brigades, as well as a new AFP Chief and Vice Chief of Staff."

19. Miranda and Ciron (1987b: 169) put the 1972 manpower figure at 62,715 and that of 1976 at 142,490. The Fact-Finding Commission cites slightly lower figures—57,100 troops in 1971 and 113,000 in 1976—amounting to a near doubling (98 percent) of the AFP (Davide et al. 1990: 52).

20. One estimate puts the approximate number of troops in 1984 at 250,000 (Hernandez 1984: 22). An even higher figure—300,000—is cited in *Business Day,* March 11, 1983.

21. Hernandez estimates the overall military budget for 1972 at $136 million and that of 1977 at $420 million. For the 1981 figures see Berry (1986: 220).

22. Bello and Rivera (1977: 7–33) argue that this increase does not include U.S. weapons sales and unauthorized aid.

23. *Veritas,* May 26, 1985, p. 15.

24. For example, the entire class of 1976 refused to sign an official indictment of classmate Victor Corpus upon the latter's defection from the AFP and his teaching assignment at the academy in December 1970. Interview with Victor Corpus, August 24, 1990, Fort Bonifacio, Pasig, Metro Manila.

25. In this regard, a curious anomaly is perhaps worthy of note: despite broadly similar backdrops, none of the 1969, 1970, or 1972 graduating years provided much in the way of critical leadership for RAM. Instead of proceeding from the assumption that there was something fundamentally different about the 1971 graduates, it appears more fruitful to shift the focus away from the reputed characteristics of this class to the specific circumstances that allowed a handful of its members to provide the necessary leadership for the reformist movement that emerged.

26. In this regard it seems fair to assume that Honasan's assignment to Defense Minister Enrile's security unit resulted from a routine rotation of appointments—a sheer coincidence. But there is little doubt that once Honasan had served under Enrile, the latter was instrumental in effecting the colonel's reassignment. Moreover, personal ties rather than pure coincidence were critical for bringing both Kapunan and Legaspi on board Enrile's security team. The appointment of another 1971 graduate, Col. Victor Batac, as a close aide to Lt. Gen. Fidel V. Ramos, however, seems to be another case of coincidences playing into the hands of the emerging RAM leadership. The physical proximity of the headquarters of the Defense Ministry and that of the Philippine Constabulary (on opposite sides across Metro Manila's main thoroughfare, Epifanio de los Santos Avenue [EDSA]) surely benefited the coordination of activities between Honasan, in Camp Aguinaldo, and Batac, in Camp Crame. Batac, of course, became the chief RAM organizer within the PC. Interviews with Marites Danguilan-Vitug, August 15, 1990, Quezon City, and Victor Corpus.

27. "PCGG Wants Wealth of 3 Generals Forfeited," *Manila Chronicle,* August 2, 1987, p. 1. Of course, "even the rebel military officers who lambasted corruption among public officials are known to have profited from illegal numbers games, gold-panning operations, and logging concessions" (Hernandez 1996: 71).

28. The first such interview, "Conversations with the Reformists," appeared in *Veritas,* May 12, 1985, p. 14. For the early days of RAM see Arillo (1986); "Open Letter to Gringo," *Philippine Star,* September 7, 1987, pp. 1 and 10; and Alfred McCoy's "RAM Boys Series" (1988).

29. As noted by Crouch (1997: 226), active military officers were barred from holding civilian government positions under the new constitution in the post-Marcos period. In this regard, Hernandez suggests that "one count of a little over a hundred... is regarded as an extremely conservative estimate by knowledgeable sources." See "'Generalizing' the Bureaucracy," *PDI,* April 15, 1997, and "Military: New Political Elite," *MC,* April 2, 1997, cited in Hernandez (1997: 57).

30. Among other notorious (former) RAM or Young Officers Union (YOU) members, Victor Batac (Philippine Military Academy [PMA] 1971) and his protégé Diosdado Valeroso (PMA 1986) were assigned to posts at PNP Headquarters in Camp Crame under Lacson.

31. In a speech to the Council of Philippine Affairs on February 21, 2001, President Macapagal Arroyo acknowledged meeting with the following top-ranking military and police officials during her tenure as vice president and, until October 2000, as a cabinet member under the Estrada administration: Armed Forces Chief of Staff Gen. Angelo Reyes, PNP Deputy Director Leandro Mendoza, Gen. Edgardo Espinosa of the AFP Joint

Command Staff College, PNP Col. Reynaldo Berroya, and Gen. Hermogenes Edbane of the PNP Directorate for Human Resource Development and Doctrination. According to Macapagal Arroyo, (former) civilian politicians Fidel V. Ramos, José "Peping" Cojuangco, and Luis "Chavit" Singson played critical roles in making these introductions. "GMA Reveals Support of 5 Military Groups," *PDI*, February 22, 2001; "Probe Macapagal-AFP 'plot,'" *PDI*, February 25, 2001.

32. As the political opposition to Estrada gained momentum in the fall of 2000, Cabinet Secretary Alfredo Lim conducted repeated DILG "loyalty checks" on governors, mayors, and local police. Meanwhile, under the command of close Estrada associate and chief of police Panfilo Lacson, the PNP remained publicly supportive of the embattled president until the day before his successor was sworn in. Indeed, Lim never broke with his president, and Lacson did so only after the chief of staff of the armed forces, Gen. Angelo Reyes, and the secretary of national defense, Orlando Mercado, had announced their defections from Estrada and joined the civilian political opposition and broader protest movement at the Edsa Shrine on January 19, 2001.

33. Some 17,000 posts are to be filled in the May 14 elections, including 13 seats in the 24-member Senate and all 250 seats in the House of Representatives. Governors, mayors, and other local posts will also be contested on this date. See also "Word War of Generals," *PDI*, January 25, 2001; "Generals Hug, Make Up: 'Credit Goes to the People,'" *PDI*, January 26, 2001; and "Coup Talk Made Admiral Walk," *PDI*, February 24, 2001.

34. "Erap Pledges P10B for AFP," *PDI*, July 2, 1999.

35. See, for example, "Ex-Generals Raise Concern over China Action in Spratleys," *PDI*, May 14, 1999, and "RP Navy 'Sinks' Sino Fishing Boat," *PDI*, May 25, 1999.

36. See, for example, "President Defends RP Air Patrol over Spratleys," *PDI*, March 26, 1999; "US Echoes Erap's Line on Spratley Row," *PDI*, May 23, 1999; "Estrada Calls for New Security Setup in Asia," *PDI*, June 4, 1999. Among those who opposed the VFA were the Catholic Bishops Conference of the Philippines (CBCP), the Bagong Alyansang Makabayan (Bayan), and many NGOs.

37. See, for example, "VFA Approval Paves Way for Glan Port," *PDI*, May 30, 1999.

38. "Communist Rebels End Talks, Expect Battle to Pick Up Soon," *PDI*, May 31, 1999.

39. Citation from Tiglao (1994). For recent reports of fighting in the mountains of the Cordilleras and Bicol see, for example, "Army Accused of Bombing Villages," *PDI*, April 12, 1999; "Balweg, Ex-Rebs, AFP Men Next in Line—NPA," *PDI*, May 3, 1999; and "Albay Villagers Flee as Army and Rebels Clash," *PDI*, May 6, 1999. With the expiration of the Joint Agreement on Safety and Immunity Guarantees on July 1, 1999, the Zamboanga-based Southern Command ordered all its units "to step up their counter-insurgency drive and arrest communist rebels." See "15 Rebs Listed as Most Wanted," *PDI*, July 9, 1999. After a flurry of reported recent small-scale NPA attacks in provincial Philippines, the AFP has warned of an upsurge of such offensives "as rebels make their presence felt during the run-up to the May 14 general elections" in 2001. "7 Troopers Killed in NPA Attack," *PDI*, February 13, 2001. See also "Negros Communist Rebels Wage War on Danding Bets," *PDI*, February 27, 2001.

40. However, the new administration has declared the Abu Sayyaf a "terrorist group" beyond the purview of any proposed peace talks. "Military Operations vs MILF Suspended," *PDI*, February 21, 2001; "MILF Insists on Talks Abroad, with 'Referee,'" *PDI*, March 3, 2001.

41. For recent reports on a similarly contentious issue, see, for example, "RP Fears China Building Structures on Scarborough," *PDI*, February 24, 2001.

42. According to one estimate, the Philippine Navy in the early 1990s counted "eleven U.S. built corvettes, thirty-two small patrol craft, and several amphibious landing ships, *all of World War II vintage*" [emphasis added]; citation from Storey (1999: 103). At the same time, "the Philippine Air Force possessed seven elderly F-5 jet fighters, only five of which were air worthy"; ibid.

43. "US Admiral: VFA No Security Blanket," *PDI*, May 24, 1999.

44. "RP, US to Hold Military Exercises in February," *PDI*, June 2, 1999.

45. "US Troops Arrive for War Games," *PDI*, February 18, 2000.

CHAPTER 7

1. A fourth controversy, over the control of radio and television frequencies, is discussed later in terms of its economic implications. It too grows out of the events of May 1992, when the military used the media to broad-

cast its own interpretation of the demonstrations. A primary reason for the effort to diversify ownership of the media is to ensure that interpretations of events cannot be so easily controlled in the future.

2. The best example is *Sayamrat sapda wijan*, August 9, 1998, pp. 7–11. In English the *Bangkok Post* gave extensive coverage to the controversy; see, for example, August 9, 1998, p. 3 and August 10, 1998, p. 2.

3. By military mindset, I do not mean the attitudes or opinions of individual soldiers, or even of leading generals. Particularly for earlier periods, such data is not available. Like Huntington, I refer to the institution, to "the values, attitudes and perspectives which inhere in the [military history] and are deducible from [its] nature" (Huntington 1957: 61).

4. Note the resemblance here to the colonial armies in neighboring countries where promotion and often admission to the officer corps were restricted by race.

5. This aspect, however, should not be overemphasized. The first military detachment King Chulalongkorn sent to Chiangmai in 1874 consisted of just 3 noncommissioned officers and 24 troops. Chiangmai was probably the most important city in the north with its own strong local nobility. See Battye (1974: 146). Most troops remained in Bangkok to ensure the safety of the king.

6. Members of the royal family initially monopolized access to advanced military training, however, so that in the early years they may in fact have been the most qualified officers.

7. The best English-language account is by Mokaparong (1972). In Thai see Kasetsiri (1992) and Nakharin (1992).

8. It is not clear whether the same individuals joined the different groups. I am arguing here that there was a continuity of attitudes that provided a sympathetic audience when the military sought support at the grassroots level.

9. The police force by then had come to include paratroops, armored vehicles, and coastal ships and was in charge not only of counterinsurgency but also of guarding much of the border. It was supported by the CIA. The army was supported by the Joint U.S. Military Assistance Advisory Group, although the relationship was not without considerable tension. See Fineman (1997) and Muscat (1990).

10. The "hearts and minds" approach was based on the premise that the war against communism was not to be won on the battlefield but by winning over the hearts and minds of the people.

11. Class Four had 59 students, Class Five had 148, Class Six had 170, and Class Seven had 136 (Table 7.2).

12. During this time certain high-profile atrocities were investigated, bringing the military into public disrepute. Perhaps the most notorious was the Ban Na Sai incident. See Morell and Samudavanija (1981: 169–72).

13. On these two factions and their ideas see Samudavanija (1982); on counterinsurgency policy see Saiyud (1986).

14. Although the counterinsurgency efforts doubtless contributed to the decline of the CPT, the conflict between China and Vietnam was probably the most crucial factor. The conflict led both sides to stop their support of the CPT. Supplies, finances, and rear bases were cut off, and the CPT radio station in southern China fell silent. This exacerbated a conflict in the party between the students who had joined in the mid-1970s and the traditional leadership over the future direction of the movement. The amnesty allowed the students a way out of a situation they increasingly found intolerable. Whatever the reasons for the destruction of the CPT, for the military it was a tremendous victory.

15. *Bangkok Post*, July 24, 1998, p. 1

16. *Bangkok Post*, July 28, 1998, p. 1; July 29, 1998, p. 2.

17. *Bangkok Post*, July 25, 1998, p. 3.

18. Companies with concessions in Burma during this period are detailed in *Sayamrat sapda wichan*, October 27, 1991, pp. 8–14.

19. *Bangkok Post*, January 25, 1999; January 27, 1999; February 9, 1999; February 24, 1999.

20. *Nation*, April 9, 1996, p. A1.

21. *Bangkok Post*, January 18 and January 19, 1999.

22. *Straits Times*, October 22, 1998; Ubonrat (1998).

23. Interview with a committee member, December 9, 1998.

24. The army's commander in chief, General Chettha Thanacharo, stated that the army planned to reduce troop strength to 80,000; *Bangkok Post*, July 30, 1998, p. 3.

25. *Bangkok Post*, May 17, 1999; *Nation*, January 4, 2000.

26. The problem was exacerbated by the power of horizontal military factions such as Class Five of the military academy. Promotion is one of the main types of patronage dispersed by factions, and for horizontal factions this meant many promotions to the same rank.

27. *Bangkok Post,* July 31, 1998, p. 3.

28. *Bangkok Post,* July 28, 1998, p. 3. A *Bangkok Post* editorial claims the number of generals has been reduced, but gives no figures; January 31, 2001, Internet edition.

29. *Bangkok Post,* August 4, 1998, p. 1.

30. According to the same press report, "the Foreign Affairs Ministry barely had a say in relations with Burma" and policy was "characterized by personal relationships." The Directorate of Intelligence reportedly was forced to "rely on newspaper clippings" during General Chettha's tenure. See *Bangkok Post,* November 29, 1998, p. 1.

31. *Bangkok Post,* January 3, 1999.

32. Interview with staff officers, December 1998. The officers said that the Santinimit teams, which propagate democracy, continue to function at a reduced level and claimed that by the late 1990s their role was only to disseminate information. A member of the parliamentary budget committee pointed out that budget cuts following the 1997 economic crisis have limited the funds available for the military to carry out development projects (interview, December 1998).

33. *Bangkok Post,* December 3, 1998, p. 1.

34. *Nation,* March 27, 1999, p. 1.

35. *Nation,* March 23, 1999.

36. *Bangkok Post,* March 23 and 25, 1999; http://www.bangkokpost.net/issues/thanom/b280399.html. Although I have not been able to confirm all the specific relationships reported in the press, it is the general pattern that is important here.

37. It has been standard practice for many years to award a 10 percent bonus to the military academy entrance exam scores of children of military officers, which helps perpetuate the dominance of military families. Civilian Defense Minister Chuan has ordered an end to this practice beginning in 2001. See *Bangkok Post,* June 1, 2000.

38. Interviews with staff generals in Bangkok, December 1998.

39. *Bangkok Post,* August 10, 1999.

40. Involvement in a drug war has led to three new enemies for the Thai military. In addition to the drug dealers themselves, identified as the United Wa State in Burma, the conflict has inevitably led to tensions with the Burmese military regime, and apparently Thai actions on the Burmese side of the border (see *Far Eastern Economic Review,* June 1, 2000, pp. 24–26). Even more troubling is the treatment of minority groups in Thai territory in the area. There are plans to resettle the minorities into new villages where they can be more easily watched and controlled. They are also to be won over by assistance in finding new ways of earning their living. One military officer has been quoted as saying, "They are all aliens . . . only our national unity counts" (Sanitsuda Ekachai, "Military's drug fight primed to backfire," *Bangkok Post,* June 29, 2000). These are the same policies that ISOC pursued against the communists in the 1960s, indicating again the continuity of tactics, attitudes, and missions.

41. This figure is derived from the military ranks that accompany the names of members of the senate on the Web page of the parliament (www.parliament.go.th) and does not include enlisted ranks.

42. Jordan (1990: 149) pointed this out and added that "two thirds of R[oyal] T[hai] A[rmy] combat power is assigned in support of Bangkok."

43. *Bangkok Post,* March 5, 2000, and April 30, 2000.

44. Army commander Surayud was quoted as saying, "Some officers still have this old belief that a coup d'etat can solve political problems. I personally do not believe in such measures." He also said he could not guarantee there would be no coups in the future (*Bangkok Post,* November 5, 2000, Internet edition).

CHAPTER 8

1. I have used the phrase "uneasy accommodation" to indicate the tension that arises between the two institutions out of recognition of their dependence on each other, on the one hand, and the potential for conflict for supremacy on the other.

2. For details see Omissi (1994).

3. This was stated to the author by Prof. Talukder Maniruzzaman, a noted political scientist of Bangladesh, in a personal interview in February 1999. According to him, Mujib was uncomfortable with Zia because the general had read the Declaration of Independence. Another opinion, however, holds that Mujib was following the advice of General Osmany, commander in chief of the Bangladesh liberation forces. See Hannan (1999: 83).

4. This was stated to the author by midranking military intelligence officers in personal interviews held in March 1999.

5. Zia had to face as many as 21 coups; in the last one, he was assassinated.

6. *Holiday* (Dhaka), December 6, 1981.

7. This was stated to the author by a former student leader, presently a member of parliament.

8. This information was gathered by the author through a series of personal interviews of mid- and senior-ranking officers between February and August 1999.

9. Probe, 1994, p. 45.

10. This was stated to the author by Major General (retired) Ibrahim, who had not only served in the CHT but was actively involved in initiating the peace process during the Ershad regime; personal interview, March 1999.

11. *Independent*, February 25, 1999.

12. This was initiated by Zia with the introduction of Bangladeshi nationalism.

13. *Daily Star*, July 2, 1999.

14. This was stated to the author by a mid-ranking military intelligence officer in a personal interview in March 1999.

15. *Independent*, July 29, 1999.

16. *Asian Age*, March 27, 1996.

17. *Bangladesh Times*, May 21, 1996.

18. *Daily Star*, May 22, 1996.

19. *Daily Star*, May 27, 1996.

20. *Independent*, August 2, 1999.

21. As an illustration see *Mirpur Papers*, April 1998.

CHAPTER 9

1. See, for example, the reform proposals outlined by ABRI's head of social-political affairs (Kassospol)—later renamed head of territorial affairs (Kaster)—General S. Bambang Yudhoyono (1998).

2. The decision was finally made on February 13, 2000, after an extraordinary public tussle between Wahid and Wiranto lasting roughly two weeks. For a useful summary see *New York Times*, February 14, 2000.

3. *New York Times*, February 2, 2000.

4. On the revolutionary origin of the armed forces and their essentially "political" nature see Said (1991) and Sundhaussen (1982).

5. On the revolutionary period see Kahin (1970). On the importance of these years in the formation of military doctrine and attitudes see Said (1991).

6. The army's changing role in this period was carefully examined by Ruth McVey (1971: 131–76; 1972: 147–81). See also Lev (1966).

7. Some analysts, including the military's own historians, have argued that ABRI was in effect forced to assume a central political role because of the weakness and incompetence of civilian politicians and institutions in the 1940s and 1950s. There is some truth in this claim, but it obscures the element of corporate and private interest that influenced ABRI's political moves as well as the role of the military leadership itself in weakening the civilian institutions it so disliked.

8. The best summary of the military's role in the 1965 "coup" and its aftermath is by Crouch (1988: chaps. 4–8).

9. See Scott (1985) and Robinson (1995).

10. On the political role of the armed forces during the early New Order period see Jenkins (1984) and Crouch (1988: chaps. 9–14).

11. A brief account of the origins of the doctrine can be found in Vatikiotis (1993: 69–71).

12. The 1982 law—UU No. 20/1982, tentang ketentuan-ketentuan pokok pertahanan keamanan Negara Republik Indonesia—has since been amended, but the dual function doctrine remains. Prior to 1982, the legal and ideological basis for military involvement in both areas had existed largely in an assortment of presidential decrees and emergency regulations promulgated during the Sukarno regime and in the immediate aftermath of the 1965 coup.

13. For a recent critique of the dual function doctrine along these lines see Dr. Indria Samego et al. (1998).

14. On Indonesia's external threat assessment see Lowry (1993).

15. This doctrine is outlined in Departemen Pertahanan Keamanan Republik Indonesia, *Doktrin Pertahanan Keamanan Negara*, Jakarta, 1991.

16. For the history of the development of this doctrine see Nasution (1965).

17. On the origins and implications of the territorial command structure see Lowry (1993: 37 and 74–78).

18. Specifically, Crouch wrote that the territorial units "watch over political developments in their areas in order to nip in the bud any opposition movement. Measures are taken to prevent political parties, NGOs, trade unions, student organizations and religious groups from challenging the regime" (1998b: 22).

19. Over the past three decades, a variety of agencies and bodies have been established to perform one or more of these functions, including BAIS, BIA, and BAKIN. By far the best study of Indonesia's military intelligence system is by Tanter (1991).

20. For details of the history, size, and mission of Kopassus and Kostrad see Lowry (1993: 40, 81–84, 93).

21. DPR (Dewan Perwakilan Rakyat); MPR (Majelis Permusyawaratan Rakyat). The armed forces also have reserved seats in the regional and subregional legislative bodies, respectively the DPRD I and DPRD II (Dewan Perwakilan Rakyat Daerah).

22. Until 1997 ABRI was allocated 100 of the 500 seats in the DPR (Crouch 1998b: 17).

23. For a good brief account of the army's involvement in Golkar and other political parties see Schwarz (1994: chap. 10).

24. In 1993, for example, ABRI had to accept the election of a civilian, Harmoko, to the top post in Golkar—a post he held, despite military displeasure, until 1998. On the tussle over Harmoko's election see Said (1998: 546).

25. According to Kristiadi (1999: 107), in the late 1990s some 80 percent of district-level Golkar heads and 25 of 27 provincial Golkar heads were ex-ABRI.

26. The figure of 4,000 was provided by the ABRI commander, General Wiranto; *Siar*, February 24, 1999.

27. For evidence of both formal and informal military intervention in the judicial system see Amnesty International (1994).

28. On the problem of impunity see Amnesty International (1994). For a straightforward description of the system of military justice see Salam (1994).

29. The term "unconventional financing" refers to the practice of securing revenues for military units through channels, including smuggling, extortion, and rent seeking as well as legal means, other than the official state budget. The origin and development of the system is well described by Crouch (1988: chap. 11).

30. See, for example, *Economist*, July 10–16, 1999.

31. As the territorial commander for Central Java in the early 1950s, for example, the future President Suharto became adept at operating within this system.

32. On unconventional financing see Kristiadi (1999) and Lowry (1993).

33. On the 1965 killings see Cribb (1990) and Robinson (1995: chap. 12).

34. On the Malari Affair and its context see Crouch (1988: chap. 12).

35. On PETRUS see Bourchier (1991).

36. See Crouch (1998b: 6). Among the ABRI-affiliated groups commonly mobilized for such purposes were the Pemuda Pancasila, Pemuda Panca Marga, and the Forum Komunikasi Putra Putri Purnawirawan ABRI.

37. On the Sudharmono dispute see Said (1998: 541).

38. Although the opposition to Habibie's appointment was not so openly expressed as the opposition to Sudharmono's in 1988, it was understood that Habibie was not ABRI's preference. Crouch (1998b: 3–4) wrote, for example, of "a general military antipathy toward Habibie" and said there was "considerable consternation" was he was nominated in March 1998.

39. Murdani was dismissed as ABRI commander in 1988, but he held the less powerful post of minister of defense and security until 1993. For a good summary of the tussle between President Suharto and General Murdani see Schwarz (1994: chap. 10). See also Said (1998: 540–46).

40. On the growing domestic and international challenge to military authority in the field of human rights see Robinson (1996: 74–99).

41. This was very clearly the case in Aceh; see Robinson (1998).

42. On the Indonesian government's response to the Santa Cruz massacre see Haseman (1995) and Amnesty International (1992).

43. For a detailed analysis of the relationship between domestic and international influences in shaping human rights policy and practice see Robinson (1996).

44. The contemporary reports of human rights organizations provide ample evidence of the disjuncture between the rhetoric of openness and the reality of continued repression during these years. See, for example, Amnesty International (1994).

45. The president issued the order for troop deployments on July 6, 1990, and further reinforcements arrived in early August 1990. The troops deployed from outside the region included two battalions of the elite Kopassus (Special Forces Command), as well as units of the Marinir Jakarta, Kujang Bandung, KODAM VII/Brawijaya, Arhanud Medan, Linud Medan, and police mobile brigades. For additional details see Lembaga Bantuan Hukum (1990: 34–35). See also *Reuters,* July 22, August 15, and November 25, 1990.

46. The author was the Amnesty International researcher for Indonesia from 1989 to 1995 and was responsible for the preparation of this report and others published by the organization during that period.

47. The origins and evolution of these features of New Order military doctrine and practice have been analyzed in some depth by Tanter, Langenberg, and others. See Tanter (1990) and Langenberg (1990).

48. Confidential personal communication from a human rights lawyer, Banda Aceh, August 1998.

49. For examples and eyewitness testimonies see Amnesty International (1993).

50. In late August 1998 Indonesia's National Human Rights Commission excavated several of the mass grave sites. Commenting on their findings, a member of the commission said, "The discovery of the skeletal remains has convinced us beyond doubt that the reports of widespread military atrocities over the past nine years in Aceh are an undisputed fact." *Jakarta Post,* August 28, 1998. For further details of these investigations and the mass graves see the commission's report "Laporan Komnas HAM: Dari Kuburan Massal Hingga Cuwak," August 24, 1998. See also *Kompas,* August 22, 1998; *Jakarta Post,* August 22, 1998; and *Waspada,* August 14, 1998.

51. From an interview with Maj. Gen. R. Pramono, *Tempo,* November 17, 1990; translation as cited in JPRS-SEA-90-034, December 16, 1990.

52. Confidential interviews with Acehnese refugees in Malaysia, October 1991; and Amnesty International (1993: 13).

53. See *Far Eastern Economic Review,* November 19, 1998, pp. 18, 25; *Gatra,* August 15, 1998, p. 38.

54. For this and other cases see Gani (n.d.: 9) and Sumatra Human Rights Watch Network (n.d.: 2–3).

55. See, for example, the paper presented by ABRI's head of social-political affairs (Kassospol)—later renamed head of territorial affairs (Kaster)—General Bambang Yudhoyono (1998) and by Lemhannas governor, General Agum Gumelar (1998).

56. On ABRI's efforts to retain its seats in the DPR see Crouch (1998b: 7).

57. Among other things, Sudrajat had implied that under the 1945 Constitution a civilian president could not be considered the supreme commander of the armed forces. When he stepped down in late January 2000, Sudrajat said that he had apologized to Wahid. *Duta,* January 26, 2000.

58. *Jakarta Post,* January 28, 2000.

59. Wiranto was suspended, though not fired, on February 13, 2000. Three months later, after undergoing seven hours of questioning by prosecutors over his role in the violence in East Timor, he announced that he would not seek to return to his cabinet post. *New York Times,* May 17, 2000.

60. *Los Angeles Times,* November 25, 1999.

61. Amnesty International commented that "the government is still unwilling or unable to take decisive action against higher level military leaders." Amnesty International, May 17, 2000.

62. On the April 2000 meeting and its implications see Kusnanto Anggoro (2000).

63. *Tempo Interaktif,* April 25, 2000.

64. *Tempo Interaktif,* May 10, 2000.

65. For a summary of the reform proposals advanced by ABRI in 1998 see Crouch (1998b: 12–16).

66. For a profile of Major General Agus and a useful outline of his reform proposals see "Civil-Military Relations—Gus Dur Versus Wiranto," *Van Zorge Report,* January 7, 2000.

67. *Jakarta Post,* December 18, 1999.

68. Madeleine Albright, "Indonesia, the United States, and Democracy," a speech delivered in Jakarta on March 5, 1999.

69. *AP,* January 14, 2000.

70. On the coup rumors see *Duta,* January 4, 2000, and *New York Times,* February 5, 2000.

71. Toward the end of 1999, General Wiranto grew increasingly impatient with antimilitary protesters, claiming that the TNI had already carried out an internal evaluation and correction.

72. What criticism there was tended to be legalistic. See, for example, "Perintah Wiranto Tembak di Tempat Langgar Hukum," *Siar,* February 23, 1999.

73. In a related move toward limiting civil society and strengthening state and military power, in early 1999 military and police authorities began to implement a controversial new law limiting free expression. The law in question was UU No. 9/1998 tentang kebebasan menyampaikan pendapat di muka umum. For an example of the use and the criticism of this new law see "48 Pelajar dan Mahasiswa ditangkap," *Kdpnet,* March 2, 1999.

74. *Straits Times,* January 23, 2000.

75. In June 2000 Minster of Defense Juwono Sudarsono reportedly urged the DPR to pass a new emergency law (UU Keadaan Daururat) to replace the 1959 regulation (UU/PRP/23/1959).

76. On the rumors of a coup see *New York Times,* February 6, 2000, and *Siar,* March 28, 2000. It is also noteworthy that some officers, including General Wiranto and Kostrad commander Lt. Gen. Djaja Suparman, openly opposed the official investigation.

77. Shortly after Suharto's resignation in May 1998, a mixture of evidence and rumor began to emerge to the effect that Prabowo had been directly involved in the kidnapping and murder of several prodemocracy activists earlier in the year and had openly challenged the new president's authority. Within a matter of days, Wiranto, apparently acting with Habibie's blessing, had transferred Prabowo from his position as Kostrad commander to a relatively powerless post with no troops under his direct command. In August, following a rare investigation by an Officer's Honor Board, Prabowo and two officers close to him were discharged from the armed forces. Although Wiranto sought to portray this decision as a sign of the military's commitment to reform, critics tended to view it as an effort to solidify his own command of the armed forces and to shift the focus of public criticism away from ABRI as a whole and toward a handful of his rivals.

78. Prominent among the Wiranto group were Major General Sudrajat, removed as TNI spokesperson in January 2000, and Lt. Gen. Djaja Suparman, removed as Kostrad commander in February. For details of the split see *Jakarta Post,* December 18, 1999; *Bangkit,* December 20–26, 1999; *Republika,* January 27, 2000; and "Civil-Military Relations—Gus Dur Versus Wiranto," *Van Zorge Report,* January 7, 2000.

79. Crouch (1998b: 3) wrote, for example, that "Prabowo had developed close ties with a radical Islamic organization, KISDI, and various martial arts organizations which could be mobilized for street demonstrations. It was also rumored that Prabowo maintained links with youth gangs...in the Tanah Abang area of Jakarta." For further allegations and details of Prabowo's links to such groups see "Awas, Aksi Kelompok Eks Tidar," *Siar,* March 10, 1999; and "Ahmad Sumargono Pojokkan Habibie dan Bela ABRI," *Siar,* March 9, 1999.

80. Among the Prabowo loyalists accused of engineering social violence was Maj. Gen. Kivlan Zein. See "Mayjen Kivlan Zein Bantah Tuduhan Gus Dur," *Siar,* March 3, 1999. The key figure in Wiranto's circle was said to be Kostrad commander Djaja Suparman. Like Prabowo, he was alleged to have links with radical Islamic groups such as KISDI and the Front Pembela Islam (FPI). See *TNI-Watch,* January 19, 2000, and *Siar,* January 25, 2000.

81. For Wahid's allegations regarding the TNI see *Republika,* January 26, 2000, and *Jakarta Post,* April 14, 2000.

82. *Jakarta Post,* October 14, 1999.

83. See International Crisis Group (2000: 9) and *Jakarta Post,* January 26, 2000.

84. In appointing Maj. Gen. Agus Wirahadikusumah to the post of Kostrad commander, for example, President Wahid was very likely attempting to limit the danger posed by this powerful unit. Rumored Ministry of

Defense plans to reduce the size of Kopassus from eleven battalions to just one would appear to have a similar objective.

85. For some early reactions to the proposal see *Jakarta Post*, December 18, 1999.

86. Crouch (1998b: 22).

87. *Washington Post*, February 19, 2000; *Los Angeles Times*, May 25, 2000.

88. This case study is based substantially on the author's personal experiences and observations while serving as a political affairs officer with the United Nations (UNAMET) from June to November 1999.

89. There is no doubt that there was pressure from the international community at this time for a resolution of the East Timor problem, though the boldness of Habibie's proposal seems to have surprised even those urging change. In late February 1999, for example, U.S. State Department policymakers, taking their cues not from Habibie but from the TNI and Ali Alatas, were still hoping to avoid a direct popular ballot and UN involvement in East Timor.

90. On July 6 the head of the UN mission in East Timor, Ian Martin, met General Wiranto to convey precisely this point. The same message was conveyed repeatedly, to no avail, to military and civilian leaders over the next two months.

91. An extraordinary 98.6 percent of registered voters cast a ballot, of whom 78.6 percent rejected the offer of autonomy under Indonesian rule.

92. Officially the decision was issued as Presidential Decree 107/1999.

93. In one of dozens of examples of TNI complicity with the militia, heavily armed elite Kostrad soldiers assigned to protect the UN compound allowed armed militia men through their perimeter and into an adjoining field where several hundred people had taken refuge and scores of UN vehicles were parked. Not only did the TNI troops fail to prevent the militia from terrorizing and firing their weapons at the refugees, they actually assisted the militia in smashing the windows of the UN vehicles and driving them away.

94. United Nations Transitional Authority for East Timor (UNTAET), "Patterns of Official Responsibility for Human Rights Violations in East Timor," Internal report, November 1999.

95. The official Indonesian inquiry alleged that six generals shared responsibility for human rights violations amounting to crimes against humanity. The six named were Maj. Gen. Zacky Anwar Makarim, Maj. Gen. Adam Damiri, Brig. Gen. Tono Suratman, Brig. Gen. Noer Muis, Brig. Gen. (Police) Timbul Silaen, and Gen. Wiranto.

96. *South China Morning Post*, January 6, 2000.

97. The main holdouts in early discussions and at the committee stage were the Partai Demokrasi Indonesia-Perjuangan (PDI-P), Golkar, Partai Persatuan Pembangunan (PPP), and Partai Keadilan and Persatuan (PKP). Some delegates even demanded a nationwide referendum on the issue before an MPR vote. The vote taken was to rescind the MPR decision of 1978 by which East Timor was formally declared a part of Indonesia.

98. The commission of inquiry visited East Timor in late November and early December 1999 and released its report at the end of January 2000.

99. Commenting on the idea of an international tribunal, President Wahid said, "We are strongly against it. We prefer to give the opportunity to the national process." TNI spokesperson Graito Usodo was even more blunt. "The last thing we want," he said, "is for outsiders to interfere in our internal matters." *Jakarta Post*, February 1, 2000.

100. Indeed, it even encouraged some to admit responsibility. Shortly before the arrival in Jakarta of UN Secretary General Kofi Annan to discuss an international tribunal, General Wiranto reportedly said "as long as I was responsible for security, I am responsible for those human rights violations in East Timor." *New York Times*, February 15, 2000.

101. *Los Angeles Times*, December 29, 1999.

CHAPTER 10

1. For a complete explication of this approach see Schiff (1995).

2. *Sun*, August 22, 1996.

3. See Enloe (1977: 23) on how the British deliberately made the Malay Regiment a communal institution.

4. *New Straits Times*, August 16, 1992.

5. When the CPM tried to take over the country by mounting a guerrilla war and embarked upon political terrorism, first against the British administration and later the federal government, a state of emergency was declared in parts of Perak and Johore in June 1948. Eventually the state of emergency was extended to the entire country by August 1948. The "emergency" ended in 1960. The threat of communist activities ended on December 2, 1989, when the government signed a peace treaty with the CPM.

6. The nation faced an external threat from Indonesia in 1963 in response to the formation of Malaysia.

7. *New Straits Times*, April 6, 1981.

8. *Asiaweek*, March 12, 1999.

9. The Internal Security Act, for example, was designed to be used on the communists and their allies during the period of emergency to obtain information and thereby prevent a repetition of subversive activities. The act continues to be used by the authorities, however, in the context of maintaining national security. See Mohd. Reduan Aslie (1990: 382–83).

10. These objectives of the MAF in the current sociopolitical context now also include assisting the police and civil authorities in the maintenance of public order and antiterrorism operations. See Prasun K. Sengupta, "Malaysia's Force Modernisation Priorities" (*ADJ*, April 2000: 12–16).

11. It is worth noting, however, that the chief of defense forces occupies a higher position than the secretary-general when it comes to the order of precedence in federal functions. See *Sun*, August 22, 1996.

12. *New Straits Times*, July 5, 1991.

13. These remarks were made at an exclusive interview with the editorial team of *Asian Defence and Diplomacy*. With respect to civilian supremacy, the general's comment on military procurement is noteworthy: he stated that the MAF's procurement policies strictly follow the eighth and ninth five-year development plans and the priorities assigned by the civilian-controlled government. See *Asian Defence and Diplomacy*, 6 (9), September 1999: 29–36.

14. *Star*, March 1, 1983.

15. *New Straits Times*, April 10, 1992.

16. Prime Minister Tun Hussein Onn appointed his brother-in-law, Gen. Ghazali Seth, as chief of armed forces in 1981. In 1987 Gen. Hashim Mohd. Ali, who is the brother-in-law of the present prime minister, Dr. Mahathir Mohamad, was promoted to the post of chief of defense forces. For more examples see Crouch (1991: 129).

17. The National Operations Council was a ten-member body composed of the chief of defense forces, the inspector-general of police, and senior Malay civil servants.

18. Remarks by the current chief of armed forces, Gen. Mohd. Zahidi bin Zainuddin. See *Asian Defence Journal (ADJ)*, April 2000: 20.

19. *ADJ*, April 1998: 23.

20. *ADJ*, April 1998: 16.

21. *New Straits Times*, July 8, 1989.

22. See Crouch (1991: 130) for further examples of ex-servicemen offered prestigious employment by the government.

23. *ADJ*, March 1993: 7.

24. *ADJ*, March 1993: 10.

25. *ADJ*, April 1998: 18.

26. See Abdul Ghani Yunus (1995: 3–4).

27. *ADJ*, April 1998: 20–21.

28. Based on interviews with senior MAF officers.

29. *New Straits Times*, January 31, 1993.

30. Comment made by A. V. Dicey, a British constitutional lawyer, quoted in *Sun*, August 22, 1996.

CHAPTER 11

1. *Pointer*, 1992, p. 1.

2. *FEER*, December 5, 1991.

3. The left-wing Barisan Socialis was the most significant opposition party to the PAP in the 1960s. In 1966 it announced that it was boycotting parliament and adopting a "back to the streets" strategy. This opened the way for the PAP to exert its complete domination of the parliament. Having denied itself access to the key political platform in the country, the Barisan then faded as a force in Singapore politics.

4. *FEER*, January 13, 1983.

5. *FEER*, January 13, 1983.

6. The Five Power Defense Arrangement, set up in April 1971, provided for consultations among the five nations of Australia, Malaysia, New Zealand, Singapore, and Britain in the event of any threat of external aggression against Malaysia and Singapore.

7. With considerably enhanced military capabilities—buttressed by the acquisition of advanced military hardware and a burgeoning defense technology industrial base—by the mid-1980s the SAF believed that it not only had the capability of repelling an attack from an external aggressor but "will be around to pick up the pieces at the end." More recently, the SAF has openly declared that should deterrence and diplomacy fail, it now has the capability to win "a swift and decisive victory over the aggressor" in a conflict.

8. *Straits Times*, June 30, 1992.

9. One such example was Brig. Gen. Tan Chin Tiong, who had begun his career as a civil servant in the Ministry of Finance. Persuaded to join the military as a full-fledged officer, he rose to the rank of deputy chief of general staff of the SAF. General Tan left the army in 1981 and is presently permanent secretary in the Ministry of Foreign Affairs.

10. Interview with General Tan in 1998.

11. Presently, the minister for defense is assisted by a second minister and two ministers of state.

12. Interview with General Choo in 1998.

13. Interview with Lim Siong Guan in 1999.

14. The Joint Staff of the SAF is headed by the chief of defense forces and includes the Joint Operations and Planning Directorate, the Joint Intelligence Directorate, the Headquarters Medical Corps, and the SAFTI Military Institute. The Manpower Division and Resources Planning Office form part of the Joint Staff, but these two offices double-report to the permanent secretary.

15. *Straits Times*, May 1, 1984.

16. *Straits Times*, November 1, 1965.

17. SAF reservists are now called "operationally ready national servicemen" in an attempt to eradicate the mistaken notion that they are backup soldiers to be summoned only after the standing force of regulars and full-time national servicemen has been deployed in battle. But given its deeply entrenched usage, the term "reservist" has retained a permanent place in the popular jargon of the Singapore public.

18. *Straits Times*, June 30, 1992.

19. *Straits Times*, July 3, 1987.

20. *Straits Times*, September 30, 1999.

21. This observation stems from a number of essays written by regular officers in the army journal the *Pointer*, lamenting the gradual erosion of "institutional moorings" and the proud traditions of the SAF. The SAF, these essays claim, has become less an institution of "robust military culture" and more a workplace of free-market ethos where personal welfare and advancement are stressed over martial values of selfless sacrifice.

22. *Straits Times*, February 1, 1996.

23. Other ex-military men in the present cabinet include Rear Admiral (NS) Teo Chee Hean (minister for education and second minister for defense), Brig. Gen. (NS) George Yeo (minister for trade and industry), and Col. (NS) Lim Hng Kiang (minister for health). All of them are SAF scholars.

24. *Straits Times*, September 7, 1981.

CHAPTER 12

1. Numerous analysts have remarked on Sri Lanka's democratic success and promise. Jane Russell's comment in her authoritative study of communal politics (1982: xiv) that "apart from a few recurring patches of anomie, since independence Sri Lanka has been a model third world country" is not exceptional. A similar com-

ment by D. E. Smith that "the Ceylonese record with the alternation in office of two major parties is quite impressive in the third world" (1970: 195) implicitly compared the island's political achievements with those of England. In a similar vein Donald Horowitz stated retrospectively that any knowledgeable observer would have predicted that Malaysia was in for serious, perhaps devastating, Malay-Chinese conflict, whereas Sri Lanka (then Ceylon) was likely to experience only mild difficulty between the Sinhalese and Tamils (1989: 18).

2. This de facto partition is marked by army camps and refugee camps for the internally displaced. Until the government's 1995 campaign against the LTTE when it captured the northern Jaffna peninsula, which had been controlled by the LTTE for many years, there were effectively two governments locked in bloody combat: one in the southern capital Colombo and the other in the northern peninsula controlled and administered by the secessionist LTTE.

3. It is this border/partition that Operation Jaya Sikurui (Victory Assured)—begun and abandoned almost two years later by the Sri Lankan army to clear the main supply route to the northern capital of Jaffna in 1997— set out but failed to erase.

4. The figure of extrajudicial killings consists largely of persons disappeared in the south during the JVP uprising in the late 1980s.

5. I use the term "Tamil-speaking" minorities to flag the linguistic basis of the conflict and to denaturalize the ethnic explanation for the conflict, especially because minority Muslims have shared Tamil sentiments of exclusion from governance and development in the postcolonial period in Sri Lanka. But as the conflict has progressed, the Muslim leadership has for various reasons, including violence by the LTTE, carved out a new Muslim ethnicity.

6. Describing multiplicity as rizomatic, Deleuze and Guattari state, "A multiplicity has neither subject nor object, only determinations, magnitudes and dimensions that cannot increase in number without the multiplicity *changing in nature* (the laws of combination therefore increase in number as the multiplicity grows)....An assemblage is precisely this increase in the dimensions of a multiplicity that necessarily changes in nature as it expands its connections" (1987: 8). The "war machine" as I define it thus encompasses and signifies the proliferating connections and interdependency between agents and cultures of violence, both military and paramilitary, and their changing dimensions.

7. Unlike the Bosnian Serbs, the LTTE has practiced ethnic cleansing in the name of its security interests rather than for ethnic purity. The distinction remains semantic, however, because the LTTE has not allowed the Muslims and Sinhalas it displaced to return to the Jaffna peninsula, which it claims as the homeland of the Tamils. The relationship between the Muslims, the LTTE, and the Tamils on the east coast partakes of a different dynamic.

8. Sri Lanka had seen strife between groups of Sinhalas and Tamils in 1958, 1977, and 1981, but the clashes in 1983 were unprecedented in scale and violence. There are two interpretations of the pogrom/riots of July 1983 that question their ethnic basis. Although violence was clearly directed by Sinhala groups and mobs against Tamil persons and property, it has been argued that the riots were pogroms organized and instigated by ultra–Sinhala nationalist segments in the government of the ruling UNP. The other interpretation of the July 1983 riots that questions the ethnic explanation contends that the violence was in fact class-coded (Gunasinghe 1989) and that many of the rioters were merely cashing in on the general disorder to settle personal vendettas or to enrich themselves in the looting. Stanley Tambiah's analysis (1997) of the events of July 1983 combined these arguments.

9. At the census conducted in 1981—the most recent decennial census in the country, because of the ethnic conflict—Sri Lanka consisted of Sinhalas (74 percent), Sri Lankan Tamils (12.8 percent), Indian Tamils (5.5 percent), and Muslims (7.5 percent) (consisting of 7.1 percent Moors and 0.39 percent Malays), and others. These groups are unevenly distributed on the island: the Tamil-speaking peoples are concentrated largely in the northern and eastern provinces.

10. At the end of December 1995 the Ministry of Rehabilitation and Reconstruction estimated that there were 1,017,181 internally displaced people in Sri Lanka, and 140,000 were displaced overseas. (Some of the latter have sought asylum status.) In December 1998, official estimates of the internally displaced were 800,000. Figures of displaced persons are controversial, however. The University Teachers for Human Rights (1994) estimated that half a million Tamils have become refugees overseas. The decennial census of Sri Lanka scheduled for 1991 was not taken because of the conflict. Estimates suggest that 78 percent of the internally displaced are ethnically Tamils, 13 percent are Muslims, and 8 percent are Sinhalas (Gomez 1994). Many displaced people, Tamils, Muslims, and Sinhalas alike, fled the Sri Lankan army and LTTE brutality.

11. In the 1980s and 1990s this process was reflected every day in debates in the national press over the Tamil homelands myth propagated by the LTTE, as well as in the rhetoric of the Sinhala Commission's paranoid nationalism generated by fifteen years of armed conflict. Much ink has been used on the invention of nationalist histories and traditional homelands myths. The history/homelands debates reveal the thinness of the line between history and nationalism, scholars and nationalists. For a good deconstructive account see Daniel (1997).

12. Interview with Sukumar Rockwood, *Weekend Express,* June 14, 1998.

13. *Sunday Times,* June 5, 1999.

14. A presidential commission headed by the defense secretary was established in 1998 to inquire into the loss of seventeen aircraft by the Sri Lankan air force in a two-year period. The committee's observations, reported in the *Sunday Times* of October 1998, read, "Certain purchases of aircraft have been made without adhering to accepted tender procedures." In July of the same year, the Colombo High Court sentenced to death five members of the security forces found guilty of the rape and murder of a fifteen-year-old schoolgirl, Krishanthi Coomaraswamy, and the murder of her mother, her brother, and a neighbor who went in search of her to the army camp. This was described as a landmark case in the judicial history of Sri Lanka: it was the first time that members of the security forces were given a heavy sentence for grave human rights violations as a result of a civil trial. The crimes had been committed in September 1996 amidst widespread cases of disappearance and other human rights violations in the Jaffna peninsula.

CHAPTER 13

1. Comments made by Ellis Joffe at the CAPS/Rand PLA conference, Washington, D.C., July 8–11, 1999.

2. In a series of reorganizations, the PLA has been able to spin off many of the noncombat units that are actively involved in these activities. In 1985, for instance, the Xinjiang Production Corps was officially separated from the ranks of the Chinese military.

3. The best account of the military aspects of Tiananmen is by Brook (1998). For a penetrating critique of Brook's book by an eyewitness military observer, see the review by Col. Larry Wortzel in the February 1994 issue of the *Australian Journal of Chinese Affairs* (now the *China Journal*).

4. The best analysis of these political control systems is by Shambaugh (1991: 544–50).

5. As an example of Jiang's perceived role in promotions see Luo Yuwen (1996). A larger promotion ceremony, involving nineteen officers promoted to full general by Jiang, occurred in 1994. Because Jiang's visits to military units are a regular occurrence—itself an important analytical fact—a comprehensive listing of these visits is impossible. For an interesting snapshot see the Federal Broadcast Information Service transcript of a ten-part China Central Television series on Jiang's visits to units aired in July and August 1996. Jiang is also alleged to personally interview all candidates at the division level and above, though the slate of candidates is undoubtedly shaped by the senior military leadership. See Lu Yushan (1994).

6. Xu Shiyou, for instance, served as commander of the Nanjing Military Region for more than 28 years.

7. I am grateful to Michel Oksenberg for reminding me of this fact.

8. For a discussion of military participation in foreign policymaking see Swaine (1996: 23–41); the author discusses the PLA's role in defense policymaking on pp. 42–58.

9. Perhaps the most vexing and least determinate aspect of Chinese military affairs involves estimates of its annual defense budget. Although observers appear to have a fairly firm grasp of what is included and not included in the official defense budget—which no one believes is the real figure—estimates of the actual budget vary widely and there is little hope of resolving the issue with any degree of certitude.

10. For a historical survey of the PLA's participation in the economy since the late 1920s see Mulvenon (2000: chap. 2).

11. The exact origins of the term "military-business complex" are unknown, but like "PLA, Inc." it has become a staple of journalistic reporting on the subject. See Mulvenon (2000).

12. Personal communication with Tai Ming Cheung, Nov. 12, 1998.

13. According to one account, the PLA was split on the issue between the senior military leadership and the combat units who supported divestiture, and the logistics units and others who were profiting from commercial activity.

14. I thank Dennis Blasko for this information.

15. "Separation of Army from Business Done," *China Daily*, Mar. 21, 1999, p. 1.

16. Apart from budgets, there is also evidence to suggest that the civilian leadership has aggressively pursued disciplinary investigations involving corruption in PLA enterprises, much to the chagrin of PLA officers who feel that the effort is gratuitous and harmful to the public reputation of the military. See Lawrence (1999).

CHAPTER 14

1. It was the Political Department (Cuc Chinh Tri) between 1946 and 1950 and the General Political Directorate (Tong Cuc Chinh Tri) after 1950 (see Tong Cuc Chinh Tri 1998).

2. "Dieu Le Dang Cong San Viet Nam, 14–20 thang 12, 1976," tr. 23–25; Nghi quyet so 11/NQ cua Bo chinh tri ve to chuc Dang va to chuc cong tac chinh tri trong quan doi nhan dan Viet Nam (trich), September 19, 1978, pp. 41–60.

3. The person in charge of political and party work was called "political commissar" (*chinh uy*) at the levels of military region, corps, division, and regiment and "political officer" (*chinh tri vien*) down to the company level.

4. "Nghi Quyet 172 QUTW cua Thuong Vu Quan Uy Trung Uong ve to chuc thuc hien che do thu truong trong quan doi nhan dan Vietnam (trich)," May 29, 1979, pp. 85–93.

5. The unit commander's title varied from level to level: *tu lenh* at the divisional level and above and *chi huy truong* at the provincial level. For the rest of the units, it was *lu doan truong, trung doan truong, tieu doan truong*, and *dai doi truong*.

6. "Nghi Quyet 172 QUTW cua Thuong Vu Quan Uy Trung Uong ve to chuc thuc hien che do thu truong trong quan doi nhan dan Vietnam (trich)," May 29, 1979, p. 91.

7. "Bao cao chinh tri va bao cao xay dung Dang cua Ban Chap Hanh Trung Uong tai Dai Hoi Dai bieu toan quoc lan thu V (trich)," March 27, 1982, p. 151; "Nghi quyet 07 cua Bo Chinh Tri ve viec doi moi, hoan thien co che lanh dao cua Dang doi voi quan doi nhan dan Viet Nam, su nghiep quoc phong va thuc hien che do mot nguoi chi huy trong quan doi," December 15, 1982, pp. 153–73; "Quy dinh cua Ban Bi Thu ve to chuc Hoi Dong Quan Su cac cap trong quan doi nhan dan Viet Nam," August 12, 1982, pp. 174–80.

8. "Quy dinh cua Ban Bi Thu ve to chuc co quan chinh tri trong quan doi nhan dan Viet Nam," August 12, 1983, pp. 202–17.

9. Ibid.

10. "Nghi quyet Bo Chinh Tri ve viec tiep tuc kien toan co che lanh dao cua Dang doi voi quan doi nhan dan Viet Nam va su nghiep quoc phong," July 4, 1985, pp. 257–66.

11. See "Dieu Le Dang Cong San Viet Nam (Do Dai hoi dai bieu Dang toan quoc lan thu VI sua doi bo sung) (trich)," 15–18 thang 12, 1986, pp. 289–91.

12. "Quy Dinh cua Ban Bi Thu ve to chuc Dang trong quan doi nhan dan Viet Nam (trich)," July 30, 1987, pp. 274–89, especially pp. 287–88. For the full text see "Quy dinh ve to chuc Dang trong quan doi nhan dan Viet Nam so 12/QD-TW ngay 30 thang 7 anm 1987," in *To chuc su lanh dao cua Dang trong Quan Doi Nhan Dan Viet Nam* (1987, 1: 8–38).

13. "Quy dinh ve to chuc co quan chinh tri trong quan doi nhan dan Viet Nam so 11/QD-TW ngay 30 thang 7 nam 1978," in *To chuc* (1987, 1: 26–38).

14. "Nghi quyet hoi nghi lan thu ba ban chap hanh trung uong khoa VII ve mot so nhiem vu doi moi va chinh don Dang) (trich)," June 29, 1992, pp. 325–33; "Nghi quyet quan uy trung uong ve quan triet va thuc hien nghi quyet hoi nghi trung uong lan thu 3 ve mot so nhiem vu doi moi va chinh don dang trong dang bo quan doi (trich)," August 27, 1992, pp. 334–47.

15. Chiefs of the General Political Directorate were Nguyen Chi Thanh (1950–1961), Song Hao (1961–1976), Chu Huy Man (1977–1987), Nguyen Quyet (1987–1991), Le Kha Phieu (1991–1996), and Pham Thanh Ngan (1997–).

16. *Jane's Defence Weekly*, September 4, 1996, p. 17.

17. *Quan Doi Nhan Dan*, March 31, 1989.

18. The cessation of aid from the Soviet Union had a major impact on the domestic economic reform process in Vietnam. As many economists have pointed out, despite the abolition of central planning in 1986 there was

no major move to liberalize the economic system until 1989, when the Soviet aid stopped. Between 1989 and 1991, the Vietnamese state was confronted with a serious fiscal crisis (Fforde and De Vylder 1996).

19. For example, the CMPC granted Military Region IV permission to construct a railroad from Minh Cam to Tien An and a communication line from Vinh to Tien An (Dam Quang Trung 1976). From 1970 to 1975, the Ta Ngan Military Region, covering the area on the left bank of the Red River, was involved in road construction, the expansion of new economic zones, land cultivation, the production of construction materials, reforestation, and fishery. Its activities expanded beyond its assigned targets, contributing substantially to the state budget and producing income to increase the salaries of soldiers. It was also able to accumulate fixed capital and an economic infrastructure, including the manufacture of bricks and tiles and fishing boats (Dang Kinh 1976).

20. See *To chuc* (1989); "Nghi quyet so 33 NQ-DUQSTW ngay 9 thang 2 nam 1989 ve day manh nhiem vu lao dong san xuat va tham gia xay dung kinh te cua quan doi, chan chinh lai to chuc san xuat va cai tien co che quan ly cac don vi lam kinh te," pp. 7–16.

21. *Chi thi so* 46/CT ngay 03 Thang 3 nam 1989 cua Chu tich Hoi Dong Bo Truong ve nhiem ve san xuat quoc phong trong kinh te quan doi, pp. 3–6.

22. Ibid.

23. Ibid.

24. *Quan Doi Nhan Dan,* July 21, 1989, p. 3.

25. *Quan Doi Nhan Dan*, May 4, 1989, p. 3.

26. For the full text see *Dien Dan*, no. 48 (January 1996): 16–23; for a detailed discussion see Vasavakul (1997).

27. This information comes from interviews conducted in 1999.

28. In fact, rural unrest in Thai Binh, according to interview information, had been led by veterans residing in villages. The VCP relied on the Vietnam Veterans' Association to help maintain future stability.

29. This form of activity follows Decision 35/HDBT of the government.

30. *Jane's Defence Weekly,* September 24, 1997, p. 13.

31. *Tai Chinh Viet Nam*, March 2, 1998, p. 4.

32. *Quan Doi Nhan Dan*, October 9, 1998, p. 1.

33. *Quan Doi Nhan Dan*, October 15, 1998, p. 3; October 16, 1998, p. 3.

34. *Quan Doi Nhan Dan*, September 28, 1999, p. 1; November 3, 1998, p. 3.

35. This information comes from interviews in 1999. It was confirmed later in a meeting in July 2000 with Mr. Vu Xuan Hong, vice president of the Vietnam-USA Society. Mr. Hong pointed out that VPA leaders supported a bilateral trade agreement with the United States.

CHAPTER 15

1. Korean Central News Agency editorial, October 20, 1998; for a summary see *Jugan Bukhandonghyang (North Korea Weekly)*, October 17–23, 1998.

2. Article 46 of the KWP bylaws, which were revised in 1980, defined the KPA as its revolutionary armed forces.

3. Central News Agency, February 16, 1997; for details see Chung (1998: 68–70).

4. On the factional composition of the South Korean military see Chapter 4 in this volume.

5. Defense Minister Choe Yong-gon, one of Kim's closest allies during the struggle against Japanese colonial rule, is known to have opposed Kim's plan of military invasion of the South for fear of American intervention (Park 1996: 287–304; Chang 1991: 152–56).

6. Mu Chong was officially purged because of failure to defend Pyongyang from UN forces and his order to execute retreating soldiers as though he were a "feudal lord" (Suh 1988: 123). Kim also feared that Peng Dehuai would help Mu Chong to challenge him because the two had formed a friendship during the Chinese civil war (J.-S. Lee 1995: 243).

7. Kim Il Sung was apologetic about the commando raid on the Blue House when he met Lee Hu-rak, who visited North Korea as Park Chung-hee's secret envoy on May 2–5, 1972. Kim said the raid was the act of extreme leftists obedient neither to his will nor the party's. He added that those responsible for the provocation had been purged (C.-S. Kim 1994: 353).

8. The "three revolutionary teams" were institutionalized by constitutional amendment in 1972 and put into action in February 1973 to oversee ideological, technological, and cultural revolution. They were dissolved in 1995 as a result of growing disapproval of their operations.

9. The thesis of *kangsung daekuk* calls for the construction of a strong and prosperous nation on three fronts: ideological, economic, and military. For the full text of an editorial on this concept see *Nodong Shinmun*, August 22, 1998.

10. Central News Agency, October 20, 1998.

11. *Nodong Shinmun*, August 22, 1998.

12. The bureaucratic compartmentalization view was expressed in a personal interview by Hwang Jang-yop, a former KWP party secretary who defected to South Korea.

13. Interview with Hwang Jang-yop and Kim Duck-hong in *Chosun Ilbo*, July 1, 1997.

14. The U.S. Arms Control and Disarmament Agency has estimated that North Korea's arms exports amounted to $3.28 billion between 1986 and 1996 (in 1996 constant prices) (USACDA 1997: 37).

15. Interview with Won Dong-hyun in Beijing, October 25, 1999.

CHAPTER 16

1. *Dawn*, October 14, 1999.

2. The address of Pakistan's founding father and first governor general, Mohammed Ali Jinnah, to the officers of the Staff College at Quetta (June 14, 1948) enumerated the responsibilities of the defense forces: "You ... are the custodians of the life, property, and honor of the people of Pakistan. ... I would like to take the opportunity of refreshing your memory by reading the prescribed oath to you:"

I solemnly affirm, in the presence of Almighty God, that I owe allegiance to the Constitution and the Dominion of Pakistan (mark the words Constitution and the Government of the Dominion of Pakistan) and that I will as in duty bound honestly and faithfully serve in the Dominion of Pakistan Forces and go within the terms of my enrollment wherever I may be ordered by air, land, or sea and that I will observe and obey all commands of any officer set over me. ...

He continued: "I want you to remember and if you have time enough you should study the Government of India Act, as adapted for use in Pakistan, which is our present Constitution, that the executive authority flows from the Head of the Government, who is the Governor General, and, therefore, any command or orders that may come to you cannot come without the sanction of the Executive Head. This is the legal position" (Government of Pakistan 1989: 264–65).

3. According to a proclamation made by Mirza on October 7, 1958, "It is said that the Constitution is sacred. But more sacred than the Constitution or anything else is the country and the welfare and happiness of its people. As Head of the State, my foremost duty before my God and the people is the integrity of Pakistan. It is seriously threatened by the traitors and political adventurers whose selfishness, thirst for power, and unpatriotic conduct cannot be restrained by a government set up under the present system." Also enlightening is the statement of Gen. Ayub Khan in his first broadcast to the nation on October 8, 1958: "This is the occasion on which I feel I should take my countrymen and women into confidence as to the army's attitude and behavior. ... We solemnly decided to build a true national army free from politics, a model of devotion to duty and integrity imbued with the spirit of service to the people and capable of effectively defending the country. Further, I always told my people that our major task is to give cover to the country behind which it could build a sound democratic system and lay the foundation of a stable future. We kept severely aloof from politics. ... Let me announce in unequivocal terms that our ultimate aim is to restore democracy but of the type that people can understand and work" (Rizvi 1987: 273).

4. From the letter sent on March 24, 1969, by Field Marshal Ayub Khan to the commander in chief of the Pakistan army, Gen. Yahya Khan: "I have exhausted all possible civil and constitutional means to resolve the present crisis. ... Calling the Assembly in such chaotic conditions can only aggravate the situation. ... It is beyond the capacity of the civil government to deal with the present complex situation, and the Defense Forces must step in" (Rizvi 1987: 280).

5. From Bhutto's address to the nation on March 4, 1972: "We have changed the colonial structure of the Armed Forces of Pakistan and injected a truly independent pattern into its vital service....And you must remember, my friends and compatriots, that the people of Pakistan and the Armed Forces themselves are equally determined to wipe out the Bonapartic influence from the Armed Forces. It is essential so that these tendencies never again pollute the political life of this country" (Rizvi 1987: 287–88).

6. From Gen. Mohammed Zia-ul-Haq's first address to the nation on July 5, 1977: "It must be quite clear to you now that when the political leaders failed to steer the country out of a crisis, it is an inexcusable sin for the Armed Forces to sit as silent spectators. It is, primarily, for this reason that the Army perforce had to intervene to save the country."

7. The Defense Committee of the Cabinet, the Defense Council, the Defense Ministry, and the Joint Chiefs of Staff Committee together constitute Pakistan's HDO. Prime Minister Bhutto announced its establishment on December 20, 1975.

8. Headed by the prime minister, the Defense Committee of the Cabinet includes the ministers of defense, foreign affairs, finance, interior, states and frontier regions, Kashmir affairs, information, communications, commerce and production, the chairman of the JCSC, the three service chiefs, and the secretaries of defense, foreign affairs, and finance.

9. With the defense minister as chair, the Defense Council's members are the minister of finance, the minister of state for defense and foreign affairs, the chairman of the JCSC, the three service chiefs, and the secretaries of foreign affairs, defense, and finance.

10. General Ayub Khan's abrogation of the constitution of 1956 was justified on the basis of Kelson's theory of revolutionary legality (*State v. Dosso;* PLD 1958, SC 533); General Zia-ul-Haq was exonerated for violating the constitution of 1973 on the basis of the "doctrine of necessity" (*Begum Bhutto v. Chief of Army Staff;* PLD 1977, SC 657).

11. *News,* September 6, 1998.

12. *Jang,* June 12, 1996.

13. *Herald,* May 1999, p. 28.

14. *Frontier Post,* November 9, 1990.

15. *Nation,* August 8, 1993.

16. *News,* July 5, 1994.

17. *Muslim,* February 5, 1993.

18. Contempt of court proceedings against General (ret.) Mirza Aslam Beg; PLD 1993, SC 310.

19. *Horizon,* July 12, 1992.

20. *News,* November 25, 1997.

21. *News,* October 18, 1999.

CHAPTER 17

1. Josef Silverstein (1977: 285–95) notes that although the word "federal" never appears in the constitution, the document lays out a de facto federal system.

2. "Burman" refers to the ethnic majority comprising roughly 65 percent of the current national population. Most ethnic Burmans live in the central part of the country and in the Irrawaddy delta. They speak the "Burmese" language. "Burmese people" are simply those who are citizens of Burma: there is no ethnic connotation in the adjective. The largest minority groups in Burma today are as follows: Shan (10 percent of the total population), Karen (7 percent), Rakhine (4 percent), Chinese (3 percent), Mon (2 percent), Indian (2 percent), along with small numbers of Assamese and Chin minority peoples.

3. The AFPFL was formed in 1945 out of a national front composed of various organizations that had banded together to fight the Japanese. Prior to independence, the bulk of its membership came from organizations allied with the Communist Party; after the two factions of the Communist Party rebelled against the AFPFL government, however, the national front was dominated throughout the 1950s by the Socialist Party.

4. British advisers had appointed Karens as commander of the armed forces (Gen. Smith Dun) and as chief of the air force (Saw Shi Sho); the chief of operations was a Sandhurst-trained Karen, Brig. Saw Kya Doe. The

quartermaster general, who controlled three-quarters of the military budget, was a Karen, Saw Donny. Although Brig. Bo Let Ya, army chief of staff and later minister of defense, was an ethnic Burman with nationalist credentials, his politics had shifted rightward during the early postwar years, and he publicly supported continued British influence, if not control, over the Tatmadaw. Karen officers and other ranks dominated nearly all the supporting services, including the staff, supply and ammunition depots, artillery, and signal corps.

5. Interview, February 1993.

6. For background on the KMT in Burma the best sources are Lintner (1994), Taylor (1973), Maung Maung (1953), and Mya Thway (1961).

7. U.S. advisers openly trained and lived among the KMT in the Shan State. Moreover, the bodies of three white men fighting alongside KMT troops against the Burma Army were discovered in 1953; on these bodies were found diaries and notebooks containing their addresses in the United States. Although the U.S. Embassy immediately claimed they were Germans, there was little evidence to support this (Lintner 1994: 113).

8. Interview with a former field commander, February 1993.

9. Interview with Col. Tin Maung Aye, April 2, 1992.

10. Interview with U Aung Gyi, May 4, 1992.

11. Nu had a long-running fascination with pop psychology and had even translated Dale Carnegie's *How to Win Friends and Influence People* into Burmese.

12. Interviews with former brigadier Maung Maung, May 3, 1992, and former brigadier U Aung Gyi, May 8, 1992.

13. According to a report on Psywar activities submitted to the 1958 Commander Officers conference, in 1958 alone the directorate published 145 posters, produced seven different radio shows that were broadcast 81 times, and sponsored 26 "returning to the light" (surrender or amnesty) ceremonies (Union of Burma, War Office, General Staff Department 1958b).

14. Interview with U Aung Gyi, May 8, 1992. In 1958, Psywar started publishing *Khit-yeh*, a magazine directed toward rural readers. Even though it was distributed free of charge, its stories read far more like propaganda and it was notably less popular than *Myawaddy*.

15. Toward that end, Ba Than launched two magazines for army personnel in the 1950s. In July 1953, Psywar began publishing the *Tatmadaw Journal (Sit-hna-loun)*, which was distributed to all units and was aimed at junior officers and NCOs. The *Military Science Journal (Sit-pyin-nya Ja-neh)* was published four times a year beginning in June 1956. Its objective was announced in the very first issue: "Throughout history, military science has progressed and changed on a daily basis. As we in Burma have sometimes ignored these changes and failed to improve our military science, we have risked becoming another's slave. Therefore it is not only every soldier's responsibility to keep on top of developments but also every citizen's responsibility." Nearly every article appearing in this journal throughout the 1950s was a translation of a foreign essay on some aspect of military affairs. Frequent sources included the *Australian Army Journal, Army Combat Forces Journal* (U.S.), *Infantry School Quarterly* (U.S.), *Statesman* (U.K.), *Air Forces Quarterly* (U.K.), *Artillery Journal* (India), *Armor* (U.S.), and *Military Review* (U.S.).

16. Discussions of the updated ideology draft at the 1958 Commanding Officers conference included papers on "psychological preparedness" (Union of Burma, Directorate of Education and Psychological Warfare 1958a). On the proposal to "stimulate, motivate, and sustain by moral action the public interest and belief in the ultimate triumph of democracy and socialism," Ba Than reported at length to the 1957 conference about his observations during a study mission to Manila (Union of Burma 1957a, 1957b). The curriculum for the first eight-week Psywar course in 1957 was based on five subjects: ideology, political economy, community development, combat psywar, and technical training (Union of Burma, Directorate of Education and Psychological Warfare 1957c).

17. This number includes officers, other ranks, and union constabulary forces (which were being absorbed into new army units).

18. In July 1999, some 112,000 students out of nearly 400,000 passed the entrance examinations for university. They joined 300,000 students who had passed the exams from 1996 to 1998 but were still awaiting the reopening of universities, which had been closed since December 1996. See Reuters, July 26, 1999, available online at: http://infoseek.go.com/Content?arn=a1150LBY246reulb-19990726&qt=myanmar&sv=IS&lk=noframes&col=NX&kt=A&ak=news1486 [accessed July 30, 1999]. An army spokesman told a conference in 1998 that the Defense Services Academy was being expanded to accommodate 1,000 cadets for each class. In the 1980s, academy intakes were probably around 150 to 200 for each class (Thein Swe 1998).

19. The OSS was founded in 1994 for two reasons: to create a new four-star-general billet to justify Lt. Gen. Khin Nyunt's promotion to general and to create a semiacademic institution similar to strategic studies think tanks elsewhere in Association of Southeast Asian Nations (ASEAN), thus giving Burma a "one-and-a-half-track" seat at ASEAN gatherings (Selth 1997).

20. According to an OSS report, "Among the Neolithic peoples, then, is a total lack of any evidence as to indicate mass mortality or mass burial that could have arisen out of inter-ethnic conflicts; for this reason, divisive inter-racial disharmony and enmity seemed anathema to the national groups in those days of yore"; reported in *Myanmar Perspectives* magazine, March 1999.

21. This delegation of authority from the junta to the regional commanders resolved serious tensions among senior military leaders. At the time of the September 1988 coup d'état, the junta members held lower ranks than the regional commanders and occupied correspondingly lower positions. The ranks of the regional commanders gave them greater status in the reorganizing regime, and their resulting rise to incipient warlordism no doubt reflects this differential. The junta attempted to address this imbalance by raising the status of positions in the newly reorganized Ministry of Defense and the high command by one or two ranks; most junta members were summarily promoted.

22. Prior to 1988, regional commanders were rotated systematically every three years. By the time a regional commander had put down roots and consolidated personal authority in a region, therefore, he would be transferred elsewhere.

23. Interview with Col. Ye Htut, September 22, 1997.

24. "Current Data on the Indonesian Military Elite: January 1, 1998–January 31, 1999," *Indonesia* 67 (April): 133–47.

CHAPTER 18

1. The only armed struggle was waged by the Indian National Army (INA) in collaboration with the Japanese Imperial army. Weary of a politicized army, the Indian National Congress leadership did not embrace the INA and prevented any of its members from joining the Indian military after independence (Cohen 1990a; Wood 1986).

2. The leadership provided by the military in December 1948 when the entire political leadership in Yogyakarta was captured by the Dutch was crucial for the survival of the revolution and the winning of independence.

3. Several reasons have been advanced to explain this outcome (Crouch 1978: 28). Though important, the military struggle was preceded by more than two decades of political agitation. Civilian leaders such as the charismatic Sukarno and the able administrator Mohd Hatta were older, much better educated, had a national following, and also had international exposure and recognition. They were in the forefront of the nationalist movement in articulating and formulating key ideas and concepts such as the *pancasila* doctrine and the 1945 constitution that defined the basis for the Indonesian nation-state and its system of government. The military leaders, on the other hand, were relatively young and poorly educated, lacking in political organization and experience. Disunited and leading a ragtag organization, the military leaders did not have comparable nationalist credentials or the mandate to speak for the entire army. Further, following the demise of Sudirman in 1950, the army leadership was taken over by a small group of mostly Dutch-trained "technocrats" who preferred to withdraw from a political role.

4. During the 1945–1949 revolutionary period there was much contention among the political elite over whether Indonesia should be a federal or unitary state, whether it should be an Islamic, communist, theocratic, or secular state, and over the nature of the constitution and the type of government. These issues appeared to be settled by August 17, 1950, when a new unitary Republic of Indonesia with a new (provisional) constitution replaced the federal Republic of the United States of Indonesia that came into being at the time of the formal Dutch transfer of sovereignty on December 27, 1949. But they were not. There was greater agreement on what Indonesia was not than what it should be (Ricklefs 1993: 233). The issues would resurface soon, creating massive political challenges for the new political leadership of the country.

5. Disenchanted with Javanese political domination and economic exploitation and perceiving the rise of the coalition under the leadership of Sukarno as likely to further tilt the distribution of power against the outer

islanders, local military commanders in resource-rich North and West Sumatra, most of whom were affiliated with the Masyumi party, took over the regional governments in December 1956. Similar developments followed in Kalimantan, North and South Sulawesi, and Maluku. All clamored for greater autonomy from Jakarta.

6. West Irian was renamed Irian Jaya after it came under Indonesian control and was renamed again as West Papua in the post-Suharto era.

7. Some analysts, such as Selig Harrison who reviewed the North Korea chapter in this volume, have a different view of this development. In their view, Kim junior had to resort to this path to power because he still had not consolidated his control of the KWP.

8. It is pertinent to note here that Kim Il Sung's faction that fought against the Japanese came to dominate the KPA.

9. "Slow March to Reform." 2000. Interview with Susilo Bambang Yudhoyono, in *Far Eastern Economic Review*, October 26, p. 36.

10. Ibid.

11. Harden, Blaine. 2000. "By Deals with Burmese Junta, Minorities Thrive." *New York Times*, November 17.

BIBLIOGRAPHY

100 Pi rongrian nairoi phrachulachomklaeo (100 Years of the Chulachomklaeo Military Academy). n.d. Bangkok: Royal Thai Army.

Abraham, Itty. 1998. *The Making of the Indian Atomic Bomb.* London: Zed Books.

Abrahamsson, Bengt. 1972. *Military Professionalism and Political Power.* Beverly Hills: Sage.

Abueva, José Veloso. 1979. "Ideology and Practice in the 'New Society.'" In David A. Rosenberg, ed., *Marcos and Martial Law in the Philippines.* Ithaca: Cornell University Press.

Acharapon Kamutphitsamai. 1997. *Kabot R.S 130: Suksa korani kanpatirup thang kanpokkhrong lae klum thahan mai* (The uprising of 1912: A case study of the administrative reformation and the new soldiers). Bangkok: Amarin Wichakan.

Adelman, Jonathan. 1982. "Toward a Typology of Communist Civil-Military Relations." In Jonathan Adelman, ed., *Communist Armies in Politics.* Boulder: Westview.

Aguero, Felipe. 1995. *Soldiers, Civilians, and Democracy: Post-Franco Spain in Comparative Perspective.* Baltimore: Johns Hopkins University Press.

————. 1997. "Toward Civilian Supremacy in South America." In Larry Diamond, Marc F. Plattner, Yun-han Chu, and Hung-mao Tien, eds., *Consolidating the Third Wave Democracies.* Baltimore: Johns Hopkins University Press.

Ahamed, Emajuddin. 1980. *Bureaucratic Elites in Segmented Economic Growth.* Dacca: University Press.

————. 1988. *Military Rule and the Myth of Democracy.* Dacca: University Press.

————. 1998. "Military and Democracy in Bangladesh." In R. J. May and Viberto Selochan, eds., *The Military and Democracy in Asia and the Pacific.* London: C. Hurst and Co. and Bathurst: Crawford House.

Ahmad, Farzand. 1992. "Domain of the Dons." *India Today,* January 31, pp. 37–41, International edition.

Ahmad, Zakaria. 1981. "The Bayonet and the Trunchoen: Army/Police Relations in Malaysia." In D. C. Ellinwood and Cynthia Enloe, eds., *Ethnicity and the Military in Asia.* New Brunswick, N.J.: Transaction Books.

Ahmad, Zakaria, and Harold Crouch, eds. 1985. *Military-Civilian Relations in Southeast Asia.* Singapore: Oxford University Press.

Ahmed, Imtiaz. 1993. *State and Foreign Policy: India's Role in South Asia.* Delhi: Vikas.

————. 1997. "Political System and Political Process in Bangladesh: Consensus on Intolerance and Conflict?" *Journal of Social Studies* 78: 71–89.

Ahmed, Moudud. 1995. *Democracy and the Challenge of Development: A Study of Politics and Military Interventions in Bangladesh.* Dacca: University Press.

Ahmed, Mushtaq. 1971. *Politics without Social Change.* Karachi: Space Publications.

———. 1972. *Government and Politics in Pakistan.* Karachi: Space Publications.

Ahmed, Rashid. 1998. "Pakistan: Hollow Victory." *FEER,* October 22, 1998, pp. 19–20.

Ahmed, S. 1995. "The Military and Ethnic Politics." In C. H. Kennedy and R. B. Rais, eds., *Pakistan 1995.* Boulder: Westview.

———. 1997. "Pakistan at Fifty: A Tenuous Democracy." *Current History* 96 (614) (December): 419–24.

Ahn, Byeong-man. 1990. "Yusinchejeeui Jeongaegwajeongghwa Yeoksajeok Euimi" (The development of the Yushin system and its historical meaning). In *Hyeondaesaereul Eoteotge Bolgeotinga* (Understanding modern Korean history). Vol. 4. Seoul: Dong-a Ilbosa.

Ahn, Chan-il. 1992. "Bukhaninminkunui Jojikkwanribangshikkwa Kunbu Elite" (The administrative system of KPA and military elite). *Bukhanyongu* (North Korea studies) 3 (2): 175–93.

Akbar, M. J. 1985. *India: The Siege Within.* New Delhi: Penguin.

Alagappa, Muthiah, ed. 1995. *Political Legitimacy in Southeast Asia: The Quest for Moral Authority.* Stanford: Stanford University Press.

———. 2001. *Military Professionalism in Asia: Conceptual and Empirical Perspectives.* Honolulu: East-West Center.

Alavi, Hamza. 1972. "The State in Postcolonial Societies: Pakistan and Bangladesh." *New Left Review* 74 (July–August): 145–73.

Albright, David. 1980. "A Comparative Conceptualization of Civil-Military Relations." *World Politics* 32 (4): 553–76.

Ali, C. M. 1967. *The Emergence of Pakistan.* New York: Columbia University Press.

Ali, S. Mahmud. 1994. *Civil-Military Relations in the Soft State: The Case of Bangladesh.* ENBS/EC Research Paper 1/6–94. Dhaka: AHQ.

Ali, T. 1970. *Pakistan: Military Rule or People's Power.* New York: William Morrow.

Alvi, H. 1983. "Class and State in Pakistan." In H. Gardezi and J. Rashid, eds., *Pakistan: The Unstable State.* Lahore: Vanguard.

———. 1990. "Authoritarianism and Legitimation of State Power in Pakistan." In S. Mitra, ed., *The Post-Colonial State in South Asia.* London: Harvester-Wheatsheaf.

Amnesty International. 1988. *Philippines: Unlawful Killings by Military and Paramilitary Forces.* New York: Amesty International.

———. 1992. *Santa Cruz—The Government Response.* London: Amnesty International.

———. 1993. *Shock Therapy: Restoring Order in Aceh, 1989–1993.* London: Amnesty International.

———. 1994. *Power and Impunity: Human Rights Under the New Order.* London: Amnesty International.

Anderson, Benedict R. O'G. 1972. *Java in a Time of Revolution: Occupation and Resistance, 1944–1946.* Ithaca: Cornell University Press.

———. 1977. "Withdrawal Symptoms: Social and Cultural Aspects of the October 6 Coup." *Bulletin of Concerned Asian Scholars* 9 (July–September): 13–30.

———. 1978. "Studies of the Thai State: The State of Thai Studies." In Eliezer Ayal, ed., *The Study of Thailand.* Athens: Ohio University Press.

———. 1988. "Cacique Democracy in the Philippines: Origins and Dreams." *New Left Review* 169 (May/June): 3–31.

————. 1991. *Imagined Communities: Reflections on the Origins and Spread of Nationalism.* Rev. ed. London: Verso.

Andreski, S. 1968. *Military Organization and Society.* London: Routledge.

Andreski, Stanislav. 1971. *Military Organization and Society.* 2nd ed. Berkeley: University of California Press.

Anek Laothamatas. 1988. "Business and Politics in Thailand: New Patterns of Influence." *Asian Survey* 28 (April): 451–70.

Angel, Robert C. 1988–89. "Prime Ministerial Leadership in Japan: Recent Changes in Personal Style and Administrative Organization." *Pacific Affairs* 61 (4) (Winter): 595–99.

Anggoro, Kusnanto. 2000. "Salah-salah, Tentara Kembali Berkuasa." *Tempo,* May 1–7.

Anwar, Dewi Fortuna. 2001. *Negotiating and Consolidating Democratic Civilian Control of the Indonesian Military.* Honolulu: East-West Center Occasional Papers, Politics and Security Series, No. 4.

Arillo, Cecilio. 1986. *Breakaway: The Inside Story of the Four-Day Revolution in the Philippines.* Manila: CTA and Associates.

Armacost, Michael H. 1996. *Friends or Rivals?: The Insider's Account of U.S.–Japan Relations.* New York: Columbia University Press.

Arya, D.C., and R.C. Sharma, eds. 1991. *Management Issues and Operational Planning for India's Borders.* New Delhi: Scholars Publishing Forum.

Asagumo Shimbunsha. 1976. *Boei Hando Bukku* (Defense Handbook). Tokyo: Asagumo Shimbunsha.

————. 1998. *Boei Hando Bukku* (Defense Handbook). Tokyo: Asagumo Shimbunsha.

Asahi Shimbun Wangankiki Shuzaihan. 1991. *Wangan Senso to Nihon* (The Gulf War and Japan). Tokyo: Asahi Shimbunsha.

Aslie, Mohd. Reduan, ed. 1990. *Tan Sri Hanif Omar: Kepolisan dan Keselamatan.* Kuala Lumpur: AMK Interaksi.

Aspinall, E. 1995. "Students and the Military: Regime Friction and Civilian Dissent in the Late Suharto Period." *Indonesia* 59 (April): 21–44.

Auer, James E. 1973. *The Postwar Rearmament of Japanese Maritime Forces, 1945–71.* New York: Praeger.

Auh, Soo-young. 1971. "The Military in the Politics of South Korea: 1961–1966: The Role of Political Institution-Building." Ph.D. dissertation, West Michigan University.

Aung Myoe, Maung. 1998. *Building the Tatmadaw: The Organisational Development of the Armed Forces in Myanmar.* Canberra: Strategic and Defence Studies Centre.

Ayoob, Mohammed. 1995. *The Third World Security Predicament: State-Making, Regional Conflict, and the International System.* Boulder: Lynne Rienner.

Badhwar, Inderjit. 1990a. "Asserting Authority." *India Today,* February 28, p. 31, International edition.

————. 1990b. "Perilous Turn." *India Today,* April 30, pp. 10–16, International edition.

Baja, Emmanuel A. 1933. *Philippine Police System and Its Problems.* Manila: Pobre's Press.

Bajpai, Kanti. n.d. "India's Nuclear Posture after Pokharan II." Unpublished manuscript. School of International Studies, Jawaharlal Nehru University, New Delhi.

Bajpai, Kanti P., P.R. Chari, Pervaiz I. Cheema, Stephen P. Cohen, and Sumit Ganguly. 1995. *Brasstacks and Beyond: Perception and Management of Crisis in South Asia.* New Delhi: Manohar.

Baldwin, Robert E. 1975. *Foreign Trade Regimes and Economic Development: The Philippines.* New York: Columbia University Press.

Ball, Desmond. 1998. *Burma's Military Secrets: Signals Intelligence from 1941 to Cyber Warfare.* Bangkok: White Lotus.

Bambrungsuk, Surachart. 1988. United States Foreign Policy and Thai Military Rule, 1947–1977. Bangkok: Duang Kamol.

———. 2001. "Thailand: Military Professionalism at the Crossroad." In Muthiah Alagappa, ed., *Military Professionalism in Asia: Conceptual and Empirical Perspectives.* Honolulu: East-West Center.

Banerjee, Ruben. 1992. "Return to Arms." *India Today,* November 30, pp. 36–37, International edition.

Baruah, Sanjib. 1994. "The State and Separatist Militancy in Assam: Winning a Battle and Losing a War." *Asian Survey* 34 (10) (October): 863–77.

Battye, Noel. 1974. "The Military, Government, and Society in Siam, 1868–1910: Politics and Military Reform During the Reign of King Chulalongkorn." Ph.D. dissertation, Cornell University.

Baxter, Craig, and Syedur Rahman. 1991a. "Bangladesh Military: Political Institutionalization and Economic Development." *Journal of Asian and African Studies* 26 (1–2): 43–60.

———. 1991b. "Bangladesh Military: Political Institutionalization and Economic Development." In Charles H. Kennedy and David J. Louscher, eds., *Civil-Military Interaction in Asia and Africa.* Leiden: E. J. Brill.

Bedlington, Stanley. 1978. *Malaysia and Singapore: The Building of New States.* Ithaca: Cornell University Press.

Bedlington, Stanley S. 1981. "Ethnicity and the Armed Forces in Singapore." In D. C. Ellinwood and Cynthia Enloe, eds., *Ethnicity and the Military in Asia.* New Brunswick, N.J.: Transaction Books.

Bello, Walden. 1987. *Creating the Third Force: U.S.-Sponsored Low-Intensity Conflict in the Philippines.* San Francisco: Institute for Food and Development Policy.

Bello, Walden, and Severina Rivera. 1977. "The Logistics of Repression." In Walden Bello and Severina Rivera, eds., *The Logistics of Repression and Other Essays: The Role of U.S. Assistance in Consolidating the Martial Law Regime in the Philippines.* New York: Friends of the Filipino People.

Benjamin, Roger, and Raymond Duvall. 1985. "The Capitalist State in Context." In Roger Benjamin and Stephen L. Elkin, eds., *The Democratic State.* Lawrence: University Press of Kansas.

Benjamin, Roger, and Stephen L. Elkin. 1985. *The Democratic State.* Lawrence: University Press of Kansas.

Bentley, G. Carter. 1993. "Mohamad Ali Dimaporo: A Modern Maranao Datu." In Alfred W. McCoy, ed., *An Anarchy of Families: State and Family in the Philippines.* Monograph 10. Madison: University of Wisconsin Center for Southeast Asian Studies.

Berger, Thomas U. 1993. "From Sword to Chrysanthemum: Japan's Culture of Anti-Militarism." *International Security* 17 (2): 119–50.

———. 1998. *Cultures of Antimilitarism: National Security in Germany and Japan.* Baltimore: Johns Hopkins University Press.

Berlin, Donald Lane. 1982. "Prelude to Martial Law: An Examination of Pre-1972 Philippine Civil-Military Relations." Ph.D. dissertation, University of South Carolina.

Berry, Nicholas Orlando. 1967. "Representation and Decision-Making: A Case Study of Philippine-American War Claims." Ph.D. dissertation, University of Pittsburgh.

Berry, William E. 1986. "The Changing Role of the Philippine Military During Martial Law and Implications for the Future." In Edward A. Olsen and Stephen Jurika Jr., eds., *The Armed Forces in Contemporary Asian Societies*. Boulder: Westview.

Bhattacharyya, Rupak. 1998. "Unrest in the Bangladesh Army on May 18–20, 1996: Implications for the Bangladesh Polity." *Journal of Social Studies* 81: 1–27.

Bhaumik, Subir. 1996. *Insurgent Cross Fire: North-East India*. New Delhi: Lancer.

Bhimaya, Kotera M. 1997. "Civil-Military Relations: Comparative Study of India and Pakistan." Ph.D. dissertation, RAND Graduate School, Santa Monica, Calif.

Bickford, Thomas. 2000. "A Retrospective on the Study of Chinese Civil-Military Relations Since 1979: What Have We Learned? Where Do We Go?" In James Mulvenon and Richard Yang, eds., *The PLA in the Post-Mao Era: A Retrospective*. Santa Monica: Rand.

Bienen, H., ed. 1971. *The Military and Modernization*. Chicago: Aldine-Atherton.

Binder, L. 1961. *Religion and Politics in Pakistan*. Berkeley: University of California Press.

Bitzinger, Richard. 1995. "China's Defense Budget: Is the PLA Cooking the Books?" *International Defense Review*, February, pp. 35–37.

Bitzinger, Richard, and Lin Chong-pin. 1994. *The Defense Budget of the People's Republic of China*. Washington, D.C.: Defense Budget Project.

Bland, Douglas L. 1999. "A Unified Theory of Civil-Military Relations." *Armed Forces and Society* 26 (1): 7–26.

Boeicho (Japan Defense Agency). 1976–98. *Boei Hakusho* (Defense white paper). Tokyo: Okurasho Insatsukyoku.

Boeimondai Kondankai (Advisory Group on Defense Issues). 1994. *Nihon no anzenhosho to boeiryoku no arikata: 21-seiki hemuketeno tenbo* (The modality of the security and defense capability of Japan: Outlook for the 21st century). Tokyo: Okurasho Insatsukyoku.

Boei Nenkan Kankokai. 1992–98. *Boei Nenkan*. Tokyo: Boei Nenkan Kankokai.

Bonner, Raymond. 1987. *Waltzing with a Dictator: The Marcoses and the Making of American Foreign Policy*. New York: Times Books.

Bo Quoc Phong. 1995a. *50 nam Quan Doi Nhan Dan Viet Nam* (50 years of the Vietnam People's Army). Hanoi: Quan Doi Nhan Dan.

———. 1995b. Qui che quan ly lao dong san xuat va lam kinh te cua quan doi (ban hanh kem theo QD 265/QD-QP ngay 31/31995 cua Bo truong Bo Quoc Phong) (Regulations on the army's production labor and economic activities promulgated following the Ministry of Defense's Decision 265 QD-QP of March 13, 1995). Hanoi: Quan Doi Nhan Dan.

Bose, Nayana. 1999. "Angels Who Bring God's Blessing." *Seminar* 479 (July): 27–31.

Bourchier, David. 1991. "Crime, Law, and Authority in Indonesia." In Arief Budiman, ed., *State and Society in Contemporary Indonesia*. Clayton, Victoria: Monash University.

Brass, Paul R. 1994. *The Politics of India Since Independence*. New York: Cambridge University Press.

———. 1997. *Theft of an Idol: Text and Context in the Representation of Collective Violence*. Princeton: Princeton University Press.

Bresnan, John. 1993. *Managing Indonesia: The Modern Political Economy*. New York: Columbia University Press.

Brillantes, Alex Bello. 1987. *Dictatorship and Martial Law: Philippine Authoritarianism in 1972*. Quezon City: Great Books.

British Embassy in Rangoon. 1953. Confidential dispatch from K. R. Oakeschott to R. W. Selby, Southeast Asia Department, Foreign Office, London, June 17. Available at the Public Record Office, Kew, UK; Document FO 371/106682.

———. 1962. Annual Appreciation of the Burma Army for the Period 1 May 1961 to 30 April 1962. Available at the Public Record Office, Kew, UK; Document FO 371/166395.

Brook, Timothy. 1998. *Quelling the People: The Military Suppression of the Beijing Democracy Movement*. Stanford: Stanford University Press.

Brooke, Micool. 1998. "The Armed Forces of Myanmar." *Asian Defence Journal*, January 13, pp. 11–16.

Bryant, C. D. 1979. *Khaki-Collar Crime: Deviant Behavior in the Military Context*. New York: Free Press.

Buck, James H., ed. 1975. *The Modern Japanese Military System*. Beverly Hills: Sage.

Bu-Cop, A. I. 1981a. "Che do mot nguoi chi huy—nguyen tac quan trong nha cua viec xay dung cac luc luong vu trang Xo-Viet" (One-command system—the most important principle of the Soviet armed forces—continued). *Quan Doi Nhan Dan*, May, pp. 55–67.

———. 1981b. "Che do mot nguoi chi huy—nguyen tac quan trong nhat cua viec xay dung cac luc luong vu tran Xo-Viet" (One-command system—the most important principle of the Soviet armed forces). *Quan Doi Nhan Dan*, June, pp. 51–60.

Budiman, Arief, ed. 1990. *State and Civil Society in Indonesia*. Monash Papers on Southeast Asia, no. 22. Clayton, Victoria: Monash University.

Bukhanyonguso. 1978a. *Bukhan Kunsaron* (On North Korea's military). Seoul: Bukhanyonguso.

———. 1978b. *Bukhan Jungse* (Trends in North Korea). Seoul: Bukhanyonguso.

———. 1983. *Bukhan Chongram: 1945–1982* (Encyclopedia of North Korea). Seoul: Bukhanyonguso.

———. 1994. *Bukhan Chongram: 1982–1993* (Encyclopedia of North Korea). Seoul: Bukhanyonguso.

Bullard, Monte. 1984. *China's Military-Political Evolution: The Party and the Military in the PRC, 1960–84*. Boulder: Westview.

Bullard, Monte R. 1997. *The Soldier and the Citizen: The Role of the Military in Taiwan's Development*. New York: Armonk.

Bunbongkarn, Suchit. 1987. *The Military in Thai Politics 1981–86*. Singapore: Institute of Southeast Asian Studies.

———. 1998. "The Military and Democracy in Thailand." In R. J. May and Viberto Selochan, eds., *The Military and Democracy in Asia and the Pacific*. London: C. Hurst and Co. and Bathurst: Crawford House.

Burke, Victor Lee. 1997. *The Clash of Civilizations: War-Making and State Formation in Europe*. Cambridge: Polity Press.

Burki, S. J. 1991. *Pakistan: The Continuing Search for Nationhood*. Boulder: Westview.

Burton, Sandra. 1989. *Impossible Dream: The Marcoses, the Aquinos, and the Unfinished Revolution*. New York: Warner Books.

Callahan, Mary P. 1996. "The Origins of Military Rule." Ph.D. dissertation, Cornell University.

Callard, K. 1957. *Pakistan: A Political Study*. London: Allen and Unwin.

Campos, Cicero C. 1983. "The Role of the Police in the Philippines: A Case Study from the Third World." Ph.D. dissertation, Michigan State University.

Case, William. 1995. "Malaysia: Aspects and Audiences of Legitimacy." In Muthiah Alagappa, ed., *Political Legitimacy in Southeast Asia: The Quest for Moral Authority*. Stanford: Stanford University Press.

Chai, Jai-Hyung. 1972. "The Military and Modernization in Korea." Ph.D. dissertation, Case Western Reserve University.

Chaloemtiarana, Thak. 1979. *Thailand: The Politics of Despotic Paternalism*. Bangkok: Social Science Association of Thailand.

Chan, Christine. 1998a. "Markets Fall as Regulators Grill J&A Chiefs." *South China Morning Post*, July 15.

———. 1998b. "More Staff Quizzed at J&A." *South China Morning Post*, July 16.

———. 1998c. "Nervous J&A Clients Bail Out." *South China Morning Post*, July 17.

Chan, Heng Chee. 1974. "Politics in an Administrative State: Where Has the Politics Gone?" In C. M. Seah, ed., *Trends in Singapore*. Singapore: Singapore University Press.

———. 1985. "Singapore." In Zakaria Ahmad and Harold Crouch, eds., *Military-Civilian Relations in Southeast Asia*. Singapore: Oxford University Press.

Chang, Joon-ik. 1991. *Bukhan Inmin Kundaesa* (History of the KPA). Seoul: Seomundang.

Chang, Myong-bong. 1998. "Choigeunui Bukhan Sahoijuui Honbopkaejungui Bunsok" (Analysis of North Korea's amended socialist constitution in 1998). *Tongilyonguronchong* (Korean journal of unification studies) 7 (2): 1–39.

Chang, Myong-soon. 1999. *Bukhan Kunsa Yongu* (Study of North Korea's military). Seoul: Palbokwon.

Chang, Yo-hua. 1992. *The Military Statecraft of Lee Teng-hui* (in Chinese). Taipei: Center for National Defense Information.

———. 1993. *Lee Teng-hui's Hegemonic Crisis* (in Chinese). Taipei: Center for National Defense Information.

Chantornvong, Sombat, and Montri Chenvidyakarn. 1991. "Constitutional Rule and the Institutionalization of Leadership and Security in Thailand." In Stephen Chee, ed., *Leadership and Security in Southeast Asia*. Singapore: Institute of Southeast Asian Studies.

Chari, P. R. 1991. "Civilian Control over the Military in India." *India Defence Review*, October, pp. 9–15.

———. 1999. "A Nuclear Doctrine for India." *The Hindu*, April 16, editorial page.

Chaudhary, G. W. 1988. *Pakistan: Transition from Military to Civilian Rule*. London: Scorpion.

Chawla, Prabhu. 1999. "Voyage of Intrigue." *India Today*, January 18, International edition.

Chawla, Prabhu, and Manoj Joshi. 1999. "Sunk!" *India Today*, January 11, pp. 19–24, International edition.

Chen, Kao. 1995. "Taiwan's Military Is Learning to Play by New Rules of the Game." *Straits Times*, June 15, p. 38.

Chen, Shih-meng, Chung-Cheng Lin, C. Y. Cyrus Chu, Ching-hsi Chang, Jun-ji Shih, and Jin-Tan Liu. 1991. *Jiegou Danggou Ziben Zhuyi* (Disintegrating KMT-state capitalism). Taipei: Zhengshe.

Chen, Shui-bian, and Chen-heng Ko. 1993. *Goufan Heihezi Baipishu* (White paper on the black box of defense). Taipei: Formosa Foundation.

Cheng Hsiao-shih. 1990a. *Party-Military Relations in the PRC and Taiwan: Paradoxes of Control*. Boulder: Westview.

———. 1990b. "The Polity and the Military: A Framework for Analyzing Civil-Military Relations in Taiwan." *Journal of Social Sciences and Philosophy* 5 (1): 129–72.

———. 1997. "The Trend of Transformation in Civil-Military Relations in Our Country, 1987–1995." In Chin-chiang Su, Thomas Peng, Cheng Hsiao-shih, Arthur Ding, Wen Yuan-hsing, Wang Ping-hung, Ho De-fen, Chou Chu-ying, Chen Ying-yu, and Chen Chih-wei, eds., *Jundui Yu Shehui* (The military and the society). Taipei: INPR.

Cheng, Tun-jen. 1993. "Taiwan in Democratic Transition." In James Morley, ed., *Driven by Growth: Political Change in the Asia-Pacific.* Armonk, New York: M. E. Sharpe.

Chengappa, Raj. 1999. *Weapons of Peace.* New Delhi: Harper Collins.

Chengappa, Raj, and Manoj Joshi. 1998. "Future Fire." *India Today,* May 25, International edition.

Cherian, John. 1999. "Concern over Dismissal." *Frontline* 16 (2) (January 16–29), Electronic edition.

Chiang, Mickey. 1990. *Fighting Fit: The SAF.* Singapore: Times Editions.

Chibber, M. L. 1979. "Para Military Forces." *USI Papers* No. 4 (September). United Services Institution, New Delhi.

———. 1986. "Introduction of National Service in India for Defence and Development." *Indian Defence Review,* January, pp. 35–44.

———. 1990. "Siachen—The Untold Story (A Personal Account)." *Indian Defence Review,* January, pp. 146–52.

Chin Kin Wah. 1974. *The Five Power Defence Arrangement and AMDA: Some Observations on the Nature of an Evolving Relationship.* Occasional Paper 23. Singapore: Institute of Southeast Asian Studies.

———. 1987. *Defence Spending in Southeast Asia.* Singapore: Institute of Southeast Asian Studies.

Chinworth, Michael W. 1992. *Inside Japan's Defense: Technology, Economics, and Strategy.* Washington, D.C.: Brasseys.

Chittagong Hill Tracts Commission. 1991. *Life Is Not Ours: Land and Human Rights in the Chittagong Hill Tracts, Bangladesh.* Copenhagen and London: International Work Group for Indigenous Affairs and Anti-Slavery International.

———. 1992. *Life Is Not Ours: Life and Human Rights in the Chittagong Hill Tracts, Bangladesh.* Copenhagen and London: International Work Group for Indigenous Affairs and Anti-Slavery International.

Cho, Hee-yeon. 1998. *Hangookeui Gookga Minjoojooeui Jeongchibyeondong* (State, democracy, and political changes in Korea). Seoul: Dangdae.

Choi, Jang-jip. 1989. *Hangookhyeondaesjeongchieui Goojowa Byeonhwa* (The structure and change of Korean politics). Seoul: Kachi.

———. 1993. *Hangookminjoojooeuieeron* (Theory of Korean democracy). Seoul: Hangilsa.

Choi, Jin-wook. 1996. *Kim Jong Ileui Dangkwon Jangahk Yungu* (A study of Kim Jong Il's party power consolidation). Seoul: Korea Institute for National Unification.

———. 1998. "Kaejung Honbop Yihu Bukhanui Kwolryok Kujowa Jungchaek Jonmang" (The prospects for North Korea's power structure and policy since the amendment of the socialist constitution in 1998). *Tongilyonguronchong* (Korean journal of unification studies) 7 (2): 41–63.

Choi, Ju-hwal. 1997. "North Korean Mass-Destruction Weapons." A prepared statement for the North Korean Missile Proliferation Hearing before the Subcommittee on International Security, Proliferation, and Federal Services of the Committee on Governmental Affairs, United States Senate, October 21.

Choi, Ju-hwan. 1992. *Bukhan Kyongjeron* (The North Korea economy). Seoul: Daewangsa.

Choi, Sung. 1997. *Bukhan Jungchisa* (Political history of North Korea). Seoul: Pulbit.

Choi, Wan-kyu. 1991. "Chogi Chosun Inminkunui Baljonkwajongkwa Dang-Kun Kwangye" (Genesis of the KPA and party-military relations). In Hyun-wook Ko, ed., *Bukhancheje Surip-kwajong: 1945–1948* (The building process of North Korea's political regime). Seoul: Institute for Far Eastern Studies, Kyungnam University.

Chu Huy Man. 1984. "Chu nhiem chinh tri va co che lanh dao moi cua Dang doi voi Quan Doi trong giai doan cach mang hien nay" (Political commissars and the new party leadership structure in the armed forces in the new revolutionary era). *Quan Doi Nhan Dan,* March, pp. 1–32.

Chu, Yun-han. 2001. "Democratic Consolidation in the Post-KMT Era: The Challenge of Governance." In Muthiah Alagappa, ed., *Taiwan's Presidential Politics: Democratization and Cross-Strait Relations.* Armonk, N.Y.: M. E. Sharpe.

Chua, Beng-Huat. 1997. *Communitarian Ideology and Democracy in Singapore.* London: Routledge.

Chuma Kiyofuku. 1985. *Saigunbi no seijigaku* (The politics of rearmament). Tokyo: Chishikisha.

Chung, Chin O. 1978. *Pyongyang between Peking and Moscow: North Korea's Involvement in the Sino-Soviet Dispute, 1958–1975.* Tuscaloosa: University of Alabama Press.

Chung, Kyu-sop. 1997a. *Bukhanoikyoui Ohjewa Oneul* (Yesterday and today of North Korea's diplomacy). Seoul: Ilshinsa.

———. 1997b. "Kim Jong Il Juogkwonui Kwonryok Jaepyonkwa Anjongsong Bunsok" (Analysis of power structure and regime stability in Kim Jong Il regime). *Tongilkyongje* (Unification economy) 28: 38–50.

Chung, Seung-hwa. 1987. *12.12 Sageon Chung Seung-hwaneun Malhanda* (Seung-hwa Chung speaks about the 12.12 mutiny). Seoul: Kachi.

Chung, Yoo-jin. 1997. "Bukhan Jeyi Kyongjekwonui Daehayeo" (On the second economy in North Korea). *Tongilyongu* (Korean unification studies) 1: 90–107.

Chung, Young-tai. 1995. *Kim Jong Il Chejewa Kunbu Yokwhal: Jisokkwa Byonhwa* (The KPA's role under Kim Jong Il regime: Continuities and changes). Seoul: Korea Institute for National Unification.

———. 1996. "Kim Jong Il Jongkwonui Chejeyujijonryak: Kunsabumun" (Kim Jong Il's regime maintenance strategy: The military sector). *Tongilyonguronchong* (Korean journal of unification studies) 5 (2): 83–113.

———. 1998. "Bukhan Kangsung Daekukronui Kunsajok Uimi" (The military implications of "Strong and prosperous nation" thesis in North Korea). *Tongilyonguronchong* (Korean journal of unification studies) 7 (2): 65–89.

"Civil-Military Relations—Gus Dur Versus Wiranto." 2000. *The Van Zorge Report on Indonesia.* January 7.

Clapham, Christopher, and George Philip, eds. 1985. *The Political Dilemmas of Military Regimes.* Totowa, N.J.: Barnes and Nobles Books.

Clausewitz, Carl Von. 1984. *On War.* Edited and translated by Michael Hoear and Peter Paret. Princeton: Princeton University Press.

Clutterbuck, R. 1973. *Riot and Revolution in Singapore and Malaya, 1945–1963.* London: Faber.

———. 1984. *Conflict and Violence in Singapore and Malaysia.* Rev. ed. Singapore: Graham Brash.

Cohen, Stephen P. 1988. "The Military and Indian Democracy." In Atul Kohli, ed., *India's Democracy: An Analysis of Changing State-Society Relations.* Princeton: Princeton University Press.

————. 1990a. *The Indian Army: Its Contribution to the Development of the Nation.* Delhi: Oxford University Press.

————. 1990b. *The Indian Army: Its Contribution to the Development of a Nation.* Berkeley: University of California Press.

————. 1998a. "Indian Perspectives on War, Peace, and International Order." Paper presented at the Conference on Conflict or Convergence: Global Perspectives on War, Peace, and International Order, Harvard Academy for International and Area Studies, Cambridge, Mass., November 13–15.

————. 1998b. *The Pakistan Army.* Karachi: Oxford University Press.

Cohen, Youssef, Brian R. Brown, and A. F. K. Organski. 1981. "The Paradoxical Nature of State-Making: The Violent Creation of Order." *American Political Science Review* 75: 901–10.

Collier, Kit. 1999. *The Armed Forces and Internal Security in Asia: Preventing the Abuse of Power.* Honolulu: East-West Center Occasional Papers, Politics and Security Series, No. 2 (December).

Collins, Joseph J. 1999. "Civil-Military Relations: How Wide the Gap?" *International Security* 24 (2): 199–203.

Colton, Timothy J. 1978. "The Party-Military Connection: A Participatory Model." In Dale R. Herspring and Ivan Volgyes, eds., *Civil-Military Relations in Communist Systems.* Boulder: Westview.

Commission of Inquiry into Involuntary Removal or Disappearances of Persons in the Western, Southern, and Sabaragamuwa Provinces. 1997. *Final Report of the Commission into Involuntary Removal or Disappearances of Persons in the Western, Southern, and Sabaragamuwa Provinces.*

Coquia, Jorge R. 1957. *The Philippine Presidential Elections of 1953.* Manila: University Publishing Co.

Coser, Lewis. 1956. *The Functions of Social Control.* London: Routledge and Kegan Paul.

Cribb, Robert, ed. 1990. *The Indonesian Killings, 1965–1966: Studies from Java and Bali.* Monash Papers on Southeast Asia, no. 21. Clayton, Victoria: Monash University.

Crisol, José M. 1954. *The Red Lie.* Manila: Agro Printing and Publishing House.

————. 1980. *The Red Lie.* Manila: Agro Printing and Publishing House. (First ed., 1954.)

Crispinin, Shawn W. 1998. "Burma: Internal Matter." *FEER*, August 13, 1998, p. 26.

Cronin, Patrick M., and Michael J. Green. 1994. *Redefining the U.S.-Japan Alliance: Tokyo's National Defense Program.* McNair Paper 31. Washington, D.C.: National Defense University, Institute for National Strategic Studies.

Crouch, Harold. 1978. *The Army in Indonesian Politics.* Rev. ed. Ithaca: Cornell University Press.

————. 1985. "Indonesia." In Zakaria Haji Ahmad and Harold Crouch, eds., *Military-Civilian Relations in Southeast Asia.* Singapore: Oxford University Press.

————. 1988. *The Army and Politics in Indonesia.* Rev. ed. Ithaca: Cornell University Press.

————. 1991. "The Military in Malaysia." In Viberto Selochan, ed., *The Military, the State, and Development in Asia and the Pacific.* Boulder: Westview.

————. 1997. "Civil-Military Relations in Southeast Asia." In Larry Diamond, Marc F. Plattner, Yun-han Chu, and Hung-mao Tien, eds., *Consolidating Third World Democracies: Themes and Perspectives.* Baltimore: Johns Hopkins University Press.

————. 1998. "Wiranto and Habibie: Military-Civil Relations Since May 1998." Paper presented at the workshop/conference, Democracy in Indonesia? The Crisis and Beyond, Melbourne and Monash Universities, December 11–12.

———. 2000. "Indonesia: Jakarta Doesn't Control the Military." *International Herald Tribune*, September 15, p. 6.

Cullinane, Michael. 1993. "Patron as Client: Warlord Politics and the Duranos of Danao." In Alfred W. McCoy, ed., *An Anarchy of Families: State and Family in the Philippines*. Monograph 10. Madison: University of Wisconsin Center for Southeast Asian Studies.

Cumings, Bruce. 1993. "The Corporate State in North Korea." In Hagen Koo, ed., *State and Society in Contemporary Korea*. Ithaca: Cornell University Press.

"Current Data on the Indonesian Military Elite." 1993. *Indonesia* 55 (April): 177–98.

Da Cunha, Derek. 1999. "Sociological Aspects of the Singapore Armed Forces." *Armed Forces and Society* 25 (Spring): 459–75.

Dahl, Robert A. 1971. *Polyarchy: Participation and Opposition*. New Haven, Conn.: Yale University Press.

Dam Quang Trung. 1976. "Bo doi quan khu 4 quyet tam hoan thanh thang loi nhiem vu tren cong truong duong sat thong nhat" (Military Region IV is determined to complete the tasks assigned on the North-South railway sucessfully). *Quan Doi Nhan Dan*, June, pp. 41–46.

Dang Kinh. 1976. "Cac luc luong vu trang Quan khu Ta Ngan phan dau hoan thanh tot nhiem vu xay dung kinh te" (Ta Ngan Military Region struggled to complete economic development tasks). *Quan Doi Nhan Dan*, June, pp. 32–40.

Dang Phong, and Melanie Beresford. 1997. *Authority Relations and Economic Decision Making in Vietnam*. Copenhagen: NIAS.

Dang The Chuong. 1984. "Su lanh dao cua Dang va che do mot nguoi chi huy trong quan doi" (Party leadership and the one-command system). *Quan Doi Nhan Dan*, January, pp. 52–63.

Danguilan-Vitug, Marites. 1990. *Kudeta: The Challenge to Philippine Democracy*. Manila: Center for Investigative Journalism.

Dang Vu Hiep. 1983. "May van de co ban trong co che lanh dao moi cua Dang doi voi quan doi va su nghiep quoc phong" (Basic problems in the new party leadership structure in the army and defense tasks). *Quan Doi Nhan Dan*, October, pp. 13–29.

———. 1996. "Quan doi nhan dan trong cuoc dau tranh chong 'dien bien hoa binh' bao ve doc lap dan toc va chu nghia xa hoi" (The People's Army in the struggle against peaceful evolution to maintain national independence and socialism). *Thong Tin Chuyen De* 52 (February): 125–30.

Daniel, Val. 1997. *Charred Lullabies*. Princeton: Princeton University Press.

Dasgupta, Swapan. 1999. "It's Their War Too." *India Today*, July 19, pp. 25–35, International edition.

Davide, Hilario G., Jr., Carolina G. Hernandez, Ricardo J. Romulo, Delfin L. Lazaro, and Christian S. Monsod. 1990. *The Final Report of the Fact-Finding Commission (pursuant to R.A. No. 6832)*. Makati: Bookmark.

Davis, Anthony, and Bruce Hawke. 1998. "Burma: The Country That Won't Kick the Habit." *Jane's Intelligence Review*, March, pp. 26–31.

Decalo, Samuel. 1976. *Coups and Army Rule in Africa: Studies in Military Style*. New Haven, Conn.: Yale University Press.

Deleuze, Guilles, and Felix Guattari. 1987. *A Thousand Plateaus: Capitalism and Schizophrenia*. Translated by Brian Massumi. Minneapolis: University of Minnesota Press.

Delfs, Robert. 1991. "Japan: To the Gulf, at Last." *FEER*, May 9, p. 19.

De Quiros, Conrado. 1997. *Dead Aim: How Marcos Ambushed Philippine Democracy.* Pasig City: Foundation for Worldwide People Power.

Desai, A. R., ed. 1986. *Violation of Democratic Rights in India.* Bombay: Popular Prakashan.

Desch, Michael C. 1996. "Threat Environments and Military Missions." In Larry Diamond and Marc F. Plattner, eds., *Civil-Military Relations and Democracy.* Baltimore: Johns Hopkins University Press.

Deshmukh, B. G. 1999. "A Systemic Failure." *Frontline* 16 (2) (January 16–29), electronic edition.

De Silva, K. M. 1997. "The Police and Armed Services." In K. M. De Silva, ed., *Sri Lanka: Problems of Governance.* Delhi: Konark.

Diamond, Larry. 1999. *Developing Democracy: Toward Consolidation.* Baltimore: Johns Hopkins University Press.

———. 2001. "Anatomy of a Political Earthquake: How the KMT Lost and the DPP Won the 2001 Presidential Elections in Taiwan." In Muthiah Alagappa, ed., *Taiwan's Presidential Politics: Democratization and Cross-Strait Relations.* Armonk, N.Y.: M. E. Sharpe.

Diamond, Larry, Juan J. Linz, and Seymour Martin Lipset, eds. 1989. *Democracy in Developing Countries.* 4 vols. Boulder: Lynne Rienner.

Diamond, Larry, and Marc F. Plattner, eds. 1996. *Civil-Military Relations and Democracy.* Baltimore: Johns Hopkins University Press.

Diamond, Larry, Marc F. Plattner, Yun-han Chu, and Hung-mao Tien, eds. 1998. *Consolidating Third World Democracies: Regional Challenges.* Baltimore: Johns Hopkins University Press.

Dickson, Bruce J. 1997. Democratization in China and Taiwan: The Adaptability of Leninist Parties. Oxford: Clarendon Press.

———. 2001. "Taiwan's Democratization: What Lessons for China?" In Muthiah Alagappa, ed., *Taiwan Presidential Polls, Democratic Consolidation and Cross-Strait Relations.* Armonk, N.Y.: M. E. Sharpe.

Dillon, Dana R. 1994. "A Southeast Asia Scenario." *Military Review,* September, pp. 51–60.

Dinh Tu Linh. 1997. "Bao ve muc tieu trong chong bao loan lat do" (Maintain objectives in riot management). *Thong Tin Khoa Hoc Quan Su,* June, pp. 19–21.

Dixit, J. N. 1997. *Assignment Colombo.* New Delhi: Konark.

Dixon, N. 1976. *On the Psychology of Military Incompetence.* London: Lowe and Brydone.

Djiwandono, Soedjati, and Yong-mun Cheong, eds. 1998. *Soldiers and Stability in Southeast Asia.* Singapore: Institute of Southeast Asian Studies.

Doan Khue. 1996. "Su nghiep cong nghiep hoa, hien dai hoa dat nuoc voi cong cuoc cung co nen quoc phong toan dan, xay dung quan doi nhan dan" (Industrialization and modernization in the strengthening of the all-people defense system and the building of the People's Army). *Thong Tin Chuyen De* 53 (March): 28–33.

Dong-a Ilbosa, ed. 1988. *Hyeondaesaereul Eoteotge Bolgeotinga* (Understanding modern Korean history). Vols. 1–2. Seoul: Dong-a Ilbosa.

Doorn, J. V., ed. 1968. *Armed Forces and Society: Sociological Essays.* Paris: Mouton.

Doronila, Amando. 1985. "The Transformation of Patron-Client Relations and Its Political Consequences in Postwar Philippines." *Journal of Southeast Asian Studies* 16 (1) (March): 99–116.

Downing, Brian M. 1992. *The Military Revolution and Political Change: Origins of Democracy and Autocracy in Early Modern Europe.* Princeton: Princeton University Press.

Dreyer, June Teufel. 1982. "The Chinese Militia." In Jonathan R. Adelman, ed., *Communist Armies in Politics*. Boulder: Westview.

———. 1986. "The Role of the Armed Forces in Contemporary China." In Edward A. Olsen and Stephen Jurika, eds., *The Armed Forces in Contemporary Asian Societies*. Boulder: Westview.

Duncan, Ian. 1997. "New Political Equations in North India: Mayawati, Mulayam, and Government Instability in Uttar Pradesh." *Asian Survey* 37 (10) (October): 979–96.

Dunlap, Charles J. 1996. *Melancholy Reunion: A Report from the Future on the Collapse of Civil-Military Relations in the United States*. Occasional Paper 11. Colorado: USAF Institute for National Security Studies.

Dupont, Alan. 1996. "Indonesian Defence Strategy and Security: Time for a Rethink?" *Contemporary Southeast Asia* 18 (December): 275–97.

Edgerton, Ronald King. 1975. "The Politics of Reconstruction in the Philippines: 1945–48." Ph.D. dissertation, University of Michigan.

Elias, Norbert. 1998. *On Civilization, Power, and Knowledge*. Chicago: University of Chicago Press.

Elkin, Jerrold F., and W. Andrew Ritezel. 1985. "Military Role Expansion in India." *Armed Forces and Society* 11 (4) (Summer): 489–504.

Ellinwood, D. C., and Cynthia Enloe, eds. 1981. *Ethnicity and the Military in Asia*. New Brunswick, N.J.: Transaction Books.

Elliott, David. 1992. "Vietnam's 1991 Party Elections." *Asian Affairs* 19 (3) (Fall): 159–69.

Enloe, Cynthia. 1977. "Malaysia's Military in the Interplay of Economic and Ethnic Change." In John A. Lent, ed., *Cultural Pluralism in Malaysia: Policy, Military, Mass Media, Education, Religion, Social Class*. Special Report 14. De Kalb: Center for Southeast Asian Studies, Northern Illinois University.

———. 1978. "The Issue Saliency of the Military-Ethnic Connection: Some Thoughts on Malaysia." *Comparative Politics* 10 (2): 267–85.

———. 1980. *Ethnic Soldiers*. Athens: University of Georgia Press.

———. 1981. "Ethnicity in the Evolution of Asia's Armed Bureaucracies." In D. C. Ellinwood and Cynthia H. Enloe, eds., *Ethnicity and the Military in Asia*. New Brunswick: Transaction Books.

———. 1983. *Does Khaki Become You? The Militarization of Women's Lives*. London: Pluto Press.

Esman, M. J. 1972. *Administration and Development in Malaysia*. Ithaca: Cornell University Press.

Evans, Peter B., Dietrich Rueschemeyer, and Theda Skocpol, eds. 1985. *Bringing the State Back In*. Cambridge: Cambridge University Press.

Evans, Rowland, and Robert Novak. 1979. "The Secret 'Swing Strategy.'" *Washington Post*, October 8, p. A21.

Fairbank, John King, Edwin O. Reischauer, and Albert M. Craig, eds. 1965. *East Asia: The Modern Transformation*. Vol. 2. Boston: Houghton Mifflin.

Fay, Peter Ward. 1993. *The Forgotten Army: India's Armed Struggle for Independence, 1942–45*. Ann Arbor: University of Michigan Press.

Feaver, Peter D. 1992. *Guarding the Guardians: Civilian Control of Nuclear Weapons in the United States*. Ithaca: Cornell University Press.

———. 1992–93. "Command and Control in Emerging Nuclear States." *International Security* 17 (3) (Winter): 160–87.

———. 1996. "The Civil-Military Problematique: Huntington, Janowitz, and the Question of Civilian Control." *Armed Forces and Society* 23 (2) (Winter): 149–78.

————. 1999. "Civil-Military Relations." *Annual Review of Political Science* 2: 211–41.

Federation of American Scientists. 1998. "Second Economic Committee." http://www.fas.org
/nuke/guide/dprk/agency/2_econ_com.htm.

Feit, E. 1973. *The Armed Bureaucrats: Military-Administrative Regimes and Political Development.* Boston:
Houghton Mifflin.

Fforde, Adam, and Stefan De Vylder. 1996. *From Plan to Market.* Boulder: Westview.

*Final Report of the Commission of Inquiry into Involuntary Disappearances of Persons in the Western, South-
ern and Sabaragamuva Provinces.* 1997. Colombo, Sri Lanka: Department of Government Printing. September.

Fineman, Daniel. 1997. *A Special Relationship.* Honolulu: University of Hawai'i Press.

Finer, S.E. 1976. *The Man on Horseback: The Role of the Military in Politics.* (2nd enlarged ed.) Harmondsworth: Penguin.

————. 1988. *The Man on Horseback: The Role of the Military in Politics.* (2nd enlarged ed., revised
and updated.) Boulder: Westview.

————. 1975. *The Man on Horseback: The Role of the Military in Politics.* New York: Penguin.

————. 1985. "The Retreat to the Barracks: Notes on the Practice and the Theory of Military
Withdrawal from the Seats of Power." *Third World Quarterly* 7 (1): 16–30.

Fishman, Robert. 1990. "Rethinking State and Regime: Southern Europe's Transition to
Democracy." *World Politics* 42 (3): 422–40.

Fitch, Samuel. 1989. "Military Professionalism, National Security, and Democracy: Lessons
from Latin America." *Pacific Focus* 4 (2): 99–147.

Fossum, Egil. 1967. "Factors Influencing the Occurrence of Military Coup d'État in Latin
America." *Journal of Peace Research* 4: 228–51.

Foucault, Michel. 1977. *Discipline and Punish.* London: Vintage.

Friedberg, Aaron L. 2000. *In the Shadow of the Garrison State: America's Anti-Statism and Its Cold War
Strategy.* Princeton: Princeton University Press.

Funabashi Yoichi. 1991. "Japan and the New World Order." *Foreign Affairs* 70 (5) (Winter): 58–74.

————. 1999. *Alliance Adrift.* New York: Council on Foreign Relations Press.

Gandhi, Mohandas K. 1960. *My Non-Violence.* Compiled and edited by Sailesh Kumar Ban-
dopadhyay. Ahmedabad: Navjivan.

Ganguly, Sumit. 1991a. "From the Defense of the Nation to Aid to the Civil: The Army in Contemporary India." In Charles H. Kennedy and David J. Louscher, eds., *Civil-Military Interaction in Asia and Africa.* Leiden: E. J. Brill.

————. 1991b. "From the Defense of the Nation to Aid to the Civil: The Army in Contemporary India." *Journal of Asian and African Studies* 26 (1–2) (January–April): 11–26.

————. 1994. *The Origins of War in South Asia: Indo-Pakistani Conflicts Since 1947.* Boulder: Westview.

————. 1997. *The Crisis in Kashmir: Portents of War, Hopes of Peace.* New York: Cambridge University Press.

Gani, Sjaifuddin. n.d. "Kasus Aceh: Teror Kontra Teror Sebagai Kondisi Umum." Unpublished manuscript.

Gardezi, H., and J. Rashid, eds. 1983. *Pakistan: The Unstable State.* Lahore: Vanguard.

Garver, John. 1996. "The PLA as an Interest Group in Chinese Foreign Policy." In C. Denni-
son Lane, Mark Weisenbloom, and Dimon Liu, eds., *Chinese Military Modernization.* London: Keegan Paul International.

George, Sudhir Jacob. 1994. "The Bodo Movement in Assam: Unrest to Accord." *Asian Survey* 34 (10) (October): 878–92.

Ghosh, Amitav. 1997. "India's Untold War of Independence." *New Yorker,* June 23 and June 30.

Ghosh, Amiya Kumar. 1996. *India's Defence Budget and Expenditure Management in a Wider Context.* New Delhi: Lancer.

Ghosh, S. K. 1987. *Communal Riots in India.* New Delhi: Ashish.

Giddens, Anthony. 1987. *The Nation-State and Violence.* Berkeley: University of California Press.

Gill, Bates. 1999. "Chinese Defense Procurement Spending: Determining Chinese Military Intentions and Capabilities." In James R. Lilley and David Shambaugh, eds., *China's Military Faces the Future.* Armonk, N.Y.: M. E. Sharpe.

Gillego, Bonifacio. 1972. "Our Police Forces as a Tool of American Imperialism." *Ronin* 1 (7) (October).

Girling, John L. S. 1981. *Thailand: Society and Politics.* Ithaca: Cornell University Press.

Godwin, Paul H. B. 1988. *The Chinese Communist Armed Forces.* Maxwell AFB, Ala.: Air University Press.

Goh, Keng Swee. 1973. "National Service and Defence Policy." In *Towards Tomorrow: Essays on Development and Social Transformation in Singapore* [in honor of Lee Kuan Yew on his 50th birthday, September 16, 1973]. Singapore: NTUC. (Government publication.)

Golay, Frank Hindman. 1998. *Face of Empire: United States–Philippine Relations, 1898–1946.* Monograph 14. Madison: University of Wisconsin Center for Southeast Asian Studies.

Goldwin, Robert A., ed. 1970. *Readings in World Politics.* New York: Oxford University Press.

Gomez, Mario. 1994. "Displaced Persons." In Law and Society Trust, ed., *Sri Lanka State of Human Rights.* Colombo: Law and Society Trust.

Goodman, L. W. 1990. "The Military and Democracy: An Introduction." In Louis W. Goodman, Johanna S. R. Mendelson, and Juan Rial, eds., *The Military and Democracy: The Future of Civil-Military Relations in Latin America.* Lexington, Mass: Lexington Books.

———. 1997. "Civil-Military in the Post–Cold War Era." *Issues of Democracy* 2 (3): 19–22.

Goodman, Louis W., Johanna S. R. Mendelson, and Juan Rial, eds. 1990. *The Military and Democracy: The Future of Civil-Military Relations in Latin America.* Lexington, Mass.: Lexington Books.

Gough, K., and H. P. Sharma. 1973. *Imperialism and Revolution in South Asia.* New York: Monthly Review Press.

Government of Bangladesh. 1986. *The Army Regulations.* Vol. 1, *Rules.* Dacca: Ministry of Defence.

———. 1994. *The Constitution of the People's Republic of Bangladesh* [as amended up to June 30]. Dacca: Ministry of Law and Parliamentary Affairs.

———. 1996. *The Constitution of the People's Republic of Bangladesh* [as amended up to April 30]. Dacca: Ministry of Law and Parliamentary Affairs.

Government of Pakistan. 1989. *Report of the Commission to Review the Working of Security and Intelligence Agencies.* Islamabad.

———. Directorate of Films and Publications. 1989. *Quaid-i-Azam Mohammad Ali Jinnah: Speeches and Statements 1947–48.* Islamabad: Ministry of Information and Broadcasting.

———. Independent Bureau for Humanitarian Issues. 1999. *Role of Armed Forces in Socio-Economic Development: Pakistan as a Case Study.* Islamabad.

———. Ministry of Defense. 1976. *White Paper.* Islamabad.

Government of Singapore. 1969. *Our Security, 1819–1969: A Nation Building Through the Armed Forces and the Police.* Singapore: Government Print Office.

———. 1985. *Questions and Answers on Defence Policies and Organisation.* Singapore: MINDEF.

———. 1988. *Civil Defence in Singapore, 1939–84.* Singapore: Institute of Southeast Asian Studies.

———. 1991. *Defence Technology Group.* Singapore: DTG.

Gow, Ian. 1993. "Civilian Control of the Military in Postwar Japan." In Ron Matthews and Keisuke Matsuyama, eds., *Japan's Military Renaissance?* New York: St. Martin's Press.

Graham, Norman A. 1991. "The Role of the Military in the Political and Economic Development of the Republic of Korea." In Charles H. Kennedy and David J. Louscher, eds., *Civil-Military Interaction in Asia and Africa.* Leiden: E. J. Brill.

Green, Michael J. 1995. *Arming Japan: Defense Production, Alliance Politics, and the Postwar Search for Autonomy.* New York: Columbia University Press.

Guhathakurta, Meghna. 1996. "Democratization in Bangladesh: The Mass Uprising of 1990 and Its Aftermath." In Kumar Rupesinghe and Khawar Mamtaz, eds., *Internal Conflicts in South Asia.* London: Sage.

Gumelar, Agum (Lt. Gen.). 1998. "Pokok-Pokok Arahan Gubernur Lemhannas Pada Diskusi Dengan Harian Kompas tentang 'Visi dan Agenda Reformasi: Menuju Masyarakat Indonesia Baru.'" Unpublished manuscript.

Gunaratna, Rohan. 1993. *Indian Intervention in Sri Lanka: The Role of India's Intelligence Agencies.* Colombo: South Asian Network on Conflict Research.

Gunasinghe, Newton. 1989. "Sri Lankan Armed Forces." In Ponna Wignaraja and Akmal Hussain, eds., *The Challenge in South Asia: Development, Democracy, and Regional Co-operation.* Tokyo and New Delhi: United Nations University and Sage Publications.

Guneratne, Rohan. 1990. *Sri Lanka: A Lost Revolution: The Inside Story of the JVP.* Sri Lanka: Institute of Fundamental Studies.

Gupta, Amit. 1995. "Determining India's Force Structure and Military Doctrine—*I Want My MiG.*" *Asian Survey* 25 (5) (May): 441–58.

Gupta, Shekhar. 1984a. "Punjab: The Elusive Solution." *India Today,* August 15, p. 64, International edition.

———. 1984b. "Crackdown in Punjab." *India Today,* June 30, p. 26.

———. 1988. "The Tired Trouble Shooters." *India Today,* February 15, pp. 82–83, International edition.

———. 1990a. "Militant Siege." *India Today,* January 31, pp. 30–37, International edition.

———. 1990b. "Lives on the Line." *India Today,* August 15, pp. 36–38, International edition.

———. 1991. "The Rule of the Gun." *India Today,* January 15, pp. 14–24, International edition.

———. 1995. *India Redefines Its Role.* Adelphi Paper 293. London: International Institute of Strategic Studies and Oxford University Press.

———. 2000. "The Winner as Underdog." *The Indian Express,* May 6, editorial page.

Gupta, Shekhar, W. P. S. Sidhu, and Kanwar Sandhu. 1993. "A Middle-Aged Military Machine." *India Today,* April 30, pp. 22–41, International edition.

Gurtov, Mel, and Byong-Moo Hwang. 1998. *China's Security: The New Roles of the Military.* Boulder: Lynne Rienner.

Gutang, Rod B. 1991. *Pulisya: The Inside Story of the Demilitarization of Law Enforcement in the Philippines.* Quezon City: Daraga Press.

Haas, Ernst B. 1980. "Why Collaborate? Issue-Linkage and International Regimes." *World Politics* 32 (3) (April): 357–405.

Hamid, Syarwan. 1996. "Implementasi Dwifungsi ABRI: Renungan 50 Tahun Kemerdekeaan RI." *Republika*, May 17.

Hamm, Taik-young. 1998. *Kukga Anboui Jongchi Kyungjehak* (The political economy of national security). Seoul: Bupmusa.

Han, Bae-ho. 1994. *Hangookjeongchibyeondongron* (Political changes in Korea). Seoul: Beopmoonsa.

Han, Seung-joo. 1974. *The Failure of Democracy in South Korea*. Berkeley: University of California Press.

———. 1983. *Je 2 Gonghwagookghwa Hangookeui Minjoojooeui* (Democracy in Korea and the Second Republic). Seoul: Jongro Seojeok.

Han, Sung-joo, and Yung-chul Park. 1993. "South Korea: Democratization at Last." In James Morley, ed., *Driven by Growth: Political Change in the Asia-Pacific*. Armonk, New York: M. E. Sharpe.

Han, Yong-won. 1984. *Chang Goon* (Genesis of the Korean army). Seoul: Bakyoungsa.

———. 1993. *Hangookeui Goonboojungchi* (The military politics of Korea). Seoul: Daewangsa.

———. 1998. "Gookgabaljeongwa Gooneui Yeokhal" (National development and the role of the military). *Hangookgooneui Visiongwa Gwaje* Seminar Paper, Hangookgookbangyeongoowon.

Hanna, Willard. 1964. *The Singapore Infantry Regiment: A Metropolitan Force Prepares for the Jungle*. New York: American Universities Field Staff.

———. 1973. *The New SAF*. New York: American Universities Field Staff.

Hannan, Mohammad. 1999. *Bangladesher Shamorik Itihash 'O Tragedyr Shenanibashe Sheikh Hasina* (Military history of Bangladesh and Sk. Hasina in the cantonment of tragedy). Dacca: Agami Prokashoni.

Hardgrave, Robert L., Jr. 1983. "The Northeast, the Punjab, and the Regionalization of Indian Politics." *Asian Survey* 23 (10) (November): 1171–81.

Harding, Harry. 1987. "The Role of the Military in Chinese Politics." In Victor Falkenheim, ed., *Citizens and Groups in Contemporary China*. Ann Arbor: Center for Chinese Studies, University of Michigan.

Hartendorp, A. V. 1958. *History of Industry and Trade of the Philippines*. Manila: American Chamber of Commerce.

Hasanuzzaman, Al. Masud. 1998. *Role of Opposition in Bangladesh Politics*. Dacca: University Press.

Haseman, John B. 1995. "Catalyst for Change in Indonesia: The Dili Incident." *Asian Survey* 35 (August): 757–80.

Hashmi, B. 1983. "Dragon Seed: Military in the State." In H. Gardezi and J. Rashid, eds., *Pakistan: The Unstable State*. Lahore: Vanguard.

Hawke, Bruce. 1998. "Exposed: Burma's Weapons Industry." *Jane's Pointer*, December 8–9, pp. 8–9.

Hawkins, David. 1972. *The Defence of Malaysia and Singapore*. London: Royal United Services Institute for Defence Studies.

Hazarika, Sanjoy. 1994. *Strangers of the Mist: Tales of War and Peace from India's Northeast*. New Delhi: Penguin.

Hedman, Eva-Lotta E. 1997. "Elections in the Early Philippine Republic: 'Showcase of Democracy' in Post-War Southeast Asia." Paper presented at the annual meeting of the Association for Asian Studies, Chicago, March.

———. 1999. "Late Imperial Romance: Magsaysay, Lansdale, and the Philippine-American 'Special Relationship.'" *National Intelligence and Security* 14 (4) (Winter): 181–94.

————. 2000a. "State of Siege: Political Violence and Vigilante Mobilization in the Philippines." In Arthur Brenner and Bruce Campbell, eds., *Murder with Deniability: Death Squads in Comparative Perspective.* New York: St. Martin's Press.

————. 2000b. "Morbid Symptoms and Political Violence in the Philippines." In Eva-Lotta E. Hedman and John T. Sidel, *Philippine Politics and Society in the Twentieth Century: Colonial Legacies, Post-Colonial Trajectories.* London: Routledge.

Hernandez, Carolina G. 1979. "The Extent of Civilian Control of the Military in the Philippines, 1946–77." Ph.D. dissertation, State University of New York at Buffalo.

————. 1984. "The Role of the Military in Contemporary Philippine Society." *Diliman Review,* January–February.

————. 1985. "The Philippines." In Zakaria Haji Ahmad and Harold Crouch, eds., *Military-Civilian Relations in South-East Asia.* Singapore: Oxford University Press.

————. 1986. "Political Institution Building in the Philippines." In Robert A. Scalapino, Seizaburo Sato, and Jusuf Wanandi, eds., *Asian Political Institutionalization.* Berkeley: Institute of East Asian Studies, University of California.

————. 1987. "Towards Understanding Coups and Civil-Military Relations." *Kasarinlan* 3 (2) (Fourth quarter).

————. 1996. "Controlling Asia's Armed Forces." In Larry Diamond and Marc F. Plattner, eds., *Civil-Military Relations and Democracy.* Baltimore: Johns Hopkins University Press.

————. 1997. "The Military and Constitutional Change: Problems and Prospects in a Redemocratized Philippines." *Public Policy* 1 (1) (October–November): 42–61.

Herspring, Dale R., and Ivan Volgyes, eds. 1978. *Civil-Military Relations in Communist Systems.* Boulder: Westview.

Hilsdon, Anne-Marie. 1995. *Madonnas and Martyrs: Militarism and Violence in the Philippines.* Quezon City: Ateneo de Manila University Press.

Hirose Katsuya. 1989. *Kanryo to Gunjin: Bunmin Tosei no Genkai* (Bureaucrats and soldiers: The limits of civilian control). Tokyo: Iwanami Shoten.

Hoadley, Stephen J. 1975. *Soldiers and Politics in Southeast Asia: Civil-Military Relations in Comparative Perspective.* Cambridge, Mass.: Schenkman.

Hoang Minh Thao. 1998. "Moi quan he giua ke hoach phat trien kinh te-xa hoi voi ke hoach dam bao kinh te cho quoc phong" (Relationship between socioeconomic development plans and economic plans for defense). *Thong Tin Khoa Hoc Quan Su,* February, pp. 16–20.

Holsti, Ole. 1998–99. "A Widening Gap Between U.S. Military and Civilian Society?" *International Security* 23 (3): 5–42.

Hong, Doo-seung. 1993. *Hangookgoondaeeui Sahoihak* (Sociology of the Korean military). Seoul: Nanam.

Honna, Jun. 1999. "The Military and Democratization in Indonesia: The Development of Civil-Military Discourse During the Late Suharto Era." Ph.D. dissertation, Australian National University.

Horiguchi, Robert Yoshinori. 1989. "The Japanese Self-Defense Force." Paper presented at the Armed Forces in Asia and the Pacific conference, Canberra, December 1.

Horowitz, Donald L. 1980. *Coup Theories and Officers' Motives: Sri Lanka in Comparative Perspective.* Princeton: Princeton University Press.

Horowitz, Donald. 1989. "Incentives and Behavior in the Ethnic Politics of Sri Lanka and Malaysia." *Third World Quarterly* 11 (4) (October): 18–35.

Hosoya Chihiro, Aruga Tadashi, Ishii Osamu, and Sasaki Takuya, eds. 1999. *Nichibei kankei shiryoshu 1945–97* (A documentary history of U.S.–Japan relations, 1945–97). Tokyo: University of Tokyo Press.

Hossain, Golam. 1991. *Civil Military Relations in Bangladesh: A Comparative Study.* Dacca: Academic.

Houtman, Gustaaf. 1999. *Mental Culture in Burmese Crisis Politics: Aung San Suu Kyi and the National League for Democracy.* Tokyo: Institute for the Study of Languages and Cultures of Asia and Africa.

Howard, Michael. 1959. *Soldiers and Governments: Nine Studies in Civil-Military Relations.* Bloomington, Ind.: Indiana University Press.

Human Rights Watch. Arms Project. 1994. *India: Arms and Abuses in Indian Punjab and Kashmir.* Vol. 6, no. 10.

Hunter, Wendy. 1997. *Eroding Military Influence in Brazil: Politicians Against Soldiers.* Chapel Hill: University of North Carolina Press.

Huntington, Samuel P. 1956. "Civilian Control of the Military: A Theoretical Statement." In Heinz Eulau, Samuel J. Eldersveld, and Morris Janowitz, eds., *Political Behavior: A Reader in Theory and Research.* Glencoe, Ill.: Free Press.

———. 1957. *The Soldier and the State: The Theory and Politics of Civil-Military Relations.* Cambridge, Mass.: The Belknap Press of Harvard University Press.

———. 1968. *Political Order in Changing Societies.* New Haven, Conn.: Yale University Press.

———. 1991. *The Third Wave: Democratization in the Late Twentieth Century.* Norman: University of Oklahoma Press.

———, ed. 1962. *Changing Patterns of Military Politics.* New York: Free Press.

———. 1996. "Reforming Civil-Military Relations." In Larry Diamond and Marc F. Plattner, eds., *Civil-Military Relations and Democracy.* Baltimore: Johns Hopkins University Press.

Hussain, A. 1979. *Elite Politics in an Ideological State: The Case of Pakistan.* Kent: Dawson and Sons.

Hussain, I. 1998. *Kashmir Dispute: An International Law Perspective.* Islamabad: Quaid-i-Azam Chair.

Huxley, Tim. 1991. "Singapore and Malaysia: A Precarious Balance?" *Pacific Review* 4: 204–13.

———. 1993. The Political Role of the SAF's Officers' Corps: Towards a Military Administrative State? Canberra: Australian National University.

———. 1995. "Singapore's Soldier-Scholars." *Asian Wall Street Journal,* February 24–25.

Huxley, Tim, and Susan Willet. 1999. *Arming East Asia.* Adelphi Paper 329. London: International Institute for Strategic Studies.

Ibrahim, Mohammad. 1999. *Shena Bahinir Abhontore Atash Bochor* (Twenty-eight years in the military). Dacca: Mowla Bros.

IDR Team. 1990. "Afghanistan and Sri Lanka: Comparison of Operational Style." *Indian Defence Review,* January, pp. 78–87.

Inayatullah. 1997. *State and Democracy in Pakistan.* Lahore: Vanguard.

Indonesia. Department of Defence and Security. 1989. Undang-Undang no. 1, 1988, tentang perubahan atas Undang-Undang no. 20, 1982, tentang ketentuan-ketentuan pokok pertahanan keamanan Negara Republik Indonesia. Jakarta: Dharma Bhakti.

———. 1995. *The Policy of the State Defence and Security of the Republic of Indonesia.* Jakarta: Department of Defence and Security.

———. 1997a. Undang-Undang bidang pertahanan keamanan (hankam), 1997. Jakarta: Mitra Info.

———. 1997b. Undang-Undang Republik Indonesia no. 28 tahun 1997 tentang Kepolisian Negara Republik Indonesia. Jakarta: BP Panca Usaha.

Indonesia Publications. 1994. *The Indonesian Military Elite*. Lanham-Seabrook, Md.: Indonesia Publications.

Ingram, James. 1971. *Economic Change in Thailand 1850–1970*. Stanford: Stanford University Press.

International Crisis Group. 2000. *Indonesia's Crisis: Chronic But Not Acute*. ICG Indonesia Report No. 2. Jakarta/Brussels.

International Institute for Strategic Studies. 1973. *The Military Balance, 1971–1972*. London: IISS.
———. 1985. *IISS*. London: IISS.
———. 1985–97. *The Military Balance*. London: IISS and Brassey's.
———. 1996. *The Military Balance 1996/1997*. London: IISS.
———. 1997. *The Military Balance 1997–1998*. London: IISS.
———. 2000. *The Military Balance, 1998–99*. London: Oxford University Press.

Investor Responsibility Research Center. 1997. *Multinational Business in Burma*. Washington, D.C.: IRRC.

Islam, Rafiqul. 1992. *Pochattarer Roktokhoron* (The bloodshed of '75). Dacca: Afsar Bros.

Jahan, Rounaq. 1972. *Pakistan: Failure in National Integration*. New York: Columbia University Press and Dacca: Dacca University Press.

Jalal, A. 1991. *The State of Martial Rule*. Lahore: Vanguard.
———. 1995a. *Democracy and Authoritarianism in South Asia: A Comparative and Historical Perspective*. Lahore: Sang-e-Meel Publications.

Jalal, Ayesha. 1995b. *Democracy and Authoritarianism in South Asia: A Comparative and Historical Perspective*. New York: Cambridge University Press.

Jang, Dal-joong. 1991. "Jabonjooeui Saneophwawa Hangookminjoojooeuieui Sahoijeok Todae" (Social structure of Korean democracy and capitalistic development). In Bae-ho Han, ed., *Hangookeui Jabonjooeuiwa Minjoojooeui*. Seoul: Beopmoonsa.

Janowitz, M. 1960. *The Professional Soldier*. New York: Free Press.

Janowitz, Morris. 1963. *The Military in the Development of New Nations*. Chicago: University of Chicago Press.
———. 1964a. *The Military in the Political Development of New Nations: An Essay in Comparative Perspective*. Chicago: University of Chicago Press.
———. 1964b. *The New Military: Changing Patterns of Organization*. New York: Russell Sage.
———. 1977. *Military Institutions and Coercion in the Developing Nations*. Chicago: University of Chicago Press.

Japan Defense Agency. 1986. *Defense of Japan 1986*. Tokyo: Japan Times.
———. 1997. *Defense of Japan 1997*. Tokyo: Japan Times.

Javate de Dios, Aurora, Petronila Bn. Daroy, and Lorna Kalaw-Tirol, eds. 1988. *Dictatorship and Revolution: Roots of People Power*. Manila: Conspectus.

Jencks, Harlan. 1982. *From Muskets to Missiles: Professionalism in the Chinese Army, 1945–1981*. Boulder: Westview.
———. 1991. "Civil-Military Relations in China: Tiananmen and After." *Problems of Communism*, May–June, pp. 14–29.
———. 1997. "Wild Speculations." In James R. Lilley and Chuck Downs, eds., *Crisis in the Taiwan Strait*. Washington, D.C.: National Defense University.

Jenkins, David. 1984. *Suharto and His Generals: Indonesian Military Politics 1975–1983*. Monograph Series, no. 64. Ithaca: Cornell Modern Indonesia Project.

Jeshurun, Chandran. 1980. *Malaysian Defence Policy.* Kuala Lumpur: University of Malaya Press.

———— ed. 1985. *Arms and Defence in Southeast Asia.* Singapore: Institute of Southeast Asian Studies.

Jin, Deok-gyu. 1981. "Rhee Syng-man Sidae Gwonryeokgoojoeui Eehae" (Understanding the political power structure of the Rhee era). In Duk-kyu Jin, Bae-ho Han, Hak-joon Kim, and Dae-hwan Kim, eds., *1950nyeondaeeui Insic.* Seoul: Hangilsa.

Joaquin, Nick. 1990. *Jaime Ongpin the Enigma: A Profile of the Filipino as Manager.* Makati: Jaime V. Ongpin Institute for Business and Government.

Joffe, Ellis. 1982. "The Military as a Political Actor in China." In Roman Kolkowicz and Andrzej Korbonski, eds., *Soldiers, Peasants and Bureaucrats: Civil-Military Relations in Communist and Modernizing Societies.* London: George, Allen and Unwin.

————. 1987. *The Chinese Army After Mao.* Cambridge, Mass.: Harvard University Press.

————. 1991. "The Tiananmen Crisis and the Politics of the PLA." In Richard H. Yang, ed., *China's Military: The PLA in 1990/91.* Boulder: Westview.

————. 1993. "The PLA and the Succession Question." In Richard H. Yang, ed., *China's Military: The PLA in 1992/3.* Boulder: Westview.

————. 1996. "Party-Army Relations in China: Retrospect and Prospect." *China Quarterly* 146 (June): 299.

————. 1997. "How Much Does the Chinese PLA Make Foreign Policy?" In David S. G. Goodman and Gerald Segal, eds., *China Rising: Nationalism and Interdependence.* London: Routledge.

————. 1999. "The Military and China's New Politics: Trends and Counter-Trends." In James Mulvenon and Richard Yang, eds., *The People's Liberation Army in the Information Age.* CF-145-CAPP/AF. Santa Monica, Calif.: Rand.

Johnson, Bryan. 1987. *Four Days of Courage: The Untold Story of the People Who Brought Marcos Down.* New York: Free Press.

Joo, Don-sik. 1997. *Munmin Jeongbu 1cheon2baekil* (Twelve hundred days of civilian government). Seoul: Saramgwa Chaek.

Joo, Young-bok. 1992. *Naega Kyukeun Chosun Jonjaeng* (My memory of the Korean War). Seoul: Koryowon.

Jordan, Ben. 1990. "The Origin, Development, and Readiness of the Royal Thai Army: A Historical Perspective." Master's thesis, Cornell University.

Josey, Alex. 1980. *Singapore: Its Past, Present, and Future.* London: Andre Deutsch.

Joshi, Manoj. 1998a. "Nuclear Shock Waves." *India Today,* May 25, pp. 12–13, International edition.

————. 1998b. "Marginal Costing." *India Today,* June 1, pp. 22–23, International edition.

————. 1999. "The Ghost of Bofors." *India Today,* March 8, International edition.

Jun, Hyun-joon. 1994. *Kim Jong Il Leadership Yongu* (Study of Kim Jong Il's leadership). Seoul: Korea Institute for National Unification.

Jun, Jinsok. 1996. "Military Politics in South Korea: The Case of Intervention in 1979–1980." Ph.D. dissertation, University of Kentucky.

Kabir, Monoar. 1993. "Socio-Political Change and Regime Transition in the Third World: A Study of El Salvador and Bangladesh." *Journal of Social Studies* 61: 1–25.

Kahin, George McT. 1970. *Nationalism and Revolution in Indonesia.* Ithaca: Cornell University Press.

Kalam, A. P. J. Abdul, with Y. S. Rajan. 1998. *India 2020: A Vision for a New Millennium.* New Delhi: Viking.

Kaldor, Mary. 1999. *New and Old Wars: Organized Violence in a Global Era*. Stanford: Stanford University Press.

Karan, Vijay. 1997. *War by Stealth: Terrorism in India*. New Delhi: Viking.

Karl, Terry Lynn. 1990. "Dilemmas of Democratization in Latin America." *Comparative Politics*, October pp. 1–26.

Kanwal, Gurmeet. 1999. "Kargil." *Seminar* 479 (July): 19

Kasetsiri, Chanwit. 1992. *Kanpatiwat khong Sayam* (The revolution of Siam). Bangkok: Praphansan.

Kasturi, Bhashyam. 1999. Review of four books. *Seminar* 479 (July): 51–54.

Katahara, Eiichi. 1990. "The Politics of Japanese Defense Policy-Making, 1975–89." Ph.D. dissertation, Griffith University.

Katzenstein, Peter, and Nobuo Okawara. 1993. *Japan's National Security: Structures, Norms, and Policy Responses in a Changing World*. Ithaca: East Asia Program, Cornell University.

Katzenstein, Peter, and Yutaka Tsujinaka. 1991. *Defending the Japanese State*. Ithaca: East Asia Program, Cornell University.

Kaufman, Robert R. 1986. "Liberalization and Democratization in South America: Perspectives for the 1970s." In Guillermo O'Donnell and Philippe C. Schmitter, eds., *Transitions from Authoritarian Rule*. Baltimore: Johns Hopkins University Press.

Kee, Won-jung. 1963. "Sowee Inminui Kundaewa Dang" (The so-called people's military and party). *Sasangkye* (Thought circle), October, pp. 156–62.

Keen, David. 1998. *The Economic Functions of Violence in Civil Wars*. Adelphi Paper 320. London: International Institute for Strategic Studies.

Kennedy, Charles H., and David J. Louscher, eds. 1991. *Civil-Military Interaction in Asia and Africa*. Leiden: E. J. Brill.

Kerkvliet, Benedict J. 1977. *The Huk Rebellion: A Study of Peasant Revolt in the Philippines*. Berkeley: University of California Press.

KESBAN: Selected Readings. 1981. Kuala Lumpur: Haigate.

Kessler, Richard J. 1988. "Development and the Military: Role of the Philippine Military in Development." In J. Soedjati Djiwandono and Yong Mun Cheong, eds., *Soldiers and Stability in Southeast Asia*. Singapore: Institute of Southeast Asian Studies.

Khan, A. 1967. *Friends Not Masters*. New York: Oxford University Press.

Khan, F. M. 1963. *The Story of Pakistan's Army*. Karachi: Oxford University Press.

Khan, G. H. 1993. *Memoirs of Lt. Gen. Gul Hassan Khan*. Karachi: Oxford University Press.

Khan, M. A., ed. 1985. *The Pakistan Experience: State and Religion*. Lahore: Vanguard.

Khong, Cho-Oon. 1995. "Singapore: Political Legitimacy Through Managing Conformity." In Muthiah Alagappa, ed., *Political Legitimacy in Southeast Asia: The Quest for Moral Authority*. Stanford: Stanford University Press.

Khosa, Asif. 1996. *The Constitution of Pakistan, 1973*. Lahore: Kausar Brothers.

Kim, Choong-sik. 1993. *Namsaneui Boojangdeul I* (Directors of the KCIA). Seoul: Dong-a Ilbosa.
———. 1994. *Namsanui Boojangdeul* (Chiefs of KCIA), Vol. I. Seoul: Dong-a Ilbosa.

Kim, Gwang-sik. 1998. "Goon-Sahoi Gwangye 50nyeon: Hoigowa Jeonmang" (50 years of civil-military relationship: The past and the future). *Hangookgooneui Visiongwa Gwaje* Seminar Paper, Hangookgookbangyeongoowon.

Kim, Gwang-woong. 1988. "Hangook Mongoon Gwanryo Elite eui Ideology wa Jeongchi" (The politics and ideology of the Korean military and civilian elite). *Kyekankyeonghyang*, Spring, pp. 30–46.

Kim, Hak-joon, ed. 1991. *Minjoohwaro Ganeungil* (The road to democracy). Seoul: Dana.

Kim, Ho-jin. 1990. *Hangookjengchichejeron* (The Korean political system). Seoul: Bakyeongsa.

Kim Il Sung. 1945 [1979]. "Haebangdoen Jokukesu Dang, Kukga, Mit Mooryuk Kunsule Daehayu" (On building the party, the state, and armed forces in the liberated fatherland). In KWP Press, ed., *Collected Work of Kim Il Sung*, vol. 1. Pyongyang: KWP Press.

———. 1966 [1988]. "Hyun Jungsewa Woori Dangui Kwaup" (The current situation and our party's mission). In Kim Il Sung, *Bukhan Nodongdang Daehoi Jooyo Moonhonjip* (Selected works of the KWP congress). Seoul: Dholbege.

Kim, Jae-hong. 1994. *Goon* (The military). Seoul: Dong-a Ilbosa.

Kim, Jung-min. 1998. "Kim Jong Il Shinjibae Chejewa shilsedeul" (Kim Jong Il's new regime and power elite). *Bukhan* (North Korea monthly) 322 (October): 60–77.

Kim, Man-kyu. 1982. *Chosunjoeui Jeongchisasangyeongoo* (Political philosophy in the Chosun era). Inchon: Inha University Press.

Kim, Se-jin. 1971. *The Politics of Military Revolution in Korea*. Chapel Hill: University of North Carolina Press.

Kim, Tae-il, and Yong-hyun Kim. 1996. "Bukhanui Kwonryok NaeBuui Dang-Jung-Kun Kwangye" (Party-government-military relations in the power structure of North Korea). *Donghyangkwa Jonmang* (Trends and prospects) 31 (Fall): 63–83.

Kim, Yong-ho. 1990. "Gonghwadangghwa Samseongaeheon" (The DRP and the constitutional amendment in 1969). In *Hyeondaesaereul Eoteotge Bolgeotinga* (Understanding modern Korean history). Vol. 4. Seoul: Dong-a Ilbosa.

Kim Yung-Myung. 1997. "Pattern of Military Rule and Prospects for Democracy in South Korea." In R. J. May and Viberto Selochan, eds., *The Military and Democracy in Asia and the Pacific*. London: C. Hurst and Co. and Bathurst: Crawford House.

"Kinh nghiem xay dung khu kinh te-quoc phong o Duc Co va Ia Grai" (Experiences in the building of an economic-defense zone in Duc Co and Ia Grai). 1998. *Quan Doi Nhan Dan*, October 15, p. 3; October 16, p. 3.

Kling, Merle. 1956. "Towards a Theory of Power and Political Instability in Latin America." *Western Political Quarterly* 9: 21–31.

Kochanek, Stanley A. 2000. "Politics of Democracy and Human Rights in South Asia." Paper prepared for Politics of Human Rights and Democratization conference, University of Illinois at Urbana-Champaign, March 31–April 2.

Kohli, Atul. 1994. "Centralization and Powerlessness: India's Democracy in Comparative Perspective." In Joel Migdal, Atul Kohli, and Vivienne Shue, eds., *State Power and Social Forces*. New York: Cambridge University Press.

Kolkowicz, Roman. 1967. *The Soviet Military and the Communist Party*. Princeton: Princeton University Press.

———. 1978. "Interest Groups in Soviet Politics: The Case of the Military." In Dale R. Herspring and Ivan Volgyes, eds., *Civil-Military Relations in Communist Systems*. Boulder: Westview.

————. 1982. "Toward a Theory of Civil-Military Relations in Communist (Hegemonial) Systems." In Roman Kolkowicz and Andrzej Korbonski, eds., *Soldiers, Peasants, and Bureaucrats.* London: George, Allen and Unwin.

Kourvetaris, G. A., and B. A. Dobratz, eds. 1977. *World Perspectives in Sociology of the Military.* New Brunswick, N.J.: Transaction Books.

Kristiadi, J. 1999. "The Armed Forces." In Richard W. Baker, M. Hadi Soesastro, J. Kristiadi, and Douglas E. Ramage, eds., *Indonesia: The Challenge of Change.* New York: St. Martin's Press.

Kuang Tung-chou. 1998. "Premier Promises to Increase Military Funding to Make Up for 'Losses' After Armed Forces Close Down All Its Businesses." *Sing Tao Jih Pao,* July 24, p. A5. In FBIS-CHI-98–205, July 24.

Kukreja, Veena. 1991. *Civil-Military Relations in South Asia: Pakistan, Bangladesh, and India.* London and New Delhi: Sage.

Kundu, Apurba. 1991. "The Indian Army's Continued Overdependence on Martial Races' Officers." *Indian Defence Review,* July, pp. 69–84.

————. 1996. "The Indian Armed Forces' Sikh and Non-Sikh Officers Opinions of Operation Blue Star." *Pacific Affairs* 67 (Spring): 46–69.

————. 1998. *Militarism in India: The Civil and Military in Consensus.* London: Tauris Academic Studies.

Kunimasa Takeshige. 1997–98. "Wangansenso toiu tenkanten" (The Gulf War as a turning point). *Sekai,* July 1997–November 1998.

Kunju, N. 1991. *Indian Army: A Grassroots Review.* New Delhi: Reliance.

————. 1993. *Olive Green Home Truths: How the Army Suffers from a Colonial Hangover.* New Delhi: Reliance.

Kwon, Oh-yoon. 1989a. "Bukhaneui Dangkun Kwankye I" (Party-military relations in North Korea I). *Bukhan* (North Korea monthly) 214 (October): 193–207.

————. 1989b. "Bukhaneui Dangkun Kwangye II" (Party-military relations in North Korea II). *Bukhan* (North Korea monthly) 215 (November): 190–94.

Kyaw Soe, Maj. n.d. "The Defence Services Institute." Unpublished manuscript. Document DR 8117. Available at Defense Services Historical Research Institute, Rangoon.

Lacaba, José F. 1982. *Days of Quiet, Nights of Rage: The First Quarter Storm and Related Events.* Manila: Salinlahi Publishing House.

Lal, Chaman. 1999. "Terrorism and Insurgency." *Seminar* 483 (November): 18–24.

Lam, Willy Wo-Lap. 1996. "PAP Undertakes Thorough 'Changing of the Guards.'" *South China Morning Post,* July 24, p. 10.

————. 1998a. "PLA to Get HK28 Billion for Businesses." *South China Morning Post,* August 3.

————. 1998b. "PLA Chief Accepts HK47 Billion Payout." *South China Morning Post,* October 9.

Lang, Kurt. 1972. *Military Institutions and the Sociology of War.* Beverly Hills: Sage.

Langenberg, Michael van. 1990. "The New Order State: Language, Ideology, Hegemony." In Arief Budiman, ed., *State and Civil Society in Indonesia.* Monash Papers on Southeast Asia, no. 22. Clayton, Victoria: Monash University.

Lansdale, Col. Edward G. 1959. Anderson–Southeast Asia Subcommittee of the Draper Committee. "Civic Activities of the Military Southeast Asia." Privileged Information, March 13. Joseph Dodge Papers, Box 3, Eisenhower Library.

Laporte, R. 1975. *Power and Privilege: Influence and Decision-Making in Pakistan.* Berkeley: University of California Press.

———. 1996. "Pakistan in 1995: The Continuing Crises." *Asian Survey* 36 (2): 179–87.

———. 1997. "Pakistan in 1996: Starting Over Again." *Asian Survey* 37 (2): 118–25.

Lasswell, Harold D. 1941. "The Garrison State." *American Journal of Sociology* 46: 455–68.

———. 1962. "The Garrison State Hypothesis Today." In Samuel P. Huntington, ed., *Changing Patterns of Military Politics.* New York: Free Press.

Lawrence, Susan. 1999. "Bitter Harvest." *Far Eastern Economic Review,* April 29, pp. 22–26.

Lawyers Committee for Human Rights. 1988. *Vigilantes in the Philippines: A Threat to Democratic Rule.* New York: Lawyers Committee for Human Rights.

Lee, Dong-hee. 1993. *Mingoon Gwangyeron* (The civil-military relationship). Seoul: Iljogak.

Lee, Dong-hoon. 1993. "Bukhanui Kunsajongchaek Kyuljungkujo Mit Kwajungkwa Kunbitongjeui Munje" (Decision-making structure and process of military policy in North Korea and arms control issues). *Sahoikwahakkwa Jungchaekyongu* (Social science and policy studies) 15 (2): 127–49.

Lee, Hang-koo. 1995. *Kim Jong Ilkwa Kui Chammodeul* (Kim Jong Il and his staff). Seoul: Shintaeyangsa.

Lee, Jong-sok. 1995. *Chosunrodongdang Yongu* (Study of the KWP). Seoul: Yoksabipyongsa.

Lee, Joon-hyeong. 1994a. *Moonminjeongboo Goongaehyeokeui Seonggwawa Jeonmang* (The accomplishment and future of military renovation under civilian government). Inchon: Center for International Studies.

———. 1994b. "Moonminjeongboohaeui Mingoongwangye" (The civil-military relationship under civilian government). *Hwanghaemoonhwa,* September, pp. 193–225.

Lee, Jung-soo. 1992. "Bukhanui Dang-kun Kwangye" (Party-military relations in North Korea). *Bukhanyongu* (North Korea studies) 3 (3): 40–61.

Lee, Ki-baek. 1982. *Hangooksashinron* (Korean history). Seoul: Iljogak.

———. 1988. *Hanbandoui Jongchiwa Kunsa* (Politics and military issues in the Korean peninsula). Seoul: Ilshinsa.

Lee, Man-woo. 1990. *The Odyssey of Korean Democracy: Korean Politics, 1987–1990.* New York: Praeger.

Lee, Min-young. 1996. *Hangookanbojeongchaekron* (Korean security policy). Seoul: Jinyoungsa.

Lee, Seon-ho. 1996. "Goonsa Anbowegigwanri Eongmang" (Problems in military and security crisis management). *Hangooknondan,* November, pp. 60–70.

Le Hong Quang. 1994. "Dau tranh chong 'dien bien hoa binh' tren linh vuc chinh tri-tu tuong" (Struggle against peaceful evolution in the political and ideological arena). *Quoc Phong Toan Dan* 5: 7–10.

Le Kha Phieu. 1996. "Can bo, chien sy LLVT kien dinh muc tieu doc lap dan toc va CNXH, duong loi ket hop hai nhiem vu chien luoc" (Cadres and soldiers shall unite in the national independence and socialist objectives and in linking the two strategic tasks). *Thong Tin Chuyen De* 52 (February): 121–24.

Lembaga Bantuan Hukum. 1990. *Laporan Observasi Lapangan di Propinsi Daerah Istimewa Aceh.* Jakarta: Lembaga Bantuan Hukum.

LeoGrande, William M. 1978. "A Bureaucratic Approach to Civil-Military Relations in Communist Political Systems: The Case of Cuba." In Dale R. Herspring and Ivan Volgyes, eds., *Civil-Military Relations in Communist Systems.* Boulder: Westview.

Le Tat Thang. 1980. "May kinh nghiem thuc hien che do mot nguoi chi huy" (Experiences in the implementation of the one-command system). *Quan Doi Nhan Dan,* October, pp. 38–45.

Lev, Daniel S. 1966. *The Transition to Guided Democracy: Indonesian Politics, 1957–1959.* Ithaca: Cornell Modern Indonesia Project.

Li, Cheng-xun. 1993. *Xianzheng Tizhi Xia Guofang Zuzhi Yu Jundui Jiaose zhi Yanjiu* (A study of the national defense organization and the military's role under the constitutional system). Taipei: Yongrang Chubanshe.

Lider, Julian. 1983. *Military Theory, Concept, Structure, Problems.* Aldershot: Gower.

Lieberthal, Kenneth. 1995. *Governing China: From Revolution Through Reform.* New York: Norton.

Lintner, Bertil. 1989. *Outrage: Burma's Struggle for Democracy.* Hong Kong: Far Eastern Economic Review.

———. 1994. *Burma in Revolt: Opium and Insurgency Since 1948.* Boulder: Westview.

———. 1998. "Velvet Glove." *Far Eastern Economic Review,* May 7, pp. 18–20.

Lo, Chih-cheng. 1999. "Arms Procurement Decision Making in Taiwan." In Ravinder Pal Singh, ed., *Arms Procurement Decision Making.* Vol. 2. Oxford: Oxford University Press.

Lo, Tien-bin. 1995. *Military Strongman Lee Teng-hui* (in Chinese). Taipei: Fuermosha Chuban.

Lockhart, Greg. 1989. *Nation in Arms: The Origins of the People's Army of Vietnam.* Sydney: Allen and Unwin.

Longer, V. 1974. *Red Coats to Olive Green: A History of the Indian Army, 1600–1974.* New Delhi: Allied.

Looney, R. E. 1994. "Budgetary Dilemmas in Pakistan: Costs and Benefits of Sustained Defense Expenditures." *Asian Survey* 34 (5): 417–29.

Lowry, Bob. 1993. *Indonesian Defence Policy and the Indonesian Armed Forces.* Canberra: Strategic and Defence Studies Center, Australian National University.

Lowry, Robert. 1996. *The Armed Forces of Indonesia.* Sidney: Allen and Unwin.

Luckham, Robin. 1996a. "Crafting Democratic Control over the Military: A Comparative Analysis of South Korea, Chile, and Ghana." *Democratization* 3 (3): 215–45.

———. 1996b. "Democracy and the Military: An Epitaph for Frankenstein's Monster?" *Democratization* 3 (2): 1–16.

Luhmann, Niklas. 1985. *A Sociological Theory of Law.* Boston: Routledge.

Luo Yuwen. 1996. "Jiang Zemin Attends CMC Promotion of 4 Generals on 23 January." *Xinhua Domestic Service,* January 23. In FBIS-CHI-96–016, January 24.

Luttwak, E. 1968. *Coup d'Etat.* Harmondsworth: Penguin.

Lu Yushan. 1994. "Jiang Zemin Hits Out in All Directions to Consolidate His Strength." *Dangdai,* July 15.

MacDougall, John A. 1983. "Patterns of Military Control in the Indonesian Higher Central Bureaucracy." *Indonesia* 33 (April): 89–121.

Mackenzie, Anne. 1987. "People Power or Palace Coup: The Fall of Marcos." In Mark Turner, ed., *Regime Change in the Philippines: The Legitimation of the Aquino Government.* Canberra: Australian National University, Department of Political and Social Change, Research School of Pacific Studies, Monograph 7.

Macmud, Benjamin. 1993. "The Malaysian Army in Transition." *Asian Defence Journal,* March, pp. 6–10.

Maeda, Tetsuo. 1995. *The Hidden Army.* Chicago: edition q, inc.

Malaysia Yearbook. 1998. Kuala Lumpur: Berita Publishing Sdn. Bhd.

Malik, I. H. 1997. *State and Civil Society in Pakistan*. London: Macmillan.

Manapat, Ricardo. 1991. *Some Are Smarter than Others: The History of Marcos' Crony Capitalism*. New York: Aletheia Publications.

Maniruzzaman, Talukdar. 1988. *The Bangladesh Revolution and Its Aftermath*. Dacca: University Press.

———. 1993. *Politics and Security of Bangladesh*. Dacca: University Press.

Mann, Michael. 1988. *States, War, and Capitalism*. New York: Basil Blackwell.

Mannan, M. A. 1992. "Warlords on the Rampage." *India Today*, September 30, pp. 62–63, International edition.

Mao Zedong. 1965. *Selected Works of Mao Tse-Tung*. Vol. 2. Peking: Foreign Language Press.

Marr, David, and Carlyle Thayer, eds. 1993. *Vietnam and the Rule of Law: Proceedings of Vietnam Update Conference, November 1992*. Canberra: Department of Political and Social Change, RSPAS, Australian National University.

Marwah, Ved. 1995. *Uncivil Wars: Pathology of Terrorism in India*. New Delhi: Harper Collins.

Mathur, Kuldeep. 1992. "The State and the Use of Coercive Power in India." *Asian Survey* 33 (4) (April): 337–48.

Maung Maung. 1947. Personal Diary (unpublished). Document CD 875. Available at Defense Services Historical Research Institute, Rangoon.

———. 1953. *Grim War Against the KMT*. Rangoon: Maung Maung.

———. 1959. *Burma's Constitution*. The Hague: Martinus Nijhoff.

May May Aung. 1997. "National Museum, the Symbol of Myanmar Pride and Honour." *Myanmar Information Sheet*, December 29. Available online at http://homepages.go.com/~myanmarinfosheet/1997/1997.htm.

May, Ronald J. 1992. *Vigilantes in the Philippines: From Fanatical Cults to Citizens' Organizations*. Philippine Studies Occasional Paper 12. Honolulu: Center for Philippine Studies, University of Hawai'i.

Mayerchak, P. 1986. "The Role of the Military in Singapore." In Edward A. Olsen and Stephen Jurika, eds., *The Armed Forces in Contemporary Asian Societies*. Boulder: Westview.

McCargo, Duncan. 1998. "Alternative Meanings of Political Reform in Contemporary Thailand." *Copenhagen Journal of Asian Studies* 13: 5–30.

McCoy, Alfred W. 1985. "Politics by Other Means." In Alfred W. McCoy, ed., *Southeast Asia Under Japanese Occupation*. Monograph Series, no. 22. New Haven, Conn.: Yale University Southeast Asia Studies.

———. 1988. "RAM Boys: Reformist Officers and the Romance of Violence," *Midweek*, September 21, pp. 29–33; "RAM Boys: The Ethos of Torture in the Theater of Terror," *Midweek*, September 28, pp. 30–34; and "RAM Boys: Coup Plots That Never Changed and Invariably Failed," *Midweek*, October 12, pp. 29–32.

———. 1989. "Quezon's Commonwealth: The Emergence of Philippine Authoritarianism." In Ruby R. Paredes, ed., *Philippine Colonial Democracy*. Quezon City: Ateneo de Manila University Press.

———. 1995. "'Same Banana': Hazing and Honor at the Philippine Military Academy." *Journal of Asian Studies* 54 (3) (August): 689–726.

———. 1999. *Closer than Brothers: Manhood at the Philippine Military Academy*. New Haven, Conn.: Yale University Press.

————, ed. 1993. *An Anarchy of Families: State and Family in the Philippines.* Monograph 10. Madison: University of Wisconsin Center for Southeast Asian Studies.

McKenna, Thomas M. 1998. *Muslim Rulers and Rebels: Everyday Politics and Armed Separatism in the Southern Philippines.* Berkeley: University of California Press.

McVey, Ruth. 1971. "The Post-Revolutionary Transformation of the Indonesian Army, Part I." *Indonesia* 11 (April): 131–76.

————. 1972. "The Post-Revolutionary Transformation of the Indonesian Army, Part II." *Indonesia* 13 (April): 147–81.

Meade, E. G. 1951. *American Military Government in Korea.* New York: King's Crown Press, Columbia University.

Mehta, Ashok. 1999. "Tackling the Tigers." *Seminar* 479 (July): 42–46.

Merrill, Kay. 1998. "Myanmar's China Connection—A Cause for Alarm?" *Asia-Pacific Defence Reporter* 24 (1): 20–21.

Migdal, Joel S. 1988. *Strong Societies and Weak States.* Princeton: Princeton University Press.

Mills, C. Wright. 1956. *The Power Elite.* New York: Oxford University Press.

Ministry of Defense, Malaysia. 1984. *The Fundamentals of KESBAN.* Pt. 1, vol. 3. Kuala Lumpur: Ministry of Defense.

Ministry of Defense, Republic of Korea. 1956. *Gookbangboosa* (History of the Ministry of Defense). Seoul: Songghwangsa.

Ministry of Defense, Singapore. 1995. *Defence of Singapore, 1994–95.* Singapore: Ministry of Defense.

Miranda, Felipe. 1985. "The Military." In R. J. May and Francisco Nemenzo, eds., *The Philippines After Marcos.* London: Croom Helm.

Miranda, Felipe, and Ruben F. Ciron. 1987a. "Development and the Military in the Philippines: Military Perceptions in a Time of Continuing Crisis." In J. Soedjati Djiwandono and Yong Mun Cheong, eds., *Soldiers and Stability in Southeast Asia.* Singapore: Institute of Southeast Asian Studies.

————. 1987b. "The Philippines: Defence Expenditures, Threat Perceptions, and the Role of the United States." In Chin Kin Wah, ed., *Defence Spending in Southeast Asia.* Singapore: Institute of Southeast Asian Studies.

Mirpur Papers. Bangladesh: Defence Services Command and Staff College, Mirpur.

Miyazaki Hiroki. 1977. "Boei-niho to Bunminn-tosei nitsuite" (On the two defense-related laws and civilian control). *Kokubo,* May, pp. 94–108.

Mochizuki, Mike. 1983–84. "Japan's Search for Strategy." *International Security* 8 (3) (Winter).

Mohd. Radzuan Haji Ibrahim. 1995. *Polis Dalam Sistem Keadilan Jenayah Di Malaysia.* Kuala Lumpur: Dewan Bahasa dan Pustaka.

Mohsin, Amena. 1992. "Bangladesh-India Relations: Limitations and Options in an Evolving Relationship." In Emajuddin Ahamed and Abul Kalam, eds., *Bangladesh, South Asia, and the World.* Dacca: Academic.

————. 1997. *The Politics of Nationalism: The Case of the Chittagong Hill Tracts, Bangladesh.* Dacca: University Press.

————. 1998. "The Chittagong Hill Tracts Peace Accord: Looking Beyond." *Journal of Social Studies* 82: 106–17.

Mojica, Proculo L. 1965. *Terry's Hunters (The True Story of the Hunters ROTC Guerrillas)*. Manila: Benipayo Press.

Mokarapong, Thawatt. 1972. *History of the Thai Revolution*. Bangkok: Chalermnit.

Monsshipouri, M., and A. Samuel. 1995. "Development and Democracy in Pakistan: Tenuous or Plausible Nexus?" *Asian Survey* 35 (11): 973–89.

Moon, Chung-in. 1989. "Democratization, National Security Politics, and Civil-Military Relations: Some Theoretical Issues and the South Korean Case." *Pacific Focus* 4 (2) (Fall): 5–22.

———. 1998. "South Korea: Recasting Security Paradigms." In Muthiah Alagappa, ed., *Asian Security Practice*. Stanford: Stanford University Press.

Moon, Chung-in, and Mun-gu Kang. 1995. "Democratic Opening and Military Intervention in South Korea: Comparative Assessments and Implications." In J. Cotton, ed., *Korean Politics in Transition*. New York: St. Martin's.

Moon, Chung-in, and David I. Steinberg. 1999. *The Kim Dae-jung Government and Sunshine Policy: Promises and Challenges*. Seoul: Yonsei University Press.

Morell, David, and Chai-Anan Samudavanija. 1981. *Political Conflict in Thailand: Reform, Reaction, Revolution*. Cambridge, Mass.: Oelgeschlager.

Mouffe, Chantal. 1979. *Gramsci and Marxist Theory*. London: Routledge.

Mrazek, Rudolf. 1978. *The United States and the Indonesian Military, 1945–1965: A Study of an Intervention*. Dissertationes Orientales 39. Prague: Oriental Institute.

MRCB. 1991. *Report on the Electoral Candidates of the 1991 Elections in Bangladesh*. Dacca: MRCB.

Mukul, M. R. Akhtar. 1998. "Hey Probhu Tumi Amake Shasti Dio" (Hey, Lord, you would punish me). *Dainik Ittefaq* (Dacca), April 14.

Mulvenon, James. 1997a. *Chinese Military Commerce and U.S. National Security*. MR-907.0-CAPP. Santa Monica, Calif.: Rand.

———. 1997b. *Professionalization of the Senior Chinese Officer Corps: Trends and Implications*. MR-901-OSD. Santa Monica, Calif.: Rand.

———. 2000. *Soldiers of Fortune: The Rise and Fall of the Chinese Military-Business Complex*. Armonk, N.Y.: M. E. Sharpe.

Muralidharan, Sukumar. 1999a. "An Unjust Dismissal." *Frontline* 16 (2) (January 16–29), electronic edition.

———. 1999b. "The Admiral Speaks Out." *Frontline* 16 (5) (February 27–March 12), electronic edition.

Murata Koji. 1997. "Boeiseisaku no tenkai" (The development of defense policy). In Nihon Seiji Gakkai, ed., *Kiki no nihon gaiko: 70 nendai* (Japanese diplomacy in times of crisis: The 1970s). Tokyo: Iwanami Shoten.

Muscat, Robert J. 1990. *Thailand and the United States: Development, Security, and Foreign Aid*. New York: Columbia University Press.

Muttukumaru, Anton. 1987. *The Military History of Ceylon*. New Delhi: Navarng.

Mya Thway, Bo. 1961. *The White Chinese: Burma's Enemy* (in Burmese). Rangoon: n.p.

Nagao Yuichiro. 1996. "Naisei no Hendo to Seigunkankei nitsuiteno ichikosatsu" (Japan's political change and civil-military relations). *Shin-boeironshu* 24 (1): 56–83.

Nagashima, Akihisa. 1998. "'Futsū no kuni' ni motomerareru seiji no shinryo" (Prudent realpolitik desired for a "normal state"). *This Is Yomiuri*, January, pp. 271–86.

Nair, Elizabeth. 1994. *Conscription and Nation-Building in Singapore: A Psychological Analysis.* Singapore: NUS.

Nakharin Mektrairat. 1992. *Kanpatiwat Sayam pho. so. 2475* (The Siamese revolution of 1932). Bangkok: Munnithi khrongkan tamra sangkhomsat lae manutsayasat.

Nalapat, M. D. 1999. "Bhagwat Felled by Bureaucratic Act." *Times of India,* January 6, p. 10.

Nasr, S. V. R. 1992. "Democracy and the Crisis of Governability in Pakistan." *Asian Survey* 32 (6): 521–37.

Nasution, Abdul Haris. 1965. *Fundamentals of Guerrilla Warfare.* New York: Praeger.

Nathan, Andrew J. 1990. *China's Crisis: Dilemmas of Reform and Prospects for Democracy.* New York: Columbia University Press.

———. 1997. *China's Transition.* New York: Columbia University Press.

Nathan, Andrew, with Yangshu Chou. 1990. "Democratizing Transition in Taiwan." In Andrew Nathan, *China's Crisis: Dilemmas of Reform and Prospects for Democracy.* New York: Columbia University Press.

Nathan, K. S. 1998. "Malaysia: Reinventing the Nation." In Muthiah Alagappa, ed., *Asian Security Practice: Material and Ideational Influences.* Stanford: Stanford University Press.

National Institute of Defense Studies. 1997. *Higahsiajiasenryakudaikan 1996–97* (East Asian strategic review). Tokyo: NIDS.

Nemenzo, Francisco. 1987. "A Season of Coups (Reflections on the Military in Politics)." *Kasarinlan* 2 (4) (Second quarter): 5–14.

"Nghi quyet cua Bo chinh tri ve quan doi lam nhiem vu xay dung kinh te (trich)" (Politburo resolution on the armed forces' responsibility in economic development—excerpt). 1976. *Quan Doi Nhan Dan,* November, pp. 2–7.

Nguyen Anh Bac. 1976. "Ve van de quan doi lam nhiem vu xay dung kinh te" (On the economic involvement of the armed forces). *Quan Doi Nhan Dan,* June, pp. 23–31.

Nguyen Kim Ton. 1997. "Xac dinh doi tuong chien dau trong chong bao loan lat do" (Classify participants in riot management). *Thong Tin Khoa Hoc Quan Su,* June, pp. 16–18.

Nguyen Nam Khanh. 1994. "May van de xay dung quan doi ve chinh tri dau tranh chong dien bien hoa binh" (Problems related to the building of the army against peaceful evolution). *Quoc Phong Toan Dan* 2: 9–13.

———. 1996. "Dau tranh chong xu huong co hoi huu khuyn—mot mat tran quan trong trong cong tac xay dung dang hien nay" (Struggle against rightist deviations—a crucial battle in party building today). *Thong Tin Chuyen De* 52 (February): 112–14.

Nhu Phong. 1983. "Hoi dong quan su va che do mot nguoi chi huy trong quan doi Xo-Viet" (Military councils and the one-command system in the Soviet armed forces). *Quan Doi Nhan Dan,* November, pp. 55–62.

Nishihara, Masashi. 1985. "The Japanese Central Organization of Defense." In Martin Edmonds, ed., *Central Organization of Defense.* Boulder: Westview.

Nishioka Akira. 1988. *Gendai no Sibirian Kontororu* (Modern civilian control). Tokyo: Chishikisha.

Noman, O. 1988. *The Political Economy of Pakistan 1947–85.* London: KPI.

Nordlinger, Eric A. 1977. *Soldiers in Politics: Military Coups and Governments.* Englewood Cliffs, N.J.: Prentice-Hall.

Nordstrom, Carolyn. 1992. "The Dirty War: Civilian Experience of Conflict in Mozambique and Sri Lanka." In Kumar Rupesinghe, ed., *Internal Conflict and Governance.* London: St. Martin's Press.

Notosusanto, Nugroho, ed. 1984. *Pejuang dan Prajurit: Konsepsi dan Implementasi Dwifungsi ABRI.* Jakarta: Sinar Harapan.

Nowak, Thomas C., and Kay A. Snyder. 1974. "Clientelist Politics in the Philippines: Integration or Instability?" *American Political Science Review* 68 (3) (September): 1147–70.

———. 1974. "Economic Concentration and Political Change in the Philippines." In Benedict J. Kerkvliet, ed., *Political Change in the Philippines: Studies of Local Politics Preceding Martial Law.* Honolulu: University of Hawai'i Press.

Nunn, Frederick M. 1992. *Latin American Professional Militarism in World Perspective.* Lincoln: University of Nebraska Press.

Ockey, Jim. 1999. "Creating the Thai Middle Class." In Michael Pinches, ed., *Culture and Privilege in Capitalist Asia.* London: Routledge.

Odom, William E. 1978. "The Party-Military Connection: A Critique." In Dale R. Herspring and Ivan Volgyes, eds., *Civil-Military Relations in Communist Systems.* Boulder: Westview.

O'Donnell, Guillermo, and Philippe C. Schmitter, eds. 1986. *Transitions from Authoritarian Rule: Tentative Conclusions About Uncertain Democracies.* Baltimore: Johns Hopkins University Press.

O'Donnell, Guillermo, Philippe C. Schmitter, and Laurence Whitehead. 1986. *Transitions from Authoritarian Rule: Comparative Perspectives.* Baltimore: Johns Hopkins University Press.

Olsen, Edward A., and Stephen Jurika, eds. 1986. *The Armed Forces in Contemporary Asian Societies.* Boulder: Westview.

Omissi, David. 1994. *The Sepoy and the Raj: The Indian Army, 1860–1940.* London: Macmillan.

Opall, Barbara. 1994. "U.S. Government Finds Tough Customer in Taiwan." *Defense News,* January 17–23, p. 1.

Osmany, Shireen Hasan. 1992. *Bangladesh Nationalism: History of Dialectics and Dimensions.* Dacca: University Press.

Otake Hideo. 1983. *Nihon no boei to kokunai seiji* (Japanese defense and domestic politics). Tokyo: San'ichi shobo.

Ozawa, Ichiro. 1994. *Blueprint for a New Japan: The Rethinking of a Nation.* Tokyo: Kodansha International.

Pabottingi, Mochtav. 1995. "Indonesia: Historicizing the New Order's Legitimacy Dilemma." In Muthiah Alagappa, ed., *Political Legitimacy in Southeast Asia: The Quest for Moral Authority.* Stanford: Stanford University Press.

Pachauri, Pankaj, and Zafar Meraj. 1990. "Drifting Dangerously." *India Today,* January 15, pp. 8–13, International edition.

Paik, Hwan-ki. 1996. "Bukhan Kunsoosanyupui Hyunhwangkwa Jonmang" (The current situation and prospects of defense industry in North Korea). *Kukbang Yongu* (Defense studies) 39 (1): 69–102.

Palit, D. K. 1991. *War in the High Himalayas: The Indian Army in Crisis, 1962.* New Delhi: Lancer International.

Paltiel, Jeremy. 1995. "PLA Allegiance on Parade: Civil-Military Relations in Transition." *China Quarterly* 143 (September): 784–800.

Panitan Wattanayagorn. 1998. "Thailand." In Ravinder Pal Singh, ed., *Arms Procurement Decision-Making.* Vol. 1, *China, India, Israel, Japan, South Korea, and Thailand.* New York: Oxford University Press.

Paredes, Ruby R., ed. 1989. *Philippine Colonial Democracy.* Quezon City: Ateneo de Manila University Press.

Park, Myong-rim. 1996. *Hankuk Jonjaengui Balbalkwa Kiwon* (Outbreak and origins of the Korean War). Vol. 2. Seoul: Nanam.

Pathak, Rahul. 1992. "Running for Cover." *India Today,* August 31, pp. 44–45, International edition.

Pathak, Rahul, and Anirudhya Mitra. 1992. "New Detonations." *India Today,* March 15, p. 23, International edition.

Peled, Alon. 1994. *Soldiers Apart: A Study of Ethnic Military Manpower Policies of Singapore, Israel, and South Africa.* Ann Arbor: University Microfilm International.

———. 1998. *A Question of Loyalty: Military Manpower Policy in Multiethnic States.* Ithaca: Cornell University Press.

Peng, Foo Choy. 1998. "J&A Probe Becomes Political." *South China Morning Post,* July 18.

Perkovich, George. 1999. *India's Nuclear Bomb: The Impact on Global Proliferation.* Berkeley: University of California Press.

Perlmutter, Amos. 1977. *The Military and Politics in Modern Times.* New Haven, Conn.: Yale University Press.

Perlmutter, Amos, and William M. LeoGrande. 1982. "The Party in Uniform: Toward a Theory of Civil-Military Relations in Communist Political Systems." *American Political Science Review* 76 (4) (December): 778–89.

Pernia, Ernesto M., Cayetano Paderanga Jr., and Victorina Hermoso. 1983. *The Spatial and Urban Dimensions of Development in the Philippines.* Working paper, Manila: Philippine Institute for Development Studies.

Pettigrew, Joyce. 1995. *The Sikhs of Punjab: Unheard Voices of the State and Guerilla Violence.* Atlantic Highlands, N.J.: Zed Books.

Pham Van. 1998. "Cong tac Dang- cong tac chinh tri trong tran then cho mo dau chien dich tien cong" (Party and political work during the initial stage of offensive campaigns). *Thong Tin Khoa Hoc Quan Su,* February, pp. 41–44.

Phan Quang Tiep. 1982. "Binh doan Truong Son voi nhiem vu xay dung kinh te ket hop voi quoc phong" (Truong Son Corps combines economic development with defense). *Quan Doi Nhan Dan,* February, pp. 32–40.

———. 1986. "To chuc quan su va lao dong san xuat" (Military organization and economic production). *Quan Doi Nhan Dan,* October, pp. 44–55.

Phan Thu. 1989. "Nhiem vu san xuat quoc phong va lam kinh te cua Quan Doi trong tinh hinh hien nay" (Defense production and economic production in the army). *Quan Doi Nhan Dan,* July 21, p. 3.

Philippine Senate Committee on Justice and Human Rights. 1988. *Report on Vigilante Groups.* Manila: Bureau of Printing (January).

"Phoi hop xoa mu chu, pho cap giao duc tieu hoc, trung hoc co so, can phai dong bo, kien tri" (Linking illiteracy campaigns with the universalization of primary and lower secondary education has to be systematic). 1999. *Quan Doi Nhan Dan,* September 28, p. 1.

Pike, Douglas. 1987a. *PAVN: People's Army of Vietnam.* Novato, Calif.: Presidio Press.

———. 1987b. *Vietnam and the Soviet Union: Anatomy of an Alliance.* Boulder: Westview.

Pillai, Ajith. 1999. "Burning Deck." *Outlook,* January 18.

Pion-Berlin, David. 1992. "Military Autonomy and Emerging Democracies in South America." *Comparative Politics* 25 (1): 83–102.

———. 1997. *Through Corridors of Power: Institutions and Civil-Military Relations in Argentina*. University Park: Pennsylvania State University Press.

Pion-Berlin, David, and Craig Arceneaux. 2000. "Decision-Makers or Decision-Takers? Military Mission and Civilian Control in Democratic South America." *Armed Forces and Society* 26 (3): 413–36.

Porter, Bruce D. 1994. *War and the Rise of the Modern State: The Military Foundations of Modern Politics*. New York: Free Press.

Porter, Gareth. 1987. *The Politics of Counterinsurgency in the Philippines: Military and Political Options*. Philippine Studies Occasional Paper 9. Honolulu: Center for Philippine Studies, University of Hawai'i.

Praval, K. C. 1990. *Indian Army After Independence*. Edited by Major Shankar Bhaduri. New Delhi: Lancer International.

Probe. 1994. *Life in the Chittagong Hill Tracts*. Dacca: BCDJC.

Przeworski, Adam. 1986. "Some Problems in the Study of the Transition to Democracy." In Guillermo O'Donnell and Philippe C. Schmitter, eds., *Transitions from Authoritarian Rule: Tentative Conclusions About Uncertain Democracies*. Baltimore: Johns Hopkins University Press.

———. 1991. *Democracy and the Market: Political and Economic Reforms in Eastern Europe and Latin America*. New York: Cambridge University Press.

Purrington, Courtney. 1992. "Tokyo's Policy Responses During the Gulf War and the Impact of the 'Iraqi Shock' on Japan." *Pacific Affairs* 65 (2) (Summer).

Purrington, Courtney, and A. K. 1991. "Tokyo's Policy Responses During the Gulf Crisis." *Asian Survey* 31 (4) (April).

Puthucheary, M. 1978. *The Politics of Administration: The Malaysian Experience*. Kuala Lumpur: Oxford University Press.

Putnam, M. C. J. 1967. "Toward Explaining Military Intervention in Latin American Politics." *World Politics* 20: 83–110.

Putzel, James. 1995. "Democratization and Clan Politics: The 1992 Philippine Elections." *South East Asia Research* 3 (1) (March): 18–45.

Radiopress. 1998. *Kitachosenno gennkyo* (Study of North Korea). Tokyo: Radiopress.

Rais, R. B. 1988. "Pakistan in 1987: Transition to Democracy." *Asian Survey* 28 (2): 126–36.

———. 1989. "Pakistan in 1988: From Command to Conciliation Politics." *Asian Survey* 29 (2): 199–206.

Rajasingham-Senanayake, Darini. 1999. "Democracy and the Problem of Representation: The Making of Bi-Polar Ethnic Identity." In Joanna Pfaff-Czarnecka, Darini Rajasingham-Senanayake, Ashis Nandy, and Terence Gomez, *Ethnic Futures: State and Identity Politics in Asia*. New Delhi: Sage.

Rajgopal, P. R. 1987. *Communal Violence in India*. New Delhi: Uppal.

Ramanathan, Usha. 1996. "Review of Annual Reports of the National Human Rights Commission: October 1993–March 1994 and 1994–95." *Seminar* 439 (July): 46–48.

Ramdas, L. 1999. "Navy, Nation, and National Security." *Frontline* 16 (2) (January 16–29), Electronic edition.

Ramli, Dol. 1965. "History of the Malay Regiment 1933–1942." *Journal of the Malayan Branch of the Royal Asiatic Society,* July, pp. 204–16.

Rancangan Malaysia Ketujuh: 1996–2000. 1996. Kuala Lumpur: Jabatan Pencetakan Negara.

Rao, B. V. P. 1999. "Small Weapons and National Security." *Seminar* 479 (July): 36–41.

Rapoport, David C. 1962. "A Comparative Theory of Military and Political Types." In Samuel P. Huntington, ed., *Changing Patterns of Military Politics.* New York: Free Press.

Rasler, Karen A., and William R. Thompson. 1989. *War and State Making: The Shaping of the Global Powers.* Boston: Unwin Hyman.

Renan, Ernest. 1970. "What Is a Nation?" In Robert A. Goldwin, ed., *Readings in World Politics.* New York: Oxford University Press.

Reno, William. 1998. *Warlord Politics and African States.* Boulder: Lynne Reinner.

Republic of Korea, Ministry of National Defense. 1999. *Defense White Paper, 1999.* Seoul: Government Printing Office.

Republic of Korea, Ministry of National Unification. 1996. *Bukhan Kaeyo* (The outlines of North Korea). Seoul: Government Printing Office.

———. 2000. *Bukhan Kaeyo* (The outlines of North Korea). Seoul: Government Printing Office.

Republic of the Philippines. 1990. *Republic Act No. 6975* (An Act Establishing the Philippine National Police Under a Reorganized Department of the Interior and Local Government and for Other Purposes). Congress of the Philippines, Fourth Regular Session, July 23.

Riaz, Ali. 1994. *State, Class, and Military Rule: Political Economy of Martial Law in Bangladesh.* Dacca: Nadi New Press.

Ricci, Maria Susana, and J. Samuel Fitch. 1990. "Ending Military Regimes in Argentina: 1966–73 and 1976–85." In Louis W. Goodman, Johanna S. R. Mendelson, and Juan Rial, eds., *The Military and Democracy: The Future of Civil-Military Relations in Latin America.* Lexington, Mass.: Lexington Books.

Ricklefs, M. C. 1993. *A History of Modern Indonesia Since c. 1300.* 2nd ed. Stanford: Stanford University Press.

Ricks, Thomas E. 1997. "The Widening Gap Between the Military and Society." *Atlantic Monthly,* July, pp. 67–78.

Riggs, Fred. 1964. *Thailand: The Modernization of a Bureaucratic Polity.* Honolulu: East-West Center Press.

Rizvi, Gowher. 1985. "Riding the Tiger: Institutionalizing the Military Regimes in Pakistan and Bangladesh." In Christopher Clapham and George Philip, eds., *The Political Dilemmas of Military Regimes.* Totowa, N.J.: Barnes and Nobles Books.

Rizvi, H. A. 1986. "The Civilianization of Military Rule in Pakistan." *Asian Survey* 26 (10): 1067–81.

———. 1987. *The Military and Politics in Pakistan.* Lahore: Progressive Publishers.

Rizvi, Hasan-Askandar. 1991. "The Military and Politics in Pakistan." In Charles H. Kennedy and David J. Louscher, eds., *Civil-Military Interaction in Asia and Africa.* Leiden: E. J. Brill.

———. 1997. "Pakistan: Civil-Military Relations in a Praetorian State." In R. J. May and Viberto Selochan, eds., *The Military and Democracy in Asia and the Pacific.* London: C. Hurst and Co. and Bathurst: Crawford House.

———. 1998. "Civil-Military Relations in Contemporary Pakistan." *Survival* 40 (2): 96–113.

Roberts, Adam. 1976. *Nations in Arms: The Theory and Practice of Territorial Defence.* London: Chatto and Windus (for the International Institute for Strategic Studies).

Robinson, Geoffrey. 1995. *The Dark Side of Paradise: Political Violence in Bali.* Ithaca: Cornell University Press.

———. 1996. "Human Rights in Southeast Asia: Rhetoric and Reality." In D. Wurfel and B. Burton, eds., *Southeast Asia in the New World Order: The Political Economy of a Dynamic Region.* London: Macmillan.

———. 1998. "Rawan Is as Rawan Does: The Origins of Disorder in New Order Aceh." *Indonesia* 66 (October): 127–56.

Roh, Ga-won. 1995. *Boansa* (The National Defense Security Command). 3 vols. Seoul: Sia.

Romero, Segundo E. 1998. "The Philippines in 1997: Weakening Political and Economic Turmoil." *Asian Survey* 38 (2): 196–202.

Rosen, Stephen P. 1996. *Societies and Military Power: India and Its Armies.* Ithaca: Cornell University Press.

Ross, Edward W. 1986. "Taiwan's Armed Forces." In Edward A. Olsen and Stephen Jurika, eds., *The Armed Forces in Contemporary Asian Societies.* Boulder: Westview.

Rueschemeyer, Dietrich, Evelyn Huber Stephens, and John D. Stephens. 1992. *Capitalist Development and Democracy.* Chicago: University of Chicago Press.

Russell, Jane. 1982. *Communal Politics Under the Donoughmore Constitution 1931–1947.* Dehiwela: Tisara Prakasakayo.

Rustamji, Khusro F. 1992. "The Paramilitary-Army Interface." *Indian Defence Review.* New Delhi: Lancer.

Rutten, Rosanne. 1992. "'Mass Surrenders' in Negros Occidental: Ideology, Force, and Accommodation in a Counterinsurgency Program." Paper presented at the International Philippine Studies Conference, Australian National University, July.

Saha, B. P. 1994. *Growing Violence in Rural Areas: A Sociological, Political, and Economic Analysis.* New Delhi: Vikas.

Said, Salim. 1991. *Genesis of Power: General Soedirman and the Indonesian Military in Politics 1945–1949.* Singapore: Institute of Southeast Asian Studies.

———. 1998. "Suharto's Armed Forces: Building a Power Base in New Order Indonesia, 1966–1998." *Asian Survey* 38 (June): 535–52.

Saiyud Koedphon. 1986. *The Struggle for Thailand.* Bangkok: S. Research Center.

Sakata Michita. 1975. "Yuji no nichibei kyogi wa hitsuyo da" (The need for Japan–U.S. consultations in the event of an emergency). *Asahi janaru,* August 8.

———. 1980. "Nihon no atarashii boei seisaku" (Japan's new defense policy). *Jiyu* 22 (6) (June).

———. 1986. "Boei seisaku no choryu o kaeru" (To change the direction of Japan's defense policy). *Sakata Michita-san o sasaeru chiisana kai* (Small Support Group for Mr. Michita Sakata), no. 8/9, May 1.

Salam, Moch. Faisal, Sh. 1994. *Peradilan Militer Indonesia.* Bandung: Mandar Maju.

Samego, Indria, Dewi Fortuna Anwar, Ikrar Nusa Bhakti, M. Hamdan Basyar, Maswadi Rauf, Riza Sihbudi, and Sri Yanuarti. 1998. *"Bila ABRI Menghendaki"—Desakan-Kuat Reformasi Atas Konsep Dwifungsi ABRI.* Jakarta: Mizan Pustaka.

Samnakngan lekhathikan wuthisapha (Office of the Executive Secretary of the Senate). Khanakammatthikan kanthahan wutthisapha (Armed Forces Committee). 1997. *Raingan*

*kanphijarana suksa botbat khong kongthap nai kanphatthana khwamsamphan kap kongthap lae rattha-
ban mitprathet phua sanapsanun matrakan raksa khwammankhong haeng chat* (Report of the examination of the military's role in developing relations with the militaries and governments
of friendly nations in order to preserve national security). Senate Committee Report.

Samudavanija, Chai-Anan. 1982. *The Thai Young Turks.* Singapore: Institute of Southeast Asian
Studies.

Samudavanija, Chai-Anan, Kusuma Snitwongse, and Suchit Bunbongkarn. 1990. *From Armed
Suppression to Political Offensive.* Bangkok: Chulalongkon University.

Samuels, Richard. 1994. *"Rich Nation, Strong Army": National Security and the Technological Transformation of Japan.* Ithaca: Cornell University Press.

Sandhu, Kanwar. 1992. "Official Excesses." *India Today,* October 15, pp. 28–33, International edition.

Sardeshpande, S. C. 1992. *Assignment Jaffna.* New Delhi: Lancer.

Sargent, Inge. 1994. *Twilight Over Burma: My Life as a Shan Princess.* Honolulu: University of
Hawai'i Press.

Sartori, Giovanni. 1976. *Parties and Party Systems: A Framework for Analysis.* New York: Cambridge
University Press.

Satha-anan, Chaiwat. 1996. *Ngoppraman thahan Thai 2525–2534* (Budget of the Thai military
1982–1991). Bangkok: Khopfai.

Sato, Hiroshi. 1993. "From Appeasement to Patronage: Politics of Islamization in Bangladesh."
Journal of Social Studies 61: 43–91.

Sattar, B. 1997. "The Non-Proliferation Regime and Pakistan: The CTBT as a Case Study."
M.S. thesis, Quaid-i-Azam University, Islamabad.

Sayeed, Abu. 1994. *Bangabandhu Hatyyakando: Facts and Documents* (Bangabandhu's assassination:
Facts and documents). Dacca: Kakoli Prokashoni.

Sayeed, K. B. 1980. *Politics in Pakistan.* New York: Praeger.

Schiff, Rebecca L. 1995. "Civil-Military Relations Reconsidered: A Theory of Concordance."
Armed Forces and Society 22 (1) (Fall): 7–24.

Schurmann, Franz. 1966. *Ideology and Organization in Communist China.* Berkeley: University of
California Press.

Schwarz, Adam. 1994. *A Nation in Waiting: Indonesia in the 1990s.* Sydney: Allen and Unwin.

Scott, James C. 1969. "Corruption, Machine Politics, and Political Change." *American Political
Science Review* 63: 1144.

———. 1972. "The Erosion of Patron-Client Bonds and Social Change in Rural Southeast
Asia." *Journal of Asian Studies* 32 (1) (November): 5–37.

Scott, Peter Dale. 1985. "The United States and the Overthrow of Sukarno." *Pacific Affairs* 58
(2): 239–64.

Seksan Prasertkul. 1989. "The Transformation of the Thai State and Economic Change
(1955–1945)." Ph.D. dissertation, Cornell University.

Selochan, Viberto. 1998. "The Military and the Fragile Democracy of the Philippines." In R. J.
May and Viberto Selochan, eds., *The Military and Democracy in Asia and the Pacific.* London:
C. Hurst and Co. and Bathurst: Crawford House.

———, ed. 1991. *The Military, State, and Development in Asia and the Pacific.* Boulder: Westview.

Selth, Andrew. 1996. *Transforming the Tatmadaw: The Burmese Armed Forces Since 1988.* Canberra:
Strategic and Defence Studies Centre.

————. 1997. "Burma's Intelligence Apparatus." *Burma Debate*, September–October, pp. 4–18.

————. 1999. "The Future of the Burmese Armed Forces." Paper prepared for the Burma Update conference, Australian National University, Canberra, August 5–6.

Sengupta, Prasun K. 1998. "The MAF and Force Modernisation Challenges in the Post-Cold War Era." *Asian Defence Journal*, April, pp. 14–32.

————. 2000. "Malaysia's Force Modernisation Priorities." *Asian Defence Journal*, April, pp. 12–16.

"Separation of Army from Business Done." 1999. *China Daily*, March 21, p. 1.

Shafqat, Saeed. 1997. *Civil-Military Relations in Pakistan: From Zulfikar Ali Bhutto to Benazir Bhutto.* Boulder: Westview.

Shalom, Stephen R. 1986. *The United States and the Philippines: A Study of Neo-Colonialism.* Quezon City: New Day.

Shambaugh, David. 1987. "China's National Security Research Bureaucracy." *China Quarterly*, June, pp. 276–304.

————. 1991. "The Soldier and the State in China: The Political Work System in the People's Liberation Army." *China Quarterly*, September, pp. 527–68.

————. 1993. "The PLA and Internal Order." In Richard H. Yang, ed., *China's Military: The PLA in 1992/3.* Boulder: Westview.

————. 1996. "China's Military in Transition: Politics, Professionalism, Procurement, and Power Projection." *China Quarterly* 146 (June): 265–98.

————. 1997. "Building the Party-State in China, 1949–1965: Bringing the Soldier Back In." In Timothy Cheek and Tony Saich, eds., *New Perspectives on State Socialism in China.* Armonk, N.Y.: M. E. Sharpe.

————. 1999. *PLA Studies Today: A Maturing Field.* Paper 26. Taipei: CAPS.

————. 2000a. "Accommodating a Frustrated Power: The Domestic Sources of China's External Posture." In David Lampton, ed., *The Making of Chinese Foreign and Security Policy in the Era of Reform.* Stanford: Stanford University Press.

————. 2000b. *Reforming China's Military.* Berkeley: University of California Press.

————. 2000c. "China's Military Views the World: Ambivalent Security." *International Security*, Winter, pp. 52–79.

Shantz, Arthur Allan. 1972. "Political Parties: The Changing Foundations of Philippine Democracy." Ph.D. dissertation, University of Michigan.

Shin, Sang-joon, and Jun Hyun-joon. 1994. *Jungkukkwa Bukhanui Jungchicheje Bikyoyongu* (Comparative study of political regimes of China and North Korea). Seoul: Korea Institute for National Unification.

Short, Anthony. 1975. *The Communist Insurrection in Malaya, 1948–1960.* London: Muller.

Shue, Vivienne. 1988. *The Reach of the State: Sketches of the Chinese Body Politic.* Stanford: Stanford University Press.

Shukla, K. S. 1988. *Collective Violence: Genesis and Response.* New Delhi: Indian Institute of Public Administration.

Sidel, John T. 1993. "Walking in the Shadow of the Big Man: Justiniano Montano and Failed Dynasty-Building in Cavite in 1935–1972." In Alfred W. McCoy, ed., *An Anarchy of Families: State and Family in the Philippines.* Monograph 10. Madison: University of Wisconsin Center for Southeast Asian Studies.

————. 1995. "Coercion, Capital, and the Post-Colonial State: Bossism in the Postwar Philippines." Ph.D. dissertation, Cornell University.

Sidhu, W. P. S. 1997. "The Development of an Indian Nuclear Doctrine Since 1980." Ph.D. dissertation, University of Cambridge, Cambridge.

Silverstein, Josef. 1958. "Politics in the Shan State: The Question of Secession from the Union of Burma." *Journal of Asian Studies* 18 (1): 43–57.

————. 1977. *Burma: Military Rule and the Politics of Stagnation.* Ithaca: Cornell University Press.

Singh, Arun. 1997. *The Military Balance: 1985–1994.* Occasional Paper, Program in Arms Control, Disarmament, and International Security. Urbana: University of Illinois.

Singh, Bilveer. 1995. *Dwifungsi ABRI, the Dual Function of the Indonesian Armed Forces: Origins, Actualization, and Implementation for Stability and Development.* Singapore: Singapore Institute of International Affairs.

Singh, Gurharpal. 1996. "Punjab Since 1984: Disorder, Order, and Legitimacy." *Asian Survey* 36 (4) (April): 410–21.

Singh, Jasjit. 1990. "SAC for India: The Credible Deterrent Option." *Indian Defence Review,* January, pp. 33–41.

————. 1998. *Nuclear India.* New Delhi: Institute of Defence Studies and Analysis and Knowledge World.

Singh, Jaswant. 1986. "Rationalisation of Security Forces." *Indian Defence Review,* January, pp. 137–41.

————. 1999. *Defending India.* Bangalore: Macmillan India.

Singh, K. Kuldip. 1998. *Overcoming Crisis in Leadership: Indian Army.* New Delhi: Mans Publications.

Singh, Mahesh Kumar. 1984. *India's Defence Strategy and Tactics: A Geographical Study.* Delhi: Shree.

Singh, Manavendra. 1999a. "After Operation Shakti." *Seminar* 473 (January): 59–64.

————. 1999b. "The Soldier's Story." *Seminar* 479 (July): 24–26.

Singh, Ravinder Pal. 1999. "Civil-Military Relations." *The Hindu,* February 26, p. 12.

Sinha, Rajeev K. 1995. *Crimes Affecting State Security: Problems and Recent Trends.* New Delhi: Deep and Deep.

Sinha, S. K. 1970. "Indian Army Since Independence." *United Services Institution of India (USI) Journal* 421 (October–December).

————. 1980. *Of Military Matters.* New Delhi: Vision Books.

————. 1984. "Honor the Soldier: Grievances Need to be Addressed." *The Statesman,* June 25, editorial page.

————. 1985. "The Ultimate Weapon." *Seminar* 308 (April).

Smith, Chris. 1994. *India's Ad Hoc Arsenal: Direction or Drift in Defence Policy.* Stockholm and Oxford: International Peace Research Institute and Oxford University Press.

Smith, D. E. 1970. *Religion and Political Development: An Analytic Study.* Boston: Little, Brown.

Smith, Martin. 1991. *Burma: Insurgency and the Politics of Ethnicity.* London: Zed Books.

————. 1995. "A State of Strife: The Indigenous Peoples of Burma." In R. H. Barnes, Andrew Gray, and Benedict Kingsbury, eds., *Indigenous Peoples of Asia.* Ann Arbor: Association for Asian Studies.

————. 1996. "Burma at the Crossroads." *Burma Debate,* November–December, pp. 4–13.

Sohn, Ho-cheol. 1998. *Hyeondaehangookjeongchi* (Current Korean politics). Seoul: Sahoipyeongron.

Song, Eui-seop. 1994. *Byeoldeuleui Gonghwagook* (The republic of generals). Seoul: Goryeo Seojeok.

Song, Gun-ho, ed. 1979. *Haebangjeonhoosaeui Insik* (Understanding the history of the Korean liberation era). Seoul: Hangilsa.

Stanley, William. 1996. *The Protection Racket State: Elite Politics, Military Extortion, and Civil War in El Salvador.* Philadelphia: Temple University Press.

Stepan, Alfred C. 1978. *The State and Society: Peru in Comparative Perspective.* Princeton: Princeton University Press.

———. 1986. "Paths Toward Redemocratization: Theoretical and Comparative Considerations." In Guillermo O'Donnell and Philippe C. Schmitter, eds., *Transitions from Authoritarian Rule: Tentative Conclusions About Uncertain Democracies.* Baltimore: Johns Hopkins University Press.

———. 1988. *Rethinking Military Politics: Brazil and the Southern Cone.* Princeton: Princeton University Press.

———, ed. 1973. *Authoritarian Brazil: Origins, Policies, and Failures.* New Haven, Conn.: Yale University Press.

Storey, Ian James. 1999. "Creeping Assertiveness: China, the Philippines, and the South China Sea Dispute." *Contemporary Southeast Asia* 21 (1) (April): 95–118.

Stout, David. 1998. "The Nation: An Army as Good as Its People, and Vice Versa," *New York Times,* July 26.

Su, Chin-chiang, Thomas Peng, Cheng Hsiao-shih, Arthur Ding, Wen Yuan-hsing, Wang Ping-hung, Ho De-fen, Chou Chu-ying, Chen Ying-yu, and Chen Chih-wei, eds. 1997. *Jundui Yu Shehui* (The military and the society). Taipei: INPR.

Subrahmanyam, K. 1990. "Armed Forces and Political Education." *Indian Defence Review,* January, pp. 108–11.

Sugiyama Takao. 1995. *Heishi ni kike* (Listen to the soldier). Tokyo: Shincho-sha.

Suh, Dae-sook. 1988. *Kim Il Sung: The North Korean Leader.* New York: Columbia University Press.

———. 1999. "Kim Jong Il Kunsa chejewa NamBuk Kwankye" (Kim Jong Il's Military Regime and North-South Relations). *Bukhan* (North Korea monthly) 332 (August): 94–103.

Suh, Dong-man. 1996. "Bukhan Dang-Kun Kwangyeeui Yoksajok Hyongsong: Hankuk Jonjaeng Ihoubuteo 1961" (The historical formation of party-military relations in North Korea: From the Korean War to 1961). *Tongilmunjeyongu* (Korean journal of unification affairs) 8 (2): 159–93.

Sukunya Bamroongsuk. 1991. "Chulachomklao Royal Military Academy: The Modernization of Military Education in Thailand (1887–1948)." Ph.D. dissertation, Northern Illinois University.

Sumatra Human Rights Watch Network. n.d. "Kondisi HAM di Aceh 1995–1997." Unpublished manuscript.

Sundarji, Krishnaswami. 1993. *Blind Men of Hindoostan: Indo-Pak Nuclear War.* New Dehli: UBS Publishers' Distributors.

Sundhaussen, Ulf. 1982. *The Road to Power.* Kuala Lumpur: Oxford University Press.

Sungsidh Piriyarangsan. 1983. *Thai Bureaucratic Capitalism.* Bangkok: Chulalongkon University.

Sun Maoqing, and Jia Chaoquan. 1998. "Zhang Wannian Praises Jiang's Leadership." *Xinhua Domestic Service,* September 3. In FBIS-CHI-98–250, September 7.

Suryadinata, Leo. 1989. *Military Ascendancy and Political Culture: A Study of Indonesia's Golkar.* Athens: Ohio University, Center for International Studies.

Swaine, Michael. 1992. *The Military and Political Succession in China: Leadership, Institutions, Beliefs.* Santa Monica, Calif.: Rand.

———. 1996. *The Role of the Chinese Military in National Security Policymaking.* Santa Monica, Calif.: Rand.

———. 1998. *The Role of the Chinese Military in National Security Policymaking.* Santa Monica, Calif.: Rand.

———. 2000. "Chinese Decision-Making Towards Taiwan, 1978–98." In David M. Lampton, ed., *The Making of Chinese Foreign and Security Policy in the Era of Reform.* Stanford: Stanford University Press.

Swaine, Michael D., and Alastair Iain Johnston. 1999. "China and Arms Control Institutions." In Elizabeth Economy and Michel Oksenberg, eds., *China Joins the World: Progress and Prospects.* New York: Council on Foreign Relations.

Tahara Soichiro. 1978. *Yuutsu naru mippei gundann* (The melancholy, closed corps). Tokyo: Ushio shuppansha.

Tahir-Kheli, S. 1980. "The Military in Contemporary Pakistan." *Armed Forces and Society* 6 (Summer): 639–53.

Takesada, Hideshi. 1998. *Kitachosenshinsobunseki* (An in-depth analysis of North Korea). Tokyo: KK Bestseller.

Tambiah, Stanley J. 1997. *Leveling Crowds: Ethnonationalist Conflicts and Collective Violence in South Asia.* New Delhi: Vistaar.

Tan, T. H. Andrew. 1999. "Singapore's Defence Capabilities, Trends and Implications." *Contemporary Southeast Asia* 21 (December): 451–74.

Tanaka Akihiko. 1995. "The Domestic Context: Japanese Politics and U.N. Peacekeeping." In Selig S. Harrison and Masashi Nishihara, eds., *UN Peacekeeping: Japanese and American Perspectives.* Washington, D.C.: Carnegie Endowment for International Peace.

———. 1997. *Anzenhosho: sengo gojunenno mosaku* (National security: An inquiry into the 50 years of the postwar period). Tokyo: Yomiuri Shimbunsha.

Tanham, George K. 1992. *Indian Strategic Thought: An Interpretive Essay.* Santa Monica, Calif.: Rand.

Tanter, Richard. 1990. "The Totalitarian Ambition: Intelligence Organisations and the Indonesian State." In Arief Budiman, ed., *State and Civil Society in Indonesia.* Monash Papers on Southeast Asia, no. 22. Clayton, Victoria: Monash University.

———. 1991. "Intelligence Agencies and Third World Militarization: A Case Study of Indonesia, 1966–1989." Ph.D. dissertation, Monash University.

Taylor, Robert H. 1973. *Foreign and Domestic Consequences of the KMT Intervention in Burma.* Ithaca: Cornell University, Southeast Asia Program.

———. 1985. "Burma in the Anti-Fascist War." In Alfred W. McCoy, ed., *Southeast Asia Under Japanese Occupation.* Monograph Series, no. 22. New Haven, Conn.: Yale University Southeast Asia Studies.

Tennakoon, Serena. 1988. "Rituals of Development: The Accelerated Mahaveli Development Program of Sri Lanka." *American Ethnologist* 15 (2): 294–310.

Tesoro, Benjamin D. 1986. *The Rise and Fall of the Marcos Mafia.* Manila: JB Tesoro.

Thayer, Carlyle A. 1985. "Vietnam." In Zakaria Haji Ahmad and Harold Crouch, eds., *Military-Civilian Relations in Southeast Asia.* Singapore: Oxford University Press.

Thayer, Carlyle. 1988. "The Regularization of Politics: Continuity and Change in the Party's Central Committee, 1951–1986." In David Marr and Christine White, eds., *Postwar Vietnam: Dilemmas in Socialist Development*. Ithaca: Cornell Southeast Asia Program.

———. 1994. *The Vietnam People's Army Under Doi Moi*. Singapore: Institute of Southeast Asian Studies.

———. 1995. "Vietnam's Strategic Readjustment." In Stuart Harris and Gary Klintworth, eds., *China as a Great Power: Myths, Realities, and Challenges in the Asia-Pacific Region*. New York: St. Martin's Press.

———. 1997. "Force Modernization: The Case of the Vietnam People's Army." *Contemporary Southeast Asia* 19 (1) (June): 1–27.

Thein Swe, Col. 1998. "Human Resource Development in Nation-Building: The Role of the Armed Forces." *Myanmar Perspectives*, July. Available online at http://www.myanmar.com /gov/perspec/7–98/hum.htm.

Thomas, Raju G. C. 1986. *India's Security Policy*. Princeton: Princeton University Press.

Thompson, Mark R. 1988–89. *Cory and "the Guy": Reformist Politics in the Philippines*. UFSI Reports 16. Indianapolis: Universities Field Staff International.

Thompson, W. Scott. 1975. *Unequal Partners: Philippine and Thai Relations with the United States, 1965–75*. Lexington, Mass.: Lexington Books.

Tien, Hung-mao. 1997. "Taiwan's Transformation." In Larry Diamond, Marc F. Plattner, Yunhan Chu, and Hung-mao Tien, eds., *Consolidating the Third Wave Democracies: Regional Challenges*. Baltimore: Johns Hopkins University Press.

Tiglao, Rigoberto. 1994. "Square One: Government-Communist Talks Break Down." *Far Eastern Economic Review*, November 10.

Tilly, Charles. 1985. "War Making and State Making as Organized Crime." In Peter B. Evans, Dietrich Rueschemeyer, and Theda Skocpol, eds., *Bringing the State Back In*. New York: Cambridge University Press.

———. 1989. "War Making and State Making as Organized Crime." In Peter B. Evans, Dietrich Rueschemeyer, and Theda Skocpol, eds., *Bringing the State Back In*. New York: Cambridge University Press.

———. 1990. *Capital, Coercion, and the State*. Oxford: Oxford University Press.

———. 1992. *Coercion, Capital, and European States, AD 990–1992*. Cambridge, Mass.: Blackwell.

———, ed. 1975. *Formation of National States in Western Europe*. Princeton: Princeton University Press.

Ting, William Pang-yu. 1982. "The Chinese Army." In Jonathan R. Adelman, ed., *Communist Armies in Politics*. Boulder: Westview.

Tinker, Hugh. 1967. *The Union of Burma: A Study of the First Years of Independence*. 4th ed. London: Athlone Press.

Tin Maung Maung Than. 1999. "Myanmar: Myanmar-ness and Realism in Historical Perspective." In Ken Booth and Russell Trood, eds., *Strategic Cultures in the Asia-Pacific Region*. London: Macmillan.

To chuc su lanh dao cua dang trong quan doi nhan dan Viet Nam (Organization of the party leadership in the People's Army). 1987–90. Vols. 1–6. Hanoi: Quan Doi Nhan Dan.

Tobe Ryoichi. 1998. *Gyakusetu no guntai* (The paradoxical military). Tokyo: Chuokoronsha.

Tong Cuc Chinh Tri. 1989. *Tai lieu ve cong tac xay dung Dang va cong tac chinh tri trong quan doi* (Documents on the building of the party and political work in the armed forces). Hanoi: Quan Doi Nhan Dan.

———. 1997. *50 nam lich su Quan Doi Nhan Dan Viet Nam* (50 years of the history of the Vietnam People's Army). Hanoi: Quan Doi Nhan Dan.

———. 1998. *Lich su cong tac Dang cong tac chinh tri chien dich trong khang chien chong Phap va chong My, 1945–1975* (History of the political work during the war of resistance against the United States, 1945–1975). Hanoi: Quan Doi Nhan Dan.

Tran Kinh Luan. 1989. "Nhung van de nong bong can tiep tuc thao go o cac xi nghiep quoc phong" (Urgent problems that need to be dealt with in defense enterprises). *Quan Doi Nhan Dan*, May 4, p. 3.

Tran Minh Thiet. 1997. "Mot so y kien ve phong chong bao loan va tac chien phong thu o cum huyen (thi) trong diem" (Opinions on riot management and defensive strikes in strategically located districts). *Thong Tin Khoa Hoc Quan Su*, February, pp. 1–5.

Tran Van Quang. 1994. "Nang cao canh giac cach mang, danh bai am muu 'dien bien hoa binh' cua cac the luc thu dich" (Elevate revolutionary vigilance to fight against peaceful evolution advances of the enemy). *Quoc Phong Toan Dan* 2: 14–17.

Trinkunas, Harold. 1998. "Crafting Civilian Control of the Armed Forces: Statecraft, Institutions, and Military Subordination in Emerging Democracies." Ph.D. dissertation, Stanford University.

———. 2000. "Crafting Civilian Control in Emerging Democracies." *Journal of Interamerican Studies and World Affairs*, Fall.

Trota, José Ricardo. 1992. *The Philippine Army 1935–1942*. Manila: Ateneo de Manila University Press.

Tully, Mark, and Satish Jacob. 1985. *Amritsar: Mrs. Gandhi's Last Battle*. London: Jonathan Cape.

Turley, William S. 1977. "Origins and Development of Communist Military Leadership in Vietnam." *Armed Forces and Society* 3 (2) (Winter): 219–47.

———. 1982. "The Vietnamese Army." In Jonathan R. Adelman, ed., *Communist Armies in Politics*. Boulder: Westview.

———. 1988. "The Military Construction of Socialism: Postwar Roles of the People's Army of Vietnam." In David G. Marr and Christine P. White, eds., *Postwar Vietnam: Dilemmas in Socialist Development*. Ithaca: Cornell University, Southeast Asia Program.

Ubonrat Siriyuwsak. 1998. *Khrongsang thang setthakitkanmuang khong rabop witthayu lae thorathat Thai lae phongrathop to sitthiseriphap* (The political and economic structure of the Thai system of radio and television and the consequences for rights and freedom). Bangkok: Chulalongkon Communication Arts.

Uchida, Kazuomi. 1980. "Naval Competition and Security in East Asia." In Jonathan Alford, ed., *Sea Power and Influence*. Hampshire: Gower.

Ueda Tetsu. 1983. *Shiren* (Sea lane). Tokyo: Kosaido.

———. 1997. *Gaidorain* (The guidelines). Tokyo: Datahouse.

Union of Burma. War Office. General Staff Department. 1951a. *Memorandum: Formation of a Military Planning Staff at the War Office (Secret), August 28, No. 101/E1/SD*. Document DR 4768. Available at Defense Services Historical Research Institute, Rangoon.

————. 1951b. *Memorandum: Organization of the War Office and Formation of an Army Council, September 23, No. 188/E1/SD.* Document DR 4768. Available at Defense Services Historical Research Institute, Rangoon.

————. 1957a. *Public Lecture and Discussion of Psychological Warfare Operations, Commanding Officers' Conference, Rangoon.* In Burmese. Document CD 1. Available at Defense Services Historical Research Institute, Rangoon.

————. 1957b. *Report of the Morale Subcommittee, Commanding Officers' Conference, Rangoon, June 18.* In Burmese. Document CD 232. Available at Defense Services Historical Research Institute, Rangoon.

————. Directorate of Education and Psychological Warfare. 1957c. *Proposed Plan and Syllabi of Instruction of the First Psychological Warfare Officers' Course, Rangoon, August 19.* Document CD 232. Available at Defense Services Historical Research Institute, Rangoon.

————. 1958a. "Psychological Preparedness" (in Burmese). Paper submitted to Commanding Officers' Conference, Rangoon, August 30. Document CD 172. Available at Defense Services Historical Research Institute, Rangoon.

————. 1958b. *Report of the General Staff Department to the Tatmadaw Conference.* In Burmese. Document CD 1. Available at Defense Services Historical Research Institute, Rangoon.

————. Chief of Staff (Army). 1962. *Chief of Staff (Army) Report to the Defense Ministry Tatmadaw Conference.* In Burmese. Document CD 341. Available at Defense Services Historical Research Institute, Rangoon.

United Nations. Department of Economic and Social Affairs. 1998. *The Demographic Yearbook.* New York: United Nations.

University Teachers for Human Rights. 1994. *Someone Else's War.* Colombo: Movement for Interracial Justice and Equality.

University Teachers for Human Rights (Jaffna). 1997. *A Vision Skewed.* Special Report 9. Pamphlet.

U.S. Arms Control and Disarmament Agency. 1997. *World Ministry Expenditure and Arms Transfers, 1997.* Washington, D.C.: U.S. Government Printing Office.

U.S. Department of State. Bureau for International Narcotics and Law Enforcement Affairs. 1998. *International Narcotics Control Strategy Report.* Washington, D.C.: Government Printing Office.

Vagt, A. 1959. *On Militarism.* New York: Meridian.

Valeriano, Col. Napoleon D., and Lt. Col. Charles T. R. Bohannan. 1962. *Counter-Guerrilla Operations: The Philippine Experience.* New York: Praeger.

Van der Kroef, Justus M. 1988. "The Philippines: Day of the Vigilantes." *Asian Survey* 28 (6) (June): 631–49.

Vasavakul, Thaveeporn. 1995. "Vietnam: The Changing Models of Legitimation." In Muthiah Alagappa, ed., *Political Legitimacy in Southeast Asia: The Quest for Moral Authority.* Stanford: Stanford University Press.

————. 1997. "Sectoral Politics and Strategies for State and Party-Building from the VII to the VIII Congresses of the Vietnamese Communist Party (1991–1996)." In Adam Fforde, ed., *Doi Moi: Ten Years After the 1986 Party Congress.* Canberra: Department of Political and Social Change, Australian National University.

Vatikiotis, Michael. 1993. *Indonesian Politics Under Suharto: Order, Development, and Pressure for Change.* London: Routledge.

"Vietnamese Army Streamlines Businesses." 1997. *Jane's Defence Weekly,* September 24, p. 13.

Villamor, Cayetano. 1958. *Policemen as Peace Officers.* Cebu City: Villamor.

Vinayak, Ramesh. 1992. "A Law Without Claws." *India Today,* April 15, p. 92, International edition.

Volgyes, Ivan. 1978. "The Military as an Agent of Political Socialization: The Case of Hungary." In Dale R. Herspring and Ivan Volgyes, eds., *Civil-Military Relations in Communist Systems.* Boulder: Westview.

Vo Nguyen Giap. 1976. "Anh dung tien quan vao mat tran kinh te, cung toan dan chien thang ngheo nan, lac hau, xay dung to quoc Viet Nam xa hoi chu nghia giau manh" (Heroically involved in the economic battle, together with the masses defeat poverty and underdevelopment and build a prosperous fatherland). *Quan Doi Nhan Dan,* November, pp. 14–45.

———. 1977a. "Tien quan manh me tren mat tran xay dung kinh te, cung toan dan chien thang ngheo nan va lac hau, xay dung dat nuoc giau manh" (Advance forcefully to build the economy and, together with the masses, defeat poverty and build a rich country). *Quoc Phong Toan Dan* 252: 1–22.

———. 1977b. "Tien quan manh me tren mat tran xay dung kinh te, cung toan dan chien thang ngheo nan va lac hau, xay dung dat nuoc giau manh (tiep theo va het)" (Advance forcefully to build the economy and, together with the masses, defeat poverty and build a rich country—continued). *Quoc Phong Toan Dan* 253: 30–57.

Vu Duc Thai. 1987. "Cum kinh te-ky thuat—mot hinh thuc ket hop kinh te voi quoc phong co hieu qua" (Economic-technical complex—a model that links economic development with defense). *Quan Doi Nhan Dan,* April, pp. 39–45.

Wada, Haruki. 1992. *Kim Il Sungkwa Manju Hangil Jonjaeng* (Kim Il Sung and his anti-Japan guerrilla war in Manchuria). Translated by Jong-sok Lee. Seoul: Changjakkwabipyongsa.

Wang Shaoguang. 1996. "Estimating China's Defense Expenditure: Some Evidence from Chinese Sources." *China Quarterly,* September, pp. 889–911.

Waseem, M. 1994. *Politics and the State in Pakistan.* Islamabad: National Institute of Historical and Cultural Research.

Weber, Max. 1964. *The Theory of Social and Economic Organization.* New York: Free Press.

———. 1978. *Theory of Social and Economic Organization.* Edited by Talcott Parsons. New York: Free Press.

Webster's New World Dictionary. 1984. Englewood Cliffs, N.J.: Prentice Hall.

Weinstein, Martin E. 1971. *Japan's Postwar Defense Policy, 1947–1968.* New York: Columbia University Press.

Welch, Claude E., Jr., ed. 1976. *Civilian Control of the Military: Theories and Cases from Developing Countries.* Albany: State University of New York Press.

Welfield, John. 1988. *An Empire in Eclipse: Japan in the Postwar American Alliance System.* London: Athlone Press.

Whitson, William, with Huang Chen-hsia. 1973. *The Chinese High Command: A History of Communist Military Politics, 1927–71.* New York: Praeger.

Wiant, Jon A. 1986. "The Vanguard Army: The Tatmadaw and Politics in Revolutionary Burma." In Edward A. Olsen and Stephen Jurika, eds., *The Armed Forces in Contemporary Asian Societies.* Boulder: Westview.

Widmalm, Sten. 1997. "The Rise and Fall of Democracy in Jammu and Kashmir." *Asian Survey* 37 (11) (November): 1005–30.

Willoughby, Charles A. 1972. *The Guerrilla Resistance Movement in the Philippines: 1941–1945*. New York: Vantage Press.

Wilson, David. 1962. "The Military in Thai Politics." In John J. Johnston, ed., *The Role of the Military in Underdeveloped Countries*. Princeton: Princeton University Press.

Wolters, Willem. 1989. "Rise and Fall of Provincial Elites in the Philippines: Nueva Ecija from the 1880s to the Present Day." *Sojourn* 4 (1) (February): 54–74.

Wood, Glynn L. 1986. "Civil-Military Relations in Post-Colonial India." In Edward A. Olsen and Stephen Jurika, eds., *The Armed Forces in Contemporary Asian Societies*. Boulder: Westview.

Wurfel, David. 1988. *Filipino Politics: Development and Decay*. Ithaca: Cornell University Press.

Wyat, David K. 1984. *Thailand: A Short History*. New Haven, Conn.: Yale University Press.

Xa Luan. 1976. "Tham gia xay dung kinh te—mot nhiem vu chien luoc cua quan doi ta hien nay" (Economic engagement—a strategic task for the army today). *Quan Doi Nhan Dan*, January, pp. 3–10.

Xiang Huaicheng. 1999. "Report on the Execution of the Central and Local Budgets for 1998 and on the Draft Central and Local Budgets for 1999." *Xinhua Domestic Service*, March 18. In FBIS-CHI-1999–0320, March 18.

"Xi nghiep det quan doi" (A military-run weaving factory). 1998. *Quan Doi Nhan Dan*, October 9, p. 1.

"Xoa mu chu, pho cap giao duc tieu hoc o bien gioi" (Anti-illitcracy and universalization of primary education at the border areas). 1998. *Quan Doi Nhan Dan*, November 3, p. 3.

Yabes, Criselda. 1991. *The Boys from the Barracks: The Philippine Military after EDSA*. Metro Manila: Anvil.

Yamaguchi Noboru. 1991. "Seiji ni okeru Gunnji no Kenkyu" (A study of the military in politics). *Chuokoron*, August, pp. 158–70.

Yamamoto Tadashi, ed. 1999. *Deciding the Public Good: Governance and Civil Society in Japan*. Tokyo: Japan Center for International Exchange.

Yan Xuetong. 1998. "China." In R. P. Singh, ed., *Arms Procurement Decision Making: China, India, Israel, Japan, South Korea, and Thailand*. Vol. 1. Stockholm: SIRPI.

Yang, Byoung-ki. 1993. "A Study on the Political Orientations and Factionalism of the Korean Military Group." Ph.D. dissertation, Yonsei University.

Yang, Richard H., ed. 1993. *China's Military: The PLA in 1992/3*. Boulder: Westview.

Yang, Sung-chul. 1994. *The North and South Korean Political Systems: A Comparative Analysis*. Boulder: Westview.

Yarrington-Coats, George. 1968. "The Philippine Constabulary: 1901–1917." Ph.D. dissertation, Ohio State University.

Yawnghwe, Chao-Tzang. 1995. "Burma: The Depoliticization of the Political." In Muthiah Alagappa, ed., *Political Legitimacy in Southeast Asia: The Quest for Moral Authority*. Stanford: Stanford University Press.

Yeo, Ning Hong. 1992. "An Exclusive Interview." *Asian Defence Journal* 2 (92): 7–14.

Yeo Jung. 1991. *Bulgemooldeun Taedongkang: Jun Inminkun Jungchiwiwoneui Sooki* (The bloody Taedong River: A memoir of the former political commissar of KPA). Seoul: Dong-A Ilbo.

Yong, Mun Cheong, and J. S. Djiwandono, eds. 1988. *Soldiers and Stability in Southeast Asia*. Singapore: Institute of Southeast Asian Studies.

Yoon Byung-ik. 1990. "Bukhane Itsoso Minkunkwangye" (Civil-military relations in North Korea). *Kukbangronjip* (National defense studies) 12: 47–65.

Yoon Pil-yong. 1989. "Yoon Pil-yong Bongyoukjeungun" (Yoon Pil-yong speaks). *Sindong-a,* December, pp. 318–40.

Yoon Sung-suk. 1996. "Contradictions of Political Liberalization in Brazil and South Korea." *Korea Observer* 27 (1) (Spring): 53–84.

Yousaf, H. 1998. *Pakistan: A Study of Political Developments 1947–97.* Lahore: Academy of Administrative and Social Sciences.

Yudhoyono, Bambang (Gen.). 1998. "ABRI dan Reformasi: Pokok-Pokok Pikiran ABRI tentang Reformasi Menuju Pencapaian Cita-Cita Nasional." Unpublished manuscript.

Yunus, Abdul Ghani. 1995. "The Malaysian Armed Forces and Vision 2020." In Abdul Razak Abdullah Baginda and Rohana Mahmud, eds., *Malaysian Defence and Foreign Policies.* Petaling Jaya, Malaysia: Pelanduk Publications.

Yusof, Nordin. 1994. *Honour and Sacrifice: The Malaysian Armed Forces.* Kuala Lumpur: Ministry of Defence.

Zagorski, Paul W. 1988. "Civil-Military Relations and Praetorianism." *Armed Forces and Society* 14 (3) (Spring): 407–32.

Ziga, Lorenzo B. 1989. "Military Checkpoints and the Rule of Law: An Unsettled Peace for Whom?" *Philippine Law Journal* 64 (3/4) (September–December): 242.

Ziring, L. 1993. "The Second Stage in Pakistani Politics: The 1993 Elections." *Asian Survey* 33 (12): 1175–85.

Ziring, L., R. Braibanti, and W. H. Wriggins. 1977. *Pakistan: The Long View.* Durham: Duke University Press.

Ziring, Lawrence. 1992. *Bangladesh: From Mujib to Ershad: An Interpretative Study.* Karachi: Oxford University Press.

Zwick, Jim. 1982. *Militarism and Repression in the Philippines.* Working Paper 31. Montreal: Centre for Developing-Area Studies, McGill University.

INDEX